STALIN

STALIN

Man of History

IAN GREY

1979
Doubleday & Company, Inc.
Garden City, New York

ISBN: 0-385-14333-8
Library of Congress Catalog Card Number 78-20030

To the memory of Larissa

ACKNOWLEDGMENTS

The main sources on which I have drawn are listed in the bibliography or referred to in the notes to each chapter. I would like, however, to pay tribute to Leonard Schapiro's *The Communist Party of the Soviet Union* and to Colonel Albert Seaton's *The Russo-German War 1941–45* and *Stalin as Warlord*, which I found especially valuable.

I place on record my appreciation for the help and facilities which I have had and without which I could not have written this book in the London Library (my thanks in particular to Miss Joan Bailey) and the British Library. To Mrs. Miriam Alman for helpful comments and to Mrs. Jakki Becker for her speedy and accurate typing, I express my gratitude.

My indebtedness to my wife for her patience and constant support increases with each book that I write and I acknowledge it with love and gratitude.

London
April 28, 1978

PREFACE

Twenty-five years have passed since Stalin died. The incessant clamor of eulogy that accompanied his name in Soviet Russia has been stilled. In the West mention of him provokes moral indignation and denigration. He is known as a malevolent despot, "the greatest criminal in history." Like an ikon standing before its oil lamp and so begrimed by the fumes that the subject is barely visible, he has faded to a dark shadow, which can be identified only with difficulty.

Stalin was, however, a ruler in the tradition of Ivan the Dread and Peter the Great. He was great in ability, in courage, and in purpose. He gave positive leadership and transformed a vast, backward agrarian nation into a modern industrial power. He was also ruthless and inhuman in his methods. Like many outstanding men, he was a complex of diverse qualities.

There has been no lack of books and reports, some sensational, some scholarly, and many inspired by malice and hatred, which have dwelt on the dark side of his rule. They have tended to obscure and distort, setting up barriers to the understanding of the man and his importance. There has been a paucity of studies of his positive achievements.

The distorted portrayal of Stalin has been in part the work of Trotsky and those who sympathize with him. Other factors have contributed also, such as the idolatry of Lenin, the bitterness of émigré social democrats, and the moral judgments of Western historians. Khrushchev's speech to the Twentieth Party Congress in 1956 and the partial rejection of Stalin by the party and the Soviet government, as well as the confused de-Stalinization policy, have added to the obfuscation.

Trotsky, a man of great ability and zeal, but also possessed by extreme arrogance, was convinced that he had been defeated and humbled as a result of the machinations of Stalin. He could never accept that Stalin had become the leader of the party and of Russia, and he devoted himself to the expression of his hatred of the man he professed to scorn. Trotsky was a fierce hater and a prolific writer, a polemicist rather than a historian, who was always ready to distort and invent evidence against his enemy.

The studies of Stalin most often quoted and followed are Trotsky's *Stalin: An Appraisal of the Man and His Influence* and the biography by Boris Souvarine, a contemporary French communist, who was sympathetic to Trotsky and equally inspired by hatred of his subject.

Prominent among Trotsky's supporters and sympathizers in the West has been Isaac Deutscher, whose emotional and intellectual kinship with him found expression in a three-volume biography. Deutscher also wrote an interesting and scholarly biography of Stalin, but in it he closely followed Trotsky's interpretation. Others, too, and notably Professor E. H. Carr, a leading authority on the Revolution and the early Stalinist era, have tended to follow Trotsky's line.

While Stalin has been execrated, Lenin has been deified. In the Soviet Union, of course, the idolatry of Lenin has reached scarcely credible heights. But in the West, too, many writers, Souvarine and Deutscher in particular, have portrayed Lenin with strong and uncritical admiration. Although a great revolutionary leader, Lenin had many shortcomings and was far from infallible. At times he was no more than an unscrupulous politician, intent on power. Moreover, it was he who fostered the terror, forced labor camps, suppression of all opposition, monolithic organization of party and state, and other aspects of the Soviet system, which are anathema to Western liberal opinion and which are popularly attributed to Stalin. Nevertheless, the elevation of Lenin seems to require the denigration of Stalin, although they were both the creators of the Soviet Union, and Stalin's contribution was by no means the less important.

Soviet dissidents condemn Stalin, but are divided over Lenin. Roy Medvedev, who still resides in the Soviet Union and remains a convinced communist and follower of Lenin, holds that Stalin was wholly responsible for the aberrations of Soviet rule. His book *Let History Judge* is a sustained attempt to indict Stalinism. Solzhenitsyn maintains that the policies of Stalin and the communist system itself are alien to Russian life, and indeed are evil aberrations, engendered by Lenin and the party. He is close to the Slavophiles in demanding a return to the traditions of Orthodox Russia and apparently to the idealized old Muscovy of Tsar Aleksei Mikhailovich. Both interpretations are in my view unacceptable, as I have sought to show in this biography.

Attempts by Western historians to understand and portray Stalin are usually strangled by ethical principles and moral indignation. They start from the premise that he was a despot who thrived on doing evil and whose sole concern was to satisfy his lust for power. They are unwilling in general to admit that he had any other purpose or indeed that he had abilities of any kind except perhaps cunning and ruthlessness.

Richard Pipes, professor of Russian history at Harvard University, for whose learning I have great respect, provides striking evidence of the almost willful refusal or inability of Western academics to write about Stalin dispassionately. Thus he has stated that "Stalin possessed no statesmanlike talents of any kind," that "Stalin's supreme gift," the ability to penetrate the worst side of human nature, "was ultimately negative," and that he encouraged Hitler to embark on war and, having done so, "entrusted the major strategic decisions to professional soldiers like Zhukov." These and similar judgments are in my view so contrary to the facts as to be perverse, but they are representative of much that has been written about him in the West.

The rise to power and rule of Iosif Stalin forms one of the most extraordinary chapters in world history. Parentage, environment, and childhood contribute nothing to an understanding of his character and his life. There were many handicaps to his attaining eminence of any kind. He was small, undistinguished in appearance, pock-marked, and with physical disabilities. He was not a Russian, but a Georgian and of the humblest parentage. He had had a sound education, but within the strictly conservative limits of an Orthodox seminary. From these inauspicious beginnings his career followed an upward trajectory until he was absolute ruler over a nation of more than 200 million people.

The qualities that set him over other men and made him the arbiter of their destinies were his great and highly disciplined intelligence, his single-mindedness, his implacable will, his courage, and
his ruthlessness. Although his formal education had been limited,
he read widely. He studied the history of Russia and other countries and was mindful of the past in the formulation of policy, in
day-by-day government, and in the conduct of the war. He ac-
quired a considerable expertise in many fields and could pass from
one subject to another with mastery, and he forgot nothing.

From the time when as a young man he became a revolutionary
and then a Bolshevik, he was single-minded in his dedication to
Marxism-Leninism. But this was to merge with another obsessive
loyalty. Living and working in Russia, he became a Russian. He
identified himself completely with his adopted country, and developed as an essentially Russian autocrat.

In his dedication to the two causes of Russia and of Marxism-
Leninism he became possessed by the conviction that he was a
man of history; he was destined to rule Russia and, following the
dogma of Marxism-Leninism, to make her secure and powerful
and to create a new society. No sacrifice was too great for this
cause, and in some future time the Russian people would reap rewards in the form of peace, justice, and plenty. The policy of "socialism in one country," the campaigns of industrialization and
collectivization, the successive five-year plans, and even the purges
were directed to this purpose. All who opposed him or were suspected of opposing him in history's grand design were enemies
and must be eliminated.

As a man Stalin was remarkable and at times bewildering. Notwithstanding his popular reputation, he was human. He was sensitive to the feelings of others and capable of great warmth. He possessed charm and a lively sense of humor. He tried to be a father
to his children, but failed. In his personal life he was highly
moral, almost puritanical. His way of life was simple, devoid of
luxury of any kind. He was a lonely man. But his sympathetic
qualities were usually overborne by his chronic mistrust and suspicion, by outbursts of savage temper, and by his ruthlessness. Para-
doxically he was not a cruel man—he did not derive pleasure from
inflicting suffering on others—but he was inhuman in his readiness

to sacrifice human life on a vast scale to enforce his policies and achieve his purpose.

Between Stalin and the Western leaders there was a fundamental difference of outlook. The liberalism and humanitarianism proclaimed in the West struck him as unrealistic for his people, who were not ready for such luxuries. But the humanitarian principles of the Western leaders struck him also as hypocritical. For example, they made an arbitrary distinction between war and peace, which he did not accept. Russia was, he considered, in a state of war not only while hostilities raged against Germany but throughout his life. Churchill evidently accepted the needless massacre of 135,000 men, women, and children in Dresden, because it was carried out in time of war. Truman did not hesitate to drop the atom bomb on Hiroshima and Nagasaki, although not essential to victory over Japan. But they were incensed by the death of twelve to fourteen thousand Polish officers and men who were anti-Russian and a real danger to the nation, and by the elimination of dissidents, who might undermine Stalin's rule. Over such incidents, as over the treatment of Poland and other major issues, a wide division in outlook was apparent between Stalin and the Western leaders.

Certain Russian traditions, evolved since the formation of Muscovy, have had an impressive continuity in Russia's history, enduring into the twentieth century. Stalin, his outlook, and his rule were firmly rooted in these traditions. In a brief prologue I have indicated the most deeply ingrained and important of these historical factors, which have direct relevance to this study.

In years to come controversy will no doubt continue to rage over Stalin. But I hope there will be more studies of the positive and dynamic aspects of his rule. Soviet Russia today is a superpower with a Navy probably already larger than the United States Navy, an Army certainly larger, and a weapon capacity at least equal. Stalin was the architect and creator of this military and economic might, which has been achieved within an astonishingly brief span of years.

One of Stalin's basic objectives was always to overcome Russia's weakness and backwardness, and to establish her equality with the West. Full achievement of this purpose has come only some years after his death. It was perhaps most strikingly symbolized at Salt II in Vladivostok in November 1974. As Raymond L. Garthoff has observed: "The most fundamental political objective [of the Russians] has been American recognition of parity of the U.S.S.R. with the U.S.—parity in the broadest political and political-military as well as strategic sense, spelling an end to the U.S.S.R.'s inferiority in its relations with the United States," and in Vladivostok this acknowledgment was formally achieved.

Power politics and the need for a balance of power are as relevant to the world of the late twentieth century as they have been in previous centuries. But they are often obscured by problems of human rights, of developing countries, and kindred matters of real and urgent concern. The West is particularly involved in these fields, and it is salutary to bear in mind that such matters are not the Soviet priorities. Machiavelli, whose *The Prince* Stalin is said to have studied closely, argued that political policies and behavior should be considered apart from Christian morality. Stalin followed this precept and was concerned with political realities apart from ideology, and his policies are still the policies of the Soviet Union. It is in understanding these policies and the national attitudes informing them that the study of the man and his era is particularly relevant and important.

This study is, then, an attempt to lift its subject from a morass of distortion, prejudice, and obfuscation in which it has become buried. I have sought to present briefly Stalin's life, his objectives and outlook, and, so far as possible with the scant material available, to portray the man. I have not tried to extenuate or even less to justify the inhumanities of his rule: They are well documented. But I have eschewed moral judgments and I have not obtruded my own political views, although as one born and brought up in the traditions of the rule of law and of parliamentary government I find Marxist dogma totally unacceptable and the outlook of most Marxists abhorrent. Thus I have tried to understand and portray Stalin in his own Russian context. I hope that I may have avoided at least in some degree what Marc Bloch described as "that Satanic enemy of history, the mania for making judgments."

Stalin himself, who was prone to invoke the name of the deity, would probably have said: "That is for God."

Stalin and his Russia present a vast and challenging field of study. The difficulties of the historian are, however, greatly increased by both the lack of materials and the unreliability of so much of what is available. Nothing is known about certain periods of his life. Speculation and rumor fill the vacuums.

Stalin himself was exceedingly reticent. Apparently he took no interest in history's verdict. Roosevelt was much concerned about his place in history. Hitler, too, worried about history's verdict. Churchill wrote voluminously to record, explain, and justify his actions for posterity. Stalin made no attempt to do so. He had a public and a private persona. The adulations of the personality cult concerned his public persona. The official biographies, published in his lifetime, by Yaroslavsky, Beria, Barbusse, and others, are also part of the cult. If, as Khrushchev stated, he carefully revised the official short biography to ensure that he was described in terms of the cult, this, too, was a matter of his public persona and part of the panoply of power. But he wrote nothing about himself, his private thoughts and motives. No one knew him, but there were those who glimpsed aspects of the man. The historian must rely on the official records, his speeches, and articles, and the writings of others.

Most of the material published in the West on Stalin has been written by those hostile or with a strong bias against him. Trotsky and Souvarine have been mentioned. This material is interesting and often of great value, but it must be treated with caution. Often it is tendentious and unverifiable. If the rules of evidence, followed in a British court of law, were applied, much would be held inadmissible.

An example is the oft-quoted statement, alleged to have been made by Stalin who "one summer night in 1923, opening his heart to Dzerzhinsky and Kamenev," said, "To choose one's victim, to prepare one's plans minutely, to slake an implacable vengeance, and then to go to bed . . . There is nothing sweeter in the world." Apart from the circumstances that this hearsay evidence was recorded with reservation by Souvarine, who had presumably been told by Kamenev, both the wording of the remark and the idea of Stalin "opening his heart" to these two men seem to me wholly out of character. The remark is normally quoted as a fact.

Khrushchev's speech to the Twentieth Party Congress and the two volumes of his memoirs are full of interest, but they, too, must be treated with extreme caution. He was concerned only to demote Stalin, while promoting and justifying himself, and he went to great lengths to do so. While he was in power, there was increasing emphasis on his military leadership during World War II, when he was a political kommissar. The six-volume *History of the Great Patriotic War of the Soviet Union 1941–1945*, published in 1961–65, contains a mass of valuable factual material, but also, while lauding Khrushchev's comparatively unimportant role, it makes only marginal critical mention of Stalin. Since his fall from power, Khrushchev's military genius has been forgotten, and Brezhnev's insignificant role in the war is being inflated. The denigration of Stalin has been halted, however, and tribute is again being paid to his wartime leadership and to other aspects of his rule.

While Stalin was alive, Russian generals did not presume to publish memoirs. The official version was that Stalin, as the great leader and Supreme Commander in Chief, had led Soviet Russia to victory. The memoirs of generals might be seen to detract from this version, and Stalin himself would have disapproved of them also as self-glorification by individual generals. They had, in fact, received considerable recognition in the form of decorations, promotion, and the great salutes which had celebrated their victories at the time, and, with the exception of Zhukov, they had retained positions of prominence.

After the Twentieth Party Congress in 1956 Soviet generals, anxious like their Western counterparts to recount their wartime exploits, to promote and justify their actions, hastened into print. So numerous were the memoirs that an American academic, Seweryn Bialer, published an anthology with copious notes and commentary. This was the time of de-Stalinization and many wrote about Stalin's errors and lack of military training. Indeed, the emphasis was on his mistakes, and his positive direction was passed over in silence, although all made clear that as Supreme Commander he maintained control over all fronts and major operations. Since the first spate of memoirs, however, the pendulum has swung towards a limited recognition of his role. In this study I have relied almost entirely on the memoirs of Zhukov, Rokossovsky, and Shtemenko, and on Vasilevsky's articles, for these men worked closely with Stalin.

Western leaders, officials, and service chiefs have provided glimpses which contribute towards a portrait of the man. The memoirs of Hopkins, Churchill, and Harriman have special value, as have the occasional insights of Birse, the interpreter. Most important of all, of course, in the portrayal of Stalin the man is his daughter's book *Twenty Letters to a Friend*, which impresses me as spontaneous and truthful. I have drawn on it heavily. Mrs. Alliluyeva's second book, *Only One Year*, falls in a different category. It was written in the United States after she had broken her links with her country, and in its judgments on her father it surely bears many marks of the influence of the new friends she had made in the West. They included Mr. Kennan and others who read the manuscript of the book, and whose basic interpretations of Stalin I reject. It remains only to note that hers was the final betrayal of her father, who might have said, in the words of King Lear,

> How sharper than a serpent's tooth it is
> To have a thankless child!

CONTENTS

Why, man, he doth bestride the narrow world
Like a Colossus . . .

The evil that men do lives after them;
The good is oft interred with their bones . . .

William Shakespeare, *Julius Caesar*

STALIN

PROLOGUE

The Russian Tradition

Certain features of Stalin's rule, which are alien to Western concepts, have been rooted in the history and outlook of the Russian people for centuries. They are part of the Russian tradition to which he was heir and which he maintained for the same reasons as his predecessors.

The most important of these traditions have been the supremacy of the state; the absolute power of the autocrat, who was the embodiment of the state, over the lives, property, and thoughts of all subjects from the highest in the land to the lowest; the feeling of vulnerability; the secretiveness and mistrust, especially of foreigners from the West; the sense of superiority and of messianism; the sensitivity to criticism; and the brutalized exercise of authority. Western travelers who visited the country in the reign of Ivan the Terrible, and observers of Stalin's Russia, have noted the same features. Their observations convey a sense of the continuity, even changelessness, of Russia's history.

The history of Russia is an epic of the unending struggle to settle the vast Eurasian plain. An extreme climate of long, very cold winters and short hot summers, an expansive plain with no natural defense barriers, and a network of mighty rivers dictated the conditions in which the nation was established. But it has been a beleaguered nation, existing on the frontiers between Europe and Asia, between settled and nomadic peoples, and under constant attack.

In the West the peoples have striven after wealth and political and economic rights. The first concern of the Russians in every generation has been for the defense of their country and their families against the invader. Invasion and war have shaped their outlook and their political system. They have accepted complete subordination to the state as they have accepted the absolute power of their autocrat, primarily because national survival demanded a centralized state and a ruler able to mobilize every human and other resource for defense.

Kievan Rus, the first step towards nationhood, endured for some three and a half centuries. But it could not stand against the destructive waves of Pechenegs, Cumans, and other nomadic tribes from Asia, or against the pressures of the Germanic tribes, driving the Lithuanians and Letts before them in the north. In search of security the Russians moved into Galicia and Belorussia, but their main migration was to the forest lands of the upper Volga and Oka rivers. There Moscow became the center of the new Russian nation. Then in the thirteenth century came the Mongol invasion.

The horde of Genghis Khan swept across the Eurasian plain, destroying all in its path. The shock of Mongol ferocity and the experience of Mongol rule in the course of the following two centuries made a profound and lasting impression on the Russians and on the emerging state of Muscovy. The authority of the Great Khan was enforced mercilessly. The Yasa, embodying the military and civil laws of the Mongol Empire, prescribed death as the penalty for most breaches of the law. Failure to pay taxes or to provide the required number of recruits and, worst of all, rebellion, brought prompt and savage retribution. Servile obedience was demanded of the Russians and other subject peoples.

In the fifteenth century the Grand Princes of Moscow threw off the Mongol yoke. But they had the formidable task of establishing the new Russian nation. It involved defending their lands, while reconquering the territory inhabited by Orthodox Russians but under foreign rule, and colonizing the vast lands to the south and east. Muscovy was under constant attack by the Khanate of Kazan, until Tsar Ivan IV conquered it in 1552, and by the Swedes, Poles, Lithuanians, and Germans in the west.

During these years, however, the most constant and debilitating drain on the strength of the young Russian nation was the unceasing war against the Tatars of the Crimean Khanate, behind whom stood their suzerain, the mighty Ottoman Empire. In their frequent, and in some periods annual, attacks, the Tatars appeared suddenly from the steppes, plundering and destroying, but concentrating mainly on taking captives to sell as slaves in the markets of the Mediterranean. Regularly the Russians manned their defenses, which in places were no more than a hundred miles south of Moscow. Gradually they established defense posts and fortified towns along this southern frontier and pressed southwards.

This struggle against the Tatars dominated Russia's history for nearly three centuries. The Russian historian Klyuchevsky observed: "If one thinks of the amount of time and the material and spiritual forces consumed in this wearying, violent, and painful pursuit of the steppe predator, one can hardly ask what the people of Eastern Europe were doing while Western Europe was achieving its triumphs in industry and commerce, in social life, in the arts and the sciences."

The Crimean Khanate was finally conquered and in 1783 incorporated into the Russian Empire. The invasions and wars which had characterized Russia's history became more intermittent. But early in the nineteenth century Napoleon invaded Russia. A terrible battle was fought at Borodino, and the French occupied Moscow, which was partially destroyed by fire. In the twentieth century Russia has experienced two devastating invasions by the Germans.

The tragedies of war have been alive in the memories of all Russians throughout their history. It is doubtful whether any other nation has suffered so constantly from the horrors of invasion. The long experience has implanted in the people a sense of vulnerability and of menace to their homelands. It is indeed difficult for Anglo-Saxons, whether in Britain or America, who have long enjoyed security, to understand the pressures of military service and the unending terror and tragedy of such a history.

"No people in the world have a greater veneration for their prince than the Muscovites who from their infancy are taught to speak of the Tsar as of God Himself," observed Adam Olearius, a seventeenth-century visitor.

The Tsar was surrounded with the magnificence and ceremonial of Byzantium. He was not merely an object of worship. He was vested with the same absolute power as the Mongol Khans. His subjects were his slaves who owed him service and obedience. The Mongol heritage was reinforced and in some ways transformed by the influence of Byzantium and the Orthodox Church, which inculcated the doctrine of Caesaropapism. The Tsar stood as head not only of the nation but also of the Church, and was God's vicar on earth. Briefly during the Time of Troubles (1605–13), when the Rurikid dynasty became extinct, when the Poles invaded the country and occupied Moscow, and Muscovy was reduced to anarchy, the faith of the people in the divine authority of their Tsars was shaken. But it revived quickly with the establishment of the Romanov dynasty in 1613. The tradition of veneration, servility, and absolute obedience to the Tsar was to endure without basic change until the Revolution in 1917. In this tradition were rooted the deification of Lenin and the power and worship of Stalin.

The chief function of the Tsar was to mobilize men and resources for defense. The people had to be organized on military lines to ensure that forces were ready on the southern frontiers and against enemies in the west. The country was vast and the process of colonizing the lands to the east and south meant that the population was scattered. A system evolved whereby everyone was in complete bondage to the autocrat. It was based on what was in effect the nationalization of the land, which was granted to the serving nobility on the condition of their service. It followed from the granting of these *pomestie*, or service estates, that the peasants, too, were bound to the land. Serfdom developed during the seventeenth century into a system of bondage, akin to slavery. All including the nobility were the slaves, or *kholopi*, of the Tsar.

In enforcing service and tax-paying obligations in a country so immense and sparsely populated, the state applied savage methods, derived from the Mongols. Execution, flogging with the knout or *batogi*, which could cause death, and other cruel punishments were commonplace. All subjects of the Tsar were liable to the same treatment. Only in the later eighteenth century were the nobility and the priesthood granted immunity from flogging. Exile and hard labor in Siberia became common sentences in the nineteenth century.

The Tsar's special police, who began in 1565 with the Oprichniki of Tsar Ivan IV and developed as the Okhrana and the Third Section of His Majesty's Own Chancery, were ubiquitous. Throughout their history the Russians, acknowledging their complete subservience to the Tsar, accepted the punishments meted out in his name. The methods of enforcing authority brutalized the nation, but aroused no protest. Indeed, the Russians felt a fervent patriotism and an exalted love for their country and its regime, believing that it was superior to those of other countries. It was an outlook which astonished Western travelers, who were appalled by the bondage, brutal treatment, and impoverished conditions endured by the mass of the people.

Nikolai Karamzin, the leading Russian historian of the early nineteenth century, wrote: "Our ancestors, while assimilating many advantages which were to be found in foreign customs, never lost the conviction that an Orthodox Russian was the most perfect citizen and Holy Rus was the foremost state in the world. Let this be called a delusion. Yet how much it did to strengthen the patriotism and the moral fibre of the nation." Karamzin himself did not consider this idea of superiority a delusion, nor did the great mass of the Russian people.

The Russians of Kiev and Novgorod had had close ties of trade and culture with the West. Then for nearly 250 years (1240–1480) they were under the yoke of the Mongol Khans, and were isolated. They knew nothing of the Renaissance, the Reformation, the explorations, and the scientific discoveries which transformed the West. Painfully in the sixteenth and seventeenth centuries the Tsars awakened to Russia's backwardness, especially in the arts of war. The English merchants who made their way to Muscovy were welcomed by Tsar Ivan IV, because he needed Western military expertise. Peter the Great (1682–1725), who fought against Russia's backwardness and isolation throughout his reign, was primarily interested in Western naval and military techniques. He recognized, however, that Russia's security could not rest on military might alone, but must be rooted in economic strength and efficient government.

The Western influence, which swept into Russia in the seventeenth and eighteenth centuries, disturbed the people. They regarded all that came from the West with the deepest suspicion. They knew nothing about the countries beyond their frontiers and were not allowed to travel. The Western experts, engaged in the Tsar's service, were obliged to live in the "Foreign Quarter" outside Moscow, so that they would not contaminate Orthodox people. Staunchly conservative Muscovites held to their practices and traditions, believing them to be superior.

The Orthodox Church strengthened them in this conviction. The Russians received Christianity from Byzantium towards the end of the tenth century. The new faith took deep root among them and profoundly influenced their outlook. The Mongol Khans had been tolerant of Christianity, and during their occupation the Russian church had developed vigorously. It played a momentous role in the founding of the Russian nation, and, while acknowledging the primacy of Constantinople as the center of Orthodox Christendom, it became strongly nationalistic.

In 1453 Constantinople fell to the infidel Turk. Already independent, the Russian church assumed the role of heir. The legend of Moscow as the Third Rome was fostered and became for the devout Russians an article of faith. This legend enhanced the authority and standing of the autocrat and the renown of Moscow. It also gave expression to the Russian sense of mission. Their church was the sole guardian of the true Christian faith. They would lead the nations of the world, and specifically of the West, to unity, brotherhood, and salvation.

In the twentieth century this messianism could no longer be expressed in terms of Orthodox Christianity or of Moscow—the Third Rome. Marxism-Leninism became the creed of which the Russians purported to be the guardians for the peoples of the West and of the world.

Along with their claim to possession of the true dogma, the Russians have continued to regard themselves as bearing a mission to lead and protect Western civilization. Russia, they have long asserted, shielded the West against the Mongol horde of Genghis Khan, against the Tatars of the Crimea, and the Turks.

This sense of mission is as strong today as in the past. In World War II Russia saved the West by defeating the fascist powers. According to Soviet pronouncements, Russians were fighting not only to defend their own country "but to free the peoples of Europe from fascism, to save the world from its barbarism and bestiality." Claims of this kind are characteristic, and they express the sense of messianic mission to lead and convert, which has been embedded in the Russian outlook since the fifteenth century.

"Russia is a European power," declared Catherine the Great, and she went on to state that Russia had always been a European country. The statement was frequently debated in the nineteenth century and remains a matter of contention. Whether true or not, the fact is that Russia has always differed strikingly in social values and traditions from the West. Visitors have always expressed astonishment and horror at the bondage, brutality, secretiveness and suspicion, the messianism, and other aspects of Russian life. Also they have usually shown a sense of superiority and at times an arrogant condescension, while George F. Kennan and other twentieth-century writers have displayed a lofty moral disapprobation towards many Russian practices.

The Russians have always been sensitive to criticism and to being patronized. Indeed, Stalin complained about the superior attitude of British naval officers, serving in North Russia during the war, towards the Red Navy. Western attitudes of moral superiority have helped intensify the mistrust, secretiveness, and even hostility of Russians towards foreigners. Moreover, as Vasily Klyuchevsky observed, they have felt that Westerners have never appreciated the long bitter struggle for survival and the other factors that have hampered Russian development. Western attitudes have, in fact, helped fortify the Russian sense of their own special strength and mission.

In their attitude to the West the Russians have been divided. The Westernizers, represented by Peter the Great and symbolized by his city of St. Petersburg, have sought to discard most of the conservative Muscovite traditions, to reform Russia, and to join fully in the Western community of nations. The Slavophiles, sometimes known as the Muscovites, embracing the great mass of the nation, have cherished the old traditions and asserted their belief in the innate superiority of the Russian people in their strength and their moral values. They have sought minimal relations with the West, convinced that Russia would develop in her own way to strength and world leadership. The conflict between these views has been consistently reflected in the rivalry between Moscow and St. Petersburg.

In adopting Russia as his country, Stalin absorbed the outlook and traditions of the Muscovites and their faith in the destiny of the Russian nation.

1

First Years
1879-88

Iosif Vissarionovich Dzhugashvili, known in history as Iosif Stalin, was born on December 9 (21), 1879, in the ancient Georgian town of Gori. Situated on the banks of the swift-flowing Kura River and surrounded by hills, Gori is the center of a beautiful district of the Tiflis province, in which the valleys are renowned for vineyards, wheat fields, and orchards. It is part of the region, known to the ancient Greeks as Colchis, where Jason and the Argonauts quested for the Golden Fleece. In these idyllic surroundings Iosif spent his boyhood.

Vissarion, his father, came from the village of Didi-Lilo, near Tiflis, where his parents, like their forebears, had been peasant-serfs. For Vissarion emancipation meant that he was free to follow his trade as a cobbler. Around 1870 he moved to Gori, where in 1874 he married Ekaterina Georgievna Geladze, daughter of a serf family from a nearby village. She was about eighteen years of age, some five years younger than her husband. They were humble working people, poor and illiterate. They set up home in a modest

domik in Soborovaya Street near the main cathedral in Gori. It
comprised a front porch and two rooms with brick floors and also
a basement. The main room was about fifteen feet square and
poorly lit by one window. It was furnished with a small table, four
stools, a small buffet with a samovar, a mirror, a trunk holding
their belongings, and a plank bed with straw mattress. Steps led
down to the cellar, where Ekaterina probably cooked on an open
fire. By Russian standards of the day it was by no means untypical
accommodation for a poor family.[1]

In this house Ekaterina bore three children, all of whom died in
infancy. The fourth child was Iosif, and on him, her Soso or
Soselo, the affectionate diminutives of Iosif, she lavished her love
and care.

Information about Vissarion is scanty. He was apparently unsuccessful in earning a living as a cobbler. In 1885 he returned to
Tiflis, taking a job in a shoe factory belonging to an Armenian
named Adelkhanov, where he had worked for a time before his
marriage.

Stalin referred only once publicly to his father when he pointed
out that as a cobbler his father was not a true proletarian since he
still had a petty bourgeois mentality.[2] He made one other public
mention of his childhood and his parents. This was in December
1931 when he gave an interview to Emil Ludwig, the popular bi-
ographer of the time. To the question "What impelled you to become an oppositionist? Was it perhaps bad treatment by your parents?" Stalin answered, "No. My parents were uneducated, but
they did not treat me badly by any means."[3] This statement
conflicts with other accounts of his childhood.[4]

Iosif Iremashvili, one of Iosif's boyhood friends, described Vissarion as thick-set in build, with black eyebrows and mustache,
stern and irascible in temperament. He was said to have been a
drunkard. Georgians had a reputation for drinking heavily. In
Georgia and in Russia "drunk as a cobbler" was a common expression.

Iremashvili, writing years later and with the hindsight and bias
of an émigré, observed that "undeserved and frightful beatings
made the boy as grim and heartless as was his father."[5]
Stalin's daughter, Svetlana, relates that her father told her how

in defense of his mother "one day he threw a knife at his father. The father rushed after him screaming and neighbours hid the boy."[6]

His mother, Ekaterina, was the dominant person in his childhood. When young she was apparently an attractive, red-headed woman. Like her husband, she spoke only Georgian, but in later years she learned to read and at least to write her name in Russian in order to be worthy of her son. He was the center of her life. Since her husband drank what he earned or could not earn enough to keep them, she had to "slave day and night to make ends meet in her poor household."[7] After Vissarion had gone to Tiflis, it was probably easier, for she had to care only for herself and Iosif. She washed clothes, baked bread, cleaned, and sewed. She kept him clothed and well fed, so that he grew into a strong healthy boy with exceptional energy and stamina.

Ekaterina was deeply religious, but it was also for social reasons that she decided that Iosif should enter the priesthood. The emancipation of the serfs had opened the gates of the theological colleges to peasant boys of exceptional ability. Ordained as a priest, he would marry and have charge of a parish; he would move up in the world and, while serving God, he would enjoy ease and security such as she had never known. This was her consuming ambition for her son, and she worked hard to achieve it.

Gori boasted four schools, including the elementary theological school in which Ekaterina managed to enroll her son. At this time he spoke only Georgian, and she arranged for him to have lessons in Russian, the indispensable language. Also she obtained for him a monthly allowance of three rubles. She earned ten rubles as a laundress and cleaner at the school. On this meager income she maintained herself and Iosif during the next five years.

Two events threatened her plans with disaster. In 1886 Iosif became desperately ill with smallpox. His tough constitution pulled him through, but his face was always to be deeply pock-marked. The second threat was the opposition of her husband, who was determined to apprentice the boy to his father's trade. "You want my son to be a priest, a church official, don't you?" he expostulated. "You'll never live to see it happen! Yes, I'm a cobbler and my son will be a cobbler like me."[8]

Stalin

One day, probably in 1889, Vissarion came to Gori and took his son away to the Adelkhanov factory in Tiflis. It was a stormy family event. His wife and neighbors tried to dissuade him, but he stubbornly insisted that his son must be apprenticed in the shoe factory. Details of the struggle over Iosif's future are not known, but Ekaterina had the last word, for the boy returned to school in Gori. [9]

Stalin never mentioned this episode, and indeed his silence generally about his father may have been due to the hatred that he felt for this man who had beaten him and his mother, and had shamed them both by his drunkenness. Though he was only eleven years old when his father died in 1890, stabbed to death in a drunken brawl, his experiences probably left only grim memories.

For his mother he felt a strong and enduring love. She was a woman of high principles, puritanical in outlook, and stubborn. She was strict and beat him at times, but no doubt she also indulged him. As a boy he was close to her and appreciated that her life was hard. It was to become extremely lonely: The son whom she adored went to Tiflis at the age of fifteen. He came home to her for short periods during the next five years, but then he virtually passed out of her life. She was to hear about him constantly, but by then he belonged to another world; he had become the great leader and ruler of Russia, remote from Georgia and even more remote from the simple surroundings of her life.

Ekaterina remained a devout woman of simple, even austere, tastes. Stalin spoke of her as "an intelligent woman" although uneducated, and he respected her, too, for her upright character. Concerned about her lonely way of life, he persuaded her to move to Moscow, and for a short time she stayed in the Kremlin. But the change was too great. She returned to the quiet warmth and the familiar ways of Georgia.

A photograph, taken in 1932, shows the face of an old lady in black Georgian costume. The mouth is firm and sensitive, but the expression of the eyes is sad and bewildered.[10] Two years later when her grandchildren paid her a visit, they found her half-seated on a narrow iron cot in her small room in the old palace in Tiflis; she had been offered more luxurious accommodation, but this was her choice. The grandchildren had little communication with her, because only one of them understood Georgian. Their visit apparently moved her deeply, for she was in tears much of the time.[11]

She never understood the high office of her son and the adulation surrounding him. When he went to see her shortly before she died, she said to him, "What a pity you never became a priest!"[12] It was the great regret of her life. Stalin used to recount the remark with approval of "her scorn for what he'd accomplished, for the clamour and world glory."[13] He, too, was little concerned with the panoply of high office, and like her he was also austere in his way of life. In 1936, aged about eighty, she died.

2

The Georgian Schoolboy
1888–94

Iosif spent five years at the Gori Theological School. His mother no doubt impressed on him the need to work hard, but he was by nature fiercely competitive; he had to excel and to prove himself better than others. He was naturally intelligent and gifted with an exceptional memory. His marks were always high, and he was regarded as the "best student," leaving the school in July 1894, aged fourteen, with a certificate of honor.[1] The school authorities recommended him for a place in the Tiflis Theological Seminary. For the son of a humble family whose father's drunkenness and sordid death were doubtless known to the priests, the recommendation was a mark of faith in the boy's ability and future.

Iremashvili described Iosif as being at this time thin and wiry with aquiline nose and narrow pock-marked face, his eyes dark, lively, and disturbing. Although small in build he was strong and the best wrestler in the school. But he was "different from other children," and disliked for his surly bullying manner.[2] Like many men of ability who are small physically and suffer from poverty, lowly birth, or physical disability, he was aggressive and eager to assert himself.[3] Iremashvili wrote that "as a child and youth he was a good friend so long as one submitted to his imperious will."[4]

While he was at school in Gori, Iosif fell seriously ill again. This time it was blood poisoning, which affected his left arm. Speaking of this illness years later to his sister-in-law, Anna Alliluyeva, he remarked, "I don't know what saved me then, my strong constitution or the ointment of a village quack."[5] It left him with a slight shortening and withering of the left arm. Trotsky noted that in later years he wore a warm glove on his left hand, even at sessions of the Politburo.[6] This further disability no doubt intensified his sense of disadvantage and his need to assert himself.

At school Iosif became a voracious reader and, according to Iremashvili, read "almost all the books" in the Gori Library.[7] Emelyan Yaroslavsky stated that at this time he read Marx and Darwin and became an atheist. When a schoolfellow spoke of God, Iosif cut him short. "You know they deceive us. There is no God. . . . I'll lend you a book to read; it will show you that the world and all living things are quite different from what you imagined, and all this talk about God is sheer nonsense."[8] This incident, if true, probably took place later when as a student at the seminary he certainly lost his faith. It is unlikely, too, that Marxist ideas were known outside a small circle of intellectuals in Tiflis at this time. It was claimed, nevertheless, that Iosif was able to obtain this and other works from a private bookshop in the town.[9]

Two years after he had started at the school there was a drastic change in teaching. Georgian had always been the language of instruction, but in 1890, as part of Alexander III's rigorously enforced policy of Russification, all instruction was given in Russian, and Georgian became officially a foreign language, taught in two lessons a week.[10]

Vano Ketskhoveli, one of Iosif's schoolfellows, wrote that "in the upper classes of Gori school we became acquainted with Georgian literature, but we had no mentor to guide our development and give a definite direction to our thoughts. Chavchavadze's poem 'Kako the Robber' made a deep impression on us. Kazbegi's heroes awakened in our youthful hearts a love for our country and each of us on leaving school was inspired with an eagerness to serve his country. But none of us had a clear idea what form this service should take."[11]

This love for their country and its literature was all the more understandable because Georgia has a romantic history and a rich cultural heritage. Iosif was attracted by the romantic Georgian heroes. He read Shota Rustaveli's classic, *Knight in the Panther's Skin*, but was most impressed by Kazbegi's stories of the mountain rebel, Koba (The Implacable). He began to use Koba as a nickname; later it was to be the name he used most frequently until about 1910, when he started calling himself Koba Stalin and then finally Iosif Stalin.

The Caucasian isthmus was on one of the ancient invasion routes. Scythians, Cimmerians, Greeks, Arabs, Mongols, Turks, Persians, and finally the Russians had occupied the land. Georgia, like Armenia, the other Christian nation in Transcaucasia, settled down under Russian rule. The Georgians saw the Tsar as their natural protector against Turks and Persians, and they looked to Moscow as the center of Orthodoxy. Moreover, the Georgian nobility and gentry were numerous and impoverished. Many seized the opportunity to go north, attracted by the glittering court of St. Petersburg and the rewards to be won in the Russian service.

Throughout these centuries, despite the destruction wrought by conquerors, the loss of lives in innumerable wars, the insatiable demands by Turks, Persians, and others for Caucasian slaves, and the migration to the north, Georgians, drawing strength from their ancient culture, managed to endure as a nation.

Georgians tend to be tall and lean with dark complexion and black hair. In temperament they are said to be wild, unpredictable, impetuous, generous and hospitable, animated in conversation, a laughing nation of poets and orators, and great drinkers of the wines they produce.

Generalizations about national character are at best approximate, but often they contain elements of truth. Iosif, however, was utterly untypical except perhaps for certain physical features. Early in his career he began to think of himself as a Russian and to scorn Georgians, perhaps because they were pleasure-loving, ebullient, romantic people who so easily lost touch with reality.

3

The Seminarist
1894-99

Tiflis, the capital of Georgia, is in the hot dusty western region of the country. It is an ancient city, with spacious squares and avenues and, leading from them, narrow crooked streets, enclosed by crowding flat-roofed houses and bazaars where traders from Turkey and Persia as well as Georgians and Armenians jostled and bargained.

At the turn of the century its population was over 150,000, of which the Armenians, Georgians, and Russians were the main elements. As the seat of the Tsar's viceroy and the government center of Transcaucasia, which embraced not only Georgia but also parts of Armenia and Azerbaijan, Tiflis was a bustling polyglot city.

The Russian government, recognizing the importance of Transcaucasia as a frontier zone, had built a military highway to strengthen its defenses. But the region was taking on a new economic significance. Oil and mining industries were developing rapidly with the aid of foreign capital and expertise. In 1867 work began on a railway from Tiflis to the Black Sea, and the line was soon extended from Tiflis to Baku on the Caspian Sea.

For the fifteen-year-old Iosif the move from Gori to this bustling city must have been a momentous change. He had always lived at home, cared for by his mother, and now he was alone in strange surroundings. Ekaterina, too, was alone, but she could take pride in the fact that her son had gained a place in the Tiflis Theological Seminary, which was held in great respect by Orthodox Georgians as their foremost institution of higher education.

Like seminaries in other parts of the Empire, its purpose was not only to provide education but also to train its students for the religious life. In the second half of the nineteenth century, however, a fever of unrest was sweeping through Europe. In Russia it erupted with special force in the seminaries.

By the time of Iosif's enrollment, the Tiflis seminary had become a center of opposition to the Russian authorities. In 1885 Sylvestr Dzhibladze, a student who was to become a revolutionary leader, was banished to Siberia for assaulting the principal, Chudetsky, who had spoken of Georgian as "a language for dogs," and in the following year Chudetsky was murdered by another student. In March 1890 the students went on strike for a week. Late in 1893 Mikhail Tskhakaya and Lado Ketskhoveli, both to become active revolutionaries, led another student strike. The police closed the seminary, and eighty-seven students were expelled.[1]

The archives of the Tiflis police, published in 1930, revealed that as early as 1873 there were reports of students reading forbidden books, and the works of Darwin, Buckle, Mill, and Chernyshevsky were mentioned.[2] A search in the seminary brought to light copies of Renan's *La Vie de Jésus* and Hugo's *Napoléon le Petit*. Three teachers were dismissed for their "liberal spirit." The police archives stressed, however, that ardent nationalism rather than liberal or revolutionary ideas was the real source of the students' unrest.

At the time of Iosif's arrival the principal of the seminary was a Russian monk, Germogenes, and the inspector Abashidze, a Georgian, eager to gain promotion from the Russian authorities. Remembering the murder of Chudetsky, they were concerned for their own safety and alarmed by the rebellious mood of the students. They enforced discipline strictly, and, ever watchful, they spied on the students and often searched the dormitories.

"Locked within barrack walls we felt like prisoners, guiltless of any crime, who were forced to spend a long term in jail," Iremashvili wrote.[3] Each day in the seminary followed a rigid routine. All gathered in the chapel at 7 A.M. for the lengthy Orthodox service. Lessons and prayers alternated during the day. With special permission, a student might go out for two hours at the end of classes, but he had to return by 5 P.M., when the gates were locked. Discipline was harsh. The punishment for small misdemeanors was solitary confinement in one of the dark cells in the basement. Persecution by the monks, poor food, and lack of fresh air and exercise broke the health and spirit of many boys.

During his first two years in the seminary, Iosif evidently impressed his teachers as an able and obedient student. He was eighth in class in the first year and fifth in the second. With his quick brain and retentive memory he was able to absorb the theological training, and he was never to lose his feeling for the rhythms and poetry of the liturgy and of the New and Old Testaments. Moreover, the curriculum included mathematics, Greek, and Latin as well as Russian literature and history. Although formal and limited in range, it provided a sound basic education.

At the same time he was learning the skills and cunning of the conspirator. He came to hate the seminary and its monks, and what he later called its "humiliating regime."[4] He was readily infected with the rebellious spirit which was rife among the students.[5] But the monks had no inkling of his real feelings until later when he no longer bothered to conceal them.

Iremashvili, who entered the seminary at the same time, evidently held Iosif in some awe. He stood apart from his fellow students and was not popular. The boy who in the Gori Theological School had felt a desperate need to assert himself over others was becoming more formidable. In the grim atmosphere of the seminary he was discovering his own strength and learning self-discipline.

At this time Iosif began reading more widely.[6] There was a circulating library in Tiflis from which he borrowed books. His read-

ing embraced not only Georgian poetry but also Russian and Western classics. Gogol, Saltykov-Shchedrin, Chekhov, and Tolstoy
became his favorite Russian writers. He read translations of Bal-
zac, Hugo, and Thackeray, whose *Vanity Fair* made an impression
on him. He also absorbed books on history, economics, and biol-
ogy. Noteworthy titles on his list were Darwin's *Descent of Man*,
Feuerbach's *Essence of Christianity*, Buckle's *History of Civilization in England*, Spinoza's *Ethics*, Letourneau's *Literary Evolu-
tion of the Nations*, and Mendeleyev's *Chemistry*. It was a bold
reading program for a young theology student. As with the liturgy
and the Bible, he did not forget what he read. Years later he
would quote and refer to many of these books.

Iosif also wrote poetry during his first two years in the seminary.
He never referred to his verses and neither acknowledged nor denied authorship. Five poems were published in the second half of
1893 and the sixth poem in the following year. They were forgotten until December 1939 when, as part of the celebrations of his
sixtieth birthday, the Tiflis newspaper, *Zarya Vostoka* (Dawn of
the East) reprinted them under the banner heading *Stikhi Yunogo
Stalina* (Verses of the Young Stalin).

The poems are romantic and strongly nationalistic in spirit. He
dedicated one to the memory of Prince Rafael Eristavi, a popular
Georgian poet, and in it he expressed his great love of his country. The other poem which claims special attention is "To the
Moon," an impassioned lyric invoking the Georgian martyrs who
had fallen to foreign oppressors. If indeed written by Iosif, the
poems are evidence of his fervor as a Georgian patriot at this
time.

In the course of his interview with Stalin, Emil Ludwig mentioned that the Czech statesman T. G. Mazaryk had claimed that
he had felt himself to be a socialist at the age of six. He then
asked Stalin what had made him a socialist and when. The reply
was: "I cannot assert that I was already drawn to socialism at the
age of six. Not even at the age of ten or twelve. I joined the revolutionary movement when fifteen years old, when I became connected with underground groups of Russian Marxists then living
in Transcaucasia. These groups exerted great influence on me and
instilled in me a taste for underground Marxist literature. . . . It

was a different matter at the Orthodox theological seminary which I was then attending. In protest against the outrageous regime and Jesuitical methods prevalent in the seminary, I was ready to become and actually did become a revolutionary, a believer in Marxism as a truly revolutionary teaching."[7]

It is more probable, however, that Iosif became a Marxist not in 1894 but two or three years later. The harsh regime had certainly antagonized him, but he always hated authority imposed on him by others. He could not accept opposition or criticism from fellow students and retaliated with sarcasm and abuse. Iremashvili considered him to be intensely ambitious and interested not in Marxism, but in dominating others.[8]

The records of the seminary show that the model student who studied diligently during his first and second years was coming into conflict with the monks. In November 1896 an assistant supervisor, Murakhovsky, noted in the conduct book:

> It appears that Dzhugashvili has a ticket to the cheap library from which he borrows books. Today I confiscated Victor Hugo's *Toilers of the Sea* in which I found the said library ticket. The principal, Father Germogenes, endorsed the entry with the ruling: "Confine him to the punishment cell for a prolonged period. I have already warned him once about an unsanctioned book, *Ninety-three*, by Victor Hugo."[9]

In March 1897 the same Murakhovsky made another entry:

> At 11 A.M. I took away from Iosif Dzhugashvili Letourneau's *Literary Evolution of the Nations* which he had borrowed from the cheap library. The library ticket was found in the book. Dzhugashvili was found reading the said book on the chapel stairs. This is the thirteenth time that this student has been discovered reading books borrowed from the cheap library. I handed the book to the Father Supervisor.[10]

For Iosif this must have been a time of uncertainty. He knew that he had no vocation for the priesthood and indeed had lost his belief in Orthodoxy. But he did not know what to do with his life. Sasha Tsulukidze and Lado Ketskhoveli, both older than Iosif, were the two remarkable men who influenced him most in this period. They were typical of the galaxy of young people who appeared in Russia at the turn of the century. All were brave, imaginative, and enterprising; but all were motivated by a bitter hatred of the existing order, believing that through destruction they were reaching towards a millennium in which the people would enjoy justice and plenty; at least the majority would enjoy it, the minority having been blown up or eliminated in some similar way.

Tsulukidze, who came of a princely family, was an intellectual with literary ability. He was devoted to the revolutionary cause and contributed articles in Georgian to *Kvali* (The Furrow) and *Iberia*, the leading publications, seeking to explain and popularize Marxist theories. When he died of tuberculosis in June 1905, all Georgian revolutionaries attended his funeral, which developed into a popular demonstration. Iosif had his friend's writings collected and published in book form in 1927 as a tribute to his memory.

Lado Ketskhoveli was very different in character from Tsulukidze, the feverish intellectual. He was a tireless and enterprising man of action. He had attended the same theological school in Gori and the seminary in Tiflis and then had embarked on a revolutionary career. After the famous strike in the seminary in December 1893 he had gone to Kiev, where he was arrested, held in prison for three months, and on his release was kept under police surveillance. In 1897 he returned to Tiflis and worked fanatically in the revolutionary underground.

The two friends encouraged Iosif's interest in Marxism. They were probably his sponsors when he joined Messame Dassy (The Third Group), the first Marxist social democratic organization in Georgia.[11] Its founders were Noi Zhordania, a former student of the seminary and later president of the independent Republic of Georgia (1918–21), and K. Chkheidze, G. Tseretelli, and Sylvestr Dzhibladze, all of whom were to hold prominent positions until as moderates they were displaced. Noi Zhordania was the leader of the group.

Messame Dassy was a legal organization, functioning with police approval. It published *Kvali*, a daily newspaper in Georgian, and *Moambeh* (The Herald), a monthly journal. Tsulukidze and Ketskhoveli were strongly critical of both publications. They wanted defiance, the excitement of conspiracy and of dramatic, violent action against the tsarist regime.[12]

Membership of Messame Dassy was nevertheless a major step in Iosif's development. Discussions with his two friends and contacts with other members of the group broadened his interest in Marxism. He was given the responsibility of running a workers' study circle. Recalling these meetings in later years, Stalin said: "I received my first lessons of practical work in the apartment of Comrade Sturua in the presence of Dzhibladze (he was also one of my teachers), Chodrishvili, Chkheidze, Bochorishvili, Ninua, and other foremost workers of Tiflis."[13] It was a new and stimulating experience for the nineteen-year-old revolutionary to be lecturing to workers. But he was still a seminarist, and the severe limits on his freedom undoubtedly irked him all the more at this time when he was finding so much to do.

In his *Memoirs*, written in Paris in the 1930s, Noi Zhordania recalled:

> At the end of 1898 I was head of *Kvali*. One day a young man appeared at the editorial offices and presented himself: "I am Dzhugashvili, a student at the Theological Seminary." Having requested that I hear him out, he began with: "I am a faithful reader of your journal and your articles. All of them have made a great impression on me. I have decided to quit the seminary and spend my time amongst the workers. Give me your advice."
>
> His decision pleased me. In the Tiflis social democratic organization there were too few propagandists. But before I gave him any advice I considered it necessary to verify the mental equipment of this young man. When I posed several questions about history, sociology and political economy, I was surprised that he had only a superficial notion concerning all of them. His political knowledge had come from the articles in *Kvali* and Kautsky's Erfurt programme. I explained that it would be difficult to function under these conditions. Our workers were curious and wanted knowledge. When they were persuaded that a propagandist was ignorant, they would turn away and refuse to listen. I advised Dzhugashvili to remain one more year in the seminary and to undertake some self-education. "I'll think about it," he replied and departed.[14]

Zhordania was probably patronizing towards the young student and, like other embittered and impotent political enemies writing their memoirs in exile, he tried to denigrate this man who had become supreme ruler. Certainly he exaggerated Iosif's lack of education. Then nineteen years old, he had shown himself to be an able student and he had read widely, interesting himself closely in Marxism and revolutionary ideas. His approach to the editor of *Kvali*, who was one of the best known political writers in Georgia at this time, nevertheless seems likely. Life in the seminary had become intolerable. Membership of Messame Dassy and the experience of talking to the study circle of workers had given him a sense of purpose. He sought advice as he felt his way towards the final decision to give himself wholly to revolutionary work.

Soviet accounts of Iosif's political activities during 1898 attribute to him an importance that could hardly be justified at this state. It was said that he had become the foremost critic and opponent of Zhordania's views, and that he was a leading force among the railway workers, organizing them to stage a major strike in December 1898.[15] But he was then still at the seminary and an apprentice revolutionary. He would have had little influence among the railwaymen and would have made no headway in opposing the highly respected leaders of Messame Dassy.

By the end of 1898, Iosif's attitude towards the seminary authorities had become insolent and defiant. In December 1898 the assistant supervisor wrote in the conduct book:

> In the course of a search of students of the fifth class by members of the board of supervision, Iosif Dzhugashvili tried several times to enter into argument with them, expressing dissatisfaction with the repeated searches of students and declaring that such searches were never made in other seminaries. Dzhugashvili is generally disrespectful and rude towards persons in authority and persistently refuses to bow to one of the masters [S. A. Murakhovsky], as the latter has repeatedly complained to the board of supervision.

Iosif's punishment was solitary confinement in the cells for five hours.[16]

Finally on May 27, 1899, the council of the seminary expelled him "for having missed his examinations for an unexplained reason."[17] The decision came as an anticlimax. The monks had not expelled him for leading a revolution among the students. He himself later stated that he had been "turned out of the theological seminary for propagating Marxism."[18] His mother was insistent that he had not been expelled and that she herself had taken him away. Speaking in 1930 to H. R. Knickerbocker, an American journalist, she said: "I brought him home on account of his health. When he entered the seminary he was as strong as a boy could be. But overwork up to the age of nineteen pulled him down, and the doctors told me that he might develop tuberculosis. So I took him away from school. He did not want to leave. But I took him away. He was my only son."[19]

It is clear that, whatever the real reason for his departure from the seminary, Iosif himself did not make the decision. But now that he was free he threw himself into the career of a dedicated professional revolutionary, and became Koba, "The Implacable."

4

Koba the Revolutionary 1899–1902

At the time of leaving the seminary, Koba's instinctive feeling of rebellion was growing into a savage need to challenge and destroy the tsarist regime. Eagerly he read all the revolutionary material he could lay his hands on and talked with others who were fired by the new spirit of revolution, but he could not yet find the kind of guidance and the answers that he needed. The writings of Plekhanov and of Lenin stimulated his ideas, but living far away in Georgia he had no real contact with the revolutionary movement.

Russian revolutionaries, living abroad, were sundered by furious, often vicious, polemics. Georgy Plekhanov, the father of Russian social democracy, considered himself the arbiter in all matters concerning the movement in Russia. He was incensed by the heresy of "Economism," which argued that workers should concentrate on improving wages and conditions. A more serious heresy, perpetrated by the "Legal Marxists," denounced violent revolution. To all orthodox Marxists this was "revisionism" and "reformism," terms of strongest communist censure. Lenin, who was emerging as the dominant leader of the Russian movement, regarded any argument that ruled out violent revolution as the worst form of apostasy.

Underlying these heresies was the basic question of the applicability of Marxism to Russia. It was a Western doctrine, conceived and rooted in the industrialized, capitalist societies of western Europe. In embracing Marxism, Plekhanov, Axelrod, Martov, Lenin, and others had accepted that Russia must reach the same stage of industrialization before there would be a mass proletariat, able to rise in revolution and assert its power.

The fact that in Russia at the end of the century the peasants comprised well over 100 million of the total population (excluding Finland) of 170 million made this goal extremely remote. From about 1892, however, under the able direction of Count Sergei Witte, Minister of Finance and Economy, industrialization developed with astonishing momentum. Plekhanov and others began to think that the goal of a mass proletariat might not be so far distant. But Lenin, impatient for action and power, realized that Marxism had to be adapted to Russian conditions.

Returning from exile in February 1900, Lenin stayed briefly in Pskov and then moved to Munich. He was eager to convene a congress to outlaw all heresies and to restore unity to the Russian social democratic movement. He was also planning to produce a paper to be called *Iskra* (The Spark). On December 24 (11), 1900, the first issue was published in Leipzig. Copies were smuggled across the frontier and it at once became influential as the voice of the Marxist movement in Russia.

Far away in Georgia, Iosif Dzhugashvili, or Koba as he now called himself, probably heard about the heresies and the wrangling among the Social Democrats abroad. He was not impressed, for he was intolerant of the émigré Marxists who lived in comfort in capitalist countries and devoted their time to internecine disputes. True revolutionaries faced risks while teaching and organizing the workers. But he was soon taking special interest in *Iskra*.

Reliable information on his life and activities is scanty for the period from May 1889, when he left the seminary, until December 1905, when he attended the Tammerfors Conference and first met Lenin. Certain historians described him as leading a vast underground revolutionary movement in these years. To them it was clear that he must have been a prodigy, like Athena who sprang from the head of Zeus, fully armed and uttering a war cry. Hostile writers seized on these early years as revealing his backwardness and inability to contribute to the movement.

Trotsky wrote of his "slowness of intellect, lack of talent, and the general colourlessness of his physical and moral countenance."[1] Souvarine, pointing to his lack of influence, rated him as having the qualifications of a noncommissioned officer.[2] At this time Koba may indeed have seemed a raw recruit, aggressive because unsure of himself in the company of intellectuals. He was a fringe member of the intelligentsia, without a professional or noble background. Among even the *paznochintsi*, an indeterminate class, his origins were humble. A bitter sense of social inferiority, intensified by his pock-marked face and deformed arm, must have been factors in his general awkwardness and aggressiveness towards others, including friends and colleagues, and in his self-effacement.

This period was, nevertheless, an important stage in his long apprenticeship. He began learning in earnest from other revolutionaries and from workers, especially the railwaymen, who were the most awakened politically. He lived a clandestine existence outside society, hounded by the police. He is espied from time to time, but then vanishes into the shadows. It was a grim, often squalid, way of life, relieved only by the sense of striving with a few comrades towards the goals of revolution and a new society. He was, however, well equipped for underground life. He had courage, self-discipline, patience, sharp intelligence, and a strong instinct for survival.[3]

After leaving the seminary he may have spent some time with his mother in Gori, regaining his health. He earned money tutoring children of wealthy families in Tiflis, and presumably lived in some worker's hovel. Among his pupils was Ter Petrosian, the audacious Armenian terrorist known as Kamo, who was to become his disciple and lieutenant.

Towards the end of December 1899, Koba started work as a clerk in the Tiflis Geophysical Observatory. According to Vano

Berdzenishvili, who had been expelled from the seminary in autumn 1899 and had begun working in the observatory in February of the following year, there were six observers. They included the brothers Vano and Lado Ketskhoveli. Vano later recalled that "we had to keep awake all night and make observations at stated intervals with the help of delicate instruments. The work demanded great nervous concentration and patience."[4] A police report at this time described Koba, however, not as an observer-meteorologist, but simply as a bookkeeper.[5]

Evidently Koba found his job at the observatory congenial. The pay was low, but for the first time in his life he had the privacy of a room of his own and, when not on duty, he was free. Iremashvili described his room as bare and austere, but his table was always piled high with books and pamphlets, among which the works of Plekhanov and Lenin were prominent.[6] He divided his free time between reading and leading discussions at meetings of workers' groups. Berdzenishvili recalled later that he "used to procure illegal pamphlets and *Iskra* and let us read them; but where and from whom he got them none of us knew."[7]

May Day 1900 was an important event for Koba. The Mayevka, as it was called, was illegal and had never been celebrated in Georgia. Koba took charge of preparations, according to Sergei Alliluyev, a railwayman who was his friend and later his father-in-law. Early in the morning small groups of workers made their way to Salt Lake in the mountains beyond the outskirts of Tiflis, giving the password to pickets posted along the route. They carried banners with revolutionary slogans in Russian, Georgian, and Armenian, and two banners bore portraits of Marx and Engels.

In a mood of elation five hundred workers sang the "Marseillaise" and listened to speeches on the international proletariat and the coming fight for workers' rights. Sergei Alliluyev mentioned only that Koba was one of the speakers.[8] Georgy Ninua, however, recorded that Koba said: "We have grown so strong that next year we will be able to conduct the Mayevka not in mountain hollows, but on the main streets of Tiflis. . . . Our red flag must be in the centre of the city, so that tyranny will feel our strength."[9]

Industrial unrest was mounting in Russia during these years,

and in Georgia the unrest had become acute. A wave of strikes
swept through the factories in Tiflis between May and July 1900,
and in August the railwaymen staged a major strike. Koba, supported by M. I. Kalinin, a metalworker who was to become President of the Soviet Union, was said to have organized and led
these strikes.[10]

In summer 1900, Viktor Kurnatovsky arrived in Tiflis. A tall,
gaunt man who bent forward in company because he was hard of
hearing, he was liked and respected in revolutionary circles.[11] He
had been an active terrorist, and while in exile he had become the
close companion of Lenin.

His arrival in Georgia coincided with an increase in revolutionary activity. Preparation went ahead for the May Day demonstration in 1901, which, as Koba had urged in the previous year,
was to be held not in the mountains, but in the center of Tiflis.
The Okhrana was, however, well informed about these plans. On
March 21 (1901) Kurnatovsky and some fifty of the leading Social
Democrats were arrested. On the same evening police raided the
rooms of Koba and his colleagues at the observatory. Koba had
been about to go to his room at the time of the search, but notic-
ing that the building was surrounded by police he had walked the
streets of the city and had returned only when it was safe.[12]

After this raid, Koba "went underground," according to the
official account.[13] It seems, however, that he worked at the observatory during the following week, which suggests that the police
were not overly concerned about him. As a precaution, however,
he moved from Tiflis and became a fugitive revolutionary, calling
himself Koba and other names, and was meagerly housed and fed
by workers and comrades who were almost as poor as he was. It
was a harsh but exciting life in which he was both hunter and
hunted.[14]

The immediate task was to press ahead with the May Day preparations. On the day, some two thousand workers gathered at the
Soldatsky Bazaar near the Aleksandrovsky Gardens in the center
of Tiflis. The police and detachments of Cossacks were waiting
with sabers drawn and whips in hand. Fighting broke out at once.
Fourteen workers were wounded and more than fifty arrested.

After the demonstration Koba eluded the police and went into hiding in Gori or the nearby mountains. He secretly visited the apartment of Iremashvili, where he talked excitedly about the violence and about the need to provoke greater violence in future demonstrations.[15]

Koba was exhilarated by the open declaration of war on the autocracy rather than by the shedding of blood. He was impatient of the unending talk and disputation which dominated the lives of so many revolutionaries: He craved action. Indeed, Lenin took a similar enthusiastic interest in "the blood-letting side of the business," and expressed the same attitude: "We must want to fight and we must learn how to fight. Words are not enough!"[16]

The news of the demonstration delighted Lenin and his comrades in Germany. *Iskra* pronounced that "the event that took place on Sunday, 22 April, at Tiflis is of historical importance for the entire Caucasus—this day marks the beginning of an open revolutionary movement in the Caucasus."[17] Though Kurnatovsky and many of the leading members of the movement were in prison and soon to be banished to Siberia, and the demonstration had been suppressed, to Lenin, as to Stalin, any violent confrontation of workers with police was of great importance, and the greater the violence and bloodshed the greater the importance of the occasion.

Lado Ketskhoveli had escaped arrest in Tiflis and had made his way to Baku. There he managed to set up a printing press in the Muslim quarter. Nina, the code name for the press, began functioning in summer 1901, but soon ran into difficulties. It was an antiquated flat-bed press, noisy to operate in secrecy; and, lacking a printer's license, Ketskhoveli was unable to obtain sufficient type, ink, and paper.

At this point Leonid Krasin, one of the most remarkable members of the Russian revolutionary movement, took it in hand. Tall and distinguished in appearance, with broad forehead and intelligent face, and possessing great charm, he was a man of driving energy and extraordinary abilities.[18]

As industrial manager in the Baku oil refinery, he gathered around him workers who shared his Marxist convictions. Sergei Alliluyev was one of his recruits, as also were most of the members of the local Social Democratic Party Committee. He was in touch

with Lenin, who made him responsible for party affairs throughout Transcaucasia. This included the smuggling of copies of *Iskra*
sent by sea from Marseille to Batum. It was a complex and wasteful system, and Krasin set about printing it locally.

Within weeks Krasin had reorganized the press, which was soon
running off copies of *Iskra* as well as *Brdzola* (The Struggle), the
first illegal revolutionary newspaper to be published in Georgian,
and *Yuzhny Rabochii* in Russian. Certain sources later claimed
that "Ketskhoveli conducted all his varied revolutionary work in
Baku under the direction of the Tiflis leadership group of the Russian Socialist Democratic Workers' Party and Comrade Stalin."[19]

The "Tiflis leadership group" comprised only Koba, Lado
Ketskhoveli, Sasha Tsulukidze, and a few others. Of them Ketskhoveli was certainly the leading force, while in the background
Krasin provided advice and probably funds. The group was already in conflict with the moderate Messame Dassy, led by Noi
Zhordania. The editorial of the first issue of *Brdzola* was concerned not with asserting socialist principles and revolutionary tactics, but with polemics against the moderates. *Brdzola* also declared that "the Georgian social democratic movement is not an
isolated, exclusively Georgian, labour movement with its own pro-
gramme. It goes hand in hand with the entire Russian movement
and consequently subordinates itself to the Russian Social Democratic Party."[20] This statement was a criticism of the majority in
Messame Dassy, who favored a separate Georgian party, associated with the Russian party but independent.[21]

Koba made some contribution to this first editorial. Later he
laid claim to authorship by including it in his *Collected Works*.[22]
In style, however, it is unlike his other writings and he probably
collaborated with others in producing it.

The next issue of *Brdzola* appeared in December 1901. Its main
article, titled "The Russian Social Democratic Party and Its Immediate Tasks," was his work.[23] Koba was not a natural writer,
but he learned to express himself with great effect. In his early articles and speeches he wrote in a rhetorical style with the rhythms
and repetitions of the Orthodox liturgy which struck familiar
chords in the minds of the workers. In later writings his style was
more simple and direct.

The first article, printed in *Brdzola*, contained the following typical passages:

> Many storms, many streams of blood have swept Western Europe in order that an end should be put to the oppression of the majority of the people by the minority; but the suffering has not yet been dispelled, the wounds have remained just as sore as before and the pain is becoming more and more unbearable every day. . . .
>
> Not only the working class has been groaning under the yoke of Tsardom. Other social classes, too, are strangled in the grip of autocracy. Groaning is the hunger-swollen Russian peasantry. . . . Groaning are the small town-dwellers, petty employees . . . petty officials, in a word, that multitude of small men whose existence is just as insecure as that of the working class and who have reason enough to be discontented with their social position. Groaning, too, is the lower and even middle bourgeoisie that cannot put up with the tsarist knout and bludgeon. . . . Groaning are the oppressed nationalities and religions in Russia, among them the Poles and Finns.[24]

The revolution must be led by the workers, for only in this way would it achieve "a broad democratic constitution, giving equal rights to the worker, the oppressed peasant and the capitalist."[25]

Here Koba was following the orthodox Marxist line. His article gathered strength when he turned to the mechanics of revolution. This, not the battle of theories, was his real interest. Of all the weapons of the revolutionary he held violent demonstrations to be the most effective. Accompanied by bloodshed, they aroused the anger of the people, turning them into militants.[26] This propagation of violence was a response to the brutality of the tsarist police and Cossacks, but it was also a reflection of the inhumanity of the revolutionary ethic. Koba, like Lenin, was not concerned about human suffering, no matter how great in scale, so long as it advanced the cause of revolution.

5

Batum, Prison, and Exile 1902-4

On November 11, 1901, Koba was elected to the first Tiflis committee of the Russian Social Democratic Labor party. This committee represented a group of twenty-five members who wanted more positive policies than those of Messame Dassy. Two weeks later Koba went to Batum. A secret police report noted: "In autumn 1901 the social democratic committee of Tiflis sent one of its members, Iosif Vissarionovich Dzhugashvili, formerly a pupil in the sixth form of the Tiflis seminary, to Batum for the purpose of carrying on propaganda among the factory workers. As a result of Dzhugashvili's activities . . . social democratic organizations began to spring up in all the factories of Batum."[1] Other sources stated that the committee virtually expelled him from Tiflis.[2]

Batum, on the Black Sea coast, was a town of some thirty thousand people, about half of whom were Turkish. The town and the subtropical coastal region had come into Russian possession only in 1878 as a result of the Russo-Turkish War. Batum was in character still a Muslim Turkish town. It had expanded rapidly, however, as a Russian industrial center. The Transcaucasian Railway, linking Baku and Batum, had been completed in 1883. Ten major industrial enterprises had been established there, including the Rothschild, Nobel, and Mantashev oil refineries. Workers numbered about eleven thousand; their pay was low and conditions were oppressive.

The social democratic movement in Batum was led by Nikolai Chkheidze, a former student of the Tiflis seminary, widely respected for his learning and his powers as an orator. He was a forceful personality, but like the majority of Social Democrats in Georgia he favored "Legal Marxism" and deplored violent revolutionary activity. He was to become chairman of the Petrograd Soviet after the February Revolution in 1917, and welcomed Lenin and his party on their arrival at the Finland station, warning him against destroying the Revolution by violence. He was brushed aside.

As a friend of Dzhibladze in Tiflis, Chkheidze probably had some notice of Koba's arrival, but this did not prepare him for the furious activity of the young revolutionary. He was horrified when he learned Koba's plans, and approached him several times personally and then through friends with pleas to abandon his militancy. Finding his pleas rejected, he condemned Koba as a "disorganizer" and a "madman."[3]

Arriving in Batum in November 1901, Koba had begun at once to organize and incite the workers.[4] On December 31, 1901, under the cover of a New Year's party held in the rooms of a worker, a new Batum social democratic organization was formed. Koba also managed to set up a simple printing press, which he later expanded with equipment brought from Tiflis; it was soon producing leaflets and manifestoes. By the end of February 1902 eleven social democratic circles had been organized among workers in the main factories. All pointed to a new force at work in Batum.

On February 27, 1902, a strike at the Rothschild oil refinery led to a march by more than six thousand workers on the offices of the military governor. Troops opened fire, killing fifteen and wounding fifty-four workers. A further five hundred were arrested. News of the violence and bloodshed spread rapidly. An official inquiry revealed that the demonstration had been spontaneous, and there was no mention of Koba or any other revolutionary leaders. But Soviet sources were to relate how Koba had organized the strike and demonstration. Yaroslavsky later wrote of him as being "in the midst of the turbulent sea of workers, personally directing the movement."[5] Another report stated that Koba organized a further demonstration at the time of the funeral of the victims.[6]

To Stalin this demonstration had been a dramatic revolutionary achievement. Lenin, too, hailed it as an event of major significance in the Caucasus. The workers and moderate Social Democrats in Batum, however, were appalled by the violence and the suffering which appeared to achieve nothing.

The police made every effort after the Batum demonstration to find the secret printing press. To escape detection Koba moved it to an Abkhazian village on the outskirts of the town where the narrow streets and crowded houses of the Muslim quarter gave cover. Workers, dressed as Caucasian women, wearing the long veil, or *chadra*, would come to the house to collect the leaflets, printed by the press. Neighbors began to suspect that the press was forging paper money and demanded a share of the proceeds. It took some time to disabuse them and persuade them to help.[7]

The Batum demonstration on March 9, the defiance of the workers, and the bloodshed, coming as the explosive culmination of unrest in industrial centers throughout Transcaucasia, stirred the police to action. They began rounding up the revolutionaries. For the first time Koba found himself under arrest. According to Yaroslavsky's account:

> On Friday night, April 5, 1902, Kotsia Kandelaki and he visited the home of Darakhvelidze, who had arranged a social gathering. Soso (Koba) was twenty-two years of age, still slender, with a black beard and moustache. He resembled a "romantic student" with dark, wind-blown hair. Someone in the party suddenly realized that the Batum Okhrana had not only surrounded the house but had also placed informers in the basement. Soso (Koba), smoking a "papirosa" and talking with Kandelaki, was unperturbed. He calmly remarked "It's nothing" and continued smoking. Shortly thereafter the police charged into the room and arrested the Darakhvelidze brothers, Kandelaki, and Soso.[8]

Imprisonment, like exile, was accepted as an inevitable stage in the career of the professional revolutionary. Tsarist prisons away from the Russian cities were usually ramshackle buildings, run in a rough-and-ready style, and the crowded Batum prison was no exception. Political prisoners were treated leniently on the whole and allowed privileges unless they were disorderly; some revolutionaries felt a compulsion to be rowdy and to make life as difficult as possible for their jailers, and this led to outbreaks of temper and violence on both sides.

Koba did not indulge in provocation. He wanted to be left to pursue his own interests. During the year he spent in Batum prison (April 5, 1902 to April 19, 1903) he was quiet and well behaved. He was self-sufficient and disciplined, rising early in the morning, keeping fit by exercise, and spending most of the day in study.[9]

Six weeks after his arrest, the police opened a file on Koba. It contained photographs, full face and in profile, and the following description: "Height: 2 arshins 4½ vershoks [approximately 5 feet 4 inches]. Body: medium. Age: 23. Second and third toes of the left foot fused. Appearance: ordinary. Hair: dark brown. Beard and moustache: brown. Nose: straight and long. Forehead: straight and low. Face: long, swarthy and pockmarked."[10]

Each detail, as set down in his file, seemed to emphasize ordinariness and what Trotsky called "the general colourlessness of his physical and moral countenance."[11] In fact, it was a distinctive, handsome face, strong in character. The police knew him as Ryaboi, "the pock-marked," and took no special interest in him.[12] They even failed to record his shortened left arm. Like others at this time and later, they misjudged this small, quiet man.

On April 19 (1903) Koba was transferred to the prison in Kutais, some eighty miles away, where he was held for some six months. A moderate Social Democrat who was in the prison at the time recalled in later years that Koba moved stealthily like a cat and only occasionally smiled in a restrained calculating manner, but never shouted or lost his temper. Already he was remarkable for the self-control and the mask of imperturbability which were to characterize him as he moved towards supreme power.[13]

Of those involved in the Batum demonstration some were

brought to trial; others, including Koba and Kandelaki, found their cases decided by administrative decree. On July 9, 1903, Koba was sentenced to three years' exile, to be passed in the Irkutsk province of Siberia in the village of Novaya Uda.

Exile to Siberia, as distinct from penal servitude, was no longer the harsh punishment that it had been in the past. The prisoners usually made the long journey under guard but by easy stages, and no longer on foot and in chains. Indeed, in February 1897, when sentenced to three years in Siberia, Lenin had obtained permission to travel independently at his own expense and without guards from St. Petersburg. He had been able, too, to break his journey in Moscow to spend a few days with his mother.

Once he had arrived at his place of exile, the prisoner could live with considerable freedom, hunting, fishing, visiting friends, and carrying on reasonable correspondence. With his small government allowance he would rent a room in the house of a local inhabitant, but he needed money from family or friends to buy special food, tobacco, and similar items. In fact, Siberia offered a quiet, healthy way of life, which suited Lenin and many other revolutionaries.

Koba made the long journey to Siberia by way of Novorossisk, Rostov, Tsaritsyn, Samara, and then to Irkutsk. It was not until November 27 (14) that he reached Novaya Uda. All his life he had lived in the heat of Georgia, and the Siberian winter must have proved an ordeal. It did not deter him, however, from making his escape, and he was soon back in Georgia, reaching Tiflis in February 1904. He went directly to the apartment of Micho Bochoridze, a Social Democrat, and there he met Sergei Alliluyev, who recalled their meeting in his memoirs. To him Koba related how he had tried to escape a few days after arriving at Novaya Uda, but was ill prepared for the cold. He was caught in a "buran," the dreaded Siberian blizzard, and nearly froze to death. He had turned back in time with frostbitten face and ears, but had finally got away on January 5 (1904).[14]

About this time Koba married Ekaterina Svanidze from the village of Didi-Lilo. She was probably the daughter of Semyon Svanidze, a Social Democrat employed on the railway. Her brother, Aleksandr, had attended the Tiflis seminary, and Iosif may have met her through the father or brother. He himself never spoke of his marriage. Revolutionaries were expected to treat such matters as private, and also he was naturally reticent about his personal life. Nearly all that is known about this first marriage comes from Iremashvili's recollections.

Ekaterina was apparently untouched by the revolutionary ideas of her father and brother and remained a typical Georgian woman for whom her husband and her child, Yakov, born in 1908, were her whole life. She was married in the Orthodox Church and was, like her mother-in-law, very devout. Iremashvili relates that "she tended to her husband with all her heart, spending her nights in fervent prayer while awaiting her Soso busy at his meetings, praying that he might turn away from ideas displeasing to God and revert instead to a quiet home life of labor and contentment."[15] She died young in 1910, and was buried with the full rites of the Church.

6

Koba the Bolshevik 1903-4

Addressing the cadets of the Kremlin Academy at a memorial service on January 28, 1924, Stalin, as Koba had then become,[1] said:

> "I first became acquainted with Lenin in 1903. True, it was not a personal acquaintance; it was made by correspondence. . . . I was then in exile in Siberia. My knowledge of Lenin's revolutionary activities since the end of the nineties and especially after 1901, after the publication of *Iskra*, had convinced me that in Lenin we had a man of unusual calibre. He was not then for me the leader of the party, he was its actual creator. When I compared him with the other leaders of our party, it seemed to me constantly that Lenin's fellow workers— Plekhanov, Martov, Axelrod and others—stood a full head below Lenin, that by comparison with them Lenin was not simply one of the leaders, but a leader of the highest type, a mountain eagle. . . . This impression became so deeply imprinted on my mind that I felt impelled to write to a close friend, living as a po-

litical exile abroad, asking his opinion. Some time later, when I was already in exile in Siberia—this was at the end of 1903—I received an enthusiastic letter from my friend and a letter, simple but profound in content, from Lenin to whom, it appeared, my friend had shown my letter. Lenin's note was comparatively short, but it contained a bold and fearless criticism of the practical work of our party and a remarkably clear and concise account of the entire plan of work of the party in the immediate future. . . . This simple and bold letter strengthened my opinion that Lenin was the mountain eagle of our party. I cannot forgive myself for having, from the habit of an old underground worker, consigned this letter of Lenin's, like many other letters, to the flames. My acquaintance with Lenin dates from that time."[2]

It was scarcely possible that Koba could have received a letter addressed to him in Novaya Uda, where, according to the official version, his stay was so brief. It is also improbable that Lenin, then in Switzerland, had heard of Koba or Iosif Dzhugashvili at this time. The story might have been a deliberate fiction, employed on a solemn occasion and carefully invoking Lenin's name to suggest that he was Lenin's true successor; the text of the address, published in *Pravda* some two weeks later, had wide circulation. Or it might have been a slip of memory after the lapse of twenty tumultuous years.

The story appears, however, to have been true in essence. In October 1904 Koba had written from Kutais to his friend Davitashvili, in Leipzig, expressing strong support for Lenin's ideas. Davitashvili showed the letter to Lenin, who commented favorably on this "fiery Colchian," Colchis being the ancient name for western Georgia.[3]

It has been suggested, also, that Koba had in mind Lenin's *Letter to a Comrade on our Organizational Tasks*, which was not addressed to him personally, but was circulated by the Siberian Social Democratic party in June 1903. Koba probably read it while in Siberia. Writing to Davitashvili he made the request, "Don't forget to send by the same person the pamphlet *Letter to a Comrade*—many here haven't read it!"[4]

The *Letter* fitted Koba's enthusiastic description. It expressed an aggressive practical approach and emphasized the importance of the Central Committee which must direct all local organizations and funds, and also the need for "the greatest possible centralization in relation to the ideological and practical leadership of the movement and the revolutionary struggle of the proletariat."[5] It made an impact on Koba, because it formulated so effectively the ideas which had been stirring in his own mind.

The year 1903, when he first properly appreciated Lenin's ideas, was momentous in his development. He had dated his acquaintance with Lenin "from the end of the nineties and especially after 1901, after the publication of *Iskra*," but he went on to say that in 1903 Lenin had made an indelible impression on him as "the mountain eagle," soaring above the other leaders.[6]

Two further events in this period were decisive for Koba. One was his reading, probably early in 1904, of Lenin's pamphlet, *What Is to Be Done?* The other event was the congress of the Russian Social Democratic Workers' party, held in July–August 1903, which ended with the division of the party into Bolsheviks and Mensheviks.

Lenin's pamphlet, published in March 1902, reads turgidly with occasional gleams of inspiration, but it is scarcely less important than *Das Kapital* itself in the Russian revolutionary movement. In it under the pretext of elucidating orthodox Marxism, Lenin was in effect Russifying the doctrine. Marx had held that the proletariat would evolve its own class consciousness and in the process would discover within itself the will and the way to revolution. Lenin's interpretation was distinctively Russian in that he demanded a party, organized on military lines, that would lead, direct, and impose Marxism and revolution on the people. This was the experience of Russian history, in which every major change had come, not in response to popular demand, but from above, imposed on the people, who stolidly obeyed. The revolutionary movement was not conceivable to Lenin in other terms. With the arrogance of the Russian intelligentsia he saw the Russian people, not as individuals, but as a mass which had to be led and compelled along certain paths for its own good. To him and his comrades, including Stalin, this Russian mass could not be left to decide a matter so important.

Lenin proposed a centralized, disciplined party of professional revolutionaries, which would direct the working class. Marx, too, had envisaged such a party, but one which was representative of the workers after the spontaneous emergence of political class consciousness among them. Lenin had no time for the concepts of party democracy, freedom of expression and criticism, or spontaneity of political movements. Democracy was anathema to him. The party must be in the vanguard, leading, teaching, compelling the workers to revolution. Left to themselves, the workers were capable only of trade-unionism and of fighting for narrow economic objectives, but the political class consciousness, which would lead to revolution, "can only be brought to the workers from the outside, that is to say from outside the economic struggle, outside the sphere of relations between workers and employers."[7]

Lenin demanded an elitist party disciplined and in complete control of the revolutionary movement. In *What Is to Be Done?* he argued that this control should vest in the émigré editorial board of *Iskra*, while the Central Committee in Russia would administer the local committees. It was, in fact, a military organization, and it assumed that there would have to be a commander in chief, a dictator.

Intolerant of opposition, incapable of accepting the leadership of another person, and driven by an obsessive hunger for power, Lenin took it for granted that he would be in command of the party. As one who knew him well noted, he possessed "unshakeable faith in himself . . . faith in his destiny, in his conviction that he was preordained to carry out some great historical mission." Indeed, he himself remarked that the idea of anyone else in the party taking the supreme position was enough "to make a cat laugh"![8]

Meanwhile the need to convene a congress of the party had become pressing. The *Iskra* group seethed with ideological and personal conflicts during 1902 as party policy was hammered out in readiness for the Second Party Congress. Plekhanov was jealous of his position as Father of Russian Marxism. Lenin had asserted himself as leader of the group and resented Plekhanov, whose support he still needed.

A further source of conflict between them was the arrival of Lev Bronstein, already known as Trotsky and nicknamed "The Pen," who burst upon the scene with "instant brilliance."[9] Plekhanov detested him from the start, whereas Lenin, who had sudden, often short-lived, enthusiasms for people, welcomed him with open arms.

Trotsky was the son of a small-scale Jewish landowner in the Ukraine. His parents were both nearly illiterate, but he early developed a passion for words, and it was as an orator and a writer that he was most outstanding. Pale in complexion, with heavy dark mustache and small goatee, and thick-lensed pince-nez to aid his weak, shortsighted eyes, he looked a typical Russian Jewish intellectual. Lenin was soon eager to co-opt this young man with the fluent pen to the editorial board of *Iskra*, a move that Plekhanov angrily opposed.

Trotsky was generally disliked for his arrogant, patronizing manner. Like Lenin he was convinced that he had a special role in history and was destined to lead. His love of power was supported by the "certainty of the rectitude of his principles."[10] But, while Lenin behaved with a certain modesty, Trotsky was vain, prickly, and overbearing. Anatoly Lunacharsky, the first Kommissar of Education, wrote of "his colossal arrogance and inability or unwillingness to show any human kindness or to be attentive to people. . . ."[11] All at one time or another felt the lash of his sarcasm and abuse and the insult of his condescension.

The congress opened in Brussels on July 30 (NS), and under pressure from the police it moved to London, where it concluded on August 10 (NS), 1903. Lenin's machinations throughout the meetings aroused hostility, but he gained a spurious majority for his program and in the process succeeded in splitting the party. Unscrupulously he made the most of his advantage, publicizing the result as a victory for the Bolsheviki (the Majority-ites) over the Mensheviki (the Minority-ites), terms which quickly became part of the language of the Revolution.

Koba may have heard reports about the London congress while he was in Siberia, and he learned the full story on his return to Georgia. It was clear that the Russian Social Democratic Workers' party had been formally established; it was clear also that the party was split between Bolsheviks and Mensheviks. Noi Zhordania, who had attended the congress, had been alarmed by

Lenin's perfidious conduct and by his conception of the party as a rigidly centralized organization, wielding supreme power. He favored a loose union of more or less autonomous groups, and on his return to Georgia he exercised his authority to ensure that Georgian Social Democrats took the Menshevik position. Indeed under his leadership and that of Sylvestr Dzhibladze the Mensheviks became by far the strongest faction in Georgia, and they remained dominant during the next twenty years.

Koba immediately took the Bolshevik position. He did so without hesitation and was to be single-minded in his dedication to the [Bolshevik] cause.[12] It was a decision demanding conviction and courage. Lenin and the Bolsheviks had little support in Transcaucasia, and the possibility of their gaining power appeared remote. The fact that his decision might doom him to permanent opposition did not deter Koba. By temperament he belonged to the opposition at this stage of his career. He was opposed to the Tsar and his regime, to the liberals and the Socialist Revolutionaries, and now to the great majority of Social Democrats. Opposition was part of his way of life: He needed enemies.

The positive reason for his support of the Bolshevik stand was his conviction that it provided the only effective approach to revolution. *What Is to Be Done?* had given rational arguments for what he believed was the right course of action. The intellectuals, like Plekhanov, Axelrod, Martov, Zasulich, and others, who spent their time abroad and had no experience of the workers or the peasants, could talk about the spontaneous growth of political consciousness, but he knew that without leadership they would never make a revolution. Lenin alone would get action and results; he was the one positive force in the midst of the theorizing intellectuals, and Koba stood at his side.

The firmness of his commitment was shown in the two letters, mentioned above, which he wrote from Kutais to his friend, Davitashvili, in September-October 1904. In the first letter he asked him to send *Iskra*, which now had a Menshevik editorial board, critical of Lenin's position. He added in explanation of his request that "though it's without a spark [*Iskra*] it's still needed; at least it has a chronicle, devil take it, and you have to know the enemy well."[13]

Koba was incensed, too, by an attack, written by Plekhanov, on *What Is to Be Done?* Plekhanov had questioned in particular Lenin's view that no reliance could be placed on the spontaneous emergence of a revolutionary outlook in the working class and that the workers had to be taught and led by the party. Plekhanov was revered by most Social Democrats, but not by the young Georgian member, who wrote scathingly:

> This man had either gone completely mad or hate and hostility are speaking in him. I think that both causes have a place here. I think Plekhanov has fallen behind on the new questions. He is haunted by the old opponents and as of old he confirms that "Social consciousness determines social life," "ideas do not fall from heaven." . . . Now what interests us is how to work out a system of ideas (a theory of socialism) from the separate ideas. . . . Does the mass give its programme to the leaders and the supporting arguments or do the leaders give it to the mass?[14]

Like Lenin, Koba found it inconceivable that the party should wait passively for the workers to awaken to consciousness of their revolutionary role. The eruptions of discontent that were to bring the nation close to chaos during the coming months confirmed both men in their view, for the masses showed themselves ready to accept economism and constitutionalism, but stopped short at revolution.

7

Overtures to Revolution 1904-5

Throughout Russia unrest among the intelligentsia, workers, peasants, and the subject nationalities mounted dangerously. Political crimes, strikes, violence, and outbreaks of arson and destruction of property in the country districts became more frequent. The Tsar and his ministers were bewildered, and they, too, shared the widespread feeling that the nation was about to be overwhelmed in a terrible paroxysm of rebellion.

War against Japan, which started in February 1904, aggravated the explosive mood of the people. The humiliating defeats suffered by the Imperial Army and, in May of the following year, by the Navy, went far to undermine confidence in the regime.

The tragedy of January 9 (22), 1905, known as "Bloody Sunday," dealt a severe blow to the authority and prestige of the Tsar when troops opened fire on a mass procession to the Winter Palace to petition him. Hostility towards the autocratic regime gained momentum. Violent outbreaks among workers and peasants threatened anarchy. Bewildered by the situation, Nicholas II made concessions, announcing in March a plan to give limited popular participation in government. But the imperial decree providing for a consultative Duma, or council, confirmed the general fear that the Tsar would make only minimal concessions. Towards the end of September a printers' strike in Moscow spread, and within a week the vast country was paralyzed by a general strike. Faced with the alternative of civil war, Nicholas II capitulated and on October 30 issued a manifesto, promising a parliamentary system of government and, in effect, the beginnings of a constitutional monarchy.

For months Russia had been like an immense volcanic zone, the surface of which was broken by countless jets of steam and gas and beneath which the earth's crust was cracking. Away in Switzerland, however, Lenin was little concerned with these tumultuous events. Since the Second Party Congress, when he had lost control of *Iskra*, he had been campaigning for the Central Committee in Russia to summon another congress at which he would, he hoped, recover his position in the party. He was meeting with strong opposition, however, for he had antagonized many of his supporters. But Lenin, indefatigable and unscrupulous, and aided by events in Russia, got his way.

On April 12 (25), 1905, the congress, called by the Bolsheviks the Third Congress, opened in London. The Mensheviks denounced it as illegal, but it served his purpose as another step towards forging a party of professional revolutionaries directly under his leadership.

All revolutionaries were disturbed, however, by the way they and their programs had been swept aside in the rush of events. The explosions of popular discontent should have provided ideal conditions for launching a revolution. But they had not been ready, and the unpalatable fact was that the nation, too, was not ready. The people wanted reform, not revolution. To Lenin, of course, it was not relevant that the people did not want revolution. He wrote of the need for stronger organization, fighting units, and a centralized party leadership. *Iskra* under Menshevik control took a different line, calling for "a wide organization based on the working masses, acting independently."[1]

The Petersburg Soviet of Workers' Deputies, set up late in 1905 on the initiative of the Mensheviks, also incurred Lenin's hostility. Nonparty in composition, the Soviet was remarkably successful in defying the authorities during its short existence (October 13 [26] to December 2 [15], 1905) in the period to be known as "the days of freedom." This success was due mainly to Trotsky, who dominated and led it.

At first, the October Manifesto, setting out the Tsar's major concessions, did nothing to calm the turbulence which was tearing the nation apart. Workers, peasants, and units of the armed forces demonstrated against the autocratic regime, while right-wing opinion reacted angrily against the manifesto as an act of betrayal of the autocracy. Landowners and others organized bands of thugs, the Black Hundreds, which attacked, often with horrible brutality, Jews and others regarded as intellectuals. Conservatives and reactionaries also formed societies to defend the old Muscovite institutions.

Russia was in the thrall of dark forces. Cities and towns became cauldrons of violence and crime. Revolutionaries and reactionary bands, terrorists, anarchists, and criminals preyed on each other and on society, as misguided idealism, brutal crime, and a sense of desperation powered the vortex which whirled the nation towards chaos.

In the midst of this turmoil the main political parties were organizing to contest the elections to the Duma, the new state council. The Constitutional Democrats, known as the Kadets, demanded a constitution or fundamental law, and some of its members wanted full parliamentary democracy on the British model, and even a republic. The Octobrists were less radical in their demands.

The Social Democrats and the Socialist Revolutionaries were thrown into confusion. All expressed furious hostility to the new liberal parties, to the Duma, and to the October Manifesto. But they had to recognize that events had displaced them and that they had no real support among the people. Nevertheless, the small hard core of Social Democrats did not lose heart, and with extraordinary tenacity they looked ahead.

Koba was apparently detached from the dramatic events of these months. Returning to Tiflis from his brief Siberian exile early in

1904, he had found new developments among Georgian Social Democrats. The Transcaucasian party organizations had held a constituent congress in March 1903 and had set up a "Caucasian Union Committee" of nine members to give leadership to the movement. At some time after his return he was co-opted to the committee.[2]

About the same time Stefan Shaumyan, an Armenian Bolshevik, was also co-opted to the committee. He at once became Koba's enemy. Shaumyan, who had studied engineering in Riga and philosophy in Germany, and had met Lenin, probably treated Koba as an uneducated provincial, and he appears to have been a vicious opponent. He is said to have denounced Koba as "a viper," and he reported to Lenin any critical remarks that Koba made about him. Rivalries and disputes among the revolutionaries and especially the Bolsheviks were seldom notable for tolerance, compromise, or courtesy, but were marked by savage vituperation and bitterness. The rivalry between the two men continued until 1918, when Shaumyan died as one of the "twenty-six commissars shot by the British," who have been enshrined as martyrs in Soviet history.[3]

During 1904 Koba was active as a member of the Caucasian Union Committee. In June he was in Baku, setting up a new Bolshevik committee, and during the summer he traveled to all the regions of Transcaucasia, leading discussion meetings and tirelessly opposing the Mensheviks at every opportunity. In September *Proletariatis Brdzola*, the illegal paper published in Georgian and Armenian by the Union Committee, contained his article "How Does Social Democracy Understand the Nationality Question?" a subject on which he was to write further as an acknowledged authority.[4]

During 1905, the year of violence and upheaval, Transcaucasia and especially Georgia were torn by even worse turbulence than Russia. Black Hundreds in Baku provoked massacres between Armenians and Turks. Arson and sabotage destroyed industrial plants. Crime and senseless violence were rife. In August a week of bloodshed in Tiflis ended in a battle with troops at the town hall in which many were killed. But the rioting continued, and only towards the end of the year was order restored.

Koba was probably involved in many of these upheavals, but working in the background. The official chronology and other sources contain scant information. In January (1905) he published in *Proletariatis Brdzola* an article on "The Proletariat Class and the Party of the Proletariat," and in May his pamphlet *Briefly About Party Dissensions* appeared in Russian, Georgian, and Armenian.[5] In it he presented a strong defense of Lenin's basic thesis that the working class would attain revolutionary consciousness only by means of the teaching and leadership of the party. He attacked Noi Zhordania, who had criticized this thesis. Zhordania published a reply, and on August 15 *Proletariatis Brdzola* carried two further articles in which Koba rejected the reply.[6]

In these hard-hitting polemics Koba showed that he had a full understanding of Marxism and of Lenin's views, and that he could be a formidable opponent. The fact that Zhordania, the most eminent Social Democrat in Transcaucasia, should have engaged in public debate with him showed that Koba was no longer a humble apprentice who could be ignored. Indeed, Zhordania, who must have known his identity, may have paused to wonder whether he had been wise to rebuff the young seminarist who had offered his services seven years earlier.

In July he published in *Proletariatis Brdzola* an article on "Armed Uprising and Our Tactics," in which he wrote that "the flame of revolution is burning more and more strongly" and stressed the need for armed rebellion. It was a cogent statement of the necessity for the Bolsheviks to plan and train "fighting bands" and to bring order and discipline into the revolutionary struggle.[7]

Koba's articles were gaining attention not only in Transcaucasia but also abroad. In July (1905) Krupskaya wrote on Lenin's behalf, requesting a copy of the pamphlet *Briefly About Party Dissensions* and the regular supply of the Russian edition of *Proletariatis Brdzola*. Lenin expressed delight with the pamphlet and the articles and their forthright expression of Bolshevik policies. Koba's rebuttal of Zhordania's reply to the pamphlet particularly pleased him, and in writing about the paper he referred to the "splendid formulation of the question of the celebrated 'introduction of consciousness from without.' "[8]

Lenin probably knew the identity of the author of the pamphlet and the articles, although they were unsigned. Koba had first come to his attention late in 1904 through the letters written from Kutais. Direct correspondence began in May 1905 when Koba as a member of the Caucasian Union Committee wrote to him about the relative strength of Bolshevik and Menshevik factions in the region. Lenin was on the lookout for supporters of this caliber and would hardly have overlooked this active Georgian.

Taking advantage of the relaxation of censorship after the October Manifesto, Koba and Shaumyan produced the Caucasian *Workers' News Sheet*. The first issue, which appeared in November 1905, contained his short article expressing in forceful terms his hostility towards the liberals and the Mensheviks and to participation in the elections to the Duma.[9] As in everything he wrote, the article was a consistent expression of the Bolshevik stand, and in this he was not echoing Lenin as his master but expressing his own ideas and outlook.

Koba was already becoming known as the stubborn champion of Bolshevism in the region where Bolsheviks were few in number. In fact, this reputation, supported by his writings, probably led to the next major step in his revolutionary career.

8

Revolution in Retreat
1905-12

In December 1905 Koba traveled to Finland to take part in the Bolshevik conference at Tammerfors. It was a momentous journey, for it brought him into direct contact with Lenin and into the mainstream of the revolutionary movement.

Koba was now twenty-six years old. He had spent all his life in Transcaucasia except for his brief exile in Siberia, and he had developed through several distinct stages. The schoolboy in Gori who had had to dominate his fellows had become a Georgian nationalist and then a rebel against authority in the Tiflis seminary. His natural rebelliousness had intensified and gained direction, as he learned about Marxism and the Russian revolutionary tradition. Reading Lenin's *Letter to a Comrade* and *What Is to Be Done?* had crystallized his sense of purpose. But although he accepted the basic correctness of Lenin's program and acknowledged his leadership, he retained a strong independence and never became a subservient disciple.

The Bolsheviks gathered in Tammerfors to discuss participation in the coming elections to the Duma and also the general move among Social Democrats towards unity. Bolsheviks and Mensheviks had drawn further apart. For this Lenin was chiefly responsible, for he constantly attacked the Mensheviks. In Tammerfors he was anxious only to ensure the solidarity of his own supporters. Koba was known to be a staunch Bolshevik, and it was probably Lenin who sponsored his presence at this conference.

In Tammerfors, the two men met face to face. Lenin's first impressions of Stalin are not known. But nineteen years later Stalin spoke of this occasion, and, despite the lapse of time and the special circumstances, his remarks, made in the address to the Kremlin Academy, are interesting.

The address, cast in simple words and carefully avoiding the grandiloquence that might have been expected, contained several elements: It was a genuine tribute to Lenin as the founder and leader of the Bolshevik party; it laid emphasis on those virtues of dedication, discipline, and humility which Stalin himself valued and wanted to impress on young Russians; and it was an effective assertion of his role as Lenin's partner and of his claim to be his natural successor.

> "I was hoping to see the mountain eagle of our Party, the great man, great not only politically but, if you please, physically, for in my imagination I pictured Lenin as a giant, stately and impressive. What then was my disappointment when I saw a most ordinary man, below average height, in nothing, literally in nothing, distinguishable from ordinary mortals. . . .

> "It is accepted that 'a great man' must usually arrive late at a meeting so that the people assembled may await his appearance with fast-beating hearts, and then before 'the great man' appears the warning goes round, 'Hush! Silence! . . . He's coming!' This ceremony did not seem unnecessary to me, for it impresses and inspires respect. What then was my disappointment when I learnt that Lenin had arrived at the conference before the delegates and, settled somewhere in a corner, was quite simply carrying on a conversation, a most ordinary conversation, with the most ordinary delegates at the conference. I will not conceal that this seemed to me rather a breach of certain essential rules. . . .

> "Only later I understood that this simplicity and modesty of Lenin, this striving to remain unnoticed or, at least, not to be

conspicuous and not to stress his high position—that this characteristic was one of Lenin's strongest features as the new leader of
the new masses, of the simple, ordinary masses of fundamental
humanity."[1]

In this same style he extolled "the irresistible force of logic" of
Lenin's speeches, and their "extraordinary power of conviction,
the simplicity and clarity of argument." He was presenting Lenin
as the hero of the party and nation, for he knew that the Russian
people, accustomed to the Tsar at the apex of their national life,
needed some readily understandable image in his place.[2]

At the time of the Tammerfors Conference, however, Lenin
was far from being the acknowledged leader of the social democratic movement. He headed only the small Bolshevik faction. To
Koba, he was not the infallible leader to be followed blindly, but
the revolutionary most outstanding for his leadership and his
sound practical approach.

What part Koba played in the conference is not known, for the
records were lost. Krupskaya acclaimed "the enthusiasm that
reigned there! The revolution was in full swing. . . . Every comrade was ready for the fight!"[3] While sharing in this enthusiasm,
he was probably content to remain in the background. It was his
first conference outside Transcaucasia, and he was cautiously
finding his feet. At the congress in Stockholm, four months later,
he was not silent.

The Fourth Congress, known by the Mensheviks as the Unification Congress, met from April 23 to May 8 (April 10–25), 1906. It
was attended by 111 voting delegates. The Russians made up less
than half of the total. The Georgian delegation of eleven, reflecting the predominance of the Mensheviks in the country, contained only one Bolshevik—Koba, using the alias of "Ivanovich."
Lenin had hoped for a Bolshevik majority, but found that the
Mensheviks could muster 62 against his 44 or 46 supporters.
Moreover, while Plekhanov, who now sided with the Mensheviks,
was treated with special respect and was promptly elected to the
Bureau or Steering Committee of the Congress, Lenin failed to
get elected. But, noting the general desire to reunify the party, he
made a display of being reasonable and declared his belief that
Bolsheviks and Mensheviks could work together.

Koba was not overawed by his first congress and the presence of the most prominent members of the party. It was to be characteristic of him that he was never overawed by people or events. Although young and without real support in Georgia, he was a convinced Marxist and revolutionary, and he was prepared to express his views forthrightly. Plekhanov was to Koba the archetypal intellectual revolutionary, living abroad and out of touch with Russian life. When Plekhanov with his dry academic manner and sharp tongue made critical remarks about Lenin, Koba was quick to castigate him.

The main issues debated by the congress concerned the support of the peasantry, the Duma elections, and expropriations. Lenin had never come to grips with the role of the peasants in the revolutionary struggle. He had taken it for granted that the peasants must follow the proletariat. After the Revolution of 1905 he was forced to revise his policy. The peasants were, he realized, crucial to the coming revolution. The Socialist Revolutionaries and the new liberal parties were attracting their support by promising them the land. Belatedly the Social Democrats had awakened to the fact that they needed a policy to win over the peasantry.

At the Stockholm congress the Mensheviks argued in favor of municipalization of the land, which meant vesting it in locally elected councils to be administered for the benefit of the peasants. Lenin and the Bolsheviks proposed nationalization by vesting the land in the central government and, so they claimed, making it the property of all citizens. Argument raged around these two proposals.

Koba had no time for debates which were so enmeshed in dialectics that the realities of the situation were forgotten. In the congress he bluntly condemned both municipalization and nationalization and proposed as a "temporary" expedient what he called distributism, which meant seizing and sharing out the land directly among the peasants. This was what they wanted and this alone would win their support. Lenin and others attacked his proposal, but he stood his ground, maintaining that it was the obvious practical policy. He argued further that in fostering rural capitalism his proposal was in accordance with Marxist doctrine and a logical advance towards the socialist revolution. And in 1917 his policy, by then endorsed by Lenin, produced the slogan "All land to the peasants," which gained the party wide support on the land and was a major factor in its victory.

Lenin had been unable also to make up his mind about participation in the Duma elections. At the Tammerfors Conference he had supported the resolution to boycott them. The Bolsheviks held, mistakenly as it proved, that the Duma was bound to be a reactionary body which they must oppose. Participation in the elections and co-operation within the Duma would lead workers to think that they could gain their objectives by parliamentary means and without resorting to revolution.

The Mensheviks were divided in their attitude and left it to local committees to decide whether or not to take part in the elections. By the time the delegates had assembled in Stockholm, the elections were nearly over, and it was clear that the Kadets had severely defeated the right-wing and reactionary parties. The Social Democrats, who had belatedly contested the elections in certain regions, had a mere eighteen seats.

Lenin now changed his mind about the boycott and in Stockholm voted for a Menshevik resolution, approving participation in the few elections still to be held. Several Bolsheviks, including Stalin, refused to follow him and abstained.

In articles published in Georgia in March before he had left to attend the congress, Stalin had clearly expounded his policy of dividing the land among the peasants and of boycotting the Duma elections. His stand against Lenin on both issues was thus not for effect, as a gesture of independence, or to establish himself in the eyes of party comrades. He was acting consistently and apparently without thought for his popularity or advancement.

An issue debated with displays of anger in the congress was expropriations. This euphemism covered robbery, often with violence, of state and private institutions, and extortion and terrorism, committed to obtain funds for the party. The Stockholm congress passed by a large majority a resolution forbidding nearly all forms of expropriation. Lenin did not openly oppose the resolution, but at once set about organizing secretly a Bolshevik Center with the main task of planning further robberies to provide him with funds. Stalin, it seems, became its agent in the

Stalin

Caucasus. The activities of this secret center were to cause a major storm.

The congress elected a new Central Committee of seven Mensheviks and only three Bolsheviks. It closed with the two factions formally united. Lenin had no intention, however, of accepting decisions merely because they had been agreed by the majority of the delegates. He told Lunacharsky that he would never allow the Mensheviks to "lead us along after them on a chain."[4]

At the end of the congress, he and several members of the "former" Bolshevik faction, but not Stalin, signed a declaration, listing the decisions which they had opposed and claiming the democratic right to urge their own views in "comradely" debate while, of course, fully acknowledging and accepting the decisions of the majority.[5] At the time of making this declaration of good faith, his secret Bolshevik Center was already at work. As one Bolshevik stated, the unification "had practically no influence on our Bolshevik affairs. We certainly did not disarm as a strong, independent revolutionary faction."[6]

The First Duma met on May 10, 1906. The Kadet party, emboldened by its large majority, demanded full constitutional government and, lacking any traditions of discussion, tolerance, or compromise, pressed its demands. The inevitable deadlock was resolved by dissolution of the Duma on July 21.

Nicholas II then appointed as his prime minister Peter Stolypin, a remarkable man whose firm but enlightened policies might have averted the collapse of the regime. In the period until the new Duma was elected, he introduced major reforms and began a transformation in the position of the peasantry.

The Second Duma, which assembled on March 5, 1907, was stormy. The crisis came on June 14 (1907) when Stolypin faced it with the demand that the parliamentary immunity of the Social Democrat deputies be waived so that they could be tried for fomenting mutinies in the armed services.[7] The Duma rejected the demand, and on June 16 an imperial manifesto, declaring that the Duma harbored enemies of the nation, dissolved it.

During 1905, the year of anarchy, the party's fighting units had carried out countless raids and expropriations, and, until the Stockholm congress, the practice had been more or less accepted by most members as part of the tactics of revolution. The Caucasus was the scene of intensive activity. No fewer than 1,150 acts of terrorism were recorded in the years from 1905 to 1908. Koba was probably involved in many of these acts, but precise information is lacking. Mensheviks inside Russia and, after 1921, abroad repeatedly condemned his activities as an expropriator. It seems, however, that the Okhrana did not connect him with these raids. Early in 1908 the Caucasian Mensheviks tried to indict him before a party court for disobeying the ban on expropriations. The party trial never took place, for he moved from Tiflis to Baku, and on March 25 he was arrested.

Subsequent official accounts of this period of his career are silent about his role in directing fighting units and robberies. Truly Russian in being sensitive to criticism, especially of the kind reflected in the remark, made privately by Rosa Luxemburg, about the "Tatar-Mongolian savagery" of the Bolsheviks, and at the same time conscious of the dignity of the regime, Soviet leaders have been unwilling to admit association with such activities.[8]

Koba, again using the name of Ivanovich, traveled to London to attend the Fifth Congress, which began on May 13, 1907. His mandate as a delegate was questioned. He was finally admitted, but with only a consultative vote, while Shaumyan was allowed a full vote. This discrimination probably aroused his resentment.

The congress was held in the Brotherhood Church in London's Whitechapel, and even this cosmopolitan city can rarely have seen such a bizarre gathering. Some delegates, like Plekhanov, wore dark tail coats and looked like respectable bankers, while the Russian worker delegates were mostly bearded and wearing Russian blouses. Others from the Ukraine and the Caucasus were exotic and romantic in their tall sheepskin hats. But more remarkable than their dress was the verbose eloquence of the delegates. They were in a country where they could express themselves freely and, speaking in Russian, there was no danger of their most inflammatory utterances attracting the attention of the police.[9]

Koba did not speak during the congress. Trotsky, doing his utmost to portray Stalin as a complete nonentity in this period, wrote that he was "still utterly unknown, not only to the party generally but even to the three hundred delegates at the Congress."[10] He claimed that he himself learned of Stalin's presence only much later when he read Boris Souvarine's biography. But Koba observed Trotsky and clearly took an instant dislike to him. He was always antagonistic towards the intellectuals, who spoke eloquently and interminably. On his return from the Congress his only public reference to Trotsky was in the *Baku Proletarian,* in which he wrote that "Trotsky displayed a 'beautiful irrelevance'" (*Krasivoi nenuzhnosti*).[11]

At the congress Martov moved a resolution and supported it with severe criticism of Lenin for continuing expropriations in defiance of the party's decisions. This resolution prohibiting all members from taking "any part whatever" in such activities was adopted by 170 votes to 35, with 52 abstentions.[12] Lenin made no reply to the Menshevik attack and he abstained from voting. But he had no hesitation in continuing expropriations.

Delegates had hardly returned from the London congress, when on June 25 (1907) a sensational bank raid took place on Erivan Square in the center of Tiflis. A cashier under escort of two policemen and five Cossacks was taking notes worth thousands of rubles to the State Bank when a gang attacked the carriage with bombs. Three of the escort were killed outright and some fifty passers-by were wounded. News of this raid and of the large sum stolen spread quickly, and it was soon known that the Bolsheviks were responsible. Coming so soon after the London congress, it caused a storm of anger in the party.

The leader of the raid was Kamo, as the young Armenian Semyon Ter-Petrosyan was called. He had been born in Gori, the son of a meat dealer. He had decided on a military career, and, fluent Russian being an essential qualification, he had taken Russian lessons from his fellow-townsman Koba, who was three years older. Koba had enlisted him as a terrorist. Kamo was well equipped for the role. He was a giant of a man, simple-minded, absolutely loyal and trustworthy to his leaders, especially to Koba, generous to his comrades, but cruel and ruthless towards all others. Soviet and other Marxist writers have described him as a legendary hero.[13]

Although shocked and angered by the Tiflis bank raid, the

Mensheviks refrained from public attacks on Lenin and his henchmen. The Transcaucasian Party Committee was less amenable to Lenin's influence, but it passed only a general resolution, condemning the Tiflis robbery.[14]

At this time Lenin was concerned about the elections to the Third Duma, which were to take place on September 14. He was now convinced of the importance of taking part. Koba had strongly advocated boycott in the past, but now supported Lenin. "In the new Duma," he wrote, "the Bolsheviks would be able to proclaim to the whole nation that there is no possibility in Russia to free the nation peacefully."[15]

The Third Duma met in November 1907 and was to continue for its full term of five years. In it the liberal-conservative Octobrists formed the dominant party. Its leader was Aleksandr Guchkov, a man of integrity, anxious to serve his country. His co-operation with Stolypin enabled this Duma to enact important reforms. The Social Democrats, led in the Duma by the fiery little Georgian Chkheidze, had only eighteen deputies of whom five were Bolsheviks, and they neither contributed to nor obstructed the sessions.[16]

By 1907 the tide of revolution, which had threatened to engulf the country, had receded. Law and order had been restored, and while there was widespread apathy, there was also hope in many quarters that the government under Stolypin's leadership and with the active support of the Duma would carry Russia into a new constitutional era.

In the period from 1907 to 1912 the Social Democratic party disintegrated. Krupskaya wrote that "we have no people at all," and in retrospect G. E. Zinoviev, who was then close to Lenin, stated that "at this unhappy period the party as a whole ceased to exist."[17] Arrests had taken some toll of the membership, but the decline in party strength was due mainly to desertion by those who lost interest or considered that the Revolution was now no more than a distant chimera.

Of those who remained in the party the majority argued for giving up illegal activities inside Russia and devoting themselves to trade-union work and especially to the Duma, which gave promise of fundamental reforms. Lenin thundered against such members, denouncing them as "liquidators," an epithet soon applied to all Mensheviks.

Struggling constantly to establish his absolute control over the remnants of the Bolshevik party, Lenin finally managed to convene a party conference to open in Prague on January 18, 1912. The conference was, in fact, unconstitutional and unrepresentative, but it acted with a show of authority. It established a distinct, independent Bolshevik party under Lenin's leadership, and it elected a Central Committee. Its members were all close to Lenin. They included Sergo Ordzhonikidze, Suren Spandarian, the Armenian Bolshevik, and Roman Malinovsky, and there were five alternate members. The committee later co-opted two further full members, I. S. Belostotsky and Iosif V. Dzhugashvili.

Malinovsky was at once brought into prominence. Lenin had heard of his activities in St. Petersburg but met him for the first time at the Prague conference. He was already convinced that this new recruit was destined to be an outstanding party leader. Lenin was a poor judge of men, and his uncritical enthusiasm for Malinovsky illustrated strikingly his lack of judgment. It showed, too, how inept he was as a conspirator, for the tsarist police were able with ease to plant their agents so that Bolshevik plans and policies were always known to them in advance. At any time Lenin's most trusted lieutenants included one or more police spies, and of them Malinovsky was the most remarkable. His treachery was uncovered after the Revolution and he was shot.

9

The Caucasian Chapter
Closes
1907-12

In the months following the Tiflis bank raid, Koba was at work in the heat and oil-stench of Baku. He was in his late twenties, lean, disciplined. Although married with a child, he was living under cover with a forged identity card, and, if not actually hunted, he was under the constant threat of arrest.

Within the revolutionary movement, too, conditions were extremely difficult. The spirit of party comradeship existed only in the struggle against the tsarist regime. Relations among members were often poisoned by bitter resentments and rivalries. Koba himself was caught up in this web of ferocious antagonisms.

An event which aroused Koba's anger was his trial by a local party court early in 1908 on the charge of organizing an expropriation in Baku. The steamship *Nicholas I* was looted, and a worker maintained that the Bolsheviks were responsible. Koba was implicated, but while the party court was hearing the case, he was arrested by the police on the charge of leading a subversive revolutionary organization. The party court apparently abandoned the proceedings and passed no judgment. The hearing nevertheless gave rise to allegations that Koba had been tried for his part in the Tiflis expropriation, and that he had been expelled from the party.[1]

Ten years later Martov published an article in the Menshevik paper, V*pered* (Forward), which had not yet been closed down. In it he stated that Stalin had been expelled from the party for being involved in expropriations. Stalin, then the powerful Kommissar for Nationalities, reacted sharply, swearing that "never in my life was I placed on trial before my party or expelled. This is a vicious libel. . . . One had no right to come out with accusations like Martov's except with documents in one's hand."[2] He insisted on taking the matter to the Supreme Court. Martov was granted time in which to collect evidence in the Caucasus. When the court resumed, however, it was found that the documents in the case had inexplicably vanished. Finally the court administered a "social reprimand" to Martov for "insulting and damaging the reputation of a member of the government."[3]

The fever of unrest which had died away in most of Russia was burning still in Baku. Workers in the oil industry continued to agitate for better pay and conditions, and at this time they won an important concession, when the employers agreed to their electing representatives to negotiate on their behalf. Koba led the campaign among the fifty thousand workers for this concession. And in this dispute he took a more moderate and practical approach than he had taken in the past.

This new approach found expression in the nine articles which he wrote on these negotiations for *Gudok* (The Whistle), the news sheet of the oil workers' union.[4] The articles were the work of a writer who was learning to express his ideas forcefully. He explained that at the time when workers broke up machinery and set fire to factories, it was an anarcho-rebellious conflict; at another time the conflict took the form of individual terrorist acts. But it was no longer sensible to destroy machines and factories, for the workers themselves suffered most from this sabotage. The need was to take control of the industries as soon as possible, as part of the struggle to eliminate poverty.[5] The immediate purpose should be to negotiate with the employers, but only if the employers gave some firm guarantees that they would meet the workers' demands. The Mensheviks argued in favor of negotiations without any guarantees or conditions. His proposals found support with the majority of the workers, who now rejected economic terrorism.

The authorities had granted immunity to the conference of workers' delegates, and it met over several months, discussing in detail the collective agreements on wages and working conditions, and arguing about politics. "While all over Russia black reaction was raging, a genuine workers' parliament was in session in Baku," wrote Sergo Ordzhonikidze, one of Koba's closest friends and later Kommissar for Heavy Industry.[6]

Away in Switzerland and depressed by reports of the death of the revolutionary movement in Russia, Lenin could only express admiration for the oil workers and their leaders, "our last Mohicans of the political mass strike," as he called them, overlooking the fact that they were not striking but negotiating.[7] At the same time he could not but take note of the Bolshevik leaders in Baku, who worked indefatigably and did not succumb to the general apathy among revolutionaries. Foremost among them were Koba, whom as Ivanovich he had met in Tammerfors and London; Ordzhonikidze; and Klimenti Voroshilov, the secretary of the oil workers' union and a close friend of Koba.

On March 25, 1908, Koba was arrested and held in Bailov prison. He was arrested not for the part he had played in various expropriations, about which the authorities appeared surprisingly to know nothing, but for being the leader of a secret subversive organization. Bailov prison, built to hold four hundred inmates, contained some fifteen hundred at this time, and conditions were harsh. General callousness and outbreaks of savagery marked the lives of the prisoners. Koba and other political prisoners formed discussion groups, and there were the usual factional rivalries and hatreds. Always they had to be careful, for the police planted agents among them, a practice which intensified the deep suspicion among the revolutionaries. Prisoners suspected of being police agents were murdered.

Koba was accustomed to such conditions, and they had developed in him a stern self-control and a ruthless attitude towards his fellows. He took advantage of prison leisure to read widely and to write articles which were smuggled out and published in *The Baku Proletarian* and *The Whistle*.[8]

On November 9 (1908) Koba was sentenced to two years' exile in Solvychegodsk in the Vologda province. On February 8, 1909, when on the way to Solvychegodsk, he became ill with typhus, and he arrived only at the end of the month. Four months later, on June 24, he escaped to St. Petersburg. Sergei Alliluyev arranged accommodation during the few days he spent in the city. From secret party headquarters he obtained a new false passport under the name of Zakhar Gregorian Melikyants. But he made no attempt to stay in St. Petersburg. He was in a hurry to return to Baku, where there was work to be done among the oil workers and where he had ready access to two newspapers for articles and propaganda. At this time, however, he was already looking beyond local party activity and thinking of the national party.

In Baku he found that party membership had dropped to two or three hundred Bolsheviks and about a hundred Mensheviks. All were infected with the general mood of hopelessness, and *The Baku Proletarian* had not appeared during his absence. He found quarters inside the Balakhlana oil field, and at once set about reviving the paper as a first step towards revitalizing the party not only in the Caucasus but also in Russia and in émigré circles.

The issue of *The Baku Proletarian* which appeared on August 27 (1909), just three weeks after his return, contained his editorial under the heading "The Crisis in the Party and Our Tasks." It was a challenging statement of the causes of decline in the party and of the action needed. In his criticisms he did not spare the émigré leaders, including Lenin. He sounded a call for positive action:

> It is not secret that our party is passing through a severe crisis. . . . The first factor which bears heavily on the party is the isolation of its organizations from the broad masses. . . . It is enough to look at Petersburg where in 1907 there were about 8,000 members and now you will find 300 or 400. . . . But not only is the party suffering from isolation from the masses, but also from the fact that its organizations are in no way linked with each other. . . . Petersburg does not know what is happening in

the Urals, and so forth. . . . The existing papers published abroad, *The Proletarian* and *The Voice*, and on the other side *The Social Democrat*, do not and can not join together the scattered party organizations. . . . And it would be strange to think that organs published abroad, remote from Russian reality, could unify the work of the party. . . .[9]

Turning to remedies, he rejected any suggestion of abandoning underground work, as this would kill, not save, the party. The proposals to transfer to the ordinary workers all party functions and in this way to free the party from instable elements of the intelligentsia had much in its favor and would certainly help to revitalize the party. It was not the answer, however, while "the old methods of party and the 'leadership' from abroad" continued.[10]

By placing the word "leadership" in quotation marks he was emphasizing the failure of Lenin and other émigrés to give dynamic direction. The practical leader in direct contact with the workers, facing hardship and anger, Koba was scornful of the émigrés not only because they lived in comfort and security, "remote from Russian reality," and failed in their task but also because all belonged to the intelligentsia, a class which he resented and mistrusted.

The immediate need was a party journal, published inside Russia, which would encourage, inform, and restore the sense of party unity among groups scattered over the vast empire. And there must be an active co-ordinating committee also inside Russia. At the same time full use must be made of the Duma and trade unions and other legal avenues for carrying on the struggle against the regime.

At this time of crisis when the party was disintegrating, Koba abandoned his previous rigid partisan position and argued for the unity of all factions. He became a conciliationist. A resolution of the Baku Committee of the party, which he wrote and which was published in the same issue of *The Baku Proletarian* as his editorial, sternly reprimanded Lenin for his quarrel with Bogdanov, a surgeon who was at the same time a Marxist philosopher and a Bolshevik, and the split within the editorial board of *The Proletarian*.[11] There had been a permissible difference of opinion, but this could not be allowed to lead to a split. It was a difference of opinion "of the kind that always has happened and will happen in such a rich and vital faction as the Bolsheviks."[12] The resolution revealed a new, almost magisterial approach, transcending local and factional limits, by the coming leader to whom the party was the all-important center of the movement.

Koba was not seeking any rift in his relations with Lenin, and he had no thought of challenging him for the leadership. He was a realist who recognized that Lenin was the only possible leader of the movement at this time. He had written honestly of the causes and had proposed cures for the existing crisis. His editorial had been unsigned and the resolution was from the Baku Committee, but he could assume that Lenin would know the identity of the writer in each case. Now in a series of "Letters from the Caucasus," written during November and December 1909 and published in *The Social Democrat* in Paris and Geneva, he demonstrated that in his basic attitude he remained wholly in agreement with Lenin.[13] The *Letters* reported briefly on relations between the nationalities in the oil fields, the unions, and in local government in the Caucasus. He castigated the local Mensheviks and their leader, Noi Zhordania, and these passages in the letters caused difficulties. The editorial board the *The Social Democrat* comprised Lenin, Zinoviev, Kamenev, and the two Mensheviks, Martov and Dan, for the party was not at this stage finally split. Strong objections were raised to the criticisms of the Mensheviks, but Lenin must have derived satisfaction from the staunch support of his Georgian correspondent.

At the same time Lenin had misgivings about him. He recognized his single-minded devotion to the Bolshevik cause, his ability, and his self-reliance. He had an acute need for young men of this caliber. But Koba also showed a strong independence, and when he presumed to criticize and disagree, Lenin considered it to be not independence, but lack of party discipline. In June 1908 in a letter to a friend in Switzerland Koba had referred to Lenin's polemics with Bogdanov as a "storm in a teacup" and had even expressed support for some of Bogdanov's philosophical views.

After the publication of Lenin's *Materialism and Empiriocriticism*, Koba wrote to another friend in Switzerland, commending the book, but also mentioning that Bogdanov had drawn attention to certain "individual faults of Ilyich [Lenin] and had correctly observed that Ilyich's materialism differs in many ways from Plekhanov's, which Ilyich, contrary to the demands of logic —for diplomatic reasons?—tries to cover up." Writing from Sol-vychegodsk on January 24, 1911, to Vladimir Bobrovsky, he commented that "we have of course heard about the 'storm in a teacup' abroad: the blocs of Lenin-Plekhanov on the one hand and Trotsky-Martov-Bogdanov on the other. So far as I know, the workers' attitude towards the first bloc is favourable. But in general the workers are beginning to look upon the emigration with disdain; 'Let them crawl on the wall to their hearts' content; but as we see it, let anyone who values the interests of the movement work, the rest will take care of itself.' "[14]

All of these comments were repeated to Lenin and they rankled. Walking with Ordzhonikidze in Paris one day, Lenin asked him if he was familiar with the expression "storm in a teacup." Ordzhonikidze knew about Koba's letters and began defending his friend. "You say, Koba is our comrade, as if to say, he's a Bolshevik and won't let us down." Lenin retorted, "But how do you close your eyes to his inconsistency? Nihilistic little jokes about a 'storm in a teacup' reveal Koba's immaturity as a Marxist."[15]

Like many political leaders, Lenin lacked a sense of humor and could be petty. He also had little understanding of the impatience felt by the party workers for the squabbles of the émigrés. In fact, Bogdanov's attempts to evolve a theory of knowledge in harmony with Marxist materialism were interesting and posed no threat to party unity, whereas Bogdanov's ultra-leftist policies were a danger and were the real reason for Lenin's break with him. Koba had read the writings of both men on the subject and his comments were pertinent. Lenin could not brook criticisms, and the touch of mockery in Koba's comments disturbed him.

Meanwhile at the end of January 1910 a further resolution of the Baku Committee, written by Koba and distributed as a hand sheet, declared that "the state of despondency and apathy" which had been paralyzing the moving forces of the Russian Revolution was passing.[16] Closely in touch with the oil workers and sensitive to the mood of the country, Koba was in advance of Lenin and other émigré leaders. The resolution proposed urgently the transfer of the (leading) practical center to Russia, the publication of a national newspaper, produced in Russia with the proposed practical center providing its editorial board, and the organization of local papers in the most important party centers. It was proposed, too, that Bolsheviks should unite with Mensheviks who supported underground work and that all others, the liquidators, should be expelled.[17]

At this time Koba was working frantically to bring about a general strike in the Caucasian oil industry. On March 23, however, he was again arrested and held in Bailov prison. Six months later he was sentenced by administrative decree to return to Solvychegodsk to complete his term of exile. Again it was lenient treatment, and this time he served out his sentence, remaining in Solvychegodsk until June 27, 1911. He was then banned for five years from returning to the Caucasus or living in St. Petersburg or Moscow. He chose Vologda as his place of residence, but on September 6 he went illegally to St. Petersburg, where he was promptly arrested and sent back to Vologda for a three-year term.

This marked the end of the Caucasian chapter of his career. The Caucasus had given him education and revolutionary experience, but he had grown beyond its narrow stage. He was to return for brief visits, but from this time he belonged to the national party.

10

Stalin Emerges
1912–13

In mid-February 1912, while still in exile in Vologda, Stalin, as he was beginning to call himself, received a firsthand report on the Prague conference, at which Lenin had established a separate and independent Bolshevik party. Ordzhonikidze had come personally to give him the news of the new party. He learned, too, that he had been co-opted as a full member of the party's Central Committee. Moreover, Lenin had acted on his insistent demands that there should be an organizing center as well as a newspaper inside Russia. The Central Committee had set up a Russian bureau with the functions of supervising and revitalizing party groups throughout the country. Stalin had been appointed a member of the bureau.

For Stalin this was the beginning of a period of frantic activity. As he had forecast, a new tide of popular unrest had begun to flow. The death of Leo Tolstoy, revered as a great writer and even more as a powerful moral force, had marked the start of a wave of demonstrations, but more important was the removal of the strong leadership of Peter Stolypin. On September 1, 1911, while attending a gala performance in the Kiev opera house in the presence of the Tsar, he was shot at point-blank range.

Stolypin had succeeded within a remarkably short time in establishing order and giving Russians promise of a more liberal way of life. Lenin and other revolutionaries recognized that he was creating conditions in which revolution would be delayed, perhaps indefinitely. Unknown to them, however, Stolypin's tenure of office had been nearing its end, and the assassin's bullet had shortened it only by a few days. Incapable of appreciating the wisdom of Stolypin's policies or of recognizing in him the savior of his regime, Nicholas II had decided to dismiss him. Under his successors the government became increasingly reactionary. The mood of the people changed, and discontent showed in demonstrations and strikes.

On February 29, 1912, Stalin escaped from Vologda, and, after a brief stop in St. Petersburg, he hastened south to Baku. Social Democrats, with a few individual exceptions, had never envisaged the permanent division of the party. Bolsheviks and Mensheviks alike took for granted that ultimately they would be united. Lenin's coup in forming his own Bolshevik party met with wide disbelief and opposition, and nowhere more than in Transcaucasia, the Menshevik stronghold. The purpose of Stalin and other members of the bureau was to persuade Social Democrats that the Bolshevik party under Lenin's leadership was the true revolutionary party.

Early in April 1912 Stalin was again in St. Petersburg, organizing production of the new Bolshevik newspaper, a task that Lenin had entrusted to him. He had been agitating for publication of a newspaper to inform and unite party groups, but now it was more urgently needed to project the new party, purged of Menshevik liquidators. Newspapers were subject to severe censorship, but even under this constraint a Bolshevik newspaper could do much to strengthen the party.

On April 22, 1912, the first issue of *Pravda* (The Truth) appeared with the editorial written by Stalin. The secretary of the editorial board was a young man named Vyacheslav Skriabin, later to be known as Molotov. The name of the new paper was deliberately taken from Trotsky's *Pravda,* published abroad, which had remained by far the most popular of the newspapers smuggled into Russia. It was a shrewd theft, for the new paper claimed many of Trotsky's readers, while controverting the policies he had been advocating. Trotsky protested angrily, and could do nothing but cease publication of his own paper.

On the day that the first issue of *Pravda* appeared, Stalin was arrested. Other members of the bureau were arrested soon afterwards. Malinovsky, the only member to remain at liberty, had done his job well, and most Bolsheviks, influenced by Lenin's vehement support of him, were slow to suspect that he was an agent of the police. When Molotov was arrested, another of Lenin's protégés, Miron Chernomazov, who was also a police agent, was appointed secretary to the editorial board in his place.

This time Stalin was sentenced to three years' exile in the Narym province of Western Siberia. He arrived there on July 18, 1912, and escaped on September 1, returning to St. Petersburg. At once he resumed control of *Pravda,* and now he found himself protecting the paper from Lenin's angry criticisms. In his editorial in the first issue Stalin had written, "We believe that a strong full-blooded movement is unthinkable without controversy—only in a cemetery can total identity of opinions be achieved!"[1] And further, the editorial proclaimed: "Just as we must be uncompromising in our attitude to the enemy, so we must make concessions to each other. War against enemies of the workers' movement, peace and comradely endeavour within the movement—that will be the guiding principle of *Pravda* in its day-by-day work."[2]

This conciliatory policy was abhorrent to Lenin. Remote from Russian realities, as Stalin had pointed out in his Baku articles, he could not appreciate the pressure of demands by Bolsheviks inside Russia for reunion of the party. At this stage in the judgment of Stalin and others living and working in Russia, *Pravda* had to be conciliatory to gain support, and circulation was soon steadily rising towards its peak of eighty thousand copies. Lenin nevertheless continued to bombard the editorial board with articles, viciously attacking the Mensheviks as "liquidators" and "conciliators." Stalin and other members of the board carefully censored his articles, and this brought angry tirades from Cracow, where Lenin had moved in order to be closer to operations without facing any of the risks of life inside Russia.

"Vladimir Ilyich was so upset," wrote Krupskaya, "when from the outset *Pravda* deliberately struck out from his articles all polemics with the liquidators."[3] Typical of Lenin's petulant outbursts was "We must kick out the present editorial staff. . . . Would you call such people editors? They aren't men, but pitiful dish rags, who are ruining the cause!"[4]

During the autumn of 1912, Stalin was directly involved in the elections to the Fourth Duma. He wrote the election manifesto for the party's candidates under the title "Instruction of the Petersburg Workers to Their Labour Deputy." It required them to publicize the demands of the workers, to promote revolution, and not to take part "in the empty game of legislation in the ruling Duma."[5]

The "Instruction" was adopted by workers in all major industries in St. Petersburg. Moreover, briefly forgetting his anger with *Pravda*, Lenin expressed himself to be so pleased with it that he published it in *The Social Democrat,* and in a letter to the editorial board of *Pravda* he wrote: "Without fail print this Instruction to the Petersburg deputy in a prominent position in heavy type."[6]

Thirteen Social Democrat deputies were elected, six Bolsheviks and seven Mensheviks. As in the previous Duma, they began at once to co-operate with each other, forming a united faction and electing Chkheidze, the Georgian Menshevik, as their leader. In doing so they were reflecting the strong demand among the workers for party unity; furthermore, as a very small minority group in a now reactionary Duma they needed to stand together.

Lenin exploded in anger. He demanded that the Bolshevik deputies publicly break from their Menshevik colleagues in the Duma. Soon after the elections, Stalin made his way to Cracow in answer to a summons from Lenin calling a meeting of the Central Committee there. Lenin lectured the committee members on the immediate need for the Bolshevik deputies to make the break. While convinced that such action was inevitable at a later date, Stalin knew that to do so forthwith would lose the Bolsheviks' support. Moreover, on returning to St. Petersburg towards the end of November, he found that the Bolshevik deputies were unwilling to meet Lenin's demand. He did not press them, nor did he publicize in *Pravda* the need for the division in the party.

Thwarted in his demands, Lenin resorted to more devious tactics. He called for another meeting of the Central Committee in Cracow, this time with the six Bolshevik deputies taking part. For Stalin and others this meant yet another frontier-crossing and breaking away from important work in Russia. It was a demonstration of Lenin's great authority that his summons was obeyed, and by the end of December 1912 all had assembled in Cracow. Meanwhile Lenin had dispatched Jacob Sverdlov to take charge of *Pravda* in Stalin's absence and to make the required changes.[7]

In Cracow at the end of December Lenin again urged on the members of the Central Committee and now particularly on the six Bolshevik deputies the importance of an immediate open split with the Mensheviks. Fired by the absolute conviction that he was right, he finally secured their agreement. Stalin had always accepted the need for an open split, but had disagreed only about the timing, and now he accepted Lenin's demand.

When the members of the Central Committee and the Bolshevik deputies returned to Russia, Stalin remained in Cracow at Lenin's request. It was the first time that the two men had been together without other members being present, but there is no record of their conversations or of their impressions of each other. In many ways they were strikingly similar. Both were small, sturdy in build, and with a slight Asiatic cast of feature; both possessed enormous strength of will, and Stalin was soon to develop the same drive to power, which was to make them the dominant leaders of the first half of the twentieth century. But there was a fundamental difference. Lenin, with his bullet head thrust forward, vibrant with nervous energy, was a dynamic personality, while Stalin, controlled and inscrutable and not yet fully conscious of his mission, appeared quieter in temperament. But he possessed an inner strength, ruthless and cold as steel—in character he was the more powerful.

Lenin was not interested in people, only in their views, and specifically in whether he could count on their support. He was nevertheless probably curious to know more about this Georgian. Stalin's record as a staunch Bolshevik and his origin as a man of the people, not a member of the intelligentsia, had told in his favor. His strongly independent cast of mind and his readiness to disagree on occasions were, however, disturbing characteristics to Lenin, who demanded subservience from his supporters. At this time, however, apart from keeping him away from St. Petersburg and leaving Sverdlov a free hand on *Pravda*, he had particular need of Stalin's assistance in finding a solution to the troublesome problem of the nationalities.

At the turn of the century the Great Russians formed less than half of the empire's total population of 124.2 million. Of the other nationalities within its frontiers the most important were the Ukrainians (22.5 million), the Poles (7.9 million), the Jews (5 million), the Letts (1.4 million), the Lithuanians (1.65 million), and the Georgians (1.35 million), while the Grand Duchy of Finland, linked with Russia through the person of the Tsar, had a population of 3 million.[8]

Nationalist movements among most of the non-Russian peoples had gathered strength, reacting particularly against the rigorous Russification policies of Alexander III. In 1905, the revolutionary year, massive demonstrations and rebellions had taken place in Poland, the Ukraine, Finland, the Baltic provinces, and the Caucasus, but this upsurge had been countered after 1907 by a Russian nationalist offensive.

On the problem of the nationalities Lenin had been confused in his thinking. He had always expressed strong support for nationalist movements as for any other activity that might help destroy the tsarist regime. He was the champion of self-determination, territorial autonomy, and the absolute right of secession, but still he thought in terms of a strictly centralized party of all workers in the Russian Empire. He gave his attention to the problem for the first time when the Bund, claiming to represent all Jews as a distinct nationality, demanded "national-cultural autonomy." He opposed the claim on the ground that the Jews were widely scattered and did not occupy a recognized territory; the correct solution was for the Jews to merge into Russian organizations. But he continued to promote the rights of Poles, Ukrainians, and other nationalities, which occupied their own distinct territories.

The real dangers of nationalism struck Lenin forcibly early in 1912, when he was living in Cracow in Austrian Poland. The Austrian Empire, like the Russian, contained numerous national minorities, and over the years the Austrian Social Democrat party had developed as a federation of autonomous groups, organized on national lines. Lenin now saw this as a serious weakness. At the same time he became aware of the division among Poles between Józef Piłsudski's Socialist party, which stood for full independence, and the Polish Social Democrat party, dominated by Rosa Luxemburg, who was an internationalist, adamantly opposed to the Polish and all other nationalist movements as irrelevant and potentially damaging to the revolutionary cause. Lenin argued against this internationalism, because it was inexpedient and would lose his party support in Russia, but he also condemned nationalism, which would weaken the party.

Lenin remained basically a Great Russian in outlook and in his assumption that the party would be Russian dominated and led. Now he became alarmed by the possibility that the Russian party might also lose its unity and decline into a loose federation of national groups, each with its own independent standpoint. The time had come to combat this pernicious threat.[9] The dilemma nevertheless remained of how to reconcile the promotion of national independence movements with the unity of the Russian party and ultimately with the centralized Russian republic, which would emerge after the Revolution.

Stalin's arrival was timely. As a Georgian he could not be charged with Great Russian chauvinism, and he came from a region in which there was one Social Democrat organization, embracing Georgians, Armenians, Russians, Tatars, and others. Recently Noi Zhordania and a group of Georgian Mensheviks had proposed the adoption of the Austrian principle of "national-cultural autonomy." Stalin was the right man to expose the falsity of the idea. He had always opposed this deviation in Transcaucasia. As long ago as 1904 he had written strongly in support of a centralized Russian party, embracing workers of all nationalities, and had attacked Georgians who favored national groups within the party. Again in 1906 he had opposed national autonomy when it was mooted by a group of Social Democrats in Kutais.

Lenin was delighted to discover that Stalin shared his view that such a trend within the party would lead to fatal weakness. In February 1912 he wrote to Maksim Gorky: "About nationalism, I fully agree with you that we have to bear down harder. We have here a wonderful Georgian who has undertaken to write a long article for *Prosveshchenie* after gathering all the Austrian and other material. We will take care of this matter."[10]

Stalin spent January 1913 in Vienna, writing his article which was published under the title of *Marxism and the National Question*.[11] In the introduction he stated his basic position:

> The wave of nationalism has been advancing more strongly all the time, threatening to engulf the working masses. . . . At this difficult stage social democracy has the great mission of repelling nationalism, of protecting the masses from the general infection, for social democracy alone can achieve it, opposing against nationalism the tried weapons of the internationalism, unity and the indivisibility of the class struggle.[12]

In the first section of the article he defined the constituent elements of a nation as community of economic life, of language, of territory, and of "national character," all of which elements must be present together. Next he explained that every true nation had the right "freely to determine its own fate," to be autonomous and to secede.[13] But he strongly criticized the Austrian program of "cultural-national autonomy," which amounted to hidden nationalism and "paves the way not only for the isolation of nations, but also for the breaking-up of the workers' movement."[14] He condemned the Jewish Bund and the Caucasian groups which pursued separatism and subordinated socialism to nationalism. The correct solution for the Jews was assimilation, and for the Transcaucasian people it was regional autonomy. Indeed, regional autonomy was the answer to the national problem in Russia, provided that in permitting freedom for the minorities to use their own languages, run their own schools and cultural activities, the workers were organized within the one Social Democrat party. He ended his article with the assertion that the final answer to the national question lay in "the principle of the international unity of workers."[15]

Marxism and the National Question was written in his clear and trenchant style. In its approach and arguments it was recognizably his own work, showing how his thoughts on the subject had developed consistently over the past eight years. Moreover, he wrote it with confidence, for he knew more about the problem than Lenin or Trotsky and Bukharin, whom he met in Vienna at this time.

Lenin was pleased with the work. In an editorial on the national program of the party he wrote that the article "stands out in first place" in recent Marxist theoretical writing on the subject.[16] It gave Stalin a new standing as a Marxist theoretician in party circles.[17]

As soon as this work was done, Stalin returned to St. Petersburg, arriving there in mid-February 1913. He found accommodation in a private apartment, and in reminiscences published many years later, his landlady recalled that he was very earnest, quiet, and considerate.[18] But his stay in St. Petersburg was brief. Jacob Sverdlov, like himself a co-opted member of the Central Committee, had been arrested on February 9 (1913), and, informed by Malinovsky, the Okhrana was now rounding up all leading Bolsheviks. On February 23 a musical evening was arranged to raise funds for *Pravda*. Stalin was uncertain about attending and asked the advice of Malinovsky, who assured him that the police would never arrest him on such a public occasion.[19] He went and was promptly arrested.

11

The Last Exile
1913-17

For five months Stalin lay in prison in St. Petersburg. Early
in July 1913 he was sent under guard by rail to Krasnoyarsk and
then by boat northwards along the Yenisei River to Monastyrskoe, a small town which served as the administrative center of
the Turukhansk region. His previous sentences of exile had been
to places not too far distant and had involved inconvenience
rather than hardship. The new sentence marked the end of such
lenience. The Okhrana had evidently decided that the Bolsheviks
had served their purpose in disrupting the Social Democrat party
and were no longer needed. Systematically the police arrested and
removed them to distant penal settlements where they could
cause no trouble.

The Yenisei-Turukhansk region in northern Siberia, part of
which lies within the Arctic Circle, is a vast, remote expanse from
which escape was virtually impossible. The savage cold, the extreme monotony of the long dark winters, the brief hot summers
when the air was thick with insects, and the greatly feared winter

storms, which struck like hurricanes, burying whole villages in whirls of snow, all intensified the sense of isolation. Life was reduced to a primitive struggle against the elements. Men went mad and the suicide rate among the exiles was high. It was a place where only men with reserves of moral and physical strength survived; and they, too, were marked permanently by the experience.

Stalin was probably in a black thwarted mood as he waited in prison to learn his fate, and then set out on the long journey deep into Siberia. Through ability, dedication, and hard work, and certainly not through tact, subservience, or flattery, he had risen in the party hierarchy to a position of authority. As a member of the Central Committee and editor of *Pravda* he had much to do, but he was being sent far away into exile and impotence. He may have felt resentful towards Lenin, Trotsky, and others who lived in security abroad, but more probably he despised them for removing themselves from the dangers of the real revolutionary struggle.

Learning that he was to join them, the colony of exiles in Monastyrskoe prepared a separate room and saved food for him from their meager provisions. In the bleak isolation of their lives, a new arrival was an exciting event, especially a member of the Russian Bureau and of the Central Committee. He would bring news of other comrades and of the latest developments in St. Petersburg and Moscow.

Headed by Sverdlov, the exiles assembled to greet him on arrival. Stalin did not respond to their welcome. He was surly in manner and evidently not prepared to talk to them. He went into his room and did not reappear. But the account of how he antagonized his fellow exiles should be treated with reserve. It is contained chiefly in the reminiscences of R. G. Zakharova, published more than fifty years later. She herself was not in Turukhansk, but heard the details from her husband, a Bolshevik in exile there from 1903 to 1913, who obviously had no liking for Stalin.[1] But with his rough manners and aggressive outlook, and his complete disinterest in personal popularity, Stalin readily made enemies at this time. While the other exiles banded together for companionship, he isolated himself except when official party business was to be transacted. According to his daughter, "He loved Siberia . . ." and "He always looked back on his years of exile as if they were nothing but hunting, fishing, and walks through the taiga."[2] But he may also have had an instinctive need for solitude in which to think about the future, sensing that he was on the threshold of a new epoch in his life.

Yakov Sverdlov, with whom Stalin was never on friendly terms, was a small, unemphatic man in appearance, but had been since 1902 an indefatigable underground worker. Lunacharsky wrote of him: "The man was like ice . . . like a diamond. His moral nature, too, had a similar quality that was crystalline, cold, and spiky. He was transparently free of personal ambition and any form of personal calculation to such a degree that he was somehow faceless. He never originated anything but merely transmitted what he received from the Central Committee, sometimes from Lenin personally."[3]

During their Siberian exile, and especially in Kureika, where they were sent to finish their term, Stalin and Sverdlov were thrown into each other's company, and they became completely estranged. Writing in March 1914 to a friend, Sverdlov commented: "I am much worse off in the new place. Just the fact of not being alone in a room. There are two of us. With me is the Georgian, Dzhugashvili, an old acquaintance whom I already know from another exile. A good fellow, but too much of an individualist in everyday life."[4] In the following May, Sverdlov wrote in another letter that "now the comrade and I are living in different quarters and rarely see each other."[5]

There is as usual only the scantiest information about Stalin's own life and outlook in this period. The Alliluyevs provide some details. Sergei Alliluyev and Stalin had become friends in Baku, and, when Sergei moved with his family to St. Petersburg, he and his wife always welcomed Stalin into their home, and helped him when he was on the run. While in Turukhansk he received from them parcels of warm clothing and gifts of money. Later in 1915 he wrote to Olga, Sergei's wife, expressing thanks and asking them not to spend their much-needed money on him. But he asked them to send him post cards, showing local scenery. "Nature in this accursed region is shamefully poor—in summer the river and in winter the snow, that's all nature offers here—and I'm crazy with longing for natural scenes, if only on paper."[6]

Svetlana Alliluyeva related that in later years he would sometimes talk about Siberia, "its stark beauty and its rough silent people."[7] He was on good terms with the local inhabitants. They showed him how to fish in the Yenisei, but instead of staying in one place, as they did, he moved about until he found a spot where the fishing was good. His catches were often so large that they believed that he had magic powers and would exclaim: "Osip [their own name for him], thou knowest the word!" On one occasion in winter he was overtaken by a snowstorm on the way home and lost his way. Coming upon two local peasants, he was surprised that they ran away from him. He learned later that his face had been so covered with snow and ice that they had thought he was a goblin.[8] Later his own daughter wrote that "my aunts told me that during one of his Siberian exiles [presumably Turukhansk] he had lived with a local peasant woman and that their son was still living somewhere—he had received little education and had no pretensions to the big name."[9]

In Siberia, Stalin fretted over his inactivity. The Bolshevik organization was disintegrating. *Pravda's* circulation fell from forty thousand copies daily to about half this number. The open break by the Bolsheviks from the Mensheviks in the Duma was a major cause of this decline. At the same time the Okhrana was arresting all Bolshevik activists, and depriving party organs of leadership. Then on August 2, 1914, the German declaration of war on Russia united the Russian people in a mood of patriotic fervor and loyalty to the Tsar. Support for the Bolsheviks and other revolutionary parties declined even further.

Within Russia, revolutionaries were divided into the defensists, who refused to oppose the national war effort, and the defeatists, who, in Lenin's words, stood for the defeat of Russia "as the lesser evil" and urged "the conversion of the imperialist war into a civil war."[10] In the Duma the Bolshevik and Menshevik deputies refused to vote for the war budget; and in August 1914 they made a public declaration, repudiating the war.

Lenin was not satisfied. He demanded that they should adopt his *Theses on the War*, which went far beyond their declaration, and required them to work for Russia's defeat. No policy was more calculated to antagonize workers and peasants at this time or to bring the full force of government repression down on the already enfeebled party. In his intransigence he seemed intent on destroying the party. The fact that he was ordering the deputies to commit treason, for which summary trial and execution were the penalties in wartime, may not have occurred to Lenin, who moved early in September 1914 from Austria to neutral Switzerland for safety.

Soon after the arrest of Sverdlov and Stalin, Lev Kamenev had arrived in St. Petersburg, now called by the Slav name of Petrograd in the wave of anti-German feeling. Kamenev had come as Lenin's personal representative on the Central Committee. He arranged a meeting of Bolsheviks to discuss the *Theses on the War* on the night of November 14. The police knew about the meeting through their agents, and arrested all present. Aleksandr Kerensky, leader of the socialist revolutionary Trudovik group in the Duma and a prominent advocate, defended them and proposed to the court that Lenin should be tried in his absence and his defeatist views made known more widely. At their trial Kamenev and the Bolshevik deputies repudiated Lenin's theses. They were nevertheless found guilty of treason, but escaped the death sentence and were exiled to Turukhansk.

Arriving in Monastyrskoe, Kamenev and the deputies found that their conduct at the trial was being heatedly discussed by the exiles already there. In July 1915 some eighteen Bolsheviks, including four members of the Central Committee, assembled and heard reports on the trial. There was a move to censure Kamenev, but Stalin and others opposed it. According to Trotsky, Lenin remained highly critical of Kamenev's behavior and demanded a public apology by him and the five deputies, which they never made.[11]

By October 1916 conditions at the front had deteriorated, and casualties were so heavy that the government announced the call-up of political exiles. Stalin was ordered to report in Krasnoyarsk. It meant traveling in winter conditions from Kureika to Monastyrskoe and along the Yenisei to Krasnoyarsk. According to Boris I. Ivanov, "When Dzhugashvili arrived at Monastyrskoe from Kereika, . . . [he] remained as proud as ever, as locked up in himself, in his own thoughts and plans."[12]

Early in 1917 Stalin had his medical examination and was rejected as unfit for service because of the deformity in his left arm and also because, as he told the Alliluyev family, the authorities considered that he would be an "undesirable element" in the Army.[13] Since, however, his sentence had only a few months to run, he was not sent back to Turukhansk, but allowed to settle in Achinsk, a small town on the Trans-Siberian railway line.

Lev Kamenev was then in Achinsk, where he had been joined by his wife, Olga, who was Trotsky's sister. Stalin was a frequent visitor to their house in the evenings. A. Baikalov, an émigré who published his recollections in Paris thirty-seven years later, was there on occasions. He recalled that Kamenev dominated the conversation and that he did not hesitate to cut short Stalin's rare contributions with slighting comments. Stalin would then sit in silence, smoking his pipe, occasionally nodding agreement with Kamenev.[14]

One can only speculate about Stalin's development during the three and a half years spent in Yenisei-Turukhansk. There is no lack of stories of his abrasive behavior, but nearly all were recorded many years later by embittered exiles. The hatreds engendered within the Russian revolutionary movement remained intense and vicious. In fact, this offensive behavior stemmed from his nature as an able and sensitive individual, deeply conscious of his humble background and other disadvantages, who had always felt a driving need to assert himself. With people of similar background he was friendly, but towards intellectuals and others who patronized him he was aggressive. But he was capable of close human relationships. Around 1904 he had married Ekaterina Svanidze and had had a child; he was warmly received by the Alliluyev family and other friends. Indeed, he was recognizably a more normal human being than Lenin.

At the time of his Siberian exile Stalin was in his mid-thirties. He could look back on achievements and valuable experiences. He had watched and listened to Plekhanov, Martov, and other leading Social Democrats, and he had worked closely with the "mountain eagle" himself. He had a sharp, critical eye and was quick to discern the strengths and weaknesses of others. He had realized that he was in no way their inferior, but an equal. It was this realization that softened his abrasiveness and that explains his plea for a spirit of comradely understanding within the party which, to Lenin's disgust, he had expressed in the editorial of the first issue of *Pravda*. It may partly explain, too, the facts that he was gaining a reputation for being a man of moderation and that at the party conference in July 1917 he was elected to the Central Committee with the third highest number of votes. Alongside this change in conduct, growing out of a new self-confidence, certain ideas were evolving in his mind which were to dominate his thinking in the years to come, and with a dynamic power that was to make him the absolute ruler over the vast Russian empire.

Since the age of nineteen he had been single-minded in his dedication to Marxist dogma and to the conception of the small party of professional revolutionaries, leading the working class in the complete transformation of society. He never wavered in his conviction that this was the only way to organize and govern people for their own welfare.

Of the other ideas which were now taking a permanent grip on his mind, the first was a profound sense of Russian nationalism. He began to think of a Russia no longer weak, undeveloped, inefficiently governed, and at the mercy of her enemies, but powerful, dynamic, and able to dominate the world. By an extraordinary process of assimilation this Georgian embraced Russia with a deep feeling for her historical traditions and strivings. He had read widely in Russian history and had studied the policies and methods of Ivan the Dread and Peter the Great, perhaps seeing himself as their heir. Moreover, the conceptions of Moscow as the Third Rome and of the messianic mission of the Great Russian people, transmuted by Marxism-Leninism, gripped his imagination, revealing themselves in his later policies.

The second idea, probably embryonic at this time and properly realized only years later when Lenin's health began to fail, was that he himself was the man of history, fated to lead the party and Russia in this momentous mission. He would regenerate and awaken this somnolent giant of a country to its destiny. This, rather than personal lust for power, was the driving motive, the grand purpose, and the main source of the tyranny of his rule.

12

1917

In his Siberian exile, Stalin was removed from the calamitous events of the war years. But news of the disasters at the front, the ferment in the cities, and the approaching collapse of the tsarist regime all added to his impatience to return to Petrograd. On learning of the amnesty for political prisoners he set out at once for the city.

The capital to which he returned was confused and chaotic, reflecting the state of the whole country. Law and order had broken down. Anarchy was at hand. But Nicholas II at the Supreme Military Headquarters in Mogilev remained unaware of the gravity of the situation. In spite of appeals and warnings from the president of the Duma and others, he believed that his troops would restore order. On March 12, however, mutiny broke out in certain senior regiments in the capital; this was the turning point. The special guards detachments, ordered from Mogilev to put down the mutiny, joined with the rebels on reaching the city. On March 15 Nicholas II abdicated.

Although the Duma was formally dissolved, its members re-fused to disperse. They elected a provisional committee which as-sumed power. But the committee was at once faced with the ri-valry of the Soviet of Workers' and Soldiers' Deputies, which had been active briefly during the Revolution of 1905 and was now hurriedly revived. The deputies were said to have been chosen on the basis of one for each thousand workers and one for each army company, and they claimed to be representative of the insurgents and left-wing elements. The Provisional Committee and the Exec-utive Committee, known as Excom, of the Soviet co-operated to a limited degree, and on March 16 agreed to set up a provisional government. Kerensky, a lawyer of great energy and ability, was to become head of this government. But although a revolutionary socialist in politics, he was moderate and humane and lacked the implacable fanaticism of Lenin, Stalin, and Trotsky, and he failed to understand the mood of the country.

Arriving on March 12 in Petrograd, Stalin went at once to the Alliluyev home, where he received a warm welcome. The whole family was present: Sergei and his wife, Olga, their son, Fedor, their elder daughter, Anna, whose memoirs provide the record of this home-coming, and the younger daughter, Nadya, then a schoolgirl aged sixteen. He answered their questions about life in Siberia, and, using his talent for mimicry, he made them laugh about the peasants who had met the train at every station from Krasnoyarsk to Petrograd. The spokesman of each group would orate grandiloquently that "holy revolution, long-awaited, dear rev-olution had arrived at last" and salute the returning political exiles as warriors from a field of battle. They seemed to think that *Revolutsiya* (Revolution) was a person and a successor to the Tsar, just as in 1825 many of the troops had believed that *Konsti-tutsiya* (Constitution) was the wife of Constantine, who was thought to be succeeding Alexander I to the throne.

On the following morning Stalin set out by tram for the office of *Pravda*. Fedor, Anna, and Nadya went with him. They were looking for accommodation nearer to the city center. When they parted, Stalin called out: "Don't forget to keep a room for me in the new apartment! Don't forget!"[1]

Party headquarters had been set up in a mansion, which had

belonged to the ballerina Mathilde Kschessinska. There he met
with a rebuff. The Bolshevik organization was coming to life
again. The Russian Bureau of the Central Committee was directing party affairs and taking in various members as they emerged
from prison or exile. On March 12, the day of his return to Petrograd, the bureau considered the question of Stalin's admission
to its membership. According to the minutes of this meeting, the
bureau received a report that he had been an agent of the Central
Committee and would be a desirable member. It is strange that
the bureau should have required a report on Stalin and that its
minutes should have described him merely as an agent of the Central Committee, when he had been a member of it and of the bureau as well as editor of *Pravda*. Then came the extraordinary decision that "in view of certain characteristics inherent in him, the
Bureau expressed itself to the effect that he should be invited with
an advisory vote."[2]

The reference to "certain characteristics" presumably concerned
his uncomradely aloofness in Turukhansk. Further, Kamenev was
to be allowed to write for *Pravda*, provided that his articles were
unsigned. The decision must have been all the more offensive,
since Muranov, a former Bolshevik deputy, who had no special
abilities or record of service to the party, but who returned from
exile with them, was admitted at once to full membership.

The leading members of the bureau at this time were Aleksandr
Shlyapnikov and Molotov. They were clearly troubled by the prospect of being displaced by Stalin and Kamenev. Shlyapnikov explained later that the bureau's attempt to exclude them from its
inner counsels arose from disapproval of their ambivalent attitude
towards the provisional government and the war.[3] It was a specious excuse, for Muranov was known to support the government
and the policy of continuing the war.

Stalin acted at once, showing a new authority. He was the senior
party member present, and in ability he towered over Shlyapnikov
and Molotov, whom he swept aside. Three days after his return he
was elected to the bureau's Presidium with full voting rights and
was appointed Bolshevik representative on the Executive Committee (Excom) of the Petrograd Soviet of Workers' Deputies. With

Kamenev he also took over *Pravda*, which had resumed publication on March 5, 1917, under the editorship of Molotov.

Stalin dominated the party during the three weeks until Lenin's return. Recognizing that Lenin's violent opposition to the war and to the provisional government would antagonize most party members and people outside the party, he pursued a moderate policy. He advocated limited support for the provisional government on the ground that the bourgeois-democratic revolution was not yet complete and that there would be a period of years before conditions were ripe for the socialist revolution. It made no sense, therefore, to work to destroy the government at this stage. In his policy towards the war he was equally common-sensed, writing that "when an army faces the enemy, it would be the most stupid policy to urge it to lay down arms and go home."[4] In response to the general demand among Social Democrats, he was even prepared to consider reunion with acceptable elements in the Menshevik party, and on his initiative the bureau agreed to convene a joint conference.

Pravda reflected this policy of moderation. Articles received from Lenin were edited, and the abusive references to the provisional government and to the Mensheviks were toned down or cut. According to Shlyapnikov, jaundiced by his summary displacement, the "editorial revolution was strongly criticized by Petrograd workers, some even demanding the expulsion of Stalin, Kamenev and Muranov from the party."[5] But, while there may have been a few radicals who took this line, the mass of the party supported the moderate policy, as was shown in the general response to Lenin's pronouncements during the following weeks.

Late on the evening of April 3, Lenin arrived at the Finland Station in Petrograd. It was a tumultuous occasion, effectively stage-managed with festoons of red banners, guards of honor, and a military band. Describing the scene, Sukhanov observed that "the Bolsheviks, who shone at organization and always aimed at emphasizing externals and putting on a good show, had dispensed with any superfluous modesty and were plainly preparing a real triumphal entry."[6] In promoting Lenin as the hero of the masses, however, the party had a special purpose. Lenin had traveled from Switzerland through Germany, aided by the enemy government.

Patriotic and anti-German feelings were still strong among Russians, and the party was anxious to counteract rumors that Lenin was a German agent, a charge which was to cause the Bolsheviks serious embarrassment in the months ahead.

"All the comrades groped about in darkness until the arrival of Lenin," one Bolshevik noted.[7] Disregarding the fanfare of welcome, he plunged at once into the business of revolution. He made an immediate impact on the party both by his implacable fanaticism and by the drastic, urgent policy that he expounded.

At the Finland Station, Lenin ignored Chkheidze and the Excom delegation who had come to greet him and at once harangued the crowd about the futility of defending the capitalist fatherland and the need to negotiate an immediate peace. On the way to party headquarters he stopped repeatedly to address the people, railing against the war, the provisional government, and the Mensheviks as "traitors to the cause of the proletariat, peace, and freedom."[8] His speeches disturbed many of his listeners. "Ought to stick our bayonets into a fellow like that. . . . Must be a German," Sukhanov overheard one angry soldier remark.[9]

Lenin was clearly out of touch with the mood of the city. But he was impatient. He sensed, after conspiring and struggling all his life, that power was within his grasp. He hammered home his policies, and, aided by the increasing anger over food shortages, the disasters of the war, and the crisis of leadership, he began to gain support. His message was simple: The party must press forward to immediate socialist revolution. He ruled out union of any kind with the Mensheviks, or support for the provisional government, or for any continuation of the war. He set out this policy in his *Theses*, which he urged upon the party conference in April.

The party was shaken by his aggressive demand for immediate revolution. *Pravda* denounced it as "unacceptable in that it starts from the assumption that the bourgeois democratic revolution is ended."[10] Kamenev, Zinoviev, and other leading Bolsheviks as well as many ordinary members opposed not only his main thesis but also his ban on relations with the Mensheviks. Inexorably he wore down their opposition and ranged the party behind him.

In May Trotsky arrived from abroad and greatly strengthened Lenin's position. They had had many disputes, but fundamentally they were in agreement. At the time of his return to Russia, Trotsky was not even a member of the Bolshevik party, but he was soon to be welcomed with enthusiasm and elected at once to the Central Committee.

From the moment of Lenin's arrival in Petrograd, Stalin slipped into the background. His moderate approach had been overruled, and, like so many others in the party, he must have pondered deeply over the new policy of immediate revolution. Apparently, however, he accepted with equanimity his own personal displacement. He had always recognized Lenin as the leader, and if he had had any thought of challenging his position, this might have been the time to do so. Far from challenging, however, he appreciated that Lenin's policy, which would have been madness earlier, was becoming practical and necessary in the growing chaos to which both the provisional government and the Soviet were contributing. He now gave Lenin his full support.

During the coming months Stalin appeared to be overshadowed also by Trotsky, Zinoviev, Bukharin, and others. Sukhanov described him as a "grey blur."[11] Trotsky with customary malice and excess described him as a "plebian democrat and oafish provincial forced by the spirit of the times to assume the Marxist tinge."[12] At this time Stalin was entrenching himself as a moderate and dependable leader, and with Kamenev he remained editor of *Pravda*. While the others were making speeches and contending for the center of the stage, he was always present, stable as a foundation stone, working within the party organization. Far from being a "grey blur," he was gaining the respect and confidence of members, as was shown at the Seventh Party Conference in late April, when he received the third highest number of votes after Lenin and Zinoviev in the secret ballot for the Central Committee.

At this conference Stalin delivered his report on the nationalities. It was no longer a matter of theory, but had become an urgent practical problem. The Finns, Poles, and Ukrainians were demanding independence or at least a degree of autonomy. Stalin spoke on the right of all nationalities to self-determination and even secession. This may have given him some difficulty, for he instinctively favored a strongly centralized and united Russian state. But he handled the session convincingly and gained the support of the conference. Grigori Pyatakov, Ukrainian by birth, and Feliks Dzerzhinsky, a Pole, had both disagreed, fearing that the disintegration of the Russian empire would damage the class struggle and the cause of revolution. Stalin defeated them in debate, but tried to reassure them that in the free socialist republic which would take the place of the empire, the nationalities would have no desire to secede.

Seeking every weapon to help him to seize power, Lenin now proclaimed his support for the Soviets of Workers', which were sharing power with and dominating the provisional government. He had been impressed by their popularity, and, recognizing that they held the real power, he reversed the policy he had advocated from Switzerland. Now he argued that the party must work to create "a republic of workers', soldiers', and peasants' deputies in the whole country." The slogan "All power to the Soviets" was born.

Alarmed by the mounting anarchy and the threats of a violent popular upheaval, and influenced by Kerensky's fervent appeals, the Excom of the Petrograd Soviet and the provisional government formed a coalition. At first Kerensky was the dominant leader in the coalition. He was still committed to continuing Russia's participation in the war, and he threw himself into whipping up support for a new military offensive. It began on July 1 and swept forward triumphantly against the Austrians. But then German troops halted the advance. The Russian armies collapsed. Thousands of desperate, undisciplined men surged eastwards. For Kerensky and other moderate revolutionaries this rout put an end to all hopes of negotiating peace from a position of strength and of restoring stable government. Russia was not fated to follow a moderate course.

A tide of violent disorder swept over the country, exploding in the "July Days." Fear gripped the city. Some twenty thousand sailors from Kronstadt and thirty thousand Putilov workers joined the general violence. Mass hysteria led to mass killings and destruction. But, as Sukhanov wrote, "The blood and filth of this senseless day had a sobering effect by evening and evidently evoked a swift reaction."[18]

The upheaval, which had seemed spontaneous, had in fact been instigated by the Bolsheviks. But its fury had taken Lenin by surprise. He had made no plans to take over the city or to depose the provisional government, and the demonstration had grown so explosively that the party could not control it.

The city reacted sharply. The provisional government, with the support of the Petrograd Soviet, accused the Bolsheviks of attempting to destroy the Revolution and reduce the country to anarchy. The Ministry of Justice released documents purporting to prove that Lenin and other Bolshevik leaders were, in fact, German agents. The accusation made an immediate impact. The Bolshevik party became the object of popular hatred. *Pravda* was closed down. Trotsky, Kamenev, and Lunacharsky were arrested, but Lenin and Zinoviev had already gone into hiding. At this time public opinion was severely critical of Lenin on political and moral grounds. Within the party, too, voices were raised accusing him of abandoning his comrades and being concerned only for his personal safety.[14]

Lenin's hiding place was the new apartment of Stalin's friends, the Alliluyev family, on Rozhdestvenskaya Street. There he occupied the room that had been kept for Stalin's use. The question now was whether Lenin and Zinoviev should surrender to trial in order to counter the criticism that they had deserted their comrades and to answer the government's charges.

On the night of July 20 (7 July) Stalin, Krupskaya, Ordzhonikidze, and others gathered in the apartment to discuss the question with Lenin. The chief fear was that if he surrendered, government agents would kill him before he reached prison, let alone trial. Stalin and Ordzhonikidze tried to negotiate with the Mensheviks in the Petrograd Soviet guarantees that, if they surrendered, Lenin and Zinoviev would be protected and given a public trial. At this time, however, when Bolshevik fortunes were at such a low ebb and when Lenin himself was the subject of virulent criticism, he would not risk his personal safety or limit his freedom of action. It became necessary to change his hiding place. Sestroretsk, a small town on the Gulf of Finland, was chosen. Great care was taken with his disguise. Stalin acted as barber and shaved off his beard and mustache. Wearing a cap and a long coat, lent by Sergei Alliluyev, Lenin looked like a Finnish peasant, as he made his way, accompanied by Stalin and Alliluyev, to the Primorsky Station, where he boarded the crowded train to Sestroretsk.[15]

With so many of its leaders under arrest or in hiding, and surrounded by hostility, the Bolshevik party was at the nadir of its fortunes. It demonstrated, however, an extraordinary resilience. The few remaining members were dedicated and unshakable. Moreover, Stalin was at liberty, and he provided a leadership which, although less dynamic and visionary than Lenin's and less dramatic than Trotsky's, was rocklike in its strength and determination.

Early in August, the Sixth Party Congress met secretly in Petrograd. In the absence of Lenin, Stalin delivered the Central Committee's report to the 267 delegates, displaying great skill and persuasiveness. Many delegates were on edge after the hysteria of the July Days and confused by Lenin's change in tactics. He had now abandoned the slogan "All power to the Soviets" because, he declared, the Soviets had become counterrevolutionary in supporting the government against the Bolsheviks.

In presenting the Central Committee's report, Stalin showed that he had moved away from his moderate policy. He now condemned the provisional government as "a puppet, a miserable screen behind which stand the Kadets, the military clique, and allied capital—three pillars of counter revolution." Before the July Days a transfer of power to the Soviets without violence might have been possible, but now "the peaceful period of the revolution has ended; the non-peaceful period, the period of clashes and explosions, has come." At the same time he was careful not to expound the new policy in the blunt terms of an ultimatum, which was Lenin's way. He was sensitive to the fact that many delegates were reluctant to cast aside the Soviets, while others still believed that it was premature to think of an immediate socialist revolution.[16] It was in large measure his achievement that the resolution approving the policy was adopted with only four abstentions.

In the discussion on the final part of the draft resolution Stalin made a spontaneous contribution which illustrated his individual approach, and pointed to his future policy. Dissenting from a proposal that revolution was possible "on condition of a proletariat revolution in the West," he said that "the possibility is not excluded that Russia will be the country that blazes the trail to socialism. . . . It is necessary to give up the outworn idea that Europe alone can show us the way. There is a dogmatic Marxism and a creative Marxism. I stand on the ground of the latter."[17]

Stalin's handling of the Sixth Party Congress raised his prestige and authority. In the elections to the Central Committee he came after Lenin, Zinoviev, Kamenev, and Trotsky in the number of votes polled. When the Central Committee elected the editorial board of *Pravda,* Stalin received the most votes and Trotsky failed to gain election. When it was decided to elect a ten-man inner cabinet of the enlarged Central Committee, Stalin again prevailed in the balloting.

In July Kerensky had become Prime Minister, and with the support of the Excom had formed a new cabinet with a majority of moderate socialists. The challenge to Kerensky's government came from the right. It was led by General Lavrenti Kornilov, a Cossack of proven bravery and ability, but his attempted coup collapsed without a shot fired.

This military challenge to the government and the threat of a reactionary dictatorship had rallied the whole city behind Kerensky. Mensheviks, Socialist Revolutionaries, and Bolsheviks formed a united front in the Soviet. The Bolsheviks were particularly active. With the committee's approval they enlisted an armed militia, which enabled them to expand the Red Guard to a strength of some 20,000 in Petrograd.

The Bolshevik party began growing in strength. The July Days and the denunciation of Lenin as a German agent had proved to be only minor setbacks. By the time of the Sixth Congress in August 1917, membership had increased to some 200,000. It was an impressive growth, but still the party represented a tiny minority in the country as a whole, and could claim the support of only 5.4 per cent of the workers averaged over twenty-five towns.[18] But, while insignificant in size, it was organized and disciplined, and in Lenin, Trotsky, and Stalin it had exceptional leaders.

Still in hiding, Lenin was now in a frenzy of impatience. He was convinced that an insurrection, led by the party, and a dictatorship of the left were immediately possible. At a meeting early in September the Central Committee had before it his demand that revolutionary detachments should arrest the government and seize power. The committee and the party as a whole believed that he was recklessly inviting a repetition of the July Days. They were acutely nervous. Lenin's proposed action was precipitous; the party and the country were not ready.

On October 20 Lenin slipped into Petrograd. With furious energy he pressed on members of the Central Committee his arguments for immediate revolution. The committee held a secret meeting on October 23, attended by Lenin and Zinoviev, and there was heated debate on Lenin's resolution that "an armed rising is inevitable and the time perfectly ripe."[19] Of the twenty-two members of the Central Committee, nine were absent, but finally, worn down by Lenin's tireless argument, all present, except Kamenev and Zinoviev, voted for Lenin's policy. The fact that he had a majority, no matter how slender, was enough. He considered now that the party was committed to action and certainly before the Congress of Soviets began on October 25.

Lenin's plan involved a tremendous gamble. He was counting on taking the government by surprise and on gaining popular support by promising prompt solutions to the problems of peace, bread, and the land. Kamenev and Zinoviev, who were not cast in a heroic mold, were alarmed. Stalin offered no opposition and supported this bid for power.

Meanwhile Kamenev and Zinoviev, apparently in a mood of panic, were publicizing their opposition and emphasizing the dangers involved. To Lenin and others it was treason to oppose and to reveal Bolshevik intentions. It was all the more culpable since the party rank and file were increasingly alarmed by their warnings. This was more than Lenin could stand. He had returned to Finland, and from his hiding place there, he demanded that the Central Committee expel them from the party.

At a meeting of the committee on October 17 (30), Trotsky advocated stern action against Kamenev and Zinoviev and branded them as traitors. He was not influenced by the fact that Kamenev was his brother-in-law; indeed, he was demonstrating that loyalty to the party stood far above personal relationships. Other members supported the case for severe punishment. It was Stalin who brought the note of moderation into the fury of the discussion. His argument in favor of tolerance flowed not from a passive, oil-on-troubled-waters attitude, nor from some incredibly far-sighted realization that he might need the support of these two comrades in the future, but from a deep concern for the unity of the party at this critical time. Summarily expelling two comrades of long standing would cause discord and solve nothing. Kamenev and Zinoviev knew that they had acted irresponsibly, and they would not repeat their mistakes. After his intervention, the proposal to expel them was dropped. Then it was decided to remove Kamenev from the editorial board of *Pravda*. This, too, was dropped, when Stalin resigned in protest and the committee refused to accept his resignation.

After Lenin's return to Finland Trotsky took charge. He was chairman of the Military Revolutionary Committee of the Petrograd Soviet, set up on October 25. Serving as the headquarters staff of the Revolution, this committee controlled the Red Guard and all military units in the city which supported the Bolsheviks. There was also a special military revolutionary "center," consisting of five members, elected or appointed on October 29. Stalin, but not Trotsky, was a member of this center, which has been described as the real organizing force of the Revolution.[20]

Trotsky was undeniably the leader and the driving force in all of the preparations and in the insurrection itself. Early on the morning of November 7, 1917, the Revolution began. Troops under the command of the Military Revolutionary Committee occupied key points throughout Petrograd. By early afternoon the insurgents had control of the whole of the city, except the Winter Palace; it was taken during the evening.

The swift, almost bloodless, capture of Petrograd set a pattern which was followed throughout most of the country. The exceptions were the Cossacks of the Don, Kuban, and Orenberg regions who resisted Bolshevik attempts to take control, and the capture of Moscow, accomplished by the Red Guards only on November 15 after severe fighting.

On November 8 Lenin appeared at the session of the Congress of Soviets. He was acknowledged as leader of the Revolution in a resounding ovation. The fact that he had not directed

the preparations or played any part in the momentous events of
the previous day was evidently not held against him. Stalin's contribution to the preparations is not known, but during the Revolution in Petrograd he was said to have been at his desk in the
party's editorial offices. Again, as with Lenin, his absence from the
scenes of action was not a cause of reproach. It is probable that
they stood back from the events so that they would be ready to
continue the struggle if the insurrection failed. It had not failed,
but the two men who were to be responsible for Russia's fortunes
in the years ahead now had to learn the realities of power.

13

Brest-Litovsk
1918

The Revolution, one of the most momentous events in history, had happened swiftly and almost without struggle.

Lenin and his supporters knew, however, that their position was precarious. The Second All-Russian Congress of Soviets had approved the new government, but the people of Petrograd and throughout the country were confused.[1] They accepted the coup because the Bolsheviks alone among the political parties seemed capable of positive action, and had promised to provide food, to solve the land problem, and to bring immediate peace. In the longer term, they were counting on the election of the Constituent Assembly, which would draft a constitution and bring to birth the new Russian republic. Only then, they believed, would order be truly restored and a new era of national prosperity launched.

One of Lenin's first acts was to select a cabinet, known as the Council of People's Kommissars, or Sovnarkom.[2] The fifteen kommissars included Lenin himself as president, Trotsky as

Kommissar for Foreign Affairs, Stalin for Nationalities, Lunacharsky for the People's Education, Shlyapnikov for Labor, Aleksei Rykov for Home Affairs, and Vladimir Milyutin for Agriculture.

The congress formally appointed Lenin's Council of People's Kommissars by decree, and then elected a Central Executive Committee of 101 members. The Bolsheviks won 62 seats on this committee, the Left Socialist Revolutionaries, who had formed a separate party, 29 seats, and other parties 10. The Executive Committee was to exercise legislative powers when the congress was not in session. In practice, Sovnarkom was soon wielding both legislative and executive functions.

On November 8 Lenin appeared before the congress. It was a time of high excitement and he received a "tumultuous welcome."[3] He read a proclamation, addressed to all peoples at war, calling for immediate peace without annexations and without indemnities. Next he read a decree, abolishing private ownership of land "immediately and without purchase," and providing for distribution of all land to those who cultivated it with their own labor.[4] This was a reversal of policy, and it introduced the proposal made by Stalin as a temporary measure eleven years earlier in Stockholm. The All-Russian Congress of Peasants' Deputies debated a proposal to merge with the Congress of Workers' and Soldiers' Soviets and, after the walkout of the more conservative deputies, it approved the merger.[5]

Lenin thus succeeded nominally in basing his government on the three main classes—workers, peasants, and soldiers. But he had not yet met the demand in Sovnarkom, in the Central Executive Committee, and within his own party for a coalition of all socialist parties. Right-wing Bolsheviks in particular were determined to force a coalition with the Socialist Revolutionaries and the Mensheviks. Zinoviev, Rykov, Milyutin, Vladimir Nogin, and Lunacharsky, who had all opposed the Bolshevik seizure of power but, after its success, had accepted office in Sovnarkom, now resigned. They and Kamenev also were even prepared to consider a Menshevik proposal that Lenin and Trotsky should be excluded from any coalition government. The agitation continued until, with the approval of the majority of the Bolshevik Central Com mittee, a statement, signed by Lenin, Trotsky, and Stalin, threatened the agitators with expulsion from the party. The threat had a sobering effect, and the question of coalition was forgotten in the tide of shattering events that followed.

The Constituent Assembly presented another challenge. The elections were to begin on November 12, the date fixed earlier by the provisional government. Lenin had always proclaimed the vital importance of the Assembly.[6] As the date of the elections approached he was increasingly troubled.

The results were far worse than he had feared.[7] The Bolsheviks won only 175 of the 707 seats. To Lenin and his close supporters the result was unacceptable, and one to be corrected by guns and bayonets.

On January 5, 1918, the Constituent Assembly held its opening session in the Tauride Palace. The Bolshevik and Left Socialist Revolutionary deputies walked out of the chamber. On the following morning, when the deputies arrived to resume the session, Red Guards barred the entrance to the palace. A demonstration of Socialist Revolutionaries was dispersed by Red Guards with rifle fire. The Constituent Assembly, so long awaited and discussed, was in effect dissolved, and the people, in a mood of apathy, appeared unconcerned.

On the same day the Central Executive Committee, appointed by the Congress of Soviets, which had a Bolshevik majority, approved the suppression of the Constituent Assembly. The justification was that it was an organ of counterrevolution. With their passion for at least a show of legality, the Bolsheviks, after rigging the elections, hurriedly convened a Third Congress of Soviets. By an overwhelming majority this Congress approved the dismissal of the Constituent Assembly.[8]

Stalin was directly involved in all of the major events of this time. He was already influential and indispensable to Lenin. He had signed the statement warning the right-wing members, who were agitating for coalition, and he had rejected the Menshevik proposal that Lenin and Trotsky should be excluded from a coalition government. He was to support Lenin strongly during the party crisis over the peace treaty with Germany. At the same time he was demonstrating his capacity for handling numerous responsibilities.

His first task was to create the People's Kommissariat for Nationality Affairs, known as Narkomnats. He was assisted by S. S. Pestkovsky, a Pole who had taken part in the October Revolution.

In a room in the Smolny Institute, Pestkovsky found a vacant table. He pushed it against the wall and pinned above it a piece of paper, inscribed "People's Kommissariat for Nationality Affairs." This table with two chairs provided the kommissariat's first office.[9]

Soon after becoming Kommissar, Stalin attended the congress of the Finnish Socialist party in Helsinki. On November 14 he addressed the congress, and declared solemnly that his government would honor its undertaking to the Finnish people. "Full freedom to shape their own life is given to the Finns as well as to the other peoples of Russia! A voluntary and honest alliance between the Finnish and the Russian peoples! No tutelage, no control from above, over the Finnish people! These are the guiding principles of the policy of the Council of People's Kommissars."[10]

This was in accordance with "The Declaration of the Rights of the Peoples of Russia," signed by Lenin and Stalin a few days after the Revolution.[11] To his audience in Helsinki, Stalin's speech was no doubt all the more impressive, because he came from one of the small oppressed nations of the Russian Empire. Subsequently, when reporting to the Central Executive Committee on the ratification of Sovnarkom's decree, recognizing Finland's independence, he deplored the fact that a bourgeois regime was in power. He went on to castigate the Finnish Social Democrat party for its "indecisiveness and incomprehensible cowardice" in failing to grasp power.[12]

For the present, however, he stood firmly by the principle of national self-determination, although criticized by Bukharin and other members for yielding to the bourgeois nationalism of the small nations. A few weeks later at the Third All-Russian Congress of Soviets, he enunciated a change, stating that "the right of self-determination [was the right] not of the bourgeoisie but of the toiling masses of a given nation. The principle of self-determination ought to be used as a means in the struggle for so-

cialism, and it ought to be subordinated to the principles of socialism."[13] This change was all the more necessary because most of
the small nations had installed governments which were non-
socialist and anti-Bolshevik.

In April 1918 he issued from Narkomnats an appeal to the Soviets of the national minorities under non-Bolshevik leadership.
He pointed out that it was essential to free the people from bourgeois leadership and to convert them to the idea of Soviet autonomy. "It is necessary to elevate the masses to the level of the
Soviet regime, and to fuse their best representatives with the latter. But this is impossible without autonomy of these outlying regions, that is without organizing local schools, local courts, local
administration, local organs of authority, local sociopolitical and
educational institutions with guaranteed full right of use of the
local native language of the masses in all spheres of sociopolitical
work."[14] This policy was soon to be interpreted in the slogan "national in form—socialist in content."

In May 1918, when opening a preparatory conference on the
creation of a Tatar-Bashkir Autonomous Soviet Republic, he expressed this centralist policy in forthright terms. A sovereign,
"purely nationalist" form of autonomy would be disruptive and,
indeed, anti-Soviet. The country needed "a strong Russian-wide
state authority, capable of quelling conclusively the enemies of socialism and of organizing a new communist economy." The central authority should, therefore, exercise all functions of importance, leaving to the autonomous regions the administrative,
political, and cultural functions, which were regional in character.[15]

Stalin was a member of the commission set up to draft the first
constitution, which was adopted in July 1918, creating the Russian
Socialist Federative Soviet Republic. The form of federalism with
national territorial units which he advocated was embodied in his
draft article 11. At this time, however, the R.S.F.S.R. had a treaty
relationship with the Ukrainian, Belorussian, and Transcaucasian
Soviet republics. This was to be changed by the 1924 constitution,
creating the Union of Soviet Socialist Republics.

Nationality affairs can have taken up only a small part of his
time. On November 29, 1917, the Central Committee of the party

had appointed a *chetvërtka,* or foursome, comprising Lenin, Stalin, Trotsky, and Sverdlov, to exercise power in all emergency matters. According to Trotsky, this inner council became a *troika,* or threesome, because Sverdlov was too deeply involved in the work of the party secretariat to be available.[16] Membership of this inner council and of Sovnarkom was for Stalin all the more demanding, because of Lenin's reliance on him.

"Lenin could not get along without Stalin even for a single day," Pestkovsky wrote. "Probably for that reason our office in the Smolny was under the wing of Lenin. In the course of the day he would call Stalin out an endless number of times, or would appear in our office and lead him away. Most of the day Stalin spent with Lenin."[17]

In this early period, Sovnarkom met for five or six hours nearly every day. Lenin took the chair and he drafted many of the decrees, which poured from these meetings. On December 29 and 30 decrees proclaimed "the eradication of every inequality in the army"; soldiers would in future choose their own officers and elect committees to supervise them.[18] Marriage and divorce laws were relaxed; the legal equality of men and women was emphasized; illegitimate children would have the same rights as the legitimate. Numerous decrees disposed of private property. The nationalization of industry began. All banks were nationalized. The eight-hour working day became law with immediate effect. Workers, through their elected committees, were to have a decisive voice in the management of industry.

The old legal system was swept away, and new courts and revolutionary tribunals were set up. Lenin had expected for a long time that such tribunals, as well as a secret police, would be needed to deal with the enemies of the regime. In December he entrusted to Feliks Dzerzhinsky, a Pole and a fanatic, the task of organizing the new All-Russian commission to fight counterrevolution and sabotage. Under its short name of Cheka, it became the dread secret arm of the regime, and it spawned as its successors the GPU, NKVD, MVD, and KGB.[19] On February 5 (1918) a decree proclaimed the separation of church and state, and confirmed the right of every citizen to freedom of belief and worship. The Cyrillic alphabet was revised, and as from February 1 the Gregorian calendar was introduced.[20]

Never since the era of Peter the Great, two centuries earlier, had there been such an avalanche of change and reform. The difference now was that the new government was intoxicated with power and desperately trying to gain popular support. Clothed in appealing humanitarian garb, its decrees seemed to herald a new age.

Lenin had declared repeatedly before October 1917 that on coming to power the Bolshevik government would propose peace on terms that the imperialist enemy would certainly reject. This would lead to revolution in capitalist countries and the outbreak of "revolutionary war." Now he realized that this policy was unrealistic. The German High Command knew that the Russian Army was demoralized, and that the new Soviet government would have to accept German terms of peace.[21]

The Soviet proposal for an armistice was quickly agreed to by the Germans, and signed at Brest-Litovsk on December 2. Negotiations for peace began in earnest on December 9. Trotsky then headed the Soviet delegation. He had come to make fullest use of the conference for revolutionary propaganda, and he fervently believed that revolution was imminent in Germany and elsewhere. At times he dominated the conference. His country in chaos, its Army mutinous and demoralized, and its new government desperately clinging to power, he was negotiating from a position of weakness against professional diplomats backed by a strong and victorious Army.

Trotsky's furious sallies made no impression on his German opponents. They knew the weakness of his position. Suddenly, on January 18, they produced a map of eastern Europe, showing the new frontiers, which deprived Russia of extensive territories. The ultimatum enraged Trotsky. He swore he would break off negotiations. Then, having received a telegram, signed "Lenin-Stalin," instructing him to return to Petrograd for discussions, he agreed to an adjournment until January 29. There is further evidence, cited by Trotsky himself, showing how closely Stalin stood to Lenin at this critical time. A certain Dmitrievsky observed that "even Lenin at that period felt the need of Stalin to such an extent that, when communications came from Trotsky at Brest and an immediate decision had to be made, while Stalin was not in Moscow, Lenin would inform Trotsky: 'I would like first to consult with Stalin before replying to your question.' And only three days later Lenin would telegraph: 'Stalin has just arrived. I will consider it with him, and we will at once give you our joint answer.' "[22]

Leaving Brest-Litovsk on January 6, Trotsky reached Petrograd. He now worked out his peace formula of "no peace no war." He would announce the end of the war and the demobilization of the Russian Army, while refusing to sign a treaty of peace. He was confident that the Germans would be unable to renew their offensive, because their troops would refuse to obey orders, and there would be revolution inside Germany. The formula would inspire the proletariats of Europe. He clung to the idea that revolution was imminent in Germany, Austria, and elsewhere.

In Petrograd, Trotsky argued forcefully for his new approach. Lenin was unconvinced. Stalin stated bluntly that there was no evidence of imminent revolution in western Europe and that Trotsky's formula was not a policy. After heated debate in the Central Committee, the decision emerged that Trotsky should prolong the negotiations and, when faced with a showdown, apply his no-peace-no-war formula.

The German delegation returned to Brest-Litovsk, determined to force an early peace. Their intention was first to sign a separate peace with the Ukrainian Rada, which would presumably compel Trotsky to come to terms. When the conference resumed on January 28 (1918), Trotsky vehemently rejected the separate Ukrainian peace. Again the Germans were unimpressed. With special ceremony on February 9, 1918, the treaty was signed by the Ukrainian representatives in Brest-Litovsk. The negotiations then turned to a lengthy exchange between Russian and German delegations on the application of self-determination in territories under German occupation.

The conference was nearing a crisis. Trotsky decided to make his announcement. On February 10 he delivered a scathing indictment of imperialism. The delegates, having heard it several times already, took it to be a face-saving preliminary to the acceptance of the German terms. Then he proclaimed his formula: "We are removing our armies and our peoples from the war . . . but we feel ourselves compelled to refuse to sign the peace treaty."²³ He followed this statement with stirring appeals to the working masses of all countries to follow the example of Russia.

The German and other delegations sat in silence, as Trotsky withdrew from the conference room. They were staggered by this preposterous declaration. On the same evening Trotsky returned to Petrograd with his delegation. He was delighted with his performance, and confident that the Germans would not dare to renew their offensive. To his colleagues he reported that he had won a diplomatic victory. Lenin, however, was far from persuaded. Six days later his fears proved well founded. The German government declared that the armistice would end on February 18, and on that day the German Army began advancing on a broad front.

In Petrograd the Central Committee frantically debated what to do. Lenin made it clear from the start that peace negotiations must be renewed without delay. The no-peace-no-war formula had not only failed but had endangered the Soviet government and the Revolution. Trotsky stubbornly argued that they should wait on the German proletariat, who were surely on the point of revolution. Lenin finally won a bare majority of support from the Committee.

A message was sent in the early hours of February 19, 1918, that under protest the Council of People's Kommissars accepted the German terms. The German reply came four days later. As Lenin had feared, the new peace terms were far harsher. The Central Committee reacted with fury. Bukharin shouted hysterically that they must fight, must wage a holy, revolutionary war to the last man, and most of those present echoed his demands.

Lenin remained calm in the midst of this emotional outburst. When he spoke, he repeated the hard facts of their predicament. He demanded that the peace treaty be signed, and he added the dire threat that "if this is not done I resign from the government!"²⁴ The significance of his threat was hardly noticed, as the members continued their debate. Finally Lenin's demands were approved. Bukharin voted against them. Trotsky, unable to accept that his negotiations had failed or to realize the gravity of the situation, abstained. Stalin supported Lenin, and it is unlikely that he ever forgot the vulnerability of the party and of the nation or the conflict within the Central Committee during these fateful days.

After stormy meetings the Petrograd Soviet and the Central Executive Committee of the Congress of Soviets voted to accept the German peace conditions in order to save the Revolution. The treaty was signed on March 3, 1918. By its terms Russia lost 1,267,000 square miles of territory, embracing 27 per cent of her agricultural land and a population of 62 million, 26 per cent of her railways, and 75 per cent of her iron and steel industry. The Bolshevik regime was saved, but never under the Tsars had the nation suffered such losses and humiliation.

For a time a storm raged over the treaty. Most Russians reacted from national pride. Among the revolutionary parties the reaction was also wildly emotional, but the sense of national humiliation was secondary to their revolt against the betrayal of the Revolution. Revolutionary war was, they argued, the only honorable course; it was possible as a partisan war, for if the Army was demoralized, the people could still fight. But Lenin and Stalin, and even Zinoviev and Trotsky, recognized that such action would spell the death of the party.

The Left Socialist Revolutionaries at once broke away from the coalition and campaigned for war against the imperialists. Within the party Bukharin and other prominent Bolsheviks were in revolt. Like the Left Socialist Revolutionaries they saw themselves as the defenders of the Revolution. Their appeals for a holy revolutionary war aroused enthusiastic responses among ordinary members. Gradually, however, Lenin's arguments gained support until, at the time of the ratification of the peace treaty at the Seventh Party Congress on March 15, 1918, Bukharin's resolution for the rejection of the treaty found few supporters.

In the course of some six months the party had been shaken by two major revolts. First, there had been the "waverers," the faction led by Zinoviev and Kamenev, who had opposed the Bolshevik seizure of power. Then, distinct from this faction, had come the left communists, led by Bukharin, who called for a return to the purity of socialist principles. In both cases there had been free debate within the party. The question was whether at such times of crisis when its survival was at issue, the party could allow itself to be crippled and weakened by internal dissensions. In the disciplined and united party that Lenin had always envisaged such freedom was a luxury, and inexorably the party moved towards monolithic unity.

14

Civil War
1918–20

The Treaty of Brest-Litovsk had presented the first real challenge to the party since the seizure of power. Party members were deeply shaken by the stark realities of Russia's weakness and isolation. They had not recovered from the shock of this experience when they found themselves overwhelmed by the Civil War. The new revolutionary regime faced annihilation in a struggle in which a dark destructive force took possession of the Russian people. A storm of violence, hatred, and slaughter swept over the land. It was to be one of the most savage civil wars in history, and, fought in the immensity of the Russian plain and involving millions of people, it was epic in scale.

The Civil War did not burst suddenly upon the country. Like the first warning tremors of an earthquake, it started far away in the south. Meanwhile in Moscow dogma and cherished policies were pushed aside as Lenin and his government concentrated all their thoughts and energies on survival. Events crowded upon each other, and the significance of many of the actions taken by

THE CIVIL WAR
AND THE INTERVENTION
1918 – 1920

Red Forces   White Forces

MILES
0   500
0   KM   500
POST WORLD WAR I BOUNDARIES

OB. R.

OB. R.

Krasnoyarsk

TO IRKUTSK
AND
VLADIVOSTOK

Tomsk

IRTYSH R.

Tyumen

TOBOL R.

GAJDA

Omsk

Ekaterinburg

SYROVY

Chelyabinsk

POSITIONS OF
CZECHOSLOVAK LEGION,
JUNE 1918

Troitsk

CECEK

burg

Orsk

SIBERIA

CHINA

ARAL
SEA

ASPIAN
SEA

N

W   E

S

IRAN   AFGHANISTAN   INDIA

the government at this time was realized only much later. This was especially true to the removal of the capital from Petrograd to Moscow in March 1918.

The decision was made hurriedly and as a matter of expediency. "If the Germans at a single bound take possession of Petrograd with us in it," Lenin argued, "the revolution is lost. If on the other hand the government is in Moscow, then the fall of Petrograd would only mean a serious part-blow."[1] But it was a change of profound importance in the history of Soviet Russia and in the life of Stalin himself.

The cities of Moscow and Petrograd had come to symbolize the schism within the Russian nation. Moscow was the ancient capital around which the nation had been brought to birth. In it was enshrined the old patriarchal Tsardom of Muscovy with its mixed Asiatic and Orthodox Christian traditions. Through the centuries Russians had looked towards it in the spirit of pilgrims. The Kremlin, or citadel, a grim, secretive fortress, its savage beauty accentuated by the golden domes of its churches, still retained its character as the residence of the Tsars, venerated, feared, and absolute in their powers, and it became the residence of the new Soviet leaders.

Petrograd, the magnificent city created by Peter the Great early in the eighteenth century, was the gateway for Western ideas and techniques, and represented Russia's kinship with the West. The people of Petrograd scorned Moscow as the center of all that was conservative and backward in Russian life. For their part the Muscovites, dismissing the Petrogradtsi as dangerous upstarts, viewed the West with suspicion and took pride in their role as the guardians of the old, self-sufficient, and superior Muscovite way of life.

In every generation there had been conflict between the conservative Muscovites and the westernizing Petrogradtsi. Peter the Great's cataclysm of change and reform, symbolized by his new capital, and then the Revolution, had sharpened the conflict. The people of Petrograd, the city of the Revolution, now prided themselves on being the innovators who had brought into Russia the great Western revolutionary doctrine of Marxism. Lenin and most of the Bolshevik leaders belonged in spirit to Petrograd. They were orientated towards the West and looked forward to the union of the international proletariat. But Stalin belonged to the Muscovite tradition, which was Asiatic rather than Western in character. He settled readily into the old city and, like the ancient Tsars, he made it the center of his life, becoming known as "the recluse of the Kremlin."[2]

On arrival in Moscow Stalin, like other members of the government, was allocated living quarters within the Kremlin. He found, however, that the Moscow Soviet had set aside two mansions in different streets, for his kommissariat, and he wanted it housed in one building. Pestkovsky relates that they tried to secure the Great Siberian Hotel. Stalin and he found a notice on the front doors, stating, "These premises are occupied by the Supreme Council of the National Economy." They tore it down and put up notices stating, "These premises are occupied by Narkomnats." The notices had been typed by Nadya Alliluyeva, who had joined the staff as a secretary. His attempt to commandeer this building was unsuccessful. "It was one of the few instances," Pestkovsky remarked, "when Stalin suffered defeat."[3]

The office of his kommissariat was the least of Stalin's concerns at this juncture. He was directly involved in the government's desperate measures to survive the tidal wave of disasters. The country was in a state of chaos. Industry was at a standstill and famine threatened the cities and towns. The peasants, now their own masters, had no interest in sending their produce without payment to the urban population. But overshadowing even these problems was the Civil War.

The first phase of the war had opened in January 1918. General Mikhail Alekseev had escaped to the south and had joined with Hetman A. M. Kaledin, who had established a Cossack regime in the Don area. There Alekseev recruited a Volunteer Army, known as the White Army, composed of former tsarist officers, cadets, and others who opposed the Revolution.

Lenin entrusted command of the Bolshevik offensives in the Ukraine and the Don region to Vladimir Antonov-Ovseenko, an ex-tsarist officer who had become a revolutionary. The Ukrainian Rada had declared Ukrainian independence. In reply to a Soviet ultimatum, sent on December 17, 1917, the Rada Secretariat had pointed out that "The Declaration of the Rights of the Peoples of

Russia," signed by Lenin and Stalin, had guaranteed the equality and sovereignty of the Ukrainians as of the other peoples of Russia. It rejected Sovnarkom's attempt to impose its authority. In an offensive against the Ukrainian nationalists Kiev was captured on February 9, 1918. Soon afterwards, however, German and Austrian troops began by agreement to occupy the Ukraine, which was regarded as independent. The Red forces had to withdraw.

Antonov-Ovseenko had sent his main forces into the Don region, where they brought about the collapse of the Kaledin regime. Alekseev's Volunteer Army was forced to retreat to the Kuban, and in the icy cold winter many lost their lives in the forlorn journey across the steppe. Reinforced by Kuban troops, the Volunteer Army, commanded now by Kornilov, attacked Ekaterinodar, where Red forces were some thirty thousand strong. After four days of savage fighting, Kornilov ordered the storming of the town on April 13, 1918. He had every hope of taking it. But the attack had to be abandoned after Kornilov himself was killed by a stray shell. Early in May German troops occupied Rostov and appointed General P. N. Krasnov as hetman. The Volunteer Army returned to the Don region, where it became the rallying point for antirevolutionaries.

The war entered a new phase in May–June 1918 as a result of a series of extraordinary events. The Czechoslovak army corps, some thirty thousand strong and comprising Czech and Slovak prisoners of war, isolated after the Russian Army's collapse, seized control of all the main towns and stations, except Irkutsk, along the Trans-Siberian railway. They had refused to take sides with the White or the Red forces, but then, finding themselves menaced by the Soviet government, and especially by Trotsky's telegrams ordering that they be either taken into labor battalions or recruited into the Red Army, they had resolved to fight their way to the east. They were well armed and disciplined, and there were no Soviet forces capable of preventing their domination of the eastward route.

Lenin, Trotsky, and Stalin now recognized that the survival of their regime depended upon the creation of a disciplined army. It was not a matter to which they had given previous thought.[4] The breakdown of the Brest-Litovsk peace conference and the renewed

German advance underlined the urgent need to raise a regular army. On March 1, 1918, the Supreme War Council was set up in Petrograd and charged with this task. But the move of the government to Moscow and the emergence of small independent units, raised by local Soviets, and other factors hampered progress. The Red Army developed slowly and in confusion.

On March 13 (1918) Trotsky, now the people's Kommissar for War, was appointed chairman of the Supreme War Council. He had long been urging conscription, strict discipline, technical efficiency, and an officer corps as necessities in a regular army. The most striking innovation on which he insisted was that, in the exceptional conditions of the revolutionary era, the technical knowledge and experience of the displaced tsarist officers must be utilized. It was an extremely controversial proposal. Officers were hated as class enemies. Many warned against the danger that such officers would betray the Red Army and desert at times of crisis. Lenin had strong doubts about relying on them. But then he learned that some forty thousand of these "military specialists" were already serving, and that the Army would disintegrate if they were withdrawn. Trotsky had his way. He had coerced officers into service and ensured their loyalty by a ruthless system of holding their families as hostages and by placing them under the close supervision of military kommissars. Many officers deserted, but many were converted to the revolutionary cause, or gave their service as a duty to the nation.

Trotsky played an outstanding role in the early phases of the war. Possessed by a demon of energy, he constantly toured the various fronts. The special train from which he operated was a reflection of the man, with his ability and his love of power and ostentation. Drawn by two engines, the train was equipped with a radio and telegraph station, printing press, electrical generator, and a garage with cars which he used to dash to critical points away from the railway line. Trotsky's staff, bodyguard, and train crew all wore uniforms of black leather. A machine-gun unit was part of its complement. They had to be on guard not only against White forces but also against guerrilla bands which ranged the country.

In its struggle for survival, the Soviet government resorted to war communism, which involved centralized government control of the economic life of the nation. An immense bureaucratic machine was hastily erected, and was soon wielding tremendous power, usually with gross inefficiency.

The food kommissariat was the most crucial of the new bureaucratic institutions. Food products had to be requisitioned from the peasants and distributed by a system of rations cards, issued strictly on a class basis. The rate of death from starvation and malnutrition was high, especially in cities and towns. The food kommissariat had absolute power and responsibility for providing the people "with articles of prime necessity and food stuffs."[5] It mobilized workers' detachments for the collection of grain. By July 1918 these detachments had more than ten thousand members. They operated on military lines, each unit containing not fewer than seventy-five men with commander and political kommissar, and armed with machine guns. Their task was to wrest the grain from class enemies, namely village bourgeoisie, speculators, and the kulak, literally "the fist," who hired labor, leased land, and was comparatively well off.

Class hatreds were intensified by a special decree, signed by Lenin and Sverdlov in June (1918), ordering the formation of Committees of the Poor, the Kombedy. They were responsible for distributing food and goods, and in particular for requisitioning surplus grain from kulaks. In practice they acted as though they had license to take what they wanted. Envy, greed, and hatred had full rein. The whole country was soon in the throes of a bread war as savage and inhuman as the Civil War. Men and women were burned alive, cut up with scythes, tortured, beaten to death.

Lenin was soon appalled by the ferocity and scale of the war that he had unleashed in the villages. On August 18, 1918, he sent a circular to all provincial Soviets and food committees, stressing that "the Committees of the Poor must be revolutionary organizations of the whole peasantry against former landlords, kulaks, merchants, and priests, and not organizations only of the village proletarians against the rest of the village population."[6] Admonitions were useless. The savagery still raged, causing untold suffering. In November 1918 the Kombedy were abolished, but the hatreds endured and the plunder of grain continued.

The Socialist Revolutionaries, the party of the peasants, had become increasingly opposed to the Bolshevik government. They had never ceased condemning the Treaty of Brest-Litovsk. They now castigated the government for causing civil war in the villages.

The Fifth All-Russian Congress of Soviets met on July 4, 1918, in the Bolshoi Theater in Moscow. The All-Russian Soviet executive committee had expelled Right and Center Socialist Revolutionaries and the Mensheviks in the previous month. The Left Socialist Revolutionaries were now the sole legal opposition party, and they planned to challenge the government.

On July 6 two Socialist Revolutionaries gained admission to the German Embassy and shot to death Count Mirbach, the German ambassador. The purpose of the assassination was to provoke the German government into denouncing the peace treaty and attacking Russia, thus forcing the Soviet government to wage a revolutionary war against Germany. The Germans were, however, fully extended on the Western Front, and in no position to renew war in the east.

On the same day the Socialist Revolutionaries attempted to take over the city with a force of several thousand men. Their troops reached the Bolshoi Theater in the evening. There they found strong Bolshevik forces on guard, and, instead of fighting, they retreated to their headquarters, where later they tamely surrendered.

The Socialist Revolutionary party was now outlawed. Fanatics among them, however, resorted to terrorism, which had been their chief political weapon before the Revolution. On August 30, 1918, M. S. Uritsky, head of the Petrograd Cheka, was shot dead. An attempt was made on the life of Trotsky. Lenin was shot and wounded by Fanya Kaplan, a young Jew. He was carried to the Kremlin, where after two anxious days he began to recover; by September 19 he was back at work.

At this time, which Lenin had called the most critical of the Revolution, when the Civil War and the bread war were reaching a climax of savagery, these acts of terrorism aroused the Bolsheviks to a frenzy. Mass terror was ordered. In Petrograd more than five hundred people were shot in reprisal for Uritsky's killing.

Fanya Kaplan was summarily executed. Petrovsky, Kommissar for Internal Affairs, issued a proclamation to all Soviets, stating: "Local Soviets should arrest all Socialist Revolutionaries at once. . . . Chekas and military departments should make special efforts to locate and arrest all those living under assumed names and to shoot without formality everyone mixed up with White Guards and other dirty plotters against the government of the working class and the poorer peasantry. Show no hesitation whatsoever in carrying out mass terror. . . ."[1]

Like a volcanic eruption of boiling lava, mass terrorism poured over the country. The Bolsheviks had always endorsed terrorism as an essential instrument of policy. Feliks Dzerzhinsky had declared in June 1918: "We stand for organized terror. Terror is an absolute necessity in times of revolution."[8] The Cheka wielded absolute power in carrying out this policy. It had over thirty thousand agents; many were criminals and brutalized, sadistic soldiers, corrupted further by license to kill, torture, and plunder.[9] In Moscow and Petrograd, and every town and village, the people lived in the midst of a fearful nightmare.

At this time of bloodshed the murder of Nicholas II and possibly also of his wife and children at Ekaterinburg on the night of July 16/17 passed unnoticed. They were merely the victims, like thousands of Russians, of the general savagery. The military kommissar of the Ural Soviet, which was responsible for the region, had gone to Moscow early in July to obtain instructions from Sverdlov. Lenin, Stalin, and Trotsky were probably consulted, and with the White armies poised to capture Ekaterinburg, they would have considered the death of the Tsar and Tsarevich unavoidable. But Nicholas II, who had failed to save Russia from revolution, had abandoned his throne by abdicating in March 1917: To the Russian people he was already dead.[10]

The summer of 1918 brought further threats to Lenin and his government. The Allied intervention, instigated primarily by Winston Churchill, but supported by the United States, France, Japan, and Italy, had led to detachments of British, French, and American troops occupying Murmansk, Archangel, Vladivostok, and other Russian towns. But this intervention did not develop in any serious form, or give real support to the White forces, as Lenin and others had feared it would. Meanwhile Soviet forces had a precarious hold on central Russia, but Siberia and, more important, the Ukraine were in anti-Soviet hands. In August, White armies captured Kazan and threatened Moscow. From the south General Krasnov's Cossack army began moving northwards to join the White forces in Kazan, and they cut the railway line between Tsaritsyn and Moscow. The northern Caucasus was the sole remaining source of grain. Loss of the region meant starvation for the people in the north.

Towards the end of May 1918, reports reached Moscow about the desperate conditions, both civil and military, in Tsaritsyn. Stalin was sent there to organize grain deliveries. Accompanied by his young wife, Nadya Alliluyeva, whom he had just married, he arrived on June 6, 1918, with two armored cars and an escort of four hundred Red Guards. On the following day he reported to Lenin that he had found a "bacchanalia of profiteering and speculation" and had taken prompt action.[11] He sacked corrupt and inefficient officials, dismissed unneeded revolutionary committees, appointing kommissars to bring order into labor and transport organization and to ensure grain deliveries to Moscow.

The Soviet North Caucasus Military District had its headquarters in Tsaritsyn. It was commanded by a former Tsarist general, named Snesarev, and a sailor named Zedin, who was an old Bolshevik. On June 14, 1918, Snesarev divided his district into three groups, each with its own commander. A few days later, probably at the instigation of Stalin, Klim Voroshilov was given command of the Tsaritsyn Group. A Donbas metalworker, employed since 1914 in the ordnance factory in Tsaritsyn, he had had no military experience. But ten years earlier he had served with Stalin on the Bolshevik committee in Baku, and the two men were close comrades. Semeon Budënny, a dashing bewhiskered former dragoon sergeant, and Stalin's friend Ordzhonikidze, as political kommissar, were also in Tsaritsyn. Voroshilov wrote later that this "group of old Bolsheviks and revolutionary workers rallied around Comrade Stalin and, in place of the helpless staff, a Red, Bolshevik stronghold grew up in the south."[12]

On July 7, 1918, Lenin sent a telegraph message to Stalin about the Socialist Revolutionary outbreak in Moscow, warning him that "it is necessary to suppress mercilessly these pitiful and hysterical adventurists, who have become an instrument in the hands of the counter-revolutionaries. So, be ruthless against the left SRs and keep us informed more often." Stalin replied that "everything will be done to forestall possible surprises. Be assured that our hand will not tremble."[13]

Tsaritsyn was coming under severe pressure. Food deliveries and the city itself were threatened. Stalin began taking a direct part in military operations. On July 7 he reported urgently to Lenin:

> I am rushing to the front. I write on business only. The line south of Tsaritsyn has not yet been restored. I am driving and shouting at everyone who needs it, and hope we will restore it quickly. You may be sure that we will spare no one, neither ourselves nor others, and we will, come what may, produce the grain. If only our military "specialists" (blockheads!) had not been idle and asleep, the line would not have been broken; and if it is restored, this will not be due to them but in spite of them. . . . In view of poor communications with the centre, it is necessary to have a man on the spot with full powers so that urgent measures can be taken promptly.[14]

Three days later, not having received an immediate reply, Stalin sent an angry message. He objected to Trotsky's highhanded action in ignoring the Tsaritsyn headquarters and dealing direct with the sectors under its command. In particular Trotsky was not to make postings without consulting the people on the spot. He went on to demand aircraft, armored cars, and six-inch guns "without which the Tsaritsyn front will not remain in being." Finally he asserted his own authority, stating that "to get things done, I must have full military powers. I have already written about this, but have received no reply. Very well. In that event I myself, without formalities, will remove those army commanders and kommissars who are ruining things. I am obliged to do this in the common interest and, in any case, the lack of a chit from Trotsky will not stop me."[15] On the following day he sent another telegram, informing Lenin that he had already taken full military responsibility and had removed commanders and military specialists who were dilatory or incompetent.[16]

Stalin's messages to Lenin were couched in forthright and even rude terms. They were, however, communications to an equal, sent at a time of crisis. Although he had respect and affection for Lenin, he did not treat him with deference. Indeed, far from taking umbrage, Lenin acted promptly. On July 19, 1918, the Supreme War Council created a War Council of the North Caucasus Military District, and Stalin was officially appointed chairman of the council.

Stalin's strong stand evidently made an impression on Trotsky. On July 24, as Kommissar for War, he sent a message, deferential in tone, affirming that the North Caucasus Military District was responsible for all military and partisan activity in the area from Voronezh on the Don River south to Baku.[17]

During July and August 1918 the Bolshevik position on the Volga continued to deteriorate. On August 13 Stalin declared a state of siege in Tsaritsyn. The position became more critical. On August 22 the military council sent orders to Zhloba, a former miner and the council's representative in the south, to advance with his Steel Division to Tsaritsyn without delay. The messenger reached Sorokin with these instructions only on September 2, 1918. Meanwhile the Don Cossacks had called off their offensive.

On August 31, 1918, Stalin wrote a long report to Lenin. He was evidently in good spirits and claimed that the Cossack forces were collapsing, a report that soon proved to be overoptimistic. He asked for torpedo boats and two submarines to be sent down the Volga, maintaining that with this support Baku, the North Caucasus, and Turkestan could easily be taken. This letter, which was written on the day after Fanya Kaplan's attempt on Lenin's life, closed with an expression of tender affection: "I press the hand of my dear and beloved Ilyich."[18]

On the same day Stalin and Voroshilov sent a telegram to Sverdlov with a message of congratulation on the escape of "the greatest revolutionary in the world, the tried leader and mentor of the proletariat, Comrade Lenin." The message called on him to respond to this despicable attempt on his life "by organizing a public, massive, systematic terror against the bourgeoisie and its agents."[19] The cult of the leader was already coming to birth.

Renewed attacks by the Don Cossacks on the Volga front again caused a crisis, showing the weakness of the Soviet forces. Confu-

sion, inefficiency, and a deep corroding suspicion undermined Red
Army operations. Another weakness was the absence of an established, centralized military command. A. I. Egorov, a former
tsarist colonel and later a commander of the Red Army on the
southern and southwestern fronts, recommended the appointment
of a supreme commander. Acting on his advice, Trotsky with
Lenin's approval made I. I. Vatsetis, also a former tsarist colonel,
commander in chief. It was a strange appointment. Vatsetis had
failed to gain promotion on completing the 1909 course at the
General Staff Academy. Trotsky himself described him as "stubborn, cranky, and capricious." Presumably he was the best man
available at the time, and although forthright in his views he
proved an indifferent commander.[20]

On September 2 the Supreme War Council was abolished, and
in its place the Revolutionary War Council of the Republic was
set up with Trotsky as its chairman. On September 18 the North
Caucasus Military District was reorganized as the South Front, a
front being in Russian terminology a formation of several armies
or an army group. Stalin was appointed chairman of its military
council, supported by Sergei Minin and Voroshilov. At the same
time all three continued to hold their posts on the military council of the Voroshilov Group, later known as the Tenth Army, in
Tsaritsyn. This duplication was to lead to confusion and conflict.

At this time Trotsky decided to move the headquarters of the
South Front to Kozlov, a railway town some four hundred miles
north of Tsaritsyn. He was influenced undoubtedly by the accessi-
bility of Kozlov for his personal train and, carried away by the
glamour of his mobile headquarters, he did not recognize that it
was a highly unsatisfactory method of maintaining over-all supervision of the rapidly changing military situation. Trotsky also appointed as the military specialist commander of the South Front a
former artillery general named P. P. Sytin, who set up his headquarters in Kozlov. The other members of the military council
stayed in Tsaritsyn.

Sytin was soon complaining to Vatsetis about the lack of co-
operation from Tsaritsyn. He was angry, too, when he learned
that Stalin, Minin, and Voroshilov had without reference to him
sent orders to I. L. Sorokin in the south concerning the organi-

zation of troops in the North Caucasus. At his request Vatsetis
canceled these orders.

Alarmed at this time by the Don Cossack advance, which was
pushing Voroshilov's forces to the east, Stalin sent urgent demands to Moscow for weapons and ammunition. He complained,
too, of Sytin's lack of concern about the South Front. The Revolutionary War Council sent Sytin with one of its members, Me-
khonoshin, to Tsaritsyn to clarify his relations with Stalin. At a
meeting on September 29, Sytin explained that he wanted the
headquarters to be at Kozlov or Balashov; Tsaritsyn was unsuita-
ble because remote from the center of operations on the Volga.
Stalin was adamant that the headquarters must remain at Tsaritsyn. Further, he, with Minin and Voroshilov, recorded that they
were "unable to recognize Sytin's full jurisdiction or the legality
of his brief."[21] The military council of the Tenth Army, comprising Stalin, Minin, and Voroshilov, was with the addition of Sytin
also the military council of the South Front. Thus in insisting on
Tsaritsyn as their headquarters and in recording a vote of no-
confidence in Sytin, Stalin and his two colleagues were acting
within their powers. They were, however, in effect opposing the
party policy of building up a centralized command structure,
which Stalin knew to be necessary.

The South Front remained unstable. On November 2, 1918,
Stalin and Minin sent a telegram to the Revolutionary War Council, asking what its intentions were, since their requests for supplies
had not been met. The conflict within the command structure
was becoming critical. The party Central Committee met to consider the problem of the insubordination of party members, and
on its instructions Sverdlov sent a message to Tsaritsyn, rebuking
the local council for disregarding the instructions of the Revolutionary War Council. Vatsetis, who received a copy of the telegram sent by Stalin and Minin, replied bluntly to them that "you
have centred your main attention on the Tsaritsyn sector at the
expense of others. . . . It has been proposed repeatedly that you
should move from Tsaritsyn to Kozlov in order to join its commander, but up to now . . . you have continued to operate independently. Such a disregard of orders . . . I consider to be intolerable."[22]

Vatsetis reported at the same time to Trotsky that Stalin's independent action was undermining the plan of campaign. He also demanded cancellation of Stalin's Order 118, which presumably contained the dismissal of Sytin. For their part Stalin and Voroshilov informed Lenin that the Central Committee should investigate Trotsky's activities which, they claimed, were jeopardizing the existence of the South Front.[23] On October 4, 1918, Trotsky gave vent to his anger in a telegram to Sverdlov, which he copied to Lenin:

> I insist categorically on Stalin's recall. Things are going badly at the Tsaritsyn Front in spite of superabundant forces. Voroshilov is capable of commanding a regiment, not an army of fifty thousand. However, I shall leave him in command of the Tenth Army at Tsaritsyn, provided he reports to the commander of the Army of the South, Sytin. Thus far Tsaritsyn has not even sent reports of operations to Kozlov. . . . If that is not done tomorrow, I shall remand Voroshilov and Minin to court martial. . . . Tsaritsyn must either submit or take the consequences. We have a colossal superiority of forces, but there is utter anarchy at the top. I can put a stop to it in twenty-four hours, provided I have your firm and clear-cut support. At all events, this is the only course I can see."[24]

This head-on conflict between two outstanding party leaders, both of whom were indispensable, faced Lenin with a difficult problem. He decided finally that he must support Trotsky and recall Stalin from the South Front. But he took great pains to avoid offending him. Sverdlov, on behalf of the Central Committee, went in a special train to escort Stalin to Moscow.[25] Furthermore, he emphasized that Stalin was not in disgrace and that his military leadership was not in question, by appointing him to the supreme Revolutionary War Council of the Republic. He also, presumably on Stalin's request, allowed him to return to Tsaritsyn for the time being.

The position at the South Front was critical. Stalin, Minin, and Voroshilov sent repeated appeals for help to Lenin and also to Vatsetis and Sytin. Vatsetis sent a reproachful reply. "From today's telegram direct to me, I see that the defence of Tsaritsyn had been brought by you to a catastrophic state. . . . You alone are responsible for the chaotic situation. . . . In view of the serious state of Tsaritsyn I am now sending reserves there. . . . Under no circumstances is Tsaritsyn to be given up."[26]

Tsaritsyn would probably have fallen on October 16 but for the timely arrival of Zhloba's Steel Division, consisting of eight infantry and two cavalry regiments. Tsaritsyn did not fall at this time, but it is far from clear who among the Red Army leaders, if any, could claim the credit for saving the city. Voroshilov wrote later that it was saved "by Stalin's indomitable will to victory," but Trotsky and others rejected this claim.[27]

On October 23, 1918, Stalin returned to Moscow. He at once displayed a readiness to co-operate with Trotsky and with others on the War Council. He was evidently anxious to expunge any impression that he was a difficult and insubordinate member of the party hierarchy. Moreover, believing firmly in discipline and centralized control, he recognized that he himself must conform and set an example. In a survey of the year's events, published in *Pravda* on October 30, he paid tribute to Trotsky for the role he had played in the Revolution as president of the Petersburg Soviet and chairman of the Military Revolutionary Committee and also as Kommissar for War and chairman of the Revolutionary Military War Council of the Republic. He was holding out an olive branch, but Trotsky did not respond.[28]

The Allied victory in the west was followed by the collapse of the Hapsburg and Hohenzollern regimes, and the first signs of revolution in their countries. Lenin, Trotsky, and other Bolsheviks who cherished hopes of an international revolutionary movement waited on developments in Germany and Austria. But their first action was to repudiate the hated Treaty of Brest-Litovsk. Next the Ukraine demanded their attention. Civil war had broken out between P. P. Skoropadsky, the Germans' puppet hetman, the Ukrainian nationalists, the Bolsheviks, and others. The vast steppelands were in a state of anarchy.

Stalin was appointed to the military council of the Ukrainian Front, which had the task of occupying the Ukraine. Soon afterwards he was elected to the All-Russian Central Executive Committee and to its Presidium. On November 30 the Central Executive Committee set up a Council of Workers' and Peasants'

Defense with Lenin as chairman, to mobilize the country's resources for war. Stalin was a member of this new council as the representative of the Central Executive Committee, and he served also as Lenin's deputy.[29]

In December 1918 the White forces in Siberia under the command of Admiral A. V. Kolchak advanced westwards. The important Urals city of Perm fell, surrendered by the Red Third Army. The White advance, if unchecked, would threaten Moscow. Kolchak also planned that detachments of his forces would join up with the White Archangel Army, north of Kotlas.

Lenin was alarmed. He sent telegrams to Trotsky, instructing him "to put pressure on Vatsetis" to reinforce Red positions in the Urals. He also informed Trotsky, who was apparently ignorant of the position, about "the catastrophic state of the 3rd Army and its drunkenness." The old Bolshevik, a former sergeant, commanding this army, was "drinking and in no fit state to restore order."[30] Lenin decided to send Stalin, but diplomatically he first asked Trotsky's opinion. Trotsky sent a telegram, agreeing that Stalin should be sent "with powers from both the party and the Revolutionary Council of War of the Republic for restoring order, purging the staff of the kommissars, and severely punishing the offenders."[31]

On January 1 (1919) Stalin, accompanied by Dzerzhinsky, set out for the Third Army. He found it demoralized and in urgent need of reinforcements. He sent his first report to Lenin four days after arrival, and this and the final report, signed in Moscow, provided an exhaustive review of the state of the army. He was blunt in his criticisms of Vatsetis, and also of Trotsky's War Kommissariat and of the Revolutionary War Council. His report showed a broad intellectual grasp of the operational and tactical requirements of an army in action. Stalin was still a tyro in military matters, but he was learning fast.

The Eighth Party Congress, held in Moscow from March 18 to 23, 1919, discussed at length the command structure and organization of the Red Army. Trotsky, who did not attend, was heatedly criticized by many delegates "for his dictatorial manners, for his scornful attitude to the front workers and his unwillingness to listen to them, for his adoration of the specialists, and for his torrent of ill-considered telegrams, sent over the heads of commanders and staffs, changing directives and causing endless confusion."[32]

Stalin would have agreed with these and other criticisms of Trotsky's highhandedness. He was probably tempted to support publicly the strong censure, moved by V. M. Smirnov, chief spokesman of the "military opposition," as it became known, on the widely detested Kommissar for War. He spoke firmly in support of Lenin, however, and in defense of Trotsky. He recognized the basic soundness of Trotsky's approach to the Red Army. "Facts show," he said, "that the concept of a Volunteer Army does not stand up to examination, that we shall not be able to defend our Republic if we do not create another regular army imbued with discipline. . . . Smirnov's proposals are unacceptable."[33]

Among members and outside the party, Stalin's reputation was growing. He was the practical leader with a capacity for work and for taking responsibility. He was not a great orator, but he always spoke with good sense. He was a man, too, who could cut his way through bureaucratic obstacles and make decisions. The high regard in which he was held was demonstrated at the Eighth Party Congress. He was high on everyone's list for election to the Central Committee. Two new subcommittees of the Central Committee were set up by the congress: the Politburo of five members to guide the party in political matters, and the Orgburo to advise in matters of personnel and administration. He was appointed to both subcommittees. In addition he was made Kommissar of State Control with responsibility for the burgeoning bureaucracy. Like the work of the Orgburo, the functions of his new kommissariat appeared to offer drudgery without the possibility of public acclaim. It was, however, essential organizational work, and in Stalin's hands both offices were to enhance his authority and magnify his power.

On May 17, 1919, Stalin arrived in Petrograd with full powers to organize the defenses of the region against attack by General N. N. Yudenich's army, which was advancing from the northwest. Remaining in Moscow, Lenin maintained control over the Revolutionary War Council and had direct contact with all the fronts.

To Stalin in Petrograd he sent a stream of telegrams, harrying, advising, demanding information. In a telegram on May 20 he expressed the hope "that the general mobilization of Petersburgers will result in offensive operations and not just sitting about in barracks."[34]

Lenin was disturbed by the speed of Yudenich's advance. He mistrusted the commanders and the troops of the Red Army in the region. On May 27 he warned Stalin to assume treachery, and as an explanation of defeat or other failure treachery was to become a phobia in the party. Stalin responded promptly. The Cheka was unleashed and soon claimed to have uncovered a conspiracy among employees of the Swiss, Italian, and Danish consulates. Stalin reported to Lenin that a counterrevolutionary plot in support of the Whites had been crushed and that the Cheka was investigating further. In a message to Lenin, dated June 4, 1919, he wrote: "I am sending you a document from the Swiss. It is evident from the document that not only the chief of staff of the Seventh Army works for the Whites . . . but also the entire staff of the Revolutionary Council of War of the Republic. . . . It is now up to the Central Committee to draw the necessary inferences. Will it have the courage to do it?"[35]

Stalin himself did not escape criticism. An old Bolshevik hostile to the Tsaritsyn group, A. I. Okulov, who was the political member of the West Front Military Council, complained to the Central Committee that due to Stalin's actions the Seventh Army was being detached from the West Front, which was under the command of D. N. Nadezhny, a former tsarist corps commander, and that it should be restored to his command. Lenin asked Stalin to comment. "My profound conviction," he replied, "is: 1, Nadezhny is not a commander. He is incapable of commanding. He will end up by losing the Western Front; 2, workers like Okulov who incite the specialists against our kommissars, who are sufficiently discouraged anyway, are harmful, because they debilitate the vital core of our army."[36] Okulov was removed from his post.

Following the repulse of the White advance on Petrograd in June, Stalin was appointed to be the political member of the Military Council of the West Front, and a new commander replaced Nadezhny.

On the East Front disagreements erupted between Vatsetis, the commander in chief, and S. S. Kamenev, the commander of the front. Trotsky supported Vatsetis, whom he had appointed, and he showed hostility towards Kamenev. On one occasion in Simbirsk, Trotsky, dressed in black leather uniform, like his personal escort, and armed with a pistol, burst into Kamenev's office and excitedly threatened him. Later, at the instigation of Vatsetis, Trotsky summarily dismissed him.

Kamenev was liked and respected. The Military Council of the East Front formally protested to Lenin. Kamenev himself went to Moscow to put his case. On May 15, 1919, he was interviewed by Lenin, who was impressed and told him to return to his command. Lenin was usually careful and diplomatic in his dealings with his closest associates, and in overruling Trotsky publicly he was expressing his strongest disapproval. He had been losing confidence in Trotsky's judgment and was increasingly impatient of his bombastic behavior. He also had no high opinion of Vatsetis, who, like Trotsky, had antagonized military as well as political workers.

The climax came in July 1919. Kamenev had worked out a plan for a further advance eastwards into Siberia. Vatsetis vetoed the plan. The East Front Military Council again protested to Lenin. Two meetings of the Central Committee considered the evidence and decided against Vatsetis. At a meeting on July 3 the committee reviewed and endorsed its decision. Trotsky in a fury, his pride affronted, declared that he would resign all his offices, but the committee rejected his resignation. It was decided further that Kamenev should be appointed commander in chief. Vatsetis was arrested, investigated for suspected treason, released, and subsequently given an appointment as a military instructor.

The Central Committee also reorganized the Revolutionary War Council, limiting its membership to six. Trotsky was included, but the other five members were not his supporters. He could no longer dominate the council and get his way. Deeply offended, Trotsky remained at the South Front for the rest of the summer. The Revolutionary War Council functioned directly under Lenin's control, and more harmoniously.

Trotsky subsequently held Stalin responsible for this major reverse in his military standing. He maintained that Stalin's antagonism towards Vatsetis was well known, and that he had supported the East Front Military Council as a means of striking at Trotsky himself. It was a reflection of Trotsky's egocentricity that he had to interpret Stalin's actions in terms of hostility towards himself. In this conflict, however, Stalin's views were those of Lenin and the other members of the Central Committee, and his overriding concern was the victory of the Red Army.

By the end of June 1919, A. Denikin controlled the whole of the Don region and his army continued its rapid advance. His forces had first spread across the Ukraine and south Russia and then they had pressed northwards. In Moscow, Lenin became increasingly anxious about the defense of the city. Kamenev, the commander in chief, had prepared a plan, concentrating strong Red forces to make a flank attack from the east. A second plan, prepared earlier by Vatsetis, and which Trotsky subsequently claimed as his own work, proposed that the armies of the South Front strike due south against Denikin's forces. The Central Committee had approved Kamenev's plan.

The Red Army's flank attack failed completely to halt the White advance. Disturbed by this failure, Kamenev reviewed his strategy and recommended that, while maintaining pressure on the enemy from the east, strong forces of reserves should be concentrated south of Moscow. The response of Lenin and the Central Committee was a striking expression of their confidence in Kamenev. He was told "not to consider himself bound by his former recommendations or by any previous decisions of the Central Committee" and that he had "full powers as a military specialist to take whatever measures he thought fit."[37]

On September 27, 1919, the Central Committee approved the plan to post strong reserves south of Moscow. It decided also to send Stalin to take charge of the South Front. This was a severe rebuff to Trotsky, who had been there during the months of disaster. For a short period Stalin and Trotsky were both at the headquarters of the South Front, but apparently they did not quarrel openly.

On October 11, 1919, Yudenich launched a surprise attack on

Petrograd, and the Red Army began to fall back in disorder. Lenin considered that the city should be abandoned, for he would allow nothing to weaken the defenses of Moscow. On October 15, however, the Politburo sent Trotsky to take charge of the defenses of Petrograd. He rallied the troops and reorganized the defenses of the city, and Petrograd did not fall. Later he was to complain bitterly that in official records Stalin had merged the first and second campaigns of Yudenich into one and "the famous defence of Petrograd is represented as Stalin's handiwork."[38]

Soon after arriving at the South Front headquarters, Stalin reported to Lenin and set out the action he proposed. He criticized Kamenev for holding to his original strategy. He argued that they must "change this plan, already discredited in practice, replacing it with a major attack on Rostov from the Voronezh area by way of Kharkov and the Donets Basin." He set out cogently his reasons and closed his report with the comment that "without this change in strategy, my work . . . will be senseless, criminal, and superfluous, giving me the right, indeed obliging me, to go off anywhere, even to the devil, but not to stay at the South Front."[39]

During the six months from October 1919 to March 1920, while Stalin was at the South Front headquarters and, as he boasted later, "without the presence of Comrade Trotsky," the Red Army succeeded in crushing the White forces. Denikin had advanced headlong, exhausting his men, and leaving himself exposed to attack in the rear. His troops were driven from Orel on October 20, 1919, and from Voronezh four days later; the morale of his force collapsed. He himself lost the confidence of his officers and the support of his Cossack allies. Early in April 1920, after nominating General Peter Wrangel as his successor, he escaped into Turkey.

In the advance of the South Front's armies against Denikin's armies, Budënny played a conspicuous role. He was a swaggering cavalryman, brave and energetic, but limited in ability. He was tireless in pressing for the formation of a cavalry army under his command. Stalin welcomed the idea of massed Red Cavalry, but Trotsky at first opposed it. He mistrusted the Cossacks, who would be the main source of cavalrymen and who were more in sympathy with the White than the Red cause. With Stalin's support, Budënny's proposal was adopted, at least nominally. Trotsky changed his mind about massed cavalry and issued his proclamation "Proletarians to Horse!" Budënny and his Red Cavalry became one of the romantic legends of the Civil War.[40]

By early January 1920, Budënny had led his cavalry to the shores of the Sea of Azov. The South Front was then divided into the Southwest Front, under Egorov's command operating against the Whites in the Crimea, and the Southeast Front, commanded by V. I. Shorin and including Budënny's Cavalry Army, which was renamed the Caucasian Front.

Shorin had been an officer in the tsarist army, but although nearly fifty years old at the time of the Revolution he had never risen above the rank of captain. High command had come to him as to many others, because no one else was available in the revolutionary camp at the time. He was disliked by Budënny and Voroshilov, who schemed to have him dismissed. Stalin supported them, and was said by Budënny to have told Ordzhonikidze, recently appointed the political member of the Caucasian Front, that Shorin was to be dismissed "for adopting an attitude of mistrust and enmity towards the cavalry army."[41] M. N. Tukhachevsky, a former second lieutenant of the Semenovsky Guards Regiment, then in his twenties, who was later designated to succeed Shorin, was to find that Budënny and Voroshilov were unruly and undisciplined, but to be handled with care because they had influential protection.

Early in February 1920, Budënny's Red Cavalry suffered a severe defeat by the Cossacks. This reverse, indicating indiscipline and poor leadership, disturbed Lenin. He at once sent a telegram to Stalin, signed by Trotsky, too, appointing him to the Caucasian Front to resolve whatever problems had led to the defeat. The telegram also directed him to make a journey to front headquarters to concert further action with Shorin and to transfer troops from the Southwest Front to his command.

Stalin was evidently tired and unwell. His reply was cantankerous. He stated that visits by individuals were in his view wholly unnecessary, adding that "I am not entirely well and ask the Central Committee not to insist on the journey." He commented further that "Budënny and Ordzhonikidze consider . . . Shorin to be the reason for our failures."[42] He prevaricated over the transfer of troops to the Caucasian Front. When Lenin sent him instructions to effect the transfer without further delay, he replied crossly that it was a matter for the High Command to ensure the reinforcement of the front. Unlike the staff of the High Command, who were all in good health, he was ill and overburdened. Apparently he felt that he had been in the south long enough and that he had completed his task there. Finally on March 23, 1920, he returned to Moscow.

Stalin was allowed only a short respite. On May 26, 1920, he was ordered to join the Southwest Front. He was in Kharkov on the following day. The Red Army's position in the south had become critical. Wrangel, who had succeeded Denikin, had restored morale and discipline among the White forces in the Crimea. He was building up the Volunteer Army to a strength of twenty thousand men, supported by ten thousand Cossacks. His forces presented a severe challenge from the south.

At this time, the Poles attacked from the west, seizing Kiev and storming over the Dnieper. Their objective was to conquer Belorussia and western Ukraine, vast territories which they had lost to Moscow in the seventeenth century. The Poles were, however, wary of any alliance with the Whites, recognizing that they would hardly accept such a loss of territory to Russia's traditional Polish enemy. The Poles were also on guard against the Soviet regime. Trotsky had publicly threatened to invade Poland as soon as the Whites had been defeated in the south.

Attacked in the south, where Wrangel made early gains, and in the west, the Red Army found itself under severe pressure. The Central Committee approved the High Command's plan that the West Front, now commanded by Tukhachevsky, should attack in northern Belorussia to compel the Poles to move troops away from the Southwest Front. It meant giving priority to the expulsion of the Poles. Egorov, commanding the Southwest Front, and his officers disagreed with this strategy. It was for this reason that Stalin was hurriedly dispatched to his headquarters.

Within a few days of his arrival Stalin had visited the Crimean Front and reported to Lenin. The situation gave rise to great anxiety. He had replaced the commander of the Thirteenth Army. He requested two divisions to reinforce the Southwest Front, for Egorov's initial offensive against the Poles had failed. Lenin in his reply firmly reminded him to copy all communications on military matters to Trotsky, the Kommissar for War. He also repeated the Central Committee decision that the Southwest Front should not yet embark on any offensive in the Crimea. Stalin at once protested against the refusal to send two further divisions and stressed the danger posed by Wrangel to the south. Lenin was not to be moved, however, and he confirmed the original plan.

Kamenev's order on June 2, 1920, was that the Cavalry Army should attack the Polish positions and seek to outflank them south of Kiev. Egorov and Stalin apparently amended the line of attack in passing the order to Budënny. The effect of this change cannot be judged.[43] The Red Cavalry attacked, forcing the Polish forces south of the Pripet Marshes to retreat hurriedly. To the north Tukhachevsky's West Front opened its offensive early in July 1920, again compelling the Poles to fall back. By the end of the month the Red Army had advanced across the frontier into northern Poland. A provisional Polish government was set up under the chairmanship of Dzerzhinsky. Tukhachevsky's four armies were drawn up on the Vistula, and the capture of Warsaw seemed imminent.

Lenin was carried away by the vision of the Red Army in Warsaw and of a communist Poland giving its full support to the revolutionary movement. He felt acutely the isolation of Russia, which with all its internal problems was bearing the socialist banner alone. This vision was shared by many within the party and gave rise to a wave of enthusiasm, as members rallied to the cry "Onwards to Warsaw!" But there were realists, Stalin foremost among them, who saw the dangers of this policy. In June (1920) he wrote that "the rear of the Polish forces is homogeneous and nationally united. Its dominant mood is 'the feeling for their native land.' . . . The class conflicts have not reached the strength needed to break through the sense of national unity."[44] It was a clear warning against accepting Lenin's facile belief that the Polish proletariat was ready for revolution.

The Politburo had, however, decided on its policy of conquering Poland in spite of the opposition expressed by Stalin and others. Stalin had hurriedly rejoined the Southwest Front which covered the southern part of the Polish lines and was at the same time on guard against Wrangel in the south. The Politburo now decided to form a special front against Wrangel under Stalin's direction. A major part of the forces of the Southwest Front would be transferred to Tukhachevsky's Western Front for the advance on Warsaw, and the remaining forces would form Stalin's special front. Angered by these instructions from the Politburo, Stalin replied churlishly that the Politburo should not be concerning itself with such details. Lenin was taken aback and asked for an explanation of his opposition. In his reply Stalin set out the organizational difficulties which the instructions entailed. Lenin was impressed by his appreciation of the situation and allowed the Southwest Front to retain its previous commitments; only three of its armies were to be transferred to the Western Front.

The basic problem was that Tukhachevsky's Western Front was separated by more than three hundred miles of the Pripet Marshes from the Southwest Front. Communications and the prompt transfer of forces over such distances were further complicated by the absence of a strong central command. Trotsky and the Supreme War Council were ignored. Kamenev, the commander in chief, issued directives but could not enforce them. The Politburo and in particular Lenin, acting independently, tried to resolve conflicts, but could not be sure that their instructions would be observed. Moreover, Lenin's instructions conflicted on occasions with plans of the commander in chief. Thus Kamenev confirmed that Tukhachevsky should outflank Warsaw from the north and west and take the city by August 12, 1920. This left the large Lublin gap unprotected between the Russian forces and the Pripet Marshes. At this time Wrangel was moving with some success, posing a threat that alarmed Lenin. On August 11 he instructed Stalin to break off operations against the Poles at Lvov and to embark on an immediate offensive to destroy Wrangel's army and seize the Crimea. On the same day Kamenev ordered the Southwest Front to send "as large a force as possible towards Lublin to assist Tukhachevsky's left flank."[45]

At this time it was believed that the Red Army had already won the battle for Warsaw. Stalin and Egorov were planning to send their cavalry not to Lublin, but to the Crimea, and they ignored Kamenev's instructions. On August 13 Kamenev sent orders that both the 12th and 1st Cavalry armies would be transferred to the command of the Western Front on the following day. Egorov felt he had to comply. But Stalin refused to sign the order and sent a telegram angrily reproaching the commander in chief for trying to destroy the Southwest Front.

Tukhachevsky's advance had been progressing slowly. But on August 16 the Poles counterattacked, concentrating on the Lublin gap, and within a few days they had shattered the West Front. On August 19 the Politburo, including Stalin, met in Moscow, still unaware that the Poles were on the point of routing Tukhachevsky's armies. The Politburo, "having heard the military reports of Comrades Trotsky and Stalin," decided that the main concentration of forces should now be directed to the recovery of the Crimea.

Responsibility for the disaster was angrily debated then and later.[46] Lenin abstained from blaming anyone, but it is clear that he himself and all the participants bore part of the blame. Lenin had been carried away by hopes of a Polish revolution and seriously miscalculated the strength of Polish resistance. Kamenev and Tukhachevsky must bear the military responsibility, since they neglected to ensure protection of their flanks before advancing. Moreover, even if Stalin and Egorov had responded promptly to orders to transfer troops from their front to fill the Lublin gap, it is doubtful whether such troops could have arrived in time and in fighting condition to have withstood the Polish onslaught.

Stalin's concern to maintain the strength of the Southwest Front was understandable. It was facing the Polish forces at Lvov, Wrangel's army to the south, and the possibility of Romanian intervention. All were serious threats, which were causing Lenin and the Politburo anxiety, and the wisdom of detaching any of its armies to reinforce the Western Front was questionable. Rightly or wrongly, however, Stalin was undoubtedly guilty of insubordination, as on other occasions in the Civil War when he was sure that he was right. But there was also an inevitability in the defeat of the Red Army. The troops were near exhaustion. They had fought heroically on Russian soil. Now they encountered the

Poles, who were defending their capital and homeland against their traditional Russian enemy, and they fought with desperate bravery.

By the close of 1920 the Civil War had ended. Wrangel, his volunteer army greatly outnumbered by the Red forces in the south, suffered a disastrous defeat. His army disintegrated, as had Kolchak's army in Siberia some months earlier. But the Whites had been doomed to failure from the start.

Lenin and his government had been able to raise the Red Army to a strength of more than 5 million men and to ensure the supply of basic munitions. There had been failures of organization, conflicts between commanders and kommissars, and frequent confusion between the headquarters of the fronts, the High Command, and the party Central Committee in Moscow. The new Soviet leaders and the Red Army were able to rise above these obstacles, and, united and fired by revolutionary zeal, they triumphed.

It is difficult, if not impossible, to penetrate the endemic confusion of the Red Army's operations in this period and the miasma of suspicions, vicious antagonisms, and conflicting claims—many of them made later—in order to evaluate the contribution of the individual Soviet leaders to the triumph. Lenin had been in command throughout the war. He had closely followed each operation, and had sent out orders, usually in the name of the Central Committee, but they were his orders. He had handled troublesome personalities, especially Stalin and Trotsky, with tact and firmness. All had accepted his supreme leadership. It was indeed during the years after the Revolution, and particularly during the Civil War, that he revealed greatness as a leader.

Trotsky's prestige had greatly diminished by the end of the war. The failure of his negotiations with the Germans and the forced acceptance of the disastrous terms of the Treaty of Brest-Litovsk had damaged his reputation. He had resigned as Kommissar for Foreign Affairs and become Kommissar for War. In the early months of the Civil War he had blazed across the sky like a comet. He had laid the foundations of the Red Army. A small vibrant figure in black leather uniform, he was gallant and ludicrous at the same time. At every opportunity he harangued the troops.

He was a fine orator, and very conscious of this talent. Often, as in Sviyazhsk in August 1918, his dramatic words and presence raised the morale of disheartened men, just as his ruthless punishments restored discipline. But he greatly overrated the power of his theatrical performances. Budënny wrote that to ordinary, often illiterate, soldiers he could be a strange figure with his waving arms and spate of words, most of which they did not understand. At times his exhortations stirred them to anger.[47] Moreover, as Lenin came to recognize, he was readily carried away by his own words, losing touch with the realities of the situation. He was also unsound in his appointments to positions of command. His stubborn support for Vatsetis had been an example. At the start of the war Trotsky had exercised wide independent authority; by the time of the Polish War he was to be found in Moscow and directly under Lenin's control.

Increasingly Lenin had come to rely on Stalin, who was in most things the antithesis of Trotsky. He rarely addressed the troops or meetings of any kind, but when he did he spoke in simple terms. He was the realist, who coldly assessed men and situations, and was usually sound in his conclusions. He remained calm and self-possessed. He was difficult only in his antagonisms towards certain people and when his advice was rejected. While demanding that others obey orders, he himself did not hesitate on occasions to be insubordinate, for he readily set his judgment above that of others. But he learned, too, that in war a supreme commander, exercising unquestioned authority, was essential to victory. He never forgot this lesson.

In November 1919 Trotsky and Stalin were awarded the new Order of the Red Banner. The award to Stalin was "for his services in the defense of Petrograd and for his self-sacrificing work at the South Front." The two awards were an indication that at the time Lenin and the Central Committee considered both men equally valuable.

In later years, when seeking every pretext to denigrate Stalin, Trotsky wrote contemptuously of his role in the Civil War. It is clear, however, from contemporary sources, including Trotsky's papers, that at the time he rated Stalin high as a military organizer. In times of crisis when party interests and the revolutionary cause transcended personal rivalries, he turned to him. During the Polish War, for example, when anxious about an attack by Wrangel from the Crimea, Trotsky recommended that "Comrade Stalin should be charged with forming a new military council with Egorov or Frunze as commander by agreement between the Commander-in-Chief and Comrade Stalin."[48] On other occasions he made or supported similar proposals to send Stalin to resolve crucial problems at the fronts. Like Lenin and other members of the Central Committee, he had come to value Stalin's abilities.

Stalin emerged from the Civil War and the Polish War with a greatly enhanced reputation. He had made mistakes but so, too, had others. To the people generally, he was still not well known. He was rarely in the public eye and, unlike Trotsky, he did not court publicity. Within the party he was known as the quiet and incisive man of action, a leader of decision and authority. In the immense task facing the government, of reorganizing the country after the years of war and revolution, he was clearly a man who would bear special responsibilities.

The experience of the Civil War made a profound impact on Stalin. It broadened his knowledge of himself and his abilities. For the first time he had responsibility on a vast scale, and he found that he could carry it and indeed was stimulated by it. But this self-knowledge came in conditions of complete brutalization. He had witnessed the bread war, when villages and whole towns were wiped out in the struggle to ensure grain deliveries to the north. He had been schooled in the principle that the party's purposes must be pursued, no matter what the cost in human lives. Now he had seen people massacred in thousands in the struggle for the survival of the party and its government. The experience implanted more deeply in him that inhumanity which was to mark his exercise of power.

15

The New Era Begins
1920

The White challenge had been crushed and the much-feared Allied intervention had failed to materialize in any serious form. But the cost of victory was horrifying. It has been estimated that in the course of the war against the Central Powers and then the Civil War some 27 million Russians perished. Most were killed on the battlefields and in the countless guerrilla engagements, but thousands died from malnutrition and disease.

The country had been ravaged and the economy was in ruins. The system of war communism had met the minimum needs of the Red Army, but in every other way it had produced disaster, hastening the economy towards chaos and collapse.

By the end of 1920, the people were starving, disease-ridden, and near exhaustion. They had endured their hardships and tolerated communist rule, while the Civil War raged, but now they were losing hope of change and improvement. Open hostility towards the Soviet leaders was widespread. In the country the peasants were already in revolt; in cities and towns the people were in

an angry mood. During the first months of 1921 the starvation
bread ration was cut by a third, and a fuel crisis was officially announced. The winter had been severe and snowdrifts had halted
food and fuel trains from the Ukraine, the Caucasus, and Siberia.
Many factories had to close down. All added to the angry desperation of the people.

Lenin and his colleagues realized the magnitude of the reconstruction which had to be tackled immediately, but were less
aware of the popular mood. At this time they were elated and
amazed by their survival. It gave them a new confidence in their
ability to deal with the formidable tasks ahead of them. They had
survived against incredible challenges; they were the new men, the
chosen men, who would change the course of history.

Stalin expressed this mood in a speech to an anniversary session
of the Baku Soviet on November 6, 1920. And he was expressing
not only the mood of the party hierarchy but also his own sense of
the destiny of the party and of Russia and his total commitment
to that destiny. He recalled the evening of October 25, 1917,

> "when we, a small group of Bolsheviks, headed by Comrade
> Lenin . . . with the Red Guard, insignificant in numbers, and at
> our disposal all in all a small, still not properly integrated, Com-
> munist Party of 200–250 thousand members, how we, this small
> group, seized power from the representatives of the bourgeoi-
> sie. . . . Three years have passed since then. And in that pe-
> riod Russia, passing through fire and tempest, has forged itself
> into the greatest socialist power in the world. . . . If at that time
> we had a small guard of Petrograd workers . . . now we have a
> famed multi-million Red Army, which threatens the enemies of
> Soviet Russia. If three years ago we had a small, not fully inte-
> grated party . . . we now have a party of 700,000 members, a
> party welded by steel, a party of members who at any moment
> can re-group and in hundreds of thousands concentrate on a
> given party task, a party which at a word from the Central Com-
> mittee, can advance against the enemy."

Stalin closed his speech with a reference to Luther's challenge to
the Emperor and the Church at the Diet of Worms in 1521,
which he paraphrased and adapted. "Russia could say 'Here I
stand on the frontier between the old capitalist and the new

socialist world, here on this frontier I bring together the strivings of the peasantry of the East with the purpose of destroying the old world. And the god of history is with me!"[1]

Faced with the stark problems of the economy and the survival of the Soviet regime, Lenin and his colleagues at first thought that the system of war communism would provide the answer. Trotsky was a fanatic exponent of this view. His plan, first presented in *Pravda* in December 1919, was approved initially by the Central Committee, but many party members argued strenuously against it. The plan provided for "the mobilization of the industrial proletariat, liability for labour service, militarization of economic life, and the use of military units for economic needs."[2] He insisted that labor must be subject to the same strict discipline as the Red Army. Wholly authoritarian in outlook and without the least understanding of or feeling for human needs and emotions, he set about imposing this discipline. The immediate result was an angry storm of protest and rebellion. The Third Red Army was on his orders redesignated "The First Revolutionary Army of Labor" and assigned to labor duties in the Urals. The soldiers deserted. Peasants, infuriated by the take-over of their districts by labor armies, burned the crops as they were gathered.

Trotsky came into direct conflict with the trade unions. He had plunged into the task of restoring the railway system, and, overruling the objections of the union, he had mobilized the railwaymen under army discipline. Then, again in the face of union opposition, he had set up his own transport authority, the Central Transport Committee, known as Tsektran. His highhanded treatment of this union and his threats that he would deal likewise with other unions infuriated unionist members of the party.

Trotsky had provoked the conflict with the unions, but there was also growing opposition to the highhanded practice of the central party organs of disregarding democratic elections and making appointments to high offices. Dispute over these fundamental issues threatened to split the party. Lenin, supported by ten of the nineteen Central Committee members, including Stalin, Zinoviev, and Kamenev, proposed some moderating of party rule. Immediate abolition of Trotsky's hated Tsektran was to be a first step. Trotsky violently opposed such "liberal" policies. He was supported by Bukharin, Dzerzhinsky, and the three members then in charge of the party Secretariat. The rift within the Central Committee could not be bridged, and it was decided to put the matter to the party at large. Zinoviev, the party leader in Petrograd, led the attack on Trotsky, whom he had always detested, condemning him as a dictator. The debate raged between the factions as all prepared for the Tenth Party Congress, due to meet in March 1921, when these questions would be resolved.

The driving sense of purpose which possessed the party leaders, and the distraction of such internecine disputes, caused them to minimize and even overlook the explosive mood of the people. Uprisings among the peasantry were too frequent to arouse special concern. But now the resourceful anarchist peasant leader Nestor Makhno had plunged the Ukraine into turmoil. Uprisings by peasants in western Siberia disrupted the Trans-Siberian Railways and further aggravated the food shortages in Moscow and other cities. Most serious of all was the rebellion of the peasants of the Tambov region, who were renowned for their turbulence. In April 1921 the Red Cavalry and special army units, commanded by Tukhachevsky, crushed the rebel forces, but it was not until the autumn that order was restored in the region.

The mood of the cities was demonstrated in February 1921 by strikes in Petrograd and elsewhere. The government declared martial law in Petrograd, and the protests were smothered in other places. But it took the mutiny in Kronstadt to make them realize the full danger of the situation.

A stronghold of Bolshevism in 1917, Kronstadt, the island naval base in the Finnish Gulf, guarding the approaches to Petrograd, rebelled against the Soviet government. The garrison of fifteen thousand sailors and soldiers, recruited from the peasantry, had been increasingly incensed by reports of forced grain requisitioning, of the brutalities of the Cheka, and the savage suppression of uprisings. Following a mass meeting of the garrison on March 1, 1921, Kronstadt rang with shouts of "Down with the Bolshevik tyranny!" and "For the Soviets—without the Communists!" The rebels proclaimed themselves to be the liberators of Russia from the new Bolshevik autocracy.

The rebels were confident that their demands would have popular support throughout the country. On the night of March 4 the Petrograd Soviet sent a demand for the immediate surrender of the garrison. Trotsky followed up this ultimatum with a threatening manifesto. Kronstadt refused to submit.

Preparations were made hurriedly to take the island fortress by storm before the ice thawed on the Neva and the Gulf. Special Cheka and communist units under the command of Tukhachevsky made three attacks and all failed. On March 16 the Soviet troops, camouflaged in white sheets, attacked again, and, after two days of savage fighting, the rebels were crushed. All who were captured were executed.

The Konstadt uprising, which had broken out on the eve of the Tenth Party Congress, unsettled Lenin and the party hierarchy. They had believed that world revolution was at hand, that the proletariat of western Europe would soon follow their leadership, and that the epic struggle of the Civil War heralded the transition of Russia to socialism. But Lenin and Stalin, and perhaps others in the Central Committee, now recognized that world revolution was far off and that the Western proletariat had no stomach for revolution. And the Kronstadt mutiny opened their eyes to the fact that inside Russia the communist leadership was the object of popular hatred. "This was the flash," Lenin acknowledged, "which lit up reality better than anything else."[3]

The immediate priority was to recover support for the party, in particular the support or at least the acquiescence of the peasants. They formed the great majority of the population, and their food production and demands dominated the economy. The party was at the mercy of the peasantry; it was a fact that Stalin was never to forget. But Lenin and, following him, Stalin also kept in mind the fundamental principle of "the dictatorship of the proletariat," which, as Lenin had stated and reiterated, justified the use of "unlimited power, based on violence and bound by no laws" in maintaining the supremacy of the party.[4]

In a desperate move to win over the hostile peasantry and the people generally, Lenin introduced at this time the New Economic Policy (NEP). The forcible requisitioning of produce from the peasants was halted. A graduated tax in kind took its place, and any future surpluses could be voluntarily delivered to the government or traded on the open market. The new incentives for free trade would probably have produced immediate results, but drought, afflicting especially the Volga basin, led to a terrible famine. Relief measures and large-scale aid from America saved many lives, but towards the end of 1921 more than 22 million people were starving to death. There seemed to be no limit to the sufferings that the Russian people were condemned to endure.

In the following year, when the harvest was abundant, agriculture produced impressive results. NEP heralded a great economic revival and a return to normal living. Initially the new policy applied to agriculture and internal trade, but it spread to industry. Private entrepreneurs, the Nepmen, emerged suddenly, injecting vitality and purpose into the devastated economy. As though to make up for the years of stagnation, the economic revival gathered an amazing momentum.

Many party members protested vigorously against this reversion to capitalism. The party as a whole was deeply shaken by this reversal of Marxist principles. Stalin keenly defended NEP. "Russia is now experiencing the same mass outburst in the development of its productive forces as Northern America experienced after its civil war."[5] Lenin rebutted criticisms of the betrayal of the revolution, claiming that, while the state retained control over the "commanding heights" of industry and foreign trade, the achievements of the Revolution were secure.

The Tenth Party Congress, meeting from March 8 to 16 (1921), marked a new era in the history of the party. The battle against the Kronstadt insurgents was raging at this time, and the delegates to the congress were both angry and intimidated by the widespread hostility towards their regime. It was a critical time when Lenin's leadership and his ruthless use of tactics of expediency were fully displayed.

The Congress approved the principles of NEP after relatively little debate. In their nervous, beleaguered mood, the delegates recognized that, however contrary to communist principles, concessions had to be made to the peasants at this time. Lenin was not greatly concerned about this retreat from dogma, which he considered temporary. Economic reforms were for him far less important than the political reforms needed to entrench the monopoly of power in the Communist party. Throughout the Congress he gave his attention primarily to the strengthening of the party political machine. He saw this as the real center of control.

In the early sessions Lenin's Platform of Ten, which purported to stand for relaxation of party dictatorship and discipline, gained the support of a large majority. Trotsky's proposals for rebuilding the economy by using the methods of war communism were heavily defeated. Lenin's resolutions on the trade unions and democratic centralism seemed to introduce a new spirit of reasonableness. One resolution declared that "it is above all necessary to put into practice . . . on a wide scale the principle of election to all organs . . . and to do away with the method of appointment from the top."[6] Another resolution emphasized that members must be able to take "an active part in the life of the party" and that "the nature of workers' democracy excluded every form of appointment in place of election as a system."[7]

Suddenly on the last day of the congress, Lenin moved two new resolutions, one on "Party Unity" and the other entitled "The Syndicalist and Anarchist Deviation in Our Party." The first denounced and outlawed all opposition groups as sources of weakness and danger, and demanded their immediate dissolution or the expulsion of their members from the party. The second resolution rejected the trade-union claims to control industry as "inconsistent with membership of the party." The trade unions were, in fact, to be merged into the state machine and to function as the servants of the state. This was no more than Trotsky had advocated, but his handling of the proposal had caused angry opposition.

The two resolutions were passed by an overwhelming majority of the delegates. It was an extraordinary reversal of their earlier decisions. Lenin's tactics had gained full acknowledgment of the absolute power of the leaders at the center. But the conduct of the delegates demonstrated also the new significance of the party. It had become an entity, something apart from the small group of leaders dedicated to revolution and communism. It had been sanctified in the furnace of the Civil War. It had overcome the Kronstadt rebellion, but it must remain vigilant. All members owed it absolute obedience and loyalty, although this might mean subjugating genuine fears and objections. They voted for Lenin's two resolutions to preserve the unity of this almost mystic concept of the party: To have rejected them would have been akin to apostasy.

Trotsky suffered an ignominious defeat at the congress, and the campaign waged against him by Zinoviev, Stalin, and others seriously damaged his reputation. His plans for the militarization of labor, for the subordination of the trade unions, and for the greater centralization of power had been overwhelmingly rejected. The adoption of NEP had also been a rebuff to his economic policies. His public conflict with Lenin had lowered his standing with members among many of whom he was personally unpopular. In the election of the Central Committee he nevertheless retained his place, but others who had supported his platform were not re-elected.

Stalin played an unobtrusive part in the disputes which dominated the Tenth Congress. He was one of the Platform of Ten supporting Lenin's proposals. He was evidently content to leave it to Zinoviev to launch the main attack on Trotsky in the pre-congress debate, but he was active in the campaign. In *Pravda* on January 5, 1921, he published an article, entitled "Our Differences," which was his first polemical article against Trotsky. He argued that "democratism" and the use of persuasion among the proletariat were essential now that the war was over and the party had to deal with the complex threats of economic collapse.[8] It was an effective polemic, but moderate in tone and without the strident vigor of Zinoviev's attacks. Apparently, however, he was more active in the background. In the course of the congress one delegate, who was a member of the Democratic Centralist group, referred to the campaign against Trotsky under the generalship of Zinoviev in Petrograd, and in Moscow led by "the military strategist and arch-democrat, Comrade Stalin."[9]

Although unobtrusive during the congress, Stalin emerged from it with greatly increased authority. In part this was due to the eclipse of Trotsky and his supporters, which led to vacancies on the Central Committee and other central organs, many of which were filled by men close to Stalin. But a more important reason was his growing mastery over the party apparatus. He alone understood how it should develop and function in order to maintain the absolute power of the oligarchy at the center. Of course, Lenin had always insisted that the party must be in exclusive control and administered efficiently. But he was somewhat scornful of administration as a form of drudgery to be entrusted to lesser men. He had more than once dismissed it as something "any housewife" could manage.[10] Trotsky saw his role as one of inspiring and driving men by oratory, and like Zinoviev, Kamenev, and Bukharin he had no patience for the back-room work of administration.

Stalin did not make this mistake. Administration and organization were inseparable and essential to the strength of the party. In running the Central Committee's Secretariat, Sverdlov had shown himself to be an outstanding administrator-organizer. Stalin himself paid tribute to him in an article, published in 1924 in *The Proletarian Revolution*. He described him as "an organizer through and through, an organizer by nature, by habit, by revolutionary training, by intuition, an organizer in all his intense activity." He had been a "leader-organizer" who had possessed the two essential qualities. The first was capacity to understand the party workers with their abilities and shortcomings, and the second was to be able to post them so that each one felt himself to be where he could most effectively carry out the party's policies.[11] In his tribute to Sverdlov he was describing something of his ideal of the party worker, as a man who submerged himself in his duties, quiet, self-effacing, and utterly dedicated.

The years from 1919 to 1922 were a period of great change and development in the party. The transition from a conspiratorial revolutionary organization into a legal governing party with not only power but responsibility had come as a shock to Lenin and other Bolshevik leaders. It was a matter now of urgently reorganizing the party apparatus so that it could meet the new demands upon it. At the same time the relationship between the party organization and the machinery of the Soviet state had to be established.

The Eighth Party Congress, in March 1919, had increased the size of the Central Committee to nineteen members and eight candidates. Two subcommittees had been set up, each comprising

five Central Committee members. The first was the Politburo
(Political Bureau), and its members from 1919 to 1921 were
Lenin, Trotsky, Stalin, Kamenev, and Nikolai Krestinsky. The second subcommittee was the Orgburo (Organizational Bureau) of
which Stalin was also a member. Lenin described the functions of
the two new organs broadly in the statement that "the Orgburo
allocates forces, while the Politburo decides policy."[12] A third
organ, the Secretariat of the Central Committee, was soon exercising extraordinary power and influence.

In the early days of the party, Krupskaya and Elena Stasova had
acted as secretaries under Lenin's personal supervision. The work
had expanded rapidly after 1917 and Sverdlov took over the Secretariat. In March 1919 he fell ill with Spanish flu and died. Krestinsky was appointed in his place.

The reorganization and expansion of the party apparatus were
accelerated by the need to establish the dominant role of the
party organs over those of the Soviet state. Lenin had declared
that the party must be "the leading and directing force" in Soviet
society.[13] This function demanded a strong and efficient party machine.[14]

The Eighth Party Congress in March 1919 had approved a special Resolution on Organizational Questions. It described the
function of party committees as being to "guide" and "control"
Soviet or government organs through directives passed to party
"factions" within them, but without involving themselves directly
in administration.

The creation of a massive, highly organized party apparatus
quickly gathered momentum. Sverdlov had handled the party administration with the help of 15 assistants and a total staff of 30.
By December 1919 the staff of the Secretariat numbered 80; three
months later it was 120; and by March 1920, 602.

The rules of party structure provided for a hierarchy of committees under the authority of the annual party congress and conference, and the Central Committee. Such committees were set up
at regional, provincial, district, and rural levels, and there were
party cells in the Red Army and in industries. Each committee
was subordinated to the committee next above it, and its membership had to be approved by its next senior committee. All an-

swered to the supreme body at the top of the pyramid, which decided who would be elected as secretary and which could replace any member of any committee.

The key to the effectiveness of this vast hierarchal network lay in the appointment of trusted party members to exercise control at every level. In the early years of the Secretariat, personnel records were far from complete, but by the beginning of 1922 a party census made it possible for the first time to record biographical data on every member. On the basis of the new records, postings could be selective. Between April 1900 and mid-February 1921 there were more than forty thousand postings, and the number grew as the party tightened its grip on the country.

Stalin's exact role in the creation of this immense party apparatus is not known, but it was significant. Indeed, he alone among the party leaders had the knowledge and patience for this kind of work. Lenin took a close interest, but, provided the development was on lines that he approved, he did not involve himself in details. Zinoviev and Kamenev were mainly concerned at this time with their roles as the party chiefs respectively of Petrograd and Moscow. Trotsky was taken up with his economic proposals. Moreover, after the rejection of his plans at the Tenth Congress in March 1921, he seemed to withdraw, as though deeply hurt, and he took no direct interest in the building of the party organization.[15]

During these years Stalin was a full member of the Central Committee, the Politburo, and the Orgburo. He had always shown a remarkable ability for shouldering a multiplicity of responsibilities. He was still Kommissar for Nationality Affairs, and from 1919 to 1922 he was also the People's Kommissar of State Control, later renamed the Workers' and Peasants' Inspection, or Rabkrin, which exercised control over the whole government machinery, becoming a "kommissariat above all kommissariats."[16]

At the Eleventh Party Congress in March–April 1922, Eugene Preobrazhensky asserted that many top party leaders were giving excessive attention to governmental matters. He went on to question whether any man, and he referred directly to Stalin, could shoulder the responsibilities of two kommissariats and also carry out his party work.

Lenin admitted the difficulty, but pointed out that there was no one else capable of dealing with these particular tasks. "These are all political questions," he said, referring to the nationality problems with which Stalin was dealing. "We are resolving them and we have to have a man to whom any national representative can go and explain in detail what the problem is. Where can we find him? I don't believe that Preobrazhensky could name any candidate other than Comrade Stalin. The same applies to Rabkrin. A gigantic job! But in order to cope with the inspection work, you have to have at the head of it a man with authority, otherwise we'll bog down and drown in petty intrigues."[17]

Krestinsky, Preobrazhensky, and L. P. Serebryakov, who had been in charge of the Secretariat since March 1920, were all closely associated with Trotsky. At the Tenth Party Congress in March 1921, they were not re-elected to the Central Committee and consequently vacated their places in the Secretariat and the Orgburo. Stalin's colleagues Voroshilov and Ordzhonikidze gained seats on the Central Committee. Molotov, already under Stalin's domination, became a full member. Two able young party workers, Valerian Kuibyshev and Sergei Kirov, both Stalin's supporters, were also elected. The three places in the Secretariat were filled by Molotov, Emelyan Yaroslavsky, and V. M. Mikhailov.

During the desperate months of the Civil War, Stalin had not been able to give time to his Kommissariat for Nationality Affairs. He returned to it actively in the spring of 1920 and quickly developed its powers and jurisdiction until it became a small-scale federal government on its own. But his handling of nationality affairs brought increasing friction in his relations with Lenin.

The policy of centralizing power in the one communist party had been clearly stated in the party rules in December 1919.[18] Communist parties in the Ukraine, the Muslim borderlands, and Georgia had been subordinated to the Russian Central Committee in the course of the Civil War, and claims to autonomy or the preservation of national identity had been brushed aside. Lenin had become disturbed, however, about the working of communist policy among national minorities. He had always had misgivings about Great Russian chauvinism, although in a party which was some 80 per cent Russian in composition, the predominance of

Russian influence was inevitable. To Stalin the policy was clear: It
was to reunite without delay as much of the tsarist empire as possible directly under Moscow's rule. Lenin accepted this principle,
but worried about the dangers of pushing the policy through in
haste, especially in Georgia. Stalin was not the man to allow exceptions, least of all in Georgia, where the despised Mensheviks
were in power.

In November 1920 Stalin went to Baku. It was his first visit to
Transcaucasia since 1912, and he had grown in authority and ma-
tured greatly during these years. In Baku he was welcomed with
enthusiasm and hailed as "the leader of the proletarian revolution
in the Caucasus and the East."[19] Ordzhonikidze, head of the Central Committee's Caucasian Bureau (Kavburo), set up in April
1920, and Stalin's strong supporter, had arranged this reception.
He was one of the group of Stalin's agents who included L. M.
Kaganovich, head of the Turkestan Bureau, S. M. Kirov, head of
the Azerbaijan Central Committee, and Molotov, head of the
Ukrainian Central Committee. Anastas Mikoyan, a young Armenian, was soon to join the group. All were eager for the complete reconquest of Transcaucasia and this meant seizing Georgia.

Early in May 1920, Ordzhonikidze, impatient for action, sent
telegrams to Lenin and Stalin, proposing that the Eleventh Army,
then in the North Caucasus under the command of Tukhachevsky, should march into Georgia. At this time the Poles were
advancing into the Ukraine. Anxious to avoid further commitments for the weary Red forces, the Politburo, in a telegram
signed by Lenin and Stalin, expressly forbade invasion and instructed him to open negotiations with the Georgian government,
led by the Menshevik Noi Zhordania. A treaty was duly signed on
May 7 (1920) by which the government of the R.S.F.S.R. formally recognized the independence of Georgia and guaranteed the
legal status of the local Communist party. Kirov went to Tiflis as
Moscow's envoy, and by diplomatic and other means he set about
undermining the Georgian government. The republic's independence could only be a temporary arrangement.

In an interview, published in *Pravda* on November 30, 1920,
Stalin stated that "the Georgia that enmeshed itself in the toils of
the Entente and was consequently deprived both of Baku oil and

of Kuban grain, the Georgia that became the main base of imperialist operations by Britain and France and hence entered into hostile relations with Soviet Russia—this Georgia is now living out
the last days of its existence."[20]

In December 1920 and again in January 1921, Ordzhonikidze,
with the support of all members of the Kavburo, sent telegrams to
Lenin urging the immediate take-over of Georgia. The reply on
each occasion was that the time was not yet ripe. Lenin's hesitation was due to many factors. The Red Army was in no condition
to wage a long campaign. The Turkish armies along the Georgian
and Armenian frontiers might attack. He feared, too, that, since
Britain had recognized independent Georgia, she might intervene
in support of the regime. Leonid Krasin was instructed to take
soundings in London, and he obtained an assurance from the
Prime Minister, David Lloyd George, that the British government would not be unduly distressed by Soviet action.

At this stage Stalin took up the Kavburo proposals, and this was
the decisive factor. He made an issue of allegations that Zhordania's government had violated the Soviet-Georgian treaty, and
argued that a revolutionary situation existed in Georgia. He proposed to the Central Committee that Ordzhonikidze be directed
to prepare an armed communist rising in Georgia and that the
Revolutionary War Council should stand ready to give military
assistance. He added a postscript to his letter which read tersely:
"I request a reply before 6 o'clock." Lenin responded promptly,
adding to the letter the words "Not to be delayed."[21] On February 15, 1921, the Red Army invaded Georgia.

Lenin continued nevertheless to feel troubled about Georgia.
Socialists abroad would be critical of the Soviet government's use
of force to overthrow a social democratic regime. At this time,
too, it was important to avoid damaging further good relations
with the West, which the Soviet government was cultivating in
the hope of attracting the massive capitalist aid urgently needed
for the revival of the Russian economy. Such factors had not troubled him unduly in respect of other national minorities, but Georgia was an exception. Early in March 1921 he sent messages to
Ordzhonikidze, urging him to try to reach a compromise agreement with Zhordania and the Georgian Mensheviks. But Zhor-

dania and his ministers had already fled from Tiflis and soon afterwards sought refuge abroad. Lenin continued to urge moderation, but Ordzhonikidze was impatient and overbearing in his methods, and Lenin's advice was ignored.

The Red Army had carried out its invasion of the country with brutality. It was followed by a swarm of officials from Moscow who took over the administration, and the Cheka exercised police functions with a crude unconcern for Georgian feelings. Ordzhonikidze set up his headquarters in Baku, and ruthlessly asserted his authority throughout Transcaucasia, especially in purging the Menshevik and anti-Soviet elements.

The Georgians reacted angrily. The conflict developed into a feud between Ordzhonikidze, supported by Stalin, and Budu Mdivani, leading the Georgian Bolsheviks, which came to a climax over the formation of the Transcaucasian federation. At first Lenin supported Ordzhonikidze and Kavburo, but gradually he became opposed to them, and in the process he turned against Stalin.

16

Lenin in Decline 1921–22

During 1921 Lenin's health began to fail. Cerebral arteriosclerosis was already obstructing the blood circulation and taking its toll. The small thick-set man whose driving energy had been inexhaustible was tiring easily. He became irascible, sensing perhaps that soon he would be unable to carry on. The interminable working hours, the day-to-day problems of party and government, the handling of fractious or overzealous members, all would be beyond his strength. He spent much of the summer resting in the village of Gorki not far from Moscow. But he found difficulty in resting; he had to be at the center, running the party and the government.

The Eleventh Party Congress was to meet towards the end of March 1922, and he prepared carefully. The sessions threatened to be stormy. Many members were critical of the dictatorship of the hierarchy and the suppression of party democracy. Indeed, in February 1922 a group of twenty-two members of the former Workers' Opposition, led by Shlyapnikov and Aleksandra Kollontai, went so far as to appeal to the Third Communist International. There was never any possibility that the International would censure the Russian party. But the action of the twenty-two members caused embarrassment to Lenin and his colleagues. In fact, they failed to appreciate that the mass of members were in sympathy with Shlyapnikov's group.

The widespread discontent erupted at the congress. Lenin attended only the opening and closing sessions. He was infuriated by the criticisms made from the floor.[1] In the past he had handled critics effectively, but now he showed his anger and made threats, and some members even laughed at him. Moreover, the congress defied him and the Central Committee in refusing to expel Shlyapnikov and Kollontai from the party. Otherwise the policies set out in Lenin's opening paper were endorsed. But on the important issue of the retention of the Party Control Commissions, the Central Committee got its way only by falsifying the voting.

The Party Control Commissions had been set up in 1920 to guard communist morals. They were separate and independent from party organs; no member of the Central Committee could serve on a control commission. They had to keep constant watch for corruption, inefficiency, and personal failings in party officials. Lenin was puritanical in the moral standards he expected and was under the illusion that through the constant vigilance of such commissions he could keep the party free from corruption.

At first the commissions acted with petty thoroughness against all members. They did not hesitate to look into complaints against the hierarchy, as in the case of the railway guard who accused Stalin of swearing and threatening him. Other party leaders found themselves under examination. Increasingly, however, the commissions investigated the critical and dissident members, and they became a means of suppressing criticism of any kind. It was for this reason that rank-and-file members wanted the commissions abolished.

At the Congress, Molotov reported on behalf of the Secretariat. He claimed that as a result of the purge of the party, some 160,000 members had been expelled or forced to resign. "Now," he stated, "those [opposition] currents and semi-formed factions do not exist."[2] The delegates were not impressed. Indeed, the sessions provided lively evidence that the spirit of opposition was far from dead. There were numerous complaints about the clumsy bureaucracy and the inefficiency of the Secretariat. Of all the organs of the Central Committee the Secretariat appeared to command least respect.

On April 3, 1922, the day after the end of the Congress, it was announced that Stalin had been appointed to the new post of General Secretary. The function of the office was to co-ordinate the work of the complex party apparatus. But it was also intended that the Secretariat would examine the membership more closely and ensure that delegates to future congresses were more carefully chosen. The obvious and indeed the only man with the knowledge, efficiency, and authority for this key post was Stalin. Kamenev as chairman of the Politburo nominated him on its behalf, and there can be no doubt that Lenin supported the nomination, which he probably initiated.[3] Molotov and Kuibyshev were appointed as Stalin's assistants. The appointment was announced in the Soviet press as a routine matter. Apparently no one, not even Lenin at this stage, paused to reflect that Stalin was now the only Bolshevik leader who was a member of the Central Committee, Politburo, Orgburo, and the Secretariat, the four closely interlinked organs which controlled every aspect of the party and of national life.

Lenin was weary after the Congress. Stormy meetings of this kind drained him of nervous energy, and, instead of recovering quickly, he had to take a long rest. Angered by this unaccustomed debility, he harried the doctors with demands for a cure. He was only fifty-two years old, an age when most men were reaching their prime, and he had a reasonable expectation of many years in power. In April 1922 he underwent a minor operation to remove a bullet lodged in his body since 1918, when Fanya Kaplan had shot him. There was evidently some hope that the operation might lead to an improvement in his condition. But on May 26, 1922, while resting at his country home in Gorki, he suffered a severe stroke with partial paralysis of the right side of his body and loss of speech.

The party and the whole nation were shocked. With the custom of centuries the Russian people looked to one man as their

ruler, the embodiment of the government and of the nation itself.
For them Lenin held the position that the Tsar had held, and at
this time, after the catastrophes of war and when every part of national life was nearing collapse, he was needed.

Within the party the shock was greatest. Lenin had created the
party. It was identified with him, and without him it was assumed
that there could be no party. The leaders were alarmed. At every
level of the membership from the Central Committee and the
Politburo down to the rank-and-file members the overriding concern was to reassure the masses and to protect the unity of the
party.

The Politburo had been the oligarchy wielding power, and although Lenin thought and acted as autocrat, he usually consulted
and sought the agreement of its members. Now within the Politburo a troika or triumvirate of Zinoviev, Kamenev, and Stalin
was formed to provide collective leadership. Zinoviev, as head of
the party in Petrograd and one of Lenin's close colleagues, was accepted at first as its leader. Kamenev, as chairman of the Politburo
and head of the party in Moscow, was also a natural member.
Stalin was the leader-organizer and represented the party apparatus. Trotsky was excluded. Zinoviev, Kamenev, and Stalin were
personally antagonistic towards him, but the main reason for his
exclusion was the fear that with his arrogant dictatorial approach
to all problems he would provoke opposition and endanger party
unity.

The triumvirate, bringing together in the absence of Lenin the
three most powerful men in the party, was accepted as a temporary arrangement. It was, in fact, the opening round in the struggle for the succession.

The party leaders worked hard to reassure the people about
Lenin's health and to instill confidence that he would soon return
to office. Stalin's short personal article, published in *Pravda* on
September 24, 1922, was particularly noteworthy. He had a remarkable gift for communicating directly with the masses, for
making them feel that he was talking as a friend and taking them
into his confidence. It was a talent that he used infrequently, but
on occasions with tremendous effect.

It was not really appropriate, he commented, to write about

Comrade Lenin resting, for he was soon returning to work. Also he had so many valued memories that he could not really write them down in a short article. But write he must, for the editors insisted. When he had seen him in July 1922 for the first time after the stroke, Lenin reminded him of one of those old warriors he had met at the front, who had fought without a break for days on end and who after a rest had come back refreshed and ready for new battles. Lenin had made the impression on him that after a month and a half's rest he was completely revived, but with traces of his former exhaustion. Lenin complained lightheartedly about the doctors' orders. "I am not allowed to read newspapers or talk about politics," he said. "But," Stalin added, "we laughed about the doctors who cannot understand that professional politicians on meeting cannot help talking about politics." A month later he found a different Lenin, now "surrounded by a pile of books and newspapers and no longer showing signs of strain and fatigue." It was "our old Lenin, peering cunningly at his visitor and screwing up his eyes."[4]

At the time when this article was written, Lenin was still seriously ill. But he was not a man to submit passively to disabilities. He strove impatiently to overcome his paralysis and to regain his power of speech. On July 2, 1922, he wrote triumphantly that "my handwriting begins to look human," and he asked for the preparation of numerous papers in readiness for his return to work. His recovery was rapid, and early in October he was again at his desk in Moscow. But he should have taken longer to recuperate. His doctors had advised him to convalesce in the warmth of the Crimea and to avoid the northern winter. He would not hear of staying away for a day longer than necessary, and, although he agreed to restrict his activities, he plunged at once into work.[5]

The return of Lenin to Moscow was welcomed by most members. But to the party leaders and especially to the triumvirate, it was a source of misgiving. Lenin had become more arbitrary and unpredictable. At this time of economic crisis and of acute unrest within the party, he might seize on some line of policy and stubbornly pursue it against all objections. At the same time he was possessive about the party: It was his creation and he was not prepared to surrender control over it even to his closest comrades.

Stalin in particular had reason to be disturbed. It seemed that illness had turned Lenin into a cantankerous, interfering old man. Even before his first stroke he had shown alarming signs of excitability and unreasonableness. A proposal, made by Sokolnikov, then Kommissar for Finance, that the state foreign trade monopoly should be relaxed had provoked a tantrum. Sokolnikov's plan was to introduce greater flexibility into foreign trade than was possible under the inexperienced administration of the Foreign Trade Kommissariat. It was a proposal that normally Lenin would have discussed rationally and calmly. Now his reaction took everyone by surprise. On May 15, 1922, he wrote to Stalin and to M. Frumkin, the Vice-kommissar for Foreign Trade, demanding that they take steps "formally to prohibit" further consideration of the proposal. Stalin answered this outburst calmly: "I have no objection at the present stage to the 'formal prohibition' of steps towards a relaxation of the foreign trade monopoly; still I think that the relaxation is becoming inevitable."[6] To Stalin this was an irritating but minor disagreement. It was, however, the forerunner of more serious conflict.

During the months of convalescence, Lenin had been able to stand back to consider the party, its apparatus, and its personalities. Probably for the first time he had recognized the extent of the power that had come into Stalin's hands. It had filled him with resentment as though he had discovered him in the act of usurping his position. Although it is usually assumed that Stalin was covertly grasping at positions of power and influence, the fact is that he was promoted mainly on the initiative of Lenin. Once appointed to his various offices he was prompt to exercise the authority necessary to carry out the work. If Lenin appreciated this, it did not diminish his resentment.

Like most men obsessed with power, Lenin saw his authority as something personal, and the thought of another wielding it was unbearable. He was the one chosen by fate to destroy the tsarist regime, to lead the Revolution, and to build a new society. At this stage, because he still believed that he would recover from his stroke and because he could not conceive of another being able to

take his place, he gave no thought to a successor. Now the possibility that Stalin might be emerging to assume that role angered
him, and he became determined to reduce his authority and even
to destroy him politically. But Stalin was already the one indispensable member of the ruling hierarchy, and, even had Lenin
been in good health, he would probably have found it impossible
to remove him.

The communists always showed concern for legal formalities:
They craved respectability. But in 1922 their earnest discussions
on a new constitution were stimulated by more than a hunger for
respectability. Relations between the R.S.F.S.R. and the other
republics were confused. The Ukraine and Georgia complained
strongly about the lack of any definition of powers and about the
supreme authority assumed by the R.S.F.S.R. in certain fields
without consultation or agreement. In 1922, also, Soviet Russia
was entering into diplomatic relations with other countries, and a
constitution was needed to enable the government in Moscow to
represent the whole country.

On August 10, 1922, the Central Committee set up a constitutional commission under Stalin's chairmanship. Its task was to
provide an acceptable definition of the relationship between the
R.S.F.S.R. and the republics, which would form the basis of a new
constitution. The commission included representatives from the
republics, but the final statement was drafted by a subcommittee,
comprising Stalin, Ordzhonikidze, Molotov, and Gabriel Myasni-
kov. It was, in fact, Stalin's project that was put forward, and
it simply reflected the relationship which had developed with
Lenin's direct participation since the Revolution. The draft was
entitled "Project of a Resolution Concerning the Relations Between the RSFSR and the Independent Republics." The main
clauses provided for the merging of the republics into the
R.S.F.S.R. as autonomous units and with the authority of the
main organs of the R.S.F.S.R. extending over the republics. This
gave effect to his vision of Soviet Russia as a centralized state in
which the government of the R.S.F.S.R. was sovereign in its
powers over the whole country.

The draft was sent to the republics for the approval of their
central committees. The Communist party of Azerbaijan, under

the firm grip of Ordzhonikidze, approved it, but the others expressed strong opposition, and none more vigorously than the Georgian. When the commission met on September 23–24, 1922, however, it showed no concern for this hostile reaction and approved the plan. On the following day Stalin sent the draft with supporting documents to Lenin in Gorki and to all members of the Central Committee, which was to meet on October 5.

Lenin was strongly critical of the draft. He had a meeting with Stalin at which he insisted that a new federation must be created with a separate government, and that all the republics, including the R.S.F.S.R., should enter it as equals. The draft plan, providing for the autonomous republics to merge with the R.S.F.S.R., would be seen as an act of Great Russian chauvinism and would provoke and strengthen nationalist movements. Stalin accepted Lenin's proposal for a union of equal republics, but rejected his demand for the creation of new organs of central government. The government of the R.S.F.S.R. already provided the necessary apparatus, and to create a new stratum of supreme organs would make for a top-heavy and confusing system.

Lenin was insistent. On September 26, 1922, he wrote a letter to Kamenev for circulation to members of the Politburo. Describing the matter as one of supreme importance, he complained that "Stalin has a slight tendency to be hasty," a remark which stung Stalin. He stated that in conversation with him Stalin had agreed to amend the draft to allow for the equal entry of all republics, together with the R.S.F.S.R., into a union of soviet republics of Europe and Asia. Stalin had not agreed, however, to the other major amendment which he demanded, and the Plenum must consider it.[7]

Stalin reacted angrily. He considered Lenin's views on the nationality question to be muddled and contradictory, and he had no patience with his concern for national sensitivities. The wording of Lenin's letter annoyed him. He circulated his own brusque comments to members of the Politburo. He dealt with Lenin's points one by one, rejecting some and dismissing others as having only editorial significance. Showing resentment of Lenin's remark about his hastiness, he commented that Lenin himself had "hastened a little" in proposing the merger of certain kommissariats with new federal organs. "There is hardly a doubt," he wrote, "that this 'hastiness will provide fuel to the advocates of independence' to the detriment of the national liberalism of Comrade Lenin."[8]

The Plenum accepted Lenin's proposals out of deference to his strongly expressed demands. He himself was not present at the session on October 6, 1922, when the matter was debated. He was suffering from toothache, but he made his views known in a note in which he wrote: "I declare war on Great Russian chauvinism, a war not for life but for death. As soon as I get rid of that accursed tooth, I shall devour it with all my healthy ones."[9] The Plenum went on to approve the revised draft. It also set up a commission of eleven members, again under Stalin's chairmanship, to draft a constitution on the basis of the principles as finally approved.

The Georgians now raised a further objection. The draft prepared by Stalin had provided for the three Transcaucasian republics to enter the R.S.F.S.R. directly. The revised draft, as approved by the Plenum, had made the provision that the three republics should first come together in a Transcaucasian federation, which would join with the other republics in forming the Soviet Union. Georgians now demanded that their country should enter the union as an individual republic like the Ukraine and Belorussia, and that the idea of a Transcaucasian federation should be abandoned. On October 16 Stalin replied that the Central Committee had unanimously rejected their demand.

By this time Stalin and others were exasperated by the Georgians, who were taking up so much time when other urgent matters needed attention. Stalin was also angry because he had learned that during his convalescence Lenin had had private talks with Mdivani and some of his colleagues. The Georgian leader was actively campaigning against Ordzhonikidze and indirectly against Stalin, and seeking special consideration for Georgia. Mdivani, who was both charming and persuasive, and was clearly struggling against Great Russian chauvinism, was gaining Lenin's sympathy.

The Georgians had some grounds for complaint about the Transcaucasian federation. Ordzhonikidze, the "fiery Sergo," had, like Stalin, identified himself completely with the Russian party.

He was, when opposed, choleric and impatient; he gave no thought to non-Russian sensitivities. On his initiative, and probably with Stalin's approval, a plenary session of the Kavburo had decided on the federation of Georgia, Azerbaijan, and Armenia. There had been no prior consultation with the central committees of the three national groups and, while Armenia and Azerbaijan subsequently acquiesced, Mdivani, on behalf of the Georgian communists, denounced the proposal.

At a meeting of the Presidium of the Georgian Central Committee, Mdivani went so far as to declare that with only three exceptions every member of the committee looked upon Ordzhonikidze as the "evil genius" of the Caucasus and requested his recall. Mdivani next sent a personal telegram to Stalin, proposing that the Kavburo's membership should be changed and complaining that "Sergo [Ordzhonikidze] is accusing the Georgian communists, me in particular, of chauvinism."[10] But Stalin, who fully approved Ordzhonikidze's activities, ignored the appeal.

In Moscow the Politburo had requested a report on the Kavburo's decision on the formation of the Transcaucasian Republic. Stalin prepared the report and drafted the Politburo decision. He sent the draft to Lenin, who confirmed his support for the federation, but proposed changes in the wording to lessen the impression that the three countries were acting under pressure from Moscow. The Politburo approved the revised draft.

Under Mdivani's direction the Georgians kept up their campaign against Ordzhonikidze and the Kavburo. Stalin's brother-in-law, Aleksandr Svandize, who was the Georgian Kommissar of Finance, wrote personally begging him to try to reconcile Mdivani and Ordzhonikidze. He added a postscript asking if he could be posted abroad as a relief from the political tensions of Tiflis, and his request was answered with an appointment as Soviet trade representative in Berlin.

The Georgians pressed on with their campaign for separate treatment. In a telegram to Lenin they denounced Ordzhonikidze. But he reaffirmed the decision that Georgia must enter the U.S.S.R. as part of the Transcaucasian federation. Stalin was furious with the Georgian leaders. On October 22 he sent a telegram to Ordzhonikidze: "We intend to put an end to the wrangle in

Georgia and to punish thoroughly the Georgian Central Committee. . . . In my opinion we have to take a decisive line and expel any or all remnants of nationalism from the Central Committee. Did Lenin's telegram come? He is furious and extremely unhappy with the Georgian nationalists."[11]

Lenin appeared, however, to be changing his position on the nationality question. He was, in fact, faced with a dilemma which he was unable to resolve. He had worked to establish a united party and a centralized state, but now he also wanted an exceptional position, including a degree of self-government, for the minorities and special protection for them against Great Russian encroachment on their rights. The two demands were incompatible. Stalin recognized the contradictions inherent in his position. He himself had identified completely with Great Russian hegemony over the party and the government. He was now irritated by Lenin's maneuvers to reconcile the irreconcilable.

The Georgians continued their campaign, and the Georgian issue began to disturb the party leaders. Kamenev and Bukharin proposed the appointment of a commission of inquiry, and the Secretariat nominated as its chairman Dzerzhinsky, who always strongly opposed the principle of self-determination. But Lenin evidently had no confidence in the chairman or members of this commission, for he asked Rykov to make inquiries in Tiflis and report to him personally.

An incident witnessed by Rykov in Tiflis and reported to Lenin infuriated him. Rykov was in Ordzhonikidze's apartment, talking with A. Kobakhidze, one of Mdivani's supporters. Ordzhonikidze came into the room, and, turning to him, Kobakhidze spoke about a white horse in Ordzhonikidze's possession and virtually accused him of corruption. Ordzhonikidze was enraged by the insult and struck him across the face. According to Anastas Mikoyan's memoirs, published after Stalin's death, the white horse was a gift from mountaineers, which Caucasian custom obliged him to accept. He had passed the horse to the official stables and rode it only on formal occasions. The accusation of corruption was unjustified and his quick-tempered reaction understandable.[12]

Lenin was incensed by the incident. He interpreted it as direct evidence that senior communist officials, carried away by Great

Russian arrogance, had not hesitated to humiliate a member of a national minority. He made no attempt to look into the circumstances of Ordzhonikidze's outburst.

This and other incidents suggested that Lenin's illness was affecting him mentally. He had become increasingly capricious and flew into rages over minor matters. A Politburo decision, made after he had withdrawn early from the session on December 7, 1922, to allow Professor Nikolai Rozhkov to reside and study in Moscow, infuriated him. Rozhkov had been a Bolshevik, but in 1917 he had joined the Mensheviks and had supported Kerensky's government. He had since given up all political activity and devoted himself to study. But he had incurred Lenin's undying hatred. Lenin harassed the members of the Politburo until, for the sake of peace, they rescinded their decision and sent the unfortunate professor to Simbirsk. It is probable that his fury over this incident and over the Georgian conflict helped to bring on the two slight strokes he suffered on December 13 and 16, 1922.

Within a few days, however, he was able to work for short spells. His special anxieties were to resolve the Georgian affair to his own satisfaction and, closely linked with it, to pursue his vendetta against Stalin. At the end of December 1922 he dictated a "Memorandum on the National Question," which was to be his last contribution on the subject:

> I am, it appears, much at fault before the workers of Russia for not having intervened with sufficient energy and incisiveness in the notorious question of "autonomization," which is officially called, it seems, the question of the Union of the Soviet Socialist Republics. . . . It is said that we needed a single apparatus. . . . Is not our apparatus the same Russian apparatus which was borrowed from tsarism and only barely anointed with the Soviet chrism? . . .
>
> In such circumstances, it is quite natural that "the freedom of exit from the Union" with which we justify ourselves, will prove to be nothing but a scrap of paper, incapable of defending the minorities in Russia from the inroads of that hundred per cent Russian chauvinist, in reality—the scoundrel and violator which the typical Russian is. . . .
>
> I think that here a fatal role was played by the hastiness and administrative passion of Stalin and also by his anger at the noto-

rious "social nationalism." Anger in general plays in politics the worst possible role.

I also fear that Comrade Dzerzhinsky, who journeyed to the Caucasus to "investigate the crimes of these social-nationals," distinguished himself in this matter only by his truly Russian attitude (it is known that assimilated non-Russians always go to excess in the matter of hundred per cent Russian attitudes) and that the objectivity of his whole commission is sufficiently characterized by the "beating" meted out by Ordzhonikidze. I think that no provocation, not even any offence can excuse such a Russian "beating" and that Comrade Dzerzhinsky is irreparably guilty of having taken a lighthearted view of this beating.[13]

After making this thunderous assault on Russian chauvinism and on Stalin and others, however, he had only trivial remedies to propose. Communist officials should observe "codes of behaviour" in the borderlands; special protection should be extended to the languages and culture of the national minorities; party control over the apparatus should be strengthened. His chief proposal was that the union of the republics must be "retained and strengthened," but that the republics should have independence except in military affairs and foreign policy. The memorandum could hardly be expected to gain Stalin's support, for he was not a sycophant, ready to suppress his opinions in an attempt to regain Lenin's favor.

17

Lenin's Last Months

Lenin was expended physically and mentally. He had devoted his life to the single purpose of leading the socialist revolution in Russia. His goal had seemed so remote that he had not expected to live to achieve it. Suddenly the war, the failure of Tsar Nicholas II and collapse of the old regime, and other factors had plunged Russia into revolution. He had seized power, but then had come the great shock. He had given long and eager thought to destroying the tsarist regime, but only in general theoretical terms to the creation of a new order. His immediate concern was to prevent power from slipping from his hands, for power was his obsession. The next stage, which was to build the Soviet state, was beyond his strength and probably his ability. Stalin had both the strength and the ability and he was ready to shoulder this immense task. It was about this time that he first began to see himself leading the party and the country.

Lenin had returned to Moscow in October 1922, intending to resume his role as leader. He had the Politburo's meetings arranged to take place not more than once a week, each meeting limited to three hours and with an agenda distributed at least one day in advance. Still he was overtaxing himself. He had to rely on others to find out what was happening. He began to suspect that a cabal had developed within the party, directed against him. In the Politburo, Zinoviev and Kamenev sided with Stalin, and Trotsky was isolated. Wherever Lenin looked, Stalin or one of his numerous supporters was in control. Angry and frustrated by his own impotence, he turned more and more against Stalin.

After the stroke on December 16, 1922, all who had worked closely with Lenin recognized that he would never again be able to undertake political responsibilities. He would struggle impatiently and with great courage to return to work, but he would have to husband his strength. At the same time the communist leaders were increasingly worried by the prospect of Lenin interfering in the affairs of party and government. He still had great prestige among the rank-and-file members and might try to undermine the position of the leaders themselves.

On December 24, 1922, Stalin, Kamenev, and Bukharin on behalf of the Politburo discussed with the doctors the regimen to be followed by Lenin. It was agreed that "Vladimir Ilyich has the right to dictate every day for five or ten minutes, but this can not have the character of correspondence, and Vladimir Ilyich may not expect to have any answers. He is forbidden [political] visitors. Friends and those around him may not inform him about political affairs."[1] Presumably these restraints were based on the opinions of the doctors, who wanted a calm routine for the invalid, avoiding in particular political controversy which would excite him. But it proved extremely difficult to enforce the restrictions. Already Lenin had exacted greater freedom to dictate to his secretaries by threatening to refuse all co-operation with the doctors. But the restrictions reflected as well as the doctors' concern the anxiety of the party leaders to prevent his ill-advised interference.

The Politburo made Stalin responsible for liaison with the doctors and, in effect, keeping a watch on Lenin. It was an invidious task. Lenin was bound to resent his guardianship. His antagonism towards Stalin would intensify. It is surprising that Stalin, recognizing these dangers, accepted the task thrust on him by his colleagues. They did not want the responsibility themselves and were probably not reluctant to see Stalin exposed to these dangers. On at least one occasion he declared that he would no longer carry on, but was prevailed upon to continue. Presumably, too, he saw the advantages of keeping closely in touch with Lenin's activities at this time.

The journal of Lenin's secretaries, kept between November 21, 1922, and March 6, 1923, contained day by day the details of his work, visitors, and health, and after December 13 it recorded his smallest actions. Lenin, his right arm and leg paralyzed, was then confined to bed in his small apartment in the Kremlin, cut off from government business and, in fact, from the outside world. The doctors insisted that he should not be disturbed, and their orders were reinforced after December 24, 1922, by the Politburo's instructions and Stalin's supervision.

Unable to relinquish the habits of power, Lenin struggled to obtain the papers he wanted, relying on his wife, Krupskaya, his sister, Maria Ilyichna, and three or four secretaries. He was obsessed with the idea that before death overtook him he must give positive instructions for the party to follow. Still he thought of himself as the leader without whom the party and the Soviet state could not survive.

Working now against time and with a paranoiac conviction of his own infallibility, he could be dangerous. The communist leaders had this danger constantly in mind, and they feared even more that he would plot against them secretly. Indeed, Lenin managed to set up a private commission to investigate events in Georgia, which he himself referred to as his "conspiracy." At the close of his life the old conspirator could not resist plotting and conniving, and even against his oldest colleagues.

Stalin was undoubtedly worried. He suspected that Lenin was working on papers and conspiring against him. The difficulty was to penetrate the wall of secrecy surrounding the invalid. The situation angered him and he could not always curb his temper. Learning that Krupskaya had written a letter, dictated by Lenin, he phoned her, angrily threatening to have her prosecuted by the

Party Control Commission for disobeying the instructions of the Politburo.

Krupskaya was deeply offended and complained to Kamenev. "Lev Borisovich," she wrote indignantly, "Stalin subjected me to a storm of the coarsest abuse yesterday about a brief note that Lenin dictated to me with the permission of the doctors. I didn't join the party yesterday. In the whole of these thirty years I have never heard a single coarse word from a comrade. The interests of the party and of Ilyich are no less dear to me than to Stalin. At the moment I need all the self control I can muster. I know better than all the doctors what can and what can not be said to Ilyich, for I know what disturbs him and what doesn't and in any case I know this better than Stalin."[2]

Presumably Kamenev said something to Stalin about being more gentle in dealings with Lenin's household. Stalin responded sharply that he would give up this impossible task and leave it to someone else to deal with these difficult people. He was persuaded to continue, and there were no further complaints. An entry by Fotyeva in the secretaries' journal on January 30, 1923, recorded that "Stalin asked me if I was not saying too much to Vladimir Ilyich. How does he manage to keep informed about current business? For example, his article on the Workers' and Peasants' Inspection (Rabkrin) shows that he knew of certain circumstances."[3]

At this time Stalin was at work on the new constitution which he presented on December 30, 1922, to the foundation congress of the Soviets of the Union of Soviet Socialist Republics. It was, he declared, "a crucial day in the history of Soviet power." In a short speech he claimed that during the past five years the regime had come through the period of wartime chaos and was now in the second period when it would deal with the economic chaos, and under the new constitution they had a united state organization and a new Russia which would tackle these problems. He had a positive approach to the immense tasks ahead and was sensitive to the criticism that the party was destructive rather than creative. "We communists are often abused for being incapable of building. Let the history of the Soviet regime during the past five years of its existence bear witness to the fact that Communists also know how to build . . . that Communists know as well how to build the new as they know how to destroy the old."[4]

By December 1922 Lenin must have realized finally that he would not be able to address the Twelfth Congress in March 1923. But he could still exert influence from his sickbed. With remarkable determination he produced between December 23 and 31 a series of notes on the future of the party, and on January 4, 1923, he added a supplement. He also dictated on December 30–31 a memorandum on the nationality question.

The heading given to the notes by his secretary, Maria Volodicheva, was "Letter to the Congress," for he intended that it would be circulated and read out to delegates. The document has become known as Lenin's Testament. In addition he wrote during January and February 1923 five articles, which the majority of the Politburo tried to suppress. For a man gravely ill and in the shadow of death it was a heroic achievement.

Much has been made of the Testament. It was not, however, an inspiring statement of the ideals and objectives of the Revolution, and was mischievous rather than constructive. It began with the statement that he would "strongly advise . . . several changes in our political system." The purpose of these changes was to strengthen the party. The first threat was that the alliance of the workers and peasants, on which the regime depended, might break down, but this was improbable, for the NEP would promote their union. The greater danger would come from a split within the party hierarchy. To guard against this happening it was essential to strengthen the Central Committee by increasing its membership. The new members must be ordinary proletarians and not members of the party apparatus, who "have already formed notorious habits and biases against which we must fight resolutely." These workers would have to be present at all meetings of the Politburo and to read all Politburo papers; by their presence they would add stability to the committee and make it possible to reorganize and improve the party apparatus.

Throughout his career Lenin had insisted on the need for a small central body of dedicated professional revolutionaries in command. He had always worked on this basis, and the Politburo of five, later seven, members was his creation. As he well knew, his proposal for an enlarged Central Committee, sitting in on all Politburo meetings, was a recipe for confusion and inefficiency. Indeed, had anyone seriously made such a proposal while he was in good health and leading the Party, he would have fought it tooth and nail.

The danger of a split in the party lay mainly in the relations between Stalin and Trotsky. Lenin wrote:

> Comrade Stalin, having become General Secretary, has concentrated enormous power in his hands and I am not sure that he will always manage to use this power with sufficient caution. On the other hand, Comrade Trotsky . . . is distinguished not only by his exceptional capabilities—personally he is perhaps the most able man in the present Central Committee—but also by his too far-reaching self-confidence and excessive absorption in the purely administrative side of things. . . .
>
> I will not further characterize the other members of the Central Committee in terms of their personal qualities. I will only recall that the October episode of Zinoviev and Kamenev was not, of course, accidental but it can just as little be held against them personally as the non-Bolshevism of Trotsky.
>
> Among the young members of the Central Committee, I want to say a few words about Bukharin and Pyatakov. . . . Bukharin is not only the most valuable and the best theoretician of the party, but is rightly considered the favourite of the whole party. But his theoretical views can only with great doubt be considered fully Marxist. . . .
>
> And then Pyatakov is a man of indubitably outstanding will and outstanding capabilities, but too carried away by . . . the administrative side of things to be depended on in a serious political question. . . .[5]

In preparing these notes for presentation to the Congress, Lenin might have shown concern to strengthen their loyalty to the party and to each other. It was evident, however, that he intended, more by innuendo than direct statement, to damage their standing and to sow discord among them. He never forgot or forgave, and was vindictive. Thus he mentioned Zinoviev and Kamenev only to remind the party that they had been too faint-hearted or cautious to support the seizure of power in October 1917. In the most general terms he praised Trotsky, and then recalled that he had stood apart from the Bolsheviks and had joined the party late, so that in effect he was a newcomer. He described Bukharin and Pyatakov, who was not a member of the Politburo, in a way suggesting that there would be great risk in entrusting them with high authority. Here as elsewhere in the "Testament" the meaning of the phrase "the administrative side of things" was far from clear. Rykov and Mikhail Tomsky, two old Bolsheviks and both full members of the Politburo, were not even mentioned. Lenin's motives in thus describing the men who would, he knew, lead the party in future contained elements of spite and jealousy.

Stalin emerged in the best light. He had done nothing to besmirch his party record. The only query was whether he could show good judgment in wielding the vast powers in his hands.

Then suddenly Lenin changed his mind: Stalin must be replaced. On January 4, 1923, Lenin dictated an addendum to his notes, condemning Stalin and proposing his removal from the post of General Secretary:

> Stalin is too coarse and this fault, fully tolerable in our midst and in the relations among us communists, becomes intolerable in the office of General Secretary. Therefore I propose to the comrades that they devise a way of shifting Stalin from his position and appointing to it another man who in all respects falls on the other side of the scale from Stalin, namely more tolerant, more loyal, more polite and more considerate of comrades, less capricious etc. This circumstance may seem an insignificant trifle. But I think that from the point of view of what I have written above about the relation between Stalin and Trotsky, this is no trifle, or it is a trifle that may take on decisive significance.[6]

The immediate cause of this outburst was presumably Stalin's rudeness to Krupskaya twelve days earlier. She had turned to Kamenev, not wishing to upset her husband, but he learned about the incident somehow, probably through Fotyeva. He dictated the note in anger, but, as his wording showed, he recognized that to propose the removal of one of the most senior and able Bolsheviks in the party merely for rudeness was unlikely to get support. In a country brutalized by civil war, famine, and other indescribable hardships, manners were an early casualty. Moreover, in his political invective, his promotion of terror, his extreme personal intolerance, and other ways, Lenin himself had done nothing to halt the demise of courtesy. Indeed, he had emphasized that a revolutionary must be prepared to "crawl on his belly in the mud" to further the cause. Stalin was hard and ruthless and he got things done. He could be brusque, rude, and outspoken, and he had a vicious temper, but he was exceedingly able and loyal to the party. Lenin himself had accepted his coarse manners in the past and had welcomed them as evidence that he was not a member of the intelligentsia, the class he hated, but a man of the people.

Once he had turned against Stalin, Lenin brooded constantly on ways in which he could damage or destroy him politically. This personal vendetta, more than noble thoughts about the future of the party, was probably paramount in his mind during his last months of partial activity. Concerned that his indictment of Stalin on grounds of his rudeness would hardly shatter the confidence and respect he commanded, Lenin decided to attack his record as head of Rabkrin, a post from which Stalin had resigned only on his appointment in April (1922) as General Secretary, and his handling of Georgian affairs.

In an article, dictated in January (1923) and entitled "How We Should Reorganize Rabkrin (A Proposal to the Twelfth Party Congress)," Lenin mounted a campaign against bureaucracy, holding up Rabkrin as a warning of its dangers. Rabkrin should be reorganized by the reduction of its staff to three or four hundred carefully chosen and experienced workers, and it should be merged with the party's Central Control Commission. Moreover, selected members of the administrative and even of the secretarial staff would have the rights and duties of members of the Central Committee, including even the right to see the papers of the Politburo and attend its meetings. He asserted that this reorganization would minimize the dangers of "purely personal and fortuitous circumstances" and presumably of a split in the leadership. This new enlarged body would carry out general supervision "irrespective of persons involved" and no one's authority, "neither that of the General Secretary nor that of any other member of the Central Committee," should be allowed to hinder or prevent their inspections.

Thus the Politburo, the inner cabinet of the party, should meet in future, observed and supervised by the presence of fifty to a hundred members of the Central Committee and also by an unspecified number of employees, including secretarial staff, of the amalgamated Rabkrin–Central Control Commission. At the same time everyone and especially those in authority would be under the constant threat of investigation. It was not a proposal to be taken seriously. But Lenin was serious. He was stating, in effect, that in his absence no one could be trusted to exercise his power or leadership, and that to this end all decision-making machinery must be so tightly interlocked and supervised as to make it impossible.

The second article, "Better Less but Better," dictated early in February 1923, contained a scarcely veiled denunciation of Stalin. "Let us speak bluntly. The Commissariat of Rabkrin does not now enjoy a shade of authority. Everyone knows that a worse-organized institution than our Rabkrin does not exist and that under present conditions nothing can be expected from this Kommissariat."[7] The criticism was overstated and unreasonable. Everyone knew that Rabkrin was neither better nor worse than other Soviet kommissariats, which had been hurriedly set up with staff who were confused by unaccustomed responsibilities.

Although he finished it on February 7, 1923, Lenin did not revise this article finally until March 2. The delay may have been due to efforts to prevent its publication. According to Trotsky, Bukharin, as editor of *Pravda*, was reluctant to publish it. Krupskaya appealed to Trotsky, who requested a special meeting of the Politburo. Stalin, Molotov, Kuibyshev, Rykov, Kalinin, and Bukharin opposed publication. Kuibyshev even suggested making up one special copy of *Pravda*, containing the article, to mollify Lenin. Trotsky and Bukharin insisted, however, that an article by Lenin simply could not be suppressed, and this argument was reluctantly accepted.[8] The article was published on March 4, 1923. It aroused no special interest.

On the following day, March 5, Lenin dictated a short letter to Trotsky and one to Stalin. The letter to Trotsky read:

> Respected Comrade Trotsky. I would very much like to ask you to take upon yourself the defence of the Georgian case in the

Central Committee of the Party. The matter is now being "prosecuted" by Stalin and Dzerzhinsky on whose objectivity I cannot
rely. Quite on the contrary. If you agree to assume responsibility
for the defence, I shall be at ease. If for some reason you do not
agree to do so, please return the materials to me. I shall consider
this a sign of your refusal. With best comradely greetings.
Lenin.[9]

The memorandum of December 30–31, 1923, was enclosed with
the letter.

Trotsky rejected Lenin's request by returning the memorandum. Before doing so, however, he secretly made a copy intending
no doubt to make use of it when a suitable occasion arose. When
Lenin's secretary, Volodicheva, phoned him to get an explicit
reply, Trotsky said that he could not accept the task because of
poor health. The incident showed Trotsky as devious and ignoble.
Clearly he was afraid of coming into direct conflict with Stalin.
He was isolated and would have had little chance of succeeding in
the Central Committee, even though he was promoting Lenin's
case. Evidently Lenin was eager to promote such a conflict
notwithstanding his anxiety, expressed in his "Letter to the
Congress," about preserving party unity.

The letter to Stalin was curt and threatening:

> Respected Comrade Stalin. You had the rudeness to summon
> my wife to the telephone and reprimand her. Although she ex-
> pressed her willingness to forget what was said, Zinoviev and
> Kamenev heard about it from her. I do not intend to forget so
> easily what was done against me, and I need not stress that I con-
> sider what is done against my wife is done against me also. I ask
> therefore that you weigh carefully whether you are agreeable to
> retract what you said and to apologize or whether you prefer to
> sever relations between us. Lenin[10]

The letter was marked "Strictly secret" and "Personal," but
copies were sent to Zinoviev and Kamenev. Lenin had asked his
secretary to take the letter personally to Stalin and to wait for his
reply. But then he delayed until Krupskaya had read it. She was so
alarmed that she begged Volodicheva not to deliver it. But Volodicheva felt she could not disobey Lenin and took the letter to

Stalin on March 7, 1923. He wrote an immediate apology, but the wording is not known.[11]

The reason for Lenin's ultimatum to Stalin is difficult to understand. Almost certainly he learned of the incident of Stalin's rudeness to Krupskaya soon after it happened, and had added the postscript to his notes. The reason for his writing in this spleenful vein two months later is not known. Possibly some subsequent incident sparked off his anger, and he was ready to misinterpret and take offense at anything Stalin did at this time.

To Stalin the letter from the leader of the party with whom he had worked closely for so many years, and for whom he had felt both respect and affection, was probably personally distressing, but it hardly threatened him politically. He had been carrying out the function of guardian of the invalid at the request of the Politburo. Krupskaya was known to be a fussy woman, possessive about her husband, and the fact that Stalin had been angry with her would not have caused undue surprise among old Bolsheviks. Although he did not feel apologetic, Stalin at once wrote an apology, for it was the only thing to do.[12]

On March 10, 1923, Lenin suffered a massive stroke which completely paralyzed his right side and deprived him of speech. He took no further part in politics.

Trotsky remained silent about his copy of Lenin's memorandum on the nationality question. At a meeting of the Politburo on March 28, 1923, he criticized Ordzhonikidze and proposed his recall from the Caucasus. But he did not refer to the memorandum. On April 16, 1923, on the eve of the Twelfth Party Congress, Fotyeva, Lenin's secretary, wrote to Kamenev, chairman of the Politburo, about it and Lenin's appeal to Trotsky to present his views. Stalin knew that the memorandum would be critical of his handling of Georgian affairs, and he might have been expected to seek some understanding with Trotsky. But he brought the matter into the open, writing to all members of the Central Committee, indicting Trotsky for keeping Lenin's notes secret for over a month and making them known only one day before the opening of the congress.

Trotsky was now on the defensive. He explained that he had copied the memorandum because he was writing an article for

Pravda and he wanted to comment on Stalin's nationality policy. He said also that he had been reluctant to release the memorandum in view of its critical comments on three members of the Central Committee. His explanation was unconvincing. He nevertheless went on to ask that the Central Committee endorse his conduct as correct.

The incident, showing him in such poor light, made him uneasy. On April 18, 1923, he wrote to Stalin, stating that on the previous day Stalin had undertaken to write to members of the committee, confirming that Trotsky had behaved properly. No letter had been sent. He threatened that, if this was not done, he would ask for a special commission to clear his name. The threat was unlikely to disturb Stalin, but he evidently decided to save Trotsky further embarrassment at this stage. On his instigation the Central Committee recorded that the memorandum had been delayed "not because of dereliction on the part of any member of the Central Committee, but because of Lenin's directives and the course of his illness."[18] The Central Committee statement also declared that Lenin had been misinformed about the ill treatment and humiliation of national minorities, but being confined to his sickbed he had believed this information and naturally had expressed anger. The statement and the memorandum were shown only to heads of delegations.

The Twelfth Party Congress, which met from April 15 to 17, 1923, was a major success for Stalin. He deflected Lenin's criticisms skillfully and handled the problems of the national minorities with authority. At the same time he advanced his own policies in such a way as to increase his appeal as a leader of moderation and ability and of unimpeachable orthodoxy.

One of the main subjects discussed was the organization of the Central Committee and of Rabkrin and the Central Control Commission. Stalin promoted Lenin's proposals to enlarge the Central Committee and to increase its control, over the Politburo. This allowed him to strengthen his own position. Of the seven members of the Politburo, elected after the previous Congress, Lenin had been removed by illness, Trotsky was isolated, and Tomsky had no influence. Stalin depended on the support of Zinoviev, Kamenev, and Rykov, and they were uneasy allies. Of

the Central Committee's twenty-seven members, fifteen were Zinoviev's supporters. By increasing the committee's membership to
forty members and nineteen candidates, which, as he emphasized,
was in accordance with Lenin's proposals, he was able to bring in
party officials whom he had promoted and who were his supporters. The changes in Rabkrin and the Central Control Commission, which were merged, also allowed him to bring in party
workers whom he could trust. In both bodies and at plenary meetings when the enlarged Central Committee and the commission
debated and voted together, he could be sure of majority support.
Lenin had, of course, emphasized that the new members of these
organs must be workers and not members of the party apparatus
with their "notorious habits and biases," but this part of his proposal was ignored.

The Congress accepted these changes without real opposition.
A few voices were raised against the suppression of criticism and
the decline of party democracy, and the continued practice of appointing instead of electing party officials. Zinoviev, who already
saw himself as the leader in succession to Lenin, responded to
such criticisms with bombast. He warned oppositionists to watch
their step, threatening that the party might well act against them
as it had acted against the Mensheviks and the Socialist Revolutionaries.

In contrast with Zinoviev's bluster, Stalin responded with an appearance of good-humored common sense. Did the pleas for more
democracy mean that crucial decisions should be made not by the
Politburo, but on the basis of discussions in twenty thousand primary party committees? All would recognize that it was essential
that decisions could be made swiftly and with secrecy, and he
warned: "You must remember that you are surrounded by enemies. Salvation may be in the ability to strike a sudden blow, to
execute an unexpected maneuver with speed."[14]

He answered other criticisms with the same dexterity, deflecting
the main points or reducing them to absurdity. Freedom of
speech and of criticism were well protected, he declared, as all delegates could hear with their own ears at the Congress. He spoke,
too, of the need for new blood in the governing organs of the

party. A department of instruction was needed in the Secretariat. It could train two or three hundred workers who could be distributed to assist local committees. His remarks sounded so reasonable that no one hearing him could doubt that he was opposed to power being vested in a few hands. "We need men with an independent viewpoint on the Central Committee, independent to be sure not from Leninism, not from the party line, no, God save us from that, but free from personal cliques, from those habits and traditions of strife within the Central Committee, which have caught on, alas, and which alarm us so much at times."[15]

On the thorny question of the nationalities Stalin was at his most skillful. He had to recognize that the strictures, especially against himself, in Lenin's memorandum were widely known among the delegates. When the memorandum was mentioned, he evaded its comments, saying that he would not quote from "teacher Lenin" in case he misquoted him. He added that he deeply regretted that Lenin could not be with them at the Congress. It was a bold performance which left critics nonplussed.

In explaining his own approach, however, Stalin was forthright and he made it plain that he could not follow Lenin's theses:

> For us, as communists, it is clear that the basis of all our work is the work of strengthening the rule of the workers, and only after this comes the question—an important question, but subordinated to the first—the national question. We are told that one should not offend the nationalities. This is entirely correct. I agree with this—they should not be offended. But to create from this a new theory that it is necessary to place the Great Russian proletariat in a position of inferiority in regard to the once oppressed nations is an absurdity. That which Comrade Lenin uses as a metaphor in his well-known article, Bukharin transforms into a whole slogan. It is clear, however, that the political basis of the proletarian dictatorship is in the first place and above all in the central industrial regions and not in the borderlands, which represent peasant countries. If we should lean too far in the direction of the peasant borderlands at the expense of the proletarian region, then a crack may develop in the system of proletarian dictatorship. This, Comrades, is dangerous.[16]

Stalin then referred to Lenin's earlier writings on the subject, emphasizing the unity and supremacy of the party, the hegemony of the industrial proletariat over the peasantry, and the priority of the class over the national principle. All delegates appreciated that in speaking of the hegemony of the "proletarian region" he meant the hegemony of Great Russia. Adroitly he drew attention to the inconsistencies of Lenin's new thesis on the nationalities. At the same time by basing his arguments on the fundamental dogma of the party he outmaneuvered the opposition, since to attack his policy they would have to challenge the dogma, which was unthinkable. They criticized the practical application of the policy, complaining of injustice and discrimination suffered in the borderlands, but in effect conceded the basic correctness of Stalin's policies. The congress thus rejected Lenin's proposals, vindicated Stalin, and endorsed his policy of Russian hegemony.

Trotsky took no part in the discussions on the nationality question, pleading that he had to prepare his report on industrial affairs. It was a brilliant report and at its conclusion he received a standing ovation. The country was facing an economic crisis and Trotsky's dramatic presentation of what he called the "scissors crisis" was convincing to the delegates.

Economic policy was beginning to dominate discussion in the party meetings. Trotsky's theses proposing more effective planning were endorsed by the Congress and then forgotten. The need for capital for industrial development was the pressing concern. Zinoviev had declared that foreign trade and loans in the forms of concessions would yield the necessary capital, but few shared his optimism. Stalin, Kamenev, Zinoviev, and Bukharin were agreed that everything must be done to promote the prosperity of the peasants, for their purchasing power would generate capital. Another view, strongly argued by Preobrazhensky, made heavy industry the first priority. This argument appealed to members who were critical of NEP because it favored the peasants at the expense of the workers. He proposed compulsory savings as the means of extracting capital from the peasants to develop heavy industry. Trotsky largely supported this position, taking a stand, like Preobrazhensky, on the dogma that "only the development of industry creates an unshakeable foundation for the dictatorship of the proletariat."[17] This was the start of a debate which continued until the end of 1927.

The Twelfth Congress had given an impression of party unity, but this was deceptive. The decline of party democracy and the dictatorial rule of the top party bureaucrats were still sources of strong resentment, and economic problems were arousing angry debate. At the time of the Congress, however, most members restrained themselves in the interest of party unity, for a Menshevik and two communist underground movements, the Workers' Truth and the Workers' Group, were active. They succeeded in organizing strikes during the summer, but in September 1922 the GPU, as the Cheka had been renamed, eradicated them.

Against this unsettled background the struggle for power between the party leaders was delayed. The alliance of Stalin and Zinoviev continued but it was fragile. Zinoviev was uneasy, especially after Stalin had managed to pack the Central Committee with his own supporters. At a meeting of a group of party leaders in the Caucasus Zinoviev spoke of the need to guard against the Secretariat becoming too powerful. When Stalin learned of this speech he at once offered to resign. The offer was refused, for they could not manage without him. An agreement was reached, however, whereby Trotsky, Zinoviev, and Bukharin would serve in the Orgburo, where they could exercise some supervision over the Secretariat. But this experiment served no purpose. All three were, strangely enough, unfamiliar with the working of the party apparatus; they made no attempt to interfere and soon stopped attending Orgburo meetings.[18]

Suddenly on October 5, 1922, Trotsky joined battle with the party leaders. He wrote to the Central Committee and to the Central Control Commission strongly criticizing the Secretariat for causing unrest in the party, and declared his intention of making his views on this and other causes of discontent known to all members. A week later, probably encouraged by Trotsky's challenge, the Declaration of the Forty-six was sent to the Politburo. It condemned "the inadequacy of the leadership" in coping with the economic crisis and criticized the "completely intolerable" management of the party. The majority of the forty-six belonged to the left wing of the party and were engaged in the higher economic organs of the state. Moreover, they had been aligned with Trotsky in the past and, although not directly connected, the two challenges were considered together.

A joint Plenum of the Central Committee and the Central Control Commission was convened at the end of October 1922. Stalin handled the matter. A resolution, passed by a large majority, censured Trotsky for making a "grave political mistake" and condemned the Declaration of the Forty-six as a "factional" move, endangering the unity of the party.[19] It was, however, a serious challenge, which could not be brushed aside by a censure resolution. Stalin readily agreed that there was need to develop democracy in the party. The Central Committee called for free discussion of the subject, and throughout the country during November 1922 party organizations and local newspapers debated it. This national debate culminated on December 5 in a Politburo resolution drafted by Stalin, Trotsky, and Kamenev, which acknowledged the demand to make the party more democratic and appeared to meet the criticisms advanced by the opposition.

Stalin, like Lenin, had no real confidence in democratic methods and no intention of introducing them in this early formative stage of the party's development. He explained his views frankly to delegates to the Thirteenth Party Congress. "I say only this, that there clearly cannot be developed democracy, full democracy . . . some comrades and organisations make a fetish of the democratic question, treating it as something absolute, outside time and space. I want to say to them that democracy is not something fixed for all times and conditions, for there are times when there is no possibility or sense in introducing democracy." He went on to explain the essential conditions for full democracy: a developed industry and economy, a working class raised in quality and culture, and military strength, securing the country against attack by foreign powers. The party had to overcome many obstacles before it could attain these conditions.[20]

Trotsky had helped in drafting the Politburo resolution of December 5 and all believed that it had his full support. It was of crucial importance because it seemed to resolve the internal party crisis and the threatened split in the leadership. There was general astonishment and alarm when three days later he published a letter in *Pravda* headed "The New Course." The letter, while appearing to endorse the terms of the resolution, was in effect a renewed attack on the party apparatus and the powerful secretaries. The party itself, he stated, must bring the apparatus under its control and develop truly democratic methods. It sounded well, but was unrealistic. Moreover Trotsky himself was known for his autocratic ways. His pleas for more democracy did not ring true, and members recognized that he was using it as a weapon against the party leaders. His attack was bound to fail, especially against Stalin.

Trotsky's letter was widely discussed, and at the Thirteenth Party Conference, meeting from January 16 to 18, 1924, he and the opposition group were condemned by an overwhelming majority. Stalin mounted a devastating attack against them. He also caused a sensation by quoting a secret clause from a resolution of the Tenth Party Congress concerning expulsion from the party for factional activity, and he asked the conference to reaffirm this clause. He threatened "decisive measures" against those who circulated "forbidden documents." The economic policy endorsed in the resolution laid emphasis not on heavy industry, as proposed by the left-wing group, but on the promotion of agricultural prosperity and on price controls. Trotsky and the forty-six were defeated and warned.

Since his stroke in March (1923) Lenin, unable to speak or write, had been removed from politics. Throughout these months he was fully rational, but helpless. On January 19 and 20, 1924, Krupskaya read aloud to him the *Pravda* reports of the Thirteenth Party Conference. She noticed that he became excited. He had a further stroke on the morning of January 21 and died in the evening.[21]

18

Lenin's Testament

On the evening of January 21, 1924, Stalin, Zinoviev, Bukharin, Kamenev, Kalinin, and Tomsky drove in sledges through the freezing night to Gorki. Lenin's body lay on a table around which fir branches had been banked. They paid their respects to the dead leader and then hastened back to Moscow to attend a formal meeting of the Central Committee. Two days later they returned to Gorki to escort the body to Moscow. There it lay in the Hall of Columns, known now as the House of the Trade Unions. During the following four days people lined up for hours in the icy cold of the exceptionally severe winter of 1924 and more than 700,000 people filed past the bier, paying their last respects just as their forebears had done in other years when the Tsars had lain in state.

An extraordinary wave of emotion swept through the country. The deep religious feeling of the Russians found expression in their threnodies and spontaneously the cult of Lenin was born.[1] Among the hundreds of delegates gathered for the Congress of Soviets there was mass weeping after Kalinin had announced the news of Lenin's death. A spate of decrees from the Central Committee reflected the popular mood. The anniversary of his death would be observed as a day of mourning; Petrograd was renamed Leningrad; the "Lenin Institute" was established to produce editions of his writings in all languages of the world; monuments to Lenin were to be raised in Moscow and other cities. The most remarkable, and to some Bolsheviks bizarre and distressing, decision was that Lenin's body should be embalmed and displayed under glass in a mausoleum by the wall of the Kremlin on Red Square. People unable to attend the funeral would be able to pay their respects and future generations could come as pilgrims to gaze upon their leader.[2]

On January 24, 1924, *Pravda* in the first issue to appear since Lenin's death published an article entitled "The Orphaned Ones" by Bukharin. The title like the content of the article was wholly Russian in spirit, for on the death of the Tsar, especially if there was doubt about the succession, the cry of the people was always that, forsaken by their "little father," they were like orphans.

Bukharin's article was a deeply emotional eulogy. "Comrade Lenin was first of all a leader . . . a leader such as history presents to humanity once in hundreds of years. . . . He was the greatest organiser of the masses. . . . It would hardly be possible in all history to find another leader so loved by his comrades-in-arms. All of them felt a special feeling for Lenin. Their feeling for him was precisely one of love."

Trotsky was in the Caucasus and did not attend the funeral.[3] He sent a short article by telegram, which was published in *Pravda*. It expressed the same fervent idolatry. "The Party is orphaned," it read. "The working class is orphaned. Just this is the feeling aroused by the news of the death of our teacher and leader."

A proclamation from the Central Committee intoned elevated sentiments about the leader of world communism, the love and pride of the international proletariat. "But," it concluded with strong religious undertones, "his physical death is not the death of his cause. In the soul of every member of our party there is a small part of Lenin. Our whole communist family is a collective embodiment of Lenin."

The most striking and for the mass of Russians the most inspiring valediction came in the speech delivered by Stalin to the Second All-Union Congress of Soviets on January 26, 1924, and published in *Pravda* four days later.[4] It took the form of an oath of loyalty and service to the party of Lenin and, although communist in terminology, it was Orthodox in spirit, evoking the repetitions and rhythms of the liturgy. Instinctively he reverted to the forms of the Orthodox Church when he needed to express his deepest faith. Although it was an exhortation to the hundreds of delegates assembled at the Congress and to the people as a whole, it was also for him, like a coronation oath, a statement of personal dedication. To the Jewish party leaders for whom the Orthodox liturgy was alien, his speech sounded theatrical and false. But to all other members, notwithstanding their commitment to the atheism of Marxist dogma, and to the masses outside the party, the poetry and music of the Orthodox service had been part of their lives and unforgettable and they responded to his oration.

"Comrades! We Communists are people of a special kind. We have been cut from special material. We are the ones who form the army of the great proletarian strategist, the army of Comrade Lenin. There is nothing higher than the honour of belonging to this army. There is nothing higher than the title of membership of the party of which Comrade Lenin was the founder and leader. Not to everyone is given the honour of being a member of such a party. Not to everyone is it given to endure the adversities and tempests involved in membership of such a party. Sons of the working class, sons of deprivation and struggle, sons of incredible hardships and heroic endeavours—these above all others must be the members of such a party. . . .

"Going from us, Comrade Lenin bequeathed to us the duty of holding high and keeping pure the great title of member of the party. We swear to thee, Comrade Lenin, that we will with honour fulfil thy command! . . .

"Going from us Comrade Lenin bequeathed to us the duty of maintaining the unity of our party as the apple of our eye. We swear to thee, Comrade Lenin, that we will with honour fulfil thy command! . . . Going from us Comrade Lenin bequeathed to us the duty of preserving and strengthening the dictatorship of the proletariat. We swear to thee, Comrade Lenin, that we will not spare our strength in order to fulfil with honour thy command!"[5]

He solemnly intoned further oaths, using the same formula, impressing on his audience and on the people as a whole these undertakings of sacred duty.

Close associates who knew about Lenin's hostility towards Stalin during the last months of his life may have questioned the sincerity of this valediction. But he was wholly sincere in his dedication to the party and to Lenin's heritage. For Lenin the interpreter of Marx, the leader who had created the party and had seized power, he had deep respect. But Lenin, at times an inept politician who could be influenced by Georgian nationalists, exasperated him.

Stalin must have felt surprised and hurt by Lenin's behavior during the last months. As yet he knew nothing of the testament which was still held secret, but he had been made aware of Lenin's personal hostility. He had served Lenin and the Bolshevik cause loyally for twenty years; he had worked closely with him as a member of the Central Committee for ten years. On occasions he had expressed disagreement, and during the Civil War when they had been under unbearable pressures, he had shown bad temper, as had Trotsky and others. Lenin had uttered no recriminations. Their relationship had always been based on trust and devotion to the cause, and he had never conspired to displace him or to undermine his authority. The reward for this loyalty was a vicious campaign to destroy his position in the party. Stalin can only have seen it as a terrible betrayal. Certainly he did not respond then or later with hostility or resentment. In fact his attitude towards Lenin was accurately expressed in his lecture to the Kremlin Military Academy on January 28, 1924.[6] Although carefully contrived to show him as the natural successor, this speech had laid stress on the qualities of the great leader, "the mountain eagle." The Lenin who had turned on him had been an ill and dying man. Nevertheless, Stalin had a tenacious memory, and this betrayal by his old leader probably contributed to the cancerous growth of suspicion and mistrust of others, which was to contort his outlook in the years to come.

The cult rapidly grew more pervasive and powerful in the months after Lenin's death. By 1929 a granite mausoleum containing his figure under glass had been completed on the Red Square and had become a place of pilgrimage, the religious center of Soviet Russia. Portraits, busts, and statues were inescapable in every part of the country. Schools, halls of rest and culture, libraries, and other establishments all had their "Lenin corner." In primitive peasant huts far from the cities a print or newspaper portrait of Lenin might be seen in place of or even alongside the traditional ikon. His writings as well as poems, hymns of praise, and worshipful studies poured from the printing presses. Lenin was the new deity; his every word was sacrosanct; his name was the compelling symbol of the unity of Soviet Russia.

Among the party leaders the Westernized Bolsheviks, including Trotsky, had written in terms of hero worship of the dead leader. They felt the same dedication to Lenin's party as the simple rank-and-file members. But in supporting the cult they had been moved, too, by practical considerations. The popular worship of Lenin would strengthen the party.

Stalin has often been held responsible for launching and promoting the cult, but, as already stated, it developed as a spontaneous expression of popular feeling. It was a feeling which he understood and shared. The Orthodox teachings of childhood and in the Tiflis Seminary had taken deep ineradicable root. He was not religious in any conventional sense, but he was not truly an atheist. He had referred to the "god of history" and believed in destiny or fate. There was, in fact, a strong religious element in his Bolshevism and in his intense feeling for Russia.

The Central Committee met usually only every second month. The Politburo—and this meant the troika of Zinoviev, Kamenev, and Stalin—continued to wield power, as during Lenin's illness. No one as yet made any open move to assume the leadership. It would have appeared arrant presumption for any individual to step into the shoes of the great Lenin. In any case, collective rule had always been held up as the party's ideal. Tensions were, however, mounting between the leaders. Zinoviev took for granted that, as Lenin's lieutenant for many years and as head of the Comintern, he was the logical successor. He was a big man, extremely able, and a brilliant orator, but fat and soft in physique and character, and given to bluster. Kamenev, bearded, handsome, and dignified, was also able, and, except when carried away by anger, milder in temperament than Zinoviev, whom he supported closely. Rykov, the old Bolshevik who had followed Lenin as chairman of the Council of Kommissars, was a likable man, respected throughout the party, but he lacked a forceful personality and no one thought of him as a potential leader. At this time Zinoviev with Kamenev as his shadow seemed the most probable successor.

Trotsky was the outsider. It was held against him that he was not an old Bolshevik but a recent member of the party. This would have mattered far less if he had not been so disliked and feared personally by all, with only a few exceptions, who had had direct contact with him. His great ability was recognized, as was also the danger that he would spread discord and strife throughout the party by his highhanded methods. Discussing the precedents of the French Revolution—a favorite preoccupation of Russian revolutionaries—they saw Trotsky as a possible Bonaparte who in his personal passion for power would destroy the revolution. Fear of Trotsky had brought Zinoviev, Kamenev, and Stalin together, and now it held them from breaking apart.

Stalin did not appear to be a contender. Unobtrusive, quiet, modest, he was plainly the party worker who attended to the essential tasks of administration and organization. But he was always accessible to members and officials, listening patiently to their problems and complaints. Boris Bazhanov, a former official on the staff of the Central Committee who claimed to have been Stalin's personal secretary, described him standing in a corner, puffing his pipe, listening for an hour or more while an agitated provincial secretary or ordinary party member poured out his troubles. His patience was unlimited and, although he rarely committed himself, he earned the gratitude of many members in this way. He was always reticent, a man of few words who kept his own counsel. Bazhanov wrote that "he did not confide his innermost thoughts to anybody. Only very rarely did he share his ideas and impressions with his closest associates. He possessed in a high degree the gift for silence and in this respect he was unique in a country where everybody talked far too much."[7]

In the Civil War he had borne heavy responsibilities and had faced dangers in a way that had brought him credit throughout the party. He had dispensed summary justice when necessary and had shown that he could be ruthless, but he had not shown the brutality for which Voroshilov, Budënny, and others were notorious. In his speeches he was moderate and reasonable. He handled criticisms with apparent good humor, and even when attacking the opposition he was less savage than Lenin or Zinoviev. In Politburo meetings he sought to be agreeable. Writing of the first Politburo meeting that he attended and a time when the struggle between the three leaders and Trotsky was tense, Bazhanov noted that "Trotsky was the first to arrive for the session. The others were late, they were still plotting. . . . Next entered Zinoviev. He passed by Trotsky and both behaved as if they had not noticed one another. When Kamenev entered he greeted Trotsky with a slight nod. At last Stalin came in. He approached the table at which Trotsky was seated, greeted him in a most friendly manner and vigorously shook hands with him across the table."[8] It was at this time that, although in opposition to him, Trotsky described Stalin to his close friend and translator, Max Eastman, as "a brave and sincere revolutionary."[9]

In what is known of Stalin's life up to this time, there is, in fact, nothing that presaged the inhuman dictator that he was to become. Future events were to cast long shadows, and historians have tended to attach a general frightfulness to his every action, but his conduct as a dedicated revolutionary was of a kind with that of Trotsky and Lenin. The change may be dated from the time of Lenin's illness, when it seems probable that he first began to see himself as the successor. Certainly before 1921 he showed no pretension to the leadership, and was content to serve. He was proud, sensitive, but not personally ambitious. After the removal of Lenin he, like many others, must have wondered about the future of the party. Of the most prominent members Trotsky, towards whom he felt strong antipathy, would endanger unity and the others were not remotely of his caliber. Thus it would seem that during 1922 or 1923 Stalin began to consider seriously that in the interests of the party and communist Russia he would have to take over the leadership, and once having reached this decision he pursued his goal quietly and implacably.

The struggle for power was waged under cover, taking the form of ideological disputes in which each participant sought to show that he was more true to Lenin's teachings than the others. For the troika the removal of Trotsky was the first priority. A new journal, *Bolshevik*, was launched with the avowed purpose of combating "Trotskyism." Stalin gave a series of lectures at the Communist University in Moscow, named in honor of Sverdlov. The lectures, under the title "Foundations of Leninism," providing the first canon of Stalinism, emphasized the importance of party unity and discipline, the party's role as leader of the masses, and the need to strengthen the union of peasants and workers. They were, in fact, the principles laid down in his "oath" speech.

From February to May 1924 the "Lenin enrollment" was carried out with much publicity. One of the resolutions of the Thirteenth Party Conference had been to mount a membership drive among "workers from the bench." The Central Committee, meeting a few days after the funeral, endorsed this decision and apparently agreed, although it was not mentioned in the conference resolution, that it should be accompanied by a purge of oppositionists. At the same time the vast party machine which Stalin had painstakingly overhauled and expanded was effective in enlisting suitable new members.

The total membership, reduced by the beginning of 1924 to 350,000 with 120,000 candidates, was increased by more than 200,000 members, mostly young and ready to obey instructions from their party secretaries. Lenin had often expressed concern about the smallness of the proletarian element in the party, and the new enrollment was proclaimed as a great advance for Leninism because the new members were mainly proletarian.

Stalin's majority support in the Central Committee and the Central Control Commission and his control over the party apparatus made his position seem unchallengeable. But five days before the Thirteenth Party Congress was to open, something happened which suddenly threatened his career. Krupskaya sent to

Kamenev the notes which Lenin had dictated between December 23, 1922, and January 23, 1923, with a covering letter explaining that she had suppressed the two notes, known as the "Testament," because Lenin had expressed the "definite wish" that these notes should be submitted to the next Party Congress after his death. In fact, Lenin had dictated the notes specifically for presentation to the Eleventh Party Congress, held in March–April 1923. Her reasons for holding them secret for so long were not stated, but in bringing them forward at this time she was clearly seeking to damage Stalin politically.[10]

On the day after receiving the package from Krupskaya, Kamenev circulated the notes to a group of six senior Bolsheviks, including Zinoviev and Stalin, who called themselves the Central Committee Plenum Commission. It decided to "submit them [the notes] to the nearest Party Congress for its information."[11] The action taken fell far short of this decision. The notes were read out to a group of some forty delegates, who met on May 22, 1924, on the eve of the Congress. Zinoviev and Kamenev were both concerned to keep Stalin in office. He was their indispensable ally against Trotsky and the oppositionists. Zinoviev declared that, while they had all sworn to carry out Lenin's wishes to the letter, they knew that his fears about their General Secretary had been baseless.

Trotsky recalled that during the discussion Stalin referred to the Lenin who had dictated these notes as "a sick man surrounded by womenfolk," a barbed reference to Krupskaya, but he did not take an active part. Trotsky himself did not contribute to the discussion. Finally by thirty votes to ten it was decided that the notes should not be published, but that their contents should be conveyed to selected delegates to whom it should be explained that Lenin had been seriously ill at the time and misinformed by those around him.

For Stalin it must have come as a bitter shock to learn for the first time the contents of the "Testament" and to have this direct confirmation of Lenin's personal hostility. He had then suffered the humiliation of being arraigned by the old leader and of being present at the discussions on the action to be taken. His position had been threatened, for the full Congress could hardly ignore the last injunctions of the leader whom all were now so ardently worshiping. It must have come as a relief for him when it was decided that the Congress would be bypassed and that the notes would not be published. Nevertheless, when the newly elected Central Committee met, he offered his resignation. He was probably confident that those he had carefully selected for election would not accept it. In the event the committee, including Trotsky, voted unanimously not to accept his resignation.[12]

19

Overthrow of
the Opposition
1924-27

Although Lenin's attempts to undermine his position had failed, Stalin was watchful and cautious during the Thirteenth Party Congress, held in May 1924. He had made careful preparations, especially in excluding oppositionists from delegations, but Trotsky and others, who had signed the Declaration of the Forty-six, were among the delegates. They might try to disrupt the Congress. Also Zinoviev and Kamenev were merely temporary allies, who would turn on him when they saw the chance. The Congress, at which he was received with "applause turning into an ovation," proved a personal triumph.

Throughout the Congress, the first to be held since Lenin's death, there was a strong general desire to exclude polemics and factionalism. Zinoviev delivered the principal report, and he avoided controversy. At the end of his speech he referred to the "growth of a new bourgeoisie" under NEP and the danger of a "new Menshevism," but he did not name Trotsky or the oppositionists. Finally he offered a peace formula to dispose of the disputes which had plagued the party during the past year.

"The most sensible step and most worthy of a Bolshevik," he said, "which the opposition could take is what a Bolshevik does when he happens to make some mistake or other . . . is to come before the party on the tribune of the Party Congress and say 'I made a mistake and the party was right.' "[1]

Zinoviev's rhetorical call for unity received "stormy and prolonged applause," giving some indication of the party's impatience with internecine disputes. Stalin followed him on the platform and delivered a businesslike report on the party's organization. He made no mention of the opposition and, as always, showed that he was the last man to provoke conflict.

Present as a nonvoting delegate, Trotsky did not have to speak. But he could not ignore Zinoviev's appeal. Nothing was more difficult for Trotsky than to believe that he might be mistaken, unless it was to confess it publicly. At this time, however, his arrogance and inflexibility involved him in an inner conflict with his strong sense of dedication to the revolution and to the party as its embodiment. This led him into a confused and emotional defense of his position.

In his speech he again stressed the dangers of bureaucracy, confirmed his adherence to the resolution of December 5, 1923, on the need to eliminate factions, and pressed for more effective planning. Most of those present had heard him make these points on previous occasions, and he was evidently unconscious of the fact that, coming from him, these reiterated demands implied criticisms of the party leaders.

"Comrades," he continued, "none of us wishes to be right or can be right against his party. The party is in the last resort always right, because the party is the unique historical instrument given to the proletariat for the fulfilment of its fundamental tasks. I have already said that nothing is easier than to say before the party 'All this criticism, all these declarations, warnings and protests, were simply a sheer mistake.' But Comrades, I cannot say this, because I do not think so. I know that one cannot be right against the party. One can be right only with the party and through the party, since history has created no other paths to the realization of what is right."

Trotsky went on in this tortuous fashion. He repeated that certain parts of the resolutions of the previous party conference were "incorrect and unjust. But," he stressed, "the party cannot take any decisions, however incorrect and unjust, which could shake by one jot our boundless devotion to the cause of the party, the readiness of each one of us to bear on his shoulders the discipline of the party in all conditions."[2]

The speech, with its painstaking avowals of the party's infallibility, was poisoned by the conspicuous sense of his own intellectual superiority and his conviction that he was right and the party wrong. Moreover, he had misjudged the timing and the audience. To the majority of the delegates his speech with its insistence on incorrect and unjust party decisions sounded as though he put himself above the party.

The fury of the Congress was now directed at him. Krupskaya made an appeal for the factions to put aside their disputes and work together. The delegates were in no mood to heed her. On the day after Krupskaya's speech, Stalin addressed the delegates. He said that he, too, was opposed to "duplicating debates about differences," and for this reason he had made no reference to them in his previous speech. But it was unthinkable that he should be silent now. He proceeded to attack Trotsky for his defiance of the resolution of December 5, 1923, and of the decisions of the Thirteenth Party Conference.

Zinoviev and Kamenev both delivered vicious attacks. Kamenev, who had a reputation for mildness, apparently harbored a deep hatred of Trotsky, whose sister he had married, and his attack was venomous. The Congress unanimously confirmed the decisions of the party conference and praised the Central Committee for its "firmness and Bolshevik uncompromisingness . . . in defending the foundations of Leninism against petty bourgeois deviations."[3]

The Congress increased the size of the Central Committee from forty to fifty-three members and from seventeen to thirty-four candidates. The new men were in the main from the provincial apparatus and Stalin's supporters. Lazar Kaganovich, one of Stalin's ablest assistants, became a member of the committee as well as both the Secretariat and the Orgburo. Bukharin was elected to the Politburo to fill the vacancy left by Lenin. Trotsky scraped through in the elections to the committee and retained his other posts.

In the Third Communist International, known as the Comintern, which had been founded in March 1919, Trotsky was still highly regarded. Many Western communists were appalled by the ferocious attacks on him. But Zinoviev, whom Lenin had appointed president of the Comintern's executive committee, was actively undermining Trotsky's position and removing his main supporters from the organization. Indeed, during the Thirteenth Congress of the Russian party, several Western communists were invited to speak, and all with the exception of Boris Souvarine, the French communist, who subsequently wrote a hostile biography of Stalin, condemned Trotsky and the opposition. At the Fifth Congress of the Comintern, held in Moscow in June–July 1924, Trotsky was again savagely attacked and called upon to appear in person to justify himself. His refusal to attend set the seal on his condemnation.

Stalin was active among Western communists in Moscow at this time. Within a few months he and Zinoviev had managed to reduce the international movement to complete subservience to Moscow. Trotsky and Lenin had founded the Comintern in the faith that it would become a world party into which the Russian party would ultimately merge. Stalin, the realist, could see little prospect of this ideal being achieved. It would happen, if at all, only in the far distant future. He insisted that in the meantime the Comintern should be under Moscow's control for tactical and propaganda purposes.

Since May 1922 the troika of Stalin, Zinoviev, and Kamenev had held power. Relations had become tense, but unity was maintained. All three paid lip service to the theory of collective leadership, but they were held together mainly by the fear that Trotsky might try to seize power. Furthermore, in the midst of the mounting cult it was still too soon after Lenin's death for anyone to attempt to assume the leadership.

The contest appeared now to be between Stalin and Zinoviev. Several incidents had sharpened their rivalry, but at this stage

Zinoviev continued to see himself as Lenin's successor. He and Kamenev were taken aback in June 1924 when Stalin publicly chided them for mistakes in communist doctrine. The mistakes, if indeed they were mistakes, concerned petty points of interpretation. The importance of the incident was that Stalin was asserting his authority within the troika.

Another significant step taken by Stalin, a few weeks later, was to post Zelensky, secretary of the Moscow party apparatus, to Central Asia, replacing him with Uglanov. This weakened the position of Kamenev as chairman of the Executive Committee of the Moscow Soviet and leader of the Moscow party organization. A meeting of fifteen senior party members, convened by Zinoviev, criticized Stalin for his "uncomradely" action. He rejected the criticism, accusing them of trying to break up the collective leadership and to introduce dictatorship in place of party democracy. By autumn an open split between the leaders was imminent, but again Trotsky kept them together.

After the mauling he had suffered at the Thirteenth Party Congress and at the Congress of the Comintern, and after experiencing the hostility of the Central Committee and the Politburo, Trotsky might have been expected to lie quiet for a time. He was, however, wholly lacking in political judgment. It was not that he miscalculated the response of other people to his actions, but that their thoughts and feelings did not exist for him. He was concerned solely with his own ideas and policies, which, he believed, transcended all others in their rightness, and he was genuinely astonished when they met with storms of protest and criticism. By contrast Stalin was keenly sensitive to the attitudes and feelings not only of members of the party but also of people outside. With his sense of timing and his political acumen he was a formidable foe.

At this time when the tide of party opinion was running strongly against him, Trotsky gave an extraordinary demonstration of ineptitude. Already in June 1924 he had published a pamphlet, intended as a salute to Lenin, but in treating the great leader as his partner and equal he had caused offense to many members. Then in September (1924), while resting in Kislovodsk in the Caucasus, he published his early articles and speeches in one volume with an introduction, entitled "Lessons of October." It was an account of the progress of the revolution with the theme of the betrayal by the "right." He dwelt on the conflict between Lenin and Zinoviev and Kamenev on the eve of the October Revolution and even wrote about mistakes made by Lenin himself.

The volume, published in October 1924, caused a sensation. By digging up the past Trotsky was seen to be attempting to indict the present leadership and to cast doubts on the infallibility of Lenin. Bukharin promptly published an article in *Pravda*, entitled "How Not to Write the History of October." This was an interim reply. Trotsky had to be answered fully and by raking up the past he had exposed himself to a devastating counterattack. Before 1917 he had engaged constantly in polemics with Lenin; as was characteristic of the revolutionaries, their exchanges were marked by virulent abuse. Kamenev, then editor of the official edition of Lenin's works, published his reply in *Pravda* and *Izvestiya* on November 26, 1924, under the title "Leninism or Trotskyism." The article, ranging over Trotsky's early career, sought to show that Trotsky had always been opposed to Bolshevism and Leninism.

Stalin's contribution was a reasoned and destructive attack. Referring to Trotsky's prominent role in October, he said that it was to be admitted that Trotsky had done well, but so had others.[4] He dealt lightly with the errors of Zinoviev and Kamenev, which were generally known, and even admitted that before Lenin's arrival in Petrograd in March 1917 "I shared this mistaken position of other comrades."[5] Nothing had antagonized members more than Trotsky's insufferable assumption that he had been right all the time. Stalin was at pains to show that he himself was human and fallible.

Examining Trotsky's main heresies, he demonstrated by quotations from Lenin's writings that Trotsky had been in direct conflict with the master at all stages. In fact, Trotsky and Lenin had been basically close in their views, but it was not difficult to find quotations to prove the opposite. The most damaging part of Stalin's attack came in quotations from Trotsky's correspondence in 1913 with Chkheidze in which Trotsky had written that Lenin was "the professional exploiter of everything that is backward in the Russian workers' movement."[6] He had also written that "the whole foundation of Leninism at the present time is built on lying and falsification."[7] Stalin closed his speech with the statement that "Trotsky has come forward now with the purpose of dethroning Bolshevism and undermining its foundations. The task of the party is to bury Trotskyism as an ideology."[8]

The speech sent a shock of horror through the party. It seemed impossible that any member, least of all a leading Bolshevik like Trotsky, could have written in such terms of Lenin. But Stalin's evidence was irrefutable. The charge that Trotsky had been all along a vicious enemy of Lenin and Leninism was accepted as proven.

A campaign was mounted "to bury Trotskyism." Newspapers throughout the country published articles and reports of local party meetings, vilifying and condemning him. A persecution fever gripped members, now oblivious of his services to the revolutionary cause. As the days passed, there was a growing amazement that he issued no denials or answers to these attacks. His uncharacteristic silence could only mean admission of guilt. On December 13, 1924, *Pravda* went so far as to publish an editorial note, stating that no communication had been received from Trotsky concerning the charges against him.[9]

The campaign against Trotsky, which had been going on for over a year, now reached its climax. He was shaken by the intensity of the new vilification. He had never expected that his "Lessons of October," which he had written to set the record straight and to warn the party that it was on a wrong course, would loose such a hurricane of protest. Under the strain his health broke down. Doctors recommended a rest-spell in the Caucasus. He refused to leave his quarters in the Kremlin. Sick, solitary, and surrounded by hostility, he awaited the meeting of the Central Committee to be held on January 17–20, 1925. He had written what is known as his letter of resignation in which, as in his speech to the Thirteenth Congress, he expressed his loyalty and submission to the party, but refused to make any confession of error.

At the committee meeting Zinoviev and Kamenev showed eagerness to make the final kill. Supported by others, they demanded the expulsion of Trotsky not only from the committee and the Politburo but from the party itself. This, the final sentence of excommunication, was opposed by Stalin. Reporting later to the Fourteenth Party Congress, he explained that "we, the majority of the Central Committee . . . did not agree with Comrades Zinoviev and Kamenev because we realized that the policy of cutting off heads is fraught with major dangers for the party. . . . It is a method of blood-letting—and they want blood—dangerous and contagious; today you cut off one head, tomorrow a second, and then a third: who would remain in the party?"[10] It was a fateful pronouncement.

The only action taken against Trotsky at this meeting of the Central Committee was to remove him from office as president of the Revolutionary War Council and Kommissar for War. For some months he had held office only nominally. M. V. Frunze, one of his chief antagonists in military matters, had been appointed Deputy Kommissar in the spring of 1924, and had virtually taken control.[11] For the time being Trotsky remained a member of the Central Committee and the Politburo, but he was a member on sufferance. He had forfeited the support and prestige he had commanded in the party. His conduct had demoralized his few supporters. He was alone.

The collective leadership of the troika now quickly broke up. Stalin and Zinoviev were recognized as the chief adversaries. Kamenev had lost his influence as head of the Moscow party organization. Zinoviev was still in a strong position. By the end of 1924, however, he had come to recognize belatedly that Stalin was not merely the unobtrusive provincial who ran the central party apparatus, but a formidable opponent. Now when the conflict between them erupted, Zinoviev found that he was outmatched and that he was struggling not for power, but for survival.

The conflict brought a flare-up of the traditional rivalry between the two cities. The Leningradtsi were in an arrogant mood and resented Moscow's pre-eminence as the center of the party organization and of the government. Conscious of their revolutionary tradition and of the fact that their city had borne the name of Peter the Great and now bore the name of Lenin, they maintained a proud independence.

Zinoviev was in control of Leningrad and, although not personally popular, had the support of the city against Stalin and the

Muscovites. The insubordination of the Leningradtsi caused Stalin considerable trouble, and it was not until the end of the following year (1926) that he brought their city finally under Moscow's control.

The struggle within the troika and the Politburo centered on the nature of NEP, which had troubled Marxists since its introduction in 1921. The difficulty arose from the fact that Marxism, a doctrine devised for an industrial society, was being imposed upon a predominantly peasant society, and the dogma provided no guidance on the problems that arose. The party leaders were not sure how to proceed. If they exploited the peasants for the benefit of the proletariat, which was considered inevitable in building a communist state, the peasants would resist with a massive silent withdrawal of their co-operation or they would rebel. The party's hold on the country was still precarious, and a major peasant rising could mean the collapse of the regime.

The alternative was to allow the peasants to produce and market their grain in a more or less free economy, encouraging them to expand production and to market increased grain surpluses. On this basis, Bukharin, Preobrazhensky, and others argued, it would be possible to promote an industrial revival. The danger was that the peasants, who were restive and constantly demanding further concessions, would seize the opportunities to exercise not only economic but also political influence. It was an obsessive fear among the party leaders that the peasants would challenge the party's monopoly of power. Lenin had feared this possibility and in introducing NEP, which gave the peasants economic freedom, had been careful to deny them political power. Between these two extremes various compromises were possible, but compromise was foreign to the Russian approach to such problems.

The Politburo was divided. Bukharin and the right-wing Bolsheviks argued in favor of maximum concessions to the peasantry. Bukharin went so far in an article in *Pravda* on April 14, 1925, as to declare to the peasants, "Enrich yourselves, develop your farms, do not fear that you will be subjected to restrictions."[12] Later he was obliged to modify this statement and then to retract it completely, but at the time it was intended to encourage grain production and to calm peasant fears for their security under the communist regime.

Stalin leaned towards this policy of appeasement of the peasants. To his practical mind there seemed no alternative at this time, but he had no fondness for the peasant with his conservative bourgeois outlook and his obsession with private ownership. He was uneasy about the encouragement given to the kulak, the prospering peasant who might become a capitalist power in the countryside.

The Fourteenth Party Conference from April 27 to 29, 1925, discussed agricultural policy at length. Stalin did not address the conference, leaving Bukharin and Rykov to present the right-wing policy. There was general agreement on appeasement of the peasantry and little opposition was heard. The conference emphasized that the economic revival of the country depended on "the marketability of agricultural production" and the promotion of industrial productivity. To gain the support of the peasantry, the over-all tax on them was sharply reduced by 25 per cent. The conference also legalized the practice, already widespread, of allowing peasants to hire labor and to lease further land, which benefited the kulaks.

The obstacles to increased marketability were well known. The great estates had been broken up and there were 24 to 25 million small holdings, cultivated by peasant households, living near subsistence level. It was an uneconomic method of cultivating the vast agricultural lands of Russia. The peasants had all known hunger, and now they consumed most of the grain, leaving only small amounts for the market. The acute shortage of manufactured goods gave no incentives for marketing produce. Moreover, they were suspicious of the communist government and greedy for higher prices, and for these reasons, too, many held back their grain.

Zinoviev was silent during the Fourteenth Conference. He was on the defensive and biding his time. Stalin had already, early in February 1925, made moves to undermine his authority in the Comintern. But the Leningrad party organization showed a sturdy independence in resisting attempts by Stalin to insinuate his men into key posts. Zinoviev's supporters began to counter Moscow's pressure by promoting left-wing policies in the *Leningradskaya Pravda* and by other means.

During the summer of 1925 the rivalry came into the open. Zinoviev and Kamenev had supported the right-wing pro-peasant policy so long as they felt secure in their places in the Politburo, but under attack from Stalin they adopted the radical left-wing position. The left-wing view laid great stress on the danger that the kulaks would rapidly grow in economic strength and, by withholding their grain, would soon be able to force the Soviets to submit to their demands. They would then revive capitalism. The correct policy was to introduce large-scale collective farms not by compulsion, but by persuasion and by offering such inducements as the supply of fertilizers, seed, and tractors. Once settled on these collective farms the peasants would readily appreciate their advantages. The left-wing policy also called for greater emphasis on industrial expansion, especially to provide for the mechanization of agriculture and, more broadly, to create a balanced socialist economy.

Zinoviev pressed his attack against the right-wing further by arguing that NEP was not a development of true Leninism, but a "strategic retreat" into capitalism. Stalin at once countered by accusing him and his supporters of pessimism. In alleging that the revolution had taken a backward step, they showed a lack of faith in the capacity of the Soviet people, who had in the glorious October Revolution shown the way to the proletariat of the world. It was an argument which kept the opposition on the defensive.

The Fourteenth Party Congress, which had been much delayed, was finally arranged to open on December 18, 1925. As part of the preparations the Central Committee met from October 3 to 10, and the opposition members—Zinoviev, Kamenev, Sokolnikov, then Kommissar for Finance, and Krupskaya—showed at once that they intended to press their policies. It was a bold and desperate move, for they knew that they would be overwhelmed by Stalin's majority in the Congress. In the Central Committee they charged that they had been obstructed in making criticisms of the official policy. Stalin was prepared to be conciliatory at this stage. Their protest was discussed and resulted in a compromise resolution which emphasized both the threat posed by the kulaks and the need to encourage the peasants. It seemed that a direct confrontation between the supporters of the two policies might be avoided.

Shortly before the Congress was to open, however, the party organizations in Moscow, Leningrad, and other parts of the country held local conferences to discuss policy and particularly to elect their delegates. The Leningrad conference rejected all the candidates whom Moscow sought to have included in their delegation. Stalin was angered by this display of independence. The Moscow conference passed a resolution severely criticizing the Leningradtsi, who responded in the same spirit. *Pravda* and the *Leningradskaya Pravda* engaged in a bitter exchange of abuse. Belatedly Zinoviev tried to make a deal that the Leningradtsi would halt their open opposition to the official policy line, if they had a guarantee that no reprisals would be taken against them after the Congress. The Central Committee rejected his proposal.

The Congress opened quietly. Stalin delivered the main political report and did not mention the opposition. He acknowledged that the kulak was a danger, but warned against exaggerating it. Any policy that antagonized the peasantry would hinder the economic progress which, as all knew, was outstanding and encouraging. But tension soon mounted. Lashevich, the first opposition speaker, could hardly make himself heard above the jeers and catcalls. Zinoviev tried to present a reasoned case, but he made a mistake in attacking Bukharin, especially for the latter's appeal to the peasants to enrich themselves. Bukharin was popular, and the attack brought delegates to his aid. Zinoviev's speech was drowned at times by noisy interruptions. Krupskaya made an appeal for party unity, but her counsels were unheeded. When Lashevich spoke strongly against "cutting off" Zinoviev and Kamenev from the party leadership, Mikoyan replied sharply that it was not a matter of "cutting off," but of Zinoviev and Kamenev submitting "to the iron will of the majority of the Central Committee."[13]

Kamenev dominated the proceedings on the fourth day. In a mood of desperation he delivered one of the most forceful speeches of his career.[14] He expounded the opposition policy. Then, towards the end of his speech, he astounded the Congress by making a personal attack on Stalin. "We are against creating the theory of a leader!" he declared. "We are against making a leader! We are against having the Secretariat combine in practice both politics and organization and place itself above the political organ."

A storm of protest drowned his speech, but Kamenev was not to be silenced. "I must say what I have to say to the end!" he shouted. "Because I have more than once said it to Comrade Stalin personally, because I have more than once said it to a group of party delegates, I repeat it to the Congress. I have reached the conviction that Comrade Stalin cannot perform the function of uniting the Bolshevik general staff!"[15]

Kamenev spoke in a fury of temper, as when he had made his vicious denunciations of Trotsky. But his attack on Stalin miscarried. He was not demanding more democracy, but the continuance of the Politburo of which he was a member. His speech, inspired by jealousy and malice, had the effect of rallying the Congress in support of Stalin, who represented party unity. Tomsky, as official spokesman, attacked the speech angrily. Kamenev had demonstrated, he said, the true nature of the opposition, which was inspired not by policies and principles, but by personal jealousies. At the same time he was at pains to deny that there was an individual leader or that there could be one. It was still too soon after Lenin's death to admit that he could have a successor. Tomsky closed with an appeal to Kamenev and Zinoviev to "apply to yourselves the lesson which you taught Comrade Trotsky" and "bow your heads before the will of the party!"[16]

On the following day Kamenev returned to the attack, but this time plaintively objecting to the fact that Stalin's wishes usually prevailed. "Comrade Stalin is evidently destined," he said, "by nature or by fate to formulate propositions rather more successfully than any other member of the Politburo. Comrade Stalin is, I affirm, the leading member of the Politburo without, however, claiming priority; he takes the most active part in the settlement of questions; his proposals are carried more often than anyone's, and these proposals are carried unanimously."[17] It sounded more like a tribute to Stalin's industry, judgment, and modesty than an attack, as was intended.

The three rapporteurs of the congress—Stalin, Molotov, and Zinoviev—wound up the proceedings. Stalin was restrained. He denied any intention of "cutting off" Zinoviev and Kamenev, but demanded that they respect the cause of party unity. He denied any claims to personal leadership. "It is impossible," he concluded, "to lead the party otherwise than collectively. It is stupid to think about any other way after Lenin; it is stupid to talk about it."[18] His speech was received "with applause turning into an ovation." The final resolution, endorsing the official policy, was carried by 559 votes to 65. It was an overwhelming personal victory for Stalin.

Stalin made no attempt at this time to dispose of Zinoviev, Kamenev, and the other oppositionists. Perhaps he was confident that they would dig their own graves. In the elections to the Central Committee all of the opposition leaders were re-elected. Subsequently the existing members of the Politburo—Stalin, Zinoviev, Bukharin, Rykov, Tomsky, and Trotsky—were reappointed, but Kamenev was reduced to candidate membership. The Politburo was increased from six to nine members, and Molotov, Voroshilov, and Kalinin, all Stalin's men, were the additional members. The Central Committee was increased to 106 and the Central Control Commission to 163 members. No major changes took place in either body, but the additional members strengthened Stalin's control over them.

The real blow which Stalin struck against Zinoviev was to remove him from the Leningrad party organization. A new editor took over *Leningradskaya Pravda* which at once ceased publicizing opposition views and faithfully reflected official policy. Then early in January 1926 Molotov led a strong delegation to Leningrad to report to workers' groups on the Congress. Ignoring local party leaders, members of the delegation appealed directly to the rank and file, addressing in all 63,000 workers and securing more than 60,000 votes in support of the official policy. In a brief intensive campaign Molotov's team brought about a massive swing of Leningrad members away from their leaders, whom they had empowered only a few weeks earlier to oppose the central authority in Moscow. The change was a further demonstration of the power of the appeal for party unity; it reflected also the inadequacy and un-popularity of Zinoviev as leader.

During 1925 Trotsky held himself aloof from party politics. He did not speak at the Fourteenth Party Congress and watched with apparent contempt the efforts of Zinoviev and Kamenev to oppose Stalin. The savaging he had suffered in the previous year had hurt him deeply and he had retreated behind a wall of silence. His one public statement, made in September 1925, was mendacious. In a book entitled *Since Lenin Died*, the American writer Max Eastman, who was a close friend of Trotsky's, published some extracts from Lenin's "Testament" and an account of the struggles within the party since Lenin's death. He had obtained this information from well-informed foreign communists, from party members close to Trotsky, and possibly from Krupskaya or even from Trotsky himself. In an article Trotsky denounced the book and its inside information as false. It was "a slander" to suggest that documents had been concealed from the Central Committee, and "a malicious invention" to allege that Lenin's "Testament" had been violated.[19]

Trotsky later claimed that he had written the article under threat from Stalin. It is more probable that without threats Trotsky lied in the hope of saving his position as a member of the inner party organs. But in publishing this denial he was throwing away his most useful weapon against Stalin. The Lenin cult had developed to the point where every word of the dead leader was law. A skillful use of the "Testament" might have damaged Stalin's position, but now Trotsky was prevented from using it.

The opposition groups remained small minorities within the party. Their leaders were motivated mainly by resentment of Stalin's towering position, by the instinct for survival, and to a limited extent by concern about the official policy, which favored the peasants. The opposition leaders were, moreover, filled with malice and hatred towards each other. Zinoviev and Kamenev had vied in the virulence of their attacks on Trotsky. Trotsky had never disguised his contempt for his opponents and had been brutally outspoken in attacking them.

It was remarkable then that the opposition leaders managed in the spring of 1926 to unite. They acted out of desperation. They knew that they could not defeat Stalin's party apparatus. They knew, too, that the OGPU, successor to the GPU, was active against rank-and-file oppositionists, although as yet police methods were not used against senior members.

To Stalin this coalition of the opposition leaders was a sinister attack on party unity, made at a time when the party's hold on the country was still precarious. He denounced the agreement reached between Zinoviev and Trotsky as "an open, straightforward, and unprincipled deal."[20] It was indeed a sordid exchange in which Trotsky withdrew his criticisms of Zinoviev, who in turn conceded that Trotsky's stand against "bureaucratism" had been justified.

Trotsky was mainly responsible for drafting the opposition platform. He took care to avoid any suggestion of an attack on party unity or of the formation of a new faction. He attributed the failings of the existing party management to antagonism between the bureaucracy and the proletariat. This was the reason for repressive measures and for the decline of party democracy, a concept for which Trotsky, when in power, had shown scant respect. The opposition proposed policies which would accelerate industrial growth, improve the grim conditions of the true industrial proletariat, and counter the threats of the kulaks and middle peasants.

The opposition presented their program in part to the Plenum of the Central Committee on April 6–9, 1926, and in full to the meeting on July 14–23, 1926. They were stirred to action by the collapse of the general strike in Britain, for which they blamed the party leaders' failure to give guidance and leadership to the British workers. Stalin countered by removing opposition supporters from positions of authority.

At the same time Stalin set about discrediting the opposition, alleging with dubious evidence that it was not really left-wing, but a right-wing bourgeois deviation. Then the opposition leaders played into his hands. They organized demonstrations in factories, demanding full party discussion of their proposals. This was a flagrant breach of discipline and an affront to party unity. Appalled by their own temerity and recklessness, the six leaders— Trotsky, Zinoviev, Kamenev, Pyatakov, Sokolnikov, and Evdoki-

mov—confessed their guilt in a public declaration and swore not
to pursue factional activity in future. They also denounced their
own left-wing supporters in the Comintern and the Workers' Opposition group. Apparently their confession was voluntary and an
attempt to salve their consciences. They had sought, they admitted naïvely, only to retain some influence within the party. Their
pusillanimous conduct exposed them and their few supporters to
reprisals.

In October (1926) the Plenum of the Central Committee, sitting jointly with the Central Control Commission, gave a severe
warning to the opposition leaders. Trotsky was dismissed from the
Politburo and Kamenev from his candidate membership, and Zinoviev was removed from the Comintern. The opposition demand
to be allowed to circulate their policy statement to delegates attending the forthcoming Fifteenth Party Conference was rejected.
A further factor, damaging to the opposition, was the defection of
Krupskaya, announced at the conference by Stalin. She had signed
the original declaration of policy of the united opposition, but
had been antagonized by the conduct of Trotsky, Zinoviev, and
the others. In a letter to *Pravda* she expressed her disgust cir-
cumspectly. The opposition "went too far . . . comradely criticism became factionalism . . . the broad mass of the workers and
peasants understood the statements of the opposition as statements against the basic principles of the party and Soviet power."
She closed with a demand for "maximum unity in action."[21]

Krupskaya had become a pathetic figure, and her influence had
declined sharply. A woman of integrity, she was dedicated to
Lenin's memory and to the service of the revolutionary cause. But
she had no understanding of politics, and she was constantly outmaneuvered by Stalin. She had loathed him since their first meeting in 1913. She had found, however, that even with her great
prestige as Lenin's widow, she was powerless. Stalin watched her
closely, knowing that she would harm him whenever opportunity
offered. Indeed, in 1926 she managed to smuggle further extracts
of Lenin's "Testament" to Boris Souvarine, the French communist. He passed them to Max Eastman, who arranged for their
publication in the New York *Times* on October 18, 1926. It was a
vindictive and futile gesture which failed to affect Stalin's posi-

tion. But now, in defecting from the opposition, she demonstrated, as she had done on previous occasions, that the sanctity of the party of Lenin and of its unity mattered to her above all else.[22]

At the Fifteenth Party Conference, Trotsky and Zinoviev finally destroyed themselves politically. Trotsky made a lengthy speech and had to ask repeatedly for more time. He was interrupted constantly by ridicule and laughter. Zinoviev groveled and begged forgiveness for his errors. He, too, was heckled and ridiculed. Both had been arrogant in power and now they were humiliated and defeated. It was left to Bukharin to make the final savage attack on them; the delegates, thirsting for blood, applauded loudly.[23]

The main discussion at the conference was not on the opposition, but on Stalin's new theory of "socialism in one country." It bore the stamp of his mind and outlook, and it marked the beginning of the Stalinist era. The Russian revolutionary drive had been losing momentum since the end of the Civil War and the process had accelerated after Lenin's death. A new policy was needed that would inspire the Russian people to undertake the superhuman task of carrying their country on from the October Revolution towards socialism and communism. That policy was "socialism in one country." Its emotional appeal was overwhelming. It aroused a new fervor in the party, and pride in the revolution spread beyond the party ranks. It was a declaration of independence from the West and of faith in the capacity of their country to forge ahead, creating its own future alone and unsupported. Backward Russia, for so long treated as lagging on the outskirts of Western civilization, would show herself to be advanced and at the center of civilization in the coming millennium.

Stalin's major contribution to Russian communist doctrine had its origins in the polemics with Trotsky after the publication of "Lessons of October." Of the heresies alleged against Trotsky, the most important was the basic theory that the success of the Russian Revolution depended on the support of revolutions in the industrial West. As a Russian nationalist Stalin instinctively rebelled against this assumption of dependence. Since the Mongol conquest in the thirteenth century, Russia had forged her own civilization, taking what she wanted from other countries but never depending on them; indeed, the ingrained Muscovite tradition insisted that Russian civilization was superior, and it was Russia's mission to lead the world.

Stalin nevertheless had to contend with the fact that Lenin had always accepted as fundamental the dependence of Russia's Revolution on world revolution or at least revolution in the industrial West. To Trotsky, the internationalist who scorned nationalism in any form, it was unthinkable that Russia could pursue a revolutionary course except as part of the world proletariat. He had simply taken this assumption for granted in "Lessons of October."

Stalin had accepted this theory. As late as April 1924, when giving his lectures on "Foundations of Leninism," he had expressly confirmed that Russia's Revolution would succeed only as part of the international revolution. But he had growing doubts. Revolutions had failed to materialize in the West, and the socialist bid for power in 1923 in Germany, on which Lenin, Trotsky, and others had pinned so much hope, had been a fiasco. It was patently unrealistic to expect revolution in the West in the foreseeable future. Did this mean that the Russian Revolution must inevitably fail or that it must somehow mark time until the rest of the world was ready?

Searching in Lenin's writings for ammunition against Trotsky, he came upon an article, written in 1915, which contained the germ of the idea of the new policy. Lenin had written that, since capitalist countries had not all developed at the same pace, it was possible that revolution would come in some countries earlier than in others, and that it might even break out first in one country. He did not mention Russia specifically, and probably had not had Russia in mind as that one country. Seizing on this tenuous statement, Stalin developed his concept of "socialism in one country," creating the impression that Lenin had envisaged and approved this possibility and, incidentally, that Trotsky had rejected it.

Stalin's idea was first considered by the Politburo in April 1925. Zinoviev and Kamenev had agreed without enthusiasm to its inclusion in the resolution to be submitted to the Fourteenth Party Congress in December 1925. It had aroused no great interest among the delegates, who had endorsed it as a matter of abstract doctrine without immediate practical application. Then in January 1926, after his triumph at the congress, Stalin wrote his article "On Questions of Leninism" in which he answered opposition criticisms and then dealt with the main obstacles to the creation of socialism in one country. The first was the backwardness of the Russian economy, which was a challenge to the faith and ability of the people. The real threat was that the capitalist powers, having entered upon a period of stabilization, might attack Soviet Russia. To counter this danger the Soviet Union must withdraw and in isolation pursue a policy of intensive industrialization. She would then prepare herself to repel any capitalist attack and at the same time surge forward irresistibly towards industrial socialism. This article was reprinted in a volume entitled "Questions of Leninism," which provided a fundamental text of the party in the years ahead.

At the Fifteenth Party Conference "socialism in one country" was discussed and approved in principle. Stalin made full use of its appeal. He taunted the opposition with being men of little faith; they had no confidence in the power of the Russian party and of the Russian people to build socialism in their own country. The policy as he presented it posed a dramatic challenge to the party and the people to embark on heroic action.

Although defeated at every stage, the opposition leaders did not give up. They seized on two events in May 1927 to renew their attacks. The first event was the murder of Chinese communists in Shanghai by Chiang Kai-shek's troops. They charged that the official foreign policy, condoning alliances with noncommunist regimes and in this case the Kuomintang, was contrary to the principles of international communism. The sufferings of brother communists in China demonstrated the failure of the party leaders. Trotsky charged further that this was a natural outcome of the "petty bourgeois theory of socialism in one country."

The criticisms made an impression on the rank-and-file members who were readily aroused by the struggles of foreign comrades. But then a genuine fear of capitalist attack caused alarm. In May 1927 the British police raided the offices of the Soviet Trade Delegation in London and found evidence of subversive communist activities. The British government reacted strongly by breaking off diplomatic relations with the Soviet Union. In Moscow this was interpreted, quite mistakenly, as the first step by Britain to a declaration of war. The opposition protested that a change of leaders was essential, if the country was to defend itself in war, and that the support of the true foreign revolutionaries, who were now being denounced as deviationists, should be enlisted in Russia's coming struggle. Stalin and his supporters answered that this was the time when party unity mattered above all else and that the oppositionists should put aside their differences and rally to the party.

The war scare died away, but the ferment continued in the party. Stalin's patience with the opposition leaders was exhausted. He had always stood against their expulsion, and at the Fourteenth Congress in December 1925 he had explained why he had opposed the demand of Zinoviev and Kamenev for the expulsion of Trotsky. Now his view was different. The party would be at risk so long as the oppositionists were active within its ranks. Lenin would never have tolerated them. He had been determined in 1917 and later to smash the Mensheviks and the SRs, and he had insisted in 1921 on the prohibition of factions within the Bolshevik party. Stalin himself had always shared his view that the party must be completely united. He had hoped that some genuine settlement might be reached. This hope was no longer tenable. The party and the regime were facing immense problems and fighting to survive. The opposition exercised a debilitating influence, which was not permissible at this crucial time.

At the Plenum of the Central Committee at the end of July 1927 he moved a resolution for the expulsion of Trotsky and Zinoviev from the committee. He could be sure of a majority in the committee, whereas in the Politburo the right-wing members —Bukharin, Rykov, Tomsky, and Kalinin—were said to oppose such drastic action. The Central Committee approved the resolution, but then it was rescinded. Ordzhonikidze, who was now chairman of the Central Control Commission, had mediated with the opposition, who once again had made a declaration of unconditional surrender. Stalin then agreed to the withdrawal of the resolution. It was clear, however, that time was running out for the opposition leaders.

In September 1927, as preparations were getting under way for the Fifteenth Party Congress, the opposition drew up the third statement of their aims and policies. Their chief purpose was to change the party leadership, eliminating the right-wing and Stalin in particular, although the statement did not specify names. Members elected by the Congress to the Central Committee "must," it declared, "be independent of the apparatus" and "closely associated with the masses," a formula which would have excluded Stalin and most of his supporters.

The opposition presented their statement to the Central Committee with the demand that it be printed and circulated to all delegates to the Congress. Expecting that their demand would be rejected, as indeed it was, they had set up a secret printing press, intending to print the statement for mass circulation. The OGPU knew in advance about their plans and seized the printing press. All who were directly involved were arrested and at once expelled from the party, but the leaders remained free for the time being. Desperate and frustrated in their efforts to publicize their views, they addressed meetings of workers. The Central Committee, meeting jointly with the Central Control Commission on October 21–23, 1927, again severely reprimanded them, but they remained members and at liberty.

On November 7, 1927, the tenth anniversary of the Revolution, Trotsky and Zinoviev promoted demonstrations in Moscow and Leningrad. The demonstrations were thinly attended and ineffectual, but they were a grave breach of party rules. Again the OGPU was ready. The police and organized bands of thugs broke up the demonstrations and many were arrested. A week later Trotsky and Zinoviev were expelled from the party. The Congress endorsed their expulsion and expelled in addition a further seventy-five oppositionists of the Trotsky-Zinoviev group, as well as fifteen Democratic Centralists. The Congress demonstrated with enthusiasm in support of the party leaders. Certain groups of oppositionists signed declarations of obedience to the decisions of the Congress and petitioned to be readmitted to membership. Trotsky himself signed several of these petitions but to no avail. Zinoviev and Kamenev petitioned to be readmitted and abjectly recanted, confessing that their opposition views had been antiparty and anti-Leninist. Their conduct was pitiful. They were told that their pleas would be considered in due course and they were left to wait. Months later they were readmitted to the party and even given minor appointments, but their political careers were at an end.

In January 1928 Trotsky and some thirty other oppositionists departed from Moscow by train to distant parts of the country. Trotsky was sent to Alma-Ata in Central Asia; for him it was the beginning of a long exile.

20

The Leader Emerges 1926–29

At some time shortly before the Fifteenth Party Congress, Stalin reached a momentous decision. It did not happen with dramatic suddenness, but came to him gradually, flowing with a terrible inevitability from the country's predicament. It was a decision demanding courage and determination and the fanatic conviction that the survival of Soviet Russia depended upon it. It was a decision to plunge the country into an era of headlong industrialization and collectivization.

Stalin had made up his mind that there was no alternative. Industry was backward and small in scale, and agriculture primitive and unreliable in output. Communist rule was threatened by the capitalist powers, who would strike as soon as they were ready, sweeping away the party, destroying the gains of the Revolution, and enslaving the nation. He had read widely and knew Russia's history. This had been her fate whenever she was weak and lacking firm leadership. But to Stalin the country had never been so enfeebled and vulnerable as in the 1920s, when the party was undermined by opposition factions and when the leadership was at the mercy of the great amorphous mass of over 100 million peasants stubbornly opposed to change and antagonistic to the communist regime and its purpose of leading the nation into a new era of strength and socialist prosperity.

There was no time to lose in building industry, collectivizing agriculture, and creating a strong economy. And always in the forefront of Stalin's mind was the imperative need to build Russia's military might so that she could stand proud and secure against the nations of the world. These had been the goals of Peter the Great, whom he admired as a hero and a model. In November 1928, addressing the Central Committee, he declared that "when Peter the Great, competing with the more developed Western countries, feverishly constructed industrial works and factories to provide supplies for the army and to strengthen the country's defence, this was an attempt to liquidate her backwardness."[1] The theme of liquidating Russia's backwardness began to recur in his speeches and articles.

Peter had been autocrat, wielding absolute power and imposing his will on the nation. This was the Russian tradition; it was what the people had always known and expected. Stalin had begun to see himself as heir to this tradition. He cast himself in the role of leader because none of the other party leaders was remotely capable of assuming it, and because he had developed a burning sense of his mission to lead Russia. Shared leadership was weak leadership, as had been amply demonstrated since Lenin's death. He must rule as the great Tsars had ruled, but he was not yet armed with the necessary power.

The policy of concessions to the peasantry to encourage grain production and marketability appeared to have been successful. Two good harvests had given outstanding yields. Adjustment of the agricultural tax and improvements in the efficiency of the state and co-operative purchasing organizations had produced results. The grain collection for the year July 1926–June 1927 amounted to 10.6 million tons, compared with 8.4 million tons in the previous year. Not only had more grain been produced and marketed, but a larger proportion of the grain had been gathered into the public sector. This meant that the export target figure of 275 million rubles was almost reached.

By the end of 1926 a mood of optimism was spreading through the party. Bukharin and Rykov, who had argued insistently for the official policy, were exultant. The left-wing opposition, led by Trotsky and Zinoviev had, they claimed, proved wrong. Rykov, presenting the report on the economy to the Fifteenth Party Conference in October 1926, declared that industry and agriculture were progressing side by side.

The opposition was taken aback by the initial success of the official policy. Zinoviev, Kamenev, Pyatakov, Sokolnikov, Trotsky, and Evdokimov went so far as to sign a declaration on October 16, 1926, which was in effect a confession of defeat and of support for the official policy. But in the conference discussions, Trotsky made the point that "the economic experience since April [the previous conference] has been too small to give us any hope of converting the comrades."[2]

Although gratified by the apparent success of the official policy, Stalin and the more perceptive members of the party were troubled by the agricultural situation. As communists they were obsessed with the kulaks, who were class enemies. Attempts had been made by progressive rates of tax and in other ways to restrict their growing wealth, but with little effect. The fact was that the kulak was not the oppressive monster denounced at party meetings, but the efficient peasant who worked hard, showed initiative, hired labor, and leased additional land, and was an important producer of the grain surpluses so desperately needed to feed the towns and for export. A resolution of the Central Committee in April 1926, however, acknowledged with grave misgiving "the inevitable strengthening of the kulaks in the present period of NEP" and referred to "the struggle of kulak elements to control the countryside."[3]

Another factor clouding the widespread optimism was the amount of grain held back and accumulated by the peasants. It was estimated that by July 1, 1926, some 6 million tons had been hoarded, a figure expected nearly to double by the end of the year. Six months later Rykov admitted that the amount of grain in peasant hands was even higher, which meant that "the tempo of development of the economy is to a significant extent retarded."[4]

Stalin was well aware that the criticisms of the Trotsky-Zinoviev opposition had validity. The official policy of promoting the prosperity of the peasants as the only way to generate capital might well have to be modified by using more forceful methods to extract this capital. It was unacceptable, too, as well as dangerous, that the workers' standard of living lagged far behind that of the prospering peasants.

In the debate leading up to the Fifteenth Party Congress, to be held in December 1927, Bukharin and Rykov continued to display optimism, but there was strong emphasis on "a more decisive offensive against the kulak." The opposition countered in their policy statement with a section, headed "Official optimism is an aid to the enemy," declaring that "capitalism in the countryside is growing absolutely and relatively, and every day sees an increase in the dependence of the Soviet state and its industry on the raw material and export resources of the well-to-do and kulak sector of the countryside."[5]

At the Fifteenth Congress the mounting crisis, threatened by a decline in grain deliveries, intensified the underlying uneasiness. The need for collectivization and industrialization was stressed. In his general report to the Congress, Stalin spoke of "a transition to collective cultivation of the soil on the basis of a new and higher technique." He gave no hint of the tremendous decision already in his mind. He was impatient for action, but the time was not yet ripe. Bukharin, Rykov, and Tomsky in the Politburo and other right-wing supporters would oppose any policy to abandon NEP and to use force against the peasantry.

The crisis, threatening famine in the early months of 1928, was due not to failure in production, but to refusal of the peasants to deliver their grain. Prosperity had brought a new spirit of independence among them and a readiness to defy the party and government. Urgent measures were introduced to avert calamity. Party workers, more than 30,000 in number, were sent to important regions to extract grain from the peasants. The party leaders themselves traveled to regions where the peasants were notably uncooperative. Stalin set out on January 15, 1928, to visit parts of Siberia. There the harvest had produced a record yield, but surpluses had been held back. He admonished and exhorted, and even threatened that grain hoarders would be prosecuted under Article 107 of the criminal code of the R.S.F.S.R., a new article added only in the previous year. Under this pressure peasants rebelled in some districts, and their hostility towards Moscow intensified. The amount of grain collected increased, but some 250,000 tons had to be imported and precious foreign exchange used to pay for it. Early in 1928 it became clear that the peasants, whose surpluses had often been extracted by brutal methods, were sowing less so that they would have no grain surplus.

Stalin had not yet revealed his new policy. Rumors had begun to spread after the defeat of the left opposition that NEP would soon be abolished. But at the joint meeting of the Central Committee and the Central Control Commission on April 6–11, 1928, these "malicious rumors" were firmly denied. Soon afterwards, however, at the meeting of the Central Executive Committee of the All-Union Congress of Soviets, Stalin introduced the draft of a new land law, severely restricting peasant rights. It met with strong opposition and was withdrawn, it was said, to allow for further discussion. The draft nevertheless revealed one part of the policy he had in mind.

At this time Gosplan, the State Planning Commission, was working on a plan for the over-all development of industry, as instructed by the Fifteenth Party Congress. The commission envisaged a gradual industrial growth based on estimates of agricultural expansion. The Gosplan economists were astounded in May 1928, when Kuibyshev as head of the kommissariat responsible for the economy suddenly demanded an expansion of 130 per cent in industry within five years. To the protest that this was impossible came the reply: "Our task is not to study economics, but to change it. We are bound by no laws. There are no fortresses which Bolsheviks cannot storm."[6] At the end of May Stalin proclaimed to the party his new policy of collectivization and rapid industrialization. He presented it as a challenge and the only course open to the nation.[7]

Bukharin, Rykov, and others supporting right-wing policy made no public comment at this time, but they were alarmed. The force used against the peasants in extracting their grain during the past months had horrified them. Stalin's new policy portended the abolition of NEP and the use of compulsion against the peasantry in place of their policy of persuasion. They knew that they could not hope to gain the support of the party against Stalin, but there might be the possibility of defeating him in the Politburo and the Central Committee.

The meeting of the Central Committee from July 4 to 12 (1928) was stormy, but the official account, published in the Soviet press at the time, maintained that a spirit of compromise had reigned. The resolution passed by the committee on the agricultural problem affirmed again that there was no thought of repealing NEP, and rumors to the contrary were dismissed as "counterrevolutionary chatter."[8] The small and middle peasants would continue to be the main grain producers. Severe restrictions on the kulaks and the brutal methods used in extracting grain from the peasantry amounted to "breaches of revolutionary legality" and were denounced.

Stalin's speeches to the Central Committee, which were only published long afterwards, revealed that he had spoken bluntly about the need for the new policy. Industrialization was moving too slowly, and to promote more rapid development it was necessary to exact "tribute" from the peasantry temporarily to generate the necessary capital. It was an "unpleasant business," but there was no other source of capital, and Bolsheviks could not shut their eyes to things merely because they were unpleasant.[9] In the Politburo and now in the Central Committee he had come into headlong conflict with Bukharin and Rykov.

On July 11, 1928, before the close of the Central Committee session, Bukharin called suddenly on Kamenev. He was in a highly excitable state and near to panic. "Do not let anyone know of our meeting!" he exclaimed. "Do not telephone; it is overheard. The GPU is following me and watching you also. . . . We consider Stalin's line fatal to the revolution. This line is leading us to the abyss. Our disagreements with Stalin are far far more serious than those we have with you. . . . He is an unprincipled intriguer who subordinates everything to his appetite for power. At any given moment he will change his theories in order to get rid of someone. . . . He will strangle us!" Several times he referred to Stalin as "the Genghiz Khan of the Secretariat."[10]

Bukharin, who had done so much to destroy Kamenev politically, now approached him secretly, because he was expecting Stalin to seek alliance with Kamenev and Zinoviev, and even with Trotsky in order to defeat the right wing. In his hysterical outburst he revealed how little he understood his adversary. In fact, Stalin was staking everything on enforcing his extreme policy. It was a bold and courageous step. It might easily miscarry, and then his opponents would turn on him savagely. Bukharin was desperate, too, because, outmatched and overruled, he felt the menace of Stalin's opposition and foresaw that, like Trotsky, he was soon to be excommunicated and crushed.

Kamenev was not carried away by Bukharin's pleas for support. He was noncommittal and decided "to wait calmly for signals from the other camp."[11] Like Bukharin, he, Zinoviev, and Trotsky still clung to their pathetic belief that they were indispensable to Stalin and that they would be recalled to play their parts in the central organs of the party. The habit of underestimating Stalin lingered. Bukharin had calculated that with the support of Yagoda, the deputy head of OGPU, of Kalinin, Voroshilov, and Ordzhonikidze, the right wing would be able to vote down the new policy. But they voted with Stalin. Bukharin alleged that he had some kind of hold over them; in fact, he dominated them by force of character and leadership.

At this stage, Stalin avoided any public break with Bukharin, Rykov, and Tomsky and their supporters. Rumors of conflict between the party leaders were still firmly denied. At this time, too, foreign delegates had gathered in Moscow for the Sixth Congress of the Comintern, which met there from July 17 until September 1, 1928. A special statement, addressed to the Comintern and signed by all members of the Politburo, including Bukharin and Rykov, denied that there were any disagreements between the Russian leaders. But the rumors persisted, encouraged by a whispering campaign directed against Bukharin.

Stalin now engineered the final defeat of the right wing through the congress of the Comintern. He himself had suffered severe criticism from Trotsky and others for supporting alliances with noncommunist elements in China and in Britain. He now abandoned this policy and those who supported it. The congress passed resolutions condemning right-wing reformists. Bukharin and other right-wing leaders had misgivings, but tamely supported the new line. The Comintern resolutions served as a prelude to a similar change in direction within the Russian party. On September 18 (1928) *Pravda* stated that the struggle against the right-wing pro-kulak forces was equally vital in Russia.

At the end of September (1928) Bukharin published in *Pravda*, of which he was still nominally the editor, an article entitled "Notes of an Economist," which brought the conflict into the open. The article was a reasoned statement of right-wing policy towards industry and agriculture. Stalin conceded that it presented a justifiable, if abstract, point of view.[12] But Bukharin and his supporters did not realize that Russia could not afford the time for slow and gradual reconstruction; it was a matter of terrible urgency. Moreover, he was convinced that peasant nonco-operation would cripple the all-important industrialization program, and also he would not accept that the party and its policies should be at the mercy of the conservative, anticommunist masses.

While still maintaining the fiction of unity among the leaders, Stalin struck against his opponents. He removed three of Uglanov's chief lieutenants in the Moscow party organization, in which the right-wing challenge was, he declared, particularly strong. But again he asserted that there was no conflict within the Politburo.[13] Bukharin and his colleagues also kept up the pretense of unity in public. But they were more and more desperate. Bukharin made a further approach to Kamenev, apparently without result, and indeed there was little that Kamenev or Zinoviev could do in their isolation. With the support of Tomsky he made an attempt in the Politburo to remove Stalin's chief allies, but this failed completely. Bukharin, Rykov, and Tomsky threatened to resign, and to avoid the crisis that this would have caused, Stalin agreed to several compromise resolutions in the Central Committee. In a speech published in *Pravda* and other papers, he again denied rumors of conflict in the Politburo.

Inexorably he pressed ahead with his plans. To the meeting of the Central Committee on November 16–24 (1928) he enunciated the principles of his policy. Socialism would be achieved in Russia, he stated, only by "catching up with and overtaking" the capitalist nations in economic and industrial development. Furthermore military strength that would ensure the security of the nation and of the Soviet regime depended on a strong and developed industry. There was no time to lose, for, as was inculcated by communist dogma, the capitalist powers were watching and waiting for the opportunity to destroy the young socialist nation.

Bukharin and the right-wing group were defenseless and defeated. Stalin displaced their key supporters and prepared to implement his policy. On November 27 (1928) Uglanov and others were sacked from the Moscow party organization. In the following month the Central Executive Committee approved a new law, depriving the peasantry of their remaining individual rights to the land.

At this time, too, Stalin was undermining the authority of Tomsky, who had always maintained strong control over the trade unions. The Eighth Trade Union Congress, meeting at the end of December 1928, duly approved the program for industrialization, which, as revised by Kuibyshev, set impossibly high targets. The congress also endorsed the demand for more democracy and freedom of criticism within the unions and for the removal of "bureaucratic officials" no matter how senior. This was aimed directly at Tomsky, who was renowned for his authoritarian methods. He offered to resign and his offer was rejected, but he was removed the following year. Power over the trade unions passed into the hands of five of Stalin's men, including Kaganovich, whom the congress elected to its presidium.

Bukharin and Rykov knew that the end was near. They and their supporters were under observation by the OGPU. Bukharin's approaches to Kamenev were known and, indeed, left-wing supporters of Trotsky who were in exile abroad had published an account of Bukharin's secret meeting. Among Russian Social Democrats there was no room for charity or forbearance towards defeated enemies, only for vicious hostility. Bukharin had never been a contender for the leadership, like Trotsky and Zinoviev. He was content to accept Stalin's primacy, but was desperately concerned about the extreme policies, especially towards the peasantry, on which Stalin was determined. He was a gentle, emotional intellectual, awed by Stalin's ruthless determination to take action which would involve wide-scale violence and possibly civil war.

In a last attempt to alert the party to the dangers as he saw them, Bukharin delivered a long speech on January 21, 1929, the anniversary of Lenin's death. It was published in *Pravda* and as a pamphlet with the evocative title "Lenin's Political Testament." He quoted Lenin to emphasize that a period of peaceful development was needed and that a "third revolution" must be avoided.

Stalin was losing patience with this debate on policies, when immediate action was needed. In February (1929) Bukharin, Rykov, and Tomsky were summoned before the party Control Commission, charged with making contact with the disgraced left-wing leader, Kamenev. They at once laid a complaint with the Politburo which, according to Stalin's subsequent report, criticized the rule of one man and "bureaucratization." They also urged a slowing down of industrialization and a halt to the setting up of collective and state farms, the restoration of private trade, and an end to the extreme measures against the kulaks. The Politburo, meeting with the Presidium of the Central Control Commission, condemned their views, especially their apparent defense of the kulaks, their conduct in approaching Kamenev and in threatening to resign, and denounced them for forming a faction.

In April 1929 Stalin delivered a lengthy attack on Bukharin at the meeting of the Central Committee. He would not allow the right-wing leaders to appear as the champions of the peasantry or of a gradual and undemanding economic policy. The right wing was, he declared, so eager for union with the peasants that they even embraced the kulaks. They were at one extreme while the Trotskyites in opposing any union with the peasants were at the other, and both extremes were wrong. He took the middle way of union with the poor and middle peasants against the kulaks. A campaign, discrediting Bukharin as a theoretician, began. The Central Committee denounced the right-wing leaders and recommended that Bukharin and Tomsky should be removed from all offices held by them. The judgment of the Central Committee was circulated within the party and not made public at this stage. But the split in the party leadership was soon widely known.

Bukharin, the "favorite of the whole party," as Lenin had called him, had been a friend and member of Stalin's family circle, but this did not protect him. Stalin abhorred weakness, passivity, defeatism. He interpreted the policies of the right oppositionists in these terms, and held them up to cruel ridicule. "Have you ever seen fishermen before the storm on a great river like the Yenisei?" he said to the joint plenum of the Central Committee and the Central Control Commission in April 1929. "I have more than once. It happens that one group of fishermen mobilizes all its forces in the face of the oncoming storm, inspires its people, and boldly heads the boat into the storm, saying 'Hold fast, boys! Tighter on the rudder! Cut through the waves! We'll win!'

"But there is another kind of fishermen who lose heart when they see the storm coming, start to whine, and demoralize their own ranks. 'Oh woe, the storm is breaking! Lie down, boys, on the bottom of the boat, close your eyes! Maybe, somehow, we'll be carried into the shore!' [*General laughter*]

"Need it be demonstrated that the Bukharin group's outlook and behaviour are as similar as two drops of water to the outlook and behaviour of the second group of fishermen, those who retreat in panic in the face of difficulties?"[14]

The meeting roared with laughter which expressed scorn for Bukharin and his weakling associates. It was this meeting that marked the end of Bukharin, Rykov, and Tomsky and the right opposition as a political force. The party was in a heroic mood. It needed positive, forthright leadership, and at this juncture it had no patience with cautious men who showed fear of the dangers.

On April 23-29 (1929) the Sixteenth Party Conference met and unanimously adopted the five-year plan for industrialization and the policy of rapid collectivization. Rykov, anxious to be restored to favor, proposed the adoption of the plan and delivered a stirring speech in support of it. Bukharin and Tomsky did not speak, but evidently voted for the new policies.

Stalin now dealt with his opponents, removing them from their various offices. Bukharin and the other right leaders were guilty of attempting to form a faction with former Trotskyites and of "collaboration with capitalist elements." To ensure that they were all discredited in the eyes of the party and of the people, they were required to make public confessions of their errors in most humiliating terms. On November 26 (1929) Bukharin, Rykov, and Tomsky made their final confession of defeat and publicly acknowledged the wisdom of Stalin's policies.

21

The New Leader
1929-34

On December 21, 1929, the nation celebrated Stalin's fiftieth birthday with unprecedented extravagance. Newspapers vied in their eulogies. Enormous portraits covered the walls of the Kremlin. Statues and busts dominated the squares and public buildings of every town. Party organizations, factories, collectives, and simple groups of people in every part of the country sent him avowals of loyalty. The slogan "Stalin is the Lenin of today" appeared on banners and was chanted at public meetings. Stalin, the Man of Steel, was commemorated in new names of cities and towns, and the highest mountain in the Pamirs was called Mount Stalin. The name and the portrait became part of the daily lives of the people. It was the beginning of the Stalin cult, which developed on a phenomenal scale.

This frenetic adulation was in part the enthusiastic work of the party machine in Moscow and of party officials throughout the country. They were praising and ensuring that the people joined in praising their chief, the General Secretary of the party. They owed their positions to him and they knew how his authority could reach into the most distant corners of the party organization. But servility and self-interest were accompanied by genuine veneration.

The demonstrations of worship were in part a spontaneous popular expression of relief and gratification that at last Russia had a strong leader. The traditions of five and more centuries were revived and gave strength to the cult of Lenin and even more to that of Stalin, who certainly encouraged the cult. Indeed, once it had gathered momentum it is doubtful whether he could have halted it. He was already in some degree a prisoner of his own power and position. But the cult was important in buttressing his authority within the party and among the people. The power of the Tsars had been their unassailable heritage and upheld by the Orthodox Church. He depended on the cult and on the almost mystical veneration of the Communist party as the foundations of his leadership.

While accepting the need for the cult, however, Stalin probably took little active part in promoting it. The Yugoslav communist Milovan Djilas, meeting him in 1945, formed the opinion that "the deification of Stalin . . . was at least as much the work of Stalin's circle and the bureaucracy, who required such a leader, as it was his own doing."[1]

Stalin was, in fact, not a vain, self-obsessed man who had to be surrounded by fawning and flattery. He detested this mass adulation of his person, and throughout his life he went to great lengths to avoid demonstrations in his honor. Indeed, he was to be seen in public only at party congresses and at ceremonial occasions on Red Square, when he was a remote figure standing on Lenin's mausoleum.[2] He had the same lack of personal vanity as Peter the Great and Lenin, but like them he had the same supremely arrogant conviction, transcending mere vanity, that he was the man of destiny, who held the key to the future and knew what was right for the people and for Russia and, as Djilas observed, "that he was carrying out the will of history."[3]

An immeasurable gulf seemed to separate the man of 1929, aged fifty, from the small boy at the theological school in Gori and the pock-marked youth who attended the seminary in Tiflis and was destined for the priesthood. At every stage of his career he had grown in stature, showing the confidence and ability to meet greater challenges. He possessed a natural authority, an inner strength and courage. He was not overwhelmed by the responsibilities that now lay upon him as sole ruler over a nation of 200 million people, and at a time when its survival was threatened. He did not play safe, evading dangers which might lead to destruction; on the contrary, although cautious by nature, he pursued his objectives with an implacable single-mindedness, undeterred by risks. Indeed, he was about to plunge the nation into a new revolution, which, as he saw clearly, might end in catastrophe.

As a person, however, Stalin had not changed greatly. He had power and position, but showed no interest in possessions and luxuries. His tastes were simple and he lived austerely. In summer he wore a plain military tunic of linen and in winter a similar tunic of wool, and an overcoat that was some fifteen years old. He also had a short fur coat with squirrel on the inside and reindeer skin on the outside, which he started wearing soon after the Revolution and continued to wear with an old fur hat until his death. The presents, many of them valuable and even priceless works of craftsmanship, sent to him from all parts of the country and, on the occasion of his seventieth birthday, from all over the world, embarrassed him. He felt that it would be wrong to make any personal use of such gifts. And, as his daughter noted: "He could not imagine why people would want to send him all these things." It was an insight into the paradoxical humility of this extraordinary man.[4]

Stalin labored to maintain direct contact with every branch of the party and of the government. It was a personal supervision that several autocrats, Nicholas I in particular, had tried, and failed dismally to exercise. Stalin was more effective, although he had to depend on a vast, cumbrous bureaucratic machine. It was a mammoth task which meant working exceedingly long hours. Early in his career he had formed the habit of working through the night and sleeping for brief spells during the day, and members of the Politburo and senior officials had to follow suit. For long periods he did not leave the office adjoining his small apartment in the Kremlin. Whenever he could in summer, however, he went to his small country house at Zubalovo, not far from Moscow. This was the home in which he lived with his wife and children, relatives and friends, and there at this time he appeared to be a relaxed family man.

From glimpses given by Stalin's daughter, the house at Zubalovo must then have had the warm and lively atmosphere of a landowner's country house before the Revolution. There were nannies and tutors, a cook and servants, and crowds of relatives and friends, living with a kind of boisterous harmony under the one roof. The mother and father, sister and two brothers of Nadya, Stalin's wife, lived there or were frequent visitors. Ordzhonikidze, Voroshilov, and Molotov and their wives, Kirov, Bukharin, and others were often in the house. There were family dinners, picnics in the woods, and the noise of children. But there were also discords, centered chiefly on Nadya, for while she ran the home, giving it much of the family atmosphere, she was unhappy and unable to adjust to the position that marriage had brought her.

Nadya had been born in Baku and brought up in the Caucasus. Within her family circle she had imbibed the revolutionary spirit. She grew to be a beautiful young woman, Oriental and at times languid in appearance, but she had no time for appearances, and was typical of her generation in her zeal to work for the socialist millennium. No doubt as a girl she had idealized Stalin whom she remembered as a revolutionary on the run, harbored by her parents, and then as the revolutionary just returned from Siberia. Marriage with such a man probably seemed to her the highest form of service to the Revolution, but there was also a true and deep attraction between them.

Nayda's mother expressed opposition to the marriage. She and her husband had known Stalin for some twenty years and had always regarded him as a close friend, almost as a son. But she herself had suffered from being married to a revolutionary. Nadya was young and romantic. She had been spoiled by her sister and two brothers. Her mother probably saw no lasting happiness for her in marriage with a hardened revolutionary like Stalin. There was, moreover, the age gap of twenty-two years between them.

Nadya married Stalin in 1918. They lived at first in the Kremlin in Moscow, and she quickly came to hate the stone-walled fortress. She had been working as a secretary in Stalin's Kommissariat for the Nationalities. After her marriage she joined Lenin's team of secretaries, headed by L. A. Fotyeva. Then she accompanied her husband to Tsaritsyn. Life in the grim, hunger-ridden city, torn by violence over grain deliveries and threatened by White forces, would have been a cruel experience for a young wife.

From the start, her married life must have been hard and lonely. Her husband was engaged at the front during the Civil War and then completely committed to the party in the continuing crises and the struggle for power. No doubt he neglected her for long periods and was frequently brusque and distracted, but he was not wholly neglectful or insensitive to her feelings. Once when she was feeling ill after a public reception, he put her to bed and comforted her. "So you love me a little after all," she said to him.[5] It was one incident, but probably typical of many incidents which in some marriages become overlaid by bitterness. Their son, Vasily, had been born in 1920, and their daughter, Svetlana, in 1926. But the marriage was under constant strain, mainly, it would seem, because of his absorption in his work. On one occasion she took the two children and went to live with her father in Leningrad, but soon she returned to Moscow.

Nadya was rarely with her children and gave them little affection. She was nevertheless a conscientious mother, who took care that they had a full program of lessons with nurses and tutors. She tended to favor Vasily, her son, possibly because his father was strict with him. She was severe towards Svetlana, who was her father's favorite. Stalin was affectionate and playful with his daughter, writing notes, addressed to her as *Khozyaika* (housekeeper/boss), in which he asked for her orders for the day. The notes, which she kept, reveal a tender concern for her health and happiness.[6]

For some reason Stalin had turned against Yakov, his son by his first marriage, who had been brought up by grandparents in the Caucasus. The time came when Alexander Svanidze insisted that his grandson should go to Moscow to study and take advantage of the opportunities available in the capital. But from the day of his arrival Stalin harried his son with criticism. He disapproved of Yakov's first marriage, of his approach to his studies, and of his character. When Yakov tried unsuccessfully to commit suicide in 1928 or 1929, his father remarked callously, "Ha, he couldn't even shoot straight!"[7] Yakov turned to his stepmother, who was only seven years older, for affection and understanding. She espoused his cause and tried to compensate for Stalin's callousness. She, too, was probably bewildered by her husband, who could be gentle, affectionate, sensitive, and charming, and could also be unfeeling and brutal.

While Stalin was probably a difficult and neglectful husband, Nadya herself was an inadequate wife and partner. She appears to have had no understanding of the extent of the burdens her husband was bearing, or of the pressures under which he worked. She hated her role of first lady of the land and apparently made no attempt to support her husband in his position. Whenever possible, she kept her identity secret. She avoided traveling by car when it might make her conspicuous. She occupied her time with lessons in French, music, and other subjects, frantically seeking to give herself the confidence of intellectual equality with those she had to meet on official occasions. She was a sensitive, emotional young woman, married to a granite-hard master of men and leader of the nation.

In the mid-1920s Stalin had devoted long and careful thought to the way ahead, and the policies on which he finally decided were to draw him farther away from his wife and family. He had a sense of purpose and ruthlessness of purpose that they lacked. He had moved cautiously towards the policy of collectivization and industrialization. He did not underestimate, nor was he awed by, these operations; already he thought on a grand scale or, as he would have said, on a Russian scale. He knew, too, what savagery would be unleashed in the forcible collectivization of over 100 million peasants. It meant a return to the cruel destruction and vicious hatreds of the Civil War. But this time it would be greater in scope. As he prepared for this conflict his courage, nerve, and determination were staggering.

It was fundamental to Stalin's outlook that communism would

be achieved in Russia not by education and exhortation, but by force. The party must drive the people into socialism, and only from experiencing the new way of life would they become converted. He accepted that initially his policies would cause widespread suffering. He was declaring war on the great mass of the population, and war involved casualties just as the victory brought rewards. He was contemptuous of Bukharin and others who shrank from the dangers and sacrifices. In each century the Russian people had endured monstrous inhumanities both in war and as a condition of every positive advance in their history. In imposing Moscow's rule on Novgorod, as part of the unification of Muscovy, Tsar Ivan IV had massacred some 60,000 of the city's men, women, and children. Peter the Great, in building his first ships at Voronezh, and later in creating his city in the marshy estuary of the Neva, had expended countless lives. The people took pride now in the unity of their country and in the magnificence of St. Petersburg, and gave no thought to the human cost. History provided innumerable precedents and had formulated an ethic which he, like previous Russian rulers, accepted.

At this time, as he prepared to hurl the nation into this terrifying revolution, Stalin was acutely aware of the dangers. It was a matter not only of his personal survival but of the realization of the policies which he believed that he alone had the vision and resolution to enforce. The popular adulation, already nationwide, gave him no sense of security and even less did it make him feel immune from treachery and betrayal. He was deeply suspicious of this homage, especially among those surrounding him. Throughout his life as a revolutionary, the party leaders, and Lenin himself in his last months, had sought to ignore and dismiss him. The sudden change in attitude of the survivors smacked of hypocrisy. His daughter observed that "he was astonishingly sensitive to hypocrisy and was impossible to lie to."[8] Behind the façade of adulation they were conspiring against him. He did not believe that he was a demiurge, as they declared, although he was convinced that he alone knew the right policies and could lead the nation.

In the midst of the new revolution, the left opposition might try to undermine his leadership, claiming that he had usurped their policies. But he had transformed these policies, and by his timing and leadership had made it possible to apply them. Nevertheless he still had an exaggerated idea of Trotsky's prestige and influence in the party, and in January 1929 he had him expelled from the country. Supporters of the left opposition, several thousand in number, had been arrested and banished to Siberia after the Fifteenth Party Congress in December 1927, and there they remained. He had no fear of Zinoviev and Kamenev. Their nerve had failed them at the time of the great October Revolution. Expelled from the party, they had made abject confessions of error and had been readmitted in June 1928. The campaign against Bukharin and the right opposition had raised their hopes of full rehabilitation, and this would ensure their good conduct. But he mistrusted them.

Bukharin, Rykov, and Tomsky had been routed, but when the pressures of the new revolution were mounting and the weaker members were quailing before the storm, they might divide the party with their appeals for moderation. They would, he suspected, quote Lenin to the effect that "there is nothing more stupid than the idea of compulsion with reference to economic relations with the average peasants."[9] This would, perhaps, rally some support, thus weakening the party at a time of crisis.

Stalin knew, however, that at such a time, when the party was in effect at war with the people, the call for party solidarity would keep members together and that any attempts to form an opposition faction would be damned as treason. But he was on guard and ready to act against former members of the right and left opposition.

This applied with special force to those of the left opposition who, following the change in policy, had accepted his leadership. A number of senior members of this faction applied for readmission to the party. It was usually granted and they received minor posts. The first of these capitulators, as they were called, was Pyatakov, whom Lenin in his "Testament" described as "a man of indubitably outstanding will and outstanding capacities."[10] In July 1929 a group, of whom Radek and Preobrazhensky were most senior, applied for readmission. The return of these men was an acknowledgment of Stalin's primacy as leader, which none of them would have envisaged or admitted as possible a few years earlier. But it also demonstrated the power of the party as the dominant force in their lives; it was the substitute for a lost religion and, to many of them, for national patriotism. The party appealed to them as a community, subsuming egotistical individualism and uniting them in a higher purpose. Expulsion from this community was spiritual and moral death, and those expelled were prepared to make any recantation and suffer any humiliation in order to be allowed to creep back into the womb of the party.

A vivid explanation of the meaning of the party to a dedicated communist was expressed by Pyatakov in 1928. In Paris, where he was then Soviet trade representative, he met Nikolai Volsky, a former Menshevik, who had been close to Lenin at one time. Volsky was a man of intellectual integrity and charity who was angered by the savage intolerance of the Bolsheviks. At their meeting, shortly after *Pravda* had reported his recantation and restoration to party membership, Pyatakov provoked Volsky by charging him with showing a lack of courage in failing to join the Bolsheviks. Angrily, Volsky replied that it was Pyatakov who lacked moral courage, for he had publicly renounced his own convictions in order to crawl back into the party. Pyatakov responded with a lengthy declaration of his faith.

In his last months, Pyatakov said, Lenin had been ill and weary, and his writings, like NEP itself, did not truly reflect his thoughts. "The real Lenin was the man who had had the courage to make a proletarian revolution first and then to set about creating the objective conditions theoretically necessary as a preliminary to such a revolution. What was the October Revolution, what indeed is the Communist Party, but a miracle! No Menshevik could ever understand what it means to be a member of such a party!"

The basic principle of Lenin's party, he continued, was that it recognized no limitations. It acknowledged no restraints, moral, political, or physical. "Such a party is capable of achieving miracles and of doing things which no other collective of men could achieve. . . . A real Communist . . . that is, a man who was raised in the party and has absorbed its spirit deeply enough, becomes himself in a way a miracle man."

From this concept of the unlimited potential of the party, there flowed his acceptance of complete submission. "For such a party a true Bolshevik will readily cast out from his mind ideas in which he had believed for years. A true Bolshevik has submerged his personality in the collectivity, the party, to such an extent that he can make the necessary effort to break away from his own opinions and convictions, and can honestly agree with the party—that is the test of a true Bolshevik.

"There could be no life for him outside the ranks of the party and he would be ready to believe that black was white and white was black, if the party required it. In order to become one with this great party he would fuse himself with it, abandon his own personality, so that there was no particle left inside him which was not at one with the party, did not belong to it."[11]

Pyatakov was carried away by emotion, but he was expressing his deep faith, and there were many others who shared his vision. Another revolutionary, Victor Serge, wrote that "every communist, every participant in the revolution, feels himself to be the humblest servant of an infinite cause. He gives complete obedience to the party. . . . It is the party that does everything. Its orders are not to be discussed."[12] At the Thirteenth Party Congress in 1924 Trotsky, too, had spoken of the party as "the unique historical instrument given to the proletariat and as the collective to which every member owed complete obedience."[13]

It is questionable whether Stalin ever regarded the party with the same religious fervor as Pyatakov and others or with the acceptance of its collective will which Trotsky acclaimed as supreme, but which he could never accept as superior to his own judgment. Stalin had been a dedicated servant of the party since its formation. He had stressed obedience and discipline as essential qualities in its members, but had himself always shown a certain independence of mind. Like Lenin, he was a leader and a politician, who formulated the collective will and guided it on the proper paths to fulfillment.

Lenin had declared in March 1920 that "Soviet social democracy is not at all incompatible with one-man management and dictatorship. The will of a class may sometimes be carried out by a dictator, who can sometimes do more all by himself and who is frequently more necessary."[14] It had been a bold statement to make to party members among whom there were frequent demands for more democracy. But he had always insisted that the party should be a militant disciplined organization, an army under his leadership. Stalin simply developed and strengthened the party and wielded full power over it on the lines clearly laid down but never fully realized by Lenin. And whether or not he was carrying out the collective will of the party, he was convinced that he was carrying out the will of history.

Stalin became *Vozhd*, or leader, not only by force of personality, ability, and ruthless determination but also because he gave positive, challenging leadership. He inspired in people the faith that their hardships and sacrifices were to be endured, because they would bring victory, security, and other rewards. Indeed it was his own faith that anything was justified that would lead to the justice and prosperity of socialism.

In his concept of "socialism in one country" he challenged the party and the people to be masters of their own fate, not dependent on foreign parties, but by heroic endeavor showing the way to the West and the world. It was a direct appeal to national pride and to the sense of messianic vocation so deeply rooted in the Russian character. The response, especially among the young members, was a wave of enthusiasm, labor, and frantic striving to achieve impossible targets. All were concentrated on the task of creating socialism in Russia and forging the way for the whole world.

Within the party the hesitation and disagreement had been not about the basic need for increased industrialization and the organization of large agricultural collectives, but about methods and tempo. Stalin himself had been unsure and for a time he had accepted the right-wing thesis that the peasants would be won over by the clear advantages of socialism. No doubt he was influenced by Lenin's warnings that any politics that antagonized the peasants would destroy the communist regime.

Stalin did not believe, however, that the peasants could ever be won over to socialism. He knew them better than any of the party intellectuals. Since his rapid tour of Siberia to wrest hoarded grain from the peasantry, he had become convinced that they must be forced into collectives. Meanwhile he was not prepared for the party to be dependent on the peasants in its great historic task of building socialism.

Another extremely important factor was his sense of urgency. He demanded immediate action, because he was convinced that the implementation of his policies was crucial to the survival of the party and of the nation. Survival meant catching up and overtaking the industrialized Western powers. Soviet Russia was weak and at their mercy, and would remain so until she had transformed her economy and built up her industrial strength.

In one of his most revealing speeches Stalin explained in challenging terms this urgent need to catch up with and overtake the West. It happened at the first all-union conference of workers in socialist industry in February 1931, when all were feeling the frenzy and pressures of the First Five-year Plan, and were longing for some relief. Stalin would permit no relief.

"The question is sometimes asked," he declared, "whether it is not possible to reduce the tempo slightly, to hold back the movement. No, it is not possible, Comrades! It is not possible to lower the tempo. On the contrary, so far as strength and opportunities allow, it is necessary to increase the tempo. Our obligations to the workers and peasants of the U.S.S.R. demand this of us. Our obligations to the working class of the whole world demand this of us.

"To retard the tempo—this means to drop behind. And those who are backward are beaten. We do not want to be beaten! No, we do not want that! The history of old Russia was, among other things, that she was constantly beaten because of her backwardness. The Mongol Khans beat her! The Turkish Beys beat her! The Swedish feudal lords beat her! The Polish-Lithuanian nobles beat her! The Anglo-French capitalists beat her! The Japanese barons beat her! All beat her—for her backwardness. For military backwardness, cultural backwardness, governmental backwardness, industrial backwardness, agricultural backwardness. They beat her because it was profitable and went unpunished. . . .

"In the past we did not and could not have a fatherland. But now, when we have overthrown capitalism and power belongs to us, to the people—now we have a fatherland, and we will defend its independence. Are you prepared for our socialist fatherland to be beaten and for her to lose her independence? If you do not want that, then you must in the shortest time liquidate her backwardness and develop the present Bolshevik tempo in the construction of its socialist economy. . . . We are fifty to a hundred years behind the advanced countries. We must make up this gap in ten years. Either we do this or they crush us!"[15]

This sense of purpose, together with those personal qualities which by some alchemy give some men mastery over their fellows, made him a dynamic leader. He acted with the conviction that Marxist dogma as interpreted by Lenin himself provided the infallible formula to achieve national strength and social justice. But this method, rooted in the Bolshevik ethic that all means were justified by the ends, transformed him into an inhuman tyrant.

22

The New Revolution 1928-34

The First Five-year Plan was a program of production targets and slogans for Stalin's assault on Russia's backwardness. It came into operation in 1928, but was approved only in April 1929 by the Sixteenth Party Conference. It set ambitious goals for industry and envisaged a massive socialization of agriculture. But the overriding importance of the plan was that it provided a challenge to the Russian nation; it summoned the people to a life of heroic endeavor. At the same time it gave cover for a brutal collectivization of agriculture. It was a bold assault on two fronts.

This First Five-year Plan was in scale and achievement probably the greatest planned economic venture in man's history. Results fell short of targets, but were nevertheless prodigious. This feat was, moreover, accomplished in four and a quarter years, for on December 31, 1932, the plan was declared to have been fulfilled. The wastage and the cost in human suffering and sacrifice were horrifying. But Stalin was convinced that the price must be paid. The party, transported by his demand for supreme effort, accepted the price. And with extraordinary endurance the mass of Russians labored and served.[1]

The programs of collectivization and industrialization were launched simultaneously. The collectivization campaign had made some progress in 1928. The number of *kolkhozi*, or collective farms, had grown in the year ended June 1, 1928, from 14,830 to 33,258 and their membership from 194,200 to 416,700 peasant households.[2] But to Stalin such a rate of increase was completely unacceptable. As the winter of 1928–29 approached, the threat of famine became serious. There were persistent shortfalls in grain deliveries. The peasants were ignoring and possibly actively challenging the Soviet government and its policies. He demanded urgent action.

During 1929 the campaign gathered impetus; it was soon to sweep across the country in a destructive wave, recalling the Mongol invasions in the thirteenth century. On December 27 (1929) Stalin proclaimed that "we have recently passed from a policy of confining the exploiting tendencies of the kulaks to a policy of the liquidation of the kulaks as a class."[3] This amounted to a declaration of total war and even sentence of death on an ill-defined section of the peasantry, some 10 million in number. It is estimated that 5 million were deported to Siberia and the Arctic region, and of them at least a quarter perished on the journey. Thousands were killed in the villages while trying to defend their property.

On January 5, 1930, the Central Committee decreed that the target of collectivizing the vast majority of peasants within the plan period was entirely practicable. Further, it referred to the completion of the collectivizing of all grain-producing regions by autumn 1932. This raised the campaign to a climax of fury. In October 1929, 4.1 per cent of peasant households had been collectivized; by March 1930, the figure was more than 50 per cent; and by July 1, 1934, it was 71.4 per cent of the farm lands and of the peasant households. The figures represented percentages of 100 million human beings. It was a development staggering in scale.

Stalin achieved this revolution in agriculture by ruthless use of force and terror. Local Soviets were directed to confiscate the property of kulaks, making it the nucleus for the commonly owned and indivisible collectives. In practice this applied to the land and livestock of all peasants who did not voluntarily join the collectives. The OGPU, which had been expanded for the purpose, was the chief instrument in enforcing the campaign. But 25,000 "workers with adequate political and organizational experience" were also sent into the countryside to act as shock troops. The Committees of the Poor, which had whipped up savage hatreds and destruction during the Civil War, were revived. They encouraged bitter antagonism between the poor and the better-off peasants, and helped to eliminate all possibility of united action against the government campaign.

The MTS (Machine Tractor Stations) were one of the many means by which peasants were coerced into collectivization. Agronomists, veterinary specialists, and mechanics were attached to each station, which served groups of collectives. In 1929 only one MTS existed. At the Sixteenth Party Congress in June–July 1930, Y. A. Yakovlev reported that two hundred stations were operating, with tractors of Russian manufacture. Tractors were desperately needed, especially after the slaughter of horses, and they were for use only on the kolkhozi. Peasants who resisted collectivization found themselves without the means to plough their land.

Party records from the Smolensk region, captured during World War II and later published, give firsthand evidence of the chaos and violence which convulsed the countryside. The records make clear that the campaign of collectivization developed into an orgy of indiscriminate arrests, rape, and looting. Attempts by party officials to restrain excesses were ignored. The slogan of many "dekulakization brigades" was "Drink! Eat! It's all ours!"[4]

In many regions the peasants fought with blind destructive fury. Murder and arson were widespread. The communists were the enemies. Party files in Smolensk recorded that "as reports of killings and arson multiplied, Party members were warned to stay away from windows when working in Soviet institutions and not to walk in the village streets after dark."[5] Inexorably the campaign continued. Regional party officials were threatened with severe disciplinary action if they failed to ensure collection of grain quotas and the entry of their peasants into the kolkhozi. Slogans, such as "Who does not join the kolkhozi is the enemy of Soviet power," faced peasants with the choice of joining or being transported elsewhere or being killed.

The peasants demonstrated the hatred they felt for the regime and its collectivization policy by slaughtering their animals. To the peasant his horse, his cow, his few sheep and goats were treasured possessions and a source of food in hard times. But faced with confiscation and transfer of their livestock to the kolkhozi, peasants chose to slaughter them. In the first months of 1930 alone 14 million head of cattle were killed. Of the 34 million horses in Soviet Russia in 1929, 18 million were killed. Further, some 67 per cent of sheep and goats were slaughtered between 1929 and 1933.

The rage of violence and destruction threatened to get completely out of control. Party leaders proclaimed the success of the campaign with state grain collections in 1929 higher by 50 per cent than in the previous year. But Stalin was disturbed by the dangers of anarchy. On March 2, 1930, he published in *Pravda* his famous article "Dizziness from Success."[6]

The time had come, he wrote, to restrain the excessive zeal of party officials and to call a halt to the forcible herding of peasants and livestock into kolkhozi. Many officials had lost sight of the Leninist principle that entry into the kolkhozi was and must be voluntary. All officials and members must observe the model character of the collective farm, which was published in the same issue of *Pravda*. The article was followed on March 14 (1930) by detailed instructions from the Central Committee "On distortions of the party line with reference to the collectivization movement," which called for greater care in handling the peasants. Many illegalities were specified; in particular the treatment of thousands of poor and middle peasants as kulaks must be stopped.

Stalin's article had the immediate effect of calming the fury which gripped many regions. At the same time the peasants grasped the significance of the statement that entry into the kolkhozi should be voluntary, and they exercised the right to withdraw. Within two months the proportion of households collectivized in the R.S.F.S.R. fell from 60 to 23.4 per cent. By June 1930 Stalin's agricultural policy faced collapse. It seemed that peasant resistance had halted the collectivization program and had defeated him.

At the Sixteenth Party Congress, held in June–July 1930, however, Stalin himself and the delegates, some 2,100 in number, were united in acclaiming the "victory of the party line." Stalin was well aware of the extent of peasant opposition and of the disasters caused by forced collectivization, but he displayed unshakable confidence in a successful outcome. He attacked the right oppositionists who had made dire predictions of the horrors that would result from the campaign against the kulaks and from enforced collectivization. "And now we are carrying out the policy of liquidating the kulaks as a class, the policy compared with which the previous repression of the kulaks was nothing. And look, we are alive and well!"[7]

In the critical conditions of June 1930, the right-wing leaders might have been expected to offer opposition. They could claim that they had forecast the disasters that would follow from the policies which Trotsky and the left-wing faction had advocated and which Stalin was now enforcing so drastically. But they declared their fervent support for Stalin and the party line. Rykov and Tomsky both made abject confessions before the full Congress that they had been totally wrong, and they pleaded for the party's forgiveness. Bukharin was absent from the Congress, but he was to abase himself on a later occasion.

The need to maintain the unity of the party again proved to be an irresistible force. Many of the delegates with firsthand experience of the disasters in the countryside acted under the same compulsion. The party had to maintain its unity, especially at this time when it was the object of popular hatred. If the party became divided and lost its grip over the country, anarchy would follow, and they would be massacred to a man by the infuriated peasants.

The solidarity of the Congress was undoubtedly inspired in part by the general need to defend the party, the Revolution, and themselves. But Stalin's leadership was the positive uniting factor. He dominated the Congress. He stood before the delegates, calm and completely in control. He was convinced that the party line was the right line. He exuded confidence and strength, which swept away their doubts and fears. Moreover, he presented the party's policies as bold endeavors which could not fail. In the euphoria which he induced, delegates stood to acclaim their leader, who had declared that "there are no fortresses which we Bolsheviks cannot storm or seize!"[8]

At the Congress Stalin made it clear that the peasants must accept collectivization. The campaign was renewed in the autumn of 1930 and with evident effect. This time the tactics used were more controlled, but the peasants found themselves harried by violence and exposed to inexorable pressures. By mid-1931, 52.7 per cent of peasant households had been collectivized; some four years later the figure had risen to 90.5 per cent.

The peasants had been beaten, starved, and plundered, and finally forced into the hated collectives. But they had wrung an important concession. This was the retention of the *usadba*, the private allotment of land, which remained in the possession of each peasant household. Private trade in food products, which had been a feature of NEP, had been forbidden in 1929, but was permitted again in the following year. The private markets, supplied from the peasant's usadba, played a vital role in the supply and distribution of food at a time when food shortages and malnutrition were ever-present threats.

The industrialization campaign had also started with a show of moderation. Stalin was intoxicated, however, by visions of Russia transformed into an industrial nation. He gave the campaign an impetus which turned it into a frantic industrial revolution. By 1927 industry had recovered to prewar levels of production. Reporting to the Fifteenth Party Congress in December 1927, Stalin had proposed that an annual rate of 15 per cent increase in output should be accepted over the next few years. By mid-1929 the fever of industrialization had taken hold on him and he was demanding a 50 per cent annual rate of increase.

The campaign was mounted on military lines, the Politburo acting as supreme headquarters. It maintained close control through the party machine and government administration over every sector of the economy. Incessant propaganda assailed the worker with a grandiose idea of the part he was playing in this heroic plan, and demanded of him ever-increasing productivity. In every factory giant progress boards were prominent, showing the output of groups and even individuals, and any who fell behind the targets were publicly criticized and harassed. Workers' brigades were ranged against each other in "socialist competition."

Party members and young people, especially members of the Komsomol (Communist Youth League), responded with enthusiasm. All were eager to express in action their faith in the party and their mission as builders of the new socialist world. Their dedicated, self-sacrificing labor was an important factor in the achievements of industry during the first plans.

The mass of the workers did not share this enthusiasm. They were weary from long hours of labor and the constant demands for higher production. Shortages of food and the drastic decline in their living standards were aggravated by the swarms of hungry peasants who invaded the cities and towns in search of work. Exhortations, proclaiming them as the vanguard of the proletariat of the world, and ubiquitous slogans, declaring that Soviet Russia was a workers' state and that the workers owned the factories, merely intensified their disenchantment. Older workers in particular resented the change in their position in the factories. The early mood of the Revolution, carrying into the period of NEP, had promoted in all workers a sense of equality and of belonging to their factories. This feeling passed, and under severe pressures they now worked in conditions far harsher than under capitalism. Absenteeism increased, as workers tried to escape factory discipline. This led to more repressive measures. In December 1932 the internal passport system was introduced, providing a means of keeping close check on all citizens in towns and factories and in frontier areas.

The basic plan objective of laying the foundations for a new, vastly expanded heavy industry was nevertheless achieved in these years. Industrial output mounted. But the great emphasis was not only on increasing production. Major decisions of industrial policy were also made. A new pattern of geographic distribution of heavy industry was initiated. The objectives were to ensure a more even allocation of industry throughout the country, to establish heavy industries near sources of fuel and raw materials, and to reduce the strain on transport. It was recognized, too, that the concentration of industry in European Russia made it vulnerable to attack from the West. Indeed, the creation of major industrial centers east of the Urals was to be one of the most important factors in saving Soviet Russia from crushing defeat in World War II.

This redistribution of industry led to the development of a second coal and steel industry in the Ural-Kuznetsk combine. Magnitogorsk, the center of the new industrial region of the Urals, began in 1931 as a collection of huts, housing the workers who were building the furnaces and rolling mills; eight years later it was a city of 146,000 inhabitants. Kuznetsk in Siberia, known after 1932 as Stalinsk, and Karaganda in Kazakhstan, grew into great industrial cities in the same brief period.

The production of large-scale industry showed a remarkable increase of 113 per cent. This fell short of the target of 133 per cent, set for the final plan year, but it was a real achievement. The main failures were in iron, steel, and coal output. Special production campaigns were mounted to make sure that these targets were realized early in the next plan period.[9]

The campaign, relying initially on the foundations laid by the industrial policies first launched in the 1880s, had soon run into difficulties. The enormous increase in the industrial labor force meant the intake of new workers from the villages who knew nothing of machinery and were strange to factory life. At every stage of production the shortage of trained workers was acute. Engineers and technicians were engaged from the United States, Germany, and France. In March 1931 a director of the Supreme Council of National Economy stated that about 5,000 foreign specialists were employed in Soviet industry. Hundreds of Soviet engineers and students were trained abroad, especially in the United States, and returned to their country to act as instructors and leaders of industry.[10]

Such hurried measures were but small contributions to the problem, which, like the plan itself, was on an immense scale. Numerous technical schools were set up at university and secondary school levels as well as in factories themselves. By 1933 some 200,000 students were studying in higher technical colleges and some 900,000 students were attending secondary technical schools, while factory schools and specialist courses were training a million workers a year. By the end of the plan period, these schools and courses were easing the shortage of engineers and skilled workers, and the second plan, which was launched without delay, benefited.

Soviet imports of machinery were limited by lack of capital, difficulty in raising foreign loans, and discrimination against Soviet exports. The fact that the plan coincided with the great world economic depression added to Soviet difficulties.

In this time of dramatic growth, attention was not limited to industry and agriculture. The transport system was antiquated, and a massive expansion was launched. Railway construction was hampered by shortages of iron and steel and only got under way during the second plan period. But spectacular attempts were made to improve the waterways, and work started on the building of a system of arterial highways.

The nation was caught up in a ferment of reconstruction and expansion, affecting every branch of life. The educational system was reformed. Special emphasis was given to discipline in schools and to inculcating respect for authority. The revolutionary tradition of defiance of the government and its officials was no longer acceptable. Stalin's new Russia demanded an obedient and disciplined people, and the young generation, which had known the anarchy of the postrevolutionary years, must be trained.

A campaign was mounted to eradicate illiteracy, which had been reduced by 1929 to 48.9 per cent of the population between the ages of eight and fifty years. Local committees were set up in January 1930 to conduct the campaign, and by 1939 the percentage of illiterates had been reduced to 18.8 per cent. Numerous social reforms were also introduced. Appalling mistakes and wastage were commonplace in all of these undertakings, but the building of a new nation had started and continued on an epic scale.

Stalin was in command through the Politburo, and he closely supervised every new development. His responsibilities were immense, but he could see real progress, justifying the efforts of the people and vindicating his policies. The nation was at the start of a mighty resurgence. But threats to its continuance troubled him. With his unresting suspicion, he was sure that within the party some were plotting to sabotage this great advance. He saw them as an evil negative force which must be destroyed. His chief fear was still that Trotsky would somehow rise like a phoenix from the ruins of his political career to reverse all that he was doing. Throughout the 1930s he maintained an intensive propaganda campaign, damning Trotsky as the most hateful and dangerous enemy of the party and the Soviet regime.

Three small groups are known to have conspired after the Sixteenth Congress to bring about changes in policy. The first group comprised a number of fairly young members, close to Stalin, who kept up a pretense of loyalty to him. T. I. Syrtsov, the leader of the group, was a candidate member of the Politburo and Prime Minister of the R.S.F.S.R. His idea was to bridge the gulf between the left and right oppositions with a group to be known by the incongrous title of the "right-wing leftist bloc." The OGPU was quick to unmask Syrtsov and his associates. All were removed from their offices, but nothing further happened to them at the time.

In the winter and spring of 1932–33, a terrible famine gripped the country, causing thousands of deaths.[11] Late in the summer of 1932, when the famine was beginning to spread through the Ukraine and the North Caucasus, and the people were in a mood of savage desperation, another opposition group was uncovered. It was led by M. Ryutin, a former secretary of the Moscow Party Committee and a supporter of Bukharin. He drew up a two-hundred-page document, known as the "Ryutin platform," in which he denounced Stalin as "the great agent-provocateur, the destroyer of the party" and as "the gravedigger of the revolution and of Russia." He pledged himself to fight for Stalin's overthrow. His policy was to slow down the pace of industrialization, to end collectivization and return to individual farming, and to restore party democracy. He sent copies of his platform to many prominent party members and to former oppositionists, including Zinoviev and Kamenev. Again the OGPU struck promptly, arresting Ryutin and his small faction, as well as many who received copies of the platform.

Stalin had hardly taken Syrtsov seriously, but he was infuriated by Ryutin's platform. The denunciation of himself was intolerable, and his proposals were the negation of all that Stalin believed in and was convinced would save Soviet Russia. But Ryutin's ideas were dangerous. In appealing for the slackening of the pace of industrialization and the abandoning of collectivization he might rally the many members who could not stomach the violence in the countryside and the sacrifices which were inevitable at this stage of the nation's development.

In the Politburo, Stalin demanded the execution of Ryutin. It was an exceptional demand: For the first time he was calling for the death penalty to be passed on a party member. Opposition within the party had been treated as mistaken, even dangerous. Opposition members had been persecuted, expelled, imprisoned, and exiled, but never formally condemned to death. It was acceptable to execute nonparty members, and thousands had, in fact, been killed. There were no inhibitions whatsoever about the death penalty except when applied within the party. Lenin had warned about such drastic action against members, for this meant following in the steps of the French Revolution, which had devoured its own children, the Jacobins. Now Stalin demanded that in these critical times any form of opposition must be treated as a treasonable act, punishable by death. And to him the Ryutin platform was treason.

Stalin suffered a shock when the Politburo rejected his demand. Of its ten members Molotov and Kaganovich would have supported him. Voroshilov and Kalinin probably wavered, but would also have voted with him. Kirov, Ordzhonikidze, Kossior, Rudzutak, and Kuibyshev probably voted against him. This division among his closest colleagues demonstrated that, notwithstanding his supreme position, the acclamation of the Sixteenth Congress and the nationwide adulation, he had opponents even within the Politburo, and he considered them to be as dangerous as Ryutin.

A few months after the Ryutin affair, the OGPU uncovered another opposition group. It was led by A. P. Smirnov, who had been elected to the Central Committee in 1912. His group included a number of old Bolsheviks and trade-unionists, who had roughly the same program as Ryutin. All were found guilty, but probably on grounds of their ineffectiveness and old age, they were treated leniently. It was Ryutin whom Stalin could not forget.

A wave of persecution had begun during the First Five-year

Plan; it was intensified after the discovery of these opposition groups. The first of the show trials had been staged in 1930. A number of economists and engineers were arrested in August. All had held high office in Gosplan or in the trade, finance, or agriculture kommissariats, and had presumably expressed doubts at some time about the feasibility of the plan. They were tried in three groups, and two of the trials were staged under the full glare of publicity. The charges were that they had plotted in the interest of capitalist enemies and that they were "wreckers" and "saboteurs." The purpose of these trials was apparently to arouse the patriotism of the people and to alert them to the dangers of enemies in their midst, who were responsible for the decline in their living standards and the failures in the industrial program. The trials were also a warning to the intelligentsia and especially to engineers, technicians, and administrators that they must serve without question. The propaganda media hammered home these lessons and warnings. The accused who had confessed were found guilty and sentenced to terms of imprisonment.

At this time, too, the party membership was thoroughly purged. Members who came under any kind of suspicion were interrogated, usually found guilty, and sentenced in secret. Between mid-1930 and the end of 1933 the party control commission sentenced 611 members and candidates for counterrevolutionary activity. In the period from 1931 to mid-1933 regional organizations, embracing 62 per cent of the party, examined nearly 40,000 allegations of political deviation, and 15,442 members were expelled.

In his campaign to eliminate all real and potential opposition, three men whom he advanced in the early 1930s played a central role. A. N. Poskrebyshev became head of his personal secretariat in 1931. A Western observer described him as "sinister-looking . . . about five feet tall, tubby, with broad shoulders, a bent back, and large head, long crooked nose and eyes like those of a bird of prey."[12] His duties are not known precisely, but he was apparently omnicompetent and he certainly maintained close liaison with the security forces. He served Stalin faithfully behind the scenes throughout his career. The second man was A. I. Vyshinsky, a former Menshevik and professor of law, who became deputy state procurator in 1933 and chief procurator in 1935, and

who was to play a prominent part in the political trials of
1936–38.

Another of the new key men was N. I. Ezhov. He emerged in
1933 as a member of the purge commission. Stalin's suspicions extended to the OGPU itself. Its first chief, Dzerzhinsky, had instilled in the security service his own fanatic devotion to the party.
But Stalin was probably unsure whether the officers and agents of
the OGPU would be sufficiently amenable to his will. Ezhov, as a
member of the purge commission and later of the Orgburo, had
full access to the secret files on all members, including the personnel of OGPU. This information and his experience fitted him
well for the role of Stalin's trusted agent and later as head of the
security forces in place of Yagoda.

The Seventeenth Party Congress, meeting from January 26
until February 10, 1934, was called by Kirov "The Congress of
Victors" and it aptly reflected the mood. The delegates were both
relieved and exultant. The party had survived triumphantly
through famine and through savage peasant opposition. The terrible famine of the winter of 1932–33 had been followed by a record harvest in 1933. Collectivization had been achieved to the extent of more than 90 per cent of peasant households, and the
peasants seemed to have given up the struggle and resigned themselves to life on the kolkhozi. The industrialization campaign had
achieved outstanding results and had laid the foundations of
heavy industry on which the second plan could build. The sacrifices in human lives and suffering were apparently behind them.
They were looking hopefully to the future.

The Congress was above all else a triumph for Stalin. He had
led the party through the dangers and horrors of these tumultuous
years. He had shown the strength, the unshakable confidence, and
the determination of a great leader. The nation was in the midst
of an upsurge of creative activity which he had inspired and was
directing. Delegates vied in praising and worshiping him. He was
"the father of the nation" and "the outstanding genius of the
age."[13] Bukharin saluted him as "the field-marshal of the proletarian forces, the best of the best." Kamenev declared: "This era
in which we live . . . will be known in history as the era of Stalin,
just as the preceding era had entered history as the time of

Lenin."[14] There seemed no limit to the extravagance of the praise showered upon him. Finally Kirov declared to the delegates that "it would be useless to think what kind of resolution to adopt on the report of Comrade Stalin. It will be more correct and more useful for the work at hand to accept as party law all the proposals and considerations of Comrade Stalin's speech."[15] With unanimous acclaim Stalin's speech was adopted as "party law."

With mordant mistrust, however, Stalin disbelieved the acclamation that now invariably greeted him. He envisaged among the crowd of delegates innumerable pockets of opposition, each awaiting the opportunity to overturn his policies and to displace him. He took the efforts of Syrtsov, Smirnov, and above all of Ryutin as proof that his suspicions were justified. He reacted by purging the party. He must remove all whom he could not trust and at the same time tighten his personal control over the security organs. The terror had its roots in his phobia about the eradication of opposition and the need for absolute obedience to the party and to himself as its leader.

Rumors, reported some thirty years later, that there was a conspiracy to remove him from the office of General Secretary to some other post have been published, but are unsupported by evidence.[16] It is possible, however, that Stalin himself considered at this time vacating the office of General Secretary. He was nearing fifty-five years of age and had borne heavy responsibilities without a break for seventeen years. It would have been reasonable for him to lay aside the administrative burdens, assuming some new position as executive head of the party and the government. If he was considering this possibility, it would explain why the Central Committee, newly elected by the congress, did not make the usual formal declaration that it had confirmed Stalin in office as General Secretary. Moreover, the fact that he was listed at this time as "Secretary" rather than "General Secretary" of the Central Committee suggests that he was downgrading the office so that his successor would not be seen to occupy the same high position.

Much has been made of these points. It has been alleged, too, that he was almost defeated in the new committee.[17] Nothing was further from the truth. His grip on the party and on its Central Committee had never been stronger. One indication was that the members of the Politburo and the Secretariat were no longer listed in alphabetical order, but in order of seniority, and his name headed the list. Such matters of protocol were of great significance in the Soviet world. Also, the newly elected committee contained several men, like L. Z. Mekhlis, N. I. Ezhov, and G. G. Yagoda, who were then trusted Stalinists, while others of whom he disapproved were dropped.[18]

If, in fact, Stalin was considering laying down the office of General Secretary, he would probably have chosen Kirov as his successor. Kaganovich had been ruthless in enforcing collectivization and was not popular. He was, moreover, a Jew, and anti-Semitism was never far below the surface among members. Molotov had served earlier in the Secretariat and had not been a success. Kirov was a Russian with typical broad face and stub nose, a good speaker, and generally popular. He had first met Stalin in May 1918 and possibly accompanied him in July to Tsaritsyn. Subsequently he was sent, probably at Stalin's instigation, to restore party rule in Astrakhan. There in the following year he came into direct conflict with Trotsky, who had ordered the evacuation of Astrakhan before it was captured by Denikin's White forces. Kirov opposed the order and appealed to Lenin, who reversed Trotsky's decision and directed that Astrakhan should be defended to the end.[19]

This successful defiance of Trotsky brought Kirov into association with Stalin, Ordzhonikidze, and Voroshilov, and he supported them strongly in the dispute with Trotsky over the timing of the invasion of Georgia. Again he worked closely with Stalin as a member of the commission of congress which drafted the resolution on the nationalities question. In 1926 he was posted to Leningrad, where he won praise for his work in purging the local party organs of left-wing elements. He had, in fact, shown himself at every stage to be a wholly dependable Stalinist.

It has been stated that after the Seventeenth Congress, which had elected him to the Central Committee, Kirov received a proposal from Stalin that he should move to Moscow. He declined this advancement and asked to be left in Leningrad. He may have preferred to be independently in charge rather than be in Moscow under Stalin's watchful eye, and the object of the jealousy of

Kaganovich, Molotov, Voroshilov, and others to whom he might be senior in status. Evidently he was allowed to stay in Leningrad until the end of the Second Five-year Plan. After a brief vacation in Sochi with Stalin and his daughter, and then a spell in Kazakhstan, dealing with famine conditions and difficulties over collectivization, he traveled back to Moscow and thence to Leningrad.[20]

Following the Seventeenth Congress there was a feeling in Moscow and elsewhere that the worst was over, and Stalin himself may have sensed the possibility of easing the pressure. Bread rationing was abolished in November 1933. Another encouraging sign was that the OGPU, feared throughout the country, was renamed the People's Kommissariat of Internal Affairs, known as the NKVD, which seemed, at least at the time, less threatening. The powers of the political police were also restricted. Opposition members were allowed to write for the press, but not to criticize party policy. Another reason for the apparent relaxing of repression was that the Soviet government was trying to present a more liberal face to the West. Trade, access to Western expertise, and loans were desperately needed, especially from Britain, France, and America, where public opinion had been antagonized by reports of repression and violence. Other minor concessions to Russian and to world opinion may have been contemplated. But then a decree imposing on every family collective responsibility for the treason of any one of its members warned that the party was maintaining its repressive vigilance.

Two events, affecting Stalin personally, reversed any slight trend that may have existed. On the night of November 8–9, 1932, Stalin and his wife and party dignitaries attended a banquet to celebrate the fifteenth anniversary of the October Revolution. In the course of the evening Stalin said to his wife in front of others, "Hey, you! Have a drink!" She was evidently in a nervous state. She was not allowed to touch alcohol and, in fact, had an obsession about the evils of drink. She constantly warned her children against it and strongly opposed her husband's practice, in Caucasian fashion, of offering them wine at dinner. The invitation to drink, or the disrespectful way he spoke to her in public, angered her. She jumped to her feet. "Don't you dare speak to me like that!" she screamed and ran from the room.[21]

Polina Molotov went out to calm her. They walked around the Kremlin Palace in the cold winter air. Nadya had been depressed and overwrought for some days. She had complained that everything bored her, that she was "sick of everything—even the children." She was then a student at the textile branch of the Industrial Academy and she was looking forward to starting work, but her depression was deep-rooted. Talking with her friend, Polina, she gradually quietened down, and she seemed calm when she went off alone to her own apartment. During the night she shot herself, using a small revolver which her brother, Pavel, had brought from Berlin.

Stalin was stunned. He could not understand why she had taken her life. He worried about suggestions that he had been a hard and inconsiderate husband, asserting that he had always loved and respected her as his wife. He asked those around him whether it had really been important that he could not always go to the theater with her. The fact that she could have made this complaint indicates how far she was from understanding and supporting him in his work.

He was hurt and angered, too, by the note she left for him. It was destroyed at once, but his daughter learned from those who read it that the note was full of reproaches and accusations not only on personal but on political grounds. This was a harrowing time when famine and violence were at their height in the countryside. She had probably heard many grim stories from fellow students at the academy. She was horrified and blamed him.

For him this last note from the woman he had considered his "closest and faithful friend" was a devastating betrayal. He was beside himself with grief and anger. "At the civil leave-taking ceremony he went up to the coffin for a moment. Suddenly he pushed it away from him, turned on his heel and left. He didn't even go to the funeral."[22] And believing that she had left him as a personal enemy, he refused to visit her grave in the Novo-Devichy cemetery. He moved to a different apartment in the Kremlin, because he could not bear to live in the rooms he had shared with her. The dacha at Zubalovo was haunted by memories and, while his children continued to go there, he had a new house built at nearby Kuntsevo, where he lived alone for the next twenty years. But he never forgot her, and in later years he had enlargements of pictures of her taken in a happy mood, in the spring and summer of 1929, hung on the walls of his Kremlin apartment and of his country house. He would talk obsessively about her, seeking to understand why she had taken her life.

Svetlana Alliluyeva, his daughter, has written that "my mother's death was a dreadful crushing blow and it destroyed his faith in his friends and people in general."[23] His mistrust of people had deepened since the last months of Lenin's life, but her death began the clouding of his mind and the numbing of his feelings.

After Nadya's death a drastic change came in the running of Zubalovo and Kuntsevo. She had engaged the staff and maintained the household, keeping the security guards in the background. The housekeeper, cook, maids, and other staff had been like members of the family. Then gradually the old staff was replaced by employees of the NKVD. Only Svetlana's old nurse remained. Stalin had been told that she was "untrustworthy" and must go, but his daughter wept bitterly at the prospect of losing her. He could not stand tears and, growing angry, gave orders that the nurse should be left in peace.[24] But the old aunts, uncles, and cousins and friends of Nadya were gradually excluded. They aroused unhappy memories. He even began to suspect them of some complicity in his wife's betrayal and death, and certain of them were arrested and imprisoned for a time.

The sudden death of Kirov in Leningrad on December 1, 1934, was the next great shock. On the night of November 30 Kirov had worked late on a report about the recent meeting of the party's Central Committee, which he was to deliver to senior officials of the Leningrad party. He arrived at party headquarters in the Smolny Institute at about 4:30 P.M. He was on his way to a colleague's office when his assassin, Nikolaev, appeared from around a corner and shot him in the back, killing him instantly. Nikolaev collapsed at the side of his victim and was seized.

Leonid Nikolaev was thirty years old at this time. He had fought in the Civil War and had been admitted to membership of the party at a young age. He was an official of the Kommissariat of Inspection in Leningrad until its abolition in January 1934. He was given some other post, but, claiming vehemently that he had been unfairly demoted, he came into conflict with party officials and was expelled from the party. He was readmitted some two months later on giving an undertaking to observe party discipline. It was clear, however, that he was unbalanced, like many people of his generation who had endured the horrors of the Civil War and the furies of the first plan period. Although a party member he evidently had a burning sense of injustice, and political assassination was a means of expressing his protest.

Stalin was informed immediately of Kirov's death. He decided to conduct the investigation personally and left Moscow by train for Leningrad on the same evening, accompanied by Voroshilov, Molotov, and Kaganovich. The murder of his close colleague had demonstrated with terrible clarity that enemies surrounded him within the party. After the death of his wife he had been obsessed with finding the reasons for her action. Her death had been a personal suicide, but Kirov's death was a political murder. He reacted violently. He could not accept the possibility that it might have been the act of a crazed individual, seeking revenge or making a personal protest. He saw conspiracy, treason, and betrayal in every act of protest.

The assassination of Uritsky and the attempt on Lenin's life by Socialist Revolutionaries in 1918 had been political acts, and part of a conspiracy to overturn Bolshevik power. He was convinced that the murder of Kirov was also rooted in political conspiracy and that investigation would uncover the assassin's links with the oppositionists and especially with Trotsky. The response of the party must be a campaign of terror and a thorough purge of the membership. He would discover the enemies and liquidate them to a man. He knew that, as a surgeon cutting away a malignant growth from a patient would also cut surrounding healthy tissue in case it, too, was infected, innocent people would suffer in the process, but such casualties were inevitable and would not deter him.[25]

23

The Terror
1934-39

The assassination of Kirov opened a dark and terrible chapter in Stalin's reign. Like the collectivization campaign, the terror developed a furious momentum of its own. Every organ of government and every segment of society were drawn into the vortex. Stalin eviscerated the party, purged all government offices, and preyed upon the people. Arrests ran into millions. Few of those who were executed or sentenced to forced labor were guilty of any crime. For some four years the terror raged.

In launching this terror and allowing it to go to such tragic extremes, Stalin was acting not from cruelty or lust for power, but from the conviction that all real or potential opposition, or, as he interpreted it, treason, must be uprooted and destroyed. It was a time of crisis, when war was threatening, and he had to act ruthlessly. He had to ensure that the party was a strongly tempered monolithic organization, capable under his leadership of meeting any challenge and of leading Russia to strength and socialism. He was absolutely single-minded in his concentration on these objectives. At the same time he was increasingly paranoid about his role as the leader, the man of history, destined to lead Russia to these goals.[1]

Another factor in Stalin's decision to unleash the terror may have come from his study of history. He read widely and was familiar with Russia's history, particularly the reigns of Ivan the Terrible and Peter the Great. Tsar Ivan had been notorious for his use of terroristic methods and for the *oprichniki*, who served as his security force. Ivan saw his duties as autocrat in terms expressed by "Ivashka, son of Semeon Peresvetov," who wrote down his political views and proposals in his "Great Petition," which he boldly presented to the Tsar. Peresvetov urged the need for a strong autocratic ruler, for the centralization of power, and for the creation of a permanent army. Two recurrent themes in his petition were the importance of justice and the equality of all the Tsar's subjects. His ideal of justice was harsh, but in keeping with Ivan's outlook and indeed with the customs of the time. "There cannot be a ruler without terror," he wrote. "Like a steed under the rider without a bridle, so is a realm without terror."[2]

The autocrats, Ivan the Terrible and Peter the Great, were the forerunners on whom Stalin directly patterned himself. They were part of the Russian tradition. Lenin had invoked their example when he had unleashed the Red Terror, set up labor camps, and demanded the ruthless suppression of all opposition. Ivan and Peter had both devoted their energies to transforming Russia into a strong and advanced nation and had not hesitated to wield power ruthlessly to this end. What they had done in the feudal era, Stalin would do in the advanced socialist era of the twentieth century. Peter had established light and heavy industry in Russia; he had taken the first steps in creating effective administrative machinery and had promoted educational and social reforms. Stalin was now directing a similar but more far-reaching revolution in Russian life. At the same time he shared Peter's belief that the people must be driven into the new era; left to themselves, they would wallow in the old traditional ways.

With Ivan, the first Russian Tsar, who had struggled to establish the absolute power of the autocrat and to make Russia strong, Stalin felt a special affinity. Ivan had been surrounded by conspirators and traitors, the princely families and boyars. He had used terror to eliminate these enemies. It was his example that encouraged Stalin in the ruthless tactics he used against the opposition.

Obsessed with possible threats to his grand design, Stalin saw enemies all around him. He had reached the stage of believing that all who failed to support him wholeheartedly or were critical of his policies were enemies and as such they were allies of the imperialist camp and potential destroyers of the new Soviet Russia. Trotsky was still the archenemy, and here again the betrayal of Tsar Ivan by Kurbsky provided a precedent; Trotsky was his Kurbsky. Trotsky was representative of the internationalism and cosmopolitanism, which were still characteristic of the old Bolsheviks, despite their acceptance of "socialism in one country." Although held now on the small island of Prinkipo by agreement with the Turkish government, Trotsky remained a threat. He was publishing *Byuleten Oppozitsii* (The Bulletin of the Opposition), which showed that up-to-date information was reaching him through his agents inside Russia. The *Bulletin's* criticisms and proposals were similar to those set out in Ryutin's platform, but the emphasis was on changing the party leadership and carried all the force of Trotsky's bitter personal hatred.

Stalin was deeply suspicious of the old party members, the old Bolsheviks, among whom Trotsky would find supporters. Many were uneasy about his methods during the First Five-year Plan. But they had no alternative policies to advance, and always at party meetings they supported the Stalinist line. They were not a direct threat and had no one around whom they could rally in opposition. Moreover, they were overawed and afraid of Stalin. But they exerted a divisive influence and he watched them with cold suspicion.

The assassination of Kirov decided him on action. He would no longer tolerate these members who, he had convinced himself, were actively or passively against him; he would liquidate them. In their place he would bring young men of the new generation, educated and trained for managerial tasks, and completely loyal to him.

Before leaving in haste from Moscow on December 1, 1934, he

approved a decree which was published on the following day and was to provide the basic authority for the terror.[3] In Leningrad the immediate action taken was that Nikolaev, who had shot Kirov, and thirteen alleged accomplices were tried in secret on the charge of organizing a Leningrad center to plot assassinations. All were found guilty and shot. A hundred or more people, arrested before Kirov's death on charges of counterrevolution, were declared guilty of terrorism and shot. In the first months of 1935 several thousand Leningrad citizens were arrested on suspicion of holding opposition sympathies and were deported to Siberia. Zinoviev, Kamenev, and their principal associates were imprisoned in Verkhne-Uralsk. A few months later they were tried in secret on the charge of plotting to murder Stalin. Two of the accused were shot, and the others, including Zinoviev and Kamenev, were sentenced to terms of imprisonment. This secret trial set an ominous precedent, for it was the first time that political opposition by party members had been tried and judged as a criminal act.[4] But this was only the beginning of the terror and the great purge.

Screening of the party membership had become a routine exercise. In 1933 members and candidate members had numbered more than 3.5 million. In May 1935, a few months after Kirov's murder, the Central Committee directed that all party documents should be verified. By January 1, 1937 the number of members and candidates was below 2 million. In three years more than 1.5 million members and candidates had lost their party standing.

During these months Stalin was moving into positions of authority several men whom he could trust in the savage period ahead. On February 1, 1935, A. I. Mikoyan, already known as a staunch Stalinist, and V. Ya Chubar, who was probably a moderate, were elected to the Politburo in place of Kirov and Kuibyshev, who had died suddenly of a heart attack on January 26, 1935. At the same time A. Zhdanov, also a Stalinist, who had succeeded Kirov in charge of the Leningrad party organization, and Eikhe, a moderate like Chubar, were elected as candidate members. The two moderates were soon to be eliminated.

Ezhov took charge of the Control Commission in place of Kaganovich. He was to give his name to the worst period of the terror. Nadezhda, wife of the poet Osip Mandelstam, recalled Ezhov as "a modest and rather agreeable person." He was small and had a lame leg which did not stop him dancing the gopak, a strenuous Cossack dance, and flirting with girls. She wrote that "it is hard to credit that we sat at the same table, eating, drinking and exchanging small talk with this man who was to be one of the great killers of our time."[5]

Kaganovich had a genius for organization and for getting results, as he had demonstrated in directing the construction of the gigantic hydroelectric project of the Dnieprogres, the symbol of the new modernized Soviet Russia. He had a roving commission as one of Stalin's toughest henchmen. On moving from the Control Commission he took over the reorganization of the Kommissariat of Transport. He had watched Nikita Khrushchev, a burly Ukrainian peasant, at work in the Ukraine and had noted his energy and his readiness to apply brutal methods in resolving problems. In the 1930s Kaganovich was in charge of the modernizing of Moscow, including the building of the Metro, the underground railway, in which Stalin took special interest—for he was determined that Moscow should outshine Leningrad and be a worthy capital of a great industrial nation. Kaganovich brought in Khrushchev to work as one of his deputies. In 1933 Khrushchev became deputy to Kaganovich in charge of the Moscow party organization. This rapid advance showed that he had become a member of the Stalinist elite.

Two other men came into positions of power at this time. Georgy Malenkov became assistant director of the cadres department of the party secretariat and was to work closely with Ezhov. The other was Lavrenty Beria, an NKVD officer who was then serving as first secretary of the party in Transcaucasia. An evil man who managed to insinuate himself into Stalin's confidence, he was one of the principal architects of the terror.

In the background and closer to Stalin than these two men was A. N. Poskrebyshev. If Stalin trusted any man, he trusted Poskrebyshev, who alone, it was said, possessed a rubber stamp of Stalin's signature which he used at his discretion. He was responsible in 1934 for setting up the Special Secret Political Section of State Security as part of Stalin's personal secretariat. It was this Special

Section, to which Ezhov, Shkiryatov, and later Malenkov belonged, that planned the great purge.

On the surface of party life all seemed calm. The severe reprisals expected after Kirov's death had been limited in scale. The threat of terror seemed to have receded. Continued improvement in food supplies, the surging expansion of industry, and the constant pressures for greater, more heroic labors distracted people from their fears of the NKVD.

Only two months after Kirov's murder, the Seventh Congress of Soviets elected a commission to draft a new constitution. Stalin was the chairman. He presented the new constitution to the Eighth Congress, and it was proclaimed in press and radio as "the most democratic in the world." It discarded Lenin's electoral system, favoring the working class, and introduced direct secret voting. This advance was possible, he declared, because the first stage of communism had been achieved. It included guarantees of the rights of all citizens, which made the dread arm of the NKVD seem even more remote. But during these months of drafting a more liberal constitution the great purge was getting under way. Arrests, usually secret and in the dead of night, were more frequent, but all maintained the pretense that life was normal.

At the end of July 1936, party organizations throughout the country received a secret directive with the ominous title "On the terrorist activity of the Trotskyite-Zinovievite counterrevolutionary bloc." It called for special vigilance in seeking out and denouncing enemies of the regime and ordered a new review of party membership.

The terror broke upon the nation in August 1936 with the sensational Trial of the Sixteen. Zinoviev, Kamenev, and fourteen other old Bolsheviks were charged with setting up a secret terrorist center under the direction of Trotsky in exile. The center, it was alleged, had planned the assassination of Kirov and was plotting attempts on the lives of Stalin, and those close to him. Stalin had anticipated the incredulity evoked by such charges against old revolutionaries and had ordered careful preparations. His purpose was not only to disburden himself of the old Bolsheviks, but also to revise the revolutionary tradition so that the new generation of leaders would be equipped in education and outlook to advance Soviet Russia.

Revolutionary assassins of the past had been glorified as heroes. The murderers of Alexander II and of numerous tsarist officials and even those who had failed in their assassination attempts, like Lenin's brother, were members of the revolutionary pantheon. Every young Russian knew their stories and how they had hurled defiance at the courts during their trials, going to their deaths like martyrs.

This tradition was no longer relevant. It might even become dangerous. Stalin considered it essential to re-educate the coming generation, giving them positive heroes in place of the destructive terrorists, who belonged to a different age. While schools instilled in young people the duties of discipline and respect for authority, the state set about creating new heroes, who would inspire them in building a new Russia. Already the press and radio were proclaiming Stakhanov, the coal miner who raised his productivity to unprecedented levels, and the airmen and Arctic explorers, who were pressing forward to new frontiers. The ideals to be inculcated were service and high endeavor.

The Trial of the Sixteen was conducted in a blaze of publicity. It demonstrated that dangerous traitors were everywhere, even among the old Bolsheviks; that they were not heroes but enemies seeking to destroy the new Russia. The trial was effective in serving these ends. It had seemed impossible that Zinoviev and Kamenev, Lenin's old comrades, who had held high office, could be sinister enemies of the new Russia. But in court each of the sixteen accused pleaded guilty to the fantastic charges laid against them. They confessed their guilt abjectly and convincingly. All were sentenced to death and shot.

In the course of the trial the accused had implicated others. The chief prosecutor, Vyshinsky, made it known that he had ordered the investigation of Bukharin, Rykov, and Tomsky. A few days later Tomsky, the old Bolshevik and trade-unionist, committed suicide.[6]

The terror seemed to falter. Tomsky's suicide and an undercurrent of opposition among older party members may have daunted Yagoda and others in charge of the investigations. Stalin was away at this time with Zhdanov at the holiday resort of Sochi on the shore of the Black Sea. He was evidently surprised by an announcement made in Moscow on September 10, 1936, that the investigation of Bukharin and Rykov had been closed, as no evidence had been found against them. On September 25, 1936, he and Zhdanov signed a telegram to Kaganovich, Molotov, and other members of the Politburo, which read: "We consider it absolutely necessary and urgent to appoint Comrade Ezhov Kommissar for Internal Affairs [NKVD]. Yagoda has obviously proved unequal to the task of exposing the Trotskyite-Zinovievite bloc. The OGPU was four years late in this matter."[7]

Ezhov's appointment on the following day as head of the NKVD began a more savage phase in the terror, the Ezhovshchina, which lasted until 1938. The older officers of the security service, some of whom had served in the Cheka under Dzerzhinsky, were replaced. A purge hysteria seized the nation. The belief that spies and traitors were active everywhere spread insidiously. Unbalanced by the relentless propaganda and by exhortations to show vigilance and fearing for their own safety, people denounced neighbors, colleagues, even members of their own families. Lines formed outside NKVD offices, as people waited patiently to file their denunciations. Terror degraded the whole nation.[8]

The second great show trial opened in Moscow on January 23, 1937. The seventeen accused were said to be the leaders of the Anti-Soviet Trotskyite Center. They had conspired with the German and Japanese governments to overthrow the Soviet regime. Their main weapon was sabotage of the economy. Again, showing Stalin's obsessive hatred, Trotsky was condemned as the evil mind behind the conspiracy.

Vyshinsky, who as prosecutor dominated the trial, appeared calm and moderate in his conduct of the case, which had been fabricated in impressive detail. The behavior of the accused eased his task. An eyewitness at the trial wrote: "All defendants seemed eager to heap accusation upon accusation upon themselves—*mea culpa maxima*. They required little cross examination by the prosecutor."[9] All were found guilty. Thirteen were shot and four were sentenced to ten years' imprisonment.

The death of Sergo Ordzhonikidze soon after this trial revealed even more starkly Stalin's ruthlessness and inhumanity. Sergo Ordzhonikidze was one of his oldest colleagues and friends. In 1912 he had spoken to Lenin about Stalin and had been instrumental in arranging his first election to the Central Committee. They had worked together to resolve the Georgian problem. Ordzhonikidze had shown himself on this and other occasions capable of brutal action. At other times, however, he could be a warm and humane companion. He accepted Stalin's leadership, but as an old comrade and also as a member of the Politburo and Kommissar for Heavy Industry he did not hesitate to speak his mind. He was said to be the only one who protested to him about the NKVD's activities and who interceded on behalf of some of those arrested. His influence had declined, however, while that of his rival and enemy, Lavrenty Beria, was mounting.

Nearly all who knew Beria detested and feared him. Ordzhonikidze considered him an unprincipled blackguard and he told Stalin so bluntly. He opposed Beria's plans whenever possible. But Beria was able in some sinister way to plant seeds of doubt and to foster suspicions in Stalin's mind. He was a master intriguer, more cunning than the blustery Sergo. It would seem, however, that independently of Beria's influence, Stalin had decided to dispense with him.

Pressure on Ordzhonikidze had been growing. Charges of "wrecking" and sabotage in industry had been a major theme of the show trials, and the incessant demand in press and radio for vigilance against wreckers directly involved him. His deputy, Pyatakov, had been found guilty of conspiracy and sabotage and shot. Many of the senior officials in his kommissariat had been arrested. He himself was now required to make a report on industrial sabotage and to recommend fresh action to be taken against spies and wreckers to the Central Committee, convened to meet on February 19, 1937, to consider the lessons to be learned from the Trial of the Seventeen.

Ordzhonikidze was in poor health. He had high blood pressure and heart trouble, but he refused to rest or to take a vacation. The terror had penetrated into his personal life. He was anxious about his elder brother, Papulia, who had been arrested by the

NKVD and was being interrogated under torture. His statements were falsified and Stalin was said to have sent him extracts with the comment: "Comrade Sergo, look what they're writing about you!"[10]

On the morning of February 17, 1937, according to Medvedev, Ordzhonikidze had a stormy meeting with Stalin. He protested angrily that the NKVD had searched his Kremlin apartment on Ezhov's orders. Stalin answered calmly that "the NKVD can even search my apartment. There is nothing strange about that."[11] Ordzhonikidze no doubt complained about the terror and the arrest of his friends and officials in his kommissariat. Both men apparently lost their tempers, and the bonds of long friendship were forgotten.

Ordzhonikidze returned to his office and worked there until 2 A.M. next morning, when he returned to his apartment. According to the testimony of his wife, Zinaida Gavrilovna, he later refused to get out of bed. He declined to see friends who called and would not eat, but spent the day writing. About 5:30 P.M. she heard a shot, and running into his room she found him lying dead, the bedclothes stained with blood. She immediately phoned Stalin, but, although his apartment was nearby, he only came later and then accompanied by other members of the Politburo and by Ezhov.[12]

On February 18, 1937, the newspapers carried the report of Ordzhonikidze's death from a sudden heart attack. The official certificate was signed by four prominent doctors, three of whom were soon afterwards arrested and liquidated. With thoroughness the NKVD arrested members of his family, except his wife, and all who had worked with him, including even the watchman at his dacha. Although rumors circulated, the report that he had died of a heart attack was generally accepted until 1956, when Khrushchev declared that it was suicide.

Suicide troubled Stalin. It was a form of betrayal. His wife had betrayed him in this way. Now Sergo Ordzhonikidze had shot himself. His protests against the arrest of Pyatakov and others had shown that he was not able to detect oppositionists and traitors close to him, but perhaps he was protesting not only from a soft-hearted and trusting nature but because he, too, supported these traitors and would have become an active enemy. Interpreting people and events in these perverse terms, Stalin felt that he had been betrayed. Once aroused, such suspicions obsessed him, poisoning his mind against his old colleague and all associated with him. It was in understanding how suspicions made his master cut people from his thoughts, treating them and all close to them as though they were already dead, that Beria was able to wield such a profound and evil influence over him.

The meeting of the Central Committee, postponed after the death of Ordzhonikidze, opened on February 23, 1937. It was an ominous meeting. Stalin spoke at length about the wrecking and spying activities of foreign agents and Trotskyites, which undermined nearly all party and governmental institutions, and damaged industry. They had infiltrated not only the lower ranks but also the most senior offices. He then castigated those present and by implication all members for their "carelessness, indifference, and naïveté," leading to their failure to unmask the "wreckers, spies, and murderers."[13]

Carried away by the party's dramatic achievements since the Revolution, they forgot that, so long as there were capitalist states, there would be saboteurs, and further that the greater the success of the Soviet Union the greater would be the efforts of capitalist class enemies to destroy it. Constant vigilance was needed to eradicate such people "under whatever flag, whether that of Trotsky or that of Bukharin." On this basis no one, not even the most dedicated worker, was beyond suspicion of wrecking. He was injecting suspicion, like a virus, into the bloodstream of the nation.

The fact that he coupled Bukharin's name with that of Trotsky indicated that Bukharin was doomed. Indeed, when Bukharin and Rykov tried to defend themselves, the meeting shouted them down. Like a wolf pack the delegates were now demanding to "arrest, try, and shoot" these old members. But Stalin gave his own ruling: "Let the NKVD handle the case."[14]

The practical action, which Stalin ordered, was the immediate appointment of two assistants to every party official from the lowest up to Union Republic level. The Central Committee itself was directed to arrange courses to train regional party workers in "problems of internal and foreign policy." Students should be enrolled for these courses in sufficient numbers to provide "not for one but for several teams capable of replacing the leaders of the Central Committee of our party."[15] He could scarcely have warned the committee members more bluntly that he was going to dispose of them, appointing new, more trustworthy men in their places. To a man they applauded his prescience. The Central Committee had the power under the party statutes to dismiss him and other members of the Politburo. But his authority over them was extraordinary. He was the embodiment of the party, that mystic union which they served, and his word was law even when it warned of their own destruction.

For the first time the party felt the full impact of terror. Some measure of this impact is seen in the facts that of the 1,966 delegates who attended the Congress of Victors in 1934, 1,108 were arrested and did not survive, while of the 139 members elected to the Central Committee 98 were shot.

Stalin was, however, looking beyond the eradication of latent opposition within the party and the government. Constantly in the forefront of his mind was the threat of war. It was a real and imminent threat. In the past Russia had been attacked when she was weak; now she was not only weak but also had embarked on the road to socialism, which gave the capitalist powers a further reason to seek to destroy her. Soviet Russia was in the vanguard of socialism and would be the first to be attacked.

Germany posed the immediate danger. From the time of the Baltic Knights up to World War I, Germany had been a dreaded enemy. German military strength in World War I had made a lasting impression on Russians of Stalin's generation. Now Germany was rearming. Since the birth of the Third Reich in 1933, expenditure on armaments had mounted from 2,000 million to 16,000 million marks five years later. Hitler made no secret of his determination to establish a German hegemony over Europe. His anti-Comintern Pact with Japan in 1936, joined a few months later by Italy, was directed at Soviet Russia.

Since 1926 when he had established his control over the armed forces, Stalin had worked to expand and modernize them. He was no longer so concerned about the role of the Army and security forces in supporting the party. The overriding priority was to prepare against attack by Germany and other powers. He was urgently building up Russia's heavy industry and military might to this end. Under the Second Five-year Plan the defense industries developed some two and a half times as fast as the rest of industry. Budget allocations for the Army and Navy rose from 1,430 million rubles in 1933 to 23,200 million rubles in 1938, and in 1940 the figure was 56,800 million rubles. Equipment was modernized and special attention given to tanks, artillery, and aircraft. In 1934 Red Army strength was increased from 562,000 to 940,000 and in the following year to 1.3 million. Three years later the Soviet armed forces had a strength of more than 4.2 million men.

By the mid-1930s the Red Army had become a more efficient and better disciplined force than at any time in the past. Tukhachevsky, with his outstanding abilities for organization and his creative approach, made a major contribution. Zhukov in his *Memoirs* paid tribute to his professionalism, his understanding of both tactical and strategic problems, and to his recognition of the importance of scientific and technical developments.[16] Tukhachevsky was supported by a number of men of similar ability. Under their leadership Soviet military thinking was being transformed.

Two committees responsible for defense were headed by Molotov and Voroshilov. Stalin was simply a member of each committee, but it was he who directed this massive build-up of the defense industries and the armed forces. Molotov and Voroshilov referred everything to him. Kuznetsov on his appointment as Kommissar for the Navy wrote that at first "in his ignorance" he took important naval matters to Molotov, as chairman of the Council of People's Kommissars and of the Committee of Defense. Molotov simply referred him to Stalin. He learned, too, that Stalin took a close interest in naval matters and that his approval was needed in everything of importance.[17]

Zhukov and others have stated that no pattern of armament could be adopted or discarded without Stalin's authority. This "certainly cramped the initiative of the Kommissar for Defense," as Zhukov remarked, but he and others were impressed by Stalin's

wide technical knowledge. The Kommissar for Armament, Vannikov, related that early in 1941 Stalin favored the 107-mm gun as
the main armament for tanks, and he surprised Vannikov when
he added that it was a good weapon, "for he knew it from the
Civil War." Vannikov had advocated the 85-mm antiaircraft gun
for the purpose, but Stalin's preference for the 107-mm proved
justified: with some modification it was found to be excellent as
an antitank weapon and remained in service.[18] Harry Hopkins,
Roosevelt's personal representative, wrote of a meeting in which
Stalin asked for a million or more American rifles, adding that he
did not need the ammunition since "if the calibre was the same as
that used by the Red Army, he had plenty."[19]

G. Hilger, a member of the German Embassy, who observed
Stalin and others at several meetings, wrote that Molotov followed Stalin's instructions closely and yielded to him in everything. Stalin himself was simple and unpretentious in manner
when dealing with the German representatives, but curt and icy
in rapping out instructions to the People's Kommissars. Hilger
was impressed by the extent of the authority Stalin wielded. Nothing could be agreed without his express approval. He was struck
also by Stalin's technical knowledge even when discussing such a
matter as the ordnance specification of the turrets for a cruiser
which Germany was building for the Red Navy.[20] Yakovlev, the
Soviet aircraft designer, wrote of Stalin's direct interest in aircraft
development and, indeed, in this as in other fields Stalin made the
final decisions. When in 1940 Yakovlev went to Germany to purchase military aircraft, he had to send his recommendations direct
to Stalin.[21]

At the same time Stalin awed and terrified many of the most
senior officers and officials who had to answer to him. Hilger noted
the submissive attitude of Marshal Shaposhnikov, Chief of the
General Staff, when speaking to him. Hopkins, too, observed the
fear with which subordinates regarded their leader.

Stalin demanded precise replies to his questions, and he was
quick to show displeasure with vague and inadequate information.
Emilyanov, a metallurgist, was present at a meeting to discuss the
advantages of cast over pressed and welded turrets for the T-34
tank. Stalin asked for further information. Emilyanov asked per-

mission to speak. Stalin turned to him and snapped, "What are you, a military man?" Emilyanov summoned up his courage and gave the answer. Stalin asked, "How would the center of gravity be changed by the new turret?" and "What was the difference in load on the front axle?" The reply that it would be "slight" angered him; "slight" was not, he said, an engineering term. Emilyanov knew the precise answer, but his attempt to speak was ignored. Stalin rejected the proposal because it was inadequately prepared, but he ordered a commission to examine it. He appointed Fedorenko, the tank general, and pointed to two other people present, including Emilyanov. He respected the true expert.[22]

Although often immersed in the details of military, naval, and governmental matters, he did not lose sight of over-all policy. In particular he was concerned about the weaknesses which, he thought, were spreading insidiously in the armed forces, as they had spread in party and government. He must eradicate all possible sources of opposition and unreliability. The danger was that in purging the armed forces he would weaken them for a time and that this in turn might encourage Germany and the capitalist powers to make an early attack. But he could not believe that all army and navy commanders would serve with the unshakable loyalty he required. The purge was inevitable and he must strike with all possible speed.

In fact, the Red Army had consistently given the party full support. During the collectivization campaign the Army, although its troops were recruited almost entirely from the peasant class, had never wavered in carrying out its orders from Moscow. In earlier purges the Army had been found to harbor fewer unworthy elements than the party as a whole. Only 4.3 per cent of army personnel had been purged in 1933, compared with 17 per cent of the civilian membership. Moreover, party membership in the Red Army was increasing rapidly. By the end of 1934 all senior commanders and 93 per cent of divisional commanders were party members.

Stalin had always shown special attention and favor to the Red Army, and he was popular with the officers and men. In particular they welcomed the stress he laid on professionalism and patriotism. They were treated as an elite with special privileges, and officers had their own dachas, cars, and servants. He showered honors on senior officers. Towards Tukhachevsky he was said to have harbored resentment and jealousy because of disagreements during the Civil War. He had, however, recognized his ability and instead of sending him to some distant command, he had appointed him to high office, in 1935 making him a Marshal of the Soviet Union. But then, suddenly, he became convinced that Tukhachevsky was a traitor.

Storm clouds had begun to gather over the Red Army early in 1937. In the Trial of the Seventeen, the evidence had implicated several commanders. Tukhachevsky continued as Deputy Kommissar of War, but he was known to be under suspicion and many shunned him. It was ominous, too, that in May (1937) the system of dual command was revived. It provided that the military commander had a political kommissar at his side, sharing the command and endorsing all orders. The Army had always resented this system, which after 1925 had given place to the single command system.

On May 1, 1937, Tukhachevsky stood at Stalin's side on the Lenin Mausoleum, reviewing the parade on the Red Square. He was nearing the peak of his career, for in the event of war with Germany—and he was convinced that it was imminent—he would probably be made deputy to the Commander in Chief. He had been appointed to represent the Soviet government in London at the coronation of King George VI. A few days before he was to depart, however, his appointment was canceled. He was relieved of office as Deputy Kommissar of War on May 20 and sent to command the Volga military district. He arrived there on May 25 and was arrested next day.

Pravda announced on June 11, 1937, that he and seven others with the rank of general were to be tried in secret. The military court, which took only one day to hear the evidence and find them guilty, included four Marshals of the Soviet Union. Voroshilov and Budënny were completely subservient to Stalin's will. Yegorov, too, had come under Stalin's influence during the Civil War. But Blyukher was an officer of independent mind, who had been severely wounded in World War I and had displayed outstanding ability and courage in commanding Red forces in the Far East during the Civil War. It is difficult to understand how such a man could have sat in judgment on a brother officer and signed the order for his execution. Presumably he accepted as proven the charges against Tukhachevsky and, if not, he was blindly following orders of the Politburo or was under Stalin's domination. Both Blyukher and Yegorov were later arrested and shot.

On June 12, 1937, it was announced that all had been found guilty of "espionage and treason to the Fatherland" and executed. Their crime, according to the press, was that they had spied on behalf of Germany and Japan and had conspired to surrender Soviet territory in the Ukraine and the Far East in return for military support to overthrow Stalin and his regime. There was indeed some evidence of a conspiracy. It was probably not enough to deceive Stalin, but it aroused his pathological suspicion, which quickly turned to conviction of their guilt.[23]

The execution of Tukhachevsky and the seven generals signaled the start of the purge of the armed forces. It struck with exceptional ferocity during 1937 and 1938. The higher commands suffered most heavily. According to reliable estimates there were 35,000 victims. They included approximately half of the total officer corps. Three of the 5 Marshals of the Soviet Union, 13 of the 15 army commanders, 57 of the 85 corps commanders, 110 of the 196 divisional commanders, 220 of the 406 brigade commanders, all 11 vice-kommissars of war, 75 of the 80 members of the Supreme Military Council were purged. Of the officers below the rank of colonel 30,000 were purged.[24]

A major purpose of this purge of the armed forces, apart from the eradication of actual and latent opposition, was Stalin's determination to rid himself of military attitudes which he considered outdated and irrelevant. He disliked defensive strategies. He envisaged massive land and sea forces which would have the capacity to attack on a scale that made defensive strategies unnecessary. Thus, the strategy generally accepted in the Soviet Navy was wholly concerned with the defense of Russia's coasts. It emphasized the use of mines, torpedo boats, submarines, and aircraft, deployed to repel invasion by sea. Virtually all proponents of this coastal defense strategy were purged. In their place Stalin promoted young officers and appointed as Kommissar for the Navy the young Admiral Nikolai G. Kuznetsov. The emphasis now was on the creation of a powerful ocean-going Navy. In 1937–38 he launched a massive naval construction program. The Third Five-year Plan (1938–42) gave warship construction special prominence in the over-all rearmament planning. The plan called for the completion of 8 battleships, 8 battle cruisers, 14 cruisers, 12 flotilla leaders, 96 destroyers, 48 escort ships, and 198 submarines. It was a program which recalled Peter the Great's naval ambitions. But war enveloped Russia before this program could get under way.

The purge was carried out by Ezhov and the NKVD, assisted actively by Mekhlis and Shchadenko. Mekhlis, a journalist and editor of *Pravda*, and a party fanatic who was devoted to Stalin, had become head of the Army's Political Administration. Shchadenko, who had been associated with Voroshilov and Budënny during the Civil War, became Assistant Kommissar of War. Both men were hated throughout the Army.

The purge appeared to take place in two stages. The period between them may have been planned to allow for the training officers to take the place of those liquidated. The new generation of officers were the men on whom Stalin was counting. He had deliberately removed nearly all of the veterans of the Civil War. They were the men who might question his commands and weaken in their loyalty to him and his policies.

The Army itself appeared to accept or at least condone the purge. Men like Shaposhnikov, Zhukov, and many others were silent not merely to save their own skins. They were dominated and even awed by Stalin, but they were also brave, highly intelligent, and patriotic professionals. They tacitly accepted that the officers who were sacrificed might have represented a threat of betrayal, or they believed that their combined opposition to Stalin would have consequences far worse for the party and the country.

The new officers had been selected and trained to be single-minded, absolutely obedient, and devoted to him. Like the new men in the party and the government, they belonged to the Soviet elite. But, hastily trained and promoted, the young officers were untried and unsure of themselves. Time was needed for them to gain the confidence of command, and it was in the furnace of World War II that they learned and that the Red Army recovered its morale and pride.

In December 1937 the first elections to the Supreme Soviet took place under the new constitution. Stalin himself was the candidate in the Stalin district of Moscow. On December 11 he addressed his constituents as a reassuring and benign politician, appealing to them not as a godlike figure but as an equal. He said that he had not intended to speak, but the chairman—Nikita Khrushchev—had "brought me here, you might say, by force and ordered me to 'give a good speech.'" He did not speak at length, claiming that Molotov, Ezhov, and others had already said what was necessary. He simply wanted to assure them that "You can depend completely on Comrade Stalin. You can depend on him to fulfil his duty to the people."[25]

It was this declaration that the people wanted. He understood the popular mood and knew that they needed the reassurance of leadership and stability at this time when they were shaken by the news that so many of their leaders were wreckers and traitors. The purge was still raging. It did not strike directly at the great mass of the people, but it filled their lives with uneasiness and fear.

In the elections 96.6 per cent of the electors cast their votes for the party candidates. The press proclaimed this as a massive vote of confidence in Stalin and the Soviet government. The election figures may have been falsified, but there could be no doubt that the nation supported Stalin. Somehow he stood above the purges and betrayals; he was the leader to whom all looked.

Confirmation of overwhelming popular support did not, however, deflect him from completing the purge program. Preparations went ahead for the third and most important of the great show trials, the Trial of the Twenty-one, which took place in March 1938. The chief accused were Bukharin, Rykov, and Krestinsky, all once members of the Politburo, Yagoda, the former head of the NKVD, who had launched the terror, and Rakovsky, who had been chairman of the Ukrainian Sovnarkom and Soviet ambassador in England and France. The charges against them included the crimes of espionage, terrorism, and wrecking, inspired and organized from abroad by Trotsky. Yagoda faced the additional charge of having murdered Menzhinsky, his predecessor in command of the NKVD, and of plotting the murder of Ezhov, his successor. It was alleged, too, that he had been an accessory to the assassination of Kirov and to the murder of Kuibyshev and Gorky. Bukharin also faced the special charge of having conspired with the Socialist Revolutionaries in 1918 to murder Lenin, Stalin, and Sverdlov.

The trial did not proceed entirely to plan. Krestinsky caused a sensation in court by retracting his confession and plea of guilty. Such defiance was unexpected, but he returned later to recant. Under cross-examination Rykov was at first vague and evasive, then firmly took the line that he was guilty in principle on all the charges, but denied knowledge of, and complicity in, any specific crime. Bukharin took the same stand more strongly, and under examination his replies often nonplussed and angered the prosecution. His general plea was: "I plead guilty to being one of the outstanding leaders of this 'bloc of Rights and Trotskyites.' Consequently I plead guilty to what directly follows from this, the sum total of crimes committed by this counter-revolutionary organization irrespective of whether or not I knew of, whether or not I took direct part in, any particular act."[26] Yagoda and others proved unamenable at times under examination. But none of the reservations or partial denials made any real impression. Bukharin, Rykov, Yagoda, and the others had all confessed their guilt. Three of the accused, Pletnev, Rakovsky, and Bessonov, were sentenced to terms of imprisonment. The others were condemned to death and shot.

The execution of Bukharin illustrated the tragedy of the old Bolsheviks. Bukharin was one of the very few among them all who could be described as likable, although he forfeited much sympathy by his vicious and destructive attacks on his former colleagues Trotsky, Zinoviev, and Kamenev. He was a brilliant speaker and a compulsive writer from whom words poured in a fluent stream. He possessed great charm and had many friends. But he was emotional and easily led. Lenin, who had called him "the favorite of the party," also referred to him as "soft wax," a man easily impressed and politically unstable. At the time of the introduction of NEP he had moved from the far left to the far right, becoming the champion of the peasants. In the years from 1924 to 1928 Stalin had allowed him to pursue his policy of persuading the peasants to produce surpluses, and of gearing industrialization to a slow rate of growth. At no time, not even in the summer of 1928 when his policy was reversed, did he speak against Stalin publicly, but privately in near hysterical outbursts he had expressed his fears to Kamenev and to Menshevik friends. In fact, he stood in awe of Stalin and was cowed by his savage power, which was inexorably moving to destroy him.

In February 1936 Bukharin had traveled with his wife to Paris on his last visit abroad. He went as a member of a three-man Soviet delegation with the purpose of buying the archives of the defunct German Social Democratic party. The archives, which included many of Marx's papers, were in the hands of Boris Nicolaevsky, an émigré Menshevik then living in Paris. Bukharin was depressed and emotional. While abroad he spoke of his fear of Stalin with a frankness unusual for a party member. André Malraux wrote that "he confided to me absently: 'And now he is going to kill me.' "[27] But he rejected suggestions that he should remain abroad. Like a man hypnotized, he knew that he had to return to his fate in Russia.

In conversation with Dan and Nicolaevsky on one occasion he spoke heatedly about Stalin. "You say you don't know him well, but we do! He is unhappy at not being able to convince everyone, himself included, that he is greater than everyone; and this unhappiness of his may be his most human trait, perhaps the only human trait in him. But what is not human, but rather something devilish, is that because of this unhappiness he cannot help taking revenge on people, on all people but especially those who are in any way higher or better than he. If someone speaks better than he does, that man is doomed! Stalin will not let him live, because that man is a perpetual reminder that he, Stalin, is not the first and best. If someone writes better, matters are bad for him because he, Stalin, has to be the premier Russian writer. . . . No, no, Fedor, he is a small-minded, malicious man—no, not a man, but a devil!"[28] It was the outpouring of an emotional and frightened man.

For his part, Stalin did not consider Bukharin a serious threat. He was a popular man, but by Stalin's code he was gutless. At the same time he was an intellectual and cosmopolitan, more Western than Russian in outlook. He was impressionable and, as an orator and a writer who became excited under pressure, he might well give influential support to an opposition movement at a time of crisis. For these reasons, rather than personal vindictiveness, Bukharin had to be liquidated.

In all of these show trials the charges were hardly credible. Stalin himself cannot have believed them and probably knew that they had been fabricated. But with his deep-rooted conviction that Trotsky's influence was a pervasive cancer, he suspected that all oppositionists were somehow linked with him. In any case he was not concerned with particular crimes. To him the accused were real or potential oppositionists and traitors. They were guilty in principle, but their trial and execution must be seen to be just. He did not mislead himself that the Russian people and world opinion would share his belief in their guilt. The show trials had to expose them as self-confessed traitors. In fact, the trials were successful in convincing the Russian people, the diplomatic corps, and opinion abroad that the accused were justly condemned. Sir Bernard Pares, the foremost Russian specialist of the day, who had devoted himself to interpreting Russia to the West, considered that the charges of sabotage had been "proved up to the hilt" and that the rest of the evidence was "convincing."[29] Joseph E. Davies, the U.S. ambassador from 1936 to 1938, considered that the guilt of the accused had been proven, adding that this was the general opinion among diplomatic observers.[30]

The chief reason for the plausibility of the trials was that the accused readily and wholeheartedly confessed their guilt. Nothing is more bewildering than these confessions in which dedicated party men declared themselves guilty of crimes against the party, which they did not commit. The NKVD had an armory of physical and mental tortures which they used freely. Families and especially children of the accused were held as hostages and their safety was bargained for a confession. There was no limit to the sadism, deceit, and corruption applied to extract confessions not only from the accused in the show trials but also from the thousands dealt with summarily by the NKVD.

The evil methods employed by the NKVD are not sufficient, however, to explain why men of courage, like Bukharin, Pyatakov, and many others, who had devoted their lives to the revolutionary ideal, should have confessed to crimes against that ideal. There was in this capacity for confession and self-immolation a Russian element, which Stalin understood. They were like the Old Believers in the seventeenth century, who, having rejected Patriarch Nikon's innovations, assembled in their log-built churches and, chanting the old liturgy, set fire to the timber, burning themselves to death. The revolutionaries of the twentieth century were members of a secular religion, embodied in the party. They had surrendered themselves to it completely and now they believed that they had no alternative but to sacrifice themselves to it. In holding and promoting views contrary to the party's policies and threatening factionalism, they had sinned and must confess. Bukharin and others among the accused had been critical of Stalin in private circles, and this, too, was sinful. Trying to explain his attitude to Stalin, Bukharin had said, "It is not him we trust, but the man in whom the party has reposed its confidence."[31] In this surrender of will, conscience, and judgment to the party lay the tragedy of these men who were betrayed by their blind doctrinaire idealism.

The purge reached out from Leningrad and Moscow into the regional organizations of the party and the government. The union republics suffered and none more severely than the Ukraine. Stalin was particularly mistrustful of the Ukrainians. They had allied themselves with the Germans in 1917 and were obdurate nationalists, ready to break from Moscow's rule. His suspicion was aggravated by Hitler's declared intention to annex the Ukraine, and he feared that Ukrainian separatism might lead again to alliance with Germany. It was a major grain-producing region and of crucial importance to the Soviet economy at this time when the industrial labor force was expanding rapidly.

In January 1938 Stalin sent Khrushchev to reorganize the party and the government there and to revive the economy which had been shattered by collectivization. It was a demonstration of his confidence in Khrushchev's loyalty and in his competence as an energetic and ruthless administrator. Two good harvests, relieving immediate anxieties about grain deliveries, appeared to justify Khrushchev's claims that he had solved the Ukrainian problem. In 1938 he was promoted to be a candidate member of the Politburo, and in the following year he became a full member.

The purge continued unabated. People were arrested in thousands and most were sentenced to forced labor. GULAG, the main administration of corrective labor camps, which was a department of the NKVD, was responsible for a vast web of camps, concentrated mainly in the far north and in Siberia. The foundations of GULAG had been laid in July 1918 by Lenin, who had ordered the setting up of the system, and within five years 355 camps had been established, containing more than 68,000 persons. The most reliable estimate of the total numbers of people "living in detention under the NKVD" during the Ezhovshchina places the figures between 7 and 14 million.[32] All were required to work at cutting timber, mining, building roads, and other heavy labor. Conditions were appalling. Food was severely rationed, and those who failed to reach their labor norms received less than the starvation minimum. Deaths from hard labor, malnutrition, and the harsh conditions, especially in winter, were appallingly high. But already the forced labor camps had become accepted officially as the system whereby political and criminal prisoners could be isolated and made to serve the state in developing the remoter regions of the Soviet Union.[33]

Early in 1938, however, Stalin became disturbed by the mounting fury of the Ezhovshchina. His purpose of liquidating the old Bolsheviks and the veterans of the Revolution and the Civil War, and other sources of opposition, had been achieved. But under Ezhov the purge had spread like a malignant plague. Everywhere people were spying and informing against each other and everywhere arrests were on the increase. Terror was raging out of control. Stalin saw the need to call a halt. He showed the same sense of timing and the same authority, which he had displayed nearly eight years earlier with his article "Dizziness from Success."

In January 1938 the Central Committee passed a resolution which heralded what was to be called the "Great Change." The title of the resolution was "Concerning the Mistakes of Party Organizations in Excluding Communists from the Party, Concerning Formal-Bureaucratic Attitudes Towards the Appeals of Excluded Members of the VKP (b), and Concerning Measures to Eliminate These Deficiencies."[34] The new orders were passed quickly to the party secretaries at every level and to the command points of the NKVD, and emanating from the Kremlin in Moscow. They were promptly obeyed. The new enemy was identified now as the Communist-careerist. He had taken advantage of the purge to denounce his superiors and to gain promotion. He was guilty of spreading suspicion and of undermining the party. A purge of careerists was launched. At the same time mass repression diminished and the rehabilitation of victimized party members began.

The real halt to the great purge came, however, in July 1938, when Lavrenty Beria was appointed Ezhov's deputy. He took charge of the NKVD at once, although Ezhov was not removed until December 1938, when he was made Kommissar for Inland Water Transport. Soon afterwards he was shot.

Many NKVD officers were tried and executed for extracting confessions from innocent people, while others were relegated to labor camps. Loyal party members, emerging from the long nightmare, were relieved by the purging of the NKVD. It confirmed their belief that fascists had insinuated themselves into the security forces and the government and that they were responsible for the cruel persecutions and injustices of the Ezhovshchina. This explanation was encouraged officially, and it absolved Stalin and the Politburo of responsibility.[35]

Directly controlling every branch of Soviet policy and deeply involved in the build-up of the armed forces and conduct of foreign policy, Stalin could not maintain detailed control over the purge. He was aware that the NKVD had arrested many who were not guilty and that of the 7 to 14 million people serving sentences of forced labor in the GULAG camps many were innocent of any taint of disloyalty. They were inevitable sacrifices, inseparable from any campaign on this scale. But he resented this waste of human material. The aircraft designer Yakovlev recorded a conversation with him in 1940, in which Stalin exclaimed: "Ezhov was a rat; in 1938 he killed many innocent people. We shot him for that!"[36]

Throughout these terrible years Stalin showed an extraordinary self-control and did not lose sight of his purpose. He knew what he was doing. He was convinced that the majority of the people liquidated were guilty in principle. And he acted with a cold merciless inhumanity. According to Medvedev, Stalin with Molotov signed during the years 1937–39 some 400 lists, containing the names of 44,000 people, authorizing their execution.[37] Stalin could not have known or studied the cases of so many people, and he had to accept the advice of men whom he disliked and distrusted like Ezhov. He would have acted, however, on the principle that such sacrifices were completely justified by the purpose being pursued. Indeed, he went further by insisting that in purging traitors, the NKVD should not leave possible secondary sources of treason. The families and everyone close to Tukhachevsky and others were all arrested and banished to Siberia. Such paranoia and fanaticism were controlled by a ruthlessly practical intellect. Sentiment and conscience played no part. All was subjugated to his purpose of building a powerful, invulnerable socialist Russia.

The few firsthand reports of meetings with Stalin about this time arouse astonishment. It is as though one is presented not with facets of a single personality, but with several different people embodied in the one amazing man. Towards the end of 1936 Joseph E. Davies, a wealthy industrialist and convinced capitalist, was appointed U.S. ambassador to the Soviet Union. While there he traveled widely and conscientiously sought to study the regime and its industrial program. He was honest and observant and won the respect of the Soviet hierarchy. Like other ambassadors he had never met Stalin, but he did see him in June 1938 when he made his formal calls on Kalinin, the President, and Molotov, the Prime Minister, before his departure. He was in Molotov's office when the door at the far end of the room opened and to his surprise he saw Stalin approaching.

In a letter to his daughter, Davies wrote: "He greeted me cordially with a smile and with great simplicity, but also with a real dignity." They had a long and frank conversation and Stalin made it clear that he sought American aid and friendship. Davies was impressed by his "strong mind which is composed and wise. His brown eye is exceedingly kind and gentle. A child would like to sit on his lap and a dog would sidle up to him. It is difficult to associate his personality and this impression of kindness and gentle simplicity with what has occurred here in connexion with these purges and shootings of the Red Generals and so forth."[38]

With his officials, senior and junior, Stalin was brief, exacting, and peremptory. He demanded obedience and dedication, and he respected efficiency and expertise. But he could show warmth and concern, as the memoirs of Zhukov, Yakovlev, and others indicate. Zhukov even wrote of him as "an imposing figure. Free of affectation and mannerism, he won the heart of everyone he talked with."[39] Moments of friendliness, like his simplicity and charm of manner, are usually dismissed as theatrical displays turned on for a purpose.[40] But he was a man, at times human and considerate, and at other times inhuman and implacable. His moments of affection and benevolence were rare occasions of genuine emotion, felt by a man, isolated by his power, by his relentless sense of mission, and by his mistrust of others.

At the end of this dark and terrible period of the purges, Stalin stood in an unassailable position. He was the father and leader of the people. They had not identified him with his repression. In the sixteenth century the Russians had blamed the boyars for the excesses of Ivan the Terrible's reign, and in later centuries they had blamed the Tsar's officials, rarely the Tsar himself. In the same way Stalin had not been blamed. He rarely appeared in public or addressed meetings in the years 1936–38. He cultivated an aloofness which encouraged the general belief that he did not know and was not responsible for the crimes of the NKVD.

Instead Ezhov had been brought into the limelight. He and his senior officers were decorated with the Order of Lenin, and the presentations were widely publicized. A resolution passed by workers of the Stalin Automobile Factory, and typical of resolutions passed in factories, offices, and schools throughout the country, expressed gratitude to the "workers of the NKVD led by their fighting kommissar, N. I. Ezhov, so indefatigable and ruthless in unmasking the people's enemies." The resolution closed with "Long live the famed and vigilant Soviet counter-espionage with its iron kommissar, Ezhov."[41] Ilya Ehrenburg, the leading journalist of the time, wrote after Stalin's death: "We thought (probably because we wanted to think so) that Stalin did not know about the senseless ravaging of Communists, of the Soviet intelligentsia." He also described meeting Boris Pasternak on a snowy night in Lavrushensky Pereulok at the height of the Ezhovshchina. Pasternak raised his hands to the darkened sky and exclaimed, "If only someone would tell Stalin about it!"[42]

Stalin had nevertheless achieved his purpose. He had liquidated the old generation of revolutionaries and intelligentsia, retaining only those whom he considered absolutely loyal and necessary. He was now advancing the new Soviet elite, who were young, tough, and devoted to him. An English economist who spent a year from mid-1936 studying in the Economic Research Institute of Gosplan in Moscow, and lived in the students' hostel of the All-Union Planning Academy, wrote that the academy was a kind of party school for training members of unimpeachable loyalty for senior posts:

> Notwithstanding all their variety of personal character, these people were very alike, so far as I knew them, in their rather simple-minded and ruthless practicality. Marxist theory and Soviet policy as expounded by Stalin suited them exactly. I could not and cannot imagine a leader better suited to them. In the opinion of one of them there were about 50,000 party members of their general status and these were the "masters of the country." The purge which throughout this period was mounting to its climax worried them not at all in any way apparent to me either for their own safety or for pity.[43]

With this new generation of selected and trained Stalinist members, Stalin transformed the managerial class in party and state. They were inexperienced and were faced with the malaise, aggravated by the years of terror, which took the form of unwillingness and fear of taking initiative and responsibility. In the armed forces, the untried young officers, and the damage done to morale, were to bring the country close to disaster. But Stalin could claim that Soviet Russia had become stronger as a result of his grandiose campaigns of industrialization, collectivization, education, and social transformation, and that the nation was better prepared to meet the grave challenge already looming.

24

Preludes to War
1939-41

The 1930s were years of mounting pressures on Stalin. Over-all policy as well as major, and often minor, decisions on industrialization, social reforms, the build-up of the armed forces, and foreign policy were referred to the Politburo. Usually they were discussed, but it was Stalin himself who made the decisions. Foreign policy was one of his special concerns. The Soviet Union was menaced in the east and west, and the conduct of foreign relations became more complex and demanding, as he sought to deflect or at least delay the inevitable war. He carried enormous responsibilities, and only a man of exceptional physical stamina, sharp and disciplined intelligence, and iron self-control could have met such demands.

In the early years of the Soviet regime Stalin had taken only slight interest in foreign policy. Lenin, working with Chicherin, the Kommissar for Foreign Affairs, and Litvinov, his deputy, and with Bukharin, Kamenev, and Trotsky, had made it his responsibility. He had assumed a doctrinaire approach. Marxist dogma denied absolutely the possibility of permanent peace between "the camp of socialism" and "the camp of capitalism."[1] The function of Soviet policy was to promote revolution in the enemy camp through the Comintern, the organ of world revolution, and by any other means.

Lenin had found, however, that as a matter of political and economic survival he had to pursue normal relations with other countries. Soviet policy sought to build a system of alliances which would end Russia's isolation from the world community of nations. Progress was slow at first. The capitalist powers were wary of approaches from a government which preached revolution and pursued subversion in their countries. The efforts of Chicherin and Litvinov were rewarded in 1921, however, by peace treaties with Afghanistan, Persia, and Turkey; and then dramatically on April 16, 1922, a treaty of mutual friendship with Germany was signed in Rapallo. Early in 1924 recognition by Britain and most of the countries of western Europe further reduced Russia's isolation.

By 1925 Soviet foreign policy had been reformulated. National interest, entailing considerable continuity with the tsarist past, became the main concern. The new policy was described as a "breathing space" and defined as "a long period of so-called peaceful coexistence between the U.S.S.R. and the capitalist countries."[2]

It was an article of faith for Stalin as a Marxist that socialism would inevitably displace capitalism. For a time he had accepted that the promotion of world revolution through the Comintern was the first objective. Soon after the Revolution he had become skeptical about the prospects of world revolution and contemptuous of the Comintern. International communism was an ideal which Trotsky, Lenin, Bukharin, and others thought realizable in the near future. Stalin was not sanguine and he was concerned with the urgent practical problems of Soviet Russia. She was the home of the Revolution, and if she collapsed or was destroyed by capitalist enemies, world revolution would recede and become no more than a dream.

Stalin's approach was basically different from the approach of the other old Bolshevik leaders. They were internationalists and cosmopolitans. Moreover, Trotsky, the foremost internationalist, was one of the many Jewish Marxists, who had no special feeling for Russia. By contrast Stalin was intensely Russian in outlook. He had adopted Russia as his homeland. His daughter wrote: "My father loved Russia deeply all his life. I know of no other Georgian who had so completely sloughed off his qualities as a Georgian and loved everything Russian the way he did. Even in Siberia my father felt a real love of Russia."[3] With the fervor of a convert he became a Russian nationalist and as chauvinistic as any of the Romanov emperors. Russia was, he believed, the nation chosen to forge communism and lead the world. He himself remained dedicated to Marxism with world revolution and socialism as the ultimate goals, but they lay in the future. Russia was his immediate, all-consuming concern.

During the late 1920s the Treaty of Rapallo was a cornerstone of Soviet policy. Stalin's nagging fear was that Germany might be reconciled with the West and drawn into alliances against Soviet Russia. His anxiety became acute in October 1925, when Germany participated in the Locarno Pact and again in the following year when Germany was admitted to the League of Nations. Communists looked on the League as a sinister capitalist organization. But Gustav Stresemann, the German foreign minister, was seeking good relations with East and West. He calmed Soviet anxieties, first by a new trade agreement, and then by the Treaty of Berlin, forging closer ties with Moscow. By 1932 Russia was taking 30.5 per cent of German machinery exports. Hundreds of German technicians and engineers were working and instructing in Russia, and German officers were training Russian troops.

The launching of the First Five-year Plan brought further changes in emphasis in Soviet policy. Reporting in July 1930 to the Sixteenth Party Congress, Stalin declared that "our policy is a policy of peace and of strengthening trade relations with all countries."[4] Trade had been regarded merely as an instrument of foreign policy in attacking the markets and influence of the capitalist powers. Now trade was recognized as essential in obtaining the machinery, technical assistance, and capital for industrialization. But the pursuit of peace was the first priority.

Fundamental to Stalin's policies, internal and external, was the conviction that war was imminent and might devastate Soviet Russia before she was able to gather strength. It was with this thought that he had demanded immediate collectivization and headlong industrialization. There was no time to lose. The Treaty of Versailles was no more than a truce between two wars. He followed events closely in the West, seeking early signs of the coming conflict.

His hope was that the war would be confined to the capitalist camp and that Russia would be able to stand aside, as the United States had done during World War I, intervening decisively towards the end. But the danger was that Russia might be directly involved. Addressing the Central Committee in January 1925, he had said: "The preconditions of war are ripening. War may become inevitable, of course, not tomorrow or the next day, but in a few years. . . . The problem of our army, of its strength and its readiness, will arise in connexion with complications in the countries surrounding us. . . . This does not mean that in any such situation we are bound in duty to intervene actively against anybody. . . . But if war begins, we shall hardly be able to sit with folded arms. We shall have to come out, but we ought to be the last to come out. And we should come out in order to throw the decisive weight on the scales, the weight that should tilt the scales."[5] As the years passed it became clear that Soviet Russia could not remain a spectator.

In his conduct of foreign policy, Stalin showed great caution, restraint, and realism. He needed time to build up Russia's industries and military strength. He was constantly provoked in the east and the west, and in ways that must have infuriated him, but he never lost sight of the overriding need to delay the outbreak of war as long as possible. It was for this reason that he placed the greatest emphasis on peace and disarmament in world affairs.

At the same time he pursued a policy of collective security. Early in the 1930s Litvinov negotiated nonaggression pacts with Poland and Finland. At the world economic conference held in London in June 1933, he proposed a multilateral treaty of nonaggression which led to the signing of treaties with all of the countries on Russia's southern and western frontiers. This was timely, for, while diplomatic relations had been restored between Russia and China in 1932, a serious threat to Soviet interests and security had come in the Far East in September 1931, when Japan had invaded Manchuria.

Stalin was determined to avoid war at almost any cost. With memories of the humiliation of Russia in the Russo-Japanese War of 1904–5, he must have found it extremely difficult to have to appease the Japanese aggressors. In the negotiations, however, he and his officials acted with "invincible restraint and impenetrable reserve" and, despite Japanese provocations, they "kept their heads and held their hands."[6]

The danger which he feared most, because war would then be unavoidable, was that the Japanese would invade Outer Mongolia, the people's republic which served as a buffer state and was virtually a Soviet protectorate. This did not happen. The sale of the Chinese eastern railway to Japan reduced tension along the frontier, but the danger of war remained. Litvinov tried to negotiate a nonaggression pact, but the Japanese rejected his approaches.

Stalin had to recognize now that the immediate threat lay in the east, not in the west. Indeed, at this time the tension between Japan and Russia was acute and both countries believed war to be inevitable. Soviet troops were hurriedly transferred and plans were put in hand to develop industries to support the Red Army in the Far East. Stalin continued to observe a policy of strict neutrality, refusing to collaborate with Britain or the United States against Japan or even to take part in the League of Nations commission, set up to investigate the situation in Manchuria. He would do nothing that might serve as a pretext for war.

In 1933 Hitler came to power in Germany and war clouds gathered over Europe. He had repeatedly expressed his hostility towards the Soviet regime and proclaimed his demands for the Ukraine and other Russian territories to meet German needs for expansion. His aggressive policies were disturbing. Throughout the first years of Hitler's chancellorship, however, Stalin made no public reference to Germany. The Treaty of Rapallo and the two subsequent pacts were still in force, and he was hoping that Germany would continue to observe them. But he watched closely for signs of Hitler's real intentions.

At the Seventeenth Party Congress in January 1934 he made

cautious reference to fascism as "a symptom of capitalist weakness." He went on to say, "Of course, we are far from being enthusiastic about the fascist regime in Germany. But fascism is not an issue here, if only for the reason that fascism in Italy, for instance, has not prevented the U.S.S.R. from establishing the best relations with that country. Nor is it a question of any alleged change in our attitude towards the Versailles Treaty. . . . We simply do not agree to the world being flung into the abyss of a new war on account of this treaty."[7]

The Nazi leaders became increasingly aggressive and abusive. Stalin remained cautious, and he did not exclude the possibility of an alignment with Germany against the capitalist West. Bukharin and others did not share the ruthless logic of his view that any alliance was acceptable if it ensured Russia's security. They would have preferred alliance with the more civilized capitalists rather than with the barbarous Germans, and at the Congress Bukharin made a savage attack on Hitler and his policies. In the event, however, Stalin's proposals for a Russo-German alignment, and a few months later for a joint guarantee of the inviolability of Finland and the Baltic states, were rejected by Hitler.

While careful to placate or at least to avoid provoking Nazi Germany, Stalin grew more disturbed by Hitler's bellicose declarations. The German-Polish nonaggression pact suggested that he was fostering Poland's claims to the Ukraine and perhaps envisaging that the two countries might somehow share the vast steppes between them.

Stalin's first concern at this time was the security of Russia's frontiers. The way was clear for a German advance through the northern Baltic, and with Polish compliance the central route to Russia was open. The treaties signed by the Soviet government in the summer of 1934 with Czechoslovakia, Romania, and Bulgaria gave some security to the southwestern frontier. But Stalin knew that the centuries-old hostility of the Poles towards Russia made them his most dangerous neighbors.

During 1934 he worked on a reorientation of Soviet policy. His plan was to forge strong alliances with the countries of eastern Europe, but this failed because of German and Polish opposition.

It was necessary to cast the net more widely. In September 1934 Soviet Russia joined the League of Nations.

Reporting to the Seventh Congress of Soviets on January 28, 1935, Molotov spoke of the "expediency of collaborating with the League of Nations, although we are not prone to overestimate the importance of such organizations."[8] He went on to condemn German racial theories and quoted Hitler's *Mein Kampf* on the "policy of territorial conquest" directed at Russia.[9] He spoke of the growing strength of the Red Army and of increased Soviet defense expenditure. He conveyed a strong confidence in the might of the Soviet forces.[10] But the Soviet leaders were desperately worried. The pace of German rearmament, supported by a highly developed heavy industry, far outstripped the rate of Soviet expansion.

In 1935 Stalin began seeking alliances with the capitalist West. For years the United States had stubbornly refused to recognize the Soviet government. Communist doctrine and propaganda about the evils and imminent collapse of capitalism had antagonized American opinion. The United States had enjoyed great prosperity during the 1920s, which was taken as proof of the superiority of capitalism and democracy. Any expression of support or sympathy for Soviet Russia was liable to be condemned as "un-American."

Confident in its wealth and strength, the United States felt no need for diplomatic relations with the Soviet Union and took a strong moral stand against communism. But trade flourished between the two countries during the 1920s. Americans traveled freely to Russia, and American engineers and technicians contributed to Soviet industrialization.

The economic depression brought a sharp change in the American attitude. Business interests began pressing for recognition of the Soviet government in the hope that it would increase trade. It was, however, the need to counter the growing dominance of Japan in the Pacific that brought the change in U.S. policy in 1933. The Roosevelt administration on coming to power was ready to act, and recognition of the Soviet regime quickly followed. The Soviet press was jubilant in hailing the new treaty with the United States. But relations were at once disrupted by disputes over the repayment of loans made to Kerensky's government, and over Soviet propaganda. The truculent behavior of William C. Bullitt, the first U.S. ambassador, aggravated the conflicts. However, a trade agreement, signed on July 13, 1935, gave promise of more friendly relations.

In March 1935 Anthony Eden, a junior minister but already regarded as the coming Foreign Secretary, visited Moscow. The fact that Sir John Simon, a senior cabinet minister, went to Berlin was not permitted to overcloud the courteous reception extended to Eden. Later Churchill wrote that Eden "established contacts with Stalin which were to be revived with advantage after some years."[11] The significance of the visit was that Stalin himself took pains to welcome a junior minister from a country which along with France had always been regarded as Russia's chief enemy. Two months later he received Pierre Laval and Eduard Beneš, and the Russo-French and Russo-Czech alliances were agreed.

Stalin's new policy alignment was reflected strikingly in Soviet foreign trade. In 1932 Germany had supplied 46.5 per cent of Russia's total imports. By 1935 the figure had dropped to 9 per cent. Britain had displaced Germany, and imports from the United States were increasing. Germany extended massive credits in seeking to recover this vital trade. In 1936 the German share of the Soviet market rose to 22.8 per cent, but it soon dropped again.

Soviet propaganda now began projecting Russia as the champion of antifascism and peace. Its revolutionary mission was suppressed and denied. The Comintern's directives to member-parties were drastically revised to support Soviet policy. The Seventh Congress of the International called for "popular fronts" to be formed by Communists with Liberal, Labor, and even Conservative parties to fight against fascism. Litvinov, who was a Jew and detested Nazism, was tireless in promoting the new policy. Stalin himself granted an interview on March 5, 1936, to the American editor Roy Howard, in which he maintained firmly that "to assert that we desire to bring about revolution in other countries by interfering with their way of life is to speak of something that does not exist and which we have never preached."[12] Such statements and the heavy barrage of Soviet propaganda made an impression on world opinion, but mistrust of the Bolsheviks and their regime remained widespread in the West, and the devious role played by the Soviet government during the Spanish Civil War intensified Western suspicion of Soviet good faith.

The Spanish Civil War presented Stalin with acute difficulties. He was opposed to the fascist regime of General Franco and, indeed, at this time he was proclaiming Soviet Russia the champion of antifascism. He feared, too, that with a fascist regime on her frontier, France would be less likely to join in an antifascist and anti-German alliance. At the same time he considered that a republican victory in which the radical left wing was dominant would lead to a revolutionary regime in Spain, and this would alarm the Western powers and damage the prospects of forging Soviet alliances against Germany. He would have preferred to avoid involvement, and he instructed Litvinov to join the committee of nonintervention. But Hitler and Mussolini both gave active support to Franco, and Stalin felt compelled to aid the republicans. Through the French Communist party he sought to involve France on the side of the republicans. This would, he calculated, have had the effect of creating a combined military front against Germany and Italy. But France and Britain feared above all else that the Spanish war might develop into a world war, and they refused to intervene. Stalin compromised by giving the republicans minimal assistance and by insisting on the purging of the extreme left elements, seeking in this way to allay Western anxieties. His handling of the situation and in particular Soviet denials of aiding the republicans in the face of irrefutable evidence had the very effects which by tortuous diplomacy he had sought to avoid.

The Berlin-Rome axis was formed in October 1936 at a time when tension between Moscow and Berlin was mounting. The Nazis were increasingly raucous in their hostility towards Soviet Russia. Painstakingly Stalin continued to avoid the least provocation that might lead to war. He was then anxiously looking to the east. A German-Japanese anti-Comintern pact was signed on November 25, 1936. It appeared to be a simple defense agreement. He suspected, however, that the two governments had agreed on a secret plan to co-ordinate action against Russia and China. His suspicion was proved correct when one of his agents procured copies of their secret correspondence. Clashes with Japanese troops on the Manchurian frontier increased his fears. Further troops were hurried to the region. A new security treaty was signed with the Mongolian Republic and in the following year a nonaggression pact was agreed with China. But the pressure on Russia mounted relentlessly.

In March 1938 Hitler seized Austria. A crisis over the Sudeten Germans in Czechoslovakia followed. The belligerence of the Nazi leaders and the threats of violence repeated by German propaganda unnerved the British and French prime ministers. They held anxious consultations with Hitler, and both governments agreed to bring pressure to bear on Czechoslovakia to surrender the borderlands in the interests of peace.

Stalin was not readily unnerved. He responded at once with proposals that Britain, France, and Soviet Russia should present a united front against Germany and prepare with the Czechoslovak High Command a combined military plan. All three powers should invoke the League of Nations and prepare to enforce the provisions of the charter in the event of German aggression. Litvinov also confirmed that the Soviet Union would stand by the terms of the mutual assistance pact of 1935 if France, too, would honor her obligations under the pact. The Soviet plan would have averted or at least delayed war for a considerable time, and it was time that Stalin was playing for desperately.[13] But France was anxious to back out of her treaty obligations, and, notwithstanding strong opposition among many Conservative Members of Parliament, the British government showed reluctance to support France if she were involved in defending Czechoslovakia. The Soviet government was not consulted or included in the Munich conference which, meeting on September 28–30, 1938, surrendered Czechoslovakia into the hands of Germany.

The Western powers failed completely to respond to the Soviet proposals for a grand alliance under the aegis of the League. Churchill observed: "The Soviet offer was in effect ignored. They were not brought into the scale against Hitler and were treated with an indifference—not to say disdain—which left a mark on Stalin's mind. Events took their course as if Soviet Russia did not exist. For this we afterwards paid dearly."[14]

Mistrust of Soviet intentions and good faith had mounted

afresh in the West. Communist propaganda had stirred new suspicions. At the time of the economic recession in the late 1930s, the Soviet press loudly predicted left-wing victory in Spain and the collapse of the capitalist system. It is indeed surprising that Stalin permitted propaganda of this kind at a time when he was urgently pursuing alliances with the Western powers. More serious in its impact on influential Western opinion was the savage purge of the Red Army which, in the opinion of many, "destroyed the confidence of Western Europe in the strength of his army and the strength of his government."[15] It completely reversed the generally favorable impression of the British and French generals who had observed Red Army maneuvers in 1936.[16] But while Stalin could easily have restrained or changed the content of Soviet propaganda, he would have regarded any change in his decision to purge the armed forces as being out of the question. He remained firmly convinced that the armed forces had to be pruned and cleansed of all unreliable elements in preparation for the coming war.

Stalin was angered and humiliated by the disdainful attitude of the Western powers. He made no public comment at the time. He was too deeply concerned about Russia's almost complete isolation, and he would say nothing that might exacerbate the position. He had no doubt about the motives of Britain and France in agreeing to the dismemberment of Czechoslovakia by Germany. Clearly they had promised Hitler a free hand in the east in return for peace in the west. As he remarked later: "One might think that the districts of Czechoslovakia were yielded to Germany as the prize for her undertaking to launch war on the Soviet Union."[17] But he was surprised by the conduct of France in failing to honor her treaty obligation to Czechoslovakia. Russia had not been guilty of bad faith; she had undertaken to stand by France in the event of war. Britain was not committed in alliance with Russia or Czechoslovakia and so could not be charged with bad faith, only with having played an ignoble role in the sacrifice of a small nation.

Stalin could not understand how two great powers, Britain and France, had allowed themselves to be so defeated in diplomacy by Hitler, except in return for guarantees of peace in the west. He overestimated the morale and military preparedness of the two countries, while underestimating the general fear and suspicion felt towards Soviet Russia. He had to accept that they were enemies and that in any case they were too infirm of purpose and degenerate to make reliable allies.

To the Russians, Neville Chamberlain, the British Prime Minister, was the archvillain. They held him in contempt, and blamed him for the collapse of the Soviet policy of collective security. They were convinced that he was encouraging Germany to march eastwards, leaving Britain and France to enjoy peace while fascism and communism destroyed each other.

Ivan Maisky, Soviet ambassador in Britain from 1932 to 1943, described Chamberlain as "undoubtedly the most sinister figure on the political horizon of Britain at that time" and as "a man of narrow views and small capabilities." Maxim Litvinov held similar opinions of him. But they were both well disposed towards Britain and knew that there were influential groups of men who shared their opinion of Chamberlain. Their reports no doubt held Stalin from closing his mind finally to the possibility of alliance with Britain.[18]

The winter of 1938–39 was a time of deepening anxiety. Stalin knew that war was drawing nearer and that Russia's armed forces were still in no state to withstand a German attack. Russia would again be "beaten for her backwardness." Brooding over diplomatic tactics to avert war, he kept every possibility in mind. The problem was where to turn for allies. The United States kept aloof, avoiding commitment of any kind. Britain and France had rebuffed his approaches. Germany, Italy, and Japan behaved with increasing arrogance and bellicosity. The Poles were fawning on Hitler and had sent Colonel Jósef Beck, their Foreign Minister, to Berlin, evidently to negotiate some anti-Soviet deal. It was probably about this time that Stalin decided to open the door to an alliance with Hitler. It was a calculated gamble, but he could see no alternatives.

Early in March 1939, the Eighteenth Party Congress met in Moscow after an interval of four years since the previous Congress. The General Secretary's review of domestic and foreign affairs was of special importance. Stalin delivered the report on March 10 in a statesmanlike performance. He spoke of the coming economic depression and the danger that it would provoke world war. Germany, Italy, and Japan were the "aggressive countries," which would seek to escape from a slump by going to war. He emphasized the economic factors in diplomacy and spoke of the economic and the potential military supremacy of Britain and the United States. He took for granted that the United States would be involved in the war; it was a bold assumption at this time, when U.S. policy was strongly against foreign commitments of any kind. He castigated Western appeasement. "The war is being waged by the aggressor states, who in every way infringe the interests of the non-aggressive states, primarily England, France, and the U.S.A., while the latter draw back and retreat, making concession after concession to the aggressors."[19] The appeasing nations were activated by fear of revolution and a spirit of neutrality, but also by the policy of allowing Russia and Germany to "weaken and exhaust one another; and then when they had become weak enough, they would appear on the scene with fresh strength and dictate conditions to the enfeebled belligerents. That would be cheap and easy."[20] But then he stressed that, although the West was seeking to push Russia into war with Germany, no "visible grounds" existed for war between them. He poured scorn on the so-called friends of Germany who were urging her to attack Russia, and who were ignored by responsible German leaders.

Concluding his report, he summarized the objectives of Soviet policy. They were, in fact, mutually incompatible. He was concerned to keep the door open to alliance with Britain, France, and the United States, yet although he roundly condemned Nazi aggression and promised Soviet support for countries subjected to Nazi threats, he did not exclude the possibility of coming to terms with Germany. "We stand for peaceful, close, and good neighborly relations with all the neighboring countries having common frontiers with the U.S.S.R."[21]

On March 15, 1939, German troops invaded Czechoslovakia. Hitler announced that he had taken Bohemia and Moravia under German protection. Slovakia was detached and became a puppet state. Stalin was expecting this violation of Czechoslovakia as the inevitable outcome of British appeasement, and he reacted promptly with a note of protest to Berlin.

In the West, public opinion was outraged by the rape of Czechoslovakia. In Britain, Chamberlain had merely expressed disapproval in the House of Commons, and was visibly shaken by the angry reaction. On instructions the British ambassador in Moscow called on Litvinov to inquire how the Soviet government would react if Hitler attacked Romania. Litvinov responded the same evening with the firm proposal that representatives of Britain, France, the U.S.S.R., Poland, and Romania should meet without delay to concert action to avert such a danger.

The British government rejected this proposal. Its proposition was that the four countries should issue a declaration that in the event of a further act of aggression they would consult. Although angered by this feeble alternative, Stalin agreed to the declaration, provided that Poland was also a signatory. But Colonel Beck, as anti-Russian as Chamberlain, refused to sign. He proposed a Polish-British mutual assistance pact, which could be broadened to include other powers if necessary.

Chamberlain and Halifax now took an irrational plunge. On March 31, 1939, the Polish-British Pact was announced, and on April 13 it was extended to include Romania and Greece. Stalin was staggered by this British undertaking to go to the aid of countries, two of which lay between Russia and Germany, and were inaccessible to Britain. If Germany attacked Poland or Romania, Britain could do nothing without the support of the Soviet Union, and in a way that was gratuitously insulting, both governments having carefully ignored the Soviet government. Churchill, Eden, and others were quick to point out the blind stupidity of Chamberlain's policy.

Next, under pressure of public opinion, the British government proposed that Soviet Russia should give unilateral guarantees to Poland and Romania. Stalin turned down this suggestion, which provided no assistance or security for Russia in the event of German invasion. He responded, however, to a French proposal for a joint Soviet-French declaration of mutual assistance, extended to Poland and Romania. On April 17, 1939, Stalin put forward the idea of a British-French-Soviet pact of mutual assistance, which would include a military convention and would guarantee the independence of all states along the Soviet frontier from the Baltic to the Black Sea. This again was a practical plan and one which would have deterred Hitler. But Chamberlain and Halifax rejected it, because it might offend Poland and Germany, and because it would commit Britain to the defense of Finland and the Baltic states. For Stalin the inescapable conclusion was that the leaders of the British government were so blinded by hostility towards the Soviet regime that not even to avert the horrors of war would they consider an alliance with Soviet Russia against Germany.

On May 3 Litvinov was dismissed and Molotov was appointed Kommissar for Foreign Affairs in his place. The change aroused speculation in the West. Litvinov had been an ardent Westerner and an advocate of collective security, and had many friends in the West. He was credited with being responsible for the Kremlin's policy of alliance with the Western powers. It was not appreciated that he had always acted strictly in accordance with the instructions of the Politburo, of which he was not even a member, and that Stalin himself directed foreign policy.

Vyacheslav Mikhailovich Molotov, the new kommissar, was hardly known abroad, but his granitelike presence and relentless pursuit of Russian interests soon made a strong impression. At the time he was already chairman of the Council of People's Kommissars (Sovnarkom), an office akin to prime minister, and one of Stalin's most trusted colleagues.

Churchill wrote of Molotov that he was a man of "outstanding ability and cold-blooded ruthlessness. . . . I have never seen a human being who more perfectly represented the modern conception of a robot. . . . His smile of Siberian winter, his carefully-measured and often wise words, his affable demeanour, combined to make him the perfect agent of Soviet policy in a deadly world."[22]

Molotov's appointment did not bring an immediate change in policy. Reporting on May 31, 1939, to the Supreme Soviet, he strongly attacked Germany and Italy and, while critical of Britain and France, he implied that it was still Soviet policy to conclude a mutual assistance pact with them. In London, Chamberlain and

Halifax were under increasing pressure to negotiate with the Soviet government. Towards the end of May the British and French
ambassadors in Moscow had delivered proposals for a tripartite
pact, subject to League of Nations procedures, but excluding a
convention on military aid and assistance to the Baltic states.
Again showing patience and restraint, Stalin responded on June 2,
1939, with a draft agreement, which maintained the purely defensive nature of the proposals, but specified the countries to be guaranteed against aggression and the extent of the commitment of
the three signatories.

Chamberlain seemed to approve. He expressed to Maisky, the
Soviet ambassador, his interest in the draft and proposed to send a
representative to Moscow to speed the negotiations. Molotov
readily agreed to receive him. But, whereas Chamberlain and
Halifax had gone in person to Berlin, they now sent a Foreign
Office official to Moscow. It seemed a deliberate affront and, as
Churchill noted, it gave "actual offence."[23] A courteous but press-
ing invitation to Halifax to visit Russia had been waved aside.
The mission achieved nothing.

Responding to public demand, the British and French governments took an initiative. Late in July 1939, Chamberlain
suggested sending a military mission to Moscow. Stalin welcomed
the proposal. It was hoped in Moscow that Lord Gort, chief of
the imperial general staff, would head the mission. Chamberlain
appointed an elderly retired admiral, who arrived in Moscow on
August 12, 1939, without instructions. This mission, too, proved
abortive. Stalin insisted that a military convention must include
provision for Soviet troops to pass through Poland in the event of
war with Germany. The Poles declared that they did not need
and would not accept Soviet aid. The British and French governments rejected the provision.

War was pressing nearer. The German Army was ready to cross
the Polish frontier. Hitler hesitated only because he feared that
Soviet Russia would stand with Britain and France in defense of
Poland. The certainty that this was the sole deterrent to Hitler
must have made it all the more galling for Stalin that his repeated
attempts to negotiate a tripartite pact had brought only rebuffs,
humiliations, and disappointments. His foremost concern was still

to gain time so that Soviet industry and the armed forces could gather strength. Reluctantly he turned now to the possibility of an agreement with Hitler.[24]

The first German approaches, suggesting a review of Soviet-German relations, were evidently made on May 30, 1939. The Soviet government returned a noncommittal reply, for at that time negotiations with Britain and France were taking place. On August 4 the German ambassador in Moscow, Schulenburg, reported:

> From Molotov's whole attitude it was evident that the Soviet government was, in fact, more prepared for improvement in German-Soviet relations, but that the old mistrust of Germany persists. My overall impression is that the Soviet government is at present determined to sign with England and France, if they fulfil all Soviet wishes. Negotiations, to be sure, might still last a long time, especially since the mistrust of England is also great. . . . It will take a considerable effort on our part to cause the Soviet government to swing about.[25]

A German note, delivered in Moscow on August 15, drew a more sympathetic response. Molotov replied that the Soviet government welcomed the German desire for a serious improvement in relations and proposed a trade and credit agreement to be followed by a nonaggression pact or a reaffirmation of the neutrality pact of 1926, and the conclusion of a protocol defining spheres of interest. On the evening of August 19, 1939, Stalin informed the Politburo of his intention to conclude a pact with Germany.

Hitler was disturbed by the continued presence of the Anglo-French military mission in Moscow. He was seething with impatience to order the invasion of Poland. On August 20 he sent an urgent telegram to Stalin, asking him to receive Joachim von Ribbentrop, the German Foreign Minister, on August 22 or at latest 23. Stalin agreed. He had made his final decision to conclude the pact with Germany.

By this date the negotiations with the Anglo-French military mission had reached deadlock and the Poles had reaffirmed their refusal to allow Soviet troops access to Polish territory. Stalin was also influenced by the fact that fighting against Japanese troops on the Manchurian frontier continued and by the probability that he would be able to negotiate a nonaggression pact with Japan, Germany's ally.

On the night of August 23, 1939, Stalin received Ribbentrop and they agreed on the text of the agreement. But the meeting was cold and far from amicable. Gauss, chief assistant to Ribbentrop, who accompanied him, recorded:

> Ribbentrop himself had inserted in the preamble a rather far-reaching phrase concerning the formation of friendly German-Soviet relations. To this Stalin objected, remarking that the Soviet government could not suddenly present to their public a German-Soviet declaration of friendship after they had been covered with pails of manure by the Nazi government for six years. Thereupon this phrase in the preamble was deleted.[26]

The pact was to last for ten years. Stalin and Hitler knew that it was a temporary expedient. They were enemies, and between them war was inevitable. But their pact had the immediate result of freeing Hitler to launch his invasion of Poland and of giving Stalin more time. "If their policy was cold-blooded, it was also at the moment realistic in a high degree," Churchill observed.[27]

On August 31, 1939, Molotov reported to the Supreme Soviet. He explained how attempts to reach agreement with Britain and France had failed. The new Soviet-German Pact was in accordance with the policy of peaceful coexistence, formulated by Lenin and endorsed by Stalin. It would end the enmity between the two countries. His long report was designed to quieten the anxieties of the Russian people. They were accustomed to think of their country as the bastion of antifascism, and were bewildered by the abrupt reversal of policy, making them allies of Nazi Germany. But all were confident that Stalin and Molotov had the situation under control. The general reaction was that it was a shrewd move to keep Russia out of war.[28]

On September 1, 1939, Hitler invaded Poland. Two days later the Anglo-French ultimatum expired, and both countries were at war with Germany. Stalin was surprised. He had expected France and Britain to back out of their treaty obligations. But war was now a reality and he stepped up Soviet preparations. The conscription age was lowered from twenty-one to nineteen, and when the new age groups were called up during the following months, the strength of the Soviet armed forces was raised to more than 4.2 million men. On September 10 partial mobilization was decreed. Meanwhile negotiations had started with Japan to end the fighting which had continued since 1938 along the frontier between the Mongolian People's Republic and Manchukuo. Molotov conducted the talks with the Japanese ambassador, and they agreed to set up a commission to define frontier.

Stalin followed the German invasion of Poland with deep uneasiness. It was a ruthless demonstration of the mechanized power and efficiency of the German Army. He knew that the Red Army was neither equipped nor trained to withstand such an attack. "Victory in war," he had pointed out in an informal meeting of the Supreme War Council, "will be won by the side that has more tanks and more highly motorized troops."[29] His army lagged far behind the German Army on both counts. Soviet defense industries were making gigantic efforts, and Russia was catching up. He needed time and every month counted.

First, it was necessary to secure the Russian frontiers against approaches through Poland and through the Baltic states. Occupation of eastern Poland, as agreed in the secret protocol with Germany, would create a defense region. But Stalin delayed for two weeks before acting on Ribbentrop's proposal, made on September 3, that, in accordance with their agreement, the Soviet forces should advance into Poland.

On the day after the truce with Japan was signed, the Red Army crossed the Polish frontier. The Polish Army and Air Force, already shattered by the German onslaught, offered little resistance. In Moscow Molotov spoke with contempt of "the internal insolvency and obvious impotence of the Polish state," which had become "a fertile field for any accidental and unexpected contingency that may create a menace to the Soviet Union."[30] He showed no magnanimity. The Poles were enemies who in changed circumstances would have treated Russia in the same fashion.[31]

Stalin was anxious about the Baltic approaches into Russia. Leningrad, with a population of 3.5 million, was only thirty-two kilometers from the Finnish border and within range of artillery fire. Treaties of mutual assistance were imposed on Estonia, Latvia, and Lithuania. Finland was not co-operative. In 1938 Soviet proposals to lease certain territory along the northern shore of the gulf were flatly rejected. On October 14, 1939, a Soviet note made firm proposals for an exchange of territory, together with a thirty-year lease of the Hangö peninsula and frontier adjustments in the Petsamo area and on the Karelian Isthmus. The Finns refused to yield at any point. Attempts to negotiate continued, but made no progress. On November 13, 1939, Stalin broke them off. His patience was exhausted. He decided to use force.

On November 30 the Soviet attack was launched, beginning the four-months-long Finnish Winter War. The Red Army deployed twenty divisions against fifteen Finnish divisions. The Finns were, however, highly trained and well equipped. The Russian troops were poorly led and trained and inadequately armed. Their losses were appalling, and by the end of the year the Finns were still holding the Red Army on all fronts.

World opinion was on the side of the Finns and strongly anti-Russian. The Soviet Union was expelled from the League of Nations. In Britain and France the governments even considered declaring war on the Soviet Union. Chamberlain expressed the view that there would be strategic advantage in fighting Hitler and Stalin simultaneously and "killing two birds with one stone." In a broadcast on January 20, 1940, Churchill declared that Finland "had exposed for the world to see the military incapacity of the Red Army."[32]

Stalin was appalled by the failures of the Finnish campaign. It was a humiliation, and he was sensitive to the contemptuous criticism and the anti-Soviet campaign abroad. The Germans secretly and Britain and France openly took pleasure in this humiliation of Soviet armed might. The fact was that by comparison with the German war machine the Red Army was lumbering and inefficient. Stalin fumed with anger and repeatedly summoned Meretskov, who had planned the campaign, to report in Moscow. He bore in mind, too, that an alternative plan of campaign, prepared by Boris Shaposhnikov, had warned that it would take several months to overcome Finnish resistance. Now, disturbed by the real possibility of armed intervention by Sweden, Britain, and

France, and angered by the continued failure of his troops, he ordered a massive assault.

During January 1940 Russian troops were concentrated for the great advance which began on February 11. The Finns were overwhelmed by weight of numbers and by constant bombardment. They sued for peace on March 8, and four days later the treaty was signed in Moscow. The territories needed to secure the Baltic approaches to Russia's frontiers had been won. Stalin did not consider occupying Helsinki or encroaching on other parts of Finland. The callousness and contempt that the Russians showed towards the Poles did not extend to the Finns, whom they respected.

The Finnish war had proved a costly and humiliating operation, but it yielded important results. Stalin was quick to recognize the weaknesses of the Soviet forces. Addressing the Chief Military Council on April 17, 1940, he stated bluntly that all commanders must study modern warfare. The traditions and experience of the Civil War were simply obstacles to the understanding of war. Sweeping reforms were introduced. Zhukov was to call 1940 "the year of the great transformation."[33]

The status and authority of officers were raised. The titles of general, admiral, and other ranks and also the ranks of NCOs were revived in place of the revolutionary titles. The single command system was restored and the political kommissars were subordinated to their military commanders. Lack of trained officers had been felt acutely during the war, and intensive courses for officers were instituted. More than four thousand officers who had been sentenced during the great purge were recalled, including men like Rokossovsky, Rotmistrov, and Tolbukhin, who were to become Marshals of the Soviet Union. Military manuals were rewritten. No trace of the old idea of equality of officers and men remained. The emphasis was on command and discipline. All of these changes bore the mark of Stalin's authority and outlook.

During these frantic months Stalin was also selecting his top military commanders. Klim Voroshilov, his close colleague from the Tsaritsyn days, belonged to the revolutionary tradition, and, as he had shown in the Finnish war, had not developed as a military commander. He was replaced on May 8, 1940, by Timoshenko as

Kommissar for Defense. Stalin used Voroshilov in other capacities, for he was popular and completely loyal. Budënny, the dashing cavalry commander, had failed to master modern warfare, but, like Voroshilov, was kept active.

Shaposhnikov was in a different category. He had gained his commission in the tsarist army in 1903 and had qualified at the General Staff Academy in 1910. He had a broad outlook and a keen analytical mind. In the 1920s he wrote *The Brain of the Army* and other basic works on military organization and strategy. He was modest and benevolent, but also a man of strict discipline. Tall and dignified, he was still in manner the tsarist officer, referring to brother officers as "old chap" (*golubchik*) and usually prefacing his orders with "Would you be so kind" or "I beg you," but he was exacting and he got results.[34] He might have seemed an anachronism in the midst of the new generation of commanders, but Stalin and others held him in high respect.

Meretskov differed from Shaposhnikov in nearly every way. He was a bluff revolutionary, who had served in the Red Guards, and was largely self-educated. In August 1940 Stalin appointed him Chief of the General Staff in place of Shaposhnikov. He showed concern for Shaposhnikov's feelings in explaining gently to him that the time had come "to show the world that there has been a complete change in the military leadership since the Finnish War." He also had in mind the need to promote younger men and the fact that Shaposhnikov's health was poor. He valued his ability, however, and retained him at this time as Deputy Kommissar for Defense with special responsibility for military engineering and fortifications. Later he was to make him Chief of Staff again.

Meretskov remained Chief of the General Staff for only a few months. Large-scale maneuvers played an important part in this period of intensive training. The first of the war games under Meretskov's direction took place in Belorussia in the late summer of 1940, and Stalin accepted the evaluation of these maneuvers. Shortly after the second war game, held at the end of the year, however, Meretskov and the senior commanders were unexpectedly summoned to the Kremlin to report personally. Stalin and other members of the Politburo and the Chief Military

Council were present. Meretskov proved incapable of evaluating the main features of the maneuvers. Vatutin, his deputy, tried to come to his aid, but Stalin silenced him. When Meretskov referred to the Soviet field regulations to support an argument, Stalin dismissed them as propaganda, adding that "here among ourselves we have to talk in terms of our real capabilities."[35] Stalin had seen through Meretskov's bluff façade of confidence and mastery.

On February 1, 1941, Zhukov became Chief of General Staff. He had been a noncommissioned officer in the tsarist army and was, like Meretskov, largely self-educated. He had gained distinction commanding armored divisions near Khalkhim Gol in the Far East in 1939. He had a natural ability, honesty, and strength of character, and he was to prove the outstanding Russian field commander in World War II. His relations with Stalin were on occasions stormy, but they were based on mutual respect. From many incidents related by Zhukov in his memoirs, written after Stalin's death, it is clear that he never questioned Stalin's authority and that he regarded him as a leader of profound wisdom and mastery of affairs, even in the military field.

Timoshenko, Kommissar for Defense, had apparently requested Zhukov's appointment. Summoned to Stalin's office, however, Zhukov was taken by surprise by Stalin's terse statement that the Politburo had decided to make him Chief of the General Staff. He protested that he had had no experience of staff work and was a field officer. Stalin listened to his protestations and then repeated curtly: "The Politburo has decided to appoint you," laying emphasis on the word "decided."[36]

A few days later, when Timoshenko told him that Stalin had asked how he was settling into his new post, and wanted him to report in person, Zhukov was disturbed. "What will he be liable to ask me about?" "Everything," Timoshenko replied, adding, "but remember he won't listen to long reports. What it takes you several hours to tell me, you'll have to tell him in ten minutes." "What can I tell him in ten minutes? They're serious questions and require serious consideration. . . ." "He knows for the most part what you want to tell him," Timoshenko said, "so try to concentrate on the key problems."[37]

Directing every aspect of the build-up of the armed forces from the selection of senior personnel to the mechanization program, especially the introduction of the T-34 tank and the new rocket mortars (*Katyusha*), Stalin did not rely on formal meetings of the Politburo, the Chief Military Council, and other bodies. He valued direct personal contacts and firsthand reports by the men responsible. At his dacha in Kuntsevo he had frequent late-night discussions with Timoshenko, Zhukov, Voroshilov, Beria, Mekhlis, Shchadenko, and others.

About this time he told Shaposhnikov to prepare a general staff paper on the probable German plan of invasion. The paper was considered by the Politburo in September 1940 and rejected by Stalin. Shaposhnikov argued that the main German attack would fall between the Baltic and the Pripet Marshes, directed at Smolensk and Moscow. Stalin was convinced that on economic grounds the German strategy would concentrate on the south because of the need for the grain of the Ukraine, the coal of the Donets, and the oil of the Caucasus. Soviet defenses were based on this appreciation of the enemy strategy. Shaposhnikov was proved more accurate than Stalin in his forecast.

In the spring and summer of 1940 the lightning advances of Hitler's forces in the West gave added urgency to Soviet preparations. The German occupation of Norway and Denmark was followed in May by the invasion of the Low Countries and the evacuation of British troops at Dunkirk. But most shattering to the Russians was the abysmal collapse of France, and the German occupation of Paris on June 14. Stalin had expected that the French Army, secure behind the Maginot Line, would be more than a match for Germany. Attention focused on Britain, now under Churchill's leadership. But mixed with admiration for her solitary stand against Germany and Italy, there was a general fear that Britain would make peace with Germany, freeing Hitler to turn eastwards.

Stalin was meticulous in observing the terms of the pact with Germany. Towards Britain he maintained a strict neutrality. But, alarmed by the fall of France, he hurriedly occupied the Baltic states and forced Romania to cede Bessarabia and Bukovina. Soviet industrial output was stepped up. Everyone was required to work longer hours.

At this time of tension an event took place in faraway Mexico, which passed almost unnoticed in Russia. The announcement in the Soviet press read: "London, August 22 (TASS). London radio reports that Trotsky has died in hospital in Mexico City of a fractured skull, the result of an attempt on his life by one of the persons in his immediate entourage."[38]

Banished from Russia in 1929, Trotsky had applied for permission to live in Germany, France, and England. None was prepared to receive this troublesome revolutionary whose activities were now dominated by a relentless hatred of the man who had defeated him and had become supreme ruler of Soviet Russia. Bereft of power, Trotsky's remarkable intellect and energy and his vitriolic pen were concentrated against Stalin and his regime.

In January 1937 he arrived in Mexico, where he had been offered asylum. He was housed in Coyoacán, a suburb of the city in what he called "the little fortress." It had heavily barred doors, electrified wires, automatic alarm signals, and mounted machine guns. Ten Mexican policemen were on duty around the house and four or five guards were posted inside. From here he continued his campaign of polemics and vituperation.

In May 1940, notwithstanding the strong defenses, a machine gun attack was made on the house. Trotsky, his wife and grandson were unharmed. Indeed, their escape seemed so miraculous that the Mexican police strongly suspected that Trotsky himself had staged the attack in order to discredit Mexican Stalinists. Trotsky insisted that "the author of the attack is Joseph Stalin through the medium of the G.P.U.," but the Mexicans were not convinced.[39] About this time Ramon Mercader, known also as Mornard-Jacson, insinuated himself into the household. On August 20, while standing by Trotsky's desk, he suddenly attacked him with an ice ax, smashing his skull.[40]

During 1940 relations between the Soviet Union and Germany remained formally correct, but were increasingly strained. Hitler had strong misgivings about the Russians being so near to the Romanian oil fields. Stalin was alarmed by reports of German troops in Finland and of German designs on the Balkans. The

ten-year pact between Germany, Italy, and Japan, signed in Berlin
on September 27, 1940, and excluding Soviet Russia, added to his
anxieties.

On November 12, on the invitation of Ribbentrop, Molotov ar-
rived in Berlin to discuss "a long-term delimitation of interests."[41]
He found that Hitler was concerned only with the division of the
British Empire between the Soviet Union and the Axis powers.
Molotov showed no interest and infuriated Hitler by firing question after question at him and demanding specific answers about
German intentions in Finland, Romania, Bulgaria, and Turkey.
Hitler was not accustomed to interrogation of this kind, and he
was antagonized by the rocklike obstinacy of the Soviet minister.
As early as the summer of 1940 he had started thinking about the
invasion of Russia, but this meeting with the persistent and im-
perturbable Molotov probably influenced him in deciding finally
to launch Operation Barbarossa.[42]

The façade of cordial relations was maintained in the first
months of 1941. But tension was mounting. In March Bulgaria
joined the Axis; Yugoslavia also agreed to join. On March 27, however, a revolt in Yugoslavia against the pro-German policy resulted
in the formation of a new government which looked to Moscow.
Stalin was quick to sign a pact of friendship and nonaggression
with the new Yugoslav regime, but could do nothing when German forces invaded the country and Belgrade was mercilessly
bombed.

On May 5 in the Kremlin Stalin addressed several hundred
young officers, newly graduated from the military academies. He
emphasized the importance of modernization and re-equipment in
building up the power of the Red Army. He went on to warn
them that the situation was grave and that a German attack in
the near future could not be ruled out. He told them bluntly that
the Red Army was not yet strong enough to smash the Germans
easily; it suffered still from shortages of modern tanks, aircraft,
and other equipment, and its troops were still under training. The
Soviet government by diplomacy and other means was striving to
delay the Germans until autumn, when the approach of winter
would postpone any attack until 1942. If Soviet tactics succeeded,
then the war with Nazi Germany would come almost inevitably

in 1942, but valuable months would have been gained. The period "from now until August" was the most dangerous.[43]

This meeting was followed by a series of desperate attempts to appease Hitler. Friendly economic and diplomatic gestures were made. Painful efforts to avoid even the semblance of provocation were continued. On June 14, 1941, TASS, the Soviet news agency, issued a communiqué emphasizing friendly relations with Germany, which was "unswervingly observing the conditions of the Soviet-German Non-aggression Pact, just as the U.S.S.R. is doing" and denying rumors, emanating from London, of an "early war between the two countries."[44] Berlin ignored these gestures. Hitler had already made his decision.

The tension in the Kremlin became unbearable during these weeks of waiting. Stalin felt the strain. He was irascible, and reports on relations with Germany could only be submitted to him "in fear and trepidation."[45] He had concentrated "all his thoughts and deeds" on averting war in 1941; he was confident, but not positive, that he would succeed.[46] In the midst of the conflicting intelligence reports and rumors he was deeply uneasy. The German Chief of Staff had issued on February 15, 1941, a special "Directive for Misinforming the Enemy" to provide cover for Operation Barbarossa. False information was leaked that German troop movements in the east were part of the "greatest misinformation manoeuvre in history, designed to distract attention from final preparations for the invasion of England."[47]

Stalin was undoubtedly influenced by this misinformation. He did not believe, however, that in the last resort Hitler would depart from the traditions of Bismarck's Ostpolitik, requiring that Germany should avoid military involvement in Russia while engaged in the west. At the same time he had an exaggerated conception of the power and influence of the German generals even to the extent of believing that, contrary to Hitler's specific instructions, they were trying to precipitate war against Russia.

Among members of the Politburo and the Soviet High Command the firm opinion was that war would be averted in 1941. Zhdanov held that Germany was taken up with war against Britain and incapable of fighting on two fronts. On March 20, 1941, General Golikov, head of military intelligence, submitted to

Stalin a report on German troop concentration in the borderlands, but expressed the opinion that the information must
have originated from the British and German intelligence services.[48] Early in May Admiral Kuznetsov, commanding the Soviet
Navy, sent a similar report to Stalin, giving information received
from the Soviet naval attaché in Berlin on the imminence of war.
Like Golikov, he nullified the value of the report by adding that
in his opinion the information was false and planted by some foreign agency.[49]

Early in April 1941 Churchill sent a personal message to Stalin,
warning him of German troop movements and the imminence of
attack on the Soviet Union. This was followed by an urgent warning given to the Soviet ambassador in London on June 18. Reports from the Soviet Embassy in Berlin and from Dr. Richard
Sorge, the brilliant Soviet spy in Japan, gave the exact date of the
German invasion.[50]

Stalin regarded these reports with skepticism. He remained
deeply mistrustful of Britain. There was, it seems, no limit to the
perfidy of which he believed Britain capable. He was convinced
that Britain and the United States were doing everything possible
to incite Hitler to attack Russia and that Britain in particular saw
a German campaign in the east as the one way to save herself
from catastrophe. He believed that the British government had
recently held secret talks with Nazi officials, seeking to reach an
agreement at the expense of Russia. The flight of Hitler's deputy,
Rudolf Hess, to Scotland on May 10–11, 1941, intensified his suspicions of British secret diplomacy.[51]

On the evening of June 21 Zhukov learned by telephone from
Kiev that a German sergeant major had crossed to the Soviet lines
and informed the Soviet commander that the German forces
would attack at dawn on the following morning.

Zhukov at once telephoned Stalin and Timoshenko. Stalin summoned them to the Kremlin. He received them alone and heard
Zhukov's report.

"But perhaps the German generals sent this deserter to provoke
a conflict," was his first response.

"No, we think the deserter is telling the truth," they replied.

Members of the Politburo arrived. He asked for their opinions, but there was no response.[52]

Timoshenko produced a draft directive, alerting all commands. But Stalin had not given up hope that it might be a false alarm. He had the directive redrafted and finally approved its dispatch. It ordered all units on the fronts of the Leningrad, Baltic, Western, Kiev, and Odessa military districts to come to immediate readiness for a possible sudden German attack. Transmission of the directive was completed by 0030 hours on June 22, 1941. At 0400 hours the invasion began.

The German forces, comprising 3 million troops in 162 divisions with 3,400 tanks and 7,000 guns, advanced in three groups: the north group towards Leningrad, the center group towards Moscow, and the south group into the Ukraine. The sixteen months that followed were for the Germans a period of immense gains; for the Russians they were months of disastrous defeats and horrifying casualties and devastation.

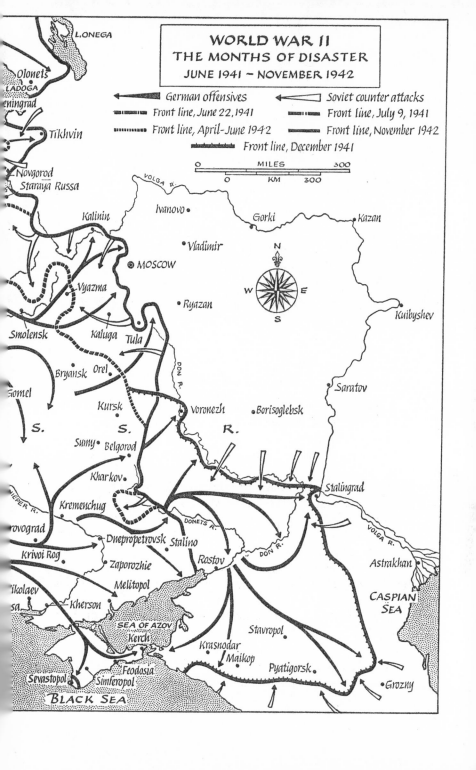

WORLD WAR II
THE MONTHS OF DISASTER
JUNE 1941 – NOVEMBER 1942

German offensives   Soviet counter attacks
Front line, June 22, 1941   Front line, July 9, 1941
Front line, April–June 1942   Front line, November 1942
Front line, December 1941

MILES 0 — 300
KM 0 — 300

L. ONEGA

Olonets
LADOGA
eningrad
Tikhvin
Novgorod
Staraya Russa

Kalinin

Ivanovo
Gorki
Kazan

Vladimir

MOSCOW

Vyazma

Ryazan

Kuibyshev

Smolensk
Kaluga Tula

Bryansk Orel
Gomel
S.

Kursk
S.
Sumy Belgorod
Kharkov

DON R.

Voronezh
R.
Borisoglebsk

Saratov

Stalingrad

Kremenchug
DONETS R.
ovograd Dnepropetrovsk Stalino
Krivoi Rog Zaporozhie Rostov
DON R.
VOLGA R.
Astrakhan

Nikolaev Kherson
ssa Melitopol

CASPIAN SEA

SEA OF AZOV
Kerch
Krasnodar Maikop
Stavropol

Sevastopol Feodosia
Simferopol
Pyatigorsk
Grozny

BLACK SEA

DNIEPER R.
VOLGA R.

25

War:
the Months of Disaster
June 1941–November 1942

By dawn on June 22, 1941, Timoshenko, Zhukov, and his Deputy Chief of the General Staff, N. F. Vatutin, were receiving frantic communications from front commanders. All reported air attacks and requested orders. Timoshenko told Zhukov to telephone Stalin.

Stalin heard his report and proposal to order troops to retaliate. There was a long silence during which Zhukov could hear the sound of his breathing on the line. Then Stalin ordered him and Timoshenko to come to the Kremlin and to tell Poskrebyshev to summon the members of the Politburo.

At 4:30 A.M. all were assembled in Stalin's office. He stood by the table, his face white, and with an unlit pipe in his hand. He was visibly shaken.

Molotov hastened into the room from a meeting with the German ambassador. He reported that Germany had declared war.

Stalin sank into his chair and sat in silence. This was one of the most shattering moments in his whole life. He had used every means at his disposal to avert this war. He had desperately willed it to be delayed at least until the following spring. He thought he had succeeded, but he had failed. Armaments were beginning to flow to the armed forces from the defense industries, and the intensive training programs were bringing daily improvements in discipline and efficiency. Six months would have made a vast difference.

Stalin knew that he had made a tragic miscalculation. The Politburo and senior military commanders, with all of whom he had discussed his decisions, had shared his views. But they were dominated by him and conscious of his intellectual superiority and his supreme authority. He was honest enough to recognize that it was wholly his responsibility. He had misjudged Hitler's intentions. Soviet Russia was threatened now with a holocaust which could sweep away the communist regime and all that it had achieved.

It was later alleged that on this evening or during the following weeks when news of terrible defeats were reaching him, his nerve snapped and he surrendered to black despair. Khrushchev stated that about this time Stalin thought the end had come. He exclaimed: "All Lenin created, we have lost for ever!" After this outburst he did nothing "for a long time"; and he returned to active leadership only after a Politburo deputation pleaded with him to resume command.[1] But Khrushchev's allegations are not supported by others who were at his side. In fact, Stalin had never been more in command than during these critical days when all seemed lost.[2]

At the dawn meeting on June 22, Stalin came out of his brooding silence to authorize Directive No. 2, calling on all military districts to attack the invaders. The order was unrealistic. The Red Army was falling back in confusion. The breakdown in communications was posing acute problems. Moscow lost touch with the forces to the north of the Pripet and with other commands.

About 1 P.M. on June 22 Stalin telephoned Zhukov and said that, since front commanders lacked combat experience and were confused, the Politburo was sending him to the Southwest Front as the representative of the Stavka. Khrushchev would join him there. Shaposhnikov and Kulik were going to the West Front. In reply to Zhukov's query as to who would manage the General Staff at this critical time, Stalin answered tersely, "Leave Vatutin in your place. Don't lose time! We'll get along somehow!"[3] He flew at once to Kiev and, joined by Khrushchev, traveled by car to Ternopol, where Kirponos, the front commander, had his command post. Already on the first day of the war Stalin was following Lenin's practice in the Civil War of sending trusted personal representatives to critical areas. For him it was not only a matter of keeping direct contact with the front and a watchful eye on unproven commanders but also a demonstration of his presence.

Shattered by the German onslaught, the Red forces fell back. Directive No. 3, sent by Stalin on the night of June 22, ordering the Southwest, the West, and the Northwest Fronts to attack, was utterly impracticable. The situation was confused and information was not reaching Moscow. Stalin himself had no conception of the speed of the German advance or the chaos in the Red Army positions.

On June 26 Stalin phoned Zhukov in Ternopol, ordering him to return to the General Headquarters at once. The enemy was approaching Minsk, and Pavlov, commanding the West Front, had evidently lost control. Kulik had disappeared and Shaposhnikov was ill. On June 28 Russian troops surrendered Minsk, the capital of Belorussia. German troops carried out a savage massacre of the inhabitants and destroyed most of the city.

Twice on June 29 Stalin came to the General Headquarters. He was in a black mood and reacted violently to the chaotic situation on the West Front. Zhukov conferred by telegraph with General Pavlov, but it was clear that the situation was hopeless. On the next day Stalin ordered Zhukov to summon Pavlov to Moscow. On his arrival Zhukov hardly recognized him; he had changed so much in the eight days of the war. Pavlov was removed from his command, and with other generals from this front, he was put on trial. All were shot.

Stalin held them responsible for the destruction of the West Front. He attached special importance to this front against which he believed the Germans would deliver their main assault. But they were, in fact, victims of the war and specifically of his own miscalculations. The most serious mistake was that the troops were not deployed in depth along the extensive western frontier with the result that the German armored divisions, advancing at speed, were able to outflank and encircle strategic positions.

The court-martial and execution of Pavlov and his senior staff also had the effect of undermining the confidence of the troops and of the people in the army's commanders. Many doubted the allegations of their treachery and feared that a new purge was being planned. This fear was increased by the decree of the Presidium of the Supreme Soviet on July 16, 1941, restoring the powers of the military kommissars. Stalin was quick to realize, however, that by this drastic action he had not stiffened morale as he had intended but had aggravated the critical uneasiness within the Red Army at a time when cool and stubborn resistance was needed. He did not repeat this mistake. In future commanders who failed were demoted, or they simply disappeared and their fate remained secret.

The need to set up military and civil command structures had been overlooked in the preparations for war. Stalin had been concentrating on the defense industries and the equipping and training of the armed forces. He personally disliked time-consuming committee work and, since all major matters came to the Politburo and finally to him for decision, he may have thought that he could dispense with supreme command organs. The outbreak of war had shown at once that many responsibilities had to be delegated.

Early on June 22, 1941, Timoshenko had submitted a draft plan to set up a High Command with Stalin as Commander in Chief. Before signing the decree on the following day, Stalin redrafted it, naming Timoshenko as Supreme Commander and establishing a General Headquarters of the High Command, which consisted of a Council of War with Timoshenko as chairman and a membership of Stalin, Molotov, Voroshilov, Budënny, Zhukov, and Kuznetsov. This arrangement, according to Zhukov, complicated the command, for there were in effect two Commanders in Chief, Timoshenko *de jure* and Stalin *de facto*.[4] The General Headquarters took the title of Stavka, the title that had been used for the tsarist supreme military headquarters. Stalin's Stavka did not,

however, have the same large support staff, but was at first merely
a group of advisers.

The General Headquarters' orders and instructions were discussed and agreed in Stalin's study in the Kremlin. It was a
large, light, austerely furnished room, paneled in stained oak, with
a long table, covered with a green cloth. Portraits of Marx, Engels,
and Lenin hung on the walls, and portraits of Suvorov and Kutuzov joined them later in the war. Stalin's desk, covered with
maps and papers, was to one side. Poskrebyshev's office adjoined
the study and next to it was a small room, occupied by security
guards. Behind the study were a lounge and signal room with all
the equipment used by Poskrebyshev to connect Stalin with the
front commanders.[5] This was the main communications center.
Stalin's office and sometimes the dacha at Kuntsevo served as the
supreme headquarters of the Soviet armed forces throughout the
war.

On June 30 the State Defense Committee (GKO) was set up. It
was the supreme organ, and its orders were executed by the Council of People's Kommissars through the machinery of the kommissariats. The Stavka, responsible for the conduct of military affairs,
was renamed the Stavka of the Supreme Command. Its council
now comprised Stalin as chairman, and Molotov, Timoshenko,
Voroshilov, Budënny, Shaposhnikov, and Zhukov as its members.
On July 19, 1941, Stalin became Kommissar for Defense, and on
August 8, 1941, he was appointed Supreme Commander in Chief
of the Armed Forces of the U.S.S.R.[6]

One of the first and most important directives of the State Defense Council (GKO), issued on July 4, was to transfer industries
to the east. The evacuation of 1,523 industrial units, many of
them enormous, including 1,360 major armament plants, was a
tremendous undertaking and in human terms a heroic achievement. But the dismantling and removal of these industries
brought an immediate drop in production. Armament shortages
were acute in the autumn of 1941 and spring of 1942. By the summer, production was reviving rapidly.

In the first fury of invasion Stalin had been taken up with the
collapse of the Soviet defenses, the organization of the High Command, and resisting the invader. For a short time he forgot the

people and the need to invoke their fighting spirit and strengthen their morale. The nation was shaken and bewildered by the sudden devastating invasion. They had believed that the Red Army would never permit an enemy onto Russian soil. Stalin himself was in some degree a victim of this propaganda. Although he knew better than anyone the weaknesses of the Red Army, he had not accepted in his heart that an invader could cross the frontiers. He had approved the *Draft Field Regulations* in 1939, which enshrined the themes that "the Soviet Union will meet any enemy attack by a smashing blow with all the might of its armed forces" and that "the military activity of the Red Army will aim at the complete destruction of the enemy and the achievement of a decisive victory at a small cost of blood."[7] This confidence had been shattered, and he knew that it was vital to rally the Russian people for the bitter ordeal ahead of them.

On July 3, twelve days after the invasion, Stalin broadcast to the nation. It was a historic speech, devoid of rhetoric, which appealed to the national pride of the people and to the sturdy Russian instinct to defend their homeland. He spoke as friend and leader, and it was this assurance that they had been waiting for. Russians everywhere and especially in the armed forces felt, as they listened, an "enormous enthusiasm and patriotic uplift." General Fedyuninsky, who was to play a distinguished role on several fronts, wrote: "We suddenly seemed to feel much stronger."[8]

"Comrades, citizens, brothers and sisters, fighters of our army and navy! I am speaking to you, my friends," were his opening words. They differed strikingly from his usual form of address, and at once united them with him. Then, with a profound instinct for the mood and needs of the people, he described their predicament, and every word burned with his own implacable will to victory.

At points Stalin exaggerated and excused, but he did not obscure the truth. "Although the enemy's finest divisions and the finest units of his air force have already been smashed and have gone to their death on the field of battle, the enemy continues to push forward." The Soviet-German Pact had been designed to give peace or at least delay the war, but Hitler had perfidiously broken their agreement and had attacked with the advantage of surprise. He would not benefit for long.

Using simple concrete language, he brought home to the people what the war would mean for them. "The enemy is cruel and implacable. He is out to seize our lands, watered by the sweat of our brows, to seize our grain and oil, secured by the labour of our hands. He is out to restore the rule of the landlords, to restore tsarism . . . to germanize [the peoples of the Soviet Union] to turn them into the slaves of the German princes and barons."

He told them bluntly that they were locked in a life-and-death struggle with a vile enemy and that they must be ruthless, utterly ruthless, in beating him. They must eradicate the chaos and panic in the rear of the lines. Then he stressed in detail the scorched-earth policy which they must follow. "In case of a forced retreat . . . all rolling stock must be evacuated, the enemy must not be left a single engine, a single railway car, a single pound of grain or gallon of fuel. The collective farmers must drive all their cattle and turn over their grain to the safe keeping of the authorities for transportation to the rear. All valuable property, including metals, grain and fuel, that cannot be withdrawn, must be destroyed without fail. . . . In areas occupied by the enemy, guerrillas, mounted and on foot, must be formed; sabotage groups must be organized to combat the enemy, to foment guerrilla warfare everywhere, blow up bridges and roads, damage telephone and telegraph lines, set fire to forests, stores and transport. In occupied regions conditions must be made unbearable for the enemy and all his accomplices. They must be hounded and annihilated at every step, and all their measures frustrated."

He expressed gratitude for the "historic utterance," made by Churchill in a prompt broadcast on the evening of June 22 when he declared: "We shall give whatever help we can to Russia and the Russian people." Stalin went on to speak of Napoleon's invasion and of Russia's victory over the French, adding that Hitler was no more invincible than Napoleon had been. Then as now the Russian people were fighting "a national patriotic war," and they were fighting for the freedom of all peoples. He called upon the Russians "to rally round the party of Lenin and Stalin."[9]

The summer of 1941 was a time of disaster. The German advance built up a terrible momentum which, it seemed, nothing could halt. The West Theater was created by Stalin on July 10 and embraced the West, Reserve, and Moscow Fronts. Timo-shenko was in command, and he found that the Germans had in a rapid pincer movement closed on Smolensk. Russian troops fought desperately, knowing that the fall of the city would leave open the way to Moscow.

Stalin flew into a fury over the fall of Smolensk on August 5, 1941. At the end of July, when the defeat was imminent, Zhukov was phoned by Poskrebyshev. "Stalin orders you and Timoshenko to come to his dacha without delay!"

Thinking they had been summoned to discuss the military situation, they were surprised to find almost all of the Politburo present. Stalin was standing in the middle of the room, wearing an old jacket and holding an unlit pipe in his hand which, Zhukov remarked, was "a sure sign of bad temper."[10]

"Now," said Stalin, "the Politburo has discussed Timoshenko's activities as commander of the West Front and decided to relieve him of his post. It proposes that Zhukov take over. What do you think of that?" he asked, turning to them.

Timoshenko was silent. Zhukov finally responded by pointing out that frequent replacement of front commanders was having a bad effect. Timoshenko had held this command for less than four weeks. He had done everything possible in the battle for Smo-lensk. The troops believed in him and it would be unjust and inexpedient to remove him at this time.

"I rather think he's right," Kalinin commented.

Stalin lit his pipe, eying the others present. "What if we agree with Zhukov?" he asked.

"You're right, Comrade Stalin," several of them chorused. "Ti-moshenko may put things right yet."

Zhukov and Timoshenko were then given permission to leave. Timoshenko was ordered to return to his front immediately.[11]

In the north the German advance was equally rapid. German troops occupied the Baltic states. On July 12, 1941, they took Pskov. Leningradtsi labored desperately to build defense works and fight off enemy attacks on the approaches to their city. By the end of August 1941 the German forces had cut Leningrad off from the rest of Russia. The morale of the people nevertheless remained high. Many of them were angry with the government, in particular with Voroshilov, Zhdanov, and Popkov, the chairman of the city's Soviet, for their shortsightedness and incompetence in preparing defenses. Some were critical, too, of the Red Army for failing to stop the German advance. The approach of the enemy and the air bombardment had apparently reduced Voroshilov to a state of panic. In September Stalin sent Zhukov to take command. He quickly brought the defenses into order. Leningrad was prepared for the long and tragic siege of winter 1941–42.

In the south the German advance was halted briefly at Lvov and other points, and then it surged forward, directly threatening Kiev. On July 29 Zhukov asked to see Stalin to make an urgent report. He was seen in the presence of Mekhlis, who was hostile to him. Zhukov spread out maps and gave a detailed survey of the situation. He then made his proposals, first to bring at least eight divisions from the Far East to strengthen the Moscow sector, and second to withdraw the Southwest Front to the east beyond the Dnieper. Stalin at once asked about Kiev. With great trepidation, knowing that his answer would provoke anger, Zhukov replied, "Kiev will have to be surrendered."

Stalin exploded. "What are you talking about? What nonsense is this? How can you think of giving up Kiev to the enemy?"

Zhukov took umbrage and replied that, if Stalin "thought that the Chief of Staff talked nonsense, then he requested his release from office and posting to the front."

"Don't be so hotheaded!" Stalin retorted. "But if that's the way you want it, we can get by without you! . . . Carry on with your job. We'll talk it over and call you."

Some forty minutes later Zhukov was summoned.

"We have talked it over and decided to release you from the duties of Chief of Staff," Stalin said. "The new Chief of Staff will be Shaposhnikov. True, his health is not too good, but we'll help him."

Stalin then asked Zhukov where he would like to go and agreed that he should take command of the counteroffensive which he had proposed on the Yelnya salient.

When Zhukov asked permission to withdraw, Stalin smiled and

invited him to sit down for a glass of tea. He valued him as a proven front commander and did not want him to go in a mood of grievance. They drank tea together, but their conversation did not flow. Zhukov's umbrage had not subsided, despite Stalin's attempts to placate him. Before they parted, however, Stalin reminded him that he was still a member of the General Headquarters of the Supreme High Command.[12]

The German High Command was agreed in August that their offensive should now be directed at Moscow. Guderian in particular claimed that a massive attack, spearheaded by his panzer divisions, would take the city. Hitler now rejected this plan and decided to turn the main German advance southwards into the Ukraine. On August 8, 1941, Guderian's group attacked the Russian Central Front near Gomel. This new advance was seen by Stalin and Shaposhnikov as part of a movement to outflank the West and Reserve Fronts and then to make a major advance from Bryansk against Moscow. On August 14 Stalin hurriedly created a new Bryansk Front, commanded by Eremenko, who had impressed him—but not Zhukov or Shaposhnikov—as an able commander. An attack from Bryansk was, in fact, what the German Commander in Chief proposed, but Hitler had not given his approval. Guderian's group was halted at the Desna River, waiting for orders to move to the east or the south. Eremenko's offensive failed, and, despite Stalin's angry messages, his troops fell back in disorder.

At the beginning of September 1941 Guderian received firm orders to advance to the south. His armored divisions moved rapidly and were soon threatening the rear of the Russian Southwest Front. Farther to the south another German force took Dnepropetrovsk, and, although Stalin had stated forcefully that the Dnieper line must be held, it crossed the river and moved northwards. Kiev was now threatened with encirclement.

On September 7, 1941, Kirponos, commanding the Southwest Front, reported the dangerous situation to Budënny and Shaposhnikov. Stalin impatiently rejected his warning. He was determined to hold Kiev and accused the front commanders of wanting to run away. Finally he gave the order for the Southwest Front to pull back to the Desna River, but he insisted that Kirponos must hold Kiev.

The order angered the front commanders, who knew the gravity of their position. Kirponos was critical of Shaposhnikov, who was "a very competent officer of the old general staff," but "he simply could not muster the courage to tell Comrade Stalin the whole truth."[13] Finally Budënny spoke by telephone with Shaposhnikov, and, failing to gain approval for a withdrawal from Kiev, he sent a signal to Stalin on September 11 protesting against Shaposhnikov's stand and stressing the danger. Budënny was at once relieved of his command. Khrushchev remained as political kommissar; evidently he had not protested as vigorously as he related subsequently. Timoshenko was appointed in Budënny's place.

On the same day (September 11), Stalin conducted a teleprint exchange with the military council of the front. He had all the facts in mind and was seeking a solution. He soon had Kirponos flustered, and he became more convinced that withdrawal was unjustified. But he did not fully understand the danger or appreciate how swiftly the German panzer divisions carried out their encirclement movements. After going over the arguments he repeated his order that Kiev must not be surrendered and bridges were not to be demolished without permission of the Stavka. He also admonished the commanders: ". . . You must stop looking for lines of retreat and start looking for lines of resistance, only resistance."[14]

Timoshenko arrived in Kiev on September 13, 1941. Three days later the Germans completed the encirclement of the city. Four Russian armies were trapped. Four generals of the front command died, and thousands of Russian troops were killed trying to break out. It was the most crushing defeat the Red Army had suffered. For the Germans it was a great tactical victory, but, as Guderian was to point out, it had the severe strategic disadvantage of delaying the German plans for taking Moscow before the winter began.[15]

Hitler's original intention had been to capture Leningrad and to occupy the Ukraine, the Donets Basin, and the Caucasus. Then Army Group Center would advance on Moscow simultaneously with Army Group North. In the first three months of the war, however, his forces made such tremendous gains that it seemed to him that Russia might collapse as ignominiously as France. He changed his plans, giving priority now to the capture of Moscow before the onset of winter. The occupation of the Russian capital would be a remarkable triumph and might bring down the Soviet government.

On October 2, 1941, Hitler issued an Order of the Day to his troops facing Moscow: "Today is the beginning of the last great decisive battle of this year." The German offensive had, in fact, already begun. Konev, commanding the West Front, had reported to the Kremlin on September 26 that a German attack was imminent. The Stavka ordered him to stand fast. The main German attack was launched from positions south of Vyazma and in the direction of Yukhnov. Communications between the Russian fronts and the Stavka were ineffective. The news, received on October 5, that German tanks were already in Yukhnov took Stalin by surprise. He had been disturbed, too, by Guderian's capture of Orel on October 2.

The advancing German forces encircled Vyazma. Stalin remained unaware of the gravity of the position until it was too late to take action. The massive setbacks and the immediate threat to Moscow would have unnerved most men, but the impact on Stalin was to strengthen his grim determination to fight. No single factor was more important in holding the nation from disintegrating at this time.

On October 5 Stalin had a teleprint conversation with Zhukov in Leningrad and ordered him back to Moscow. He was worried then by the German break-through south of Vyazma and entry into Yukhnov. He sent Zhukov to investigate the situation. On October 10 he telephoned Zhukov at the front headquarters and appointed him commander in place of Konev, who was to become his deputy. On Zhukov's suggestion, however, he agreed that Konev should take command of the Kalinin sector.

During these desperate months Stalin was constantly observing the front commanders with a suspicious appraising eye. Few of them had had adequate military training or combat experience. The most senior among them had come to prominence during the Civil War, and they had yet to master the techniques of modern warfare. Fighting against the swift and devastatingly efficient

German armies quickly exposed their weaknesses. Commanders who showed panic or indecision were to him not unfortunate men who could not stand the strain, but a danger to the country and even traitors to be dealt with accordingly. In the savagery of this struggle for survival there was no time for excuses or sympathy. He demanded of his commanders decision, courage, and positive leadership; they had to give strength to the troops who were equally untried and who on some fronts had fled in panic. At the same time, mindful of the lessons of the Civil War, he exercised close control over them, often inhibiting initiative and at times vetoing sensible action which at Kiev and other points might have avoided disaster. Several commanders were so afraid of him that they shrank from reporting setbacks, because he might hold them culpable and punish them as traitors.

Zhukov, Timoshenko, and Shaposhnikov had proved their worth and on them he relied. Zhukov and Timoshenko were of the rough sergeant-major breed, peasants in origin who had learned by experience and had become outstanding field commanders. In particular, he valued Shaposhnikov, the former tsarist officer with the clear disciplined mind, and when illness removed Shaposhnikov from the Stavka, his place was taken by Vasilevsky, who had been a staff captain in the tsarist army and who had similar ability and clarity of mind. But the fighting and defeats of the summer and winter of 1941 were also bringing forward a number of brave and competent commanders.

Stalin himself was at all times the Supreme Commander in Chief, but he was to entrust increasing authority to Zhukov and to men like Vasilevsky, Malinovsky, Rokossovsky, Vatutin, and Bagramian.

As the enemy closed on Moscow, fear gripped the city. Already on October 12–13 the State Defense Committee had ordered the evacuation to the east of many government offices, scientific and cultural organizations, and the diplomatic corps. By the end of the month some 2 million people had gone from the city. Air raids had started in July and had continued, but confident that they would soon take Moscow, the Germans did not press their air attacks.

Within the city the people grew more desperate as they learned of the enemy approach. The mass evacuations and fear of German occupation brought a mood of panic. People stampeded at the railway stations, trying to board any train to the east, and sought other means of escape. And the widespread rumors that Stalin and the Politburo had already fled the city raised the panic to a climax.

On October 17 the secretary of the Central Committee broadcast to the nation that Stalin himself was in Moscow, and he sternly denounced rumors that Moscow would be surrendered. On October 19 a state of siege was proclaimed. Spies, diversionists, and panic-mongers were liable to be brought before special NKVD tribunals and summarily punished. Stalin's presence, and the fact that the German advance was slowing down, helped to restore order.

On November 6, 1941, Stalin addressed the delegates attending a special celebration of the twenty-fourth anniversary of the Revolution, held this year underground in the Mayakovsky Station of the Moscow Metro, secure from air raids. His speech was broadcast and promptly published. He did not address the people frequently; a speech by him was a special event, particularly at this time, when the capital was in danger.

The *Blitzkrieg* had already failed in Russia, he declared. He expressed supreme confidence in the strength of the Red Army and the resistance of the Russian people. The reverses suffered had been due to the perfidious breach of the Soviet-German Pact and the unexpectedness of the German attack. Another reason for the Russian setbacks was their shortage of tanks and aircraft, and he called for massive increases in production.

Soviet Russia was not alone in the war against Hitlerite Germany, he declared. Britain and the United States had expressed their support. They were not yet real allies. "One of the reasons for the reverses of the Red Army is the absence of a second front in Europe against the German-Fascist troops," he said. "The fact of the matter is that at present no armies of Great Britain or the United States of America are on the European continent, waging war against the German-Fascist troops, and so the Germans are not required to split up their forces and fight on two fronts in the West and the East. . . . The situation at present is that our country is carrying on the work of liberation single-handed without any military assistance against the combined forces of the Germans, Finns, Rumanians, Italians, and Hungarians."[16]

Denouncing the Nazis as imperialists, Stalin spoke with angry scorn of German arrogance, the strident *Übermensch* propaganda, and the savage, often bestial, treatment of prisoners. He proclaimed the greatness of Russia in words which appealed to the patriotism of his countrymen and sharpened their hatred of the enemy.

"And it is these people without honour or conscience, these people with the morality of animals, who have the effrontery to call for the extermination of the great Russian nation—the nation of Plekhanov and Lenin, of Belinsky and Chernyshevsky, of Pushkin and Tolstoy, of Gorki and Chekhov, of Glinka and Chaikovsky, of Sechenev and Pavlov, of Repin and Sigrikov, of Suvorov and Kutuzov! The German invaders want a war of extermination against the peoples of the Soviet Union. Very well then! If they want a war of extermination, they shall have it! Our task now . . . will be to destroy every German to the very last man who has come to occupy our country. No mercy for the German invaders! Death to the German invaders!"[17]

On the following morning Stalin reviewed the traditional parade on Red Square. The troops whom he addressed were on their way to the front. The distant thunder of artillery to the west gave his speech a dramatic immediacy. Again he was appealing to the patriotism of the people. They were fighting for Russia, their homeland, and the enemy was approaching the gates of Moscow, the mother of ancient Muscovy and the capital of Soviet Russia.

"The war which you are fighting," he declared, "is a war of liberation, a just war! May you be inspired in this war by the heroic examples of our great ancestors. . . . May the victorious banner of the great Lenin inspire you! Death to the German invaders! Long live our glorious country, its freedom, its independence! Under the banner of Lenin—forward to victory!"[18]

Stalin was speaking with passion and sincerity. Far from appealing to the love of Russians for their country as an expedient to rally them in defense of the party and the regime, he was speaking from the depth of his being. Soviet Russia was Holy Russia, and Moscow was Matushka Moskva. Russia was his country, and he believed that the harsh years of building and reconstruction and now the savagery of war would in due course yield victory to the Russian people in the form of justice, freedom, and prosperity.

The texts of the two speeches circulated rapidly among the troops and civilians. Aircraft dropped copies in occupied territory. Every Russian read them avidly. They brought a dramatic and extraordinary uplift in the morale of the troops and of the civilian population. The upsurge of national feeling and the veneration of Stalin were inseparable. He had given expression to their love for their native soil and their hatred of the cruel and arrogant enemy.

The British and American support to which Stalin had referred in his speech of November 6, 1941, had been followed promptly with offers of help. A British military mission flew to Moscow. Stalin and Molotov discussed with the British ambassador the terms of an Anglo-Soviet declaration. But in his speech of July 3 and in his first letter to Churchill, Stalin sounded the theme which was to dominate and overcloud relations with the Allies: A second front should be opened on the continent without delay. Churchill explained in his reply that this demand was unrealistic. He made a number of proposals, including the basing of British fighter squadrons near Murmansk, naval operations in the Arctic, and the shipping of aircraft, munitions, and other supplies to Russia. Stalin demanded more. His attitude was that Russia was fighting the war alone and Britain, her only ally at this stage, owed her help.

Underlying his relations with Churchill was his continuing mistrust of the British. Churchill was, of course, quite different from the perfidious Chamberlain, and the British government had discarded the policy of securing peace in the west by encouraging Hitler to wage war in the east. But Stalin saw the British as a subtle and devious people. Among the Soviet forces and the people, too, the belief was that the British were saving their men and leaving the Russians to do all the fighting.

As winter approached in 1941 the question on the minds of Churchill and Roosevelt was how long Russia could stave off defeat and collapse. British and American military opinion, with only a few dissenting voices, was that Russian resistance would soon be crushed. It was to form his own view that Harry Hopkins arrived in Moscow on July 30, 1941, as Roosevelt's personal representative. Hopkins, the President's closest adviser, was an extraordinary man. Frail and ill but with a personal dynamism, a trenchant mind, and complete dedication to the Allied cause, he quickly reached a close understanding with Stalin. He was to play a major role in future relations.

His first meeting with Stalin at this time of disaster on all Russian fronts, when Western leaders were daily expecting news of Russia's collapse, made a strong impression on Hopkins:

> He welcomed me with a few swift words in Russian. He shook my hand briefly, firmly, courteously. He smiled warmly. There was no waste of word, gesture, or mannerism. It was like talking to a perfectly-coordinated machine, an intelligent machine. The questions he asked were clear, concise, direct. . . . His answers were ready, unequivocal, spoken as if the man had had them on his tongue for years. . . . If he is always as I heard him, he never wastes a syllable. If he wants to soften an abrupt answer . . . he does it with that quick, managed smile . . . a smile that can be cold but friendly, austere but warm. He curries no favour with you. He seems to have no doubt. He assures you that Russia will stand against the onslaught of the German army. He takes it for granted that you have no doubts either. . . . He laughs often enough, but it's a short laugh, somewhat sardonic perhaps. There is no small talk in him. His humour is keen, penetrating. . . .
>
> No man could forget the picture of the dictator of Russia as he stood watching me leave—an austere, rugged, determined figure in boots that shone like mirrors, stout baggy trousers, and snug-fitting blouse. He wore no ornament, military or civilian. He's built close to the ground, like a football coach's dream of a tackle. He's about five feet six, about a hundred and ninety pounds. His hands are huge, as hard as his mind. His voice is harsh, but ever under control. What he says is all the accent and inflection his words need.[19]

Stalin gave Hopkins an optimistic picture of the Russian positions. He forecast that the fronts would be stabilized before Moscow, Leningrad, and Kiev by the beginning of October at the latest. His assurance to Hopkins that Kiev would be held was probably a factor in the disastrous decision to forbid an early withdrawal from the city. His estimate of the situation may have contained an element of bluff or it may simply have reflected his refusal to accept the prospect of further major defeats. He was under severe strain at this time, and Hopkins noted that he was chain-smoking during their meeting of almost four hours.

Hopkins was profoundly impressed by Stalin as a man and by his determination to wage the war to the end. "Give us anti-aircraft guns and aluminium, and we can fight for three or four years," Stalin had said. Writing to Churchill early in September 1941, however, Stalin frankly expressed his deep anxieties. The loss of Krivoi Rog and other places "has confronted the Soviet Union with mortal danger. . . . The only way out of this more than unfavourable position is to open a second front this year somewhere in the Balkans or in France . . . and simultaneously supply the Soviet Union with 30,000 tons of aluminium by the beginning of October and a minimum monthly aid of 400 aeroplanes and 500 tanks (small or medium).

"Without these two kinds of aid the Soviet Union will be either defeated or weakened to the extent that it will lose for a long time its ability to help its allies by active operations at the front against Hitlerism."[20]

A few days later he wrote that, if a second front was not possible at present, Britain should land twenty-six to thirty divisions at Archangel or in the south to fight the common enemy.[21] The suggestion of British troops on Russian soil could only have been made in a mood of desperation.

Hopkins' report led to meetings in Moscow to discuss "apportionment of our joint resources," at which Lord Beaverbrook represented Churchill and Averell Harriman represented Roosevelt. The meetings with Stalin started on September 28 as the German offensive burst against Moscow. The discussions at the first meeting were cordial. The second meeting was difficult. Harriman noted that "Stalin seemed discourteous and at times not interested, and rode us pretty hard." Of this two-hour meeting Beaverbrook wrote: "Stalin was very restless, walking about and smoking continuously, and appeared to both of us to be under intense strain."[22] At this very time Vyazma was being encircled and Guderian's panzer group was taking Orel, both devastating setbacks.

The third meeting was again cordial. The Russian demands for equipment, machinery, and raw materials were almost totally agreed. Beaverbrook, always ebullient and an outspoken supporter of all aid to Russia and even of an early second front, infected the meeting with his enthusiasm. His pro-Russian outlook and his admiration and confidence in Stalin made him a welcome guest.[23]

The offensive against Moscow came to a halt early in October 1941. At once the Germans prepared for a second onslaught. They were war-weary and ill equipped for the Russian winter, but they were also brave and disciplined. The Russians frantically strengthened their defenses and brought up reserves. Within fourteen days 100,000 officers and men, 300 tanks, and 2,000 guns were moved into position. On both sides there was a grim determination to win this battle.

At one stage during these defense preparations Zhukov reported to Stalin that the enemy were concentrating forces against the Volokolamsk sector. Stalin at once ordered counterblows. He could not endure waiting for the enemy to attack; he had to take action. Zhukov protested that counterblows would disrupt the defense preparations in the sector and would have no impact on the already-strengthened enemy positions. Stalin was adamant. The attacks were made and failed.

On October 13, 1941, heavy fighting began on all the main routes to Moscow. In places the enemy came within fifteen miles of the city. On October 17 Shaposhnikov and the general staff were evacuated from Moscow. Stalin remained with two assistants, Vasilevsky and Shtemenko. Like everyone left in the city, Stalin was acutely worried by the apparently irresistible advance of the Germans. He telephoned Zhukov at the front. "Are you sure we'll be able to hold Moscow?" he said. "It hurts me to ask you. Answer me truthfully, as a Communist."

"We'll hold Moscow by all means," Zhukov replied, "but we'll need at least two more armies and another 200 tanks."

"It's good that you are so confident," Stalin responded. "Phone the General Staff and arrange for the assignment of the two reserve armies you're asking for. They'll be ready by late November. But we have no tanks yet."[24]

By the end of October the German advance was slowing to a

halt, but on November 15, 1941, they launched a new offensive, advancing almost to the outskirts of the city. They advanced no farther.

Stalin showed marked signs of stress towards the end of November. He was ill tempered and refused to listen to his front commanders. On November 30 he telephoned Zhukov, asking if he knew that Dedovsk, a town twenty miles to the west, had been captured. When Zhukov answered that he did not know, Stalin snapped that the commanding general should know all that was happening on his front. He ordered him to take command of a counterattack to recover the town. Zhukov made urgent inquiries and learned that not Dedovsk but an insignificant village, called Dedovo, had been occupied. He telephoned to explain the mistake. Stalin was furious and would not listen. He ordered Zhukov, Rokossovsky, and Govorov, both front commanders, to take personal command of a rifle company and two tanks to retake the village.[25]

As soon as the German attack came to a standstill, Stalin, Zhukov, and Timoshenko at once began planning a winter counteroffensive. On November 29 Zhukov telephoned Stalin to make his report on the situation on the West Front. He then requested two reserve armies to enable him to push the enemy from their advance positions in the north and south of the front. Stalin questioned whether the Germans might not be holding reserves ready to defend these positions. Zhukov assured him that they had been "bled white." Stalin said he would discuss the proposal. A few hours later Zhukov learned that not two but three armies were being transferred to his command and that he was to report his plans next day. According to Zhukov, this was the start of the planning of a massive counterattack on the Moscow front.

In the early hours of November 30 Stalin telephoned Zhukov and proposed that the whole of the West Front should go over to the offensive. Zhukov expressed concern about lack of air support and of tanks, especially the new T-34 tank, which had proved its superiority. Stalin replied that he could not have tanks, but that he should at once arrange for stronger air support. Meanwhile Timoshenko had attacked and recovered Rostov. With Stalin's ready approval he was preparing to attack the flank of the German center. Zhukov reported his plan of attack to Vasilevsky, and Stalin gave his immediate agreement.

At this time Konev, commanding the Kalinin Front, was causing Stalin concern. He was not showing an offensive spirit, and he raised objections to the proposed counterattack. Stalin expressed himself strongly by telephone and told him to stop his hair-splitting tactics and to get on with the offensive. On December 1, 1941, at 0330 hours Stalin and Vasilevsky signed the orders to the Kalinin Front. Three days later Vasilevsky, as Stalin's personal representative, was at Konev's side at the front headquarters to ensure that he carried out the offensive with full determination.

On December 2 Stalin received General Anders, a Pole who had served in the tsarist army and who had been held until recently in prison by the NKVD. Anders' task was to recruit a Polish army to fight alongside the Russians. It was a plan that Stalin had accepted with reluctance; he could never trust Poles. He received Anders courteously but without the warmth that he had shown Hopkins or was to show to Anthony Eden two weeks later. Eden found him more relaxed and without the signs of strain he had noticed in the previous September, when the crucial struggle for Moscow was drawing near.

The winter counteroffensive, launched on December 4–5, was strikingly successful at first. By mid-January 1942 the Germans had been hurled back from Moscow, in some places as far as two hundred miles. The Red Army was hampered, however, by shortages of tanks and motorized transport, and in the severe winter weather their advance slowed down.

The Battle of Moscow had been an epic event. Zhukov considered that it marked the turning point in the war.[26] It had involved more than 2 million men, 2,500 tanks, 1,800 aircraft, and 25,000 guns. Casualties had been horrifying in scale. For the Russians it had ended in victory. They had suffered the full impact of the German *Blitzkrieg* offensive, and, notwithstanding their losses and the acute shortages of equipment, they had been able to mount an effective counterattack. They had begun to destroy the myth of German invincibility that had been undermining morale. They had, moreover, relieved Moscow.

Stalin had been impatient to go over to the offensive. He

worried about the fighting spirit of his commanders. Any weakness on their part would quickly infect the troops. Often his demands for attack were unrealistic and even dangerous. He considered the myth of the invincible invader more dangerous. He believed in hurling fresh troops into battle, for only then would they learn that they could beat the Germans. When, towards the end of February 1942, Zhukov's advance was stopped by enemy resistance, he proposed breaking off the offensive and consolidating his positions. Stalin responded with the order: "Attack! If you have no results today, you will tomorrow; even if you achieve nothing except the pinning down of the enemy, the result will be felt elsewhere."[27]

At a meeting of the State Committee of Defense on January 5 (1942) Shaposhnikov, recovered from his illness and again serving as Chief of Staff, outlined the plans for an immediate, grand counteroffensive from Leningrad in the north to the Black Sea in the south. It was Stalin's plan. "The Germans are taken aback after their defeat before Moscow. They have prepared badly for the winter. Now is the time to take the general offensive!" he said.[28] Zhukov and others expressed misgivings. Stalin would not listen. He said that he had discussed the offensive with Timoshenko, who was in favor of it, and he added: "We must pound the Germans to pieces as soon as possible so that they won't be able to mount an offensive in the spring."[29]

An immediate counteroffensive on all fronts was an exceedingly bold undertaking. The official Soviet history of the war, written while Khrushchev was in power, was critical of this grand design without mentioning Stalin by name. It was overambitious. "The army still lacked the organizational experience and knowledge for an offensive operation on such a large scale."[30]

Stalin had overruled such criticisms at the meeting of the State Defense Committee. If the Army lacked knowledge and experience of mounting massive offensives, it had to learn now in the furnace of war. If the plan was overambitious, it was also a reflection of his leadership and outlook; he thought and planned on a grand scale. He was obsessed, too, with the need to drive his commanders and troops to attack and to learn to crush the enemy. He infected them with his iron determination to clear the invader from Russian soil.

The counteroffensive brought results. On the Leningrad and Moscow Fronts the Russian gains, although small in area, were important in relieving the two cities of immediate danger. The new lines were stabilized by the spring of 1942, and the Germans did not succeed at any time during the war in advancing beyond these lines.

As spring approached in 1942 Stalin and the general staff were convinced that the main enemy objective would be the capture of Moscow. Shaposhnikov urged Stalin to build up reserves by adopting a policy of strategic defense. Stalin agreed, but he could not desist from attack, and indeed he approved several major offensives.

Hitler had, in fact, decided not to renew his offensive against Moscow. His plan was now to attack to the north from the area of Kursk and then to drive eastwards towards Voronezh. In order to mislead the Soviet High Command, false information was given out that the German spring offensive would be on Moscow.

In March 1942 Timoshenko put forward a plan for a major offensive against the enemy concentrated near Kharkov, with the objective of driving the enemy from the Ukraine as far westwards as Kiev. Shaposhnikov and the general staff condemned the plan. Stalin nevertheless authorized Timoshenko to carry out as much of it as he could, using only his own resources. He overruled Shaposhnikov's objections and asked if he really meant that they should stand still, waiting for the enemy to attack first. Zhukov sided with Shaposhnikov, while stressing still that the one offensive should be undertaken by the West Front. Vasilevsky agreed strongly with Shaposhnikov, stating later that Stalin's strategy involved a disastrous dissipation of forces. He wrote, "Many might rightly censure the general staff for failing to tell Stalin the negative consequences of his plans, but would do so only if they did not know the difficult conditions under which the general staff had to work."[31] He added that the lesson learned was applied with benefit in the following year at Kursk. Meanwhile in the midst of conflicting views, a decision had to be taken. Stalin supported the attacking strategy and allowed Timoshenko to go ahead with his plan. It was a disastrous decision.

The summer of 1942 was to be a time of terrible defeats in the south. After the capture of Kiev in September 1941 the Germans had swept eastwards, occupying the whole of Western Ukraine, and most of the Crimean Peninsula, except for Sevastopol, which lay under siege. Stalin was eager to relieve Sevastopol. In March he sent Mekhlis, head of the Main Political Administration of the Red Army, to the Crimea. He trusted Mekhlis, who was hated, however, by all Red Army officers, and especially for his activities during the purge. Arriving at the headquarters of Kozlov, the front's commander, Mekhlis at once replaced Tolbukhin, the front's Chief of Staff, and according to Shtemenko, "true to his usual practice, instead of helping, he began capriciously to shuffle round other senior commanders and staff."[32] Instead of preparing defenses and planning to resume the offensive, Kozlov and Mekhlis "wasted time on lengthy and fruitless sessions of the War Council."[33] On May 8, the day of the German attack, Mekhlis sent a telegram to Stalin, beginning: "This is not the time to complain, but I must report so that the Stavka will know the front commander for what he is" and went on to state that the unpreparedness of the front was wholly Kozlov's responsibility. Stalin had no time for such disclaimers. "You are adopting the strange position of a detached observer, who accepts no responsibility for the affairs of the Krimfront [Crimean Front]," he replied. "That is a very comfortable position, but one which absolutely stinks. On the Crimean Front, you—you—are no detached onlooker, but a responsible representative of the Stavka, responsible for all the successes and failures of the Front and obliged to correct errors by the command on the spot."[34]

Attacked by Manstein's Eleventh Army on May 8, Kozlov's Crimean Front was routed. A further setback was the surrender of Sevastopol on July 4, 1942. This followed only after savage fighting which cost the Germans 24,000 lives and even higher casualties on the Russian side. Rather than surrender, officers and kommissars committed suicide; and in the caves in the overhanging cliffs the defenders, with the women and children taking refuge there, blew themselves up. It was a heroic, tragic defeat.

The failure of the Crimean Front and the surrender of Sevastopol infuriated Stalin. He recalled Mekhlis to Moscow, severely reprimanded and demoted him. Kozlov, two army commanders, and other officers of the front were not again entrusted with commands.

The German strategy was now to drive eastwards. The capture of Stalingrad was not at this stage an objective, but Hitler demanded that his forces should reach the city "or at least control the area by the fire of heavy weapons."[35]

On June 28, 1942, Army Group South attacked, forcing a gap between the Russian Bryansk and Southwest Fronts, and moving rapidly towards Voronezh. The Germans met with stubborn resistance. But they did not press their attack on Voronezh, and, turning southwards, moved down the right bank of the Don towards Stalingrad.

Replacement of the commanders of the Bryansk and Voronezh Fronts had become necessary. Discussion of the new appointments took place in Stalin's Kremlin office. Vasilevsky, newly appointed Chief of Staff in place of Shaposhnikov, who had been finally incapacitated by illness, and Vatutin, his deputy, were present. It was at once agreed that Rokossovsky should take command of the Bryansk Front. Stalin rejected the names proposed for the Voronezh Front. There was a long silence as all tried to think of a suitable commander. Suddenly Vatutin stood to attention. "Comrade Stalin, nominate me to command the Voronezh Front," he said. Stalin showed complete surprise. "What, you?" he exclaimed, and frowned. Vatutin, a lieutenant general of artillery, had joined the Red Army in 1920 and had not held a command except briefly during the Battle of Moscow. Finally, breaking his silence and turning to Vasilevsky, Stalin asked, "What do you think?" Vasilevsky spoke up for Vatutin. After further thought Stalin said reluctantly to Vatutin: "If Comrade Vasilevsky is satisfied with you, I will not oppose it." Vatutin was to serve with great distinction as a front commander.[36]

To the south the enemy groups advanced rapidly. Timoshenko's Southwest Front and Malinovsky's South Front made hurried withdrawals to avoid encirclement. Stalin had learned from his mistakes of the previous year in ordering Soviet forces to stand fast at Kiev and Vyazma.

By the end of July 1942, the Germans had conquered the whole of the Donbas, the source of 60 per cent of Soviet coal and the center of the southern industrial region. The loss of this region filled the nation with despair. The people had been told repeatedly after the Battle of Moscow that the enemy had been exhausted and that the Red Army would now go over to the offensive and drive out the invader. But still the Germans advanced, and now they were approaching Stalingrad. What appalled the Russian people most, however, was the news, which circulated rapidly, that at Rostov, Novocherkassk, and elsewhere officers and men of the Red Army had run away when attacked, abandoning their weapons and equipment. Severe disciplinary measures were enforced. Many were shot for desertion or flight in the face of the enemy, and generals and other officers were demoted and punished.

Strong criticism of the Red Army appeared in the press and was heard everywhere. The Army had always been held up as the pride of the nation, but now officers and troops were made to feel the bitter disappointment of their countrymen whom they had failed. At the same time, while there was a general call for iron discipline and sacrifice, strenuous efforts were made to raise the status of officers and to appeal to their honor and patriotism. The need to build up a corps of officers, carefully selected and trained, who could give leadership, was constantly in the forefront of Stalin's mind. The Orders of Alexander Nevsky, of Suvorov, and of Kutuzov were instituted as decorations for officers only. The old revolutionary ideals of officers and men being equal comrades and of soldiers' committees running the Army had long ago been discarded. But on October 9, 1942, Stalin took the step of abolishing the system of dual command whereby the political kommissars countersigned the commanders' orders. Kommissars were warned against indiscriminately shooting troops for cowardice or disobeying orders, and were told to limit themselves to political work. The enforcement of discipline was a matter for officers, not for kommissars. The relationship of officers and men was now based on the best traditions of the tsarist army.

In the midst of the exhortations to officers and men to fight to the death in defense of their motherland, Stalin's Order of the Day—"Soviet Soldiers! Not a step back!"—made a deep impact. The order was read out to the troops on all fronts. Ilya Ehrenburg wrote:

> It was not about decorations but about the indisciplined abandoning of Rostov and Novocherkassk, about confusion and panic; things could not go on like this; it was time everyone came to their senses. "Not a step back!" Never before had Stalin spoken with such frankness and it created an enormous impression. A *Red Star* war correspondent said to me: "A father tells his children: 'We are ruined; we must learn to live differently now.' There was neither irony nor admiration in the way he uttered the word 'Father'; it sounded like a plain statement of fact."[37]

A new Stalingrad Front was created on July 12, 1942. The German advance continued, but more slowly as Russian resistance stiffened. Early in August, forces from Army Group South reached the outer defense ring of the city, and ten days later the German Sixth Army, commanded by Paulus, was ready to cross the Don. By August 14, 1942, the whole of the territory within the Don bend was in German hands, except for isolated Russian bridgeheads in the north. German forces were now advancing on Stalingrad from the south, the northwest, and the north.

At this time of crisis Churchill arrived in Moscow for his first meeting with Stalin. He had made the journey primarily because he felt a duty to give the news personally that there would be no second front in the west in 1942. "It was," he wrote, "like carrying a large lump of ice to the North Pole." He was also keenly interested in meeting Stalin and visiting "this sullen, sinister Bolshevik State."[38]

Stalin was curious to meet Churchill, an avowed enemy of Soviet Russia, who had actively promoted the Allied intervention twenty-three years earlier. The meeting brought together two men of contrasting background and outlook. Churchill, descendant of the Duke of Marlborough and popularly elected war leader with great histrionic talents, reveled in the high drama of war, while hating the suffering and sacrifices which it brought. Stalin, coming from the humblest origins, had by ruthless ability become the national leader, Supreme Commander in Chief, and father of the Russian people. For him war was part of the savage struggle he had always known in Russia. He accepted as inevitable the terrible casualties. The Russian land was being ravaged and Russia was fighting for survival. It was a predicament that Britain, sheltered by the sea, had not known for centuries.

The first meeting, which lasted four hours, took place on August 12, 1942. Stalin, Molotov, and Voroshilov faced Churchill, Harriman, the President's representative, and the British ambassador. The first two hours were "bleak and sombre."[39] Frowning, Stalin listened to Churchill's careful explanation why the British and Americans could not attempt a landing on the French coast before 1943. Stalin rejected the explanation. He thought of Britain and the United States as the two most highly industrialized nations in the world, and both had powerful navies. If the Russian defense industries—so recently established, and many of them uprooted and evacuated since the war began—could overcome seemingly insuperable obstacles and turn out tanks and weapons in increasing quantities, surely these two industrial giants could achieve the output needed for a landing on the coast of France. He was convinced that they could do it, if, that is, their hearts were in it. Again his suspicion grew that the devious British were prevaricating and leaving the fighting to the Russians: They would act when the Germans had been weakened on the eastern front.

Angrily he asked Churchill why the British were so afraid of the Germans. Troops must be blooded in battle. He rejected Churchill's comment that Hitler had not invaded England because of the hazards of the operation. He suspected that British caution was grounded in fear of heavy casualties. Churchill and his generation were haunted by their losses of men in World War I. It was not an argument likely to move Stalin, who was keenly aware of the far greater Russian casualties in World War I and the even greater casualties suffered since the German invasion, which continued as they talked.

Churchill then revealed details, still secret, of the offensive which the British and Americans were planning in the Mediterranean, known as Operation Torch. Stalin listened intently and with growing excitement. "May God prosper this undertaking," he said. He asked questions and gave a concise summary of the importance of the operation. "I was deeply impressed with this remarkable statement," Churchill wrote. "It showed the Russian Dictator's swift and complete mastery of a problem hitherto novel to him. Very few people alive could have comprehended in so few minutes the reasons which we had all so long been wrestling with. He saw it all in a flash."[40]

At their meeting on the following evening there were further recriminations over the Second Front. A long aide-mémoire, signed by Stalin, accused the Allies of failing to honor their undertaking to make a landing on the French coast in 1942. Stalin asserted that the British Army was afraid of the Germans. Churchill became very angry and delivered a heated defense of his countrymen. Before his speech could be translated, Stalin, unbending, declared that he liked the spirit of Churchill's reply. There were many sharp exchanges, but also many signs of the warm comradeship that was developing between them.

Stalin repeatedly revealed a teasing sense of humor. When, in telling him about Operation Torch, Churchill stressed the vital need for secrecy, Stalin grinned and said that he hoped nothing about it would appear in the British press. Molotov was the embarrassed butt of a joke by Churchill, who referred to him going off from Washington to New York for a day by himself. Stalin laughed merrily. "It was not to New York he went," he said. "He went to Chicago where the other gangsters live."[41] Churchill spoke of the Duke of Marlborough's genius as a military leader who had put an end to a menace to Europe's freedom, a menace as great as Hitler's. Stalin listened and then remarked mischievously: "I think England had a greater general in Wellington, who defeated Napoleon, the greatest menace of all time." He went on to display considerable knowledge of the Napoleonic wars and especially of Wellington's Spanish campaign, which was directly relevant to the Second Front, now demanded by the Russians.[42]

After an official dinner in the Kremlin on August 14, 1942, there was a more informal final meeting on the following evening. Churchill was saying good-bye when Stalin proposed that they go to his apartment for a farewell drink. He led the way along corridors into a narrow street, still within the Kremlin, and into another building, followed by Churchill and A. H. Birse, the British interpreter, and two or three NKVD guards. Stalin's apartment comprised a dining room, work room, bedroom, and a large bathroom, all very simply furnished. There was no trace of luxury. An elderly housekeeper in white overalls, wearing a head scarf, was setting the table. Svetlana, Stalin's daughter, then aged fifteen, entered the room, kissed her father, and was presented to Churchill. He noted that Stalin "looked at me with a twinkle in his eye, as if, so I thought, to convey, 'You see, even we Bolsheviks have family life.' "[48] Molotov joined them and it was 2:30 A.M. when the homely, pleasant occasion came to an end. At dawn Churchill flew from Moscow to return to London.

26

Russian Recovery November 1942– December 1943

As the battle for Stalingrad approached, Hitler began to ascribe to the city an importance far transcending its strategic and economic value. It was Stalin's city, the symbol of Soviet Russia. He became so obsessed with the capture of Stalingrad and with the humiliation and defeat of his great foe that he lost sight of his grand strategy. He angrily rejected the advice of his Chief of Staff to break off the offensive before winter began. He was deaf to reason, and he exposed his armies in the east to a disastrous defeat which was the start of Germany's collapse.

Stalin insisted that Stalingrad must be held. He may have seen it as the symbol of his own authority. He may have feared, too, that after the long succession of defeats, relieved only by the Battle of Moscow, the fall of Stalingrad would seriously damage Russian morale at the fronts and in the rear. But the chief reason for his determination to hold Stalingrad was strategic. He was convinced that the capture of the city was part of a German plan to envelop Moscow from the east, cutting the capital off from the

Volga and the Urals, and by taking it to end the war in 1942. The German drive to seize the oil centers of Grozny and Baku was, he believed, mainly intended to distract the Russian Stavka from the defense of Moscow. In fact, he misjudged Hitler's intentions and for some time remained unaware that the assault on Moscow had been postponed.

On August 23, 1942, the Germans began the final stage of their attack on Stalingrad. Stalin was tense and ill tempered at this time. He was evidently plagued with doubts about the fighting spirit and the competence of the city's defenders. He sent a radio message to Eremenko, calling on him to stand firm: "The enemy forces involved are not large and you have sufficient resources to annihilate them; concentrate the air forces of both fronts; mobilize the armoured trains and bring them forward on the city loop line; lay smoke to confuse the enemy and strike home by night and by day, using every gun and rocket launcher that you have. Above all, do not give way to panic! Have no fear of this insolent foe and do not lose faith in victory!"[1]

At the time when this message was sent Stalingrad was already ablaze from incendiary bombs. Communications between the Front and Moscow were disrupted. Vasilevsky, sent as the Stavka representative to oversee operations, was unable to telephone Stalin with his daily report on August 23. When, on the night of August 24, he got through, he met with a spate of "insulting, painful, and mostly undeserved abuse, directed not only at the Chief of General Staff but at all Red Army Commanders." Vasilevsky had difficulty in convincing the Supreme Commander that the city was still in Russian hands.

In this mood of mistrust of his front commanders, Stalin recalled Zhukov from the West Front and on August 27 appointed him Deputy Supreme Commander. At this time the crucial southwest part of the Stalingrad Front was, it seems, removed from the control of Eremenko and Khrushchev and brought under Moscow's direction.

Fighting with great bravery and determination, the Germans pressed forward. They met with heroic resistance by the Russian defenders. Shortages of weapons and equipment had contributed to past Russian defeats, but by the end of the summer an increasing flow of armaments was coming from the factories beyond the Urals. Reserves of troops were also massing to the east of the Volga. The invaders, far from Germany, were now beginning to suffer from shortages, and their ranks were being decimated in the savage fighting.

On September 13, 1942, the Germans made an attempt to capture Mamai Hill at the center of the city. The plight of the Russian defenders was critical. Stalin at once ordered Rodimtsev's 13th Guards Division into action. Rodimtsev's men pushed back the enemy and recaptured Mamai Hill.

Stalin followed the battle closely. He had daily reports from Zhukov and other commanders at the front. He authorized the bringing up of reinforcements and ordered counterattacks. On September 12 he called Zhukov to Moscow to discuss the situation. Zhukov reported on the strength of the enemy positions, and Vasilevsky spoke about the fresh German units arriving in the Stalingrad sector from the Kotelnikovo direction.

"What does the Stalingrad Front require to be able to smash the enemy corridor and join the Southwestern Front?" Stalin asked.

"A minimum of one more fully-fledged combined army and tank corps, three tank brigades, and at least 400 howitzers. Besides, for the time of the operation an additional concentration of not less than one air army is necessary," Zhukov replied. Vasilevsky agreed with his estimate.

Stalin listened carefully. They were men whose views he respected. He took out the map, showing the positions of the General Headquarters' reserves, and studied it in silence.

Zhukov and Vasilevsky stepped away from the desk and, speaking quietly, agreed that apparently they would have to find "some other solution."

"And what other solution?" Stalin asked suddenly, looking up from the map.

Zhukov was taken by surprise, not realizing that he had such acute hearing. They went back to the desk and talked briefly about a large-scale operation. Then Stalin sent them away to the general staff to produce a plan and to report to him at nine the next evening.

Working through possible variations of strategy, Zhukov and Vasilevsky finally agreed on a plan. It was to continue wearing down the enemy by active defense at Stalingrad, while preparing a massive counteroffensive.

Next evening, shaking hands with them on their arrival in his office, Stalin exclaimed angrily: "While hundreds of thousands of Soviet people are giving their lives in the struggle against fascism, Churchill is bargaining over a score of Hurricanes. And these Hurricanes of his are junk—our pilots don't like them!" And then he continued calmly in the same breath, "Well, what are your views? Who's going to report?"[2]

This was, according to Zhukov's account, supported by Vasilevsky, the beginning of the great counteroffensive, called Operation Uranus. It was planned as a pincer movement by two main armored thrusts, one from the north by Vatutin's Southwest Front and Rokossovsky's Don Front, and the other from the south by Eremenko's Stalingrad Front.

Zhukov and Vasilevsky flew between the Volga-Don region and Moscow to consult with Stalin and in the later stages of the planning to brief the front commanders. In the course of some sixty days from the conception of the plan the Russians concentrated in the Stalingrad-Don area a total of a million men, supported by 13,500 guns and mortars, and over three hundred rocket batteries, as well as some 1,100 aircraft.[3] It was a brilliant feat of planning and organization, carried out by Zhukov and Vasilevsky, under the active direction of Stalin at every stage; it was crowned by a resounding victory.

Stalin maintained personal control over the organization and reserves of the Air Force. All tactical air forces had been transferred from the ground armies to the fronts early in the summer of 1942. Increasingly, however, the air forces of the fronts were combined for special air strikes, and the Stavka's representative, overseeing these operations, made a personal report to Stalin daily. Stavka air reserves were limited at first, but Stalin carefully built them up. Nikitin, a deputy commander in chief of the Air Force, wrote that Stalin kept a check on aircraft production, "daily noting in his own notebook" the deliveries of new planes. He personally allocated equipment to air forces. Having witnessed the effectiveness of the Luftwaffe, he attached the greatest importance to the air support for the Stalingrad offensive. Only five days before the operation was to begin, he was prepared to suspend it temporarily, if the Air Force was not yet adequate in strength.[4]

Zhukov and Vasilevsky were assigned to co-ordinate the fronts for the offensive. On November 17, 1942, however, Stalin withdrew Zhukov and sent him to prepare offensives to be made in the north by the Kalinin and West Fronts, and designed to prevent the Germany Army Group Center from detaching forces to go to the aid of Paulus at Stalingrad and Manstein to the south.

Vasilevsky was left with the heavy responsibility of co-ordinating the three fronts at Stalingrad. He was surprised when making his daily telephone report to Stalin, on November 17, to receive an order to return at once to Moscow. Stalin had received a personal letter from Volsky, commander of the IV Mechanized Corps, expressing the view that "the plan was unreal and doomed to failure." Volsky, who had commanded the 37th Cavalry Regiment, was known and respected. Stalin asked Vasilevsky to comment. He answered firmly that the offensive was soundly planned and should go ahead. Stalin at once spoke to Volsky by telephone and "to the amazement of everybody present," he did not dismiss him or even reprimand him for lacking confidence, but spoke in a kindly manner, reassuring him. Stalin then told Vasilevsky to forget the incident, adding that "the final decision regarding Volsky would be made in accordance with his performance during the next few days."[5] Volsky performed with distinction and was later appointed commander of the 5th Guards Tank Army.

The heavy duties of Chief of the General Staff were complicated for Vasilevsky by the fact that Stalin frequently sent him away to the fronts. Vasilevsky tried to find a deputy, but this presented special difficulties. "Stalin was a careful and mistrustful person, particularly of new faces,"[6] he observed. In May 1942 he suggested that Vatutin, who was at that time Chief of Staff of the Northwest Front, be brought back to Moscow. "Why?" asked Stalin. "Isn't he any good at the front?" Soon afterwards, however, Vatutin was appointed commander of the Voronezh Front.

Vasilevsky searched again. Finally he chose A. I. Antonov, who had been a junior officer in the tsarist army, and who was then Chief of Staff of the North Caucasian Front. Zhukov was to describe him as "a peerlessly able General and a man of great culture and charm."[7] Reluctantly Stalin agreed to the appointment. The unfortunate Antonov found, however, that Stalin avoided direct dealings with him. He asked to be relieved of his post, and, despite Vasilevsky's intervention, he was sent to the Voronezh Front as deputy Stavka representative. He served there with such marked ability that three months later he was back in Moscow as Deputy Chief of the General Staff. Stalin had learned to accept him.

On the morning of November 19 Vatutin and Rokossovsky launched their attack from the north. On the following day, after a few hours' delay due to thick fog, Eremenko advanced from the south. By November 23 they had met near Kalach, encircling the German Sixth Army and a corps of the Fourth Panzer Army.

Stalin at once directed Vasilevsky to concentrate on the launching of Operation Saturn, which involved a bold offensive to draw a second ring around the enemy trapped at Stalingrad. The Russian forces were then to occupy the whole of the territory within the Don-Donets corridor, so that with Rostov in Russian hands the escape route of the Germans in the Caucasus would be closed.

Two days later from the Southwest Front, Vasilevsky reported directly by telephone to Stalin on strengthening the Voronezh and Southwest Fronts against German counterattacks. The reinforcements he proposed were heavy, but Stalin agreed that they were necessary. He then instructed Vasilevsky to concentrate on the Don and Stalingrad Fronts. Vatutin would remain responsible for the lines of the outer circle down to the Chir, and Eremenko would be responsibile for the rest of the circle. Stalin said that he was giving Voronov command of Operation Saturn. Vasilevsky was evidently taken aback by these changes in responsibility. He asked for his orders in writing and Stalin sent them at once by teleprinter.

The Germans had hurriedly reorganized their forces in the south, creating Army Group Don under the command of Field Marshal Manstein. By skillful tactics he managed to fight his way to within twenty-five miles of Paulus' lines. Paulus made no attempt to break out and join him, presumably because Hitler had ordered him to stand fast. Russian forces halted the German advance. On December 24 a counteroffensive, approved by Stalin on December 19, hurled Manstein back to Kotelnikovo and then sixty miles farther to the southeast. Manstein gave up his attempt to relieve Paulus. He concentrated now on guarding the Rostov-Taman gap so that the German forces in the Caucasus and the Kuban could escape.

To the west, Operation Saturn, amended because of Manstein's offensive, and known now as Maly (Little) Saturn, was successful, advancing 150 miles in five days. In the north Zhukov co-ordinated offensives forced the Germans from the Vyazma salient and made a seven-mile gap in the enemy lines blockading Leningrad.

At a meeting of the General Defense Committee in late December, Stalin pointed out that one man only should direct the final destruction of the enemy forces encircled at Stalingrad, and there were two front commanders. "Who gets the mission?" he asked. Someone suggested Rokossovsky. Stalin turned to Zhukov, who replied that both commanders were worthy, but that Eremenko would feel very hurt if Rokossovsky got the job. "It's not the time to feel hurt," Stalin answered curtly, and told Zhukov to inform Eremenko of the decision. Eremenko was extremely hurt. He tried to phone Stalin, but was told by Poskrebyshev that he had to approach Zhukov. Finally Zhukov tried to intercede. "Stalin was none too pleased and said a directive should be issued at once to place the three armies of the Stalingrad Front under K. K. Rokossovsky." The directive was issued on December 30.[8]

Paulus and his troops rejected two calls to surrender. But, completely cut off and without supplies, they had no hope of survival and finally on February 2 they surrendered. Zhukov stated that total enemy losses in the Volga-Don-Stalingrad area were 1.5 million men, 3,500 tanks, 12,000 guns, and 3,000 aircraft.[9] Russian losses were probably far higher. It had been a decisive battle, fought with incredible ferocity and courage by Russians and Germans, and it had completely turned the tide of the war.

On February 4, 1943, Rokossovsky and Voronov were summoned from the fronts to the Kremlin. Stalin greeted them warmly and congratulated them on their victory. And, as Rokossovsky commented, this was an occasion when he "could literally charm a person by his warmth and attention."[10]

At the time when the Battle of Stalingrad was raging, Stalin found himself beset with family problems. He had tried to be a father to his two children, Vasily and Svetlana, but inevitably he had been remote from their everyday lives, and he had also made the mistakes commonly made by fathers. He had been strict with his son, seeking to bring him up as a disciplined and hard-working citizen. Vasily turned into a lazy, pleasure-loving young man, given to drink. His mother had indulged him, and since her death there had been no lack of people eager to fawn on the son of Stalin. Indeed at the age of twenty-four he was appointed a general of the Air Force, a promotion unlikely to have been made by Stalin; but he was not entrusted with any war duties. He had made sporadic attempts to live up to the image expected of him, but, lacking the ability and character, he always lapsed into drinking bouts and bad habits. Feeling that there was nothing that he could do, Stalin, apart from occasional explosions of anger, washed his hands of him.

Svetlana, grown to be a pretty red-headed girl, was his great comfort. But she was at school, and during the desperate months of war when he was involved throughout the night, snatching brief rest on the couch in his office, he saw little of her. Their walks in the woods at Zubalovo and meals together were things of the past, and he missed her company. She was a lonely emotional girl, living a quiet life of routine lessons and visits with her few friends, accompanied always by her father's NKVD guard, General Vlasik. The shadow of her father's position enveloped her and she felt imprisoned by it.

One day in October 1942 Svetlana was at the dacha at Zubalovo, where her brother had invited a number of his friends. Among them was Aleksei Kapler, a film producer in his forties, married, and a Jew. Svetlana became deeply infatuated with him. He was gentle, fatherly, and highly intelligent. He brought her books, especially novels of Hemingway, which were hard to come by and were eagerly read in Soviet Russia. Together they went to private viewings in the Ministry of Cinematography of films like

Disney's *Snow White and the Seven Dwarfs*, *The Young Lincoln*, and early Hollywood classics. Overwhelmed by the attention of this cultured man of the world, she believed herself to be in love with him. Kapler himself appears to have been captivated by this lonely sixteen-year-old girl, Stalin's daughter, and by her eager curiosity about books, music, and films. It was an innocent affair.

Stalin received NKVD reports of his daughter's new friendship, and it distressed him deeply. Puritanical in matters of personal morality, he suspected the worst and could not understand how his daughter could have allowed herself to be attracted by this middle-aged Jew, who should have been at the front like all true men instead of playing about with films and trying to seduce young girls. If his wife had been alive, she could have handled the matter. He was probably on the point of speaking to his daughter several times, but Stalingrad and the great counteroffensive demanded his full attention.

Suddenly on the morning of March 3, 1943, as Svetlana was getting ready for school, he burst into her room. He was in a rage, and both she and her nurse looked at him in fear. "Where— where are they all?" he exclaimed. "Where are all these letters from your 'writer'?

"I know the whole story! I've got all your telephone conversations right here!" He patted his pocket as he said it. "All right! Hand them over. Your Kapler is a British spy! He's under arrest!"

Svetlana took from her desk the letters, inscribed photographs, notebooks, and the new film script on Shostakovich, which Kapler had given her, and handed them to her father.

"But I love him!" she protested at last.

"Love!" he shouted and for the first time in his life he slapped her, twice across the face.

"Just think, nurse, how low she's sunk!" he went on. "Such a war going on and she's busy the whole time . . ."

He spoke with bitterness and anger. He had lost his daughter to a middle-aged filmmaker. He was undoubtedly overwrought from the strains of months of working long hours under the pressures of war, but he was also a lonely isolated man, and he probably felt a keen sense of betrayal. In her way his daughter had betrayed him as her mother had betrayed him. For months father and daughter were estranged and did not see each other.[11] Kapler was removed by a five-year sentence to Vorkuta, where he was allowed to work in the theater.

Impatient after the Battle of Stalingrad to liberate all Russian territory, Stalin had ordered an advance on a broad front. It was intended that the Red Army should reach the Dnieper by the spring of 1943. This objective was overly ambitious, but on many fronts the winter offensive achieved important gains.

The Stalingrad victory and the rapid advances along the whole front had bred overconfidence among the front commanders. Stalin shared, too, in the general elation, declaring in his Order of the Day on November 7, 1942, that soon "there will be a holiday in our street!"[12] But with his instinctive wariness he knew that excessive optimism was dangerous. It was necessary to caution not only the armed forces but the civil population, who were exulting over the victories and the liberation of occupied territories.

On February 23, 1943, the twenty-fourth anniversary of the Red Army, Stalin's Order of the Day proclaimed: "The enemy has suffered defeat, but still has not been conquered," and he called on the Soviet Army, Navy, and Air Force to redouble their efforts.[13]

The warning was timely. Manstein had mounted a counteroffensive on February 19. Moving northeastwards, he retook Kharkov and Belgorod, and was soon threatening Rokossovsky's Center Front, but then he was halted.

Towards the end of March a pause came in the fighting, which lasted until early July 1943. It was a period of furious preparation for the summer campaign. The Kursk salient was to be the arena for this crucial trial of strength. Holding Orel in the north and Belgorod to the south of the salient, the Germans believed themselves to be in a strong position to carry out a decisive pincer movement, which would reverse their losses of the winter of 1942–43.

Soviet industry had, however, achieved phenomenal results since the great evacuation of the autumn and winter of 1941–42. The industrial expansion had brought a dramatic improvement in the equipment of the Red Army. Moreover, it was not only in quantity but also in quality that the Russian forces now had the upper hand.

Stalin took a direct interest in the development of weapons, and indeed his approval was needed before any prototype or major change went into production. The improved T-34 medium tank and the IS heavy tank were, the Russians claimed, the most effective tanks in the war, and most German officers admitted their superiority.[14] The Russian artillery, and especially the rocket artillery, had a devastating fire power. By 1943 Russian rifles and machine guns had a more rapid rate of fire and greater endurance. The leading aircraft designers, Tupolev, Yakovlev, and Lavochkin, who reported directly to Stalin on their work, produced more effective planes, and gradually he had built up under his control a powerful air force. The main deficiency was motor transport, and this was met partially by the supply of American trucks and jeeps.[15]

The war had forged a new generation of young and dynamic commanders. A large proportion of the best-trained officers and troops of the Red Army had been lost during 1941–42, but by 1943 this loss had been made good by men with battle experience. The new generals were mostly under forty and were professional, rather than political, in outlook. An example was General Cherniakhovsky, who commanded a tanks corps at the start of the war and in spring 1944, at the age of thirty-six, was made commander of the 3rd Belorussian Front. When Rokossovsky had asked for the removal of Zaporozhets, a trusted old Bolshevik who was the political member of the Sixtieth Army, because Cherniakhovsky found it impossible to get on with him, Stalin immediately had Zaporozhets recalled. It was men like Cherniakhovsky who could take bold action and accept responsibility, and who were the professionals, whom Stalin had promoted.

As the summer approached in 1943, the build-up of Russian and German forces and armaments at Kursk mounted in intensity. Stalin became increasingly strained and worried during these weeks. His obsession, which Zhukov shared, was still the defense of Moscow. Both considered that the German strategy might be to strike northeast from Kursk and envelop the capital from the east. But the immediate problem was whether to mount a pre-emptive attack against the German positions north and south of the salient. Stalin had received conflicting proposals from his senior commanders. His own instinct was always to attack. Now he hesitated. On April 12, 1943, he called a meeting to consider the tactics to be adopted. Zhukov, Vasilevsky, and the general staff argued strongly against a pre-emptive strike; the Soviet forces should let the enemy attack and wear himself down against their impregnable Kursk defenses. Stalin was, however, unsure even now about the capacity of the Red Army to withstand a mass German attack. He had in mind the fact that Russian offensives had succeeded against the Germans in winter conditions. A summer offensive might present unforeseen problems. At the meeting he listened to the different views, but reached no decision.

Vatutin from the Central Front, supported by Khrushchev, began pressing for a pre-emptive offensive. Rokossovsky from the Voronezh Front sent a report in which he argued that the enemy should be left to attack first and to break his strength against the Soviet positions. Pressure on Stalin to make a decision increased. Vasilevsky wrote that it took all the efforts of Zhukov, Antonov, and himself to dissuade the Supreme Commander from adopting the repeated proposals of Vatutin to take the offensive.

According to Zhukov, Stalin reached a firm decision in mid-May to await the German attack. It would be met with fire of all types from defenses in depth, with air attacks, and with counterblows from operational and strategic reserves; after wearing the enemy down, a counteroffensive would be launched in the Belgorod-Kharkov and the Orel directions.[16]

The long wait for the opening of the enemy offensive had everybody on edge. This was the underlying factor in a fearful scene in the Kremlin office, when Stalin lost his temper. He had received a personal letter, written by a group of fighter pilots, complaining about the fabric paint used on the wings of the Yak-9 interceptor planes, which caused them to break up in flight. At once Stalin sent for Vasilevsky, Voronov, and Yakovlev, the designer. He swore at them all, calling them "Hitlerites." Yakovlev, who had had long and close relations with Stalin, wrote that he had never seen him in such a rage, and that he himself was trembling with fear. They undertook to have all planes repaired within two weeks; it was an impossible undertaking, but it appeared to mollify him. He ordered, nevertheless, that the military prosecutor's office should investigate the matter and find the traitors responsible.[17]

In the early hours of July 5, the Germans attacked, striking south from Orel and north from Belgorod, intent on encircling the Soviet Central and Voronezh Fronts within the Kursk salient. For eight days the battle raged. It involved a clash of tanks and artillery on a scale never before known in the history of warfare. The German forces suffered appalling losses and could make no impression on the Russian positions. On July 13 Hitler gave orders to break off the offensive.

The Russian counteroffensive was launched on July 12 as soon as the German drive had lost its impetus. At a meeting of general staff, front, and army commanders, called by Stalin in his Kremlin office some days earlier, Antonov gave a clear exposition of the plans of action. Stalin asked a few questions and expressed his approval. Bagramian, who then commanded the Eleventh Guards Army, wanted to propose modifications to the plan as it affected his role on the left flank. He hesitated to speak in the presence of the Supreme Commander. All were rolling up their maps and the meeting seemed to be over when Stalin suddenly asked if anyone had contrary views. Bagramian said he had. Stalin looked at him, an expression of surprise on his face, and told him to speak. Bagramian felt so nervous that he had to take a grip on himself. All present unrolled their maps again. He explained how he saw the part to be played by his army in the coming offensive and the changes he recommended. Silence followed. He was expecting his proposals, coming from an army commander, to be squashed by the Supreme Commander, the general staff, and the front commanders, whom he called the "great trinity." Stalin and the others studied their maps, and then Stalin told him his proposals were accepted subject to minor changes.

According to Zhukov and Vasilevsky, Stalin was always prepared to listen to views contrary to his own, provided they were based on facts and presented lucidly. But his attitude towards the general staff and his commanders had changed after the successful counteroffensives at Stalingrad. Indeed he went so far as to declare that front commanders should themselves decide the timing of their counteroffensives. But the habit of command was deeply ingrained and he always took control.

During the counteroffensives from the Kursk salient he was constantly pressing Zhukov and Vasilevsky and the front commanders to attack without delay. Towards the end of July both men firmly insisted that the Voronezh and Steppe Fronts needed eight days to replenish stocks before mounting their counterattacks. Stalin finally yielded to their insistence that the plan could be ruined by haste. Zhukov wrote subsequently: "Today, after Stalin's death, the idea is current that he never heeded anybody's advice and decided questions of military policy all by himself. I can't agree with it. When he realized that the person reporting knew what he was talking about, he would listen, and I know cases when he reconsidered his own opinions and decisions. This was the case in many operations."[18]

The strategy in the south, after the enemy had been smashed at Belgorod-Kharkov, brought some conflict of views. Stalin rejected the proposals, put forward by Vatutin and supported by Khrushchev, that the Voronezh, Southwest, and West Fronts should press southwards deep into the Ukraine to recover the industrial and agricultural lands, and from there prepare for the invasion of Romania and Hungary. He objected that this strategy would leave Kiev in enemy hands and the German Army Group Center, which stood only some two hundred miles from Moscow, could not be left intact. His own strategy, which was adopted, was to strike from Poltava to recover Kiev and then to advance to separate Army Group Center from Army Group South, thus threatening both groups with envelopment. This strategy was to provide the basis for the great Russian victories in central and southeastern Europe in 1943–44.[19]

The nation was elated by the victory at Kursk and by the counteroffensives. The morale of the troops was transformed, and there was no more talk of the invincibility of the enemy. The Red forces had at Stalingrad halted the German advance. In the battle of the Kursk salient they had not only crushed the German summer campaign but had also destroyed the German capacity to mount another major offensive. From this time onwards the Germans could only retreat, following a defensive strategy. The Russians renewed their westward drive with furious energy, confident that they were now invincible.

While sharing this confidence of the Red Army commanders, Stalin did not underestimate the German Army. He remained on guard against overoptimism and any slackening in discipline. As Supreme Commander he kept a close control over operations and did not hesitate to censure even the most senior commanders. Zhukov and Vatutin received a strongly worded telegram when the Voronezh Front failed to envelop the enemy at Kharkov and suffered severe casualties in the German counterattack. They were guilty of "dissipating their forces by attacking everywhere to cover as much ground as possible."[20]

Vasilevsky, chief of the general staff, received a shattering reprimand on August 17, 1943, which read:

> Marshal Vasilevsky. It is now already 0330 hours 17 August and you still have not seen fit to send to the Stavka a report on the outcome of operations on 16 August and your appreciation of the situation. . . . Nearly every day you forget this duty. . . . Again you have been pleased to ignore your responsibility to the Stavka by not reporting. It is the last time that I give you notice that in the event of your allowing yourself to forget your duty you will be removed from the post of Chief of the General Staff and recalled from the front. I. Stalin.[21]

Vasilevsky, shaken by this rebuke, claimed that he had never failed to send his report, although for good reasons his report of August 16, 1943, was a few hours late in arriving. At once he phoned Antonov in the Kremlin, who told him that Stalin was disappointed by the results of the offensives. He added that Vasilevsky's report was already in Stalin's hands when he dictated the message. He may have been in a perverse mood, or have considered that Vasilevsky was growing lax, or he may have been concerned to remind him of the Supreme Commander's authority. Vasilevsky accepted the reprimand, writing later that "the absence of any indulgence towards us was in the interest of the conduct of the armed struggle."[22]

In October 1943 the Red Army crossed the Dnieper at various points. Kiev was liberated on November 6 and Zhitomir two days later. The advance was less spectacular in the north, but on September 25 Smolensk was retaken and Moscow was freed completely from the threat of attack. By the end of 1943 the Red Army had recovered more than half the territory conquered by the Germans in their great eastward advance of 1941–42. But most of Belorussia, the western Ukraine, and the Baltic region were still in German hands.

As the Russians pushed westwards, liberating lands occupied by the Germans, they uncovered evidence of the unbelievable savagery and inhumanity of the German treatment of prisoners of war and the civilian population. Reports of enemy atrocities had been published since early in the war, but the liberation of vast territories revealed the terrible scale of German barbarity. The Russians, although inured to purges and forced labor camps, were inflamed with a bitter hatred of the enemy.

Russian prisoners had been deliberately starved to death. This followed from the instructions that German troops were to feed off the land and that all possible food surpluses must be sent to Germany where rationing was severe. But this extermination policy was justified also on the grounds that Russians were *Untermenschen*, an inferior species to be treated as animals, and that the "Jewish-Bolshevik system" must be destroyed.

It has been calculated that between June 1941 and May 1944 the Germans took 5,160,000 prisoners in Russia. Of them 1,053,000 were finally liberated. But more than 3,750,000 men were exterminated in massacres, by starvation, and by exposure. Penned together in the open air without shelter of any kind and without food, they quickly perished in the cruel cold of autumn and winter. The number of Russian civilians, including women and children, done to death in similar ways, certainly exceeded this figure; the full toll will never be known.[23]

Kharkov, the first large city to be liberated, had a population normally of some 900,000, which had been swollen to some 1,300,000 by the influx of people fleeing before the invaders. As the Germans approached, thousands fled farther to the east. Some 700,000 were in the city when it was captured and only half of them survived. Of the others, 120,000, mainly young people, were sent to Germany as slave labor. Between 70,000 and 80,000 died of hunger and exposure. Some 30,000, including 16,000 Jews, were executed. Orel's population of 114,000 was no more than 30,000 on liberation. The Germans had murdered some 12,000 and had sent more than 20,000 away as slave labor.[24]

Every occupied Russian city, town, and village suffered the same grim fate. The Jews were the first to be killed and then the Russians were dealt with in various brutal ways. At Babyi Yar, near Kiev, 100,000 Jews were massacred. The Germans concentrated their fiendishness on the Jews and Russians. They treated the Ukrainians and the Moslem peoples differently, regarding them as actual or potential enemies of the Soviet regime. Belatedly, towards the end of 1942, they made some attempt to modify their treatment of Russian prisoners of war, offering them the alternatives of death by starvation or other means, or service in the Russian Army of Liberation, known as the Vlasov Army.[25] Most Russians refused to serve under Vlasov and chose death. A few in Dachau and other concentration camps managed to survive.

Against this background Stalin ordered draconian measures to apply to all Russian prisoners of war who survived capture and German treatment, against Russian civilians who survived, and against Ukrainians and all Moslem nationalities. He knew that there were dissident elements among the Russians who had escaped the mesh of his purges and who could be cajoled or coerced by the enemy to fight against Soviet Russia. All Red Army officers and men knew the fate of shooting or starvation as *Untermenschen* that awaited them, if they allowed themselves to be taken captive by the Germans. This was constantly publicized among them. He could not believe that any Russian would lay down his arms and surrender on such terms. It followed that every Russian, especially an officer, taken prisoner was considered to have "voluntarily surrendered to the enemy"; he had betrayed his country; he was a coward or a potential or actual collaborator, who deserved his fate. If he survived he was considered to be devoid of pride and patriotism, or there was presumed to be some sinister anti-Soviet reason for his survival. This was the stark reasoning for the treatment of Russians who were liberated or returned by some other means. They were interrogated. They had to explain why they had allowed themselves to be captured instead of fighting to the death.

Usually they were sent to labor camps, and their families were punished by a two-year term of imprisonment.

Yakov, the son by his first marriage, whom he had virtually disowned for some unknown reason, had entered the Frunze Military Academy in 1935. He was a senior lieutenant in the 14th Howitzer Regiment and went with his unit to the Belorussian Front the day after war started. In July 1941 he was taken prisoner. Stalin, with his obsessive suspicion, refused to believe that even Yakov had been so dishonorable as to surrender. He seized on the idea that someone must have tricked or betrayed him. He came to believe that Iulya, Yakov's wife, was guilty. She was arrested in autumn 1941 and held in prison until spring 1943. The Germans identified Yakov and tried to make propaganda of the fact that he was in their hands, but Stalin refused to co-operate in any way.

Towards the end of the winter of 1943–44 after the Battle of Stalingrad, Svetlana paid one of her rare visits to her father. He told her then that "the Germans have proposed that we exchange one of their prisoners for Yasha. They want me to make a deal with them. I won't do it! War is war!" She added: "I could tell by his tone that he was upset. He wouldn't say another word about it."[26]

In summer 1945, when the war was over, and she was making another of her rare visits, he spoke again of Yakov. "The Germans shot Yasha," he said. "I had a letter of condolence from a Belgian officer." She observed that he spoke with an effort and did not want to say any more.[27] Svetlana, who loved her half brother, felt that after his death her father felt some warmth for this son and realized that he had been harsh and unfair. But she wrote, too, that "it was very like my father to wash his hands of members of his own family, to wipe them out of his mind and act as if they didn't exist."[28]

Civilians taken prisoner by the invaders were on their liberation required to account for their activities under the German occupation and to explain why they had survived, when so many others had been massacred or had perished. Thousands of civilians escaped as the enemy approached and joined the partisan or guerrilla movement. Stalin had ordered the formation of mass partisan opposition to the enemy.[29]

Brave men and women formed partisan groups, operating behind the enemy lines. They endured terrible hardships and perished in large numbers, but in many places they made conditions insupportable to the enemy. They were defending the motherland, while those who were simply captured contributed nothing and were perhaps actively or passively on the side of the enemy. The nation was fighting for survival. There was no time or readiness to consider the problems of individuals. All must be prepared to fight and die.

As the Germans advanced southwards and into the Caucasus, Stalin showed increasing concern about the loyalty of the Cossacks and the Moslem peoples. In the early stages of the war after the loss of the western Ukraine and the Baltic states, the fighting had taken place mainly in east Ukrainian and Great Russian territory, where the people, if not always enthusiastically pro-Soviet, were loyal to Russia. But Stalin was alert to the dangers of disaffection. In August 1941 he had as a precaution deported the Volga Germans to Kazakhstan and northern Siberia.[30]

The Cossacks since the early days of the Muscovite state had been unpredictable in their loyalties. They had, however, in the nineteenth century shown steady allegiance to the tsars, and they were known for their brutal suppression of peasant revolts, workers' demonstrations, and other forms of internal unrest. The Cossacks, like the Moslem peoples of the Caucasus and Central Asia and the Tatars of the Crimea, had suffered during the collectivization campaign and had reason to be anti-Soviet.

The Germans, overestimating the extent of the latent disaffection among the Cossacks, tried ineffectually to organize them in an anti-Soviet movement. The Cossacks were exempted from *Üntermensch* status and were encouraged to enlist in the German Army. By late 1943 some 20,000 Cossacks, or men calling themselves Cossacks, were fighting in German-sponsored units. This was, however, only a very small percentage of the Cossack population of the Kuban, Terek, and the Don, most of whom staunchly resisted the Germans.[31]

Towards the Moslem peoples, the Germans pursued a benign, almost paternalistic policy. The Karachai, Balkars, Ingush, Chechen, Kalmucks, and Tatars of the Crimea all displayed pro-

German sympathies in some degree. It was only the hurried with-drawal of the Germans from the Caucasus after the Battle of Stalingrad that prevented their organizing the Moslem people for effective anti-Soviet action. The Germans boasted loudly, how-ever, that they had left a strong "fifth column" behind them in the Caucasus.[32]

The fact that these peoples were prepared to betray Soviet Rus-sia infuriated Stalin, and he was absolutely ruthless in eradicating any possible "fifth column" which might imperil the rear of the Red Army. He was determined also that these peoples should never enjoy the fruits of victory and that they should be punished. By decrees of the Supreme Soviet at the end of 1943 and in the spring of 1944 the Moslem communities were uprooted and de-ported to the east. The decrees were carried out with such brutal-ity that the six nationalities were almost liquidated.[33]

27

Conference in Teheran November 28– December 1, 1943

Stalin, Churchill, and Roosevelt met together for the first time in Teheran towards the end of November 1943. In Churchill's words the meeting "probably represented the greatest concentration of worldly power that had ever been seen in the history of mankind."[1] They discussed their immediate war strategy and the postwar settlement to ensure peace and stability in talks that were frank but amiable and gave promise of close understanding and co-operation in the years ahead.

Anglo-Soviet relations had been under severe strain since Churchill's visit to Moscow in August of the previous year. He had then told Stalin that there would be no Second Front in 1942. This allied decision had been followed by shortfalls in armament deliveries by the North Russian convoys. The British Navy had gravely mishandled convoy PQ 17 in what Churchill described as "one of the most melancholy naval episodes in the whole war."[2] In a letter dated July 17 Churchill stated that the convoys would be suspended for a time, and Stalin responded angrily. He wrote a letter on July 23, 1942, which, far from being "rough and surly," as Churchill described it, was a blunt but dignified protest, made at a time when the Red Army was threatened with a devastating defeat at Stalingrad and desperately needed Allied supplies.[3]

Churchill's visit had led to better understanding at the time, but, notwithstanding the Prime Minister's vehement assurances, Stalin had remained suspicious that the British were leaving the fighting for as long as possible to the Russians. His suspicion sharpened, and Anglo-Russian relations declined further, as the battle for Stalingrad approached. Wendell Willkie, visiting Moscow as the President's personal representative, suggested that the United States had been willing to launch the Second Front in 1942, but that Churchill and the British military staff had raised obstacles. Soon after his departure, Soviet propaganda organs started an anti-British campaign. It reflected the deep disappointment of Russians over the absence of the Second Front. Britain was also a convenient scapegoat for the Russian defeats suffered as the invader had swept across Russia towards Stalingrad. Stalin publicly stated that "help from the Allies to the Soviet Union had so far been of little effect," and demanded "the full and timely fulfilment by the Allies of their obligations."[4] He was prompt to welcome the Allied North African landing, about which Churchill had given him advance notice. He paid generous tribute to the "first-class organizers who had accomplished this difficult military operation."[5] But this was not the Second Front.

Victory at Stalingrad brought some relief from the terrible anxiety which had weighed upon Stalin. He became more cordial towards his allies. The North African campaign and the bombing of Germany showed that they were no longer inactive. But as the crucial battle of the Kursk salient approached, his anxiety mounted. Russians everywhere were loudly critical of the Allies for failing to open the Second Front.

In his Order of the Day on May 1, 1943, Stalin referred in warm terms to the Allied victory in North Africa on which he had sent congratulatory messages to Churchill and Roosevelt, and to the bombing of Germany as "heralding the formation of a Second Front in Europe."[6] This was for all Russians the overriding need.

An official statement, issued on the second anniversary of the German invasion, went so far as to declare that "without a Second Front, victory over Germany is impossible."[7] Rumors that the Germans had approached the Allies with proposals for a separate peace intensified Russian suspicions. Stalin had in his Order of the Day on May 1, 1943, denounced German talk of peace and rumors in the Western press, "as though it is not clear that only the complete destruction of the Hitlerite armies and the unconditional surrender of Hitlerite Germany can bring Europe to peace."[8]

At this time, Stalin dissolved the Comintern. It had always represented for the Western powers the direct threat of militant communism. He had inherited the Comintern from Lenin, who had founded it in 1919 as the organ for fomenting world revolution. To Stalin, the opponent of internationalism and author of "socialism in one country," the Comintern was an encumbrance, and at this critical time it was inimical to Russian interests. He explained that its abolition was "correct and timely." It would put an end to lies spread by Nazi propaganda, that the Russian Communist party interfered in the affairs of other countries and conspired "to Bolshevize them." It would facilitate the work of freedom-loving countries, irrespective of political and religious beliefs, in joining together in the struggle against fascism.[9] The disbanding of the Comintern was welcomed in the West as clearing the way for real understanding with Soviet Russia.

While official Soviet references to the Allies were cordial in the early months of 1943, Stalin's letters to Churchill and Roosevelt were forthright. He was critical of Anglo-American delays in the North African campaign, as a result of which "the Germans transferred twenty-seven divisions, including five Panzer divisions, from France, Belgium, Holland and Germany herself to the Soviet-German front." He was not enthusiastic about the proposed landing in Sicily, which "cannot replace the Second Front in France." He reminded them that the Second Front had been admitted as a possibility in 1942 and as a firm expectation in spring 1943, and emphasized the urgent need to launch the operation not later than the early summer.[10]

In May 1943 the build-up for the gigantic trial of strength at

Kursk was reaching its climax. Stalin was tense as he waited for the Germans to open their offensive. At this critical time Churchill and Roosevelt informed him that the Anglo-American Second Front had to be postponed until spring 1944. Stalin exploded in anger. He was massing at Kursk a force of men and heavy armaments far greater than was required for the invasion of France, but these two mighty industrial powers constantly made excuses for delaying this crucial invasion. He saw the latest postponement as an act of blatant bad faith. In his letter of May 24 he stated firmly that "the preservation of our confidence in the Allies is being subjected to severe stress."[11]

Victory at Kursk relieved the pressure on Stalin. The Second Front was no longer a matter of life and death. His mistrust of the Allies was, however, deep-rooted, and no man was more tenacious in harboring mistrust. At the same time he was earnestly seeking a real understanding with them, believing that peace and world stability after the war would depend on the three powers remaining united. Primarily for this reason he was eager to have an early meeting. He had declined, however, proposals that they should meet early in 1943 on the grounds that he could not be away from Moscow and the conduct of military operations. This explanation was regarded with skepticism by the Allies, who did not appreciate that as Supreme Commander he was directing the Russian war effort personally. In August Stalin stated that a conference of the three heads of government was "absolutely desirable" and agreed that an exploratory meeting of foreign ministers should take place in Moscow in October.[12]

Relations with Britain nevertheless worsened further in the autumn of 1943. The North Russian convoys had been suspended since March. Russia still had urgent need of Allied supplies. Molotov sent through the British ambassador a peremptory demand for the resumption of convoys. Churchill promised to send four convoys, the first to sail on November 12, but as always his undertakings were hedged with a complex of provisos.

Churchill for his part demanded relaxation of the restrictions imposed on British naval personnel serving in North Russia. This demand offended Stalin. He responded so sharply that Churchill refused to accept his reply and returned it personally to the Soviet ambassador. Stalin objected, with some justice, that there were already too many British naval personnel in North Russia. He expressed his real objection frankly to Eden, which was, as Eden reported, "that if only our [British] people had treated his people as equals, none of these difficulties would have arisen, and if our people would treat his people as equals we could have as much personnel as we liked."[13]

The foreign ministers' conference, held in Moscow from October 19 until November 1, was cordial. Eden and Cordell Hull welcomed the opportunity to discuss postwar policies with Stalin and Molotov. Hull was especially pleased with an agreed statement, which was an important step towards a United Nations organization. He had feared that Russia might become isolationist after the war, and Stalin had the same fear about the United States. Eden and Hull both reported that the conference had provided real evidence that Soviet Russia wanted continued friendship and co-operation with Britain and the United States.[14]

Eden was nevertheless aware of the danger of conflict over the future of Europe. In fact, Stalin had already decided that as a matter of national security Russia must assert her dominant influence over the whole of eastern Europe. This was an essential barrier against another invasion from the west, especially from a resurgent Germany. Churchill and Eden saw the dangers of dividing the continent into two rival camps, and they feared that Russian occupation of eastern Europe would be the first step to domination of the whole continent. But interpreting Stalin's policy as a policy of aggrandizement, they failed to appreciate his obsessive anxiety to secure his western frontiers and to guard against Germany.

During the talks of the foreign ministers in October 1943 Eden tried to forestall this development of postwar spheres of interest. In one session he passed a note to Hull: "I am sorry to take your time, but behind all this is a big issue: two camps in Europe or one." But, notwithstanding the expressed American view, Hull did not appreciate the British concern on this score.[15]

During the conference, Eden secured Stalin's agreement to a heads of government meeting in Teheran. Stalin had been adamant that he could not leave Russia, but he finally accepted the venue of Teheran, from which direct communication with Moscow and the fronts by telegraph and telephone was practicable. Indeed, he was determined to establish cordial relations with the allies. When, on October 27, Eden, on Churchill's telegraphed instructions, asked for a special meeting, Stalin received him warmly, although, as he had probably foreseen, Eden's message was that the Second Front had to be postponed from the spring to the summer due to unforeseen difficulties in Italy. The senior British officer who accompanied Eden wrote that Stalin appeared "perfectly happy once he had received Eden's assurance that a short postponement and not a cancellation was involved."[16]

On November 25, 1943, Stalin, accompanied by Molotov and Voroshilov and his personal NKVD bodyguard, boarded his train at a siding near Kuntsevo. He traveled by train to Stalingrad and Baku, flying from there to Teheran. Shtemenko, the general staff liaison officer with the Supreme Commander in Chief, carried maps of all the fighting zones. At stops on the journey he spoke to the general staff in Moscow and obtained the most recent information to mark on his maps. It was his responsibility to brief Stalin every morning and evening on the state of the fronts. In Teheran, Stalin had a villa in the grounds of the mansion occupied by the Soviet Embassy, which had been the tsarist embassy. Shtemenko and his cipher staff were allocated a room there, next to the signal center. On the evening of his arrival, Stalin inspected the room and, finding it too small and dark, ordered it to be changed. From Shtemenko's room Stalin spoke by direct line with Vatutin and Rokossovsky at the fronts and with Antonov in Moscow. Here Shtemenko received drafts of orders, telephoned or telegraphed by Antonov, for Stalin's signature. He held the signed documents and telegraphed the authorized versions to Moscow.[17] While in Teheran, Stalin maintained his usual direct control over Russian operations on all fronts.

The conference sessions took place on four afternoons, starting on November 28, in the Soviet Embassy. Stalin wore the uniform of a Marshal of the Soviet Union. Birse, the British interpreter, observed that he "looked grey and more careworn than when I had seen him in Moscow, although he seemed more affable and at times his manner was almost gay."[18] General Deane, who had ac-

companied Cordell Hull to Moscow in the previous month, observed that, while the British and American parties numbered
twenty or thirty and had with them their service chiefs with staff,
Stalin had with him only Molotov and Voroshilov, and his interpreter, Pavlov. He consulted with them from time to time, but he
alone spoke in the conference and he spoke with absolute authority, for, as Deane noted, "there was never the slightest indication
that he would have to consult with his government."[19]

Addressing the conference, Stalin spoke quietly and at times
curtly. He had a highly disciplined mind and expressed himself
with utmost economy. Nothing aggravated him more than woolly,
long-winded oratory. He lost patience several times with Churchill, who talked at length and, while he had brilliant flashes, could
not resist orating. At one stage after Churchill had spoken too
long Stalin growled, "How long is this conference going to last?"[20]
But he exercised great patience and was at pains to be genial.

The discussions ranged widely during the conference sessions
and the informal luncheons and dinners which took place each
day. Stalin was concerned about the immediate war plans of the
Allies and in particular the launching of the Second Front, named
Operation Overlord. He was also thinking ahead to the settlement
of Europe after the war, the future of Poland and Germany, and
the maintenance of peace.

Churchill and Roosevelt talked about operations in the eastern
Mediterranean, about bringing Turkey into the war, and sending
Anglo-American naval forces into the Black Sea. Stalin brought
the discussion back to the prime purpose of defeating Germany by
the invasion of France. To disperse and weaken Allied effort in a
series of operations throughout the Mediterranean would be mistaken. All should be concentrated on Operation Overlord. The
plan to capture Rome should be abandoned if necessary to provide greater Allied troops for the invasion of southern France.
Churchill, always ready to shoot off on tangents and plan diver-
sions, talked a great deal about possible operations in the Balkans.
Stalin's patience with him began to wear thin. At the close of the
session on November 29, Stalin looked directly at Churchill across
the table and said: "I wish to pose a very direct question to the
Prime Minister about Overlord. Do the Prime Minister and the

British staff really believe in Overlord?" Churchill replied, "Provided the conditions previously stated for Overlord are established when the time comes, it will be our stern duty to hurl across the Channel against the Germans every sinew of our strength."[21] It was a Churchillian reply, opening with a proviso and wrapped in rhetoric. Stalin wanted a simple "Yes," but he made no comment.

Meetings of Chiefs of Staff to discuss military operations during the conference had been agreed. Stalin had objected at first that he saw no point in such separate meetings. He himself had come to discuss such matters. But he did not press his objection, and said that Voroshilov would "do his best." The military committee met on November 29, attended by Voroshilov, Sir Alan Brooke, Charles Portal, William Leahy, and George C. Marshall. Brooke dominated the meeting. He had a powerful mind, incisive speech, and the same kind of impatience as Stalin. He had met Voroshilov in Moscow in a previous year and had summed him up as "an attractive personality, a typically political general who owed his life to his wits." When at the meeting Voroshilov started pressing Stalin's views, revealing his own lack of military expertise, Brooke was terse with him. He had shown the same curt impatience in dealing with him in Moscow, and this was to have repercussions.

After dinner, hosted on the first evening by Roosevelt, Churchill drew Stalin aside to discuss what would happen after the war. Eden joined them. "Let us first consider the worst that might happen," said Stalin, and he outlined the problem which concerned him deeply and which was to underlie his policies in the postwar years. It was that Germany would recover from this war within fifteen to twenty years and with a revival of nationalism would start another war. This was the fear that obsessed him, and he was determined that Russia should never again be subjected to the torment and destruction that she was now suffering. Churchill spoke of the duty of the three powers to enforce German disarmament, to isolate Prussia, and to impose some union of the southern German states. Stalin thought that this would not be enough. They then spoke briefly about Poland and her problems, which were to be discussed in plenary session and were to bedevil Allied relations.[22]

Shortly before the session of November 29 began, there was a brief but impressive ceremony in the conference room of the Soviet Embassy, when the Stalingrad Sword of Honour was presented. It was inscribed in English and in Russian "to the steel-hearted citizens of Stalingrad. The gift of King George VI in token of the homage of the British people." The ceremony was brief. The British lieutenant commanding the guard of honor handed the magnificent sword to Churchill, who, turning to Stalin, stated that he had been commanded by the King to present to him the Sword of Honour for transmission to the city of Stalingrad. Birse, who was standing close to Stalin, saw that he was deeply moved as he took the sword, kissed the hilt, and handed it to Voroshilov. Unfortunately, Voroshilov fumbled and nearly dropped it, but managed to pass it to the Russian lieutenant of the ceremonial guard. Stalin spoke briefly, expressing his appreciation, and shook Churchill by the hand.[23]

During the next session discussions turned again to Poland. Stalin was determined to strengthen his western frontiers in every way possible. He had to resolve the problem of Poland, which had nurtured more than three hundred years of hostility towards Russia. He was increasingly concerned about the hostile Polish government in London. On July 30, 1941, Soviet Ambassador Ivan Maisky had signed an agreement with Władysław Sikorski, the leader of the London Poles, who undertook to mobilize from among Polish prisoners in Russia an army to be commanded by a Pole, but under the Russian Supreme Command, to fight against the Germans. Formation of the Polish Army in Russia under the command of General W. Anders progressed. By December 1941, it had enlisted 73,415 Poles. The Russians strongly suspected, however, that this army, led by anti-Russian officers, would never fight at the side of the Red Army against the enemy. Indeed, the Russians stated that during the critical months of 1941, when their help would have been valuable, the Poles constantly found excuses for not being sent to the front. When Churchill proposed that the Poles should be allowed to leave Russia by way of Iran to fight on the Western Front, Stalin readily agreed. Their departure on the eve of the Battle of Stalingrad was seen by Russians as desertion in the face of the enemy and as a demonstration of Polish hatred of Russia.

Stalin knew that the age-old hostility between the two nations would not suddenly disappear, but he did not intend to permit a hostile Poland, led by anti-Russian leaders like Sikorski and Anders, to be restored on Russian frontiers. Early in 1943 the Russian policy began to emerge. Poland's eastern frontier would follow the Curzon line, and in compensation the Poles were to extend westward at the expense of Germany. The Soviet press began a campaign against the Polish government in London, and the Union of Polish Patriots was established in Russia. This attempt to organize a pro-Russian government to take over from the well-entrenched Polish government in London seemed at the time unlikely to succeed.

In April 1943 the Germans announced that they had discovered at Katyn near Smolensk mass graves containing the bodies of 12,500 Polish officers and NCOs. It was alleged that the Russians had massacred them in the spring of 1940. Soviet denials did not remove strong suspicions that NKVD troops were responsible. The Soviet government broke off relations with the London Poles, castigating them as imperialists and German agents, and strengthened its support for the Union of Polish Patriots. A Tadeusz Kościuszko Division, some fifteen thousand strong, was recruited among Poles who recognized that they must bury old enmities and learn to live with Soviet Russia. By October 1943 this division was fighting alongside Red Army troops.

At the Teheran conference Stalin frankly stated his ideas about the settlement of Poland after the war. Churchill and Eden both accepted his proposals to make the Curzon or the Oder line the frontier and to incorporate Lvov into the Soviet Union. But at this stage the discussions were tentative, for, as Churchill was to write, "nothing would satisfy the Poles."[24]

Churchill and Roosevelt besought Stalin to be generous to the Finns, who were now fighting at the side of the Germans. He conceded that, unless compelled by Finnish obstinacy, he would not make Finland a Soviet province, but insisted that he would exact some compensation in the form of territory and indemnities. Churchill remarked that "there is still ringing in my ears the famous slogan: 'No annexations and no indemnities.'" This was the slogan which Lenin and Trotsky had used in seeking peace with

Germany after the Revolution. He added, "Perhaps Marshal Stalin will not be pleased with me for saying that." Stalin grinned broadly and answered: "I have told you that I am becoming a Conservative!"[25]

On November 30, Churchill's sixty-ninth birthday and a day which he was to describe as crowded and memorable, he had a private meeting with Stalin in the morning. He had become disturbed by the Russian suspicion that he would prefer to abandon Overlord in favor of an invasion of the Balkans. But also he had been uneasy about Roosevelt's reserve since arriving in Teheran. Roosevelt, with whom he had taken pains to build up a special relationship, had refused private meetings with him during the conference on the grounds that Stalin might feel that they were concerting action and policy against him. It was a specious excuse, for Stalin was well aware that they had long been in close contact, and indeed expected the two English-speaking powers to act together. Roosevelt was, in fact, more concerned to demonstrate to Stalin that he was not under Churchill's influence, as many of his own people believed. This was probably the main reason for his jokes and jibes at Churchill's expense about "colonialism" and "imperialism," which he thought would appeal to Stalin. But also he had the mistaken idea that he could handle Stalin rather as he handled members of the U. S. Congress. Churchill was further disturbed because for security reasons Roosevelt was accommodated not in his own embassy but in the Soviet Embassy, and so appeared to be in ready personal contact with Stalin.

Disconcerted by Roosevelt's attitude and the American wariness towards him in Teheran, and disturbed by Stalin's openly expressed suspicion of his determination to pursue Operation Overlord, Churchill asked for a private meeting with Stalin to explain himself fully. The meeting lasted less than half an hour. Churchill explained that he fully supported Overlord, but was opposed to an American plan for an amphibious operation in the Bay of Bengal against the Japanese. Stalin emphasized the importance of the Allied invasion of northern France and confirmed that a Russian offensive would be launched to coincide with it. He added that the Red Army was war-weary and was depending on the success of the operation. He asked about the date fixed for Overlord, but

Churchill said that this would be revealed at lunch time, when they would be alone with Roosevelt. It was then stated that it would be in May. Stalin showed great pleasure and relief.

The dinner on that evening was hosted by Churchill in celebration of his birthday. It was Stalin's first visit to a British Embassy. The NKVD took elaborate security precautions, thoroughly searching the premises, interrogating the servants and posting armed guards at all entrances and on the roof. It was nevertheless a jovial occasion. Birse, the British interpreter, had been told to stay close to Stalin and look after his wants. A warm relationship had already been established between the British major and the Soviet Supreme Commander.

At table Birse was seated on Stalin's left. He later wrote:

> Stalin, who sat uncomfortably on the edge of his chair, looked with anxiety at the display of different-sized knives and forks before him, turned to me and said: "This is a fine collection of cutlery! It is a problem which to use. You will have to tell me, and also when I can begin to eat. I am unused to your customs." This small incident showed a human, unexpected side of his character, I think. His fear, if he had any, of doing the wrong thing soon vanished, for the proceedings became increasingly friendly and jovial. He settled himself deeper into his chair, and took my advice to eat and drink when it pleased him. After formal toasts to King George VI, President Kalinin, and President Roosevelt, Churchill proposed one to "Roosevelt the Man" and another to "Stalin the Great." The President toasted Churchill, and so did Stalin. Eden toasted Molotov, and so it went on in true Russian fashion. Towards the end of the meal he asked me whether it would be in order for him to drink the health of our waiter. I said I was sure he could do so, and that the man would be very happy. He then called the Persian servant, poured him out a glass of champagne, and wished him and his comrades good luck. The Persian seemed quite overcome, and at a loss what to do with his glass. I told him to drink it on the spot. It is hard to say whether Stalin's gesture was spontaneous or done to impress the Persians. . . .[26]

An awkward incident occurred during the toasts. The President proposed a toast to General Sir Alan Brooke, chief of the Imperial General Staff, and before he had finished speaking, Stalin rose and said he would finish the toast. He then spoke in a way inferring that Brooke had failed to show real feelings of friendship towards the Red Army, that he lacked appreciation of its fine qualities, and he hoped that in future he would show greater comradeship towards the soldiers of the Red Army.

Brooke was taken by surprise. "I had, however, seen enough of Stalin by then to know that if I sat down under these insults, I should lose any respect he might ever have had for me, and that he would continue such attacks in the future." In his reply to the toast, Brooke turned to Stalin and said, "Now, Marshal, may I deal with your toast. I am surprised that you should have found it necessary to raise accusations against me that are entirely unfounded. You will remember that this morning while we were discussing cover plans, Mr Churchill said that 'in war truth must have an escort of lies.' You will also remember that you yourself told us that in all your great offensives your real intentions were always kept concealed from the outer world. You told us that all your dummy tanks and dummy aeroplanes were always massed on those fronts that were of an immediate interest, while your true intentions were covered by a cloak of complete secrecy.

"Well, Marshal, you have been misled by dummy tanks and dummy aeroplanes, and you have failed to observe those feelings of true friendship which I have for the Red Army, nor have you seen the feelings of genuine comradeship which I feel towards all its members."

Stalin's face was inscrutable as his interpreter, M. Pavlov, translated Brooke's words. At the end he turned to Churchill, and "with evident relish" he said, "I like that man. He rings true. I must have a talk with him afterwards." Brooke went up to him after dinner and again expressed surprise at these accusations. Stalin replied at once that "the best friendships are those founded on misunderstandings" and shook him warmly by the hand. Churchill wrote later, "In fact, Stalin's confidence was established on a foundation of respect and goodwill which was never shaken while we all worked together."[27]

Churchill himself stood in awe of Stalin and, as his personal physician observed, was often unnerved in his presence.[28] He found himself confronted by a swift, highly expert and disciplined intelligence, by a Russian-Asiatic outlook, an enigma which he could not understand, and above all by the reality of absolute and ruthless power, which he had never encountered. On a number of occasions Stalin made teasing remarks which Churchill took in good part. But at dinner on the first evening of the conference, he was not sure at one point whether Stalin was serious or joking, and he overreacted.

Talking of the punishment to be inflicted on the Germans after the war, Stalin said that the German general staff must be liquidated and that since German military might depended on some fifty thousand officers, they should all be shot. He may have been serious, but, in fact, Field Marshal Friedrich von Paulus and other officers, taken prisoner at Stalingrad and elsewhere, had been accorded respectful treatment.

Churchill responded vehemently that "the British Parliament and people would not tolerate mass executions." Stalin mischievously repeated that "fifty thousand must be shot!" Churchill blazed with anger. Eden made signs and gestures to assure him that it was all a joke, but he ignored them. Roosevelt tried to bring good humor back to the occasion by suggesting that not 50,000 but 49,000 should be shot. "I would rather," growled Churchill, "be taken into the garden here and now and be shot myself than sully my own and my country's honour by such infamy!"

At this point Roosevelt's son, Elliott, an uninvited guest who had joined the company after dinner, ineptly made a speech stating that he agreed with Stalin's plan and that he was sure the U. S. Army would support it. Churchill got up from the table and walked into the adjoining room. A minute later he felt hands clapped on his shoulder and turned to find Stalin and Molotov grinning broadly. They assured him that it had only been a joke. Churchill wrote that "Stalin has a very captivating manner when he chooses to use it." He returned to the table, but he was never to be fully convinced that Stalin had been joking.[29]

Stalin dominated the conference. He was brief and incisive in his comments, clear about his objectives, patient and inexorable in pursuing them. Brooke considered that he had an outstanding military brain, and observed that in all his statements he never once failed to appreciate all the implications of a situation with quick, unerring eye, and "in this respect he stood out compared with Roosevelt and Churchill."[30] The head of the U.S. military mission in Moscow had noted that no one could fail to recognize "the qualities of greatness in the man."[31] Combined with this essential greatness, there was a charm and at times a human warmth which seemed to belie the awesome ruthlessness which he would display in pursuit of what he saw as Soviet Russia's interests.

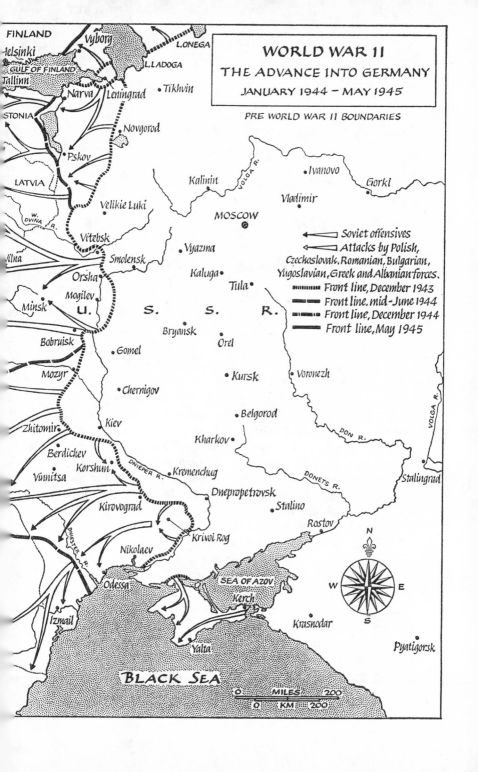

WORLD WAR II
THE ADVANCE INTO GERMANY
JANUARY 1944 – MAY 1945

PRE WORLD WAR II BOUNDARIES

FINLAND
Vyborg
L.ONEGA
Helsinki
GULF OF FINLAND
L.LADOGA
Tallinn
Narva · Leningrad
Tikhvin
ESTONIA
Novgorod
Pskov
Kalinin
Ivanovo
Gorki
LATVIA
Vladimir
VOLGA R.
W. DVINA R.
Velikie Luki
MOSCOW
Vitebsk
Vilna
Vyazma
← Soviet offensives
Smolensk
Kaluga
← Attacks by Polish,
Orsha
Czechoslovak, Romanian, Bulgarian,
Mogilev
Tula
Yugoslavian, Greek and Albanian forces.
Minsk
U.   S.   S.   R.
Front line, December 1943
Bryansk
Front line, mid-June 1944
Bobruisk
Gomel
Orel
Front line, December 1944
Mozyr
Front line, May 1945
Kursk
Voronezh
Chernigov
VOLGA R.
Zhitomir
Kiev
Belgorod
DON R.
Berdichev
Kharkov
Korshun
DNIEPER R.
Kremenchug
Vinnitsa
DONETS R.
Stalingrad
Dnepropetrovsk
Kirovograd
Stalino
Krivoi Rog
Rostov
N
DNIESTER R.
Nikolaev
Odessa
SEA OF AZOV
W   E
Kerch
Izmail
Krasnodar
S
Yalta
Pyatigorsk

BLACK SEA

0   MILES   200
0   KM   200

28

Advance into Germany January 14, 1944– May 9, 1945

At the beginning of 1944 the Russian forces were massed in twelve fronts, extended over a distance of nearly two thousand miles from the Gulf of Finland to the Black Sea. Stalin's first purpose was to liberate Leningrad completely from blockade, to knock the Finns out of the war, and to reoccupy the Baltic states. The swift and devastating advance of the Ukrainian fronts, however, forced him to concentrate mainly on operations in the south, but all fronts gained dramatic victories.

The political impact of the Red Army's advance in the north was hardly less important than the military gains. In February the Finns opened negotiations for an armistice. Stalin offered moderate terms. He may have had in mind the pleas of Churchill and Roosevelt for generous treatment of the Finns, but he was also anxious to encourage the Romanians and other satellites to break with their German ally. The Finns were, however, unsure of the real intentions of the Russians. They protested that they were unable to disarm the German troops in Finland, as Molotov demanded, and they were unwilling to allow Red troops into their country to enforce this and other conditions. In March they broke off negotiations, but the armistice was clearly only postponed.

In December 1943 Stalin had summoned Zhukov and Vasilevsky to Moscow to plan a winter offensive by the four Ukrainian fronts. Stalin had spells of bad temper during these months, when the massive victories being won might have been expected to produce a benign humor. The strain of war was probably the basic reason for his irascibility. For two and a half years without a break of a single day he had personally directed Russian military operations and had controlled the immense Russian war effort. In the midst of the military and supply problems he was aware of the rivalries and jealousies among his commanders, many of whom were rough, brutal, and independent by nature, like Konev, Timoshenko, Eremenko, Meretskov, and others. Among them there was keen rivalry to gain victory and to receive the salute of the guns of Moscow which with the decree of the Presidium proclaiming their deeds was the supreme accolade. Stalin had instituted this system, but he was aware that rivalries and the rush for glory could lead to rash and ill-prepared offensives. At no time in the war was there greater need for a strong Supreme Commander, and he asserted his authority, permitting no argument or challenge to his orders.

The outbursts of temper, which seemed more frequent early in 1944, were quickly brought under control. When the 4th Ukrainian Front in the south, commanded by F. I. Tolbukhin, was held by the enemy at the Nikopol bridgehead, A. M. Vasilevsky, the Stavka representative, decided that the attack must be broken off to prevent heavy and wasteful casualties. He spoke with Stalin by telephone, proposing this course and the strengthening of the 3rd Ukrainian Front for an outflanking movement at Nikopol. Stalin was angry and abusive. He considered that Tolbukhin should have captured the bridgehead. Vasilevsky attempted to argue, and Stalin "threw down the phone" in a fury.[1]

On the following day Vasilevsky was summoned to the telephone. Calmly Stalin discussed his proposals. He spoke also with the commander of the army facing the bridgehead, who confirmed that a direct attack would fail unless supported by an attack from the north by the 3rd Ukrainian Front. Stalin then gave orders to reinforce the front as Vasilevsky had proposed.

At the time of the encirclement of two German corps within the Korshun salient, Stalin was angered by reports that the enemy was breaking out to the north through the lines, held by Vatutin's 1st Ukrainian Front. He telephoned Konev for an immediate report. Showing great confidence, Konev asserted that "Comrade Stalin should not worry himself, as he [Konev] had taken all necessary measures to prevent the enemy's escape by posting Rotmistrov's tank army in the area between the two fronts."[2] Konev's initiative impressed Stalin, who said he would consult the Stavka. He subsequently confirmed his approval of Konev's actions.

At this time Zhukov was in bed with a severe attack of flu. On the morning of February 12 he was awakened to speak by telephone with the Supreme Commander. Stalin was annoyed that he was unable to give him an immediate up-to-the-minute report of the enemy attempt to break out from the Korshun salient. Curtly he told him to check and report. Zhukov hurriedly discussed the situation with Vasilevsky and then reported by telephone. Stalin listened and then told him that Konev had asked for command of all forces engaged in smashing the enemy within the salient, while Vatutin would command the outer ring of the encirclement. Zhukov raised objections. Stalin hung up the telephone.

A few hours later Zhukov received the directive of the Supreme Commander. Konev was given command of operations against the Korshun enemy group, while Zhukov himself was charged with responsibility for co-ordinating the operations of the 1st and 2nd Ukrainian Fronts and preventing any attempts to relieve the enveloped enemy forces. Vatutin complained to Zhukov about the unfairness of this decision, but both men knew that they had to accept it without argument.[3]

On February 18, 1944, the guns of Moscow saluted Konev and the 2nd Ukrainian Front. It was the great ceremonial salute of the nation in recognition of a major victory. There was no mention in the Presidium's decree of Vatutin and the 1st Ukrainian Front which had shared in the operation. Moreover, Konev was made a Marshal of the Soviet Union, joining in rank Zhukov and Vasilevsky, who had been promoted a year earlier.

Soon afterwards Vatutin was mortally wounded in an ambush by Ukrainian nationalist partisans. A brave, able, and dedicated soldier, he had served his country well, especially during the months since July 1942, when with great temerity he had asked Stalin to give him command of the Voronezh Front. He was buried in Kiev, but in Moscow the guns fired a salute of twenty salvos in his honor; it was the salute which he had not received after the Korshun victory.

In March 1944 Milovan Djilas, a member of the Yugoslav mission to Moscow, visited Konev's headquarters. An austere man, he was censorious about the drinking party and banquet arranged for him and his colleagues. The drinking was heavy and for the visitors, faced with the interminable toasts, an ordeal. But those on duty or in contact with the front did not drink.

Konev, a tall blond man of fifty with an energetic bony face, gave Djilas a brief description of the campaign at Korshun. He told him with relish how "some eighty or a hundred thousand Germans had refused to surrender and had been forced into a narrow space, tanks smashed their heavy equipment, and machine-gun posts, while the Cossack cavalry finally finished them off. 'We let the Cossacks cut them up for as long as they wished. They even hacked off the hands of those who raised them to surrender!' the Marshal said with a smile." It was an illustration of the bitterness and savagery of the fighting on the Russian fronts.

Sitting at Konev's side later, Djilas asked why Voroshilov, Budënny, and others who had held high command had been removed from their posts. "Voroshilov is a man of inexhaustible courage," Konev answered, "but he was incapable of understanding modern warfare. His merits are enormous, but—the battle has to be won. . . . Budënny never knew much and he never studied anything. He showed himself to be completely incompetent and permitted awful mistakes to be made. Shaposhnikov was and remains a technical staff officer."

"And Stalin?" Djilas asked.

Taking care not to show surprise at the question, Konev replied after a little thought, "Stalin is universally gifted. He is brilliantly able to see the war as a whole and this makes it possible for him to direct it so successfully."

Djilas remarked that "he said nothing more, nothing that might sound like the stock glorification of Stalin. He passed over in silence the purely military side of Stalin's direction. Konev was an old Communist, firmly devoted to the government and the party but, I would say, with his own firm views on military questions."[4]

Stalin appointed Zhukov commander of the 1st Ukrainian Front after the death of Vatutin, and he himself assumed the function of co-ordinating the operations of the two Ukrainian fronts. The campaign began to recover the Crimea. There had been proposals for sealing off the peninsula across the Perekop Isthmus, leaving the reconquest until later, while the Red Army kept up the momentum of its advance westwards and into Romania and Hungary. Stalin had vivid memories of the threat posed from the Crimea by Wrangel in 1920, and now saw the danger of the Germans breaking out and attacking the rear of the Ukrainian fronts. He ordered that the Crimea be recovered forthwith. The campaign opened early in April 1944 and in the following month, after the destruction of the German Seventeenth Army, Sevastopol was liberated.

On June 6, popularly called D-day, the Anglo-American invasion of Normandy—the long-awaited Second Front—was successfully launched. In Russia a new spirit of goodwill towards the Allies was expressed by Stalin in a statement published in *Pravda*. He was generous in his tribute to the operation of forcing the Channel and carrying out massed landings in northern France as "unquestionably a brilliant success for our Allies. One must admit that the history of war does not know of an undertaking comparable to it for breadth of conception, grandeur of scale, and mastery of execution."[5]

A pause followed on all fronts as the Russians prepared for their summer offensives. The first was launched on June 23 into Belorussia north of the Pripet Marshes. By this date the Anglo-American landings were well established. In Italy the Allies had advanced beyond Rome. The Germans were under severe pressure in every theater of war. The Russian offensive benefited from the Allied operations, but it was Hitler's stubborn insistence on rigid, rather than elastic, defense that aided them most of all.[6]

Stalin worked obsessively on the plans for the Belorussian offensive. He discussed them with all commanders, sometimes individually, sometimes together. He was in frequent communication with the fronts and the Stavka representatives, on occasions telephoning them several times a day. Modifications were worked out in detail by the general staff and brought to him each time for confirmation. It was as though he had made a special resolution not to underestimate the enemy and to take extra care now, when the tide had turned and the Russian armies were sweeping from victory to victory. He, too, was impatient to expel the Germans and to crush them on their own soil. But he would not allow slackness in preparations or overoptimism which led to risky ventures. The careful planning brought results. The great pincer movement trapped some 100,000 enemy troops at Minsk. Army Group Center was virtually destroyed with a loss of more than 200,000 men. By mid-July the Red Army had driven the Germans from Belorussia and had swept into northeastern Poland.

To the south of the Pripet Marshes, Konev launched a massive offensive on July 14, taking Lvov thirteen days later. On July 6 Stalin ordered Zhukov to come to Moscow, and two days later, accompanied by Antonov, he went to Kuntsevo. Stalin wanted to know whether they considered the forces of Konev and Rokossovsky adequate for them to reach the Vistula. Zhukov's view was that they were certainly adequate. Zhukov urged the transfer of some formations to reinforce Vasilevsky so that he could occupy East Prussia and hold down Army Group North on the shores of the Baltic. Stalin rejected this proposal. The priority was, he decided, to secure the Lvov region and eastern Poland. The Germans would fight to the last to hold East Prussia, and Vasilevsky might find himself tied down there.[7]

Two miles from Lublin, the Russians came upon the vast murder-camp of Maidanek with its complex of gas chambers, incinerators, and disposal units. Here the Germans had killed and cremated Jews, Russians, and Poles in groups of 200 to 250. Some 2,000 people had perished daily, and a total of a million and a half people had gone to their death. All Red Army troops in the vicinity of Lublin were ordered to visit the camp so that, impressed by the inhumanity of their enemy, they would allow no feelings of pity or charity to sway them in their task of destroying the Nazi regime.[8]

After advancing some 450 miles in five weeks, Rokossovsky's troops were fatigued and his front was suffering from the problems of overextended supply lines. At this time, moreover, the Germans in front of Warsaw were reinforced by three panzer divisions, rushed up from the south. In the first weeks of August they delivered a counterattack, halting the Russian attempts to advance from their bridgeheads over the Vistula. Nearly six months were to pass before the Russians were ready to launch a major offensive from these positions.

Rokossovsky's advance to the outskirts of Praga, the suburb of Warsaw on the opposite bank of the broad Vistula, made liberation seem at hand. Already on July 24, however, General T. Bor-Komorowski, commanding the Armya Krajowa (AK), the Polish underground army in Warsaw, had decided to order an uprising before the Red Army could reach the city. He was fanatically anti-Russian. He was determined that the Poles should liberate their own city and prepare the way for the London government to take power, excluding the Polish communists. For these reasons and also from stubborn pride he avoided all contact with Rokossovsky and the Russian High Command, refusing even to consider co-ordinating action with the Red Army.

The people of Warsaw were, however, expecting Rokossovsky's forces to cross the river and come to their aid. Moscow radio had broadcast on July 29 the usual appeal, sent to occupied territories, for the people to rise against the enemy as the Russians approached. They were bewildered when no Russian crossing was attempted and the Russian guns fell silent.

On August 1 Bor-Komorowski's underground army of 40,000 men attacked the Germans in the city. They were poorly armed and lacked supplies, but they fought bravely. The battle raged for sixty-three days, but the uprising was savagely crushed. Over 200,000 of the city's inhabitants were killed. The Germans expelled the 800,000 survivors and razed the city to the ground.

The uprising and what Churchill called the "Martyrdom of Warsaw" aroused controversy. The Allied leaders suspected that Stalin had ordered the Red Army to halt at the Vistula and that he was callously leaving the city to its fate. The London Poles actively fomented these suspicions in Britain and the United States. In fact, Rokossovsky's forces had been halted and were in no position to cross the river and liberate the city.

Stalin considered the uprising ill timed and misconceived. He was opposed to co-operation with Bor-Komorowski and the AK, whose hatred of the Russians was well known. He appreciated Rokossovsky's military difficulties. But also at this time when he was actively creating a new pro-Russian regime which would displace the Polish government in London, he was concerned to foster cordial Russo-Polish relations. He was anxious, too, to avoid alienating his Western allies.

On the capture of Lublin on July 23 a manifesto had proclaimed the formation of the Polish Committee of National Liberation. It claimed to have been appointed by representatives of the peasant party and other democratic elements in Poland and to be recognized by Poles abroad, including the Union of Polish Patriots and the Polish Army in Russia.

Soon after the start of the uprising, Churchill, misinterpreting Russian inactivity at the Vistula, sent a cable to Stalin, informing him that British planes were dropping supplies to the Poles and seeking assurances that Russian aid would soon reach them. Stalin's reply was noncommittal and suggested that the extent of the uprising had been grossly exaggerated. Under pressure from the London Poles, Churchill asked Eden on August 14 to send a message to Stalin through Molotov, urging him to give immediate help to the Warsaw Poles. Two days later Vyshinsky informed the U.S. ambassador that the Soviet government would not allow British or American aircraft to land on Soviet territory after dropping supplies in the Warsaw region, "since the Soviet government does not wish to associate itself either directly or indirectly with the adventure in Warsaw."[9] But on September 9 this decision was reversed. Moreover, from September 13 Soviet planes flew over Warsaw, bombing German positions and dropping supplies to the insurgents.

Churchill busily sought ways of increasing aid to the Warsaw Poles. Supported by Roosevelt, he tried to bring further pressure to bear on Stalin referring to the impact on world opinion of their abandoning the anti-Nazi Poles. Stalin was angered by Churchill's activities, which he interpreted as an attempt to promote anti-Soviet forces on Russia's frontier. He was concerned to build a strong buffer zone in eastern Europe. An essential element in the plan was a friendly Poland, closely allied with Russia, and to him this meant a communist Poland. This buffer zone was to him a matter of crucial importance, for he was obsessively concerned with the possibility of a revival of German militarism and a new invasion of Russia in twenty to thirty years.[10]

Towards the end of July, Stalin called a meeting of the Stavka to consider future strategy. One point raised by Stalin was the role of the Stavka representatives at the fronts. Commanders had complained about them taking operations out of their hands. Zhukov said that the Stavka representatives should have the right to assume full responsibility. Shtemenko observed later that "Zhukov with his powerful personality did so anyway."[11] After discussion it was agreed that Zhukov and Vasilevsky alone should have the power to take control over operations at the fronts, and this decision was embodied in a decree.

Stalin had been awaiting the opportunity to strike against Germany's remaining allies. Indeed, at the beginning of the year when the Finns had first opened negotiations, he had hoped that the Romanians would soon break free of their ally, but the Germans kept a firm grip on the country. On August 20, however, Red forces advanced from Moldavia and Bessarabia into Romania, and quickly overwhelmed the two German and two Romanian armies. Romanian troops no longer offered resistance, and in places they turned their guns on their German allies. The King dismissed the two Antonescus, who were responsible for the pro-Axis policy, and accepted the Soviet armistice terms. On August 31 the Romanians, supported by Russian troops, liberated Bucharest.

Towards Bulgaria, Stalin had acted with restraint. Recognizing the weakness of the regime and the widespread pro-Russian feeling, he had not declared war on Bulgaria, even when the Germans established a military and naval base there. But, as the Red Army swept into Romania, he was provoked, especially when the Bulgarians allowed German ships to escape from their ports on the Black Sea. On September 5 the Soviet government declared war, and three days later Tolbukhin's armies invaded the country. They were welcomed by the Bulgarians, and a new government promptly declared war on Germany.

Meanwhile the Finns, too, had come to terms. The Russian offensive along the Karelian Isthmus early in June had pushed them back to their own frontier. The Red Army made no attempt, however, to invade Finland. Stalin wanted an armistice with Finland and the expulsion of German troops from the country. He did not envisage Finland as part of his western defense zone. It was his policy to treat the whole of Scandinavia as a neutral bloc with which Russia would maintain cordial relations. On August 25 the Finns proposed an armistice, which was finally signed in Moscow on September 15. The terms were severe, but not punitive.

Late in September an offensive against Warsaw, now held by strong German forces, aroused Stalin's anger. It was an incident, demonstrating his absolute command over all Russian forces and especially over the top commanders. He had given orders for troops of the 1st Belorussian Front to outflank Warsaw to the north. The Russians met with heavy artillery fire and suffered many casualties. Rokossovsky related that he called off the offensive and reported by telephone to Stalin, who confirmed the decision. According to Zhukov's memoirs, however, it was he who telephoned Stalin, requesting permission to halt the offensive and go over to the defensive in order to give the troops a respite and to allow time for reinforcement. Stalin was displeased. "You and Rokossovsky will please fly to General Headquarters tomorrow for face-to-face discussion," he said abruptly.

On the afternoon of the following day Zhukov and Rokossovsky reported to the Supreme Commander. Antonov and Molotov were also present. Zhukov wrote, "I spread out my map and began explaining the situation. I noticed that Stalin was restless. He would come up to look at the map, then would step back, then approach again, eyeing me and Rokossovsky in turn. He even put his pipe aside which was a sure sign that his composure was slipping, and that he was displeased with something."

"Comrade Zhukov," Molotov interrupted, "you are suggesting

that the offensive be stopped now when the defeated enemy is unable to stand up to our pressure. Is that sensible?"

Zhukov explained that the enemy had organized his defenses and brought up reserves and was holding the Russian offensive.

Stalin asked Rokossovsky's opinion.

"I'd say the troops need a respite to organize themselves after a long and strenuous period of fighting," he answered.

"I suppose the enemy could use a respite to no less advantage than we would," Stalin observed. He then asked Zhukov for his proposals for an offensive on Warsaw.

Zhukov asserted that the present offensive would yield nothing but casualties. He proposed that the city should be taken by encircling it from the southwest. Stalin was growing angry. He interrupted Zhukov and told him and Rokossovsky to go to the waiting room "and think some more."

Twenty minutes later he recalled them to his office and told them that the front could go over to the defensive, as they had proposed. "As for future plans, we'll discuss them later. You may go now," he said curtly.

Zhukov observed, "Rokossovsky and I parted silently, each preoccupied with his own thoughts."

On the following day Stalin telephoned Zhukov. "What would you say to General Headquarters taking control over all fronts in future?"

Zhukov took this to mean the abolition of the post of Stavka representative and expressed the view that it would be practicable since there were now fewer fronts.

"You're saying that without feeling offended?"

"What is there to be offended about? I hope neither Vasilevsky nor I will find ourselves unemployed," Zhukov replied.

Stalin then told him that he was to take command of the 1st Belorussian Front, operating in the Berlin strategic zone, and continue as Deputy Supreme Commander in Chief. He proposed to transfer Rokossovsky to command of the 2nd Belorussian Front.[12]

Stalin valued Zhukov as the most able of the Soviet commanders. At the same time he recognized that he was an extremely powerful personality, often stubborn in pressing his views.

Between them a strong relationship existed with periods of tension, in which Stalin was always dominant. But, while at times he appeared hard on Zhukov, he took pains to do him justice and make full use of his abilities.

On July 29 Stalin himself telephoned to congratulate him on the award of his second Gold Medal of Hero of the Soviet Union, the highest and most coveted award. Kalinin, President of the Soviet Union, also telephoned to congratulate him and advise him that "yesterday the State Committee for Defence, acting on Stalin's proposal, decided to decorate you for the Belorussian operation and the liberation of the Ukraine."[13]

A few months later, however, Zhukov was again in trouble with the Supreme Commander. The incident again revealed Stalin's concern to assert his authority and the command structure, while maintaining the standing and dignity of senior officers.

The Stavka published a regular bulletin, setting out "the lessons learned at the front in the course of the fighting." Stalin found time to study each issue as soon as it was published. During the autumn of 1944 he noted that Voronov had issued two army regulations, both countersigned by Zhukov, without his knowledge or, as he stated it, "without the knowledge of the Stavka." Antonov knew nothing about it and was given two days to investigate. Stalin became more incensed when it emerged that the two Marshals did not appreciate the difference between an *Ustav* (Regulation) and a *Prizak* (Order).

The Politburo was summoned. "Since it would be improper for the general staff to do this to two generals of such rank," the Politburo must issue an appropriate order. Thereupon he dictated the order, stating:

> One. Marshal Zhukov, without sufficient checking, without summoning or consulting the people at the front and without notifying the Stavka, confirmed and enacted the *Ustav*.[14]
>
> Two. I reprove Chief Marshal of Artillery Comrade Voronov for his light-hearted attitude to artillery regulations.
>
> Three. I make it encumbent upon Marshal Zhukov to display circumspection in deciding serious questions.[15]

As under the Tsars, no one from the highest to the lowest in the land was immune from reprimand, removal, and severe punishment by the supreme ruler.

The surrender of Finland made it possible to plan the major offensive to clear the Baltic region. The German Army Group North presented a threat to the flank of the Russian armies, when they advanced on the final drive on the Warsaw-Berlin axis. Stalin took an especially close interest in directing these operations. Early in July the Red Army forces were about to envelop Army Group North, and he issued a series of directives for the operation. But the Germans skillfully avoided encirclement and prepared strong defenses in depth.

To the south early in October, Tolbukhin's armies advanced through Romania and joined with the Yugoslav partisans of Tito's committee of national liberation. On October 20 they entered Belgrade. The plan now was to mount an offensive from the south against the German and Hungarian forces concentrated in the region of Budapest and to advance northwards into Germany. Although threatened more immediately from the east, Hitler was determined to halt the Russian advance through Hungary, and he reinforced his armies at Budapest.

On October 30 Malinovsky's 2nd Ukrainian Front launched a powerful drive on Budapest. By November 4, advance columns had reached the suburbs of the city. There they were halted. Stalin had been of the opinion that Budapest could be taken quickly. In forming this opinion he was influenced by a personal telegram, sent by the malign Mekhlis from the 4th Ukrainian Front, stating that the Hungarians were completely demoralized. He had approved plans, drawn up hurriedly by the general staff, which he himself passed to Malinovsky by telephone, and he ordered the immediate capture of the city. Malinovsky repeatedly asked for more time to make essential preparations. Stalin was adamant. Only when he received a report from Timoshenko on the strength of the enemy positions did he agree to call off the offensive. At the same time he adopted a new plan to encircle Budapest from the north. But the city had still not fallen at the end of the year.

As the Russians swept westwards in a victorious horde, Churchill became increasingly worried about the spread of Soviet influence. Romania and Bulgaria were already under Soviet domination, and he was concerned about the future of Poland, Greece, and Yugoslavia. Adding to his anxiety was the fact that, as he wrote, the United States was "very slow in realising the upsurge of communist influence which slid on before, as well as followed, the onward march of the mighty armies, directed from the Kremlin."[16]

Churchill proposed visiting Moscow in October (1944) for preliminary discussions. Stalin at once extended a warm invitation. Churchill had written to him earlier about Roosevelt's plans to visit western Europe and had suggested a meeting in The Hague. Stalin was not prepared, however, to leave Moscow. In conversation with the British and American ambassadors he had "grumbled about his health," saying that he never kept well except in Moscow and that even his visits to the front did him harm; his doctors were averse to his flying, and it had taken him a fortnight to recover from Teheran.[17]

Accompanied by Eden and service chiefs, Churchill arrived in Moscow on October 9 and received a tremendous welcome. Stalin had never been more charming and friendly. Churchill and his colleagues noted, too, that all the Russians appeared to be more friendly than at the time of his visit two years earlier. Then the terrible defeats and losses suffered in the German advance, and doubts about the Second Front, had darkened their attitude towards the Allies. Now pride in the victories of the Red Army had wrought a dramatic change. The deep, vigilant suspicion of Russians towards the West appeared to have been allayed.

At the Bolshoi Theater a gala performance of ballet and the Red Army choir was arranged. Churchill was moved, as he stood in the box, by the prolonged ovation that greeted him from the enormous audience. Stalin's entry into the box gave rise to an "almost passionate demonstation."[18]

The British ambassador, Sir Archibald Clark Kerr, had at an earlier meeting persuaded Stalin to dine at the embassy, the building standing across the river from the Kremlin, which Stalin must have seen countless times from the windows of his office. The dinner was to be one of the highlights of Churchill's visit. Several days before the dinner the NKVD descended on the embassy in force, searched every corner, and posted guards inside and outside the grounds. The streets from the Kremlin to the embassy were closed to traffic on the night of the dinner and troops lined the route.

Stalin arrived wearing a long gray military overcoat and a peaked cap with a red band. Underneath he was wearing a Marshal's uniform with a single decoration on his chest. Molotov, wearing ornate diplomatic uniform, went upstairs with Stalin, accompanied by the ambassador. Vyshinsky arrived and quipped to Birse, the interpreter, as he pointed to the guards: "I see the Red Army has had another victory. It has occupied the British Embassy."[19]

Stalin was in a relaxed mood and evidently looking forward to the English-style dinner, which he had first experienced at the embassy in Teheran. At one point he stared incredulously at the life-size portraits of the Royal Family on the walls of the dining room, which included a portrait of George V. Turning to Birse, who was sitting next to him, he said, "Isn't that our Nicholas II?" Birse had to remind him that the two monarchs had been cousins and that the resemblance between them had been striking.[20] After dinner, as they withdrew to another room, the guns of Moscow began firing a salute in honor of the capture of Cluj in Romania, and the embassy was lit up by celebratory fireworks from the walls of the Kremlin.

The talks between Stalin and Molotov and Churchill and Eden produced only limited results. The Polish problem was intractable. Seeking to avoid upsetting his ally, Stalin made some gestures towards a compromise, but he remained adamant that the Soviet government could not tolerate in Poland a government that was actively hostile to Soviet Russia. He agreed nevertheless at their first meeting that Stanisław Mikolajczyk, head of the London Poles, with two of his ministers, should be invited to Moscow at once for discussions with representatives of the Lublin Committee. Their meetings were fruitless. They could not agree on the division of powers between them in a future government, and on other points both sides were unyielding.

At this first meeting, judging that Stalin was in a sympathetic mood, Churchill said: "Let us settle about our affairs in the Balkans. Your armies are in Romania and Bulgaria. We have interests, missions, and agents there. Don't let us get at cross-purposes in small ways."

Churchill records:

> While this was being translated I wrote out on half a sheet of paper: Romania-Russia 90%, the others 10%; Greece-Great Britain 90% (in accord with the U.S.A.), Russia 10%; Yugoslavia 50–50%; Hungary 50–50%; Bulgaria-Russia 75%, the others 25%.
>
> I pushed this across the table to Stalin, who had by then heard the translation. There was a slight pause. Then he took his blue pencil and made a large tick upon it and passed it back to us. It was all settled in no more time than it takes to set down. . . . The pencilled paper lay in the centre of the table. At length I said, "Might it not be thought rather cynical if it seemed we had disposed of these issues, so fateful to millions of people, in such an offhand manner? Let us burn the paper." "No, you keep it," said Stalin.[21]

In preparation for the military meetings with the British, Stalin had instructed Antonov to produce a brief and present it himself. Stalin was not satisfied, however, with the draft, sent to him at Kuntsevo, and began rewriting parts of it. He laid stress on the Soviet interest in holding Hungary as the center of Europe. For this reason, he wrote, they must convince the Allies that Soviet strength on the Balkan flank was stronger than it was in fact and that their main strategy in this theater was to smash Hungary and invade Germany from the south.

Sir Alan Brooke, chief of the Imperial General Staff, found Antonov friendly and ready to talk except in the presence of Stalin, when he appeared to lose his confidence and to be unsure how much to say. At a meeting on October 14, after Brooke had reported on Allied operations in Burma and Europe and General Deane had spoken on U.S. strategy in the Pacific, Antonov described Soviet operations. Eden found his report clear and fluent, but noted that he continually looked to Stalin for confirmation.[22] Stalin interrupted him frequently and answered questions. Finally, losing patience with Antonov's hesitance, Stalin took over from him.

On the next evening the discussion was on the war in the Pacific. Averell Harriman, the U.S. ambassador, and General Deane were attending the talks on behalf of their President. They reiterated American concern that Russia should join in the war against Japan as soon as possible. Stalin at once gave the assurance that Russia would begin hostilities within three months after the defeat of Germany, and that for this purpose the thirty Red Army divisions there would be raised to sixty divisions. This was subject, however, to the United States providing reserve supplies and to the clarification of "the political aspects of the Soviet Union's participation." He agreed also that U.S. forces would be able to use the naval base and airfields at Petropavlovsk, but they would have to use the Pacific, not the Trans-Siberian route.[23]

At this point Brooke asked whether the Trans-Siberian railways could maintain the necessary supplies for the sixty Red Army divisions. Antonov looked to Stalin for the answer, although Brooke felt sure that he knew it. Stalin did not respond, and Antonov explained that the railway could meet the supply needs of the Red forces. Then Stalin intervened and gave what Brooke called "an astonishing presentation of technical railway detail" with the conclusion that the Trans-Siberian Railway would not be able to maintain adequate supplies. Brooke observed that more than ever before he was impressed by Stalin's military ability.[24]

The third military meeting was confined to the Soviet and U.S. representatives. Stalin outlined the strategy which would be followed by his forces in the Far East. He then presented a list of the supplies, amounting to more than a million tons in bulk, which the United States was to provide. These supplies comprised food, transport, and fuel for two months for 1.5 million troops, 3,000 tanks, 5,000 aircraft, and 75,000 vehicles. Stalin obviously considered that, since the United States was so eager for Soviet participation in the war against Japan, he was entitled to exact all he could in supplies. His approach was rooted in the feeling that the immensely wealthy United States had endured none of the devastation and suffering of war on its own territory; Soviet Russia had made all the sacrifices and was entitled to demand maximum support.

In their political talks Churchill and Eden felt that they had reached general agreement on the partitioning of Germany, the treatment of war criminals, and other matters. Churchill did not raise the points in dispute with the Soviet government concerning the United Nations organization, which was under active consideration by the three powers. At Roosevelt's request he left this subject for discussion at a meeting of the three leaders to take place later in November. Apparently bypassing Churchill completely, Roosevelt had dealt directly with Stalin in arranging this meeting, and Churchill learned about it from Stalin.

Departing from Moscow, Churchill and Eden considered that their visit had been worthwhile. They had been received with an impressive display of goodwill, and, while there were still unresolved problems, they had reached a general understanding and felt that they could count on Stalin's will to co-operate.

By the end of 1944 preparations had been completed for a massive advance from the Vistula. Stalin had directed the planning, which had as its primary objective the capture of the important industrial region of Upper Silesia. This called for an advance of over one hundred miles from the Russian positions. But Stalin was looking beyond this goal to the Oder River and to Berlin, involving an advance of nearly three hundred miles.

In preparation for this winter campaign he had reorganized the main fronts, ensuring that his three most outstanding offensive generals held the key commands. Konev remained with the 1st Ukrainian Front, but Zhukov took over the 1st Belorussian Front in the center, and Rokossovsky was transferred to command of the 2nd Belorussian Front. Farther to the north I. D. Cherniakhovsky, commanding the 3rd Belorussian Front, was to advance into East Prussia. Zhukov and Konev were thus leading the main offensive. But Stalin decided that as Supreme Commander he personally would co-ordinate the operations of the four main fronts.

The build-up of troops and equipment for this offensive was stupendous in scale. The two fronts, commanded by Zhukov and Konev, alone had 2.2 million troops with 32,143 guns and mortars, 6,460 tanks and self-propelling guns, and they were supported by 4,772 aircraft.[25] The tanks included a large number of the lat-

est "Iosif Stalin" tank, described as a monster heavily armored
and carrying a 122-mm gun.

On the Western Front in December, the Anglo-American
forces found themselves seriously threatened by Field Marshal
Karl von Rundstedt's counteroffensive in the Ardennes. On January 6, 1945, Churchill sent a message to Stalin asking whether the
Allies could "count on a major Russian offensive on the Vistula
front or elsewhere during January." Stalin responded promptly.
Preparations had been made, but the offensive had been delayed
until the weather conditions were favorable. "Nevertheless, taking
into account the position of our Allies on the Western front,
GHQ of the Supreme Command has decided to accelerate the
completion of our preparations and, regardless of the weather, to
start large-scale offensive operations against the Germans along
the whole of the central front not later than the second half of
January."[26]

Eisenhower, the Supreme Allied Commander, decided to send
his deputy, Air Marshal Sir Arthur Tedder, to Moscow to explain
the Allied predicament. Tedder arrived in Moscow early in January. Simple in manner, concise in speech, experienced and professional, Tedder was a man after Stalin's heart. At the end of his detailed description of the Allied operations and the battle of the
Ardennes, Stalin exclaimed: "That's what I like. A clear, businesslike statement without diplomatic reservations." Birse noted
that "throughout the talk Stalin was like a boy listening to and
enjoying a tale of military adventure."[27]

The Russian offensive was launched at 10 A.M. on January 12,
1945. Konev's force of ten armies advanced so rapidly that within
ten days they were sweeping through Upper Silesia and fighting
on the banks of the Oder River. Two days later Zhukov opened
his offensive, and the advance of his 1st Belorussian Front was
even more spectacular. He liberated Warsaw, and by January 29
his forces had encircled Poznan and had reached the outskirts of
Frankfurt. Rokossovsky's 2nd Belorussian Front had swept across
northern Poland, while farther north Cherniakhovsky's front had
advanced deep into East Prussia and by the end of the month was
poised to strike at Königsberg.

Early in February 1945 Stalin, Roosevelt, and Churchill met in conference at Yalta on the Black Sea coast. At this time the Russians were making spectacular advances on all fronts and had reached the Oder. In the West, however, the Allied armies were recovering from the Battle of the Bulge and had yet to cross the Rhine. But nothing in the discussions as reported by Churchill and Stettinius suggested that Stalin's attitude towards his Allies was influenced by Russian military successes. He was in no way overbearing, nor did he attempt to take a strong line. Indeed, the three leaders talked frankly and achieved a wide measure of understanding and agreement, except on Poland.

The American delegation stayed at the Livadia Palace, which had been the Black Sea residence of the Tsars. Here the plenary sessions were held every afternoon. The British delegation was housed in the Vorontsov Palace. Military talks and meetings of the three foreign ministers took place in the Yusupov Palace, a large villa higher up the mountainside. In addition to the formal sessions there were private talks between the three leaders and the customary informal and formal lunches and dinners. The Yalta Conference was described as a "high-speed, high-powered conference," and for none was it more arduous than for the interpreters.

Birse, the British interpreter, has related that at the final dinner, Stalin stood up, glass in hand, and said, "Tonight and on other occasions, we three leaders have got together. We talk, we eat and drink, and we enjoy ourselves. But meanwhile our three interpreters have to work and their work is not easy. They have no time to eat or drink. We rely on them to transmit our ideas to each other. I propose a toast to our interpreters!" Then he walked around the table, clinking glasses with each of them. In raising his glass Churchill declared, "Interpreters of the world, unite! You have nothing to lose but your audience!" This parody on the communist slogan appealed to Stalin, and it was some minutes before he could stop laughing.[28]

On another occasion Stalin was affronted by what he considered disrespect, and an incident was avoided only by an appeal to his sense of humor. This happened at a luncheon when Roosevelt, although advised by Churchill to refrain, told Stalin and the whole company that he and Churchill referred to him in their secret telegrams as "Uncle Joe." Stalin took offense. "When can I leave this table?" he said angrily. Byrnes saved the occasion by reminding him that everyone spoke of Uncle Sam, and that Uncle Joe was not offensive. Accepting the name as a term of affection, Stalin calmed down.[29]

At the first plenary session on February 5 the future of Germany was discussed. All agreed that Germany should be dismembered after unconditional surrender. On Roosevelt's proposal the foreign ministers were directed to produce a plan within a month for the division and control of the country. Earlier Stalin had objected to France sharing in this process, but now he yielded to Churchill's pleas and agreed that France should administer an occupation zone and have a place on the control commission. A special committee was set up to meet in secret in Moscow to examine the complex problem of German reparations.

The second session considered the world organization for peace. At Dumbarton Oaks discussion of the question of voting rights in the Security Council had ended in deadlock. A compromise proposal, put forward by Roosevelt, was now discussed. His proposal was that each member of the council should have one vote. Conflicts would be divided into two categories, one requiring economic, political, or military sanctions, and the other for disputes which could be settled by peaceful means. Sanctions could be applied only if the permanent members of the council were unanimous. Herein lay the right of veto which was to become a crucial factor in the functioning of the council.

Stalin took a keen interest in this proposal and sought with blunt honesty to clarify the position. "The greatest danger," he said, "is conflict among ourselves, because if we remain united the German menace is not important. Therefore we must now think how to secure our unity in the future and how to guarantee that the three great powers (and possibly China and France) will maintain a united front."[30] He then spoke of the Russo-Finnish War and the fact that Britain and France had managed to expel Russia from the League of Nations. He wanted guarantees against a repetition of such a situation. When the conference resumed on the following day Stalin announced that the Soviet government accepted the new voting procedures, requiring the unanimity of the three powers.[31]

At Dumbarton Oaks the Soviet government had demanded that the republics of the Soviet Union should be founder members, each with a vote. Britain and the United States had questioned this demand as excessive. Now in Yalta, Molotov announced that the Soviet government would be content if three of the republics—namely, the Ukraine, Belorussia, and Lithuania—or at any rate two became founder members. On these and several other major issues Stalin showed his readiness to compromise. Churchill wrote in a report to London on February 8 that "in spite of our gloomy warnings and forebodings, Yalta has turned out very well so far."[32]

The Polish problem brought discord into the conference. Roosevelt observed that Poland "has been a source of trouble for over five hundred years" and Churchill was to record that Poland "was the first of the great causes which led to the breakdown of the Grand Alliance."[33]

Stalin explained his policy on Poland clearly. Throughout history Poland had attacked Russia or had served as a corridor through which enemies had invaded her. Germany had used this corridor twice in the past thirty years. Russia wanted a strong Poland who could herself guard this corridor. He did not add expressly, but it was obvious, that he would not tolerate a revival of the old regime, now represented by the London government, comprised of men who were the sworn enemies of Russia. On this problem a fundamental difference divided the Allies. Stalin was concerned for Russian security. Churchill and Roosevelt maintained that they were upholding democratic principles.

In seven of the eight plenary sessions Poland was discussed. Preliminary agreement was reached on Poland's frontiers; the final delimitation of the western frontier was to await the peace conference. But argument continued about the composition of the Polish government. Finally it was agreed that the Lublin committee provisional government should be "reorganized on a broader democratic basis, with the inclusion of democratic leaders from Poland itself and from Poles abroad." A further provision was that Molotov and the United States and British ambassadors should consult with all Polish leaders with a view to reorganizing the government on these lines. It was agreed also that "the Polish provisional government of National Unity shall be pledged on the holding of free and unfettered elections as soon as possible on the basis of universal suffrage and secret ballot."[34]

The war in the Far East had not been included on the agenda. The Americans, however, fearing that it might last a further two years, were eager for Russian participation. Roosevelt raised the subject with Stalin on February 8. Stalin confirmed that Russia would enter the war against Japan two to three months after Germany's surrender. His terms were the preservation of the status quo in Outer Mongolia and the restoration of Russia's position in the Far East, as it had been before the Russo-Japanese War of 1904–5. These terms were agreed, and Roosevelt undertook to obtain the agreement of Chiang Kai-shek.

In the course of informal meetings the three leaders achieved closer understanding of each other's outlook and problems. Stalin attached great importance to these informal relations. He went out of his way to express his faith in their alliance and his anxiety "that it should not lose its character of intimacy, of its free expression of views. In the history of diplomacy I know of no such close alliance of three great powers as this, when allies had the opportunity of so frankly expressing their views." He believed fervently that the alliance of the great powers and the United Nations were the foundations upon which future world peace could be built.[35] But when on February 11 the three leaders parted they realized that they would not all meet again. Roosevelt was frail and ill and was clearly nearing death. Stalin and the Russian people as a whole held him in high respect, seeing in him a statesman and a friend. For Churchill, too, they had respect and even affection, acknowledging that he was a great war leader, but they had also an abiding mistrust of him and the British.

The advance of the Red Army westwards continued, but the Germans were defending their ground with fanatic bravery. Stalin was angered by the failure to take Königsberg. Between Zhukov and Rokossovsky there was a brief failure in co-ordination, which called for Stalin's intervention, and he sent Vasilevsky to the fronts as his representative. He demanded the prompt destruction of the enemy so that the Russian forces there could be available for the advance on Berlin. He also told Vasilevsky that he should prepare to serve as Commander in Chief in the Far East in the near future. But on the evening of February 18 he telephoned to tell him that Cherniakhovsky, the gallant young commander of the 3rd Belorussian Front, had been killed in action, and that he was to take over his command. The fighting in East Prussia continued to be exceptionally savage and it was not until mid-April that the Germans were cleared from the region.

In Hungary the fighting was also severe. Budapest was taken on February 13. The Russians then swept northwards into Austria and on April 13 occupied Vienna. While preparing for the advance into Austria, however, Tolbukhin, commanding the 3rd Ukrainian Front, had realized that the enemy Army Group South was preparing an offensive against his front. He was particularly disturbed by reports that the Sixth SS Panzer Army had been transferred from the west to strengthen the offensive.

On March 6 the Germans attacked with "exceptional ferocity." Tolbukhin asked permission to withdraw his front to the east of the Danube if necessary. He was, according to Shtemenko, in poor health and in any case not as ruthless and determined as the other Marshals. Shtemenko was in Stalin's office when Tolbukhin telephoned. Stalin thought for a minute about his request, and then, speaking calmly, he said: "Comrade Tolbukhin! If you are thinking of extending the war by five or six months, then please do withdraw your troops behind the Danube. It will, of course, be quieter there. But I doubt whether that is your intention. Therefore you must defend the right bank and stay there yourself with your headquarters. I am sure that the troops will do their duty and fulfil their difficult task. All that is necessary is that they should be commanded properly."[36] Tolbukhin stood his ground, crushed the enemy offensive, and advanced to Vienna.

Angry exchanges took place between Stalin, Roosevelt, and Churchill during the first months of 1945. They revealed Stalin's unresting suspicion and his readiness to challenge the good faith of his allies with insulting frankness. The first incident concerned an approach made by General Karl Wolff, commander of the SS in Italy, to the American intelligence service in Switzerland. Two "exploratory meetings" with him took place, and he was told that negotiations for a separate peace could not be considered. The Soviet government was informed, and it at once charged the Allies with denying facilities for a Soviet representative to be present.

On the basis of reports from his own intelligence service, Stalin became convinced that the British and the Americans were negotiating a separate surrender in southern Europe. Bluntly he accused Roosevelt and Churchill of breach of faith and falsehood. Both leaders were angered by this attack on their integrity, and they responded vigorously. Stalin was clearly shaken to find that his accusations had caused such deep offense. He ended his letter on April 7 to Churchill with the explanatory words: "My messages are personal and strictly confidential. This makes it possible to speak one's mind clearly and frankly. This is the advantage of confidential communications. If, however, you are going to regard every frank statement of mine as offensive, it will make this kind of communication very difficult. I can assure you that I had and have no intention of offending anyone." This was, so Churchill remarked in a note to Roosevelt, "as near as they can get to an apology."[37]

When, in April, Heinrich Himmler, the Nazi leader, offered through Count Folke Bernadotte, the head of the Swedish Red Cross, to surrender the German forces in Norway and Denmark to British, American, or Swedish troops, the British ambassador in Stockholm reported the offer promptly to London. Churchill informed Stalin at once by cable and stated that his proposed reply to Himmler was that nothing less than unconditional surrender to the three major powers would be acceptable. Stalin cabled his agreement, adding the words: "Knowing you, I had no doubt that you would act in this way." Churchill felt that at last he had gained a degree of trust from Stalin, and he replied, "I am extremely pleased to know that you had no doubt how I would act and always will act towards your glorious country and yourself."[38] But the goodwill and trust were to be short-lived.

Towards the end of March rivalry erupted between the Allies over the capture of Berlin. At Yalta the three leaders had agreed on their policies on the division of Germany, but had not discussed the co-ordination of the strategy of the Red Army and the Anglo-American forces. Eisenhower and Montgomery had agreed some months earlier that their chief political and military aim should be the capture of Berlin. On May 27 Montgomery reported to Churchill that he was advancing towards the Elbe with the capture of Berlin as his objective, and Churchill was entirely in agreement with this purpose. On May 28, however, Eisenhower, without reference to the Combined Chiefs of Staff or to Air Marshal Tedder, his deputy, sent a message through General Deane to Stalin. In it he stated that his strategy was now to cut through the German defenses and to make contact with the Red Army, after which the Anglo-American armies would concentrate along an axis from west to southeast in the direction of Dresden.

Stalin informed Deane that he agreed with Eisenhower that Berlin no longer had the same strategic importance as before and that the proposed Anglo-American plan would harmonize well with Soviet operations. The Red Army would advance towards Dresden to join with the Allied forces. He stated further that the Soviet offensive would open in mid-May, but the timing might have to be altered.[39]

Churchill raised a storm over the changed Allied strategy, complaining bitterly that it was wrong and that it had not been discussed. Eisenhower recorded that Churchill "was greatly disappointed and disturbed because my plan did not first throw Montgomery forward with all the strength I could give him from the American forces in the desperate attempt to capture Berlin before the Russians could do so. He sent his views to Washington."[40]

Like Churchill, Stalin attached enormous political significance to the capture of Berlin. But he and all the Russians had a burning sense of their right to conquer the German capital. They had suffered far more than the Allies in the war and had borne the brunt of the fighting. It would have been for them an unbearable anticlimax if the Germans had surrendered the city to the British and Americans.

Stalin was particularly worried that the Germans might come to terms with the Allies and then concentrate their remaining forces on his eastern front. Immediately after giving Deane his reply to Eisenhower's message, he summoned Zhukov to Moscow from the 1st Belorussian Front. Zhukov arrived on the following day and went directly to the Kremlin. In answer to Stalin's question he said that he and Konev would be able to launch their offensive on Berlin in two weeks. He was not sure, however, that Rokossovsky could prepare so quickly, since his front was still engaged in liquidating the enemy in the Danzig and Gdynia region.

"Well, then," said Stalin, "we shall have to begin the operation without waiting for Rokossovsky. Even if he's a few days late, that's no trouble."[41]

Stalin then showed him a report that German agents had approached the Allies with proposals for a separate peace. The possibility could not be ruled out, he said, that the Germans might let the Allies into Berlin. "I believe Roosevelt will not violate the Yalta agreement, but as for Churchill, he can do anything," he added.[42]

Before dawn on April 16 Zhukov's and Konev's fronts opened the offensive. Relentlessly they pressed forward, and the German forces, defending Berlin frantically, could not hold them. By April 23, Russian troops had broken into the city. Savage fighting continued in streets and buildings. The climax of the battle came on April 30, the day on which Hitler committed suicide, when the Russians stormed the Reichstag. On May 2 all resistance in the city ceased. Six days later Field-Marshal Wilhelm Keitel, representing the German High Command, surrendered to Marshal Zhukov. Czechoslovakia had still not been completely liberated, but on May 9 Prague finally fell. This day was proclaimed Victory Day.

On the evening of May 9 Stalin broadcast to the nation. He expressed the pride, elation, and relief which all Russians felt. Like them, he had fought the war not as a communist or the leader of the proletarian vanguard; he had put ideology aside and fought as a nationalist and a patriot, defending Holy Russia. He paid tribute to the Red Army, and also to the Allied forces, but he was addressing his own people:

> The great sacrifices we made in the name of the freedom and independence of our Motherland, the incalculable privations and sufferings experienced by our people in the course of the war, the intense work in the rear and at the front, placed on the altar of the Motherland, have not been in vain, and have been crowned

by complete victory over the enemy. The age-long struggle of the Slav peoples for their existence and their independence has ended in victory over the German invaders and German tyranny. . . . I congratulate you on victory, my dear men and women compatriots![43]

At a grand reception in the Kremlin in honor of Red Army commanders on May 24, Stalin spoke again. Giving rein to his love of Russia and her people, he paid a fervent tribute to the Great Russian nation, "because it is the most outstanding nation of all the nations of the Soviet Union . . . not only because it is the leading people but also because it possesses a clear mind, a staunch character and patience." He then made the frank admission that the Soviet government had made many mistakes; it amounted to an admission of his own mistakes. But even during the desperate months of 1941 and 1942, when the Red Army was in full retreat, the Russian people had not told its government to go, and had not thought of making peace with Germany, but had shown its confidence in the government and its readiness to make sacrifices until victory had been won. "Thanks to it, the Russian people, for this confidence!"[44]

The climax of the celebrations came on June 24, when the great Victory Parade took place in the Red Square. It was a day of torrential rain, but this did not diminish the grandeur of the occasion. Rokossovsky commanded the parade, and Zhukov took the salute. Standing on the Lenin Mausoleum, Stalin appeared as a small remote figure, but, as hundreds of German regimental banners were flung down on the steps of the mausoleum and at his feet, he dominated the scene.

It was in a real sense his victory. It could not have been won without his industrialization campaign and especially the intensive development of industry beyond the Volga. Collectivization had contributed to the victory by enabling the government to stockpile food and raw materials and to prevent paralysis in industry and famine in the towns. But also collectivization, with its machine-tractor stations, had given the peasants their first training in the use of tractors and other machines. Collectivized farming had been "the peasants' preparatory school for mechanized warfare."[45] The raising of the general standard of education had also contributed by providing a vast reserve of educated men who could readily be trained.

It was his victory, too, because he had directed and controlled every branch of Russian operations throughout the war. The range and burden of his responsibilities were extraordinary, but day by day without a break for the four years of the war he exercised direct command of the Russian forces and control over supplies, war industries, and government policy, including foreign policy.

As he himself acknowledged, he had made mistakes and miscalculations, some with tragic consequences and heavy casualties. The first and perhaps the greatest of his mistakes was his political misjudgment of German plans to invade Russia. He had obdurately refused to believe that Hitler would launch his invasion in June 1941, and, seeking to buy time by placating him, he had taken none of the obvious defense measures.

Again he has been held solely responsible for the terrible Russian losses of 1941 and 1942, and criticized for not following the traditional Russian strategy of retreating into the vastness of the Russian plain. This had been the strategy followed by Peter the Great in the Northern War and by Mikhail Barclay de Tolly and M. I. Kutuzov against Napoleon. They had drawn the enemy deeper and deeper into Russia, extending his lines of communication, weakening him, and committing him to a winter campaign.

Defenses organized in depth, however, would hardly have halted the surge of the highly mechanized *Wehrmacht* in 1941. It had effortlessly crushed the Polish Army, which some British military experts in 1939 had rated above the Red Army in efficiency and morale. It had conquered France and expelled the British from the continent. Acutely aware of the inadequacies of the Russian defenses and the weakness of the Red Army in 1941, Stalin knew that they could not withstand a German attack. He gambled for time so that his urgent mechanization and training programs could build up the Red Army's strength. He lost the gamble.

Stalin knew the military history of his country and well understood the strategy of falling back and using its great spaces. By temperament, however, he was positive and aggressive, eager to attack rather than defend, and this was characteristic of his conduct of Russian strategy throughout the war. He was at the same time capable of tremendous self-control, as he demonstrated in waiting for the Germans to attack in the battle for Kursk, and in general during 1943–45 he was constantly on guard against premature and ill-prepared offensives.

A chief reason why during 1941–42 he was constantly demanding offensive action, although it often involved terrible casualties, was that in these disastrous months, when Russia seemed near to collapse, he subordinated military considerations to the need to uphold the pride and fighting spirit of the nation. He was unsure of the morale of the Red Army and of the Russian people. Attempts to direct and control an orderly withdrawal of forces and the evacuation of the civilian population would have led, he feared, to panic-stricken flight, as had happened to the tsarist army in 1916–17. The *bolshoi drap*, or great panic, which had swept through Moscow in October 1941 as the Germans approached, was the kind of failure in morale which might have spread throughout Russia, leading to complete collapse. Facing Napoleon, Kutuzov had calmly ordered the evacuation of Moscow and had abandoned the city to the French, knowing that the whole nation was loyal to the Tsar and would obey orders. Stalin did not have this certainty. In the event, the Germans had plunged deep into southern Russia, overextending their supply lines and committing themselves to winter warfare, for which they were not equipped. But at every stage he had fought to halt them, as he had halted them before Moscow. He had demanded attack and had inspired his commanders with his own spirit of aggression and will to victory. It was indeed his implacable will which more than any other factor held the nation from collapse in the tragic days of 1941–42.

Stalin has also been held guilty of bringing upon Russia the disasters of 1941–42 by his purge of the Red Army. Although tragic and wasteful, the purge probably had little effect, and certainly less than is often stated.[46] Although many senior army commanders were purged, it was in this category that the Red Army was generally superior to the Germans, even in the years 1941–42.

German superiority was marked among junior officers and
NCOs.[47]

From the first months of the war Stalin gathered around him
able senior officers, rejuvenating the High Command. He chose
them on merit, and, an astute judge of men, he was constantly
raising fairly junior officers to high rank. By the time of the battle
of Moscow, he had selected his key commanders in Zhukov, Vasilevsky, Rokossovsky, Konev, and Voronov. To them were added
by the time of the Battle of Stalingrad Vatutin, Eremenko,
Malinovsky, Meretskov, Cherniakhovsky, and others.

Stalin was unchallenged as Supreme Commander. His most
able generals, like Zhukov, Rokossovsky, Konev, and others, who
were outstanding among the generals of all countries involved in
the war, accepted his authority unquestioningly. In fact, he dominated them not by virtue of office but by force of character and
intellect. He inspired deepest respect and also affection. At times
he exploded in anger, demanding immediate action; at other
times he spoke gently, encouraging and inspiring confidence.

With his disciplined mind and tenacious memory he developed
considerable military expertise and technical knowledge. Western
officers and engineers present at discussions with him were impressed by his quick and accurate understanding. Alan Brooke,
chief of the British general staff, remarked on several occasions
on his mastery of military matters. His own commanders considered their reports carefully before submitting them, for he would
unfailingly put his finger on any weakness or loose thinking in
their presentation. In the early months of the war, when, fearful
of a general collapse, his overriding concern was to keep the nation fighting, he paid little heed to the views of his generals. As
the war continued, however, he treated them with greater respect.
Moreover, as Zhukov stated, he was always prepared to reverse his
own opinions when presented with sound reasons. But he made
the final decisions.

Although immersed in the day-by-day crises of the war, he constantly had the future in mind; he believed he was fighting and
building for the future. An essential element in that future was
the creation and maintenance of a powerful army, navy, and air
force, which would guard Russia against another devastating war.

This demanded discipline and leadership, and even in the darkest period of the war he did not lose sight of the need to create an officer corps, imbued with patriotism and professional pride, and providing responsible leadership. Earlier in 1942 he had taken several steps, such as the institution of special decorations for officers, which were designed to raise their status and authority. After the great victories of Stalingrad and Kursk, when there was an upsurge of Russian patriotism, he had revived other tsarist practices. Epaulets, once the hated symbol of the officer class, were reintroduced, and the uniforms of officers became more splendid. Nine Suvorov schools were set up, modeled directly on the tsarist cadet schools, to train an officer elite. The curriculum required a high standard of general education and included tuition in good manners and even dancing. Officers graduating from these academies were to be highly trained and dedicated professional soldiers and also gentlemen, as the graduates from West Point and Sandhurst were expected to be.

A revealing insight into Stalin's attitude came in the course of a dinner, given by Churchill in Potsdam in July 1945. Stalin was sitting next to Birse, whom he now knew well and for whom he had a real affection. Birse remarked that "he seemed glad to be able to talk between the speeches to someone who understood him without the aid of an interpreter. He said he liked these English dinners; they were simple and at the same time dignified. Then, looking round the faces opposite, he singled out General Marshall and remarked: "That's a man I admire. He is a good general. We have good generals in the Soviet army, but so have you and the Americans. Only ours still lack breeding and their manners are bad. Our people have a long way to go."[48]

Shrewd, observant, and honest, he knew the qualities he wanted in his officers. They included modesty, humility, and discipline, which, speaking soon after Lenin's death, he had impressed on the cadets of the Kremlin Military Academy. But he wanted also manners and breeding. It was noteworthy that among those who worked closely with him during the war, a disproportionate number, who included Shaposhnikov, Vatutin, Vasilevsky, Antonov, and Rokossovsky, had had training in the tsarist army and presumably possessed something of this quality of good manners which he valued. In his own conduct, according to foreign and other observers, he displayed great modesty, simplicity, and courtesy, until angered or confronted with what he regarded as deceit or a threat to his authority, and then he could become abusive and coarse.

It was his victory, above all, because it had been won by his genius and labors, heroic in scale. The Russian people had looked to him for leadership, and he had not failed them. His speeches of July 3 and November 6, 1941, which had steeled them for the trials of war, and his presence in Moscow during the great battle for the city, had demonstrated his will to victory. He was for them a semimystical figure, enthroned in the Kremlin, who inspired them and gave them positive direction. He had the capacity of attending to detail and keeping in mind the broad picture, and, while remembering the past and immersed in the present, he was constantly looking ahead to the future.

Military experts have criticized his direct control over and participation in military matters and have condemned many of his decisions, especially in 1941–42. One foreign expert, not notably sympathetic to Stalin as a man, has perhaps given the fairest judgment:

> If he is to bear the blame for the first two years of war, he must be allowed the credit for the amazing successes of 1944, the *annus mirabilis*, when whole German army groups were virtually obliterated with lightning blows in Belorussia, Galicia, Romania, and the Baltic, in battles fought not in the wintry steppes, but in midsummer in Central Europe. Some of these victories must be reckoned among the most outstanding in the world's military history.[49]

29

The Potsdam Betrayal and the End of the Grand Alliance July 1945–March 1946

The leaders of the three Allied powers—Stalin and Churchill were joined now by Harry Truman, the new President of the United States—met in Potsdam in July 1945. They came to resolve the problems of postwar Europe and to establish through the United Nations a new era of peace and stability in the world. But the spirit of co-operation and common purpose, which had been remarkable at Teheran and Yalta, died in Potsdam. The attitude of the United States and Britain towards Soviet Russia had changed. The symbol of the change was the terrible new weapon of the atom bomb in the armory of the West. To Stalin the Potsdam conference was a time of betrayal.

The three nations had celebrated the surrender of Germany with feelings of triumph, achievement, and relief. But their elation was overcast by the magnitude of the postwar problems and above all by the needs of their own countries. The United States had emerged from the war relatively unscathed and with an awareness of her great economic and military power. Britain, facing the ruin of her economy and a disintegrating empire, was but a shadow of the great imperial nation she had once been. Soviet Russia had suffered most terribly.

Casualties at the fronts and in German-occupied territory had been horrifying in scale. Few Russians were without bereavements. Stalin stated that 7 million Soviet citizens had lost their lives in the war, but the losses were probably closer to 20 million.[1] The mass of the people were living in grim conditions, still severely rationed for food, clothing, and housing, and working long hours. Many had died from overwork and undernourishment. By 1945 more than half of all workers in industry were women, and agriculture depended almost entirely on female labor.[2] The Russian people were now hoping that life would become easier, that food and other goods would be more plentiful, and that somehow the victory for which they had labored and suffered would bring rewards.

The economy was near collapse. At least a quarter of all Soviet property had been destroyed. Nearly 2,000 towns and 70,000 villages had been razed, and 25 million people were homeless. Soviet industry had achieved a prodigious output of tanks, guns, aircraft, and other materials, but this obscured the fact that industry as a whole had suffered disastrously. Some 31,000 factories, including the major industries in Kharkov, Krivoi Rog, Zaporozhie, Rostov, Odessa, Leningrad, and Stalingrad, had been destroyed.[3]

As early as 1943 Stalin had begun thinking about the reconstruction of the country after the war. Russia could, of course, rebuild her industries and revive agriculture, depending wholly on her own resources. This would mean that the people would continue living in the same harsh conditions. He was counting on massive reparation payments from Germany and her allies to compensate in some degree for the destruction they had caused. He had exacted from the Finns an undertaking to repay 300 million dollars in reparations over six years. But when at the Yalta conference he had raised the subject of German reparations, Churchill in particular had made objections.[4]

Stalin gave close thought to the possibility of substantial long-term credits from the United States to assist in financing Soviet reconstruction. By this means the Russian people would be spared the pressures and hardships they had endured in the industrialization campaign and during the war. Many communists were horrified by the thought of such dependence on a capitalist power; others saw in it a threat to Soviet security. Stalin evidently considered that the value of such assistance would outweigh these and other objections. He was concerned with the recovery and security of Russia rather than with ideology.

Early in 1945 Molotov discussed with Harriman, the U.S. ambassador in Moscow, the possibility of financial aid, and on being told that it would require an act of Congress, he asked that Congress might deal with it before the end of the war. Again on February 5, 1945, Molotov, in conversation with Stettinius, "expressed the hope that the Soviet Union would receive long-term credits from the United States."[5] Earlier in the war several prominent American industrialists, and especially Donald M. Nelson, had discussed in Moscow the possibility of a large loan. Stalin had expressed keen interest and had given Nelson a list of Soviet priorities. A strong body of opinion in Washington favored financial aid to Soviet Russia. Henry Morgenthau, Secretary of the Treasury, discussed Soviet credits several times with Harriman and wrote to the President on January 1, 1945:

> We are not thinking of more lend-lease or any form of relief but rather of an arrangement that will have definite and long-range benefits for the United States as well as for Russia. I am convinced that if we were to come forward now and present to the Russians a concrete plan to aid them in the reconstruction period it would contribute a great deal towards ironing out many of the difficulties we have been having with respect to their problems and policies.[6]

Other counsels prevailed, however, and no U.S. credits were provided. On succeeding to the presidency after Roosevelt's death, Truman, in fact, cut off lend-lease supplies. Stalin already had misgivings about Truman, who in 1942 had seriously proposed in the Senate that the United States alternate aid to Hitler and to Stalin in such a way as to ensure that Russia emerged as the exhausted victor.[7] Indeed, promptly after May 8, 1945, celebrated in the West as Victory in Europe Day, lend-lease supplies were abruptly halted, although the Soviet Union was committed to joining in the war against Japan. This act, and particularly the manner in which it was done, caused deep offense in Moscow.[8]

When, however, on May 26 Truman sent a personal representative to Moscow with assurances that he intended to pursue Roosevelt's policy of co-operation, Stalin extended a warm welcome to him and all the more because the envoy was Harry Hopkins, whom he trusted. The chief purpose of Hopkins' mission, lasting from May 26 to June 6, was to seek some solution to the Polish question. In the United States and Britain the Poles were active propagandists who exercised a strong and insidious influence. Impassioned and unshakable in their hatred of Russia, they would never concede that Poland had to come to terms and learn to live with her mighty neighbor. They worked indefatigably in promoting anti-Russian and anticommunist feeling in the West, and their contribution to the breakdown of the Grand Alliance and to the ensuing cold war was considerable.

In January 1945 the Armija Krajowa was converted into an underground army on the orders of the Polish government in London. General L. Okulicki headed this Polish underground which waged guerrilla war against Russians in Poland. The London government and the church in Poland worked to intensify anti-Russian feeling. In the early postwar months the Polish underground assassinated more than a hundred Red Army officers and men. Indeed Alexander Werth, who was one of a large group of Western press correspondents who visited Poland at this time, witnessed a special anti-Russian demonstration, staged for their benefit by the underground, in which two unfortunate Russian soldiers were shot outside their hotel.[9] In March, Okulicki and fifteen other underground leaders were arrested and taken to Moscow. An outcry was aroused in the West.

On his arrival in Moscow Hopkins interceded with Stalin on behalf of the Polish underground leaders. In June 1945 they were tried in Moscow for assassinating Red Army personnel and were given lenient sentences. Churchill evidently regarded them as brave patriots and had proposed making their release a condition before further discussions could take place with the Soviet government. Hopkins ignored this proposal.[10] He persuaded Stalin to invite Mikolajczyk and two London Poles, as well as prominent Poles in Poland who did not support the Lublin Committee, to come to Moscow for talks. As a result a new Polish provisional government was set up, and on July 5, 1945, the United States and Britain formally recognized it. They were not satisfied with this compromise government, but realized that Stalin had come far to meet their objections and that they must accept it, pending their meetings in Berlin.

While in Moscow, Hopkins received instructions from Stettinius to raise directly with Stalin a matter which had brought to a standstill discussions at the San Francisco conference on the United Nations organization. Molotov had instructed Gromyko, the Soviet delegate, to insist that a matter in dispute could not even be discussed by the Security Council except with the unanimous agreement of the five permanent members, unless the dispute was one that could be settled by peaceful means. This new proviso extended the power of veto beyond the limits agreed at Yalta. At Hopkins' meeting with Stalin, Molotov attempted to justify his instructions to Gromyko. Stalin told him not to be ridiculous and at once accepted the American position.[11]

As the date of the Potsdam meeting approached, Stalin became more concerned about Russia's security. His fear remained that Germany would recover rapidly and, thirsting for revenge, would strike in a third attempt to conquer Russia. Roosevelt had told him in Yalta that U.S. troops would be withdrawn from Europe in two or three years. This left Britain as the only ally against a resurgent Germany, for he did not count France. But the war had seriously weakened Britain, and it remained to be seen how quickly she would recover. Moreover, he still had a deep mistrust of the British.

Stalin believed firmly in the need to maintain the alliance with the United States, but saw that this might prove impossible. American expansionist policy, promoted by the fear that the American economy would suffer a disastrous depression if expansion of overseas markets did not continue, would surely lead to conflicts. Another threat was the assumption, held by most Americans as an article of faith, that the United States with its free capitalist system was the epitome of all that was progressive in the world,

while Soviet communism was a menacing evil. This national outlook could become dangerous, because it was backed by the
knowledge that the United States was without rival in might,
while Soviet Russia was ravaged and weak.

Stalin had no doubts that communism was superior to capitalism and that Soviet Russia would overtake the capitalist world by
peaceful competition. He needed peace and stability for reconstruction and development of the Soviet economy. The greatest
threat to Soviet growth was war. Russia had suffered too much
from wars, and another war, especially with modern weapons,
might destroy the Soviet regime and retard Russian development
for a hundred years or more. Nevertheless, Marxist dogma proclaimed that war was inevitable between the socialist and capitalist camps, and he gave every priority to making his country strong
and secure.

Long before the end of the war Stalin had adopted the policy of
ensuring Soviet domination over eastern Europe to provide a barrier against aggression from the West. Communist parties and
pro-Soviet elements were promoted in Czechoslovakia, Romania,
Bulgaria, and Yugoslavia. Poland was the weak link in this defense chain, but with time a pro-Soviet communist regime could
be built up there. The disturbing factor was that the Western allies refused to accept that eastern Europe was a zone of Soviet
influence and that Russia had a legitimate interest in creating a
defense barrier in the west.

Churchill in particular was disturbed by the spread of Soviet
power in eastern Europe. He saw it as the prelude to a bid to
dominate the whole of Europe. He refused to accept that Stalin
was concerned to build only a defense barrier. To Truman, who
was not knowledgeable in international relations, he wrote on
May 12, 1945, that an "iron curtain" had been drawn down upon
Russian-occupied Europe and that he envisaged the advance of
the Russians "to the water of the North Sea and the Atlantic."
Two months later on July 18 he was assuring Stalin in conversation that he wanted to see Russian ships passing through the
Dardanelles and the Kiel canal and sailing the oceans of the
world. On another occasion he remarked to Stalin that "it looked
as if Russia was rolling westwards." Stalin firmly rejected the alle-

gation, stating that he had no such intention and was on the contrary withdrawing his troops from the west, starting with 2 million men within the next four months.[12]

The Potsdam conference began on July 17, 1945, with signs that the spirit of goodwill and co-operation, forged at Teheran and Yalta, would continue. Stalin appeared to be in a genial and relaxed mood. He gave a private dinner for Churchill, who wrote that "his easy friendliness was most agreeable."[13] Churchill himself appeared untroubled about the outcome of the British general election and reveled in the exchanges and private talks that such high-level conferences afforded him. Truman was the newcomer. Churchill called on him on the morning after his arrival and "was impressed with his gay, precise, sparkling manner and obvious powers of decision."[14]

The momentous news of the explosion in the Mexican desert of an atom bomb, developed by a team of American and British scientists, was given privately to Churchill on the first day of the conference. His immediate reaction was that the might of the Western powers had been enormously enhanced and that of Soviet Russia correspondingly reduced, and further that Soviet participation in the war in the Far East was no longer necessary or desirable. The Far East would become a region of Western, predominantly American, influence, from which Soviet Russia, notwithstanding her Pacific coast line and her long historic interest in the region, could be excluded. It was this basic attitude which Stalin sensed and which seemed to justify his mistrust of Churchill.

Truman and his staff reacted in the same way. The Americans had pressed Stalin to assist in bringing the Japanese war to an early end. At Yalta they had expressed relief and pleasure when Stalin had promised to enter the war within three months of the defeat of Germany and they had readily agreed to his terms. As late as May 8, 1945, Hopkins on his mission to Moscow had sought and obtained Stalin's reassurance that the Red Army would assist in defeating Japan.

Suddenly two months later, with the atom bomb at their disposal, the Allies were rejecting Russian aid and furiously planning to bring about Japan's defeat before Russia could declare war. In this way they could evade Stalin's terms, which included the return to Russia of the territories lost to Japan in the war of 1904–5, a matter of great national pride to Stalin and his generation.

Truman asked Churchill's advice on the best way to break the news of the new weapon to Stalin. Churchill wrote that Stalin had been "a magnificent ally in the war against Hitler and we both felt that he must be informed of the New Fact which now dominated the scene, but not of any particulars."[15] It was decided that the President would mention it informally after one of the sessions.

A week later Truman with his interpreter approached Stalin after the plenary meeting and told him about the new bomb of extraordinary power. Churchill was about five yards away, watching intently. Stalin appeared delighted and he asked no questions. It seemed that he had no idea of the significance of the new weapon.

Stalin may not have understood immediately from Truman's informal statement the dramatic importance of the event, but he was quick to sense the change in the Allies' attitude towards Russia. One American general wrote that "we were in a position to be tough and indifferent."[16] It was not a reasoned approach on the part of the British and Americans, but an attitude bred of exasperation with Russian secretiveness, suspicion, and demands, and bred also of arrogant confidence that they now possessed power far exceeding that of Soviet Russia and could do and say what they pleased. The possibility that the Russians would develop atomic weapons of their own and themselves "get tough" was not considered, or was considered to be remote, for it was assumed that they were too backward in technology to make such a sophisticated weapon.[17]

The change in the attitude of his allies disturbed Stalin. It confirmed his worst fears and suspicions, and it offended him deeply as an act of ingratitude and rejection. Russia had, he believed, saved the West from Nazi barbarism just as in the thirteenth century Russia had shielded Europe against the Mongol horde of Genghis Khan. To him and to all Russians it was clear that, if Russia had not destroyed German armed might, Hitler would have conquered Britain and have carried the war into

North America. Russia deserved the gratitude and respect of the Allies, not their arrogance and condescension. No one was more sensitive about affronts to Russian national pride than Stalin, and at Potsdam the Allies caused deep and abiding offense.

Discussions ranged widely during the thirteen plenary sessions of the conference. Many matters were held over for decision at the peace conference or by the council of foreign ministers. The Americans and British expressed strong criticism of Soviet policy in the liberated countries, especially Romania and Bulgaria. The Russians replied with criticism of British conduct in Greece. Accusations were made that Russia was violating the terms of the Yalta agreement. But it was on Germany and Poland that disagreement was most serious.

The three powers had recognized the Polish provisional government. Dispute now concerned Poland's western frontier. The Poles had to be compensated for territory lost along the frontier with Russia. Churchill vigorously opposed the extension of the western frontier, as proposed by Stalin, to the Oder and Western Neisse. But after the British general elections in which Churchill and his party were defeated, Clement Attlee, the new British Prime Minister, supported Truman and accepted Stalin's proposal.

The Allies had agreed earlier that Germany should be divided into four zones, administered respectively by the United States, Britain, Soviet Russia, and France, and that all four would share control over Berlin as a fifth zone. Germany would not have a central government, and matters affecting the country as a whole would be decided by the Allied Control Commission. This was in accord with Stalin's policy of insisting that Germany should not be dismembered, but should remain united under the strict control of the four powers.

The Russian demand for reparations had been accepted in principle at Yalta. The special commission set up to examine the subject failed to reach agreement. At Potsdam Stalin pressed constantly for acceptance of a figure for reparations. The Allies refused to be committed. They were incensed by reports that the Russians were already removing from occupied territories machinery and other property which were not accepted as booty of war.

Various practical difficulties forced the Western Allies to abandon their policy of treating the German economy as a whole. James Byrnes, the new United States Secretary of State, finally proposed that each power should satisfy its reparations claims from its own zone. Some 40 per cent of the value of German industrial equipment deemed unnecessary for a peace economy was in the Soviet zone. Byrnes proposed further that 10 per cent of such industrial equipment in the western zones should be given to Soviet Russia, who could also request additional equipment from the U.S. and British zones in exchange for food or coal.

Stalin and Molotov argued against this arrangement, although in some ways it was favorable to them, because it would lead to the breakup of Germany. In the end they accepted it as part of a package in which they were conceded the right to collect German assets throughout eastern Europe, as well as other demands. But their proposal for joint administration of the Ruhr was rejected, and the Western Allies excluded them from their occupation zones. The policy of maintaining Germany as a unit under Allied control collapsed. Germany was divided between east and west.

On July 25, 1945, in the midst of the conference, Churchill and Eden departed from Berlin to be in London for the results of the general election. Stalin had told Churchill earlier at a private dinner that all his information from communist and other sources had confirmed his belief that the Conservatives would be returned with a majority of about eighty seats. Churchill had answered that he was not sure how the soldiers had voted. Stalin assured him that the Army preferred a strong government and would therefore vote Conservative. It seemed to Churchill that Stalin wanted to maintain contact with him and with Eden rather than with Attlee, whom he knew as a small, reserved, humorless man, and some strange Foreign Secretary. But Churchill's government was severely defeated.

Four days later Attlee returned to Potsdam as Prime Minister, accompanied by Ernest Bevin, the new Foreign Secretary. Bevin, a trade-union leader, was a big man with a warm personality, but uneducated and ill equipped for the office of Foreign Minister. In Potsdam he was openly aggressive towards the Russians, treating the negotiations as though they were a confrontation between a trade union and employers. Attlee was increasingly curt. Truman and his staff became truculent.[18] The Americans and British were united in their confidence that they were negotiating from a position of overwhelming strength and that they had no need to be conciliatory or understanding.

The chasm between Soviet Russia and the two Allies widened, as the Americans sought ways of forestalling Russia's entry into the war against Japan. The Soviet government had denounced its neutrality pact with Japan on April 5, 1945, and had evaded Japanese approaches for Soviet mediation to negotiate peace. Meanwhile Roosevelt's undertaking to obtain the agreement of Chiang Kai-shek to Stalin's conditions for Soviet participation in the war had led to Soviet-Chinese talks, lasting two weeks before the Potsdam conference. The talks continued from August 7 to 14, 1945, and it was apparent that Chiang Kai-shek was prolonging them on American instructions. Again an ultimatum demanding immediate unconditional surrender by the Japanese was issued on July 26, 1945. The Russians complained that they had not been consulted, and when they asked that publication of the ultimatum be delayed for three days, they were informed that the text had already been released. Stalin was particularly incensed because he was convinced that while Japan was ready to surrender, she would fight to the end against unconditional surrender.

On August 6, 1945, the atom bomb was dropped on Hiroshima. Stalin and most Russians recognized at once the awesome significance of the event. Truman had merely told him of a "super bomb," and according to Molotov the word "atomic" was not mentioned.[19] Japan was already on the point of capitulating and would probably have laid down arms within a few days even if the bombs had not been dropped on Hiroshima and then on Nagasaki and even if Russia had not declared war. Stalin realized that the Americans had made use of the bomb primarily to impress and threaten Russia. Indeed, Byrnes acknowledged later that the bomb was needed not so much against Japan as to "make Russia manageable in Europe."[20]

The Russians felt now that they had emerged from the tragic war against Germany only to find themselves threatened from the West with a new and terrible weapon. Stalin was acutely aware

of the vulnerability of Russia. He is reported to have summoned
five of the foremost Soviet scientists and to have ordered them to
develop a Soviet atom bomb in the shortest possible time and regardless of cost.[21]

The Soviet forces under the command of Vasilevsky advanced
swiftly into Manchuria. They were seasoned troops with superiority in equipment, and the Japanese could not halt them. Vasilevsky's orders were to seize the areas specified by Stalin at Yalta
before the Americans could reach them. He dismissed the declaration of surrender by the Japanese emperor on August 14, 1945,
and on August 17 sent his own ultimatum to the commander of
the Japanese Kwantung Army, calling for his surrender by August
20. During these days Soviet airborne troops seized Dairen and
Port Arthur and penetrated into northern Korea, while the Soviet
Pacific fleet occupied southern Sakhalin and the Kurile Islands.

On September 2 Stalin broadcast to the nation. It was the day
on which the final surrender of Japan was signed on board the
U.S. warship *Missouri*, a ceremony to which he had sent an unknown general. In his broadcast Stalin dwelt on the war of
1904–5. "Russia was defeated in that war," he said. "As a result
Japan grabbed Southern Sakhalin and firmly established herself in
the Kuriles, thus padlocking our exits to the Pacific. . . . This defeat of the Russian troops in 1904 left a bitter memory in the
minds of our people. Our people waited and believed that this
blot would some day be erased. We, people of the older generation, have waited forty years for this day. Now this day has
come."[22]

Stalin went on to say that peace had come at last and that
Soviet Russia was no longer threatened by Germany and Japan.
He paid tribute to the armed forces of the United States, China,
and Britain. But it was the speech of a Russian patriot, taking
pride in having reversed a historic defeat and finding in it some
compensation for the rebuffs to Russian national pride at Potsdam.

Relations with the Western powers declined sharply in the following months. Stalin believed that the menace of American
domination was pressing inexorably on Russia. At the meetings of
foreign ministers in London, Moscow, and Paris to draft the peace

treaties and discuss postwar problems, Molotov was constantly attacked by Byrnes and Bevin for installing totalitarian regimes in Romania, Bulgaria, Hungary, and Yugoslavia. Molotov insisted that Russia was entitled to the security of having friendly governments in the countries of eastern Europe. He argued that the Western powers had no right to impose their conception of democracy on other countries. But the Western powers claimed the right, because they had military power, because they were confident that democratic elections in those countries would result in the formation of anticommunist governments, and because they were determined to halt any extension of Soviet influence beyond central and eastern Europe.

In Iran a conflict developed which Stalin saw as a sinister demonstration of the American menace. British and Soviet forces had occupied Iran early in the war to forestall any attempt by the pro-German Shah to aid the enemy in an invasion of Russia from the south. American forces later joined the Allies, and Iran was kept open for the transport of war supplies to Russia. Towards the end of the war the Allies agreed on a date for the withdrawal of the occupation forces. British and American troops withdrew, but Soviet forces lingered. The Western Allies accused the Russians of seeking to establish a pro-Soviet regime in Iran. The Soviet reply was that Russian troops were needed in Iran to bring pressure on the government to grant oil exploitation rights, for Russia was desperately short of oil as a result of German damage to her oil fields.

American and British demands for the withdrawal of the Soviet units threatened a major clash. Stalin was unwilling to press the dispute too far and finally recalled his troops. The Americans at once stepped in with dollar aid to Iran and sent military and other advisers. Quickly Iran was brought under American domination as complete as the Soviet domination of Romania and Bulgaria. Stalin regarded this as an act of American aggression. Iran was far removed from the United States, but on Russia's frontier, and the Americans were setting up military installations. Pressure by the Western powers also forced the Russians to give up their demands to share in the control of the Dardanelles and access to the Black Sea.

Stalin had counted on the co-operation of the three powers in maintaining world peace and stability. He had endorsed the charter of the United Nations, which had as a basic purpose the prevention of nations forming blocs and holding peace and the balance of power between them. Churchill's "Iron Curtain Speech," made at Fulton, Missouri, in the United States on March 6, 1946, alarmed and appalled him. It proclaimed the division of the world into the communist and Western blocs, and it advocated a strong political and military "fraternal association" of the United States, Britain, and the Commonwealth to maintain the balance of power and ensure peace. It was a declaration of hostility, falling short of war. Stalin denounced the speech in measured terms as "a dangerous act, calculated to sow seeds of dissent and hinder collaboration among the allied nations. It has harmed the cause of peace and security. Mr Churchill has now adopted the position of a war-monger."[23]

Stalin understood that, although no longer Prime Minister, Churchill was expressing the views of the American and British governments. Truman had shared the platform with him at Fulton. The British Labour party had expressed disagreement, but the Labour government was following the policy which he advocated.

In the United States dissenting voices were raised. Henry Wallace, Secretary of Commerce, declared: "We should be prepared to judge [Russia's] requirements against the background of what we ourselves and the British have insisted upon as essential to our respective security. We should be prepared, even at the expense of risking epithets of appeasement, to agree to reasonable Russian guarantees of security." But this and other statements by Wallace were not acceptable to Truman and Byrnes or to public opinion generally in America, where the sense of power and of the mission to defend freedom were dominant. Byrnes insisted on the resignation of Wallace and threatened to resign himself if Truman did not back him. Wallace resigned.[24]

The peace conference in Paris and the meetings of the council of foreign ministers were protracted. Stalin and Molotov were relying on obstructionist tactics to avoid being continually outvoted by the Anglo-American bloc. Treaties with Italy, Hungary,

Finland, Romania, and Bulgaria were signed, however, in February 1947.

The most angry and lengthy negotiations concerned Germany. Stalin was determined to exact maximum compensation from the enemy who had devastated Russia. He pressed his demand for 2 billion dollars in reparations to be paid by Germany from capital, current production, and by labor. The Western powers rejected the figure as too high and insisted that reparations could be paid only from capital. In a mood of growing exasperation they opposed other Soviet demands, which they interpreted as blatant communist aggrandizement.

Underlying Stalin's demands, however, were his continuing fear of German resurgence and a third attempt to conquer Russia, and his suspicion now that the Western powers would aid Germany in recovering her economic and military strength and use her as an ally against Russia. This was the real and most alarming danger. The decision of the British and Americans to merge their zones of occupation intensified his fears.

Interpreting Soviet policy as wholly concerned with communist expansionism, the Western powers became more aggressive. On March 12, 1947, Truman proclaimed his doctrine of the containment of Soviet Russia. This policy was strongly influenced by the ideas of G. F. Kennan, a state department officer whose views on Russian affairs were then highly regarded. He argued that communism was an evil creed, alien to Russian traditions, and that the Soviet leaders depended on the use of force to remain in power.[25] There was little hope that politicians of the caliber of Truman and Byrnes, Attlee and Bevin, would recognize that this and other militant anti-Soviet policies were driving the Soviet leaders to the wall and that their threats merely strengthened popular support for the regime they were seeking to destroy.[26]

Complementary to the doctrine of containment was the Marshall Plan, launched in the summer of 1947. It was a bold and generous policy to promote the rapid economic recovery of Europe. In the announcement of the plan there had been no reference to its application to Russia. At a press conference, however, Marshall himself stated that he saw no reason why Russia should not be included. The U. S. Congress, in the mood of the time, would undoubtedly have raised obstacles in the way of Russia's benefiting. But, prompted by his party and acting on the assumption that the Marshall Plan was open to Russia, the British Foreign Secretary invited Molotov to Paris to discuss possible Russian participation.

Stalin's attitude was extremely cautious. He had been disappointed in earlier hopes of American aid. Now he was on guard against American domination. He was suspicious of the motives of the Western powers, which had become so openly hostile to Soviet Russia. Promptly he decided that Russia would have nothing to do with the plan. It was part of American expansionist policy and of the Truman doctrine of containing and destroying communism. Moreover, he brought pressure on Poland, Hungary, and Czechoslovakia, who had accepted the plan, to withdraw.

The division between the communist and Western blocs was now seen an unbridgeable. Stalin was convinced that the Western bloc, led and supported by the economic and military might of the United States, was intent on the destruction of Soviet Russia and the communist world. His policy was to develop eastern Europe as an integrated bloc under Moscow's absolute control, politically and economically independent of the West. The Western powers interpreted this to mean that Moscow was planning a general offensive against them and was even considering military action. The "cold war," a tragic period of recriminations, exaggerated suspicion on both sides, and bitter animosity, had begun.

In the course of the next three years the two blocs came dangerously close to military conflict. Stalin consolidated the Soviet bloc, eliminating all noncommunist elements and transforming their regimes into people's democracies, regarded as a traditional stage before socialism. Economic integration followed with the setting up of Comecon (Council for Economic Mutual Assistance), embracing the Soviet Union, Czechoslovakia, Bulgaria, Hungary, Romania, and Poland. When the Yugoslav communists asserted their independence of Moscow, Stalin in a fury denounced them for betrayal of the revolutionary cause. He went so far as to have the Yugoslav Communist party expelled from the Cominform (Communist Information Bureau), the modified form of the Communist International, which he had revived in September 1947.

The climax in the anti-Soviet policies of the Western powers came for Stalin on April 4, 1949, when the North Atlantic Pact was signed. It provided for a military alliance of twelve countries and established the North Atlantic Treaty Organization to maintain a combined military force. This military alliance was declared to be wholly defensive, but to Stalin and all Russians it was obviously offensive in intention. The inclusion of the Federal Republic of Germany as an equal member three years later was a horrifying development.

Work on the buildup of heavy industry and military strength in the Soviet Union and throughout the Soviet bloc was intensified. In June 1948 Stalin attempted to secure complete control over Berlin by preventing deliveries of food and goods by land and water from the West. The Allies countered by airlifting supplies to the city. He was not prepared to provoke a war and in September 1949 allowed a return to the use of the land and sea routes. But in the United Nations, and especially in the discussions on international control of atomic energy, it was plain that a great chasm of mistrust and hostility separated Soviet Russia from the countries of the West.

Two events gave Stalin and his people encouragement in this tense period. The first was the explosion of a Soviet atom bomb in September 1949, and the second was the establishment of the communist regime, under Mao Tse-tung's leadership, over the whole of China. Possession of the atom bomb was important to Russian morale. Stalin and others in the Kremlin had actively feared that the United States might use atomic weapons against Russia, and there were influential voices in Washington urging that this was the way to deal decisively with the Soviet government.

Also important to Russian prestige and confidence was the fact that China, with its population of nearly 600 million people, had become part of the communist bloc, of which Soviet Russia was the accepted leader. Moreover, the United States now considered her security in the Far East to be threatened by the emergence of this mighty communist power. War in Korea brought the blocs close to a major conflict. The Americans, deciding to make Japan the cornerstone of their anticommunist policy, pressed agreement on a peace treaty with Japan, which the Soviet government refused to sign. For the time being the position of the two blocs in the Far East was deadlocked.

Nothing disturbed Stalin more profoundly, however, than the Anglo-American policy of establishing western Germany as an economic and military power. He was opposed particularly to the integration of a German army into the North Atlantic Treaty Organization and the defenses of the Western powers. This was to him the most sinister aspect of the Western offensive against Russia. In March 1952 he proposed that the four Allied powers should meet without delay to discuss a German peace treaty. He conceded many points in the exchange of notes that followed his initiative. He was prepared to agree that Germany should have her own armed forces for defense purposes, but insisted that she be barred from joining an alliance directed against any power which had taken part in the war against her. He accepted the principle of free elections throughout Germany. But the exchange ended in the rejection of Stalin's proposals. The Western powers would not yield. It was clear to Stalin that Russia was a beleaguered country, threatened by the Western capitalist powers, and that she must prepare for war.

30

The Great Resurgence
1946-53

Stalin was physically tired by the time of the Potsdam conference. The strains of the war had taken their toll. He was not a cold, nerveless man, unaffected by crises and challenges; he was emotional and tense, as his moods and outbursts of temper showed. He also had great self-control, stamina, and resilience. It was noted at Potsdam that he appeared worn, although relaxed and genial in temper. According to his daughter, Svetlana, he fell seriously ill soon after the ending of the Japanese war, but in December 1945 he was able to receive Byrnes and Bevin when they came to Moscow for the meeting of foreign ministers. Like the whole nation he needed a period of rest, but there was to be no rest.

The problems of postwar resettlement and reconstruction were immense. Within a few months of the end of the war eight million men were being demobilized from the armed forces. Four and a half million people returned from German slave-labor and other camps. Eight million people had been evacuated beyond the Urals and were now flowing westwards in search of their homes. But a gradual return to better conditions of peacetime, for which all longed, was not permitted. All who were able were soon to be pressed into the great reconstruction, which called for a fury of labor such as they had known during the First Five-year Plan.

Stalin had become convinced after the Potsdam conference that Soviet Russia was threatened. American imperialism confronted her in the west, the Far East, and the south. The United States was a super-power economically and militarily. Russia was in no condition to stand against or compete with her.

Fourteen years earlier, Stalin had declared: "The history of old Russia was, among other things, that she was constantly beaten because of her backwardness." The danger now was that, weak and backward as a result of the war, Russia would be beaten yet again. He was determined that this would not happen.

Russia had triumphed in the war and emerged as the world's second great power. Twice before in her history—after Peter the Great's victory at Poltava in 1709 and after the defeat of Napoleon in 1812—Russia had gained a similar great power status. In each period she had relapsed into weakness. He would permit no relapse this time. Soviet Russia would rebuild her shattered economy by her own efforts and remain a great power.

On August 19, 1945—significantly a few days after the dropping of the atom bomb on Hiroshima—Stalin gave orders to Gosplan to prepare a reconstruction program. The result was the Fourth Five-year Plan, adopted by the Supreme Soviet on March 18, 1946. The plan laid down priorities and prescribed an astonishing tempo for postwar development. Heavy industry had first priority as the basis for the complete reconstruction of the economy and for a strong and permanent armament industry.

The plan called for an over-all increase in industrial output by 1950 of 48 per cent above prewar levels. It specified new construction and output to be achieved in each branch of heavy industry. The planned increases in the consumer industries and agriculture were comparatively modest. The targets to be achieved within five years appeared impossibly high for a country devastated by war and a people who had suffered terrible casualties and who continued to endure food and housing shortages and austere living conditions. Moreover, the work had to be carried out entirely within their own resources, except for the contribution made by reparations.

The plan included provision for the first stage of Stalin's twenty-year naval construction program. He was determined to resume his prewar policy which would ensure that Russia had a navy in keeping with great power status. With a planned delivery of some 200,000 tons of warships annually the Navy was to have 1,200 submarines, 175 destroyers, 35 cruisers as well as battle cruisers and aircraft carriers. In the years 1945–50, however, the main danger appeared to arise from the massive amphibious assault capacity of the American and British navies. America's monopoly of nuclear weapons posed a grim threat, but it was not seen as so immediate because of the lack at this stage of an adequate delivery system. Priority was therefore given to coastal defense forces. By the end of the 1940s, however, Stalin had resumed his prewar program of creating an ocean-going navy.

The plan called for heroic endeavor and bore the stamp of Stalin's implacable determination. He was driven still by the vision of Soviet industrial output exceeding that of the West and particularly of the United States. This long-term goal, he explained at the beginning of 1946, would require "perhaps three new five-year plans, if not more," and he stressed that the target figures for steel, coal, and oil had to be achieved within the current plan.[1] Again, as in the first industrialization campaign, he was presenting the Russian people with a challenge which, driven by his will, they had to meet.

The achievements in the plan period were remarkable, although greatly exaggerated by Soviet propaganda. Progress in the first year was hampered by severe drought and by the many problems of resettling and retraining labor in difficult conditions. Indeed, compared with 1945, over-all industrial output fell by 17 per cent in 1946. Thereafter output mounted rapidly. The investment plan for 1946–50 was reported to have been surpassed by 22 per cent. In the Ukraine, where enemy destruction had been almost total, mineral output reached the 1940 level; the great Dnieper Dam was rebuilt and by March 1947 was generating electricity, and industries producing consumer goods also achieved impressive increases in output. By 1950 the Soviet industrial system was stronger than before the war, and it was also ready for the arms race then beginning. The recovery in agriculture was, however, disastrously slow.[2]

Inseparable from the reconstruction of the Soviet economy was the need to safeguard and entrench the rule of the Communist party. Stalin believed that the party, too, was vulnerable. It was challenged by the capitalist camp and it was endangered internally. He saw the possibility of a serious threat in the fact that so many Red Army officers and men had seen with their own eyes the wealth of Western countries. They would make unfavorable comparisons with conditions in Russia, which had not yet attained these standards. Stories of Western life would spread among the people, who were expecting to enjoy the rewards of victory. A dangerous discontent might spread among them and war-weariness might lead to apathy. In the past the Russian people had been prone after a period of great national effort to slip into idleness. He would not allow any such decline. At this time they must redouble their efforts and labor to build a Russia with economic and military strength greater than ever before. Only then would they enjoy the rewards of victory.

Another danger was that Western liberal ideas might have infected some among the many thousands of Russians who had had contact with the West. This infection could lead to subversive movements which would undermine the party. In the previous century, after the defeat of Napoleon, officers and men of the imperial army who had marched into France had, on their return, spread discontent and unrest. Moreover, many officers had been inflamed by liberal ideas. The leading Decembrists, whose rebellion had shaken the autocracy in 1825, had been young officers carried away by ideas of Western reforms. Stalin could recall from his own experience how the Bolsheviks, a small minority inspired by Marxist dogma imported from the West, had seized power in 1917. Mindful always of the lessons of history, he was on the watch for the least sign of such alienation.

In the great postwar reconstruction the party itself would be the powerful weapon against subversion and apathy. It had grown impressively in membership during the war. Some 2 million members had been admitted in 1942 alone. This growth had been encouraged as part of a policy of broadening the base of the party, particularly by recruiting within the armed forces. War casualties had decimated membership. By the beginning of 1945, however, there were 5,760,369 members, and by October 1, 1952, the figure was 6,882,145. The Komsomol, or Young Communists, had numbered 15 million in October 1945. The figure had dropped to some 9 million in March 1949, but by August 1952 it was about 16 million.

The policy of mass recruiting had the purpose of restoring confidence in the party among the people and in the armed forces after the calamities of the first months of the war. But this growth had brought changes in the character of the membership. The priority given to enlisting proletarian and peasant members had been abandoned in the 1930s. But mass recruitment had led to an increase in the number of factory workers and peasants in key positions of authority, able to encourage and drive the people towards attainment of the plan targets.

Stalin himself attached importance to the recruitment of the new generation of intelligentsia. He had consistently advanced this new Soviet elite since before the war, and he looked on them as the coming leaders. This policy was strikingly reflected in the postwar membership of the party. By 1952 between a third and a half of the members were under thirty-five years in age and about three-quarters were under forty-five. The old generation had been almost totally eliminated by time, by the war, and not least by the purges.[3]

A renewed emphasis on the role of the party was notable in a speech which he made on February 9, 1946, the day before the elections for the new Supreme Soviet. Only five months earlier, on September 2, 1945, in an address to the nation on the surrender of Japan, he had spoken as a fervent patriot, exulting over the recovery of Russia's Far Eastern possessions, and he had not mentioned the party or communism.[4] But on February 9, 1946, his speech dwelt on Marxism and the role of the party. Crisis in the capitalist camp had caused World War I, and a further crisis had erupted in World War II. For the Russian people the recent war had been a tragedy, but it had also been "a great school of experience and testing," which had proved the strength of the social and state system of the Soviet Union and of its armed forces. The nation would be prepared for new challenges in the future.

Victory would be won not by bravery alone. It required a strong armament industry and ample supplies of every kind. The industrialization program had proved its value, and he quoted examples of wartime output to support his claim. Then, giving the main target figures, he expounded the party's plan to raise industrial and agricultural production to new heights. He spoke gravely, without needing to raise his voice to give expression to his iron will, and his speech was punctuated constantly by enthusiastic applause. He ended with an expression of gratitude to the people for their faith in him, and this brought an impassioned ovation.[5]

Stalin's position was supreme and beyond challenge. He was Prime Minister and also in effect General Secretary of the party. He felt no need to convene the All-Union Party Congress, which under the statutes was the source of all authority and was required to meet every three years. No congress had met since 1939, and another was convened only in October 1952. The Plenum of the Central Committee met seldom. The Politburo met rarely in formal session, but most of its members gathered fairly regularly at the dacha in Kuntsevo.

Since the Battle of Stalingrad, the Soviet press and other media had extolled him as the great leader and father of the nation. Every time his name was mentioned, it was as "our beloved father," "our dear guide and teacher," "our dear and well-beloved Stalin," and "the greatest leader of all times and of all peoples." There was no limit to the eulogies in what came to be known as "the personality cult." Although he lived and worked most of the time at his dacha in Kuntsevo, a window in the Kremlin always remained lit throughout the night. Anyone walking on Red Square could see it and know that, as reiterated by the radio, "He lives, thinks, and works for us." He was already a myth, a god.

On July 29, 1952, *Pravda,* describing events on "Aviation Day" at Tushino airport, reported:

> Two o'clock in the afternoon. Comrade I. V. Stalin ascends the governmental rostrum, hailed by cheers which for a long time

refuse to abate. The Soviet people welcome the appearance of the wise leader, the great educator, the inspired strategist. Comrade Stalin cordially salutes the crowd. The ovations grow stronger, expressing the unlimited devotion and ardent love of the Soviet people for Iosif Vissarionovich Stalin. . . . Hundreds of thousands of people greet Stalin in a transport of enthusiasm. . . .

A small figure on the rostrum, remote from the vast crowd, Stalin accepted this adulation on the few special occasions when he felt obliged to appear before the people. He authorized and condoned this public worship, which had mounted in a dramatic crescendo since the war. It was necessary in support of his power and position. It was like the rich panoply of church and state which had surrounded the Tsars, elevating them above everyday life and enveloping them in majesty and power. But, while accepting such demonstrations of loyalty and the paeans of praise, he was detached and uninfluenced. He took nothing for granted, not even the loyalty of the people. They had been loyal to the Tsar, but then had rejected him. It could happen to him, to any national leader. With his gnawing mistrust and his reading of history, he believed that real or potential enemies were always lurking among them.

While in his public appearances he acknowledged the extravagant tributes paid to him, in his personal relations with people he behaved with modesty and dignity. Averell Harriman, who met him on numerous occasions, wrote:

Publicly Stalin had permitted the most abject adulation of himself and accepted without hesitation every tribute and gift offered him, believing it was good propaganda. But privately he combined great dignity with an almost unpretentious modesty. In 1942 when I accompanied Churchill to Moscow to see him, we found him wearing for the first time the uniform of Marshal of the Soviet Union, a title he had just assumed. Churchill admired the uniform and congratulated Stalin on his elevation, but Stalin brushed the compliment aside with an unassuming manner. "They said I ought to accept the position of head of the armed forces in order to improve the morale of the troops," he said modestly. Just who "they" were was not made clear.[6]

Modesty and dignity, combined with professionalism, were the qualities he had always admired. He had sought to inculcate them in the new generation of the Soviet elite. Among the Allied leaders the men he had particularly respected were the American General Marshall and the two British service chiefs Alan Brooke and Tedder, who embodied these qualities. With his own people he was severe when they displayed lack of modesty. Zhukov was, he recognized, the most outstanding among the Soviet commanders, and he had received the fullest public recognition. But Zhukov, a strong, ebullient personality, was at times boastful. At a meeting of the Supreme Military Council in 1946, over which Stalin presided, he castigated "one of our most important soldiers [presumably Zhukov] for immodesty, unjustified conceit, and megalomania."[7]

Zhukov's removal from the office of Deputy Supreme Commander in March 1946 and his relegation to comparatively minor commands were probably due in large part to this defect in character. Stalin retained most of his senior commanders in high offices. Vasilevsky was made Chief of General Staff in November 1948 and Minister of Defense four months later. Konev served as Commander in Chief of the ground forces from June 1946 until March 1950 and then became Inspector General. Govorov, too, served as Inspector General for a time. Rokossovsky was appointed Soviet Commander in Chief in Poland and then Polish Minister of Defense. Bagramian, Malinovsky, Meretskov, and Tolbukhin were given major commands.

While retaining these commanders, Stalin kept a watchful, suspicious eye on each of them and indeed on all who were in positions of power. The cancer of mistrust had become a monstrous growth in the postwar years. He relied completely on no one. Men like Molotov, Beria, Voroshilov, Mikoyan, and Kaganovich who had worked closely with him over many years found themselves suddenly removed to a distance, deprived of his confidence, and even under threat of arrest. The smallest spark could ignite his suspicions and bring upon the unfortunate individuals disgrace and even death. The communist system in Russia had not found a means of removing men from power without fabrications of treason, or sentences of imprisonment, exile, and execution.

Stalin was now husbanding his strength. He was unhealthily sallow and physically in decline, but mentally he was alert and completely in control of national policies. Among those in authority under him, rivalries, maneuvering for position and power, and unspoken concern for the succession were taking place. He undoubtedly observed and even fostered these rivalries, but in a way designed to prevent any individual gathering too much power into his hands. At times he promoted attacks and criticisms of individuals as though warning them not to take their office for granted—or else to spur them to greater efforts. Like Lenin, he had come to regard his position as personal and beyond the grasp and power of any of those surrounding him. Although in his seventies, he felt that death was still far off, and he took no steps to name a successor. He could find no one to whom he could entrust the policies which were to him of paramount importance.

Two men who had long been prominent in the hierarchy and were regarded as possible successors were Malenkov and Zhdanov. Malenkov had held a position of power since the time of the great purges. He was responsible for party organization and for the promotion and demotion of key officials. He acted on Stalin's behalf in party affairs and served on the State Committee of Defense. Small, plump, and with a Mongol cast to his features, he was able and intelligent, his dark eyes mirroring his agile mind. But early in 1945 Stalin called Zhdanov to Moscow from Leningrad, where he had served throughout the siege. Although in poor health and suffering from a heart ailment, Zhdanov was ambitious and tough. Presumably Stalin considered that Malenkov had become complacent or too secure. Zhdanov at once launched a strong attack on Malenkov's work as chairman of the Committee on Rehabilitation of Liberated Areas and on his management of the dismantling of German industry. The attack was so effective that Malenkov was forced to retire into the background. Suddenly in July 1948, however, Stalin recalled him. A few weeks later Zhdanov died. Restored to office Malenkov began to think of himself as heir-apparent, but he had other rivals.

On Stalin's direction, or at least with his approval, Malenkov made an attack on the handling of party policy in the Ukraine. It was in effect an attack on Khrushchev. He had been first secretary of the Ukrainian party since 1938. In the war he had served as a political officer with the Red Army as it retreated to Stalingrad and then as it had advanced westwards and liberated the Ukraine. Malenkov now demanded stronger party controls over the collective farms of the steppelands. The peasants of the Ukraine had always hated the collective system, and in the hope that at the end of the war the system would be abolished, they had been expanding their private holdings by seizing land belonging to the collectives. On March 19, 1946, a joint resolution of the Council of Ministers and the Central Committee directed that all land and equipment alienated by the peasants should be restored to the collectives. Within a year some 14 million acres were recovered. Malenkov also criticized corruption and inefficiency among local party and government officials.

A Council on Collective Farms was given responsibility for restoring order and strengthening party control in the Ukraine. But in 1946 the whole of this vast region suffered a terrible drought and the harvest failed. Party mismanagement in the Ukraine was blamed. Khrushchev was again under attack. In March 1947 Lazar Kaganovich, Stalin's chief trouble shooter, was sent to the Ukraine, where he took over the office of first secretary, leaving Khrushchev as chairman of the local council of ministers. But somehow Khrushchev survived this crisis, and when later in 1947 Kaganovich returned to Moscow, he again became first secretary of the Ukrainian party.

The sinister figure in the background was the Georgian Lavrenty Beria. He was described as "somewhat plump, greenish, and pale, and with soft damp hands . . . and bulging eyes behind his pince-nez."[8] In character a blend of Iago and Cassius, he had a soft insinuating manner, and he knew how to play on his master's sick suspiciousness. Svetlana hated Beria, and years earlier Stalin's wife had urged his dismissal. He was, in fact, hated by everyone, and, possibly reasoning that this would preclude his joining any cabal and so guaranteed his loyalty, Stalin had retained him in charge of the Ministries of State Security and Internal Affairs since 1938, and had made him responsible also for secret atomic and scientific projects, while allowing him to rule over Transcaucasia as though it were a private empire.

Stalin nevertheless was aware of the extent of his power. He was about to curb Beria's influence when war broke out. During the war he relied on him in security matters. Indeed, he gave him the rank of Marshal of the Soviet Union, an appointment bitterly resented by officers of the Red Army, who remembered the part he had played in the purge of the Army. Moreover, in 1946 Beria was made a full member of the Politburo, probably in acknowledgment of his important responsibility for secret scientific research and the development of Russia's atomic bomb. But at this time Aleksei Kuznetsov, a secretary of the Central Committee, was given the responsibility for supervising the security apparatus. Kuznetsov was not one of Beria's men and in giving him the task of supervising Beria's special domain, Stalin was warning Beria that he could and possibly would be replaced.

In March 1949 changes in the most senior Soviet ministries were announced. Molotov was replaced by Vyshinsky as Minister of Foreign Affairs. Bulganin was succeeded by Marshal Vasilevsky as Minister of Defense. Mikoyan was replaced by Mikhail Menshikov as Minister of Foreign Trade. The retired ministers were well known as members of the Stalinist old guard. All were or were made deputy prime ministers of the Soviet Union. It seemed to be a fairly routine reshuffle, but it was the beginning of an ominous period in which no minister or official could feel secure.

Molotov, who had been Foreign Minister since 1939, and Stalin's loyal colleague since 1917, was without ambitions for greater power. His dismissal and the sudden mistrust of his master must have hurt him deeply. He suffered a further blow when his wife, Polina, was arrested and exiled to Kazakhstan. Unlike most wives of top Soviet officials, Polina had pursued her own career and had been well known in Moscow as a hostess. She had been a member of the Central Committee and Minister of Fisheries, and she had founded the Soviet perfume industry. But she was Jewish and alleged to be involved in "Zionist conspiracies." The Central Committee stripped her of all party functions, and she was tried in secret. Possibly, however, the real reason for her exile was that she had been the close friend of Nadya, Stalin's wife. He could not bear to be reminded of her by Polina in whom Nadya had confided. But in his last years Stalin seems to have become more resentful and vindictive towards those close to him who enjoyed the companionship of their wives. Kalinin, President of the U.S.S.R., was parted from his wife and she was imprisoned for some years. The wife of Poskrebyshev was arrested and imprisoned. Molotov, Kalinin, and Poskrebyshev nevertheless continued to serve their master without protest and with complete loyalty, although they knew that they themselves were under a cloud.

Stalin's malice and mistrust struck not only against his oldest colleagues but also against certain of the most prominent of the new generation of the Soviet elite. As in the past, his suspicion, once aroused against an individual, was inexorable. The victim was often relegated to a black corner of Stalin's mind and, when finally dealt with, was erased from his memory as though he had never existed. It was this capacity for cutting a person off and eliminating him from his mind that spared him the pangs of remorse. The suicide of his wife, Nadya, was the exception; she haunted him until his death.

In 1949–50 a purge, known as the Leningrad Affair, led to the execution by firing squad of a number of senior party officials who had been brought into prominence by Zhdanov. The instigators of the conspiracy against these men appear to have been Malenkov, Beria, and Viktor Abakumov, who had been head of Smersh, Red Army counterintelligence, during the war and was Minister of State Security from 1946 to 1952. They were evidently intent on destroying opponents who had supported Zhdanov against them. The conspirators succeeded in poisoning Stalin's mind against Nikolai Voznesensky, Aleksei Kuznetsov, and Mikhail Rodionov.

Voznesensky was an outstanding representative of the new professional elite, advanced by Stalin into the place of the old intelligentsia whom he had cleared away in the great purge. He was a professor of economics when Zhdanov placed him in charge of economic planning for Leningrad in 1935. Three years later, at the age of thirty-five, he was appointed head of Gosplan with over-all responsibility for Soviet economic planning. While still holding this onerous post he became in 1941 a Deputy Prime Minister of the U.S.S.R. and a candidate member of the Politburo. During the war he was deputy chairman of the State Defense Committee. After the war, while still directing Gosplan, he was made a full member of the Politburo. In 1948 he won the Stalin Prize for his short book *The War Economy of the U.S.S.R.*, which Stalin himself read in manuscript and, after making some corrections, had approved for the prize. Voznesensky was clearly one of Stalin's coming men and possibly, so it was rumored, was being prepared for the succession. In March 1949, only a few months after winning the Stalin Prize, he was suddenly dismissed from all appointments and arrested.

Aleksei Kuznetsov had been second secretary of the party in Leningrad from 1937 until 1945. As a member of the war council he had played an important part in the defense and final liberation of the city. He succeeded as first secretary when Zhdanov was recalled to Moscow. Then in 1946 he was appointed to the secretaryship of the Central Committee and entrusted with supervision of the security services. This meant his supervising Beria himself, and it was probably Beria who engineered his downfall. Mikhail Rodionov had worked closely with Zhdanov earlier, but had not held any office in Leningrad. He had become Prime Minister of the R.S.F.S.R. at an early age.

In September 1950 the Military Collegium of the Supreme Court sentenced Voznesensky, Kuznetsov, Rodionov, and their accomplices to death for treason. Moreover, the records of the case were sent to each member of the Politburo, who duly approved the findings and the sentence and signed to that effect.[9]

On October 5, 1952, the Nineteenth Party Congress opened in Moscow. Stalin was present, but took no part in the proceedings except to deliver a short closing address. Molotov gave the opening speech, but Malenkov delivered the key report, which Stalin himself had always delivered since 1924, and this seemed to mark him clearly as the successor. It was, however, Stalin's report that he delivered, for it embodied his policies. He was still the unchallenged leader, venerated and infallible. The Congress gave expression to this fact in the stormy standing ovation that greeted his appearance and by the fulsome references to him in every speech.

In two of the resolutions, which seemed no more than formalities, he was signifying that the party was firmly established and no longer needed to rely on old traditions to the same degree. The party was renamed the Communist party of the Soviet Union and the words "of Bolsheviks" were dropped. After all, the title Bolsheviks, meaning "Majority-ites," was no longer relevant to a party which ruled supreme and unopposed. The Politburo, a title with long Leninist associations, was renamed the Presidium. More important, the Presidium was enlarged to twenty-five full members and twelve alternate members. His purpose in making this change was to bring younger members into the top leadership. The party was now composed of the young, but the old members remained in office: The old men did not readily surrender power and position.

Stalin himself resigned as General Secretary of the party, an office he had held since 1922, although he had not used the title since the 1930s. This did not, however, diminish his authority and full control. But at this time he seemed conscious of his failing strength and torn between securing the strong continuity of the party leadership, and at the same time clinging to power. He still had work to do in ensuring that his policies were fully implemented, but he was determined to advance the new generation of professional Stalinist leaders. This meant removing the old guard, and he knew that, unless he compelled them, they would never stand aside. At the same time corrosive mistrust made him question the honesty and commitment of others, young and old. They would be seduced by power and position and forget the real purposes to be served. All his life he had been involved in the savage struggle for power and he trusted no one.

At the Congress Stalin sat through the opening and Malenkov's report. All eyes were upon him. Their worshipful respect set him apart. He was a small gray-haired old man, failing in strength, and completely alone, isolated by their adulation and by the terrible power which he held. He led a solitary existence. His permanent residence was the dacha at Kuntsevo, but he had other dachas, not far away at Semenovskoe and Lipki. He felt truly at home only in the dark, dense forests of pine and silver birch trees which surrounded these places. In the summer he would work in the garden of the dacha, and in winter, when the sun shone, he would sit by the windows, working on papers and receiving officials. Often now he spent the whole day at the dacha and did not go to his Kremlin office. Towards the end of each summer he traveled south and spent two months in one of the villas always kept ready for him in the Caucasus.

Because it was believed that he lived under the constant threat of assassination, he was enveloped by security precautions. When he traveled between the Kremlin and Kuntsevo, five black limousines drove at speed through the city, where all traffic was halted. The drivers frequently overtook each other, changing the order in which they traveled. No one could tell which limousine contained him behind its curtains. Special security guards were permanently posted at the dacha, and elaborate measures, including searchlights, made the place like a prison camp. His journeys to the south were carried out like military exercises. Much of this security was probably imposed on him by zealous officers, like Vlasik, intent on expanding their authority and importance, but it also reflected his own chronic suspicions.

Dinners at Kuntsevo, attended by Malenkov, Beria, Bulganin, Khrushchev, and other old colleagues who were not in disfavor, provided his only social life. They were working dinners at which policy matters were discussed and decided, but then they became evenings of heavy eating and drinking, reminiscing, and coarse banter. Djilas, the Yugoslav communist, described one dinner at Kuntsevo which he attended in January 1948. He noticed a decline in Stalin and felt that there was a growing tension between him and Molotov. He also deplored the scale of the eating and drinking. Fastidious, severe, and often self-righteous, he was critical of all that he saw. He had idolized Stalin as the great communist leader and could not get over the disappointment of finding him to be a Russian politician who at times revealed his peasant origins.

The dinner evenings at Kuntsevo, when he talked over state affairs and as an old man reminisced, were the only occasions when he relaxed, although then only partially. He often recalled the war; he missed the high drama of those years. He horrified Djilas when at a dinner in 1944, the second that Djilas attended, he contradicted a remark that the Germans would need fifty years to recover from the war. "No," he replied, "they will recover and very quickly. It is a highly-developed industrial country with an extremely skilled and numerous working class and technical intel-

ligentsia. Give them twelve to fifteen years and they'll be on their
feet again." Standing up and hitching his trousers, he added:
"The war will soon be over. We shall recover in fifteen or twenty
years and then we'll have another go at it!"[10]

At Kuntsevo as in his Kremlin office, Stalin felt his loneliness,
but did not admit it. He desperately missed his wife, Nadya, who
had died nearly twenty years earlier. He blamed her suicide on her
family, Polina Molotov, and the evil influence of Michael Arlen's
novel *The Green Hat*, which she had been reading. In 1948, for
the first time, he talked openly with Svetlana about her mother,
and it was apparent that memories of her troubled him deeply.

The one person whom he loved and who might partially have
filled the gap in his life was his daughter. She was, however, emotional and self-centered and without any capacity for devotion and
self-sacrifice. Since the incident of her schoolgirl infatuation with
Aleksei Kapler, she had felt estranged from her father. When in
July 1941 she telephoned to tell him that she had graduated, he
told her to come to see him. He was pleased with her diploma,
but disapproving of her plan to go to university for a degree in literary studies. "You want to be one of those bohemians. . . . No,
you'd better get a decent education. Let it be history. . . . Study
history. Then you can do what you want."[11]

During the war their meetings were infrequent. In May 1944
Svetlana went to Kuntsevo to tell her father that she wanted to
marry Grigori Morozov, a student at the Institute of International
Relations. He was Jewish, and Stalin, who had something of the
traditional Russian prejudice against Jews, and who was at this
time deeply suspicious of the burgeoning Zionist movement, disapproved. His main criticism, however, was that the young man
was not serving his country. "It's terrible at the front," he said,
"and look at him, he's sitting it out at home!"[12] But he did not
forbid the marriage, as Svetlana had feared. "Yes, it's spring. To
hell with you. Do as you like!" was his final comment.[18] He refused to meet her husband or to allow him in his house, but he
gave them an apartment outside the Kremlin. When Svetlana became pregnant, he relaxed his ban. "You need the country air," he
said, and allowed them the use of the dacha at Zubalovo, but he
never met Morozov.

Stalin was pleased when in the spring of 1947 his daughter's marriage broke up. He had never approved of her husband, but he was affectionate with Iosif, his grandson. Meetings between father and daughter again became rare, months passing without any contact. In August 1947 he invited her and her son to join him in Sochi. It proved an uneasy holiday. She found difficulty in communicating with him and could not adjust to his habits of sitting up most of the night and sleeping part of the day. She was bored by the dinners when Malenkov, Beria, Bulganin, and the others came. The effort needed to show her affection and to give him her companionship was apparently beyond her capacity.

Again weeks went by without contact between them. In the spring of 1949 Svetlana married Yury Zhdanov, son of Andrei Zhdanov, at one time seen as a possible successor to Stalin himself. This pleased her father, who knew the family and respected the son. Apparently he thought that his daughter and son-in-law might move into the second floor which had been added to the dacha at Kuntsevo. Svetlana herself observed that "as he'd got older my father had begun feeling lonely. He was so isolated from everyone at this time, so elevated that he seemed to be living in a vacuum. He hadn't a soul he could talk to."[14] She and her husband refused, however, to move into the dacha, and in the summer of 1948 she declined his invitation to join him in the Caucasus. Stalin was deeply hurt, and when in November 1948 she spent a short time with him in the south, he was in an angry mood.

Traveling back to Moscow by train with him, Svetlana was again shaken and depressed by his isolated way of life. It was a special train, carrying him and the security guards, who cocooned his existence. Every station had been cleared. When the train halted, Stalin would walk along the platform to chat with the engine crew. She was convinced that he had not ordered such arrangements, and he would curse the generals and colonels of the bodyguard who got in his way. "It was the system of which he himself was a prisoner and in which he was stifling from loneliness, emptiness, and lack of human companionship."[15] But she realized that he, too, was at fault. "He saw enemies everywhere. It had reached the point of being pathological, of persecution mania, and it was all a result of being lonely and desolate."[16] At this time the campaign against "rootless cosmopolitans" and against Zionists was under way. Arrests of people within her family circle dismayed Svetlana. She protested to her father, but was angrily rebuffed.

For another long period she did not see her father. Her second marriage and living in the Zhdanov household made her very unhappy. During the winter of 1949–50 she was pregnant and suffering severely from a kidney ailment. In a state of self-pity and depression after the birth of her daughter, she wrote to her father for comfort. He replied promptly, with the last letter she was ever to receive from him:

> Dear Svetochka! I got your letter. I'm very glad you got off so lightly. Kidney trouble is a serious business. To say nothing of having a child. Where did you get the idea that I had abandoned you? It's the sort of thing people dream up. I advise you not to believe your dreams. Take care of yourself. Take care of your daughter, too. The state needs people, even those who are born prematurely. Be patient a little longer—we'll see each other soon. I kiss my Svetochka. Your "little papa." May 10th 1950.[17]

Stalin took his last holiday in the south in the autumn of 1951. He did not leave Moscow again and lived at Kuntsevo most of the time. Svetlana with her two children visited him on the November 7 anniversary in 1952 and again on his seventy-third birthday on December 21. He looked unwell then and was obviously suffering from high blood pressure, but he would not see doctors and he treated himself with old peasant remedies. He had always enjoyed tobacco and for at least fifty years had rarely been without his pipe or cigarette, but suddenly he gave up the habit.

On this as on other occasions Svetlana felt she should visit him more often. Friends urged her to telephone him. She hesitated because he would often answer curtly, "I'm busy!" But she knew that he welcomed her visits and liked to see her children. Behind his growling manner there was real concern for them, especially after her divorce from her second husband. Often he would offer her money, knowing that she depended on the allowance of a university student and was short of money. When as a graduate student of the Academy of Social Sciences she received a higher allowance, he would give her money for the children and for the daughter of his first son, who had been shot by the Germans. At the same time he was always insistent that she should work and pay her way, and that she should never be what he called a "parasite."

The campaign against Western influences had led to the denunciation of many intellectuals, especially Jews, as "rootless cosmopolitans." It culminated in 1952 in the execution of a number of Jewish writers. This purge was followed by the "Doctors' Plot," which was first made public by *Pravda* on January 13, 1953. A Dr. Lydia Timashuk had sent a private letter to Stalin, alleging that the treatment prescribed by certain eminent doctors, including Vinogradov, who had been Stalin's physician, amounted to the murder of leading citizens. These doctors had, it was alleged, caused the premature death of Andrei Zhdanov, and they were administering similar treatment to Marshals Voroshilov, Konev, and Govorov, to General Shtemenko, and others.

Stalin had strong doubts about Timashuk's allegations. But at the time he was in a fever of suspicion about Zionist and Titoist conspiracies, planted and fostered by a network of American and British agents. He believed, too, that among his old colleagues there was a plot to displace him or at least curtail his powers. He reacted violently. He would not allow doctors near him, although he knew his health was failing. He dismissed Poskrebyshev, his trusted secretary for so many years. Vlasik, head of his personal security since the Civil War, was imprisoned. They, like Molotov, Beria, and others, waited fearfully for the great new purge that seemed about to break upon them. But they were spared.

31

Death
March 5, 1953

Death came suddenly. On the evening of Saturday February 28, 1953, Malenkov, Beria, Bulganin, and Khrushchev had dined at Kuntsevo. Stalin had been in a good humor and the evening had been jovial. When Sunday March 1 passed without his usual call, summoning them or discussing business by telephone, all were surprised.

Svetlana telephoned Kuntsevo on the Sunday. The duty officer told her: "There's no movement right now." This meant that her father had not stirred, and, as she knew, it was forbidden to disturb him.

Later on the Sunday night the duty officer of the guard telephoned Malenkov, Beria, Bulgania, and Khrushchev at their dachas. Stalin had not rung for his dinner. He feared that something had happened, but the guards did not dare to go into his room. All four rushed from their dachas to Kuntsevo. Voroshilov and Kaganovich were summoned. When they gained entrance to his room, they found Stalin lying fully dressed on a rug. He was in a coma.

Doctors were called. They diagnosed a cerebral hemorrhage, brought on by arteriosclerosis and high blood pressure. The communiqué announcing his illness to the nation emphasized that the medical treatment was under the close surveillance of the Central Committee of the party. In fact, the six members of the Presidium present had organized guard duty, taking it in turns two at a time to watch over him and the doctors day and night.

On Monday morning Svetlana was called from class at the academy and told that Malenkov wanted her to come to Kuntsevo. Khrushchev and Bulganin were waiting for her in the drive to the dacha. Both were in tears. They took her to her father's room, which was crowded with doctors, nurses, and equipment, and the members of the Presidium. She kissed her father's face and hand and, sitting at his side, continued holding his hand. From time to time he opened his eyes, but they were unseeing and he did not regain consciousness. His heart and constitution were strong, but the hemorrhage was spreading and he was fighting against suffocation. On the fourth day he regained consciousness briefly, but was severely paralyzed. A nurse gave him a drink from a spoon. He pointed to one of the many blown-up photographs of children which he had taken to pinning on the wall of his room. This picture showed a small girl feeding a lamb. He seemed to be trying to make a joke of his situation.

The death throes began. His face changed and turned black as he struggled to breathe. It was a terrible fight against death. He raised his left arm, and to his daughter it was a menacing gesture, as though he were trying to bring a curse upon all present. Then he died.

Voroshilov, Bulganin, Kaganovich, Malenkov, and Khrushchev were sobbing. Beria alone showed no grief. All departed to make preparations, and only Svetlana, Bulganin, and Mikoyan remained by the body. An old nurse prepared the room. Then, after a time, the staff began filing in to take leave of their master. It was a Russian leave-taking. Valechka, the housekeeper who had looked after him for eighteen years, fell to her knees and, laying her head on his chest, wailed aloud as peasant women did, and no one attempted to quiet or to stop her. The household staff were devoted to him. He was considerate and kind to all who served him, and at Kuntsevo only the generals and commanders of the guard felt his anger.

Early in the morning of March 6, Moscow radio announced the death of Stalin. A vast crowd began filling the Red Square; most of the people were sobbing quietly. Later in the afternoon the body, which had been brought to the Kremlin during the night, was placed in the Hall of Columns. It lay on a raised bier, surrounded by banks of flowers, and it was uncovered. The crowd had greatly increased, and by the late afternoon the line of mourners was reported to stretch for ten miles. In their thousands Russians from Moscow and distant regions filed past the bier in a slow, unending procession, taking leave of their father.

In every part of the country from Vladivostok in the east to Leningrad in the west, from Archangel in the north to Astrakhan in the south, houses and windows were draped in red flags, hung with black crepe. Even in the numerous labor camps, crowded with men and women who had suffered from the savage repression of his rule, there were displays of grief. A nation of over 200 million people was united in the solemn quiet of mourning for their leader who had guided and driven them through harsh trials and a savage war and who, they knew instinctively, had sought to serve them and Russia.

NOTES

1. V. Kaminsky and I. Vereshchagin, "Detstvo i yunost vozhdya: dokumenty, zapisi, rasskazi," *Molodaya Gvardiya*, No. 12 (1939); hereafter cited as Kaminsky and Vereshchagin. E. Yaroslavsky, *Landmarks in the Life of Stalin* (London, 1942), p. 7; hereafter cited as Yaroslavsky.

   A marble pavilion was erected over the house by Lavrenti Beria in the 1930s to preserve it as a national shrine. A plaque states: "Here the Great Stalin was born on 21 December 1879 (NS) and spent his life until 1883."

   Svetlana Alliluyeva, Stalin's daughter, saw the mausoleum and adjoining museum in 1951, and wrote, "Under the marble canopy you can barely see the little hovel which ought to have been left as it was and could perfectly well have told its story without the marble. Everything was treated as a relic." *Twenty Letters to a Friend* (London, 1967), p. 213.

   The mausoleum was completely neglected after Stalin's death, and in 1962 it was closed for repairs. Laurens Van Der Post, *Journey into Russia* (London, 1964), p. 98; Harrison Salisbury, *Stalin's Russia and After* (London, 1955), p. 95.

   The removal of statues and pictures of Stalin from places of prominence has been enforced throughout the Soviet Union since 1956. The exception has been Georgia, where the people take pride in having produced the great leader and resent his demotion. Yielding to Georgian feeling, the Soviet government has allowed monuments to remain.

   An American journalist, Robert Kaiser, reported in April 1973 that the mausoleum and the large Stalin museum adjoining it were open and the tall statue of Stalin was still standing on its gray marble base in the center of Gori. *The Guardian* (London), April 9, 1973.

2. Iosif Stalin, *Sochineniya* (Moscow, 1946–55), Vol. 1, pp. 314–15; hereafter cited as Stalin, *Sochineniya*.

3. Ibid., Vol. 13, p. 113.

4. The most convincing account is by Iosif Iremashvili, entitled

Stalin und die Tragödie Georgiens, published in Berlin in 1932. Iremashvili was born in Gori about the same time as Stalin. They were friends at school and later in the Tiflis Seminary. He became a schoolteacher in Tiflis. In May 1921 he was arrested by Bolshevik secret police and held in prison. His sister obtained a personal interview with Stalin and begged for her brother's release. He granted her plea, but since Iremashvili, who was a Menshevik, refused to join the Bolshevik party, he was deported in October 1922 to Germany together with sixty-one other Georgians. Although a political opponent, forced to live in exile, Iremashvili evidently tried to write impartially about his childhood friend, but his memories are obviously colored by subsequent events.

Landmarks in the Life of Stalin, by Emelyan Yaroslavsky, and *The Childhood and Youth of the Leader,* by Vladimir Kaminsky and Ivan Vereshchagin, both published in Moscow after the great purges, were contributions to the official portrait of the great leader. To what extent, if at all, he was directly responsible for the statements in these official biographies is not known. All three sources have to be treated with caution.

5. Iremashvili, p. 12.
6. Svetlana Alliluyeva, *Only One Year* (London, 1969), p. 340.
7. Yaroslavsky, p. 10.
8. Kaminsky and Vereshchagin, p. 44.
9. *Pravda,* October 27, 1935.
10. *The Photographs of Margaret Bourke-White* (London, 1973).
11. Svetlana Alliluyeva, *Twenty Letters to a Friend* (London, 1967), pp. 213–14.
12. Ibid., p. 165.
13. Ibid.

CHAPTER 2

1. I. Iremashvili, *Stalin und die Tragödie Georgiens* (Berlin, 1932), p. 11.
2. Ibid., p. 8.
3. It has been suggested that at this school he became aware of class differences and class hatreds. Isaac Deutscher, *Stalin* (London, 1961), p. 6.
4. Iremashvili, p. 5.
5. A. S. Alliluyev, *Vospominaniya* (Moscow, 1946), p. 36.
6. Trotsky also quotes Souvarine's comment that cachexia of the left arm, in addition to two toes grown together, provides "proof of alcoholic heredity on his father's side." The two disabilities hardly

provide "proof" of anything. Leon Trotsky, *Stalin*, ed. and trans. Charles Malamuth (London, 1968), p. 6.
7. Iremashvili, p. 18.
8. Yaroslavsky, pp. 4–10.
9. Kaminsky and Vereshchagin, p. 47.
10. Iosif and his schoolmates are said to have demonstrated against this change. Iosif was the leader and was punished, but evidently mildly, and he was still recommended for the seminary in Tiflis. Iremashvili, p. 8.
11. Yaroslavsky, pp. 9–10.

CHAPTER 3

1. *Istoriya Klassovoi Borby V. Zakavkazi* (Tiflis, 1930), Vol. 1, p. 92.
2. Ibid.
3. I. Iremashvili, *Stalin und die Tragödie Georgiens* (Berlin, 1932), p. 16.
4. Yaroslavsky, p. 15.
5. Kaminsky and Vereshchagin, pp. 65, 67.
6. Ibid.
7. E. Ludwig, *Stalin* (New York, 1942), p. 19; Stalin, *Sochineniya*, Vol. 13, p. 113.
8. Iremashvili, pp. 17–22.
9. Yaroslavsky, pp. 16–17.
10. Ibid.
11. *Priveli Dassy* [The First Group] had been founded by Ilya Chavchavadze, the leader of advanced liberal opinion among the Georgian nobility.
   Meori Dassy [The Second Group], led by G. Tseretelli, was an organization of the Georgian intelligentsia, devoted to the theories of the western European utopian socialists. L. Beria, *On the History of the Bolshevik Organizations in Transcaucasia* (London, 1939), p. 203.
12. Ibid., pp. 11–12.
13. Stalin, *Sochineniya*, Vol. 8, p. 174.
14. N. Vakar, "Stalin po vospominaniyam N.N. Zhordania," *Poslednyia Novosti* (Paris), December 16, 1936, p. 2.
15. Kaminsky and Vereshchagin, pp. 77–79.
16. Yaroslavsky, pp. 16–17; Kaminsky and Vereshchagin, p. 67.
17. Ibid., p. 86; Yaroslavsky, p. 17.
18. Ibid.
19. H. R. Knickerbocker, "Stalin, Mystery Man Even to His Mother," New York *Evening Post*, December 1, 1930.

CHAPTER 4

1. L. Trotsky, *Stalin* (London, 1968), p. 54.
2. B. Souvarine, *Stalin* (London, n.d.), p. 42.
3. It has been suggested that during these months Koba was enlisted as an agent of the tsarist police. The Okhrana, as the tsarist security forces were known, permeated Russian society and was efficient, particularly in the use of *agents provocateurs*, and it had been infiltrating revolutionary organizations with great effect. But the evidence that he was in the pay of the Okhrana is circumstantial and unconvincing. Certainly he would not have hesitated to become a double agent if it had meant obtaining money to keep himself alive, to further the revolutionary cause or even his own interests. Like Lenin, he was concerned not about means but ends, and he accepted as a tenet of faith the principle, expressed by Nechaev, that "in this struggle the revolution sanctifies everything alike." E. H. Carr, *Bakunin* (London, 1937), p. 380.
   The proposition that Koba-Stalin was an agent of the Okhrana, with every scrap of evidence and every possible conjecture in support of it, is expounded by E. E. Smith, *The Young Stalin* (London, 1968), to which I am indebted.
4. Yaroslavsky, p. 25.
5. Smith, p. 69.
6. Iremashvili, p. 24.
7. Kaminsky and Vereshchagin, p. 89.
8. S. Alliluyev, *Proidenny Put* (Moscow, 1946), pp. 46–49.
9. Kaminsky and Vereshchagin, p. 89.
10. L. Beria, *On the History of the Bolshevik Organizations in Transcaucasia* (London, 1939), p. 22; Alliluyev, *Proidenny Put*, pp. 51–59; H. Barbusse, *Stalin*, trans. V. Holland (London, 1935), pp. 17–18.
11. A. S. Alliluyev, *Vospominaniya* (Moscow, 1946); *The Alliluyev Memoirs*, trans. and ed. D. Tutaev (London, 1968), p. 47.
12. Kaminsky and Vereshchagin, p. 95.
13. Beria, p. 23.
14. Stalin, *Sochineniya*, Vol. 1, pp. 417–18; A. B. Ulam, *Stalin* (London, 1973), p. 40.
15. Iremashvili, p. 28.
16. N. Valentinov, *Encounters with Lenin* (London, 1968), p. 20.
17. Beria, p. 24.
18. N. K. Krupskaya, *O Krasine*, quoted by Michael Glenny in "Leonid Krasin: The Years Before 1917. An Outline," *Soviet Studies*, Vol. 22 (October 1970), p. 193.

19. L. Beria, *Lado Ketskhoveli Sbornik* (Moscow, 1938), pp. 12–13.
20. L. Beria, *On the History of the Bolshevik Organizations in Trans-caucasia* (London, 1939), p. 36.
21. I. Deutscher, *Stalin* (London, 1949), pp. 38–39.
22. Stalin, *Sochineniya,* Vol. 1, pp. 3–10.
23. Ibid., pp. 11–31.
24. Ibid., pp. 11, 21–22.
25. This defense of the rights of all classes and the championing of a democratic constitution in which the capitalists would have equal rights with the workers and peasants reads strangely. In the Fore-word to his *Works,* written in 1946, however, Stalin explained that he had "accepted then the thesis familiar among Marxists, according to which one of the chief conditions for the victory of the socialist revolution was that the proletariat should become the majority of the population." Ibid., Vol. 6, p. 23; pp. xiv–xv.
26. Ibid., pp. 26ff.

CHAPTER 5

1. L. Beria, *On the History of the Bolshevik Organizations in Trans-caucasia* (London, 1939), pp. 24–25; Yaroslavsky, p. 37; *Ba-tumskaya Demonstratsiya 1902 goda* (Moscow, 1937), pp. 53, 73.
2. An account, published nearly thirty years later, stated:

> From his earliest days of activity among the workers, he [Koba] attracted attention by his intrigues against the real leader of the social democratic organization, S. Dzhibladze. He was warned, but took no notice and continued to spread slanders intending to discredit the authorized and recognized representatives of the social democratic movement, thus attempting to manage the local organization. He was brought before a party court of honour and found guilty of unjustly slandering Dzhibladze and was by unanimous vote excluded from the Tiflis social democratic organization. [*Brdzolis Khma,* quoted by E. E. Smith, p. 89.]

According to S. T. Arkomed, a Social Democrat who was present at the meeting on November 11, 1901, a member, not named but described as "a young indiscriminately-energetic and wholly-intelligent comrade," spoke bluntly against workers being elected to the committee because they lacked education and experience to further revolutionary work. Arkomed wrote further that "the aforementioned young comrade transferred his activity from Tiflis to Batum, whence the Tiflis comrades heard reports about his incorrect behaviour and his hostile and disorganizing agitation against the Tiflis organizations and its workers." S. T. Arkomed, *Rabochee Dvizhenie i Sotsial Demokratiya na Kavkaze* (Geneva, 1910), p. 74.

It has been assumed by Trotsky and most subsequent writers that the unnamed comrade was Koba. To the present writer, it seems that Koba was unlikely to have spoken in such terms; he would have regarded workers as closer to himself and more readily influenced and led than intellectuals.

3. Noi Zhordania wrote later that Koba was suspected by workers of serving as an *agent provocateur*, especially in instigating the strikes and demonstrations in Batum, and further that the Okhrana arrested him in order to counter such rumors and to maintain his cover so that he would still be of use to them. N. Vakar, "Stalin po vospominaniyam N.N. Zhordania," *Posledniya Novosti* (Paris), December 16, 1936, p. 4.
4. *Batumskaya Demonstratsiya 1902 goda*, p. 152.
5. Yaroslavsky, p. 26.
6. Stalin, *Sochineniya*, Vol. 1, p. 419.
7. *Batumskaya Demonstratsiya 1902 goda*, pp. 150ff.
8. Yaroslavsky, p. 28; E. E. Smith, *The Young Stalin* (London, 1967), p. 102.
9. *Batumskaya Demonstratsiya 1902 goda* (Moscow, 1937), pp. 134–36.

One incident, variously interpreted, occurred soon after his arrest. On a visitors' day he pushed through the bars of his cell two notes, one to be delivered to Iremashvili, his old school friend, in Gori, and the other to Elisabedashvili, a fellow revolutionary, in Tiflis. The note to Iremashvili asked him to see his mother and to tell her to say in reply to any questioning by the police that her son, Soso/Koba, had been in Gori all summer and winter until March 15 (1902), thus providing him with an alibi, if charged with participating in the Batum demonstration. The note to Elisabedashvili simply urged him to carry on with his revolutionary work. The notes reached both men, presumably taken by couriers arranged by Koba, but at some stage the police intercepted them or learned of them through an informer. Koba's mother and Iremashvili himself were questioned and Elisabedashvili was arrested. Trotsky later expressed "amazement at the carelessness with which Koba subjected two of his comrades to danger," and others have maintained that, acting in collusion with the police, Koba deliberately compromised both men. L. Trotsky, *Stalin* (London, 1968), p. 34; Smith, pp. 104–6.
10. Smith, p. 102; B. Souvarine, *Stalin* (London, n.d.), p. 46.
11. Trotsky, p. 54.
12. Smith, pp. 103–4.

13. G. Uratadze, *Vospominaniya gruzinskogo sotsial-demokrata* (Stanford, 1968), p. 66, quoted in Ronald Hingley, *Joseph Stalin* (London, 1974), p. 30.
14. Sergei Alliluyev, *Proidenny Put* (Moscow, 1946), p. 109. See also Smith, pp. 112–23, postulating that Koba was never sent to Siberia and that his journey was a fabrication by the Okhrana to protect a valued agent.
15. Koba probably grieved over the death of his devoted young wife, but Iremashvili's description of his theatrical behavior at the funeral is far from convincing. "At the cemetery gate, Koba firmly pressed my hand, pointed to the coffin and said: 'Soso, this creature softened my stony heart. She is dead and with her my last warm feelings for all human beings have died.' He placed his right hand over his heart: 'It is all so desolate here inside, so unspeakably desolate!'" Iremashvili states that the marriage took place in 1903. Iosif was then in prison, but the tsarist authorities are known to have allowed prison chaplains to solemnize marriages. He states also that Ekaterina died in 1907, but Yakov, the son of Iosif and Ekaterina, who was to be brought up by her sisters, was born in 1908. It is probable that his wife died in 1910. Smith, pp. 126–29, 392; I. Iremashvili, *Stalin und die Tragödie Georgiens* (Berlin, 1932), pp. 30–39; Svetlana Alliluyeva, *Twenty Letters to a Friend* (London, 1967), p. 110.

CHAPTER 6

1. Stalin used many names, but most frequently called himself Koba, until January 1913 when he signed an article "K. Stalin"—Koba the Man of Steel.
2. Stalin, *Sochineniya*, Vol. 6, pp. 52–53.
3. Ibid., Vol. 1, p. 396; R. C. Tucker, *Stalin as Revolutionary 1879–1929* (New York, 1973), pp. 122–23.
4. Stalin, *Sochineniya*, Vol. 1, p. 61; Tucker, pp. 122–23.
5. V. I. Lenin, *Sochineniya* (Moscow, 1941–57), Vol. 7, pp. 5, 9, 21; hereafter cited as Lenin.
6. Stalin, *Sochineniya*, Vol. 6, pp. 52–53.
7. Lenin, Vol. 4, pp. 107–13.
8. N. Valentinov, *Encounters with Lenin* (London, 1968), p. 114.
9. A. V. Lunacharsky, *Revolutionary Silhouettes* (London, 1967), p. 59.
10. Ibid., p. 67.
11. Ibid., p. 62.
12. Trotsky and others have stated that Koba began as a Menshevik and joined the Bolsheviks only in 1904. This statement is based

on a police report, dated 1911, alleging that Koba worked in the Social Democrat organization from 1902, first as a Menshevik, and then as a Bolshevik. This is clearly an anachronism, since the terms "Menshevik" and "Bolshevik" only came into existence after the party's Second Congress in July–August 1903. L. Trotsky, *Stalin* (London, 1968), pp. 50–51, 55; I. Deutscher, *Stalin* (London, 1949), p. 50; Tucker, pp. 98–99.

13. Stalin, *Sochineniya*, Vol. 1, p. 56.
14. Ibid., p. 57.

Chapter 7

1. L. Schapiro, *The Communist Party of the Soviet Union*, 2nd ed., (London, 1970), p. 670.
2. F. Makharadze, *Ocherki revolyutsionnogo dvizheniya v Zakavkazi*, quoted in R. C. Tucker, *Stalin as Revolutionary 1879–1929* (New York, 1973), p. 98n.
3. A brief account of the circumstances of the execution will be found in *The Transcaucasian Episode 1918–19*, by C. H. Ellis, who took part in operations in the region at this time.
4. Stalin, *Sochineniya*, Vol. 1, pp. 32–55.
5. Ibid., pp. 62–73, 89–130.
6. Ibid., pp. 138–72.
7. Ibid., pp. 131–37.
8. Lenin, Vol. 11, p. 386.
9. Stalin, *Sochineniya*, Vol. 1, pp. 193–95.

Chapter 8

1. Stalin, *Sochineniya*, Vol. 6, pp. 54–55. I. Deutscher wrote of the "characteristically vivid crudeness" of this speech, a description which, bearing in mind the time and circumstances of its delivery, is unacceptable. I. Deutscher, *Stalin: A Political Biography* (London, 1961), p. 78.
2. Stalin, *Sochineniya*, Vol. 6, pp. 55ff.
3. N. K. Krupskaya, *Reminiscences of Lenin* (London, 1959), p. 141.
4. L. Schapiro, *The Communist Party of the Soviet Union*, 2nd ed. (London, 1970), p. 74, note 2.
5. Ibid., p. 74.
6. V. Bonch-Bruevich, *Bolshevistskie izdatelskie dela v 1905–07 gg Moi Vospominaniya* (Leningrad, 1933), pp. 17–18.

7. Schapiro, pp. 99–100.
8. In 1931, when interviewing him, Emil Ludwig mentioned rumors concerning "armed attacks which you are said to have organized in your youth to obtain money for the Party. How much truth was there in these stories?" He asked also Stalin's opinion of Stenka Razin as an "ideological highwayman," suggesting an analogy with the Bolsheviks. Stalin talked at length about the historical factors in early peasant rebellions, but turning to stories of his own role in expropriations he laughed and handed Ludwig a pamphlet which would, he said, give him the whole story; it proved to contain nothing on the subject. Emil Ludwig, *Stalin* (New York, 1942), pp. 42–43.
9. Angelica Balabanov, *Memoirs*, quoted in B. D. Wolfe, *Three Who Made a Revolution* (Boston, 1948), p. 385.
10. L. Trotsky, *Stalin* (London, 1968), pp. 90–91.
11. Stalin, *Sochineniya*, Vol. 2, p. 51. This might also be rendered as "beautiful extravagance." The two words are used with irony or sarcasm.
12. Schapiro, p. 98.
13. Deutscher, following Krupskaya and Trotsky, describes Kamo in terms both heroic and endearing. He was "warmhearted, romantic, resourceful, and untiring"; he was "an exceedingly sensitive person, somewhat naive, and a tender comrade."

   On Erivan Square, Kamo's bombs killed three men and wounded some fifty passers-by. His exploits were numerous and must have caused hundreds of deaths and the wounding and maiming of literally thousands of innocent men, women, and children. Deutscher, p. 88; Trotsky, pp. 104–8.
14. Stalin is usually regarded as having been responsible for the Tiflis raid. A biography of Shaumyan, published in Moscow in 1965, has suggested, however, that he, not Stalin, was the chief organizer. The original plan was the work of Krasin in St. Petersburg, who discussed it with Lenin, then in hiding in Kuokkala. It is certainly plausible that Krasin would have been more inclined to entrust such an exploit to Shaumyan, a fellow engineer who had traveled abroad, rather than to an unknown Georgian. V. D. Mukhadze, *Shaumyan* (Moscow, 1965), p. 123; Adam B. Ulam, *Stalin: The Man and His Era* (London, 1974), p. 94.
15. Stalin, Vol. 2, p. 56; Ulam, p. 96.
16. It is indeed one of the ironies of history that men like Stolypin and Guchkov, who followed an honorable code of conduct, seeking to eliminate injustices and to create a prosperous society, are little known, while Lenin, Stalin, Bogdanov, Krasin, Trotsky, Ter-Petrosyan, and others like them, who worked through terror, murder, deceit, and ruthless disregard for all who were not on their side, are lauded as heroes. Clearly historians as a whole are

on the side of the victors and, for all their moral strictures about Stalin, condone the law of might.

17. Wolfe, *Three Who Made a Revolution*, p. 486.

CHAPTER 9

1. It is alleged that Koba denounced Shaumyan to the Okhrana, the most detestable betrayal that a revolutionary could commit, and further that he must have been a police agent. But Koba was far away in exile on both occasions when Shaumyan was arrested. Moreover, after his first arrest he was promptly released, and he was arrested a second time on the denunciation of M. E. Chernomazov, a police agent infiltrated into the Bolshevik ranks, who committed suicide in 1917. His sentence of exile to Astrakhan after his second arrest was far more lenient than the sentence on Koba who was sent to the icy north. B. Souvarine, *Stalin* (London, n.d.), pp. 110–11; A. B. Ulam, *Stalin: The Man and His Era* (London, 1974), pp. 97–98.
2. B. D. Wolfe, *Three Who Made a Revolution* (Boston, 1948), p. 471.
3. Ibid.
4. Stalin, *Sochineniya*, Vol. 2, pp. 81–127.
5. Ibid., pp. 110–11.
6. I. Deutscher, *Stalin: A Political Biography* (London, 1961), p. 101.
7. Lenin, Vol. 16, p. 368.
8. L. Trotsky, *Stalin* (London, 1968), pp. 117–21; S. Vereshchek, *Stalin v tyurme: vospominaniya politicheskogo zaklyuchonrogo Dni* (Paris), pp. 22, 24 (January 1928).
9. Stalin, *Sochineniya*, Vol. 2, pp. 146–47.
10. Ibid., p. 150.
11. Ibid., pp. 166–68.
12. Ibid., p. 165.
13. Ibid., pp. 174–96.
14. Robert C. Tucker, *Stalin as Revolutionary 1879–1929* (New York, 1973), p. 149.
15. I. Dubinsky-Mukhadze, *Ordzhonikidze*, 2nd ed., (Moscow, 1967), pp. 92–94.
16. Stalin, *Sochineniya*, Vol. 2, p. 197.
17. Ibid., pp. 198–99.

CHAPTER 10

1. Stalin, *Sochineniya*, Vol. 2, p. 248.
2. Ibid., p. 249.

3. Bertram D. Wolfe, *Three Who Made a Revolution* (Boston, 1948), p. 471.
4. Ibid., p. 544.
5. Stalin, *Sochineniya*, Vol. 2, p. 251.
6. Ibid., pp. 398–99.
7. A. S. Alliluyev, *Vospominaniya* (Moscow, 1946), pp. 185–87.
8. At this time the population was increasing at a dramatic rate. The total from the census of 1897 was 124.2 million; thirteen years later it was approximately 160.8 million. W. H. Parker, *An Historical Geography of Russia* (London, 1968), pp. 308–9; H. Seton-Watson, *The Decline of Imperial Russia 1855–1914* (London, 1952), pp. 30–31.
9. Lenin, Vol. 22, pp. 223–30.
10. Lenin, Vol. 48, p. 162. *Prosveshchenie* (Enlightenment) was the theoretical journal of the party at this time.
11. Stalin, *Sochineniya*, Vol. 2, pp. 290–367.
12. Ibid., p. 291.
13. Ibid., p. 312.
14. Ibid., p. 331.
15. Ibid., p. 367.
16. Lenin, Vol. 48, p. 169; Vol. 24, p. 223.
17. Trotsky stated in his *Stalin* (p. 137) that *Marxism of the National Question* was only nominally Stalin's work, for it was wholly inspired by Lenin, written under his unremitting supervision, and edited by him line by line. Without being so explicit, Deutscher and other historians have attributed this essay to Lenin, relegating Stalin's role virtually to that of amanuensis. I. Deutscher, *Stalin* (London, 1961), pp. 116–17. Souvarine (*Stalin*, p. 134) wrote with a typical sneer that "his article is the work of a diligent pupil, good for a man of his education."

   Other historians have pointed to the fact that much of the essence of the essay may be found in an article published by Stalin in 1904, and before Lenin had given real thought to the subject. Professor Richard Pipes considers from a textual analysis that it is improbable that Lenin wrote or dictated the article. Nor is there any evidence that Stalin returned to Cracow from Vienna to submit his work to Lenin for approval, as alleged by Trotsky. But in establishing that Stalin was truly the author, Professors Pipes and R. H. McNeal are grudging, as though fearing to praise. The former, for example, writes that "it is as awkward as most of Stalin's prose," and the latter that it is "a not too intelligent restatement of old arguments, replete with errors in fact and in reasoning." Robert H. McNeal, "Trotsky's Interpretation of Stalin," *Canadian Slavonic Papers*, No. 5 (1961); Richard Pipes, *The Formation of the Soviet Union* (Cambridge and New Haven, 1954), p. 41.

As stated earlier in this study, I find that Stalin's writings are usually clear and effective in conveying his message. The influence of the seminary is apparent in the rhythms and repetitions of his prose, but this quality made his writings more acceptable to the workers. He was not an intellectual, concerned with style; he was a working revolutionary and a communicator.

In conversation with M. Djilas some forty years later, Stalin spoke of the work as "Lenin's view. Ilyich also edited the book." He did not state that Lenin was its author.

18. Yuri Trifonov, *In the Light of the Fire* (Moscow, 1966), p. 53. This tribute to Stalin's thoughtfulness was apparently written after Khrushchev's denunciation, by a woman whose son and daughter had both been sentenced to exile.

19. A. S. Alliluyev, p. 117.

CHAPTER 11

1. Roy A. Medvedev, *Let History Judge* (New York, 1971), pp. 5–6.
2. Svetlana Alliluyeva, *Twenty Letters to a Friend*, trans. Priscilla Johnson (London, 1967), pp. 75, 130.
3. A. Lunacharsky, *Revolutionary Silhouettes* (London, 1967), p. 107.
4. E. Gorodetsky and Yu. Sharapov, *Sverdlov. Zhizn i deyatelnost* (Moscow, 1961), pp. 84–86.
5. Ya. M. Sverdlov, *Izbrannie Proizvedenii* (Moscow, 1957), pp. 276–77; Medvedev, p. 6.
6. A. S. Alliluyev, *Vospominaniya* (Moscow, 1956), pp. 117–18.
7. Alliluyeva, p. 75.
8. Alliluyev, pp. 167, 189–90.
9. Alliluyeva, *Only One Year* (London, 1969), p. 339.
10. Lenin, Vol. 21, pp. 1–4, 17.
11. L. Trotsky, *Stalin* (London, 1968), pp. 177–78.
12. Medvedev, p. 7.
13. Alliluyev, p. 191.
14. R. C. Tucker, *Stalin as Revolutionary 1879–1929* (New York, 1973), p. 161. Like so many recollections of Stalin, written decades later, this is questionable. Kamenev was mild, indecisive by nature, but vindictive and at times carried away by anger. Stalin was incisive, but taciturn and quick to take umbrage. While Kamenev probably talked constantly, he would not have treated his companion in such a cavalier manner, nor would Stalin have tolerated it.

CHAPTER 12

1. A. S. Alliluyev, *Vospominaniya* (Moscow, 1956), pp. 165–69.
2. "Protokoly i resolutsii Byuro Tsk RSDRP (6) Mart 1917," *Voprosy Istorii KPSS*, No. 3 (1962), p. 143.
3. A. G. Shlyapnikov, *The Year 1917: Second Book* (Moscow and Petrograd, 1923), p. 179.
4. Ibid., p. 183.
5. Ibid.
6. N. N. Sukhanov, *The Russian Revolution 1917* (London, 1955), p. 270.
7. W. H. Chamberlin, *The Russian Revolution 1917–21* (London, 1935), Vol. 1, p. 116.
8. Sukhanov, p. 276.
9. Demonstrations against Lenin quickly became widespread. Slogans, "Down with Lenin" and "Back to Germany," began to appear. Sukhanov wrote that "on 14–16 April (Old Style) all the papers carried a resolution of the immemorially revolutionary sailors of the Baltic Fleet crew who had been at the station as a guard of honour: 'having learnt that Comrade Lenin came back to us in Russia with the consent of His Majesty the German Emperor and King of Prussia [*sic*]' the sailors wrote, 'we express our profound regret at our participation in his triumphal welcome to Petersburg [*sic*]. If we had known by what paths he had returned to us, then instead of the enthusiastic cries of "Hurrah!", exclamations of indignation would have resounded: "Away with you! Back to the country you have passed through to us!"'" Ibid., pp. 276, 287–88.
10. *Pravda*, 21 (8) (April 1917), cited by L. Schapiro, *The Communist Party of the Soviet Union*, 2nd ed. (London, 1970), p. 165.
11. Sukhanov.
12. L. Trotsky, *Stalin* (London, 1968), p. 194.
13. Sukhanov, p. 451.
14. N. N. Sukhanov's reaction was probably representative of feelings within the party. He had often disagreed with Lenin, but had always revered him as "Lenin the genius." Now he wrote: "The masses mobilized by Lenin, after all, were bearing the whole burden of responsibility for the July Days. . . . Some remained in their factories or in their districts—isolated, slandered, in sick depression and unspeakable confusion of mind. Others were under arrest—awaiting retribution for having done their political duty according to their feeble lights. And the 'real author' abandoned his

army and his comrades, and sought personal salvation in flight."
Sukhanov, pp. 290, 471.

15. A. S. Alliluyev, pp. 183–84.
16. *Shestoi s'ezd RSDRP (b) August 1917 gode* (Moscow, 1958), p. 114, cited by R. C. Tucker, *Stalin as Revolutionary 1879–1929* (New York, 1973), Vol. 1, p. 174.
17. Ibid., pp. 174–75.
18. Schapiro, p. 173.
19. Ibid., p. 171.
20. Ibid., p. 176, note 2.

CHAPTER 13

1. This has been called the "heroic phase" of the Revolution, when the party and the people were in harmony and the party was in a real sense democratic. Such claims are remote from the realities of the situation. I. Deutscher, *Stalin, A Political Biography* (London, 1961), p. 174.
2. J. Bunyan and W. W. Fisher, *The Bolshevik Revolution 1917–18. Documents and Materials* (Stanford, 1934), p. 133. The title "Kommissar" was adopted to avoid "Minister" with its bourgeois associations.
3. N. N. Sukhanov, *The Russian Revolution 1917* (London, 1955), p. 628.
4. Bunyan and Fisher, pp. 128–32.
5. Ibid., pp. 211–15.
6. L. Schapiro, *The Communist Party of the Soviet Union*, 2nd ed. (London, 1970), p. 182.
7. Ibid., pp. 182–83.
8. Bunyan and Fisher, p. 385.
9. S. Pestkovsky, "Vospominaniya o rabote v Narkomnatse 1917–1919 gg," *Proletarskaya Revolyutsiya*, No. 6 (June 1930), pp. 124–31; L. Trotsky, *Stalin* (London, 1968), p. 245.
10. Stalin, *Sochineniya*, Vol. 4, pp. 1–5.
11. Bunyan and Fisher, pp. 282–83.
12. Stalin, *Sochineniya*, Vol. 4, p. 24.
13. Ibid., pp. 31–32.
14. Ibid., pp. 75–76.
15. Ibid., pp. 87–89.
16. Trotsky, pp. 240–41.
17. S. Pestkovsky, p. 128. While conceding that "at that period, Lenin had great need of Stalin," Trotsky sought to diminish the importance of the part he played, alleging that Stalin "really had no definite duties" and, having more free time than anyone else,

was the only one available. He, Trotsky, was busy "at meetings or in Brest Litovsk"; Sverdlov was overburdened with the work of the party organization; Zinoviev and Kamenev were opposing Lenin at this time. Stalin therefore became, in Trotsky's words, "chief of staff or a clerk on responsible missions under Lenin." Trotsky, pp. 241, 247.

18. Bunyan and Fisher, pp. 298–99.
19. Ibid., pp. 295–98.
20. The Gregorian calendar in use in the West was introduced in place of the Julian calendar, which was thirteen days behind in the twentieth century.
21. There is strong evidence that the Bolsheviks had been receiving secretly substantial funds from the German government primarily to support their policy of taking Russia out of the war. It is unlikely, however, that this German support influenced Lenin's decision to accept the German peace terms. Schapiro, pp. 177–79, 186n.
22. After quoting this and other reports of Lenin's reliance on Stalin, Trotsky proceeds to explain that Lenin attached no special importance to Stalin's advice. Lenin was, he states, punctilious about consulting his colleagues of the inner council, and Stalin, having few real commitments, was the one most readily available. Trotsky, pp. 244, 248–49.
23. J. Wheeler-Bennett, *Brest-Litovsk: The Forgotten Peace March 1918* (London, 1938), pp. 251–52.
24. Ibid., p. 257.

CHAPTER 14

1. J. Bunyan and W. W. Fisher, *The Bolshevik Revolution 1917–18. Documents and Materials* (Stanford, 1934), p. 530.
2. Nadezhda Mandelstam, *Hope Against Hope* (London, 1971), trans. Max Hayward, p. 147.
3. S. Pestkovsky, "Vospominaniya o rabote v Narkomnatse," *Proletarskaya Revolyutsiya*, No. 6 (June 1930), pp. 129–30.
4. D. Footman, *The Civil War in Russia* (London, 1961), pp. 13–17.
5. J. Bunyan, *Intervention, Civil War, and Communism* (Baltimore, 1936), pp. 466–67.
6. W. H. Chamberlin, *The Russian Revolution 1917–21* (London, 1935), Vol. 2, p. 44.
7. Bunyan, p. 240.
8. Ibid., p. 227. Lenin stated in June 1920 that the terror and the death penalty had been unavoidable and temporary measures, but

terror appears to have been endemic in the revolutionary movement. *The Anti-Stalin Campaign* (New York, 1956), p. 28.
9. Chamberlin, Vol. 2, p. 79.
10. Mystery surrounds the events at Ekaterinburg on July 16–17,
1918. The official account, which has been generally accepted
over the past fifty years, was written by Nicholas A. Sokolov, who
carried out an on-the-spot investigation a few months after the assassination. This account states that the imperial family and their
four remaining staff were murdered, and that their bodies were destroyed by fire and acids at disused mines nearby.
   What is extraordinary is that Sokolov's report and the supporting works almost certainly present a false version, suppressing and
distorting evidence to prove that the whole family perished in
Ekaterinburg on July 16–17. The first critical examination of the
official report was by John F. O'Conor (*The Sokolov Investigation*, New York, 1971). The most recent book on the subject is
The File on the Tsar, by A. Summers and T. Mangold. Their
final hypothesis is that Nicholas and his son, Aleksei, were probably shot in Ekaterinburg, but that the mother and four daughters
were removed to Perm, where they vanished. The mystery will
probably never be unraveled.
11. Stalin, *Sochineniya*, Vol. 4, pp. 116–17.
12. K. E. Voroshilov, *Stalin i Krasnaya Armiya* (Moscow, 1938), p.
13.
13. Stalin, *Sochineniya*, Vol. 4, pp. 118, 420. Voroshilov wrote subsequently that on his arrival in Tsaritsyn, Stalin quickly sized up the
situation. He carried out a reorganization of the troops outside
the city and "a ruthless purge of the rear, administered by the
iron hand." K. E. Voroshilov, *Stalin and the Armed Forces of the
U.S.S.R.* (Moscow, 1951), pp. 18–19.
   The danger of socialist revolutionary action and mistrust of the
military specialists also kept him on his guard. When an engineer
named Alekseev arrived with his two sons from Moscow and was
suspected of counterrevolutionary activities, Stalin gave the order
"Shoot them." It transpired that they were, in fact, anti-Soviet
agents. Many others were summarily executed. At this critical
time, when the Bolsheviks were fighting for survival, all who
aroused the least suspicion were eliminated.
14. Stalin, *Sochineniya*, Vol. 4, pp. 118–19.
15. Ibid., pp. 120–21.
16. Among the first to be removed was Snesarev, the local commander. Stalin placed him and most members of the headquarters
staff under arrest. Trotsky sent a telegram, demanding their
release, but Stalin scored it through with the order "to be dis-
regarded." Voroshilov, p. 19. Subsequently a commission investi-

gated the charges against Snesarev as a result of which he was released and posted to another sector. His staff, who were held on a barge in mid-Volga, perished when the barge suddenly sank. Roy Medvedev, *Let History Judge* (New York, 1971), p. 13.

17. Writing later and seeking to diminish Stalin's military responsibilities, Trotsky stated that "he headed only one of twenty armies," namely, Voroshilov's Tsaritsyn Group, which was untrue. L. Trotsky, *Stalin* (London, 1968), p. 270; A. Seaton, *Stalin as Warlord* (London, 1976), p. 28.

18. Stalin, *Sochineniya*, Vol. 4, p. 127.

19. Ibid., pp. 127–28.

20. Seaton, pp. 36–37.

21. Ibid., p. 35.

22. Ibid., p. 38.

23. Stalin, *Sochineniya*, Vol. 4, p. 453.

24. Trotsky, pp. 288–89.

25. According to Trotsky, Sverdlov arranged a meeting between Stalin and Trotsky on the train en route to Moscow. They talked about the Red commanders and about Trotsky's intentions. " 'Do you really want to dismiss all of them?' Stalin asked me in a tone of exaggerated subservience. 'They're fine boys.'

" 'Those fine boys will ruin the Revolution, which can't wait for them to grow up,' I answered him. 'All I want is to draw Tsaritsyn back into Soviet Russia!' " Trotsky, p. 289.

26. Seaton, p. 39.

27. Voroshilov, p. 27; Seaton, p. 40.

28. Trotsky and subsequently Deutscher interpreted this eulogy as a subtle attempt to belittle Trotsky's rule and to portray him as simply the executor of Lenin's idea. The references to Trotsky were omitted from Stalin's collected works. Stalin, *Sochineniya*, Vol. 4, pp. 148–51, for the text of the *Pravda* report.

29. Trotsky, pp. 291–92.

30. Seaton, p. 42.

31. Trotsky, p. 293.

32. Seaton, p. 46.

33. Stalin, *Sochineniya*, Vol. 4, p. 249.

34. Seaton, p. 49; Lenin, Vol. 50, p. 317.

35. Trotsky, p. 308.

36. Ibid.

37. Seaton, p. 58.

38. Trotsky, p. 308.

39. Stalin, *Sochineniya*, Vol. 4, pp. 75–77. There is some mystery about the dating and purpose of this report. In Stalin's *Works*, published in 1947, it is dated October 15, 1919, at Serpukhov, but as first published in *Pravda* on December 21, 1929, it was un-

dated. On October 15 Stalin attended a meeting of the Politburo in Moscow and, while it is possible that he wrote the report after his return to headquarters on the same day, it has been suggested that he wrote it some time in November and left it undated so as to be able to claim credit for originating the successful strategy. Voroshilov quoted this report as showing him to have been the chief architect of victory.

This strategy was not new, but merely an adaptation of Vatsetis' original plan. The Central Committee had considered it before adopting Kamenev's plan. Stalin might have claimed to have revived the plan and to have pressed for its immediate implementation, but Lenin and other members of the Central Committee were aware of the facts. In short, it is doubtful whether he would have taken the trouble to antedate his report for this purpose. Seaton, pp. 59–61.

40. Ibid., p. 62.
41. Ibid., p. 63.
42. Ibid., p. 64.
43. According to Voroshilov, reporting to the Eighteenth Party Congress, this order was "the child of Stalin's military genius." He was, of course, partisan and his claim an overstatement. Seaton, p. 67.
44. Stalin, *Sochineniya,* Vol. 4, pp. 323–24.
45. Seaton, p. 71.
46. While Lenin himself refused to blame any specific person, others showed no compunction. Tukhachevsky suggested in 1923 that the defeat was due to the delay by the Southwest Front in sending the cavalry to secure the Lublin gap. Egorov attempted in 1929 to refute "the legend of the disastrous rôle of the South West Front." Another explanation, put forward in 1935 by Rabinovich, held that Trotsky's "basically incorrect directive" forced the 1st Cavalry Army to abandon the capture of Lvov. In 1963 Todorsky, in his eulogy of Tukhachevsky, blamed the Southwest Front, and Stalin specifically. During Khrushchev's time, Rotmistrov and others also held Stalin mainly responsible. Stalin himself maintained in 1921 that Smilga, the political member, and Shvarts, the chief of staff of the West Front, had been at fault in encouraging Tukhachevsky to take an overoptimistic view of the position. Trotsky, p. 277; Seaton, p. 75.
47. S. M. Budënny, *Proidenny Put* (Moscow, 1958–65), Vol. 1, pp. 243–45.
48. Seaton, p. 68.

CHAPTER 15

1. Stalin, *Sochineniya*, Vol. 4, pp. 390–93. The speech strongly echoes in spirit the savage minatory poem "The Scythians," written by Aleksandr Blok in January 1918.
2. W. H. Chamberlin, *The Russian Revolution 1917–21* (London, 1935), Vol. 2, p. 293.
3. I. Deutscher, *Stalin, a Political Biography* (London, 1961), p. 220.
4. L. Schapiro, *The Communist Party of the Soviet Union*, 2nd ed. (London, 1970), p. 208.
5. Stalin, *Sochineniya*, Vol. 5, p. 124.
6. Schapiro, p. 213.
7. Ibid., p. 214. Thus with promises of greater freedom from central control and discipline in the party, and other conciliatory measures, the complaints of the opposition groups were apparently met. But Lenin had no intention of submitting to party democracy or of sharing the monopoly of power. Indeed he was actively working on plans which would completely nullify these resolutions. He was concerned, too, as he stated early in the proceedings, "to put an end to opposition, to put the lid on it."
8. Stalin, *Sochineniya*, Vol. 5, pp. 8–10.
9. R. C. Tucker, *Stalin as Revolutionary 1879–1929* (New York, 1973), p. 218.
10. Schapiro, p. 246.
11. Stalin, *Sochineniya*, Vol. 6, pp. 277–78.
12. Schapiro, p. 244.
13. Ibid., p. 245.
14. Ibid., p. 247.
15. A. B. Ulam, *Lenin and the Bolsheviks* (London, 1966), p. 575.
16. Schapiro, p. 242.
17. Tucker, Vol. 1, p. 208.
18. Schapiro, p. 227.
19. R. Pipes, *The Formation of the Soviet Union* (Cambridge, Mass., 1964), p. 230.
20. Stalin, *Sochineniya*, Vol. 4, p. 410.
21. Tucker, pp. 231–32.

CHAPTER 16

1. L. Schapiro, *The Communist Party of the Soviet Union*, 2nd ed. (London, 1970), p. 218.

2. R. C. Tucker, *Stalin as Revolutionary 1879–1929* (New York, 1973), p. 219.
3. Medvedev has made a case for stating that Lenin did not propose the creation of the post of General Secretary and did not nominate Stalin for it. The plenum of the Central Committee after the Eleventh Congress was presided over by Kamenev, who proposed Stalin's appointment after the Politburo had approved it. Medvedev suggests that the appointment was "presented to Leinin as a *fait accompli.*" R. Medvedev, *Let History Judge* (London, 1972), pp. 17–18.
4. Stalin, *Sochineniya*, Vol. 5, pp. 134–36.
5. L. A. Fotyeva, in *Problems of the History of the Communist Party* (Moscow, 1957), No. 4, p. 149. His senior secretary, L. A. Fotyeva, recorded that between October 2 and December 16, 1922, he wrote 224 letters and memorandums, received 171 official visitors; he took the chair at thirty-two meetings of government bodies and made three major speeches. It was a routine that could not continue.
6. Tucker, p. 241; Lenin, Vol. 45, p. 548. Four years later when the legend of Lenin's infallibility was being forged, Trotsky criticized Stalin for having opposed Lenin on this issue. Stalin then stated that he had been wrong, adding, "But I did not persist in my error and, after discussing it with Lenin, at once rectified it." Stalin, *Sochineniya*, Vol. 9, pp. 74–75.
   According to the memoirs of Fotyeva, Lenin's secretary, first published in 1964, Stalin held to his opinion and did not rectify it as he stated. To a further letter by Lenin on the subject, written on October 13, 1922, soon after his return to Moscow, Stalin added a note that "Comrade Lenin's letter has not made me change my mind." L. A. Fotyeva, *Iz vospominaniya of V. I. Lenine Dekab 1922–Mart 1923* (Moscow, 1964), p. 28; Tucker, p. 242.
7. Lenin, Vol. 45, pp. 211–13.
8. Stalin's letter has not been published in full. A partial text was published by Trotsky in *The Stalin School of Falsification* (New York, 1962), pp. 66–67.
9. Lenin, Vol. 33, p. 335.
10. Tucker, p. 255.
11. Ibid., p. 259.
12. A. Mikoyan, *Dorogoi Borby* (Moscow, 1971), p. 433.
13. R. Pipes, *The Formation of the Soviet Union: Communism and Nationalism 1917–1923* (Cambridge, Mass., 1964), pp. 283–84.

CHAPTER 17

1. The Record Book of the Secretaries attending V. I. Lenin in *Problems of the History of the CPSU* (Moscow, 1963), No. 2, p. 68.
2. M. Lewin, *Lenin's Last Struggle* (London, 1968), pp. 52–53.
3. Ibid., pp. 72–73.
4. Stalin, *Sochineniya*, Vol. 5, pp. 156–59.
5. Lenin, Vol. 45, pp. 343–48.
6. Ibid.
7. *Pravda*, March 4, 1923; Lenin, 5th ed., Vol. 45, p. 387.
8. L. Trotsky, *The Stalin School of Falsification* (New York, 1962), p. 72.
9. R. Pipes, *The Formation of the Soviet Union* (Cambridge, Mass., 1964), pp. 288–89.
10. Lenin, Vol. 54, pp. 329–30.
11. Lenin's sister, Maria Ulyanova, reported to the Central Committee in 1926 at a meeting when Zinoviev raised the subject of Lenin's letter that Stalin had, in fact, sent an apology. Ibid., p. 674.

    The text of Lenin's letter was first made public in Khrushchev's de-Stalinization speech to the Twentieth Party Congress in 1956.

    Trotsky related in his autobiography that after reading the letter Krupskaya went to Kamenev in great distress and said, "Vladimir has just dictated to his stenographer a letter to Stalin, saying that he breaks off all personal relations with him." According to Trotsky's recollections of what Kamenev told him, she went on to say that "he would never have decided to break off personal relations, if he had not thought it necessary to crush Stalin politically." L. Trotsky, *My Life* (New York, n.d.), p. 485.

    Referring to Trotsky's account of how he learned from Kamenev about Lenin's letter to Stalin, A. Ulam has pointed out that Trotsky gives the date as March 6, 1923, but the letter was not delivered until March 7, by which date Kamenev was on his way to Tiflis. Trotsky makes no mention of Lenin's appeal to him to take up the Georgian affair in the Central Committee. A. Ulam, *Stalin* (London, 1974), p. 223; L. Trotsky, *My Life* (New York, n.d.), pp. 483–86. See Robert H. McNeal, *Bride of the Revolution: Krupskaya and Lenin* (Ann Arbor, 1972), pp. 225–27.
12. Cf. I. Deutscher, *The Prophet Unarmed: Trotsky 1921–1929* (New York, 1959), p. 92.
13. Ulam, p. 224.

14. The Twelfth Congress of the Russian Communist Party (b) Sten-
    ographic Report, p. 200; Ulam, p. 226.
15. Ibid.
16. R. Pipes, *The Formation of the Soviet Union: Communism and
    Nationalism 1917–1923* (Cambridge, Mass., 1964), pp. 290–91;
    Stalin, *Sochineniya*, Vol. 5, pp. 264–65.
17. L. Schapiro, *The Communist Party of the Soviet Union*, 2nd ed.
    (London, 1970), p. 280.
18. Ibid., p. 282.
19. Ibid., p. 283.
20. Stalin, *Sochineniya*, Vol. 6, pp. 7–8.
21. Soon after the announcement of Lenin's death, rumors began cir-
    culating in Moscow that he had been poisoned. Schapiro, p. 286.
    Fifteen years later Trotsky wrote a sensational article entitled,
    "Did Stalin Poison Lenin?"
       In his biography of Stalin, Trotsky related that at a Politburo
    meeting attended by Zinoviev, Kamenev, and Trotsky himself
    late in February 1923, Stalin reported that Lenin had sent for
    him before his death and had asked for poison. Trotsky ex-
    claimed, "Obviously we cannot even consider carrying out this
    request! Guetier [Lenin's physician] has not lost hope. Lenin can
    still recover." Stalin answered, "not without a touch of an-
    noyance," that "I told him all that. But he wouldn't listen to
    reason. The Old Man is suffering. He says he wants to have
    poison at hand . . . he'll use it only when he is convinced that his
    condition is hopeless." The members parted "with the implicit
    understanding that we could not even consider sending poison to
    Lenin." L. Trotsky, *Stalin* (London, 1968), pp. 376–77.
       Trotsky's account is improbable. The secretaries' journal, which
    was carefully kept, records that after December 23, 1922, Lenin saw
    only his immediate circle, his secretaries, and the doctors, but
    none of his former political colleagues. Lenin's changed attitude
    would have made Stalin the last person to be called to perform
    such an act of mercy. The title of Trotsky's article in which he
    first revealed this "secret" suggested murder, whereas on reflection
    he described Stalin as being called on as a friend to render a last
    service. This, like so much of Trotsky's evidence against Stalin, is
    tendentious and unreliable. Robert H. McNeal, *Bride of the Rev-
    olution* (London, 1973), pp. 235–36.

CHAPTER 18

1. Lenin, like Marx, always expressed dislike and even contempt for
   all forms of ostentation and hero worship, especially towards him-

self. He was devoid of ordinary vanity, but his boundless confidence in his own ability, rectitude, and importance, in fact, transcended vanity.

Krupskaya was alone in protesting sincerely against the cult. In an open letter, published in *Pravda* on January 30, she made an appeal. "I have a great request to you," she wrote, addressing the workers and peasants. "Do not permit your grief for Ilyich to take the form of external reverence for his person. Do not raise memorials to him, name palaces after him, splendorous festivals in commemoration of him. . . . To all this he attached so little importance in his life, all this was so burdensome to him. . . . If you want to honour the name of Vladimir Ilyich, build crêches, kindergartens, houses, schools, libraries, medical centres, hospitals, homes for the disabled etc., and, above all, let us put his precepts into practice." Robert H. McNeal, *Bride of the Revolution* (London, 1973), pp. 241–42.

2. Stalin is said to have been mainly responsible for the decision to embalm. N. Valentinov related that Bukharin told him—as so often the evidence is hearsay and unsatisfactory—that the proposal to preserve Lenin's body was first raised by Stalin and Kalinin at a meeting of the Soviet leaders late in 1923. Stalin said that the suggestion had come from "comrades in the provinces," who felt that cremation was contrary to Russian religious traditions as being symbolic of punishment after death and that the body should be preserved. Stalin was said to have expressed support for this suggestion, adding that science had discovered methods of embalming that would preserve the body in lifelike condition for a lengthy period. Bukharin, Kamenev, and others expressed opposition to what was tantamount to reviving the Orthodox practice of preserving the remains of saints as holy relics. Bukharin recalled that Lenin himself had spoken strongly against venerating the memories of dead party leaders. But Stalin and Kalinin had their way. N. Valentinov, *Novaya Ekonomicheskaya Politika i kriziz partii posle smerti Lenina. Gody raboty v VSNKh vo vremya NEP. Vospominaniya* (Stanford, 1971), pp. 90–92, quoted in R. C. Tucker, *Stalin as Revolutionary 1879–1929* (New York, 1973), pp. 282–83.

In the event Lenin's body was subjected to what most people would consider to be horrifying desecration. Stefan F. Possony, *Lenin: The Compulsive Revolutionary* (London, 1966), pp. 437–48.

3. Trotsky's absence from the funeral was conspicuous. He had left Moscow a few days earlier for treatment in the Caucasus. He was probably suffering from undulant fever. He claimed that he received the news of Lenin's death in Tiflis in a coded message

from Stalin on the evening of January 21. He then alleged that he was told on January 22 that the funeral would be on January 26, when it was actually to be held on January 27. Even if his statement was true and he believed that the funeral would be on the earlier date, he could still have reached Moscow in time by train. Trotsky, *Moya Zhizn* (Berlin, 1930), Vol. 2, pp. 249–51; I. Deutscher, *The Prophet Unarmed: Trotsky 1921–1929* (New York, 1959), p. 133.

4. A. B. Ulam, *Stalin* (London, 1974), p. 235; I. Deutscher, *Stalin: A Political Biography* (London, 1961), p. 270.

5. Stalin, *Sochineniya*, Vol. 6, pp. 46–51. In 1964 it became known that Krupskaya had prepared a speech to deliver to the special session of the All-Russian Congress. The speech, found in the archives as a fair copy in her own hand, was strikingly similar in its ritualistic, exhortatory style to Stalin's "oath" speech. Robert H. McNeal suggests that Dzerzhinsky's commission, which was responsible for the funeral and other arrangements, decided that Stalin alone should proclaim Lenin's legacy on this occasion. Krupskaya was allowed to address the Supreme Soviet on January 26, 1924. She then delivered a personal speech, possibly composed in haste and while under great strain; it had nothing of the careful structure and content of the suppressed version. It was nevertheless found by many of those present to be the most moving of all the speeches at this forum. For the text of the suppressed speech, see McNeal, pp. 239–41.

6. Stalin, *Sochineniya*, Vol. 6, pp. 52–64.

7. B. Bazhanov, *Stalin der Rote Diktator* (Berlin, 1931), pp. 20–21, quoted in Deutscher, p. 274.

8. Ibid., p. 13.

9. Max Eastman, *Since Lenin Died* (London, 1925), p. 55.

10. Krupskaya sent the package to Kamenev, presumably because she regarded him as a friend and he was chairman of the Politburo. Stalin and his office were responsible for the agenda and documentation of the Congress, but she obviously could not approach him. Trotsky might have used the notes more forcefully than Kamenev. She had, however, written a friendly letter to Trotsky soon after Lenin's death, seeking a reconciliation. Her gesture had brought no reply, not even the courtesy of an acknowledgment. McNeal, pp. 243–44.

11. B. D. Wolfe, *Khrushchev and Stalin's Ghost* (New York, 1957), pp. 258–59.

12. Several accounts refer to Lenin's notes being read out to a plenary session of the Central Committee. Bazhanov claimed to give an eyewitness account of the meeting. From the records, however, it is definite that the Central Committee did not meet between Jan-

uary 1924 and the opening of the Congress on May 23. Trotsky called the meeting on May 22 a "senoren convent" (meeting of elders), a reference to the meetings held at the time of the Dumas before the Revolution. E. H. Carr, *A History of Soviet Russia: The Interregnum* (London, 1954), pp. 359–61; L. Schapiro, *The Communist Party of the Soviet Union*, 2nd ed. (London, 1970), p. 287; L. Trotsky, *The Suppressed Testament of Lenin* (New York, 1935), pp. 11–12, 17; I. Deutscher, *Stalin* (London, 1961), pp. 272–73; McNeal, pp. 245–46, 317.

CHAPTER 19

1. E. H. Carr, *The Interregnum 1923–24* (London, 1954), p. 362.
2. Ibid., p. 363.
3. Ibid., p. 365.
4. Stalin, *Sochineniya*, Vol. 6, p. 329.
5. Ibid., p. 333.
6. Ibid., p. 350.
7. Ibid., p. 352.
8. Ibid., p. 357.
9. Trotsky had, in fact, prepared a fifty-four-page memorandum with the title *The Purpose of This Explanation*. It was intended for publication, but it remained among his papers and was found only after his death. E. H. Carr, *Socialism in One Country, 1924–26* (London, 1959), Vol. 2, pp. 28–29.
10. Stalin, *Sochineniya*, Vol. 7, pp. 379–80.
11. Schapiro, p. 287.
12. Ibid., p. 296.
13. Carr, *Socialism*, Vol. 2, p. 136.
14. Ibid.
15. Ibid.
16. Ibid.
17. Ibid.
18. Ibid.
19. Schapiro, p. 301.
20. Ibid., p. 304.
21. Robert H. McNeal, *Bride of the Revolution* (London, 1973), p. 262.
22. Krupskaya was subjected to campaigns of slander, and at times when taking an opposition stand at party meetings she was severely heckled. But, although provoked by her self-sacrificing zeal, Stalin was careful to avoid overt action that would have made her a martyr. He is said to have threatened to discredit her as Lenin's widow and political helpmate. He is quoted as having said, "I shall make someone else Lenin's widow." McNeal, pp. 258–60.

23. Trotsky and Krupskaya might have helped each other greatly in the years after Lenin's death, but in his monumental arrogance and insensitivity he failed her. I. Deutscher, *The Prophet Unarmed: Trotsky 1921–29* (London, 1959), pp. 301–2; A. B. Ulam, *Stalin* (London, 1974), pp. 269–71.

CHAPTER 20

1. Stalin, *Sochineniya*, Vol. 11, pp. 248–49.
2. E. H. Carr and R. W. Davies, *Foundations of a Planned Economy 1926–29* (London, 1969), Vol. 1, p. 11.
3. Ibid., p. 23. A further difficulty was that the party could not agree on defining a kulak. Lengthy theoretical discussions were devoted to the question of "differentiation." The opposition, Trotsky in particular, made great play of the issue. For practical purposes the three categories of peasants were the kulaks, who hired labor, leased land, and were comparatively well off, the middle peasants, who did not hire labor and were self-supporting, and the poor peasants, who had small holdings but hired themselves out as laborers. The divisions, particularly between the kulaks and the middle peasants, were far from clear.
4. Ibid., p. 25.
5. Ibid., p. 39.
6. L. Schapiro, *The Communist Party of the Soviet Union*, 2nd ed. (London, 1970), p. 368.
7. Stalin, *Sochineniya*, Vol. 11, pp. 87, 93.
8. Schapiro, p. 369.
9. Ibid.
10. Ibid., pp. 369–70; B. Souvarine, *Stalin* (London, n.d.), pp. 482–84.
11. Schapiro, pp. 370–71.
12. Stalin, *Sochineniya*, Vol. 11, pp. 245–90.
13. Ibid., pp. 222–38.
14. Ibid., Vol. 13, pp. 17–18.

CHAPTER 21

1. Milovan Djilas, *Conversations with Stalin* (London, 1962), p. 98.
2. Svetlana Alliluyeva, *Twenty Letters to a Friend* (London, 1969), pp. 211–12.
3. Djilas, p. 98.
4. The flow of gifts became an avalanche in December 1950, when his seventieth birthday was celebrated. He had them all sent to a Museum of Gifts, opened in Moscow. Alliluyeva, pp. 54–55, 215.
5. Ibid., p. 116.

6. Ibid., pp. 105–7.
7. Ibid.
8. Ibid., p. 212.
9. Naum Jasny, *The Socialized Agriculture of the U.S.S.R.* (Stanford, 1949), p. 30.
10. Lenin, Vol. 45, pp. 343–48.
11. L. Schapiro, *The Communist Party of the Soviet Union*, 2nd ed. (London, 1970), pp. 384–85.
12. Victor Serge, *The Year One of the Russian Revolution* (New York, 1972), p. 367.
13. Similarities between the Jesuit Order and the Communist party have been noted. See, for example, Lewis A. Coser, "The Militant Collective: Jesuits and Leninists," in *Social Research: An International Quarterly of the Social Sciences* (New York), Vol. 40, No. 1 (Spring 1973), pp. 110–28.
   Both were militant collectives, exacting complete obedience and the subjugation of the individuality of its members. But there the similarity ends. The Jesuits were trained and disciplined over a long period; they owed obedience not only to their superiors and to the General of the Order, but also took special vows of obedience to the Pope. The Jesuit Order belonged to the Church, and its General was appointed by the Pope. Lenin conceived his party as an army of totally dedicated revolutionaries under his leadership. In theory, he was merely the executant of the will of the party; in practice, the position would be reversed. He did not live to forge the party into the united, disciplined organ that he had always envisaged. This was left to Stalin. E. H. Carr, *The Interregnum 1923–24* (London, 1954), p. 363.
14. N. Valentinov, *Encounters with Lenin* (London, 1968), pp. 135–36.
15. Stalin, *Sochineniya*, Vol. 13, pp. 38–39.

Chapter 22

1. Stalin's policies in this period have been condemned on many grounds. Academics have discussed certain aspects under the inept title of "Was Stalin really necessary?"
   The collectivization program, which had as one of its basic purposes the squeezing of the peasantry to provide the capital resources for rapid industrialization, has been a special target. Thus Professor James R. Miller has stated that "collectivization was not necessary for the industrialization drive and it was not optimal either. It was instead a disaster just like a hurricane or any other natural disaster. Economically no one gained from collectivization, including those promoting rapid industrial development."
   Many of the policies and events of this savage era can be criti-

cized and condemned. Stalin's policies must be considered, however, against the Russian background, the mood and conditions of the people, the position of the party, and, above all, Stalin's outlook and understanding of the situation. Taken together, his policies had the effect of whipping the nation into a great frenzy of constructive action, which was his purpose. See, for example, James R. Miller and Alex Nove, "A Debate on Collectivization. Was Stalin Really Necessary?" *Problems of Communism*, July–August 1976.

2. Naum Jasny, *The Socialized Agriculture of the U.S.S.R.* (Stanford, 1949). Chapters 13–16 contain a detailed description of the kolkhoz system.
3. Stalin, *Sochineniya*, Vol. 12, p. 169.
4. L. Schapiro, *The Communist Party of the Soviet Union*, 2nd ed. (London, 1970), p. 390.
5. Merle Fainsod, *Smolensk Under Soviet Rule* (Cambridge, Mass., 1958), p. 241.
6. Stalin, *Sochineniya*, Vol. 12, p. 191–99.
7. *The 16th Congress of the C.P. of the U.S.S.R. (b) Stenographic Report* (Moscow, 1931), p. 293, quoted in A. B. Ulam, *Stalin* (London, 1973), p. 335.
8. Stalin, *Sochineniya*, Vol. 13, p. 42.
9. Naum Jasny, *Soviet Industrialization 1928–52* (Chicago, 1961), pp. 97–99); Maurice Dobb, *Soviet Economic Development Since 1917* (London, 1948), pp. 255–60.
10. Max Beloff, *The Foreign Policy of Soviet Russia 1929–41* (London, 1947), p. 31. See also Jasny, pp. 97–99; Vladimir Naleszkiewcz, "Technical Assistance of American Enterprises to the Growth of the Soviet Union 1929–32," *The Russian Review*, January 1966; W. H. Chamberlin, *The Soviet Planned Economic Order* (Boston, 1931), p. 82.
11. Jasny, p. 323.
12. T. Szamuely, "The Elimination of Opposition between the 16th and 17th Congresses of the CPSU," *Soviet Studies*, Vol. 22, No. 3 (January 1966).
13. A. H. Birse, *Memoirs of an Interpreter* (London, 1967), p. 99.
14. Ulam, p. 371.
15. Ibid., p. 373.
16. Ibid., pp. 371–72. Medvedev has written that a considerable number of old Bolsheviks formed an illegal bloc at the Seventeenth Congress, comprising basically secretaries of *oblast* or provincial committees and secretaries of the non-Russian central committees. At the beginning of or before the Congress a group of party officials, it is alleged, talked with Kirov about the need to replace Stalin. But Kirov would not agree to get rid of Stalin or to be elected General Secretary himself.

17. Roy Medvedev, *Let History Judge* (London, 1971), pp. 155–56.
18. Medvedev has stated that dissatisfaction with Stalin was expressed in the election of the Central Committee by the Seventeenth Congress, when Stalin received fewer votes than any other candidate. In view of the overwhelming support for Stalin, expressed throughout the Congress, this allegation is hard to credit. Indeed, A. Ulam has pointed out that the allegation is based on ignorance of the voting procedures of the Congress. He has added that there is every reason to believe that the election of the Central Committee, including the new Stalinist members, was unanimous. Medvedev, p. 156; Ulam, p. 374.
19. J. Biggart, "The Astrakhan rebellion. An incident in the career of Sergei Mironovich Kirov," *Slavonic and East European Review*, April 1976.
20. Medvedev quotes an old Bolshevik, Durmashkin, to the effect that there was "a barely perceptible estrangement between Stalin and Kirov" in 1934, because Kirov repeatedly opposed Stalin in Politburo meetings. The source of Durmashkin's memory of this change in their relationship is not stated, although he is said to have known Kirov well. Medvedev, p. 157.
21. Alexander Barmine, a Soviet diplomat who defected to the West, claimed that he had learned from Nadya's brother the story of her death. It happened at Voroshilov's dacha, neighboring Stalin's, that she made critical remarks before the whole company about the brutal treatment of the peasantry. Stalin was furious and publicly abused her in foul terms. Later that night she shot herself.

    Soon afterwards, according to Barmine and others, who often wrote not from personal knowledge, but from the rumors which circulated in Moscow, Stalin married Rosa, a sister of Kaganovich. This third marriage, if, in fact, it ever existed, was never referred to publicly. A. Barmine, *One Who Survived* (New York, 1945), p. 264.

    Boris Nicolaevsky stated that Stalin shot his wife. He was another of the émigrés who recorded rumors as facts. B. Nicolaevsky, *Power and the Soviet Elite* (New York, 1965), p. 70.
22. Svetlana Alliluyeva, *Twenty Letters to a Friend* (London, 1967), pp. 122–23.
23. Ibid., p. 147.
24. Ibid., pp. 134–36.
25. In his "Secret Speech" to the Twentieth Party Congress, Khrushchev referred to Kirov's assassination in vague terms, implying Stalin's direct involvement. "It must be asserted," he said, "that to this day the circumstances surrounding Kirov's murder hide many things which are inexplicable and mysterious and demand a most careful examination. There are reasons for the suspicion that

the killer of Kirov—Nikolaev—was assisted by someone from among the people whose duty it was to protect the person of Kirov. A month and a half before the killing, Nikolaev was arrested on the grounds of suspicious behavior, but he was released and not even searched. It is an unusually suspicious circumstance that when the Chekist assigned to protect Kirov was being brought for an interrogation on December 2, 1934, he was killed in a car 'accident' in which no other occupants of the car were harmed. After the murder of Kirov, top functionaries of the Leningrad NKVD were given very light sentences, but in 1937 they were shot. We can assume that they were shot in order to cover the traces of the organizers of Kirov's killing."

In October 1961 Khrushchev stated publicly to the Twenty-second Party Congress: "Great efforts are still needed to find out who was really to blame for his death. The more deeply we study the materials connected with Kirov's death, the more questions arise. . . . A thorough enquiry is now being made into the circumstances of this complicated case." Nothing has yet been released from this inquiry.

The émigré Kremlinologist, Boris Nicolaevsky, pronounced that "Khrushchev's secret report at the 20th Party Congress makes it superfluous to collect legal evidence, so to speak, proving Stalin's involvement in the murder of Kirov [sic]. Although many points in the story of this murder still are obscure, even simply with regard to fact, the personal role of Stalin nonetheless emerges with sufficient clarity. . . ."

Nicolaevsky also stated that "the most important part of Khrushchev's speech is, of course, his recital of facts about Stalin's crimes. But here, too, one has to be cautious, since not everything can be taken at face value. There are many distortions—the general picture which Khrushchev tries to draw is not only inaccurate but often mendacious."

Many other writers have stated or implied, with similar absence of logic, that Stalin was directly responsible for the murder of Kirov. There is, however, no evidence to support the charge. Boris Nicolaevsky, *Power and the Soviet Elite* (New York, 1945), pp. 69–97, 204; *The Anti-Stalin Campaign and International Communism* (New York, 1956), pp. 25–26; R. Conquest, *The Great Terror* (London, 1971), pp. 72–96; but see, too, A. B. Ulam, *Stalin* (London, 1974), pp. 380–82, 387–88.

CHAPTER 23

1. Khrushchev observed twenty-two years later in his "Secret Speech," concerned with exposing the misdeeds of the master to

whom he owed his career and whom he had served obediently for some twenty-five years, that "Stalin was convinced that this [his misdeeds] was necessary for the defence of the interests of the working class against the plotting of their enemies and against the attack of the imperialist camp—the interest of the victory of socialism and communism. We cannot say that those were the needs of a giddy despot. He considered that this should be done in the interest of the Party, of the working masses, in the name of defence of the Revolution's gains. In this lies the whole tragedy!" *The Anti-Stalin Campaign and International Communism* (New York, 1956), p. 85.

2. Ian Grey, *Ivan the Terrible* (London, 1964), pp. 81–82.
3. Roy Medvedev, *Let History Judge* (London, 1972), p. 161.
4. Stalin presumably obtained the support of the Politburo for this basic change in party practice. The more moderate members of the Politburo either approved or felt compelled to acquiesce. Professor L. Schapiro suggests that Kuibyshev in the Politburo and Maksim Gorky outside it may have tried to restrain Stalin. Yagoda was later charged with poisoning both men. He may have done so on Stalin's orders or may have been forced to confess to these crimes in order to divert suspicion from the guilty agents or, most probably, it was one of the many charges fabricated for the show trial. The sudden death of Kuibyshev on January 26, 1935, and the attacks on Gorky's writings, hitherto held to be beyond criticism, have been quoted as evidence of Stalin's action against them. L. Schapiro, *The Communist Party of the Soviet Union*, 2nd ed. (London, 1970), p. 434.
5. Nadezhda Mandelstam, *Hope Against Hope* (London, 1971), pp. 322–33.
6. On methods of torture and of extracting confessions, see W. G. Krivitsky, *I Was Stalin's Agent* (London, 1939), pp. 211–32; Merle Fainsod, *How Russia Is Ruled* (Cambridge, Mass., 1965), pp. 437–38; Schapiro, pp. 422–26; A. V. Gorbatov, *Years off My Life* (London, 1964).
7. Medvedev, p. 171; *The Anti-Stalin Campaign*, p. 29.
8. Krivitsky, p. 272.
9. Joseph E. Davies, *Mission to Moscow* (London, 1942), pp. 36–37.
10. Medvedev, p. 193.
11. Ibid., p. 194.
12. Ibid., pp. 195–96.
13. A. B. Ulam, *Stalin* (London, 1974), p. 430.
14. Medvedev, p. 196.
15. Ulam, p. 431.
16. G. K. Zhukov, *Memoirs* (London, 1971), p. 113.

17. N. G. Kuznetsov, "Pered Voinoi," in *Oktyabr*, September 1963, p. 174; A. Seaton, *Stalin as Warlord* (London, 1976), p. 86.
18. Ibid., p. 87.
19. R. E. Sherwood, *The White House Papers of Harry Hopkins* (London, 1948–49), Vol. 1, p. 329.
20. G. Hilger, *The Incompatible Allies* (New York, 1953), pp. 290, 301–3.
21. A. S. Yakovlev, *Tsel Zhizni* (Moscow, 1966), p. 192.
22. Seaton, p. 88.
23. A full examination of the Tukhachevsky affair is contained in John Erickson, *The Soviet High Command 1918–41* (London, 1962), pp. 461–66, 481–88, 737. Tukhachevsky and the generals have been completely rehabilitated. Khrushchev in his speech to the Twenty-second Party Congress spoke of the alleged plot of the generals. Fainsod, p. 436. Sir Winston Churchill confirmed that Beneš told him of passing of the documents implicating Tukhachevsky. W. S. Churchill, *The Second World War* (London, 1948), Vol. 1, p. 225. See also A. I. Todorsky, *Marshal Tukhachevsky* (Moscow, 1965); N. U. Koritsky et al., eds., *Marshal Tukhachevsky: Vospominaniya Druzei i Soratnikov* (Moscow, 1965); I. Deutscher, *Stalin: A Political Biography* (London, 1961), who suggested that the generals had indeed planned a coup. The evidence of this conspiracy had been planted, however, by Hitler's Gestapo in the form of forged documents, which were passed to Czechoslovak agents who in January 1937 put them in the hands of President Beneš. In good faith he sent the documents to the Soviet government. Later revelations suggested that the NKVD had fabricated the evidence and that an émigré Russian general, named Skoblin, who was a double agent, had been responsible.
24. Raymond L. Garthoff, *How Russia Makes War* (London, 1954), pp. 220–21.
25. Ulam, pp. 462–63.
26. R. Conquest, *The Great Terror* (London, 1971), p. 528.
27. Stephen F. Cohen, *Bukharin and the Russian Revolution* (London, 1974), p. 365.
28. Professor Robert C. Tucker's interpretation of this speech and particularly his reference to Stalin's "need to have his greatness acknowledged by others" are in my view quite wrong. Robert C. Tucker, *Stalin as Revolutionary 1879–1929* (New York, 1973), pp. 424–25.
29. L. Schapiro, *The Communist Party of the Soviet Union* (London, 1970), p. 432.
30. Joseph E. Davies, *Mission to Moscow* (London, 1942), p. 39.
31. The problem of confession is discussed at length by Arthur

Koestler in *Arrow in the Blue* (London, 1945) and by Conquest, pp. 77–210.

32. F. Beck and W. Godin, *Russian Purge and the Extraction of Confession* (London, 1951), pp. 67–68; David J. Dallin and Boris I. Nicolaevsky, *Forced Labour in Soviet Russia* (London, 1948), p. 86; see also Fainsod, pp. 458–61, and A. Solzhenitsyn, *The Gulag Archipelago* (London, 1975), Vol. 2, p. 595.

33. The practice was not new in Russia. Peter the Great had used prison labor to man his naval galleys, to build his capital, and on other projects. For over two centuries, exile to Siberia and, for the most serious crimes, the severe punishment of *katora*, or hard labor, usually served on construction work, were accepted methods of colonizing and developing sparsely settled regions. The Soviet labor camps were, however, organized on a far greater scale and run more ruthlessly.

34. *VKP(b) v Rezolyutsiyakh*, Vol. 2, pp. 671–77; Fainsod, p. 442.

35. F. Beck and W. Godin, *Russian Purge and the Extraction of Confession* (London, 1951), pp. 189–91. Beck and Godin were the pseudonyms of two former prisoners of the NKVD. Their account of the purge is notable for lack of bitterness, for impartiality, and for the descriptions of prisoners and their conditions.

   One of the most remarkable and moving accounts of a dedicated Communist who was a divisional commander in the Red Army and was arrested, interrogated, tortured, and sentenced as an enemy of the people to fifteen years' forced labor in Siberia is by General A. V. Gorbatov, *Years off My Life* (London, 1964). He was released on the eve of war and returned to the Army. He fought with great bravery and was much decorated. He became in 1945 commandant of the Soviet Zone of Berlin.

36. In quoting this remark, Medvedev adds the comment that "Yakovlev seems to believe even today that Stalin did not know what Ezhov was doing behind his back." A. S. Yakovlev, *Tsel Zhizni* (Moscow, 1966), p. 179; Medvedev, p. 293.

37. Ibid., p. 294. The source of this information is not stated.

38. Joseph E. Davies, *Mission to Moscow* (London, 1942), p. 280.

39. G. K. Zhukov, *Memoirs* (London, 1971), p. 283.

40. See, for example, Ulam, pp. 560–62.

41. Ibid., p. 456.

42. Ilya Ehrenburg, *Novyi Mir*, No. 5 (1962), p. 152.

43. Jack Miller, "Soviet Planners in 1936–37," *Soviet Planning*, ed. Jane Degras and Alex Nove (Oxford, 1964), pp. 118–19.

CHAPTER 24

1. Introductory Declaration to the Soviet Constitution of July 6, 1923. See D. A. Gaiduk, *History of the Soviet Constitution 1917–57* (Moscow, 1957), p. 226; M. Beloff, *The Foreign Policy of Soviet Russia* (London, 1947), Vol. 1, p. 2.
2. *KPSS v rezolyutsiyazh*, Vol. 2, p. 74; L. Schapiro, *The Communist Party of the Soviet Union*, 2nd ed. (London, 1970), p. 353.
3. Svetlana Alliluyeva, *Twenty Letters to a Friend* (London, 1967), p. 130.
4. *Political Report to the 16th Party Congress* (London, 1930), p. 32; Beloff, p. 28.
5. Stalin, *Sochineniya*, Vol. 7, pp. 13–14.
6. Beloff, p. 78.
7. Iosif Stalin, *Problems of Leninism*, 11th ed. (Moscow, 1939), pp. 465–67.
8. J. Degras, ed., *Soviet Documents on Foreign Policy* (London, 1953), Vol. 3, p. 106.
9. Ibid., pp. 111–12.
10. Ibid., pp. 114–15.
11. W. S. Churchill, *The Second World War* (London, 1948), Vol. 1, p. 104.
12. Ibid., p. 166.
13. Ibid., pp. 234–51.
14. Ibid., pp. 239–40.
15. J. E. Davies, *Mission to Moscow* (London, 1942), pp. 116, 129–38.
16. Giffard Martel, *The Russian Outlook* (London, 1947), pp. 13–39.
17. Stalin, *Problems of Leninism*, p. 604.
18. Ivan Maisky, *Who Helped Hitler?* (London, 1964), p. 67 and *passim*; Maxim Litvinov, *Notes for a Journal* (London, 1955), p. 222 and *passim*.
19. Stalin, *Problems of Leninism*, p. 576.
20. Ibid., p. 603.
21. Ibid., p. 574.
22. Churchill, Vol. 1, p. 288.
23. Ibid., p. 304.
24. Ibid., p. 306.
25. Ibid., p. 305.
26. Ibid., p. 306.
27. Ibid., p. 307.
28. A. Werth, *Russia at War* (London, 1964), pp. 46–47.
29. G. K. Zhukov, *Memoirs* (London, 1971), p. 187.

30. Degras, p. 375.
31. Some 14,500 Polish troops, including 8,000 officers, surrendered to the Red Army. They were disarmed and interned in three prisoner-of-war camps in Katyn Wood near Smolensk. Nothing more was heard of them until the spring of 1943 when extensive mass graves were unearthed at Katyn.

    Responsibility for the Katyn massacre has never been established beyond doubt. The Nazis discovered the mass graves in April 1943. They invited the International Red Cross to carry out an impartial investigation, which would, they claimed, establish Russian guilt. The Red Cross declined to act without Russian participation and this was refused. The Germans carried out investigations and published the results, which indicted the Russians. Later in 1943, when the Red Army recaptured the Smolensk region, the Russians conducted their own examination, which, they asserted, established German guilt.

    At the Nuremberg trial, one of the charges against Göring was that he had ordered the Katyn massacre. In his defense he produced the published German report on investigations at Katyn. Russians and Poles produced no counterevidence, and the charge was allowed to drop. It is widely accepted in the West that the Russians were responsible. Werth, pp. 661–67; Churchill, Vol. 4, pp. 678–81.
32. D. Clark, *Three Days to Catastrophe* (London, 1966), p. 37.
33. *Istoriya Velikoi Otechestvennoi Voiny Sovetskogo Soyuza 1941–45*, Vol. 1 (Moscow, 1961), p. 277; hereafter cited as IVOVSS.
34. A. Seaton, *Stalin as Warlord* (London, 1976), p. 92.
35. Ibid., p. 93; G. K. Zhukov, *Memoirs* (London, 1971), p. 185.
36. Ibid., p. 187.
37. Ibid., pp. 207–8.
38. Werth, p. 97.
39. I. Deutscher, *The Prophet Outcast: Trotsky, 1929–40* (London, 1963), pp. 495–509.
40. Mystery surrounds the assassin. He was probably the son of Caridad Mercader, a prominent Spanish communist. But neither at this trial nor during twenty years in prison, when he was interrogated by police, doctors, judges, psychoanalysts, and others, was his identity or his connections established beyond all doubt.

    Ramón Mercader was made a Hero of the Soviet Union in 1977. He died of cancer in Havana, Cuba, on October 18, 1978, at the age of sixty-four. Ibid., pp. 495–509. See also L. A. S. Salazar, *Murder in Mexico* (London, 1950).
41. Churchill, Vol. 3, p. 586; Werth, pp. 105–6.
42. Ibid., pp. 104–9.
43. Ibid., pp. 122–23.

44. IVOVSS, Vol. 1, p. 404; Degras, Vol. 3, p. 489.
45. Seaton, p. 95.
46. Zhukov, p. 222.
47. Ibid., pp. 222–23.
48. Ibid., pp. 228–29.
49. Ibid., p. 229; Seaton, p. 95.
50. Churchill, Vol. 3, pp. 320–23; *The Anti-Stalin Campaign and International Communism* (New York, 1956), pp. 44–45; F. W. Deakin and G. R. Storry, *The Case of Richard Sorge* (London, 1966), pp. 228–31.
51. Averell Harriman and Lord Beaverbrook had meetings with Stalin in Moscow on September 28–30, 1941. At one of these meetings Harriman noted:

> Stalin asked about Hess and seemed much interested in Beaverbrook's amusing description of his talk with Hess and his size-up of the situation. Stalin indicated that he thought Hess had gone not at the request of Hitler, but with the knowledge of Hitler, to which Beaverbrook agreed.
>
> The net [*sic*] of Beaverbrook's statement was that Hess had come thinking that with a small group of British aristocrats a counter-Churchill government could be set up to make peace with Germany which would be welcomed by the majority of the British. Germany, with British aid, would then attack Russia. Stalin relished the amusing and detailed comments by Beaverbrook who was in his best form as a raconteur.

In his notes on this part of the conversation, Beaverbrook wrote that Stalin said that the German ambassador, who was still in Moscow at the time of the Hess flight, had told him that Hess was crazy—but Beaverbrook expressed the view that Hess was not. Robert E. Sherwood, *The White House Papers of Harry Hopkins* (London, 1948), Vol. 1, p. 392.
52. Zhukov, pp. 232–33.

Chapter 25

1. *The Anti-Stalin Campaign and International Communism* (New York, 1956), p. 50.
2. G. K. Zhukov, *Memoirs* (London, 1971), pp. 235–36.
3. Ibid., p. 238.
4. Ibid.
5. Ibid., pp. 280–81.
6. Zhukov states that Stalin assumed this position on August 8, 1941. Others state that his role as Supreme Commander in Chief

was not announced until months later; in fact, not until after the Battle of Stalingrad, and that he signed orders of the day as Kommissar of Defense. Ibid., pp. 237–38.

7. IVOVSS, Vol. 1, p. 441.
8. I. I. Fedyuninsky, *Podnyatie po Tregove* (Moscow, 1961), quoted in A. Werth, *Russia at War 1941–45* (London, 1964), p. 149.
9. Stalin, *Sochineniya*, Vol. 15 (Stanford, 1967), pp. 1–10; W. S. Churchill, *The Second World War* (London, 1948–54), Vol. 3, p. 332.
10. Zhukov, p. 276.
11. Ibid., pp. 276–77.
12. Ibid., pp. 287–89.
13. A. Seaton, *Stalin as Warlord* (London, 1976), p. 112.
14. Zhukov, pp. 298–300.
15. The official *Soviet History of the War* states that the Red Army had 677,085 men on the Southwest Front at the beginning of the battle for Kiev, and that 150,541 broke out of the encirclement. The Germans claim that they took 665,000 prisoners.

    Timoshenko, Budënny, and Khrushchev escaped by air. Stalin, Timoshenko, and Shaposhnikov have been strongly criticized for refusing to allow Budënny to withdraw as he proposed, and as Zhukov had argued earlier. Withdrawal would probably have saved many Soviet divisions. Stalin was reluctant to withdraw. He was by nature a man who had to attack, but he was also concerned about the effect of the fall of Kiev on army and civilian morale. Moreover, he had given assurances that Kiev would be held. IVOVSS, Vol. 2, pp. 108–11; H. Guderian, *Panzer Leader* (London, 1952), pp. 225–26; Werth, pp. 207–8; Seaton, pp. 109–16. See also p. 406 below.
16. Stalin, *O Velikoi Otechestvennoi Voine Sovetskogo Soyuza* (Moscow, 1943), pp. 16–33.
17. Ibid., pp. 27–28.
18. Ibid., pp. 36–37.
19. R. Sherwood, ed., *The White House Papers of Harry Hopkins* (London, 1949), Vol. 1, pp. 344–45.
20. *Correspondence Between the Chairman of the Council of Ministers of the U.S.S.R. and the Presidents of the United States and the Prime Ministers of Great Britain During the Great Patriotic War of 1941–45* (Moscow, 1957), Vol. 1, p. 21.
21. Ibid., p. 24.
22. Sherwood, Vol. 1, p. 390.
23. At this third meeting Beaverbrook noted Stalin's "doodling habits," while Litvinov was translating Russian into English. "Stalin occupied himself by drawing numberless pictures of wolves on paper and filling in the background with red pencil." Ibid., p. 391.

24. Zhukov, pp. 339–40.
25. Ibid., pp. 342–43.
26. Ibid., p. 363.
27. Seaton, p. 140.
28. Zhukov, pp. 352–53.
29. Ibid.
30. IVOVSS, Vol. 2, p. 359.
31. Seaton, p. 144.
32. Ibid., p. 146.
33. IVOVSS, Vol. 2, p. 406.
34. John Erickson, *The Road to Stalingrad* (London, 1975), p. 348.
35. A. Seaton, *The Russo-German War 1941–45* (London, 1941), p. 269.
36. Seaton, *Stalin as Warlord*, p. 150; A. M. Vasilevsky, *Delo vsei Zhizni* (Moscow, 1974), p. 200.
37. Ilya Ehrenburg, *Men, Years–Life*, Vol. 5; *The War 1941–45* (London, 1964), pp. 75–76.
38. Churchill, Vol. 4, p. 428.
39. Ibid., p. 430.
40. Ibid., p. 434.
41. Ibid., p. 447.
42. A. H. Birse, *Memoirs of an Interpreter* (London, 1967), p. 103.
43. Churchill, Vol. 4, p. 446.

CHAPTER 26

1. A. Seaton, *Stalin as Warlord* (London, 1976), p. 156.
2. G. K. Zhukov, *Memoirs* (London, 1971), pp. 381–85.
3. IVOVSS, Vol. 3, p. 20.
4. Zhukov, p. 405; Seaton, p. 161.
5. Seaton, p. 163; A. M. Vasilevsky, *Voenny Ist. Zhurnal*, October 1965, p. 25.
6. Vasilevsky, pp. 281–82; Seaton, p. 177.
7. Zhukov, p. 478.
8. Ibid., pp. 420–21.
9. Ibid., p. 423.
10. K. K. Rokossovsky, *Soldatsky Dolg* (Moscow, 1968), p. 192.
11. Svetlana Alliluyeva, *Twenty Letters to a Friend* (London, 1967), pp. 183–93.
12. I. Stalin, *O Velikoi Otechestvennoi Voine Sovetskogo Soyuza* (Moscow, 1943), p. 16.
13. Ibid., pp. 86–88.
14. IVOVSS, Vol. 3, pp. 60–61; B. Liddell Hart, *History of the Second World War* (London, 1970), p. 486.

15. Ian Grey, *The First Fifty Years* (London, 1967), pp. 356–57, 522–23.
16. Zhukov, p. 445.
17. S. M. Shtemenko, *Generalny Shtab v Gody Voiny* (Moscow, 1968–73), Vol. 1, p. 167; A. S.. Yakovlev, *Tsel Zhizni* (Moscow, 1966), pp. 330–32; Seaton, p. 183.
18. Zhukov, p. 464.
19. Seaton, p. 184.
20. Ibid., p. 188.
21. Vasilevsky, p. 338; Seaton, p. 188.
22. Ibid.
23. A. Dallin, *German Rule in Russia* (London, 1957), p. 427.
24. A. Werth, *Russia at War* (London, 1964), pp. 607–8.
25. A. A. Vlasov, born in a peasant family in the Nizhni Novgorod province, had fought with the Red forces in the Civil War. He had not suffered in the purges of 1937–38 and, promoted to the rank of lieutenant general after his service at the front in the battle of Moscow, he was one of the rising young Soviet generals. In summer 1942, however, he was taken prisoner on the Volkhov Front. To the Germans who advocated organizing an anti-Soviet movement in occupied territory, Vlasov was the kind of man needed. He had a good record, and was a natural commander, although apparently not outstanding in intelligence.

Vlasov agreed readily to collaborate with the Germans and issued to all Soviet officers and to "comrades of the Soviet intelligentsia" an appeal to join him in striving "with all the strength and means to overthrow the universally-hated Soviet regime." The plan was to create an army of liberation by bringing thousands of Soviet nationals under the unified command of this ex-Soviet general, but the plans were never realized. The army of liberation became primarily a propaganda weapon, and its impact was the opposite of what the Germans expected. Russian hatred of the Germans had been brought to white heat. Any Russian who collaborated was equally hated as a traitor. Far from undermining loyalty to the Soviet regime, Vlasov and his supporters were the objects of bitter contempt.

Ex-Soviet citizens serving in this army in 1943–44 numbered about half a million, of whom a large number were Ukrainians, Belorussians, Cossacks, and from the Caucasus.

Vlasov and eleven others were tried, found guilty of "treason to the Motherland," and hanged. George Fisher, *Soviet Opposition to Stalin* (Cambridge, Mass., 1952), pp. 32–33, 36–38, 53, 115–20.
26. Svetlana Alliluyeva, *Twenty Letters to a Friend* (London, 1967), p. 173.

27. Ibid.
28. Ibid., p. 174.
29. Iosif Stalin, *O Velikoi Otechestvennoi Voine Sovetskogo Soyuza* (Moscow, 1943), p. 13.
30. The Volga Germans had been encouraged to settle in Russia by Empress Catherine II, and they became a flourishing community. Remembering the response of the Sudeten Germans to Nazi appeals, Stalin considered them a risk and ordered their removal, but as a precaution rather than a punishment. They were nevertheless treated harshly. NKVD troops descended suddenly on the Volga German Republic, and gave the people only a few hours in which to get ready for the long journey by cattle truck. Many died of hunger and hardship on the way. On arrival at their destinations in uninhabited regions of Kazakhstan and Siberia, the survivors were given agricultural tools and left to build a new life. R. Conquest, *The Soviet Deportation of Nationalities* (London, 1960), pp. 96–97.
31. Dallin, p. 300.
32. Werth, p. 581.
33. Khrushchev in his "secret" report to the Twentieth Congress spoke of these mass deportations.

> At the end of 1943 . . . a decision was taken to deport all the Karachai. . . . In the same period, at the end of December 1943, the same lot befell the whole population of the Autonomous Kalmyk Republic. In March 1944 all the Chechen and Ingush peoples were deported and the Chechen-Ingush Autonomous Republic was liquidated. In April 1944 all Balkars were deported to far-away places from the territory of the Karbardino-Balkar Autonomous Republic which was renamed the Autonomous Kabardin Republic. The Ukrainians avoided meeting this fate only because there were too many of them and there was no place to which to deport them. . . .
>
> Not only a Marxist-Leninist but also no man of common sense can grasp how it is possible to make whole nations responsible for inimical activity, including women and children, old people, Communists and Komsomols, to use mass repression against them and to expose them to misery and suffering for the hostile acts of individual persons and groups of persons. [*The Anti-Stalin Campaign and International Communism* (New York, 1956), pp. 57–58.]

After Stalin's death five of the Moslem peoples were allowed to return to their homes. The Crimean Tatars and Volga Germans were not permitted to return. Werth, p. 581.

CHAPTER 27

1. W. S. Churchill, *The Second World War* (London, 1952), Vol. 5, p. 307.
2. Ibid., p. 237.
3. Ibid., Vol. 4, p. 421.
4. Iosif Stalin, *O Velikoi Otechestvennoi Voine Sovetskogo Soyuza* (Moscow, 1943), pp. 55–56.
5. Ibid., pp. 77–78.
6. Ibid., p. 90.
7. A. Werth, *Russia at War* (London, 1964), p. 674.
8. Stalin, p. 92.
9. Ibid., pp. 98–99.
10. Churchill, Vol. 5, pp. 667–68.
11. Werth, p. 729.
12. Churchill, Vol. 5, p. 247.
13. Ibid., p. 244.
14. Ibid., pp. 261–66; Cordell Hull, *Memoirs* (London, 1948), Vol. 2, pp. 131–32; J. R. Deane, *The Strange Alliance* (London, 1947), p. 23.
15. W. A. Harriman and E. Abel, *Special Envoy to Churchill and Stalin* (London, 1976), p. 245.
16. H. L. Ismay, *The Memoirs of General the Lord Ismay* (London, 1960), p. 327.
17. S. M. Shtemenko, *Generalny Shtab v Gody Voiny* (Moscow, 1968–73), Vol. 1, pp. 190–94.
18. A. H. Birse, *Memoirs of an Interpreter* (London, 1967), p. 156.
19. Deane, p. 43.
20. Ibid., p. 44.
21. Churchill, Vol. 5, p. 329.
22. Ibid., p. 317.
23. Birse, pp. 157–58.
24. Churchill, Vol. 5, p. 357.
25. Ibid., p. 352.
26. Birse, pp. 160–61.
27. Churchill, Vol. 5, pp. 341–42.
28. Lord Moran, *Winston Churchill, the Struggle for Survival* (London, 1966), pp. 54–65, 125–44, 225–27; cf. R. Lewin, *Churchill as Warlord* (London, 1973), pp. 159–61.
29. Churchill, Vol. 5, pp. 329–30.
30. A. Bryant, *Triumph in the West* (London, 1959), p. 90.
31. Deane, p. 43.

CHAPTER 28

1. A. Seaton, *Stalin as Warlord* (London, 1976), p. 193.
2. Ibid.
3. G. K. Zhukov, *Memoirs* (London, 1971), pp. 507–9.
4. M. Djilas, *Conversations with Stalin* (London, 1962), pp. 50–54.
5. A. Werth, *Russia at War 1941–45* (London, 1964), p. 855.
6. B. Liddell Hart, *History of the Second World War* (London, 1970), p. 578.
7. Zhukov, pp. 536–57.
8. Werth, pp. 884–98.
9. W. S. Churchill, *The Second World War* (London, 1948–54), Vol. 6, pp. 114–18. The Warsaw uprising is still a matter of controversy. The latest contribution is *Nothing But Honour: The Story of the Warsaw Uprising 1944*, by J. K. Zawodny (London, 1978), which fails to present the full story. Among the major factors which are minimized or ignored are, first, that Rokossovsky's forces, exhausted after their rapid advance, were halted by the German offensive; the second factor concerns General Bor-Komorowski. He lacked the training and experience for high command, and he gravely miscalculated the situation. Not only did he deliberately reject all idea of co-ordinating the uprising with the Red Army, but he also failed to secure firm undertakings of Allied support.

   On learning of the uprising General W. Anders, commander of the Polish II Corps in Italy, denounced Bor-Komorowski's action as "a serious crime" and "madness."

   It was, indeed, a terrible tragedy and one for which Stalin and the Red Army have been unfairly criticized. It left scars on Russo-Polish relations which took many years to heal. But it also had the effect of making many Poles realize that they must show realism and come to terms with Russia. For the Polish government in London it was a political and military defeat from which it never recovered. In fact, contrary to Bor-Komorowski's intentions, the uprising and its aftermath facilitated the formation of a communist regime in Poland.

   The most balanced account is *The Warsaw Rising of 1944*, by Jan M. Cienchanowski (Cambridge, 1974).
10. Rokossovsky in his memoirs, *Soldatsky Dolg* (Moscow, 1972), pp. 280–83, suggests that as commander of the 1st Belorussian Front he was responsible for the decision not to attempt to go to the aid of the Poles in Warsaw. Further he states that "Stalin wanted to give all possible help to the insurgents and to ease their plight."

Zhukov wrote later that he himself had ascertained that the Red Army had done all it could to help the insurgents "although the uprising had not been in any way coordinated with the Soviet command. At that time—both before and after our forced withdrawal from Warsaw the 1st Belorussian Front continued to render assistance to the insurgents by air—dropping provisions, medicines and ammunition. I remember there were many false reports on the matter in the Western press that could have misled public opinion." Zhukov, p. 551.

11. S. M. Shtemenko, *Generalny Shtab v Gody Voiny* (Moscow, 1968–73), Vol. 2, pp. 75–76.
12. Zhukov, pp. 551–53.
13. Ibid., p. 543.
14. Here he defined the difference between Ustav and Prikaz.
15. Shtemenko, Vol. 2, pp. 19–20; Seaton, pp. 225–26.
16. Churchill, Vol. 6, p. 181.
17. Ibid., p. 188.
18. Ibid., p. 208.
19. A. H. Birse, *Memoirs of an Interpreter* (London, 1967), p. 174.
20. Ibid.
21. Churchill, Vol. 6, p. 198.
22. A. Eden, *Memoirs—The Reckoning* (London, 1965), p. 488.
23. J. R. Deane, *The Strange Alliance* (London, 1947), pp. 345–47.
24. A. Bryant, *Triumph in the West* (London, 1959), pp. 307–8. Colonel Seaton has observed that on the basis of the figures given by Stalin in this presentation the daily supply and the stockpiling of three months' maintenance reserves were well within the capacity of the Trans-Siberian Railway. Antonov, not Stalin, was correct in his report. Seaton, p. 233.
25. IVOVSS, Vol. 5, p. 57.
26. Churchill, Vol. 6, pp. 242–44.
27. Birse, p. 177.
28. Ibid., pp. 184–85.
29. Churchill, Vol. 6, p. 345.
30. Ibid., pp. 310–12.
31. E. R. Stettinius, *Roosevelt and the Russians* (London, 1950), pp. 140–42, 160.
32. Churchill, Vol. 6, p. 314.
33. Ibid., pp. 320, 325.
34. Ibid., p. 338.
35. Ibid., pp. 308–18.
36. Shtemenko, Vol. 2, p. 275; Seaton, p. 244.
37. Churchill, Vol. 6, pp. 386–98.
38. Ibid., p. 468.
39. IVOVSS, Vol. 5, p. 257; Deane, p. 158.

40. D. D. Eisenhower, *Crusade in Europe* (London, 1948), pp. 436–40; Churchill, Vol. 6, pp. 402–9.
41. Zhukov, p. 588.
42. Ibid., pp. 588–89.
43. Iosif Stalin, *War Speeches* (London, 1946), pp. 135–36.
44. Ibid., p. 139.
45. I. Deutscher, *Stalin* (London, 1961), p. 550.
46. Cf., for example, John Erickson, *The Road to Stalingrad* (London, 1975), pp. 5–7. The Eurasian plain was ideal for the highly mechanized German forces and the application of high-speed warfare. Stalin knew that the Red Army, as equipped in 1941, had no chance of halting a German attack, the power and speed of which had been demonstrated in the conquest of Poland. (The Polish Army was, incidentally, rated highly by Western observers, and it had not been purged.) Stalin had sought to buy time, and his gamble failed. In these circumstances it is doubtful whether the presence of Rokossovsky and the other officers so tragically purged could have made any difference to Russian misfortunes in the first months of the war.
47. A. Seaton, *The Russo-German War* (London, 1970), p. 85.
48. Birse, p. 209.
49. Seaton, p. 271.

CHAPTER 29

1. According to James W. Brackett, *Demographic Trends and Population Policy in the Soviet Union*, prepared for the Joint Economic Committee, Congress of the United States, Washington, D.C., 1962, pp. 509–10, "Between 1941 and 1946 the Soviet Union experienced an absolute decline of between twenty-five and thirty million persons. . . . Some indication of the military losses can be had by comparing pre-war and post-war populations by sex. There were probably about 95 million males and 105 million females in mid-1941. At the beginning of 1950 the estimates show only 78 million males and 102 million females. The net declines of 17 million males and 3 million females would suggest that male military losses may have approached 15 million."
2. IVOVSS, Vol. 5, p. 376.
3. Ibid., p. 384.
4. W. S. Churchill, *The Second World War* (London, 1948–54), Vol. 6, p. 308.
5. E. R. Stettinius, *Roosevelt and the Russians* (London, 1950), p. 115.
6. Ibid., p. 116.

7. W. A. Williams, *The Tragedy of American Diplomacy* (Cleveland and New York, 1959), pp. 156–57.
8. Ibid., pp. 280–81.
9. A. Werth, *Russia at War* (London, 1964), p. 1016.
10. W. S. Churchill, Vol. 6, pp. 506–7.
11. Stettinius, pp. 281–82.
12. Churchill, Vol. 6, pp. 498–99, 551.
13. Ibid., p. 548.
14. Ibid., p. 545.
15. Ibid., p. 554.
16. J. R. Deane, *The Strange Alliance* (London, 1947), p. 268.
17. General Deane was writing about the attitude of the Americans attending the chiefs of staff meeting in Berlin. It became the attitude of British and Americans at all levels. Deane considered that their "tough and indifferent" approach succeeded and that "the conference marked the high point of Soviet-American military collaboration." Deane, p. 268.
18. James F. Byrnes, *Speaking Frankly* (London, 1948), p. 79 and *passim.*
19. Werth, p. 1034.
20. W. A. Williams, *The Tragedy of American Diplomacy* (Cleveland and New York, 1959), p. 69; J. F. C. Fuller, *The Second World War* (London, 1948), pp. 390–97; B. Liddell Hart, *History of the Second World War* (London, 1970), pp. 691–98.
21. Werth, p. 1038.
22. Ibid., p. 1041.
23. *Pravda*, March 13, 1946.
24. Byrnes, pp. 239–43; Williams, p. 171.
25. Ibid., p. 187.
26. Ian Grey, *The First Fifty Years* (London, 1967), p. 530.

Chapter 30

1. Maurice Dobb, *Soviet Economic Development Since 1917* (London, 1948), p. 304.
2. A. Nove, *An Economic History of the U.S.S.R.* (London, 1969), pp. 287–93.
3. L. Schapiro, *The Communist Party of the Soviet Union*, 2nd ed. (London, 1970), pp. 528–29.
4. Stalin, *Sochineniya*, Vol. 15, pp. 212–15.
5. Ibid., Vol. 16, pp. 1–15.
6. A. Harriman, *Peace with Russia?* (London, 1959), p. 113.
7. S. M. Shtemenko, *Generalny Shtab v Gody Voiny* (Moscow, 1968–73), Vol. 2, p. 500.

8. M. Djilas, *Conversations with Stalin* (London, 1962), p. 100.
9. Soon after the death of Stalin the cases against these men were declared to have been fabricated, and they were posthumously rehabilitated. In December 1954 the Military Collegium of the Supreme Court of the U.S.S.R. met in Leningrad and passed sentence of death on Abakumov and a number of his assistants for fabricating "the so-called Leningrad Affair." *Pravda*, December 24, 1954.
10. Djilas, pp. 105–6.
11. Svetlana Alliluyeva, *Twenty Letters to a Friend* (London, 1967), p. 195.
12. Ibid., p. 198.
13. Ibid., p. 197.
14. Ibid., p. 203.
15. Ibid., p. 205.
16. Ibid., p. 207.
17. Ibid., p. 209.

BIBLIOGRAPHY

Listed below are the main works which I have consulted and which have contributed directly or indirectly to this study. Articles from various journals and other sources are referred to in the notes to chapters.

Alliluyev, A. S. *Vospominaniya.* Moscow, 1946.
Alliluyev, S. *Proidenny Put.* Moscow, 1946.
Alliluyeva, S. *Twenty Letters to a Friend.* Translated from the Russian. London, 1967.
——. *Only One Year.* Translated from the Russian. London, 1969.
Anti-Stalin Campaign and International Communism, The. A selection of documents edited by the Russian Institute, Columbia University. New York, 1956.
Barbusse, H. *Stalin.* Translated from the French. New York, 1935.
Barmine, A. *One Who Survived.* New York, 1945.
Beck, F., and Godin, W. *Russian Purge and the Extraction of Confession.* Translated from the German. London, 1951.
Beloff, M. *The Foreign Policy of Soviet Russia 1929–41.* Vol. 1, 1929–36. London, 1947. Vol. 2, 1936–41. London, 1949.
Berdyaev, N. *The Origin of Russian Communism.* Translated from the Russian. London, 1937.
Beria, L. *On the History of the Bolshevik Organizations in Transcaucasia.* Translated from the Russian. London, 1939.
Birse, A. H. *Memoirs of an Interpreter.* London, 1967.
Bolt, R. *State of Revolution.* A play. London, 1977.
Bortoli, G. *The Death of Stalin.* Translated from the French. London, 1975.
Budënny, S. M. *Proidenny Put.* 2 vols. Moscow, 1958–65.
Bunyan, J. *Intervention, Civil War, and Communism in Russia, April–December 1918. Documents and Materials.* Baltimore, 1936.
Bunyan, J., and Fisher, H. H. *The Bolshevik Revolution 1917–18. Documents and Materials.* Stanford, 1934.
Bychevsky, B. V. *Front Commander: L. A. Govorov.* Moscow, 1973.
Byrnes, J. F. *Speaking Frankly.* London, 1948.
Carr, E. H. *The Bolshevik Revolution 1917–23.* 3 vols. London, 1950–53.
——. *The Interregnum 1923–24.* London, 1954.

——. *Socialism in One Country 1924–26.* 3 vols. London, 1958–64.
——. *The Soviet Impact on the Western World.* London, 1946.
Carr, E. H., and Davies, R. W. *Foundations of a Planned Economy 1926–29.* 3 vols. London, 1969–76.
Chamberlin, W. H. *The Russian Revolution 1917–21.* London, 1935.
——. *Russia's Iron Age.* London, 1935.
Chaney, O. P. Jr. *Zhukov.* London, 1972.
Chuikov, V. I. *Nachalo Puti.* Moscow, 1959.
Churchill, W. S. *The Second World War.* 6 vols. London, 1948–54.
Cohen, S. *Bukharin and the Bolshevik Question.* London, 1974.
Conquest, R. *The Soviet Deportation of Nationalities.* London, 1960.
——. *Power and Policy in the U.S.S.R.* London, 1961.
——. *The Great Terror.* London, 1968.
Crankshaw, E. *Khrushchev's Russia.* London, 1959.
——. *Khrushchev.* London, 1966.
Dallin, A. *German Rule in Russia.* London, 1957.
Dallin, D. J. *The Changing World of Soviet Russia.* New Haven, Conn., 1956.
Dallin, D. J., and Nicolaevsky, B. *Forced Labour in Soviet Russia.* London, 1948.
Davies, J. E. *Mission to Moscow.* London, 1942.
Deakin, F. W., and Storry, G. R. *The Case of Richard Sorge.* London, 1966.
Deane, J. R. *The Strange Alliance.* London, 1947.
Degras, J., ed. *Soviet Documents on Foreign Policy.* 3 vols. London, 1951–53.
——. *The Communist International 1919–43.* Documents. Vol. 1, 1919–22. London, 1956. Vol. 2, 1923–28. London, 1960. Vol. 3, 1929–43. London, 1965.
Deutscher, I. *The Prophet Armed: Trotsky 1879–1921.* London, 1954.
——. *The Prophet Unarmed: Trotsky 1921–29.* London, 1959.
——. *The Prophet Outcast: Trotsky 1929–40.* London, 1963.
——. *Stalin: A Political Biography.* Paperback ed. London, 1961.
——. *Russia After Stalin.* London, 1953.
Djilas, M. *Conversations with Stalin.* Translated from the Serbo-Croatian. London, 1962.
Dobb, M. *Soviet Economic Development Since 1917.* London, 1948.
Eisenhower, D. D. *Crusade in Europe.* London, 1948.
Eremenko, A. I. *Stalingrad.* Moscow, 1961.
——. *V Nachale Voiny.* Moscow, 1964.
Erickson, J. *The Road to Stalingrad: Stalin's War with Germany.* London, 1975.
——. *The Soviet High Command: A Military-Political History 1918–41.* London, 1962.
Fainsod, M. *Smolensk Under Soviet Rule.* Cambridge, Mass., 1958.

——. *How Russia Is Ruled.* Rev. ed. Cambridge, Mass., 1963.
Fischer, L. *The Life of Lenin.* London, 1965.
——. *The Life and Death of Stalin.* London, 1953.
Fisher, G. *Soviet Opposition to Stalin.* Cambridge, Mass., 1952.
Florinsky, M. T. *Russia.* 5th ed. New York, 1959.
Footman, D. *The Civil War in Russia.* London, 1961.
Frankland, M. *Khrushchev.* London, 1966.
Garthoff, R. L. *How Russia Makes War: Soviet Military Doctrine.* London, 1954.
——. *Soviet Military Policy: A Historical Analysis.* London, 1966.
Gorbatov, A. V. *Years off My Life.* Translated from the Russian. London, 1964.
Guderian, H. *Panzer Leader.* Translated from the German. London, 1952.
Harriman, A. *Peace with Russia?* New York, 1959.
Herling, G. *A World Apart.* Translated from the German. London, 1972.
Hingley, R. *The Russian Secret Police: Muscovite, Imperial Russian and Soviet Security Operations 1565–1970.* London, 1970.
——. *Joseph Stalin: Man and Legend.* London, 1974.
Hyde, M. *Stalin: The History of a Dictator.* London, 1971.
Ingram, K. *History of the Cold War.* London, 1955.
Jasny, N. *The Socialized Agriculture of the U.S.S.R.* Stanford, 1949.
——. *Soviet Industrialization 1928–52.* Chicago, 1961.
Kaganovich, L., et al. *The Life of Stalin: A Symposium.* London, 1930.
Karasev, A. V. *Leningradtsi v gody blokady.* Moscow, 1959.
Kennan, G. F. *Russia Leaves the War: Soviet-American Relations 1917–20.* London, 1956.
——. *Russia, the Atom, and the West.* London, 1958.
——. *Russia and the West Under Lenin and Stalin.* London, 1961.
——. *Memoirs: 1950–1963.* London, 1973.
Kerensky, A. *Memoirs: Russia and History's Turning Point.* London, 1966.
Konev, I. S. *Year of Victory.* Translated from the Russian. Moscow, 1969.
Krivitsky, W. G. *I Was Stalin's Agent.* London, 1939.
Krupskaya, N. K. *Memories of Lenin.* Translated from the Russian. London, 1930.
Kuznetsov, N. G. "Pered Voinoi" in *Oktyabr,* Moscow, 1965.
Lenin, V. I. *Polnoe Sobranie Sochineniya.* 4th ed. Moscow, 1941–57.
——. *Letters.* Trans. and ed. Elizabeth Hill and Doris Mudie. London, 1937.
Liddell Hart, B. H., ed. *The Soviet Army.* London, 1956.

——. *History of the Second World War.* London, 1970.
Lunacharsky, A. V. *Revolutionary Silhouettes.* Translated from the Russian. London, 1967.
McNeal, R. H. *Bride of the Revolution: Krupskaya and Lenin.* London, 1973.
Maisky, I. *Who Helped Hitler?* Translated from the Russian. London, 1964.
Mandelstam, N. *Hope Against Hope.* Translated from the Russian. London, 1971.
——. *Hope Abandoned.* London, 1974.
Manstein, E. von. *Lost Victories.* Translated from the German. London, 1958.
Medvedev, R. *Let History Judge. The Origins and Consequences of Stalinism.* Translated from the Russian. London, 1972.
Murphy, J. T. *Stalin 1879–1944.* London, 1945.
Nicolaevsky, B. I. *Power and the Soviet Elite.* Ed. Janet D. Zagoria. London, 1966.
Nove, A. *Stalinism and After.* London, 1975.
——. *An Economic History of the U.S.S.R.* London, 1969.
Orlov, A. *The Secret History of Stalin's Crimes.* New York, 1953.
Paloczi-Horvaih, G. *Khrushchev: The Road to Power.* London, 1960.
Pavlov, D. V. *Leningrad 1941: The Blockade.* Translated from the Russian. London, 1965.
Payne, R. *The Rise and Fall of Stalin.* London, 1966.
Pipes, R. *The Formation of the Soviet Union: Communism and Nationalism 1917–1923.* Cambridge, Mass., 1954. Rev. ed. 1964.
——. *Russia Under the Old Regime.* London, 1974.
——. *Karamzin's Memoirs: Old and New Russia.* Cambridge, Mass., 1959.
Pistrak, L. *The Grand Tactician: Khrushchev's Rise to Power.* New York, 1961.
Pospelov, P. N. (chairman of the Editorial Committee). *Istoriya Velikoi Otechestvennoi Voiny Sovetskovo Soyuza 1941–45.* 6 vols. Moscow, 1961–63.
Possony, S. T. *Lenin, the Compulsive Revolutionary.* London, 1966.
Rigby, T. H., ed. *The Stalin Dictatorship: Khrushchev's "Secret Speech" and other Documents.* Sydney, 1968.
Rokossovsky, K. K. *Soldatsky Dolg.* Moscow, 1972.
——. *Velikaya Pobeda na Volge.* Moscow, 1965.
Romanov, A. I. *Nights Are Longest There.* Translated from the Russian. London, 1968.
Salisbury, H. E. *Moscow Journal: The End of Stalin.* Chicago, 1961.
——. *A New Russia?* New York, 1962.
——. *The Siege of Leningrad.* London, 1969.
Schapiro, L. *The Communist Party of the Soviet Union.* 2nd ed. London, 1970.

——. *The Origin of the Communist Autocracy: Political Opposition in the Soviet State. First Phase, 1917–1922.* 2nd ed. London, 1977.

Seaton, A. *The Russo-German War 1941–45.* London, 1971.

——. *Stalin as Warlord.* London, 1976.

Sherwood, R. E. *The White House Papers of Harry Hopkins.* 2 vols. London, 1949.

Shirer, W. R. *The Rise and Fall of the Third Reich.* London, 1960.

Shtemenko, S. M. *Generalny Shtab v Gody Voiny.* 2 vols. Moscow, 1968–73.

Shulman, M. D. *Stalin's Foreign Policy Reappraised.* Harvard, 1963.

Simmons, E J., ed. *Continuity and Change in Russian and Soviet Thought.* London, 1956.

Smith, E. E. *The Young Stalin.* London, 1968.

Smith, H. *The Russians.* London, 1976.

Solzhenitsyn, A. *Lenin in Zürich.* Translated from the Russian. London, 1976.

——. *Gulag Archipelago.* 2 vols. Translated from the Russian. London, 1974–75.

Souvarine, B. *Stalin.* London, n.d.

Stalin, I. V. *Voprosy Leninizma.* 11th ed. Moscow, 1939.

——. *O Velikoi Otechestvennoi Voine Sovetskovo Soyuza.* Moscow, 1943.

——. *Sochineniya.* Vols. 1–13, Moscow, 1946–51. Vols. 14–16. Stanford, Calif., 1967.

Stettinius, E. *Roosevelt and the Russians.* London, 1950.

Sukhanov, N. N. *The Russian Revolution 1917.* Ed. abridged, and trans. Joel Carmichael. London, 1956.

Szamuely, T. *The Russian Tradition.* London, 1974.

Todorsky, A. I. *Marshal Tukachevsky.* Moscow, 1965.

Trotsky, L. *The Suppressed Testament of Lenin, with Two Explanatory Articles.* New York, 1935.

——. *The History of the Russian Revolution.* 3 vols. London, 1932–33.

——. *The Revolution Betrayed.* London, 1937.

——. *Moya Zhizn.* Berlin, 1930.

——. *Chto i kak proizoshlo.* Paris, 1929.

——. *Stalin.* London, 1968.

Tucker, R. C. *Stalin as Revolutionary 1879–1929.* New York, 1973.

Ulam, A. B. *Stalin: The Man and His Era.* London, 1974.

——. *Lenin and the Bolsheviks.* London, 1966.

Voroshilov, K. E. *Stalin and the Armed Forces of the U.S.S.R.* Moscow, 1951.

Werth, A. *Russia at War 1941–45.* London, 1964.

——. *Russia: Hopes and Fears.* London, 1969.

Wheeler-Bennett, J. *Brest-Litovsk: The Forgotten Peace March 1918.* London, 1938.

Williams, W. A. *The Tragedy of American Diplomacy.* New York, 1959.

Wilson, E. *To the Finland Station.* London, 1941.

Wolfe, B. D. *Three Who Made a Revolution.* London, 1956.

——. *Khrushchev and Stalin's Ghost.* New York, 1957.

——. *Strange Communists I Have Known.* London, 1966.

——. *An Ideology in Power.* London, 1969.

Yakovlev, A. S. *Tsel Zhizni.* Moscow, 1966.

Yaroslavsky, E. *Landmarks in the Life of Stalin.* London, 1942.

Zhukov, G. K. *Memoirs.* Translated from the Russian. London, 1971.

INDEX

Émigrés (émigré Marxists), xi,
66–67, 69–70, 81, 493. *See also*
specific individuals
Emilyanov (metallurgist), 278–79
Engels, Friedrich, 29, 32
Engineers, and industrialization, 254,
257
England. *See* Great Britain
Eremenko, A. I., 333, 356, 358, 360,
361, 393, 422, 512
Eristavi, Prince Rafael, 20
Essence of Christianity (Feuerbach),
Stalin's reading of, 20
Estonia, 311–12
Expropriations, 57, 58–59, 60–61,
63–64
Ezhov, N. I., 258, 260, 283, 284,
289–90, 291–92; described,
268–69; and Ezhovshchina terror
and purges, 268–69, 270, 272 ff.,
282, 283, 288, 289–90, 291–92

Factory schools, 253–54
Factory workers (*see also* Workers):
post–World War II recruitment
into Communist party of, 447
Famine (1932–33), 255, 258
Far East (*see also* specific countries;
developments): post–World War
II, 441–42, 444; pre–World War
II, 297, 301–2; and Russo-Japanese
War (1904–5), 47, 297, 414, 432,
436
Farming (farmers). *See* Agriculture;
Collectivization; Kulaks; land;
Peasants
Fascism (antifascism), World War
II and, 7, 289, 298, 300–1, 337,
358, 377
Fedorenko (tank general), 279
Fedyuninsky, General, 329
Feuerbach, Ludwig A., 20
Fifteenth Party Conference and
Congress, 214, 215, 217, 219, 221,
223, 224, 225, 251
Fifth Party Congress, 59–60
Finland, 53–55, 92, 97, 98, 103;
Grand Duchy of, 76; and repara-
tions, 426; and Russia and Winter
War, 311–12, 314, 412; surrender
and armistice and, 392–93, 400,

401, 404, 439; Tammerfors Conference, 27–28, 53, 55; and World
War II, 296, 298, 307, 311,
312–13, 317, 318, 333, 384,
392–93, 412, 426, 439
Finland, Gulf of, 392
Five-year Plans, xiv, 231, 244–45,
444–46; First, 244–45, 246–64,
267, 295, 444; Second, 277; Third,
282; Fourth, 444–46
Floggings, tsars and, 5
Food production and shortages, 143,
145, 146–47 (*see also* Grain);
Civil War (1918–20) and, 118,
119, 121; collectivization and,
222–32, 243, 246 ff., 251, 252,
261, 270 (*see also* Collectivization); famine (1932–33), 255,
258
Forced labor camps, 288, 289, 443,
487
Foreign policy (foreign relations),
Stalin and, xv–xvi, 289 (*see also*
specific agreements, aspects, conferences, countries, developments,
events, individuals, meetings);
post–World War II, 425–42, 444;
Potsdam and end of Grand Alliance, 425–42; pre–World War II,
289, 293–321
Foreign trade (trade relations), 162,
184, 254, 261, 295, 299–300
Foreign Trade Kommissariat (1922),
162
Fotyeva, L. A., 173, 176, 180, 237,
484
"Foundations of Leninism" lectures
(Stalin), 195
Fourteenth Party Congress, 205,
216–17, 218; Conference, 207–12
Fourth Party Congress (Unification
Congress), 55–58
France, 120, 155, 253, 256, 317,
330, 446; and French Revolution,
256; and German occupation, 433;
and intervention (*see* Allied intervention); and Napoleonic wars, 3,
330, 352, 420, 444, 446; and Second Front, 377–78, 381–82,
385–86, 396; trade with, 261; and
World War II, 300, 301, 302,